Jesus' Final Victory

Scriptural references are based on
the New International Version
and the King James Version.

Scripture taken from the HOLY BIBLE, NEW INTERNATIONAL VERSION®. Copyright © 1973, 1978, 1984 International Bible Society. Used by permission of Zondervan. All rights reserved.

The "NIV" and "New International Version" trademarks are registered in the United States Patent and Trademark Office by International Bible Society. Use of either trademark requires the permission of International Bible Society. Italics and brackets used in quotations from Scripture have been inserted by the author.

Larry W. Wilson

Wake Up America Seminars, Inc.
P.O. Box 273
Bellbrook, Ohio 45305

(937) 848-3322

www.wake-up.org

Cover Credit:
Special thanks to Ali Ries
for composing the artwork.
© Casperium Graphics

Copyright © November 2011
All rights reserved.

TABLE OF CONTENTS

Introduction	....	7
Prophecy 1	The Metal Man (Daniel 2:29-45)	35 **P1**
Prophecy 2	The Little Horn Power (Daniel 7:1-12)	43 **P2**
Prophecy 3	The Antichrist (Daniel 8:1-12)	63 **P3**
Prophecy 4	The Seventy Weeks (Daniel 9:20-27)	81 **P4**
Prophecy 5	Wars Between the North & South (Daniel 10:1-12:13) ...	97 **P5**
	Epilogue	118
Introduction to Revelation	....	125
Prophecy 6	The Six Seals (Revelation 4:1-6:17)	129 **P6**
Prophecy 7	The 144,000 (Revelation 7:1-8:1)	171 **P7**
Prophecy 8	The Six Trumpets (Revelation 8:2-9:21)	183 **P8**
Prophecy 9	The Two Witnesses (Revelation 10:1-11:19)	221 **P9**
Prophecy 10	The Baby Jesus (Revelation 12:1-6)	281 **P10**
Prophecy 11	The Rise of Babylon (Revelation 12:7-14:5)	291 **P11**
Prophecy 12	The Eternal Gospel (Revelation 14:6-15:6)	345 **P12**
Prophecy 13	The Seven Bowls (Revelation 15:7-16:21)	397 **P13**
The Angel's First Visit (Revelation 17)	....	417
Prophecy 14	The Second Coming (Revelation 18:1-19:10)	433 **P14**
Prophecy 15	The Day of the Lord (Revelation 19:11-20:10)	451 **P15**
Prophecy 16	The Earth Purified (Revelation 20:11-21:1)	467 **P16**
Prophecy 17	The New Heaven and New Earth (Revelation 21:2-21:8) ...	479 **P17**
The Angel's Second Visit (Revelation 21:9-22:21)	....	483
Appendix A	The Importance of 1994	503
Appendix B	The Israel of God	519
Appendix C	The Seven Churches	541
Appendix D	God Does Not Give Up	587

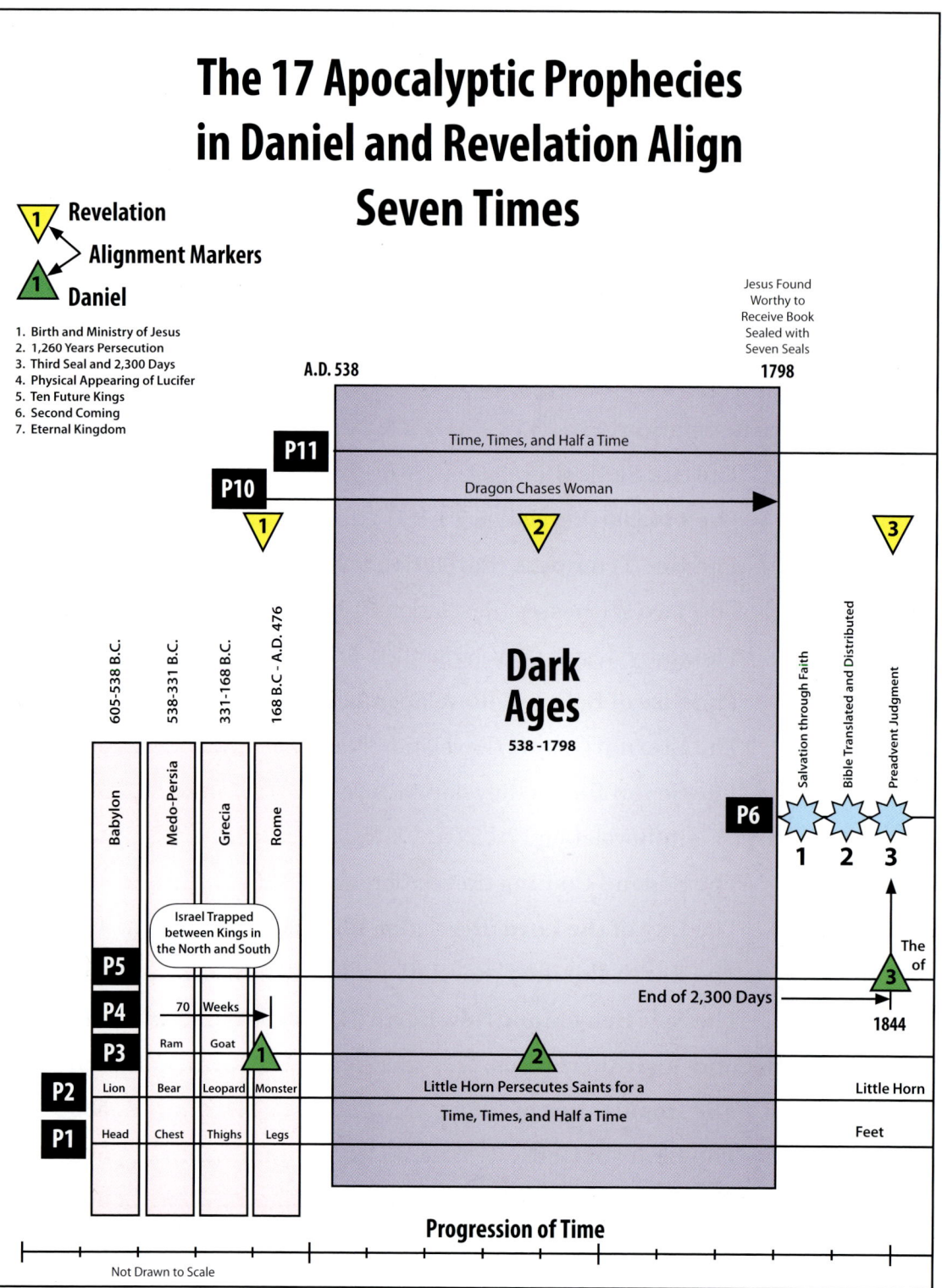

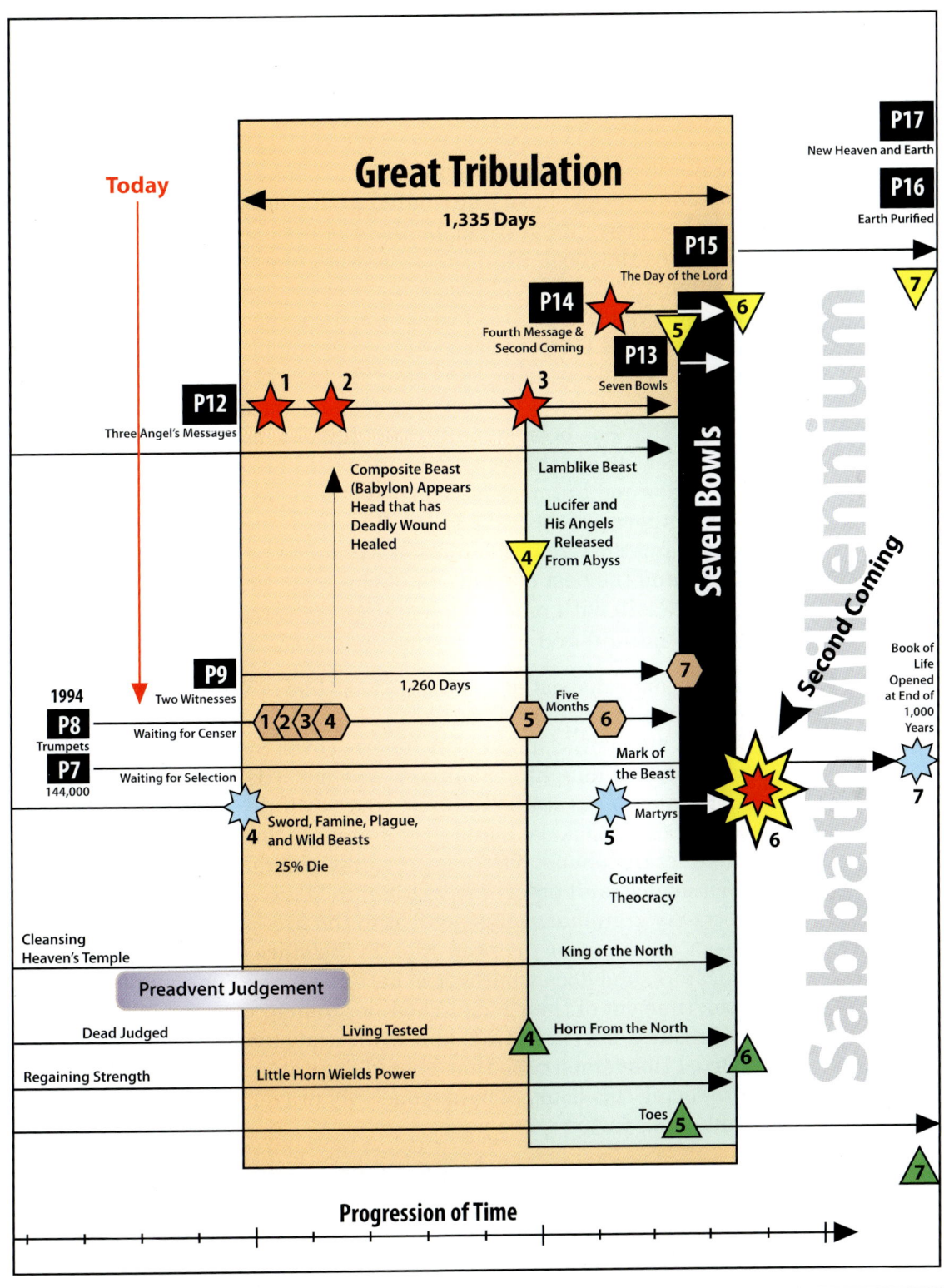

Jesus' Final Victory

In Appreciation

I am indebted to many people who have made this book possible. Generous people have contributed to this ministry without realizing that their gifts have made the production of this book possible. In a way, this book represents the work of a lifetime. It contains a summary of my prophetic study over the past forty years. Of course, even though this book is finished, the message is incomplete because God's truth continues to unfold. His truth is marching on. We are nearing the end of this world and one of the purposes of this book is to show that God has been executing a plan; a plan that has been steadily unfolding for more than twenty-six centuries. Soon, this rebellious planet will experience overwhelming chaos and unimaginable destruction. On that day, the power and authority of Jesus Christ will become apparent all over the world and the Great Tribulation will follow. It will be the worst of times and the best of times all at the same time! Jesus is returning to Earth with redemption and utter destruction – redemption for the faithful and utter destruction for the wicked.

This book is dedicated to my mother, Gladys Wilson, who introduced me to Jesus as a young boy, to my wife Shirley, who has shown me many aspects of Jesus' love over the past forty-one years, to our daughter Shannon, who has asked a thousand questions, and to my staff: To Suzy, who faithfully sees that materials are proofed, packaged, and distributed; to Shelley, who faithfully answers the phone, writes letters, fills orders, produces the *WUAS Newswatch,* and proofs my writing; to Marty, who faithfully corrects my grammar, holds my feet to the fire, pays the bills, and keeps our finances in order, repairs the office computers and duplicators, and does whatever is necessary; to Velma and Gail who took time out of their busy schedules to help with the onerous task of proofing and correcting; and to all who have financially supported this ministry so that I could dedicate a few thousand hours producing this book, "Thank you." My prayer is that you may find a blessing within these pages.

Introduction

This book is unlike any book you have read on the subject of apocalyptic prophecy because it is based on a discovery that revolutionizes prophetic interpretation. About thirty years ago, I concluded there were hundreds of different interpretations on Bible prophecy because down through the centuries, expositors have treated Bible prophecy as a work of art rather than a work of science. The essential difference between artwork and science is that artwork does not conform to natural laws. Artwork is subject to whim, bias, ability, and perspective. So, artwork is not easily reproducible. For example, if two artists were put in separate rooms and given verbal instructions, the possibility that the artists would produce identical artwork would be almost zero. On the other hand, if two scientists were put in separate rooms and given verbal instructions on conducting the same experiment, the possibility that their results would almost be identical would be very high. Because science conforms to natural laws that are self evident, science is methodical and reproducible. I have offered this comparison because I believe I have made a discovery that produces a whole new approach to prophetic study.

Why the Experts Disagree

There is a simple reason for the confusion that besets Bible prophecy. Prophetic expositors arrive at different conclusions because there are as many different methods of interpretation as there are people. *Methods of interpretation* is a phrase that defines a controlling set of ideas or views that a person has in mind *before* he or she actually begins to interpret prophecy. Doctrinal beliefs, spiritual presuppositions, religious assumptions, concepts about the role and authority of Scripture, the use of external authority, and church traditions produce controlling ideas or parameters. Consider the influence that methods of interpretation actually have: A Catholic scholar, a Baptist scholar, and a Pentecostal scholar can read the same Bible verses and interpret them differently. Each scholar will form an opinion on prophecy that is in harmony with his doctrinal beliefs because everyone reads and understands the Bible with different biases and baggage. Bias and baggage can be called, "methods of interpretation," "presuppositions," "rules of interpretation," or "hermeneutics." Bias and religious baggage produce very strong paradigms and these paradigms build barriers that often keep people from having meaningful discussions. Perhaps the following parable will illustrate the controlling power that paradigms can exert.

The Parable of the Math Teacher

Once upon a time, there was a math teacher who surrendered his life to the Lord. Later, he felt called to serve as a missionary in a foreign land. Eventually, he was invited to teach math in a college in a distant city called Overspent.

During the first week of college algebra, the teacher discovered a puzzling situation. His students could not solve a single math problem correctly. In fact, all of the students gave identical answers for each math problem that he gave them. He asked the students to explain how they entered college – given the fact they did not have the skills necessary to resolve basic math problems. The students said their high school teachers did not require them to work through math problems because highly educated and spiritually guided math teachers long ago had solved all math problems and all that they needed to do was to memorize the answers.

The teacher was shocked.

The next day, the teacher set out to remedy the problem. He put this equation on the board: $3c + 5 = 20$. He asked the students to solve for c. All of the students reported that c was equal to 3. When the teacher asked how they arrived at 3, they said they had always been taught that the variable c *always* equals 3. The teacher could not believe his ears. He demonstrated on the chalkboard how c was resolved, and he proved that $c = 5$ using simple *rules* of substitution. The students became angry. They were insulted by this "outsider" because he showed no respect for their high school elders and their traditional way of solving math problems.

The students told the teacher that if he had written $3e + 5 = 20$, their answer would have been 5 because the variable e always equals 5. They had been taught that a always $= 1$, b always $= 2$, c always $= 3$, etc. The teacher responded by saying that when it comes to math, a variable's name does not determine its value. It does not matter whether a variable is called "e," "c," or "x." When it comes to resolving a math problem, the *process* must conform to valid rules or the answer will be erroneous. The students could not bear to hear any more of this heresy, so they rose up as one man and stormed out of class. The math teacher was stunned. He wondered how he could help his students. They knew nothing about working through math problems or that math is controlled by the *four self-evident rules* of addition, multiplication, subtraction, and division. He thought to himself, "They think they have been properly informed, and they are afraid to consider answers that are contrary to the traditions taught by their elders." Perplexed by their hostility, he wondered what he could do to get the students to put aside their traditions so that they could consider a mathematical process that would enable them to accurately resolve math problems.

The next day, the teacher plainly said to his students: "Please hear me out. You have been misled. Your knowledge of math is worthless. Memorizing the answer to a math problem is not a substitute for properly working through a legitimate process to reach the correct answer. If you follow the four rules that govern basic math, you can test and validate your answers in many different ways. More importantly, others who know nothing about you or your elders can also reach the same conclusions and they can test the validity of your answers because accurate math solutions are not a matter of opinion, they are a matter of fact. *Accurate solutions are proven true when self-evident rules declare them to be true!*" Once again, the students became hostile. The teacher had condemned their traditions and their beloved elders. He had insulted them and their high school teachers. They threw desks and chairs at the teacher. During the riot, they beat and kicked him until he died.

When the bell rang at the end of class, the students went away happy. They were relieved that the offending teacher had been silenced. They petitioned the dean of the college to provide a math teacher who would teach according to their elders and their wish was granted and the rest of the school year went very well.

Years later, many of these students graduated from Overspent City College and some of them went to work for the revered elders of the city. Later on, the city faced an enormous financial crisis and all of the elders and college graduates could not stop the city from going bankrupt. When the auditors showed up, no one in the accounting department could figure out what went wrong – literally.

There are four lessons to be learned from this silly parable. First, for most of us, religious traditions and the opinions of respected leaders are usually more important than truth itself. Traditions are familiar and predictable, whereas truth can be disruptive, humiliating, and socially divisive. Second, it is impossible to be "a defender of tradition" and at the same time, be "a seeker of truth." These mind sets stand in opposition to each other. When a person is content with what he knows, leave him alone. There is nothing further that you can offer him. Third, if someone challenges the folly of a tradition, he or she will surely suffer for it. Last, if we reject or ignore the truth, failure cannot be avoided. We may arrogantly defend our ignorance, but ignorance will not save us from the outcome that truth demands.

The Bible Will Tell Us Things That We Don't Want to Believe

Experts widely disagree on Bible prophecy because every expositor has a different paradigm. The essential problem, of course, is that false presuppositions and false doctrines cannot produce valid conclusions. A valid rule is a rule that is always true. For example, 2 + 2 always equals 4 because the laws of addition, subtraction, multiplication, and division demonstrate the answer is true. Similarly, a valid rule will not have an exception even in Bible prophecy. If there is an exception in math, no one can determine if the answer is true or false. If there is an exception to a rule in Bible prophecy, no one has the authority to speak for God and tell the rest of the world when the rule should be applied or ignored. To illustrate this matter, consider a rule which some people advocate:

"A day in Bible prophecy *always* equals a year."

If this rule has no exception, the 1,000 years in Revelation 20 should be translated as 365,242 years. (365.242 days per year x 1,000 years = 365,242 years)

The day/year rule cannot be always valid because it puts the Bible in a state of internal conflict. Certain time periods in Daniel and Revelation must be translated as a day for a year (for example, the seventy weeks of Daniel 9 must be translated into 490 years), but there are other time periods like Revelation 13:5 where the rule "a day for a year" is not valid.

Faulty rules can produce unrealistic hopes and reality can produce bitter disappointment. Logic and reasonableness do not alone ensure prophetic validity. The Baptist preacher William Miller believed that Jesus would return in 1844, but his followers were bitterly disappointed. Many Christians believe that a pre-tribulation rapture is imminent, but as you read this book, you will learn that a pre-tribulation rapture cannot occur. Valid rules of interpretation will not support a pre-tribulation rapture and they do not support the idea that a rapture is necessary so that all Israel can be saved. The Bible teaches that after the cross, the Israel of God is no longer biological! Every believer in Christ has been made an heir of Abraham[1] and the the book of James teaches that the twelve tribes consist of believers in Christ![2]

For thousands of years, people believed Earth stood still and the Sun orbited the Earth. After all, everyone could plainly see that the Sun traveled across the sky! Then, along came an obscure mathematician who said that the Sun stood still. Even though Copernicus *proved* that the Sun was not moving, he was severely punished for speaking out against the traditions of the elders and telling the truth. History declares that advocates of advancing truth are frequently punished. (Even Jesus was crucified for speaking the truth.) Nevertheless, God's truth never stands still. The honest in heart always experience great joy whenever they find or receive more truth! The ongoing discovery of truth is a process that enables the Bible to reveal to us what we do not know and things we do not want to believe – at first. Unfortunately, many Christians do not want additional truth. Many people are content with their traditions (the familiar and predictable) and they are quick to discredit anything that is different before carefully analyzing it. Perhaps the greatest problem that human beings face today is that we cannot predict what our response to truth will be until more truth arrives and challenges our thinking and traditions.

No Escape: Faulty Interpretations until Daniel is Unsealed

The book of Daniel contains 533 sentences. Daniel wrote the book about twenty-six centuries ago, but unlike the other sixty-five books in the Bible, the book of Daniel was sealed up "until the time of the end." The angel, Gabriel, said to Daniel, **". . .Go your way, Daniel, because the words are closed up and sealed until the time of the end."**[3] The phrase, "Closed up and sealed until the time of the end" means that God hid something in the book of Daniel that would remain "top secret" until the time of the end arrived. I am convinced that the book of Daniel has been unsealed and the time of the end has arrived.

Introduction

The secret information that God encoded into the book of Daniel is something like the "Rosetta Stone." French soldiers accidently discovered and unearthed a stone in 1799 near Rosetta, Egypt. The stone bore a message written during the second century B.C. The message was written in two forms of Egyptian script – demotic and hieroglyphic. When archeologists examined the rock, they were thrilled because the inscriptions would help solve a very perplexing mystery. Prior to 1799, archeologists could not read many clay tablets that had been unearthed because no one could decipher the hieroglyphics. When the Rosetta Stone was discovered and translated, the demotic inscriptions on the stone enabled Thomas Young (1773-1829) and J.F. Champollion (1790-1832) to decipher the hieroglyphics of ancient Egyptians.

In a similar way, God buried a set of four self-evident rules in the book of Daniel 2,600 years ago. By God's grace, I accidently stumbled into this buried treasure. (Of course, the passage of time will prove or disprove the validity of my claim.) These four rules of interpretation shattered my prophetic thinking and I believe in due time they will shatter centuries of prophetic exposition and tradition. Because these four rules have been discovered, I believe that most previous prophetic interpretations are faulty and incomplete. In fact, after I began to personally apply the four rules in my study, they destroyed my own prophetic understanding which was faulty and incomplete. (Even after many years of study and effort since my discovery of the four rules, my conformity to the four rules remains a work in progress.) The four rules buried in the book of Daniel govern four prophetic components: God's use of time, language, chronology, and fulfillment. I believe God put these rules in the book of Daniel to dethrone the traditions and errors that the final generation maintains are true. *A revelation of greater truth is God's gift to the honest in heart.*

Predictable results go with the discovery of greater truth. The arrival of greater truth separates people who exalt tradition from people who love truth. When greater truth appears, the honest in heart rejoice to see it, while those defending the traditions of their elders will rise up and punish those who embrace it. Jesus said to His disciples, "They will put you out of the synagogue; in fact, a time is coming when anyone who kills you will think he is offering a service to God. They will do such things because they have not known the Father or me."[4] I know the parable of the math teacher is silly, but the moral of the story is consistently true. Jesus said,

"Remember the words I spoke to you: 'No servant is greater than his master.' If they persecuted me, they will persecute you also. . ."[5]

Three Levels of Information

As you might expect, God buried His secrets within the book of Daniel very well. However, when God wants truth to be revealed, He enables ordinary men and women to discover the extraordinary things He has hidden. Through the ages, we find this discovery process at work: *On or about the time of fulfillment, elements of prophecy are understood.* For example, when the day came to understand the timing of Christ's birth, wise men from the East figured it out.[6]

The apostle Paul also noticed the phenomenon of advancing truth. Consider his words: Surely you have heard about the administration of God's grace that was given to me for you, that is, the mystery made known to me by revelation, as I have already written briefly. In reading this, then, you will be able to understand my insight into the mystery of Christ, *which was not made known to men in other generations* as it has now been revealed by the Spirit to God's holy apostles and prophets. This mystery is that through the gospel the Gentiles are heirs together with Israel, members together of one body, and sharers together in the promise in Christ Jesus."[7]

The book of Daniel offers three levels of knowledge. They are:

1. Dramatic stories of faith
2. Visions revealing God's plans
3. Apocalyptic architecture

The first (and easiest) level of knowledge found within the book of Daniel contains dramatic stories of faith in God. These stories of faith and loyalty to God were recorded to benefit all generations. However, Earth's final generation will benefit the most from these stories of courage since the fiery trials in the first chapters of the book of Daniel are mini-parallels of coming events. For example, in Daniel 3 we read about Shadrach, Meshach, and Abednego facing the mandatory worship of a golden *image which the king of Babylon set up.* In Revelation 13:15, we read about the inhabitants of the world facing the mandatory worship of an *image which the king of modern Babylon will set up.* God placed these parallels and their outcomes in the book of Daniel for our encouragement.

The second (and more difficult) level of knowledge within the book of Daniel concerns the meaning of the visions found there. God gave King Nebuchadnezzar and Daniel visions that faithfully predicted the passage of time and the fulfillment of all that would occur. Students of prophecy have generally understood Daniel's visions for hundreds of years, so we cannot say that Daniel's visions were sealed up until "the time of the end." However, an element within the book of Daniel was sealed for the final generation and that element uniquely applies to the people who *will live at the end of the world.*

The Book Unsealed

The third (and deepest) level of knowledge found within the book of Daniel is *the architecture of apocalyptic prophecy.* The prophecies in Daniel conform to a structure or pattern that controls their timing and meaning. This structure also exists in Revelation! In other words, when we understand how the architecture of Daniel functions, we will immediately understand how the architecture in Revelation functions!

Daniel's architecture produces four self-evident rules. These four rules are like a combination to a safe. When the four rules are properly applied, the door to understanding swings open and the prophecies make perfect sense! This point is extremely important. Portions of Daniel and much of Revelation have been a mystery for centuries. Now that the rules are available, both books make sense *just as they read.*

When the four rules found in Daniel are applied to Daniel and Revelation, a comprehensive story unfolds that is completely harmonious with everything the Bible reveals about God's love, character, and ways. Even more fascinating, all of the details in each prophecy perfectly harmonize and they synchronize with other prophecies describing the same event. The four rules force all of the prophecies in Daniel and Revelation into a huge matrix that organizes events in an orderly, timely, and predictable manner.

To visualize this matrix, think of the seventeen prophecies in Daniel and Revelation as a wedding cake having seventeen layers. The foundation pieces are the largest pieces and naturally, they are found at the bottom of the cake. Smaller layers are stacked on top of the larger layers. In Daniel and Revelation, the toothpicks that hold the seventeen layers of the cake together represent specific events that hold and align the seventeen layers. The "toothpick events" are important because two or more prophecies often describe the same prophetic event. Because the same event is described in two different ways within two different layers (prophecies), a precise alignment of the prophecies is not only possible, but also essential for understanding the big picture.

Private Interpretation

I consider an interpretation of prophecy which does not conform to valid rules as a "private interpretation." The word "private" as used in this context does not mean obscure. Millions of people believe and endorse a private interpretation. A private interpretation is an interpretation that cannot be tested with valid rules. Of course, every person is free to believe whatever he wants to believe, but our beliefs have nothing to do with God's actions. Most of the world did not believe it would rain in Noah's day, but it had no affect on God's action.

The joy of every Bible student is to search for "the whole truth and nothing but the truth!" Even if we have valid rules of interpretation, we have no guarantee that we will correctly apply them. Said another way, it is one thing to know the laws that govern algebra, but it is another matter to correctly solve algebraic problems. When valid rules of interpretation are used, the prophecies in Daniel and Revelation will make sense *just as they read,* because the Bible is its own interpreter. On the other hand, a private interpretation requires a promoter, an interpreter – someone having superior knowledge or authority. A private interpretation produces a layer of explanation that separates the student from the Bible. Valid rules do not require an interpreter and allow the Bible to speak for itself.

Consider again the difference between art and science. A private interpretation (art) makes it all but impossible for people to independently arrive at the same conclusion without the coaxing of a guide or interpreter. A valid set of rules (science) enables people to arrive at a similar conclusion *without* knowing anyone else or listening to an expositor. Many Christians believe whatever their leaders say about prophecy without actually validating the conclusions for themselves. Lay people usually "go along" because they have no solutions of their own, and their church organization endorses a particular view which aligns with church doctrines and paradigms. Because the average Christian does not study prophecy and the subject of Bible prophecy is complicated, it is just easier to play "follow the leader."

What do you think? Should the Bible speak for itself or should it have an interpreter? I have concluded after many years of study that the Bible does indeed speak for itself and the Bible is its own interpreter. I do not accept the idea that external authority exists or that it is even necessary.

Who but God Has the Authority to Declare Chronological Order?

The visions within Daniel behave in a predictable way. Once this behavior is detected, it keeps us on track. It helps us decipher prophecies and enlightens us with information that we could not otherwise know. For example, one consistent behavior that occurs throughout the book of Daniel is that each prophecy has a beginning point and an ending point in time, and the events within each prophecy occur in the order in which they are given. This chronological behavior may sound simple, but it has profound ramifications. Consider the results of violating this behavior. If the events given within a particular prophecy do not occur in the order given, who has the authority to declare the order of events? Does anyone other than God have the authority to change the order that He created?

The chronological behavior found in Daniel's prophecies is the basis for Rule One. I have distilled this behavior into the following words (rule): *Each apocalyptic prophecy has a beginning point and an ending point in time and the events within each prophecy occur in the order they are given.* Be assured, I am not inventing a rule. I am expressing a consistent behavior that recurs without exception throughout the book of Daniel (as well as the book of Revelation).

When the fulfilled elements in Daniel and Revelation are aligned with widely published historical records, the validity of Rule One proves true *every time*! The prophecies in Daniel began unfolding more than 2,600 years ago. Some of the prophecies in Revelation began unfolding 2,000 years ago. These lengthy periods of time contain a sufficient sample to validate the four rules that spring from Daniel's architecture. The book of Daniel also provides a historical foundation for some of the prophecies in Revelation. Since prophecies in Revelation run parallel to prophecies in Daniel we can link them together and establish the timing of events mentioned in both books. So, the use of Daniel's architecture, like the hieroglyphics on the Rosetta Stone, enables us to resolve many prophetic mysteries that would otherwise be impossible to resolve.

I have arbitrarily made the rule governing chronology "Rule One" because establishing the chronological order in each prophecy eliminates a great deal of speculation and aligning the seventeen prophecies in Daniel and Revelation is "Job One." The importance of this rule cannot be overstated. Draw a time line on a big sheet of paper and place all of the events specified in Daniel and Revelation on this time line. If you attempt this, you will immediately confront the question of chronological order. Rule One is deceptively simple. It is also incredibly powerful. It demolishes two thousand years of prophetic speculation and tradition. Think about this: *If God has not declared the chronological order of events within each apocalyptic prophecy, there is no chronological order in apocalyptic prophecy.* If there is no order, apocalyptic prophecy remains in the realm of art. On the other hand, if God has declared chronological order, apocalyptic prophecy becomes a science and there is prophetic certainty ("the more sure word of prophecy") instead of endless chaos and cancelling views.

If apocalyptic prophecy is art, everyone has the same license and authority. Everyone is permitted to define and create whatever prophetic order and interpretation they want. This ongoing process has produced a cloud of confusion and as a result, many Christians treat prophecy with contempt. Worse, there is no general agreement among Christians on the next prophetic event.

When apocalyptic prophecy is regarded as art, church groups will turn to some external authority in an attempt to clarify their prophetic understanding. This authority can be the writings of founding fathers, a prophet, or even church tradition. Like the math teacher, Jesus confronted the traditions of His people and He was considered a blasphemer because the Jews put their religious traditions (art) above God's Word (authority)![8]

Because there is chronological order within apocalyptic prophecy, we can determine which prophetic event has been fulfilled and what prophetic event will come next. We have twenty-six centuries of prophetic progression and fulfillment since the book of Daniel was written. Looking backwards from our day, world history proves *there is chronological order* in the prophecies of Daniel and Revelation. This is good news because the final generation can know and understand prophecies that previous generations could not discover! Remember, God's greatest gift to the honest in heart is greater truth. This gift will never end throughout eternity! During the Great Tribulation God will swing a powerful magnet of truth over a junk pile called Earth and the honest in heart will be attracted and captured by its power and the rest of mankind will feel nothing. This is how the sheep will be separated from the goats.

What about the Other Three Rules?

Please consider the remaining three rules.

Rule Two: A prophecy or prophetic element within a prophecy is not fulfilled until all of the specifications are met. This includes the order of the events given within the prophecy. (Fulfillment)

Rule Three: Apocalyptic language can be literal, symbolic, or analogous. To reach the intended meaning of a passage, the student must consider (a) the context, (b) the use of parallel language in the Bible, and (c) a relevant text that defines the symbol if an element is thought to be symbolic. (Language)

Rule Four: The presence or absence of the Jubilee Calendar determines how God measures time. If a prophetic time period occurs during the operation of the Jubilee Calendar (1437 B.C. - 1994), time is translated as a day for a year; otherwise, translation is not permitted. (See Appendix A for further study of the Jubilee Calendar.) (Timing)

Issues and Answers

Because apocalyptic prophecy involves many facets, several issues need to be addressed before we jump into this study. Please take a few minutes and thoughtfully consider each of the following issues. Later on, as you near the end of this book, I also hope you will review these matters again. I have identified these issues *before* you begin reading in hopes they will accelerate your investigation and pique your interest in apocalyptic prophecy.

1. This Book Is a Commentary, Not a Paraphrase or a Translation

According to the dictionary, a paraphrase is an attempt to clarify the meaning of an author's words by restating the author's original idea with different words. On the other hand, a translation is quite different. A translation is a direct conversion of the equivalent sense from one language to another. I mention this distinction *so that you will understand that this book is not a paraphrase or a translation.* This book is a commentary. This book contains only my current understanding of Daniel and Revelation.

Through the years, I have experimented with different teaching techniques such as translating, paraphrasing, and interlacing. (Interlacing is the practice of inserting words within brackets [attempting to make the Bible text read more easily].) Some people dislike interlacing because they feel that I am distorting the integrity of the text. My response (attempting to be humorous) has been, "What difference does it make if I distort the text before you read it or after you read it?" When it comes to Bible *commentaries*, all commentaries stem from human opinion and none have divine authority, for if they did, they would not be commentary. As far as I am concerned, the Bible does not have or require external authority. It stands on its own. As Christians, we do not worship the Bible, we worship God the Father, Jesus Christ,[9] and the Holy Spirit, who are one in purpose, plan, and action.[10] Since there are distinct differences between a translation, a paraphrase, and a commentary, please regard this book as a commentary.

This commentary has not been designed to thoroughly prove every point. Rather, it was designed to increase your interest in Daniel and Revelation and your faith in God. Above all else, we cannot forget this: Soon, everyone on Earth will witness the amazing fulfillment of Daniel and Revelation. Once the Great Tribulation begins, it will be very easy for ordinary people to determine which commentaries on Daniel and Revelation were based on valid rules of interpretation and which were not. The truth will be self-evident and speak for itself.

The better we understand God's Word, the more clearly we comprehend God's love, ways, and plans. *Contrary to what many people think, the primary objective of apocalyptic prophecy is not future telling.* The primary objective of Bible prophecy is to understand God and how He operates. I have no intention of corrupting the intended meaning of Bible prophecy. I take the warning given in Revelation 22:18,19 very seriously. I understand that God will deal harshly with anyone who knowingly and willingly corrupts the message in Revelation by adding to it or taking away from it. On the other hand, like any other human being, I am fallible and I appreciate the promise in Revelation 1:3 which says that everyone who studies and tries to understand what Revelation means will be blessed. So, consider this commentary a stepping stone. It was written by one Bible student to help other Bible students understand the prophecies in Daniel and Revelation as quickly as possible.

Additive Nature

The study of apocalyptic prophecy is somewhat like math. Both are additive in nature. Algebra I precedes Algebra II for good reason. So, please read this book in chronological order. Do not jump around looking for answers to your questions until you clearly understand the operation of the rules of interpretation that I am following and the chronology of the elements within the prophecies. When you find a conclusion in this book with which you disagree or that is different from what you have believed, it is important that you refer to the apocalyptic chart on pages 4 and 5 and note the prophecy and chronological time of the event under consideration. Compare my conclusions with other events in other prophecies that occur at the same time. In fact, you should often refer to the chart so that you can see how each story progresses chronologically. Once you see how all seventeen prophecies connect and align with each other, you will then see the intricate relationships that exist between the prophecies.

Finally, if you disagree with my conclusions, do not waste precious time arguing with me. Direct your energy toward the ultimate prophetic challenge: Write your own commentary. Present your conclusions to the world. Post your rules of interpretation openly so that everyone can test your rules as well as your fidelity to them! Distribute several thousand copies of your book. See what happens! If your message is true, the Lord will bless you. Hurry – Jesus is coming soon. If you think His return is as near as I do, then share the good news!

2. Five Prophecies in Daniel and Twelve Prophecies in Revelation

All apocalyptic prophecies have a special characteristic – "Each prophecy has a beginning point in time, an ending point in time, and the events within each prophecy are listed in the order in which they will occur." According to Rule One, there are seventeen apocalyptic prophecies in the books of Daniel and Revelation. When the five prophecies in Daniel and the twelve prophecies in Revelation are correctly aligned, they produce one time line of clearly discernable events that occur in chronological order. The beauty of this time line is that we can easily determine our chronological position in God's plan for man's salvation.

Some of the seventeen prophecies began centuries ago. Nine sequences will begin in the near future and six are currently underway. All seventeen prophecies interlock with each other and together, they form a solid matrix that might be compared to a homemade car ramp constructed of layers of planks. As we move forward in time, we rise higher and higher on the ramp. To better visualize this ramp, consider this illustration: A man wants to change the oil in his car, but he cannot get to the oil pan because the car sits too low to the ground. He needs two ramps to elevate the front wheels of his car. To make a ramp, the man cuts seventeen pieces of timber of varying lengths. He sorts the planks so that the longest piece will be on the bottom and the shortest will be on the top. Then, he takes the longest board and nails the next longest board to it so that the second board lays a few inches away from the leading edge of the first board. The man continues to stack and nail the boards together until he has created a ramp of seventeen boards. After making two such ramps, he drives his car up the ramps and changes the oil!

The point in this illustration is threefold: First, when the ramps are completed, each group of seventeen boards work together as one unit. Similarly, the books of Daniel and Revelation produce one cohesive story. Second, the seventeen boards are deliberately arranged so that the man's car rises higher and higher as he drives forward up the ramp. In other words, each board increases the height of the ramp because they are stacked on top of each other. Similarly, as we near the end of time, our understanding of God's plans become brighter and clearer. Finally, the nails that hold the seventeen boards together are indispensable. The nails keep the boards properly aligned. So it is with the seventeen prophecies in Daniel and Revelation. They are "nailed together" by prophetic events. A prophetic event in one prophecy will align with a description of the same event in another prophecy, and soon, by "nailing" all of the prophecies together, nothing can move. The end result is that we have a solid platform (the more sure word of prophecy) that can withstand the full weight of scoffers and critical investigation.

According to the *Merriam Webster Dictionary*, an apocalypse is a divine or glorious revelation. For this reason, the last book of the Bible is often called *The Apocalypse* or *The Revelation*. The title given to the last book in the Bible suggests something will be revealed to the world that is otherwise unknown. This "something" is Jesus Christ. Jesus Christ is far different from the icon that most Christians talk about. Jesus is much larger and more complex than most Christians understand. During the Great Tribulation, Jesus Christ will be fully revealed to the world in truth and righteousness and this is why the last book of the Bible is called "The Revelation of Jesus Christ!"[11]

In a sense, all sixty-six books of the Bible qualify as a "revelation," because they are inspired. The Bible as a whole reveals wonderful things about God and His love for mankind that would otherwise be unknown. Daniel and its counterpart, Revelation, are unlike the other books in the Bible, because they were reserved for the final generation. They are special because they contain new information about Jesus Christ and His forthcoming actions. They tell the conclusion of a story that began thousands of years ago in Heaven. Jesus' ministry on Earth is a part of the story, but it is only part of the story! Think of it this way: If Christ's death on the cross is "the greatest story ever told," then what is revealed when Christ brings an end to sin and gathers His children must be the *grandest* story that can be told!

3. There Are Five Types of Prophecy in the Bible

Many Christians are confused about Bible prophecy in general because there is so much of it. Consider this: The Bible contains five distinct types of prophecy and each type must be interpreted according to its own rules. The five types of Bible prophecy are:

A. Messianic Prophecies

These prophecies are associated with the work and ministry of Jesus. There are more than 450 Messianic statements or prophecies in the Bible. Some prophecies concern His first advent and others, His second advent. Here are a few examples: Isaiah 53, Psalm 22, Matthew 26:64, John 14:1-3, and 1 Thessalonians 4:13-18.

B. Judaic Prophecies

The covenant between God and the ancient nation of Israel contained many promises and prophecies. Contrary to the beliefs of many people today, these promises and prophecies were conditional. God's covenant with Israel was contingent on Israel's behavior.[12] Bible history shows that Israel repeatedly rebelled against God and broke His covenant. This behavior explains why God destroyed Jerusalem and the temple in A.D. 70.[13] Many people believe that God will fulfill all of the prophecies and promises that He gave to ancient Israel, but a careful study of Daniel will reveal that this is not possible. The unconditional nature of apocalyptic prophecy proves that the conditional promises made to ancient Israel have been abolished and they cannot be fulfilled! (See Appendix B.)

God's covenant with ancient Israel ended with the expiration of the seventy weeks in A.D. 33. Over the centuries, Israel would not cooperate with God, therefore God annihilated the nation of Israel in A.D. 70. Knowing this would be the case, Jesus initiated a new covenant that *redefined* Israel prior to His death on the cross. The new Israel of God now consists of believers in Christ.[14] God redefined Israel during the seventieth week so that He could fulfill the promises that He made to Abraham. The end result is that Abraham's descendants are no longer biological. According to the new covenant, those who live by faith, as Abraham did, are Abraham's "seed" (the Greek word for seed is *sperma*).[15] A study of Deuteronomy 28, Galatians 3, Ephesians 2, Romans 9-11, and Hebrews 4 confirms that God never fails to keep His word, even if He has to cut off the dead branches and "graft in" another group of people to fulfill His promises. A good example of a Judaic prophecy is found in Deuteronomy 28. Judaic prophecies are important today because they help us better understand the new covenant which contains "better promises" and prophecies.[16]

Millions of people make the mistake of merging old covenant promises and prophecies with new covenant promises and prophecies, and the result is total confusion. The promises and prophecies God gave to ancient Israel had to be abandoned because Israel became obstinate. After 1,400 years of dealing with Israel, God abandoned biological Israel and created a new Israel. The books of Daniel and Revelation are based on the new covenant. This is one reason why Daniel was sealed up until the time of the end. God gave the information in the book of Daniel while His covenant with ancient Israel was still intact. *If* Israel had properly responded to God's grace during the seventy weeks and *if* Israel had embraced Messiah and ushered in the kingdom of God when Jesus appeared on Earth, the prophecies given in the books of Ezekiel, Jeremiah, and Isaiah would have been fulfilled as promised. If Israel had embraced Messiah, there would not have been a new covenant or even a New Testament, but sadly, Israel rebelled and God had no choice but to start over with a redefined Israel. (Please see Appendices B and D.)

C. Day of the Lord Prophecies

Many "Day of the Lord" prophecies are scattered throughout Scripture. These prophecies predict the end of wickedness and the vindication of God's people. Elements within these prophecies are often general enough that we can find parallels at different times in human history. For example, Isaiah 24 and Ezekiel 7 predict the destruction of Israel which parallels the destruction of Earth at the end of Earth's history. Matthew 24 is a "Day of the Lord" prophecy. This prophecy has components in it that deal with the destruction of Jerusalem (A.D. 70), as well as the end of the world. Statements about each time period are given in one prophecy because there are obvious parallels between the two events. However, the Day of the Lord prophecies do not have multiple fulfillments. The words of Jesus in Matthew 24 that pertained to the fall of Jerusalem have been fulfilled and statements that pertain to the end of the world will be fulfilled.

D. Local Prophecies

Local prophecies apply to specific people, places, and times. For example, the prophecy concerning Nineveh (Jonah 1) is a local prophecy. Local prophecies require a messenger to explain or proclaim the prophecy. In Nineveh's case, Jonah was the messenger. Before the flood, God chose Noah as a local messenger. At the time of the First Advent, God chose John the Baptist as a local messenger. Even though the messages of local prophets belong to specific times and places, timeless principles sustain their value. Since the behavior of God is constant, local prophecies also offer important parallels for our consideration. Jesus said, **"As it was in the days of Noah, so it will be at the coming of the Son of Man."**[17]

E. Apocalyptic Prophecies

Only the books of Daniel and Revelation contain apocalyptic prophecies. These prophecies are chronological in nature, that is, these prophecies outline a specific sequence of events that occur in their order over time. An apocalyptic prophecy is identified by two elements: First, there is a beginning point and an ending point in time. Second, the events given in each prophecy occur in the order given. *This never fails.* The fulfillment of apocalyptic prophecy is unconditional. All that God has said under the new covenant will surely come to pass. An easy to understand example can be found in Daniel 2. King Nebuchadnezzar's vision outlines a sequence of seven kingdoms which would rise to power in their order.

Sometimes, the sequence or structure of apocalyptic prophecy is defined by numeric order. This helps to keep everything in chronological order. For example, in Revelation 8, the second trumpet occurs *after* the first trumpet. Chronological order is *always* maintained in apocalyptic prophecy, otherwise no one can determine the order of events. Think about this: *If God has not declared the order of events in each prophecy, who on Earth has the authority to tell the rest of the world the order that God intended?*

I have introduced the five types of prophecy in the Bible for this compelling reason: Each type of prophecy has a unique set of rules and considerations. Each type requires distinctive treatment. When different types of prophecy are mixed or merged together, the Bible becomes unstable, internally conflicted, and impossible to understand because each type of prophecy requires a different set of rules to reach its intended meaning.

4. Valid Rules of Interpretation Are Essential

Rules of interpretation have nothing to do with a person's religious beliefs. Valid rules of interpretation are derived from self-evident patterns that are observed within apocalyptic text. Patterns exist in every science. For example, Dr. Georg Ohm discovered a distinct set of patterns within electricity and he quantified his observations by writing down a set of rules which we call "Ohm's law." Dr. Ohm did not invent electricity or the patterns he observed; rather, he merely discovered the architecture and behavior of electricity and Ohm's law has proven to be very helpful ever since!

Rules such as the law of gravity or Ohm's law are not explicitly stated in nature. In fact, the only laws explicitly stated and written by God in the history of fallen man are the Ten Commandments![18] Valid rules are derived from careful research and observation. When a pattern is detected that has no exception, the pattern becomes a rule. When it comes to solving the unknown in science, valid rules are required.

Consider one more example: Sir Isaac Newton researched the effects of gravity through different experiments. After observing that objects *always* fall at the same rate of speed, Sir Newton developed a mathematical formula expressing his discovery. *Sir Isaac Newton did not make up the rule that governs gravity.* Sir Isaac Newton merely discovered what God had made and he expressed the behavior of gravity in a manner that allowed others to calculate and understand the effects of gravity.

I have belabored the importance of valid rules because this commentary is based on four rules of interpretation. If these four rules are valid, one harmonious story will unfold from the books of Daniel and Revelation. The Bible is not internally conflicted. One part of Scripture does not cancel another part of Scripture. Truth is proven by the harmony that comes from the sum of all its parts – if we are willing to dig deep enough to resolve the *apparent* conflicts that veil truth.

5. God's Timing Is Not Arbitrary

Some people argue that God's sovereignty is eliminated if we say that certain prophetic events must be fulfilled *before* the Second Coming occurs. This argument has no merit if we understand that God Himself is the source of apocalyptic prophecy. He has declared what will come to pass and the order as well! God has set the time for the end of sin according to His own authority.[19] God has revealed this schedule to the final generation through the book of Daniel and we can be sure that with God, timing is everything!

Some people argue that the urgency expressed by ancient prophets should not be taken seriously. They say, **"With God, a day is as** a thousand years and a thousand years as a day."[20] They bolster their argument saying that words like *near* and *soon* should be understood from God's perspective. They conclude that a thousand years can exist between two verses because with God, time is nothing. Again, this argument has no merit because God has placed eighteen segments of time within the seventeen prophecies so that students of prophecy may align them and understand the timing of His plans. *When the time arrives for the fulfillment of a prophecy, words like "near" and "soon" mean exactly what they say.*

One silly argument often used to diminish the importance of apocalyptic prophecy is this: "The last days of Earth's history began at Calvary; therefore, we have been living in the last days since Jesus was on Earth." This 2,000 year old argument makes no sense. The book of Daniel was not unsealed at the cross. If Daniel had been unsealed at the cross, the apostles would have understood important dates like 1798 and 1844. We know from their writings that they had no idea that 2,000 years would pass before Jesus returned. Jesus kept them in the dark on this matter. He said, **"I have much more to say to you, more than you can now bear. But when he, the Spirit of truth, comes, he will guide you into all truth. He will not speak on his own; he will speak only what he hears, and he will tell you what is yet to come."**[21]

From time to time, people accuse me of being a false prophet, a kook, a cultic leader, etc., because I insist, on the basis of apocalyptic prophecy, that we are living in the last days of Earth's history. History says that twenty-one civilizations have come and gone, and *the fact that our present civilization is in shambles does not prove that Jesus is coming soon.* Even though it is a fact that civilizations come and go, the rise and fall of civilizations have nothing to do with God's predetermined timetable for this planet. Outside of apocalyptic prophecy, it is impossible to know God's plan for planet Earth.

Rightly understood, apocalyptic prophecy is a firm foundation. Through the centuries, many people have declared prophecies to be fulfilled, but many such claims have proven to be false. Remember, a fulfillment requires two affirming actions: First, all of the specifications concerning the event must be met, and second, the event must occur in the order given in the prophecy. If this system of checks and balances is ignored, the result will be prophetic confusion and uncertainty.

6. Differences between Prophetic Truth and Prophetic Faith

There is a distinct difference between prophetic truth and prophetic faith. Prophetic truth refers to those prophecies or those portions of a prophecy that have been fulfilled. Prophetic faith, on the other hand, anticipates events that are yet to be fulfilled. Since no one can prove that a particular interpretation will come to pass, our prophetic faith must be carefully built upon valid rules of interpretation. Let me state this again. *Until prophecy is fulfilled and prophetic faith becomes prophetic fact, our prophetic faith must be built upon valid rules of interpretation.*

How can we know if an apocalyptic prophecy has been fulfilled? By definition, a fulfillment is a full-filling of the specifications. A fulfillment only occurs when all of the specifications of a prophecy are met. Every specification must be satisfied before a prophecy can be declared fulfilled, including the chronological order stated in the prophecy. For example, some people claim the fourth trumpet of Revelation 8 has been fulfilled. If this claim is valid, not only would the advocates of this assertion have to demonstrate how the specifications of the fourth trumpet were met *but* they would also have to demonstrate how the specifications on the first three trumpets were fulfilled! Remember, Rule Two states *a prophecy or prophetic element within a prophecy is not fulfilled until all of the specifications are met. This includes the order of the events given within the prophecy.*

7. Additional Information Is Included

The books of Daniel and Revelation also contain information besides apocalyptic prophecy. They include historical information, discussion regarding the visions, and stories of personal experiences. For example, we learn why Daniel was taken to Babylon and how his three young friends were tested to the point of death for refusing to bow down to a golden image. In the book of Revelation, we also find information that is not apocalyptic such as historical data, information about Jesus, reasons why John was on the isle of Patmos, the condition of the seven churches in Asia Minor at the time of John's exile (See Appendix C.), and commentary on various aspects of John's visions. Even though the books of Daniel and Revelation contain information other than apocalyptic prophecy, only the portions that have a beginning point in time and an ending point in time, with a sequence of events between these two points, qualify as apocalyptic prophecy.

8. Five Essential Bible Doctrines

To appreciate all that apocalyptic prophecy offers, you also need to have a basic understanding of five essential Bible doctrines. If you do not correctly understand these doctrines, Revelation's story will be difficult to grasp. In fact, I have found that prophetic divergence between church groups is largely caused by something other than prophecy itself! The culprit is doctrine.

Many scholars and pastors prefer to keep the books of Daniel and Revelation shrouded in mystery by claiming these are books of symbolism. In other words, they are theological putty. While the books of Daniel and Revelation do contain a few symbols, there is no mystery. When God uses a symbol He always defines the symbol with a relevant text so that there is no confusion or arguing about the meaning of the symbol! Think about this: If every student of prophecy is free to define symbols as desired, we are back to private interpretation and total confusion. Competing views only cancel out each other. On the other hand, if a symbol is clearly defined, God has spoken and there is no room for confusion. This is the basis for Rule Three which states *apocalyptic language can be literal, symbolic, or analogous. To reach the intended meaning of a passage, the student must consider (a) the context, (b) the use of parallel language in the Bible, and (c) a relevant text that defines the symbol if an element is thought to be symbolic.*

"Experts" often manipulate symbolism into whatever form they need or want and poorly informed laymen will accept this manipulation if it generally agrees with what they already believe. Rule Three removes the "silly-putty" from symbolism. When God declares something is symbolic, He declares the meaning of the symbol. This simple fact enables the Bible to speak for itself and it defeats the age-old argument that Daniel and Revelation are just books of symbols that no one can understand. If more people understood Rule Three, the Bible would be understood with greater clarity and authority.

Bible doctrines can *assist or resist* our efforts to reach the intended meaning of apocalyptic prophecy. Suppose a student of prophecy embraces this popular doctrine: *When a person dies, he goes immediately to Heaven or hell to spend eternity.* If the student embraces this doctrine, Revelation 20 will not make any sense because by using this logic, Cain, the first murderer, has been burning in hell ever since his death. Why would God resurrect Cain at the end of the 1,000 years (according to Revelation 20) only to throw him back into the lake of fire? Taking this one step further, why are the wicked resurrected at the end of the thousand years if they are already burning in hell? Even more perplexing is this question: "How could Cain be sent to hell before Judgment Day arrived?" The Bible teaches that God has appointed a specific time for human beings to be judged.[22] Finally, what about this question: If the wages of sin is burning in hell throughout *eternity,* how could Jesus pay the penalty for our sins when He was resurrected after spending only three days in the tomb?[23] We see from these questions that a correct interpretation of Revelation 20 requires a correct position on what happens at death, the judgment of mankind, and the penalty for sin. The matter of doctrine has been presented because the books of Daniel and Revelation build upon five essential Bible truths. These five truths are:

1. The enduring nature and sovereignty of God's law (The Ten Commandments)
2. The return of Jesus and the destruction of the wicked (The Second Coming of Jesus)
3. God's use of parallel temples (Services in the earthly temple shadow services in Heaven's temple)
4. The terms and conditions of salvation (Salvation through faith in Christ alone)
5. The condition of man in life and death (At death, the soul ceases to exist. There is a pre-Advent judgment. The righteous will be resurrected at the Second Coming and the wicked will continue to "sleep" until the end of the 1,000 years.)

These five themes can be examined at length in my book, *Jesus: The Alpha and The Omega.* This book can be freely downloaded from the internet at www.wake-up.org or a printed copy can be purchased.

9. Ignore Chapter and Verse Designations

The original manuscripts of Daniel and Revelation did not include chapter and verse designations. Translators appended these "numerical helps" later to facilitate Bible study. Translators reasoned that students could quickly locate a sentence or group of sentences for further investigation if chapters and verses were added to the text. These well-intentioned numbers can create a minor problem. Most people think of a chapter in the Bible as a complete unit; therefore, it is easy to overlook the actual layout of the seventeen prophecies. Do not be confused with the fact that prophecies can begin and end anywhere within a chapter or that they can begin in one chapter and continue several verses into the next chapter. Apocalyptic prophecy ignores the chapter and verse designations inserted by translators.

10. Some Big Points and Little Points

No one can accurately explain every detail in Daniel and Revelation – and this includes me. I have had to change my thinking several times in my quest to understand these two books and I expect I will have to change my thinking in the future. No human being can know everything there is to know about God or His Word. So, we should never stop moving toward a better understanding of God's truth. To the scholars who scoff at the idea that ordinary people can correctly understand God's Word, I ask, "If it is impossible for ordinary people to correctly understand the Word of God, why did He give it to *us*?"[24]

Prophetic truth has several dimensions with which to grapple. For example, we may correctly identify the timing of the fifth trumpet before it happens, but wrongly interpret the event. Conversely, we may correctly interpret the event and wrongly calculate the time of its occurrence. Nevertheless, we may be sure that when the time comes, God will see to it that every person hears and understands His truth. God will accomplish this amazing feat during the Great Tribulation through His 144,000 servants. A person cannot *refuse to love the truth* and be saved if he does not first have the clearest evidences of truth set before him.[25]

We do not have long to wait before we know whether we live at *the appointed time of the end*. I believe the Bible makes it clear that events of global consequence will soon take place. Obscure prophetic matters will soon become clear as the noon day sun when final events begin to unfold. Life as we know it is about to make an abrupt turn, and on that day, the majesty and sovereign authority of Jesus Christ will begin to dawn on this planet. God's plan for the termination of sin can be understood *in advance* because the purpose of apocalyptic prophecy is the revelation of Jesus Christ. God wants His people to understand Him and His actions. We cannot love someone we do not know and cannot understand. When we see and experience the fulfillment of apocalyptic prophecy, our faith in God will be strengthened, not destroyed, even though the times will be very difficult. Jesus said, **"I have told you now before it happens, so that when it does happen you will believe."**[26]

Reach Your Own Conclusions

As you read through this commentary, keep in mind that my conclusions are a work in progress. Therefore, if you determine the four rules to be valid, let your interpretation of Daniel and Revelation be your own. If this volume proves to be helpful, great! If you can prove the four rules are false and you have a better set of rules, please share them with me. I would like to review them and the story they produce. After all, you and I will soon face the same common denominator regardless of what we believe. His name is Jesus Christ.

No prophetic conclusion is complete until *all* of the pieces of the puzzle have been included and properly assembled. This is perhaps the most difficult part of prophetic study: *The student has to understand all apocalyptic prophecies to be confident about the synthesis of his conclusions.* The amount of information involved in this endeavor is huge and because of this, I am often accused of stating ideas without substantiation. I freely confess that this occasionally happens because some of my conclusions are substantiated by other facts not directly involved with the matters at hand. Given the breadth of some themes, it is not helpful to explore supporting tangents at the time of presentation. If all tangents on a given topic are explored, the matter becomes so tedious or expansive that the volume of information can be overwhelming.

There are three ways to investigate this huge story. First, you can read and reread this volume. The second and third reading will be much more helpful than the first reading because the initial threshold for understanding the harmony of these concepts is quite high. Second, you can freely download numerous companion materials from our website at www.wake-up.org or you can purchase them in printed form if you wish. Last, if you are not able to make sense of the material presented in this volume, there is solace in knowing that God will soon reveal these matters to the world anyway. However, given the dramatic events that are going to soon occur, some exposure to the prophecies right now is far better than the hysteria and terror that will surely overtake the world when God's wrath begins. Understanding part of God's plans and purposes for the Great Tribulation is a privilege. Take advantage of it! Remember, the apostle Paul said, **"Do not treat** [Bible] **prophecies with contempt."**[27]

I hope that you will find this book helpful. Be sure to test my conclusions against the rules. Once you see the architecture in Daniel and Revelation and understand *how* God designed the seventeen prophecies, you will no longer need this commentary to help you understand *what* the prophecies say. With a little effort on your part, you will be able to help others see the wonderful story that now shines from the books of Daniel and Revelation.

Larry Wilson

June 2011

References

1. Galatians 3:28,29
2. James 1:1; 2:1
3. Daniel 12:9
4. John 16:2,3
5. John 15:20
6. Matthew 2:1,2
7. Ephesians 3:2-6, italics mine
8. Mark 7:8,9
9. John 5:22,23
10. John 10:30
11. Revelation 1:1
12. Exodus 19:5; Leviticus 18:28, 26:3; Deuteronomy 7:12
13. Matthew 23:38; 24:2; Luke 21:23; 1 Thessalonians 2:14-16
14. See Appendix B.
15. Galatians 3:28,29
16. Hebrews 8:6
17. Matthew 24:37
18. Exodus 20:3-17
19. Daniel 8:19; 11:27,29; Acts 1:7
20. Psalm 90:4; 2 Peter 3:8
21. John 16:12,13
22. 2 Corinthians 5:10; Ecclesiastes 12:14; Acts 17:31; Daniel 7:9,10
23. 1 Corinthians 15:4
24. John 16:13
25. 2 Thessalonians 2:10
26. John 14:29
27. 1 Thessalonians 5:20, insertion mine

Prophecy 1

The Metal Man

Daniel 2:29-45

Beginning Point in Time About 605 B.C.

Ending Point in Time: Second Coming of Jesus

Summary: The essence of this prophecy can be summed up in three sentences. Six kingdoms will follow the kingdom of Babylon. When Jesus establishes His kingdom on the new Earth (the seventh kingdom) it will not coexist with the kingdoms of man. He will create a new Heaven and a new Earth and His kingdom will endure forever.

Introduction: This prophecy forms the foundation upon which all other apocalyptic prophecies have been built. The chronology of seven world empires is laid out in very simple terms. The number seven indicates this is a complete story. Even though the vision says nothing about the amount of time required for fulfillment, approximately twenty-six centuries have passed since this prophecy began. A short discussion on the rules of interpretation is provided at the end of this prophecy.

The Sequence

{29} "As you were lying in your bed, O king, you were troubled about the future of your kingdom. The Most High God, the Revealer of Mysteries, saw your concerns and He has blessed you with a sweeping panorama of things to come.

Dan. 2:29

As for thee, O king, thy thoughts came into thy mind upon thy bed, what should come to pass hereafter: and he that revealeth secrets maketh known to thee what shall come to pass.

Jesus' Final Victory

Prophecy 1 - The Metal Man

Dan. 2:30

But as for me, this secret is not revealed to me for any wisdom that I have more than any living, but for their sakes that shall make known the interpretation to the king, and that thou mightest know the thoughts of thy heart.

{30} This mystery was revealed to me, not because I have greater wisdom than your wise men, for I am but a young man. The God of Heaven has revealed your dream to me so that you, O king, might know the meaning of your vision.

Dan. 2:31-33

Thou, O king, sawest, and behold a great image. This great image, whose brightness was excellent, stood before thee; and the form thereof was terrible. This image's head was of fine gold, his breast and his arms of silver, his belly and his thighs of brass, His legs of iron, his feet part of iron and part of clay.

{31} As you looked, there before you stood a large statue – an enormous statue of a metal man, awesome in size and gleaming in appearance. {32} The head of the statue was made of gold, its chest and arms of silver, its belly and thighs of bronze, {33} its legs of iron, its feet partly of iron and partly of brittle clay.

Dan. 2:34-35

Thou sawest till that a stone was cut out without hands, which smote the image upon his feet that

{34} You saw a rock cut out of a mountain,[1] but not by human hands.[2] The rock struck the statue at its feet of iron and clay and {35} the metal man was destroyed. The metal man was ground to powder[3] and the wind swept the powder away without leaving a trace, but the rock became a huge mountain that filled the Earth."[4]

Discussion

{36} "That was your dream, and the God of Heaven has revealed the meaning to me.

{37} "You, O king, are the king of kings. The God of Heaven has given you a kingdom and a throne. You have not achieved this preeminence according to personal prowess or talents. The God of Heaven has given you dominion, power, might and glory. {38} He has placed mankind, the beasts of the field and the birds of the air under your control. Wherever they live, He has made you ruler over them all. Your kingdom is represented by the head of gold.

---

were of iron and clay, and brake them to pieces. Then was the iron, the clay, the brass, the silver, and the gold, broken to pieces together, and became like the chaff of the summer threshingfloors; and the wind carried them away, that no place was found for them: and the stone that smote the image became a great mountain, and filled the whole earth.

Dan. 2:36
This is the dream; and we will tell the interpretation thereof before the king.

Dan. 2:37-38
Thou, O king, art a king of kings: for the God of heaven hath given thee a kingdom, power, and strength, and glory. And wheresoever the children of men dwell, the beasts of the field and the fowls of the heaven hath he given into thine

Prophecy 1 - The Metal Man

hand, and hath made thee ruler over them all. Thou art this head of gold.

Dan. 2:39
And after thee shall arise another kingdom inferior to thee, and another third kingdom of brass, which shall bear rule over all the earth.

Dan. 2:40
And the fourth kingdom shall be strong as iron: forasmuch as iron breaketh in pieces and subdueth all things: and as iron that breaketh all these, shall it break in pieces and bruise.

Dan. 2:41
And whereas thou sawest the feet and toes, part of potters' clay, and part of iron, the kingdom shall be divided; but there shall be in it of the strength of the iron, forasmuch as thou sawest the iron mixed with miry clay.

Dan. 2:42
And as the toes of the feet were part

{39} "Your kingdom will pass away and another kingdom, represented by the chest of silver will swallow up your kingdom as it rises to power, but the Medo-Persian Empire[5] will be inferior to your kingdom as silver is inferior to gold. Then, a third kingdom will arise and swallow up the Medo-Persians. This kingdom will be known as Grecia.[6] This kingdom, represented by the thighs of bronze, will rule over an even larger portion of Earth.

{40} "Later, a larger kingdom will swallow the Grecian Empire. The fourth kingdom will be called Rome[7] and it will be as strong as iron – a metal that is stronger than bronze, silver, or gold. This empire will be renowned for its use of iron weapons and it will crush everyone who defies its demands. Nevertheless, the kingdom of Rome will also pass away.

{41} "Then a fifth kingdom will appear upon the face of Earth. This kingdom will engulf Rome, but it will be different than the earlier empires. Instead of one sovereign authority, Europe will fragment into a mixture of strong nations and weak nations. Even though men will attempt to reconsolidate the world into one sovereign authority, strong nations will not be able to eliminate all of the weak nations because God will not permit it. For centuries, the kingdom represented by the feet will remain a mixture of strong and weak nations, even as iron cannot be mixed with brittle clay.

{42} "Before the Rock destroys the kingdoms of men, a sixth kingdom – also made up of iron and clay will appear. The kingdom is represented by ten toes. At the time of this kingdom, the whole world will be divided into ten sectors and ten kings will rule as puppet kings under the Antichrist, Lucifer.[8] Some kings will be strong as iron and other kings will be weak, like brittle clay.

{43} "The fifth and sixth kingdoms represent a fragmented world. There will be a mixture of strong and weak nations, and even though some nations will make treaties and form alliances with others in an effort to consolidate power, they will not remain united very long because iron does not mix with brittle clay.

{44} "During the days of Lucifer's puppet kings,[9] the Rock of Ages, Jesus Christ, the Son of God, will descend to Earth in clouds of glory. He will utterly destroy the kingdoms of men and no trace of them will remain whatsoever.[10] A thousand years later, Jesus will create a new Heaven and a new Earth and the meek will inherit the Earth.[11] The heirs of Abraham will live forever in Christ's kingdom which will endure forever.

{45} "This is the meaning of the vision of the Rock which was cut out of the holy mountain. The Rock and His coming kingdom are not of human origin. Human hands will have nothing to do with the establishment of God's kingdom. Just as Moses ground the golden calf into dust at Mt. Sinai,[12] the Rock of Ages will descend from Heaven at the appointed time and totally destroy the kingdoms of man. No trace of this sinful order will be seen again. The Most High God who rules over Heaven and Earth has shown King Nebuchadnezzar what will take place in days to come. The dream is true and the interpretation is certain."

Dan. 2:43
of iron, and part of clay, so the kingdom shall be partly strong, and partly broken.

Dan. 2:43
And whereas thou sawest iron mixed with miry clay, they shall mingle themselves with the seed of men: but they shall not cleave one to another, even as iron is not mixed with clay.

Dan. 2:44
And in the days of these kings shall the God of heaven set up a kingdom, which shall never be destroyed: and the kingdom shall not be left to other people, but it shall break in pieces and consume all these kingdoms, and it shall stand for ever.

Dan. 2:45
Forasmuch as thou sawest that the stone was cut out of the mountain without hands, and that it brake in pieces the iron, the brass, the clay,

the silver, and the gold; the great God hath made known to the king what shall come to pass hereafter: and the dream is certain, and the interpretation thereof sure.

The Rules of Interpretation

Consider how the Rules of Interpretation (discussed in the Introduction) are observed in this prophecy:

Rule One says an apocalyptic prophecy has a beginning point and ending point in time and the events within the prophecy occur in the order given. Notice how this prophecy begins at the time of Nebuchadnezzar, king of Babylon (605 B.C.) and ends at the Second Coming. There are seven chronological elements within this prophecy: Head, Chest, Thighs, Legs, Feet, Toes, and Rock. Geographically speaking, each kingdom swallows up the previous kingdom as time progresses. This progression continues until the whole world becomes involved during the kingdom of the ten toes. During the time of "these kings" (actually ten kings - Revelation 17:12), Jesus will return and destroy the whole world.

Rule Two says a fulfillment only occurs when all of the specifications are met, and this includes the order stated in the prophecy. History confirms the fall of Babylon to the Medes and Persians. The Medo-Persian Empire fell to the Grecians, and centuries later, the Grecians fell to the Romans. It is important to notice that some prophetic elements in this prophecy have been fulfilled. Chronologically speaking, we are living in the feet of the image, but this prophecy will not be fulfilled until the Rock of Ages destroys the kingdoms of men at the Second Coming. We can say that this prophecy has been "under way" for about twenty-six centuries!

Rule Three says Apocalyptic language can be literal, analogous, or symbolic. There are symbolic elements in this prophecy because *relevant* Scripture defines the symbols. For example, Daniel told the king that the head of gold represented the Babylonian Empire and that the chest of silver represented a kingdom that would succeed Babylon, etc. Many people, unaware of Rule Three, distort Scripture by declaring things to be symbolic which God has not made symbolic. The key point is that when God creates a symbol, He clearly defines the meaning of that symbol. When people use definitions for symbols for which God has not provided a relevant text, personal bias, confusion, and manipulation result. The Bible either speaks for itself or it does not, for who on Earth has the authority to speak for it?

Rule Four is not used in this prophecy.

References:

1. Psalms 15:1; 43:3; 68:16; Daniel 9:16 Note: In ancient times, the grand and lofty heights of mountains were believed to be the dwelling places of various gods. Even Israel's God descended to Mt. Sinai, and later, dwelt on Mt. Moriah. (Exodus 19:18; 2 Chronicles 3:1; Psalm 121:1)

2. Joel 2:1-11; Revelation 19:11-21 Note: To draw close to their gods, ancient peoples often worshiped on the highest hills or mountain tops. (1 Kings 14:23; Jeremiah 3:6; Ezekiel 18:15) The idea of a rock cut out of a mountain without human hands was both elegant and simple. God (the holy mountain) would send His Son (a divine rock, a piece of Himself, not of human origin) to destroy the kingdoms of men and establish a divine kingdom. This vision declares two profound truths: First, God raises up kingdoms and He takes them down when they become hopelessly degenerate. Second, at the appointed time, Jesus will return and destroy the kingdoms of man to establish His own. *The kingdoms of men and the kingdom of God will not coexist.*

3. Exodus 32:20; Deuteronomy 9:21; Jeremiah 4:11-25; Matthew 13:36-42; Revelation 19:19-21

4. Revelation 21:1-8,27

5. Daniel 8:20

6. Daniel 8:21

7. Luke 3:1; Romans 1:15

8. Revelation 17:12

9. Revelation 17:12-14; 19:19

10. Revelation 16:17-21; 19:15-21

11. Matthew 5:5

12. Exodus 32:20

Prophecy 2

The Little Horn Power

Daniel 7:1-12

Beginning Point in Time: About 605 B.C.

Ending Point in Time: The Second Coming of Jesus

Summary: The essence of this prophecy can be summarized in four sentences. God has linked events in Heaven with events on Earth so that we can determine our chronological position within His expansive plans. Therefore, the fall of the papacy on Earth (1798) is synchronized with the exaltation of Jesus in Heaven. After Jesus receives sovereign power, He will open the books of record (1844) and judge the dead. Afterwards, the papacy will recover and speak boastfully until it is destroyed with fire.

Introduction: This vision covers the same time span as the vision in Prophecy 1. This vision amplifies Daniel 2 using a technique called "repetition and enlargement." When this prophecy is properly aligned with Daniel 2, Daniel 8, and Luke 3, it is easy to demonstrate from Scripture that the four beasts in this vision represent the chronological empires of Babylon, Medo-Persia, Grecia, and Rome. Secular history also affirms the chronological progression of these empires. Because the Bible and secular history are in harmony and because Prophecy 1 and Prophecy 2 are in harmony, we have a prophetic foundation that is "rock solid."

Some people have trouble with the claim that this prophecy represents four world empires because they believe the empires of Babylon, Medo-Persia, Grecia, and Rome were not *world* empires. For example, the empire of Babylon did not rule over China or India or Africa in its day. Therefore, they maintain that Babylon was not a true global empire. The problem with this viewpoint is that the book of Daniel deals with the world as it pertains to the advancement of God's truth and His people. The book of Daniel does not include the *whole* world until the *whole* world becomes involved with God's truth and His people! If you study maps of these ancient empires you will discover that Babylon was swallowed by a larger empire, and Medo-Persia was swallowed by a larger empire, and Rome was also swallowed by yet a larger empire (the feet of the metal man represents Europe). This geographically expanding progression of kingdoms continues until the entire world is involved. The kingdom represented by the toes in Daniel 2 is the first kingdom in this prophecy that geographically includes the whole world.

Prophecy 2 adds several new elements to the information provided in Prophecy 1. For example, this prophecy inserts a period of 1,260 years into the kingdom represented by the feet of the metal man. This huge block of time is important to the final generation because it forces this prophecy out of antiquity in one giant step. This prophecy teaches that 1798 is a very important year, both in Heaven and on Earth. Further, this prophecy proves that God's lengthy plan to destroy the metal man and establish His kingdom on Earth is still on track. Think about this: Even though this prophecy spans more than 2,600 years, it contains an end time nugget of information that will prove to be indispensable when the final generation arrives.

The Little Horn Power - Prophecy 2

The Sequence

{1} In the first year of Belshazzar (the last king of Babylon) I was about eighty-five years of age. I received a vision one night and this is the substance of my dream: {2} In my vision I looked, and I saw the four winds of Heaven churning up the Mediterranean Sea. {3} As I watched, four enormous beasts, each different from the others, came up out of the sea.

> **Dan. 7:1-3**
> *In the first year of Belshazzar king of Babylon Daniel had a dream and visions of his head upon his bed: then he wrote the dream, and told the sum of the matters. Daniel spake and said, I saw in my vision by night, and, behold, the four winds of the heaven strove upon the great sea. And four great beasts came up from the sea, diverse one from another.*

{4} The first beast (Babylon) looked like a lion, but it had powerful wings like an eagle which allowed it to swiftly catch and devour its prey. As I watched, the lion's wings were torn off and it could no longer fly and conquer its neighbors. The lion then focused on fortifying his kingdom. He paid no attention to warnings about arrogance and self-sufficiency. Over time, the lion became pompous and disgusting in God's sight even though Nebuchadnezzar finally recognized the sovereign authority of the Most High God.[1]

> **Dan. 7:4**
> *The first was like a lion, and had eagle's wings: I beheld till the wings thereof were plucked, and it was lifted up from the earth, and made stand upon the feet as a man, and a man's heart was given to it.*

{5} Then, I saw a second beast which looked like a bear. As I watched, I noticed that one shoulder was higher than the other.

> This feature indicates that one side of this kingdom (the Persians) would ascend higher than the other (the Medes) and "shoulder" greater responsibility.[2]

> **Dan. 7:5**
> *And behold another beast, a second, like to a bear, and it raised up itself*

Jesus' Final Victory

Prophecy 2 - The Little Horn Power

on one side, and it had three ribs in the mouth of it between the teeth of it: and they said thus unto it, Arise, devour much flesh.

Dan. 7:6

After this I beheld, and lo another, like a leopard, which had upon the back of it four wings of a fowl; the beast had also four heads; and dominion was given to it.

Dan. 7:7

After this I saw in the night visions, and behold a fourth beast, dreadful and terrible, and strong exceedingly; and it had great iron teeth: it devoured and brake in pieces, and stamped the residue with the feet of it: and it was diverse from all the beasts that were before it; and it had ten horns.

Dan. 7:8

I considered the horns, and, behold, there

When the bear came up out of the sea, it had three ribs between its teeth.

These ribs represented the carcasses of Lydia, Egypt, and Babylon – three nations which resisted the bear's quest for dominion.

The Most High God told the bear, "Rise up, eat your fill of flesh, and rule the world" and it did. For awhile, the bear could not be stopped.

{6} After this, I saw a beast that looked something like a leopard, but it had four great wings like a bird. Because it had four wings, it could travel farther and faster than the lion. It was given power over the bear and it subdued its enemy very quickly. This beast (Greece) also had four heads. I later learned this empire would be divided into four sectors and each sector would have its own king.

{7} After seeing the lion, bear, and leopard, a fourth beast stood before me. This beast was unusual, terrifying, and very powerful. This beast did not resemble any animal I had seen before. It had large iron teeth that crushed and devoured its victims. It utterly destroyed its enemies as it subdued them, so that nothing remained. This monster was ruthless in its conquest and it had ten horns protruding from its head.

{8} While I was thinking about the ten horns, a little horn began to grow out of the monster's head. The little horn grew up among the ten horns and as the little horn grew in size, it uprooted three of the original ten horns. The little horn continued to grow in strength. It received power and authority to rule over the seven remaining horns. The little horn (actually, the eighth horn) had eyes and a mouth like a man. The eyes indicated that it could see (comprehend) things the other horns could not understand and its mouth spoke boastfully. The eighth horn was filled with arrogance and self-exaltation.[3] It claimed to speak for God and the other horns acquiesced to its authority.

{9} Then, I looked up. I saw an enormous courtroom in Heaven. In the middle of the courtroom was a great white throne and twenty-four lesser thrones[4] were arranged in a circle around it. As I watched, I saw a being enveloped in brilliant light enter the courtroom and the Ancient of Days, God the Father, took His seat. His clothing was so bright that I could not make out the details. His presence was as white as snow and the hair of His head was gloriously bright – like fluffy wool. His throne sparkled with lights, it looked like it was on fire. Glorious angels surrounded the thrones in concentric rings that looked like rings of fire.

{10} A huge procession of radiant angels filed into the courtroom. The procession looked like molten gold; a flowing river of fire. Thousands upon thousands of heavenly beings attended the Father and ten thousand times ten thousand angels stood reverently before Him. After this huge assembly stopped moving, the court was seated and the proceedings began. Immediately, the Ancient of Days issued a restraining order on behalf of His saints. At that moment, God broke the power of the eighth horn so that it could not persecute God's saints any longer. Then, Jesus came before the Father and after a special investigation occurred,[5] Jesus was found worthy to receive The Book of Life which was sealed with seven seals. A short time after this, when the third seal was broken, the books of record were opened and Jesus began to examine the recorded life of each person who had died. At the end of His thorough review, Jesus made a decision about each person.[6] Jesus determined who would receive eternal life and who would not.

---

came up among them another little horn, before whom there were three of the first horns plucked up by the roots: and, behold, in this horn were eyes like the eyes of man, and a mouth speaking great things.

Dan. 7:9

I beheld till the thrones were cast down, and the Ancient of days did sit, whose garment was white as snow, and the hair of his head like the pure wool: his throne was like the fiery flame, and his wheels as burning fire.

Dan. 7:10

A fiery stream issued and came forth from before him: thousand thousands ministered unto him, and ten thousand times ten thousand stood before him: the judgment was set, and the books were opened.

> **Dan. 7:11-12**
> *I beheld then because of the voice of the great words which the horn spake: I beheld even till the beast was slain, and his body destroyed, and given to the burning flame. As concerning the rest of the beasts, they had their dominion taken away: yet their lives were prolonged for a season and time.*

> **Dan. 7:13-14**
> *I saw in the night visions, and, behold, one like the Son of man came with the clouds of heaven, and came to the Ancient of days, and they brought him near before him. And there was given him dominion, and glory, and a kingdom, that all people, nations, and languages, should serve him: his dominion is an everlasting dominion, which shall not pass away, and his kingdom that which shall not be destroyed.*

{11} Then my gaze was redirected to Earth. I saw the eighth horn speaking boastful words against the Most High God a second time.[7] I kept watching this horn and its host, the monster beast, until they were destroyed. They were thrown into a lake of fire at the Second Coming.[8] {12} I should also mention that when the governments represented by the lion, the bear, and the leopard were stripped of their authority, the people who made up these empires were not destroyed. Their descendants after them continued to live until the Second Coming.

Discussion

{13} After this sequence of events ended, I saw another scene that related to the proceedings that took place in Heaven's courtroom. I saw a glorious man who did not look like an angel. Instead, He looked like me, a son of man. Many angels accompanied Him. He approached the Ancient of Days and was led into His presence. {14} After a thorough investigation, He was found worthy to receive divine authority, glory, and sovereign power.[9] A time will come when His sovereignty fills Earth, and all peoples, nations, and men of every language will worship Him.[10] His dominion will be an everlasting dominion that will not pass away, and His kingdom is one that will never be destroyed.

The Little Horn Power - Prophecy 2

{15} After watching these glorious scenes, I was deeply troubled. I wondered how this vision related to my people who were languishing as slaves in Babylon. I wanted to know how the scenes I had seen related to the promise that God would return my people to Jerusalem after seventy years.

{16} So, I approached an angel who was standing in the heavenly courtroom and asked him to explain the true meaning of this vision. He gave me this explanation:

{17} "The four great beasts you saw are four empires that will appear on Earth. Starting with the lion, these empires will rise out of a sea of humanity."

> In other words, each empire will rise out of existing nations, languages, and peoples.[11] Each empire will rule over an increasingly larger portion of Earth than the one before it. The four winds (mentioned in verse 2) represent God's four judgments.[12] When each empire becomes hopelessly decadent, God will use His four judgments to eliminate the current kingdom and establish another.

{18} "At the appointed time, the Most High God will purify Earth and give the whole world over to His saints and they will possess it forever – yes, forever and ever."

{19} I was full of questions. I especially wanted to know the meaning of the monster beast, the fourth beast, which was different from all the others – having unbreakable iron teeth and indestructible bronze claws – the beast that crushed and devoured its victims and trampled whatever was left under its feet. {20} I also wanted to know about the ten horns that were on the head of this beast and the little horn that uprooted three of the ten horns. I

Dan. 7:15
I Daniel was grieved in my spirit in the midst of my body, and the visions of my head troubled me.

Dan. 7:16
I came near unto one of them that stood by, and asked him the truth of all this. So he told me, and made me know the interpretation of the things.

Dan. 7:17
These great beasts, which are four, are four kings, which shall arise out of the earth.

Dan. 7:18
But the saints of the most High shall take the kingdom, and possess the kingdom for ever, even for ever and ever.

Dan. 7:19-20
Then I would know the truth of the fourth beast, which was diverse from all the others,

exceeding dreadful, whose teeth were of iron, and his nails of brass; which devoured, brake in pieces, and stamped the residue with his feet;And of the ten horns that were in his head, and of the other which came up, and before whom three fell; even of that horn that had eyes, and a mouth that spake very great things, whose look was more stout than his fellows.

Dan. 7:21-22

I beheld, and the same horn made war with the saints, and prevailed against them; Until the Ancient of days came, and judgment was given to the saints of the most High; and the time came that the saints possessed the kingdom.

Dan. 7:23

Thus he said, The fourth beast shall be the fourth kingdom upon earth, which shall be diverse

wanted to know the truth about the eighth horn because it had eyes like a man and a mouth that spoke boastfully, insulting God's authority.

{21} During my vision, I saw the eighth horn making war against the saints for a long period of time and it kept on defeating them {22} until the Ancient of Days took His seat and issued a restraining order. After He issued the restraining order, the eighth horn lost its ability to hurt the saints of God. Over time, it became clear that the restraining order was temporary. The eighth horn *regained* its power and resumed its persecution of God's saints. As it regains power, it will continue to speak boastfully and insult God's sovereign authority again. I learned that the eighth horn will not cease its opposition against God, His truth, and His saints until fire destroys it at the Second Coming. There will be no rest for God's saints until false religion is destroyed and Jesus establishes His kingdom. Then, and only then, will the meek have peace on Earth.

{23} The angel told me that the monster beast will be the fourth empire to appear on Earth. This kingdom will be called Rome. Rome's governance will be different from the previous kingdoms of Babylon, Medo-Persia, and Grecia. Rome will hire mercenary soldiers and even though it will not have a monarch, its ruler will exercise power over life and death. Rome will become renowned for its use of iron weapons and this kingdom will control a larger territory than any empire before it. God will give Rome the power to devour its enemies, crushing any tribe or nation that defies its authority. When the Roman Empire fills up its cup of sin, God will remove Rome's power – even as empires before it were removed from power.

{24} The angel continued, "The ten horns on the monster beast represent ten ethnic kings who will rise up from within the Roman Empire. These kings will hate the ruling government at Rome. Over time, these kings will break the Roman Empire apart, piece by piece, and they will terminate Rome's authority by A.D. 476. These tribal nations will be called: Goths, Ostrogoths, Vandals, Burgundians, Franks, Lombards, Alameni, Suevi, Anglo-Saxons, and Heruli. After Rome's power is broken into fragments, a different type of king, represented by the little horn, will rise. Unlike the tribal kings represented by the ten horns, the eighth horn will be a religious king whose throne will endure for more than twelve centuries.

"Shortly after the sixth century A.D. begins, Emperor Justinian will endeavor to reunify the old Roman Empire by creating the Holy Roman Empire. To purify and unify the empire, Justinian will give special authority to the pope in A.D. 533. This authority will give the pope (and his appointed prelates) power to determine who is an orthodox Christian and who is a heretic, but three of the original ten kings will hate the church because of religious differences. The Heruli, Ostrogoths, and Vandals will show no respect for Justinian or church authorities in Rome. These tribal nations will be uprooted by A.D. 538 and the pope will begin to exercise civil authority in A.D. 538. This process explains how the eighth horn will dominate the other seven for 1,260 years. (See Additional Note at the end of this chapter.)

{25} "The eighth horn rising out of the fourth beast represents the Roman Catholic Church. Its leaders will falsely think that they can usurp God's sovereign authority. The church will insult the Most High God by creating and imposing false doctrines on its subjects. The special authority Justinian granted to the church will establish a church/state precedent which the church will use to persecute those who refuse to obey its doctrines. Wielding absolute authority over Christians in Europe, the hierarchy of the Roman Catholic Church will think that it has the authority to change the

from all kingdoms, and shall devour the whole earth, and shall tread it down, and break it in pieces.

Dan. 7:24
And the ten horns out of this kingdom are ten kings that shall arise: and another shall rise after them; and he shall be diverse from the first, and he shall subdue three kings.

Dan. 7:25
And he shall speak great words against the most High, and shall wear out the saints of the most High, and think to change times and laws:

> *and they shall be given into his hand until a time and times and the dividing of time.*

day of worship which the Most High God has plainly declared to be the seventh day of the week.[13] The Catholic Church will also decide to eliminate the second commandment from the Ten Commandments. By dividing the tenth commandment into two parts, the Catholic Catechism will give the *illusion* that it contains ten commandments.[14] The Ancient of Days will permit the Roman Catholic Church to persecute His saints for a time, times, and half a time – 1,260 years (according to Rule Four[15]). Be assured that God will look after His saints while they are in the wilderness. He has prepared a place for them.

You may wonder why God allows the eighth horn to have power over the saints for 1,260 years. Strange as this may sound, persecution keeps the faithful – *faith-full*. Persecution separates nominal Christians from thoughtful and prayerful Christians. Persecution makes the Word of God come "alive" and for the honest in heart, truth becomes more important than the traditions of men. Persecution purifies the heart and soul and the Comforter brings great peace to the faithful.

> **Dan. 7:26**
> *But the judgment shall sit, and they shall take away his dominion, to consume and to destroy it unto the end.*

{26} "The 1,260 years will end when the court is seated and the power of the Roman Catholic Church is temporarily terminated.

Naturally, human beings cannot see what is taking place in Heaven, so God has linked events in Heaven with events on Earth. I like to call this linkage the "Heaven-Earth Linkage Law." When prophetic events transpire on Earth, "linked events" occur in Heaven. For example, when the 1,260 years allotted to the eighth horn comes to an end, the courtroom scene described in verses 9 and 10 will occur in Heaven. We know this because the Father will issue a restraining order against the eighth horn. As a result, the power of the Roman Catholic Church will abruptly end. The church will lose control over the nations of Europe. The pope will be captured and exiled to France in February 1798. This event on Earth is linked to the restraining order the Father issued in Heaven.

The little horn will later recover from the deadly wound it received in 1798.[16] A treaty (actually the Lateran Pacts of 1929) will be ratified in June 1929 and Vatican City will be returned to the papacy. Over time, the Roman Catholic Church will regain world respect and recognition. By the twenty-first century, the church will have diplomatic ties with more than 178 nations. This international prominence will play an important role during the Great Tribulation.

During the devastating judgments described as the first four trumpets of Revelation 8, the religions of the world will come together in an effort to appease God so that His wrath will cease. World leaders will select the pope to be the leader of a new government. Because the world will be in an extreme crisis, Babylon (the new government) will achieve world control without firing a single bullet. Babylon will create laws mandating moral behavior and the worship of God. Some of Babylon's laws will be contrary to the Ten Commandments, specifically, the fourth commandment. Babylon, under the leadership of the pope, will persecute those who refuse to obey its laws for forty-two months.[17] Even though the saints will be persecuted and millions will die as martyrs for their faith,[18] Babylon will come to a horrible end. Jesus will annihilate His enemies at the Second Coming.

{27} "Ultimately, the powers of darkness will prevail until the end, but do not be discouraged. Jesus will destroy them and create a new Heaven and a new Earth. Then, the world will be handed over to the saints. God's children will love, worship, and willingly obey their King forever."

We know that the courtroom scene in Heaven occurred in 1798 because there is a "linked" event on Earth. The power of the papacy was broken that year. A few years later (1844), Jesus opened the books of record (this date will be discussed in Prophecy 3) and began to judge the dead.

{28} This is the end of the matter. I was deeply troubled because I had never heard anything like this. This vision was so different from what I expected about the future that my face turned pale. I kept these things to myself, for I did not want my closest friends to think I had lost my mind.

Dan. 7:27
And the kingdom and dominion, and the greatness of the kingdom under the whole heaven, shall be given to the people of the saints of the most High, whose kingdom is an everlasting kingdom, and all dominions shall serve and obey him.

Dan. 7:28
Hitherto is the end of the matter. As for me Daniel, my cogitations much troubled me, and my countenance changed in me: but I kept the matter in my heart.

The Exaltation of Jesus

A few words about the exaltation of Jesus are necessary. Many people do not appreciate the importance of Daniel 7:13,14 because they do not understand *the process* that Jesus voluntarily endured to redeem mankind. A book could be written on this amazing topic, but the essence of Christ's humiliation and exaltation is this: When Adam and Eve sinned, Jesus went to the Father and offered to die in their place. Remember, Adam and Eve were to be executed on the day that they sinned.[19] Even before the creation of life, the Father foreknew that sin would occur.[20] Therefore, He had a plan of redemption that could be implemented when necessary.[21] The Father would have implemented the plan of redemption for the rebellious angels had they been willing to repent, but they defiantly refused. Lucifer and the angels who followed him committed the unpardonable sin, making redemption impossible. (See Prophecy 12.)

God's plan to redeem mankind is intricate because He resolves several issues at the same time. It takes some effort to sort out these issues and understand their purposes. For example, God does not want sin to occur again, so God is resolving the current problem of sin in such a way that no one will ever want to sin again! God has allowed sin to mature because He wants everyone to see how the malignant curse imposes increasing decadence and degeneracy on each succeeding generation. God wants the universe to see what sinners will become and do; when sin is given enough time. God also wants the universe to understand that He is a God of love and His laws and actions always spring from love for His children. God wants the universe to understand that He will not use His foreknowledge to manipulate any outcome that is favorable to Himself. He also wants everyone to know that His subjects really do have the power of choice.

When Jesus went to the Father and offered to pay the price for their sin, the Father revealed the huge price that redemption required. I am sure that Jesus listened thoughtfully, and after hearing the terms required for man's redemption, He submitted to three conditions. Whatever the Father wanted Jesus to become, He would become. Jesus agreed to become a man. Whatever the Father wanted Jesus to do, He would do. Jesus would live as an inferior among sinners (poor and having no human father), resist every temptation, die a horrible death, and cease to exist. Finally, whatever the Father wanted Jesus to say, He would say – no matter the consequences. Jesus agreed to speak the Father's words – no matter what.[22] When Jesus accepted these terms and conditions, the Father made a covenant with Jesus.[23] *If* Jesus perfectly carried out the Father's plan, the Father would (a) resurrect Jesus from the second death,[24] (b) give Jesus authority over His church,[25] (c) give the saints and the world to Jesus,[26] and (d) show the universe that Jesus is His equal – that Jesus is Almighty God just as the Father is Almighty God.[27] Incidently, this last item explains why the last book in the Bible is called "The Revelation of Jesus Christ."

The price for the redemption of sinners is unbelievably high. Jesus had to forfeit His eternal life for sinners and cease to exist. Jesus humbled Himself on the day that sin began by becoming a subject (a son) of the Father.[28] This is why Jesus is called, "The Son (subject) of God." Four thousand years after Adam and Eve sinned, Jesus took a deeper step into humility. Jesus not only became a man, He became the object of endless ridicule. Later, Jesus stooped even lower. He died on the cross as a criminal. Jesus could give nothing more. He gave up everything He had, even His eternal life for our redemption. On the basis of Jesus' sinless life and perfect conformity to His will, the Father "righteously" resurrected Jesus and took Him to Heaven. The Father coronated Jesus as man's high priest.[29] For the past 2,000 years, Jesus has presided over His church in much the same way that Melchizedek presided over his subjects.[30]

The humiliation and exaltation of Jesus is important to understand. When the power of the little horn was broken (1798), Jesus went before the Father and after being found worthy, He was promoted to the throne of God. Instead of sitting at the right hand of the Father as a prince and High Priest, Daniel 7:13,14 indicates that Jesus was coronated as a co-regent king with the Father and given sovereign power! In Prophecy 6, we will learn that Jesus was also found worthy to receive the book sealed with seven seals (The Book of Life) when He was given the seven attributes of sovereign power.[31] Think about this. Sovereign power can only be bestowed once. Once a person has sovereign authority, how can he be given greater power?

The Father gave Jesus sovereign power in 1798 because Jesus began a new phase of work in Heaven that requires sovereign power. The Father needed someone to (a) resolve the sin problem on Earth, (b) exonerate the character and government of God, and (c) judge each sinner compassionately. The worthiness of Jesus for this task is beyond question. He is the only person in the universe who can perfectly complete all three tasks.

Jesus began exercising sovereign power in 1798. He has to accomplish several objectives which the Father requires Him to do. For example, as sovereign king, Jesus is free to fulfill the requirements of each of the seven seals according to His own wisdom and authority. Jesus is free to glorify the Father according to His own wisdom and He is free to resolve many questions about God's government that could not be answered otherwise. Jesus can pass eternal judgment on human beings as He desires. He is free to conduct Heaven's business in whatever way He deems appropriate as long as He produces the objectives which the plan of redemption requires. At the end of the 1,000 years,[32] Jesus will complete His special work. He will fully exonerate the character and ways of God and in turn, the Father will glorify Jesus before the universe as a co-eternal God. Jesus went into the depths of humiliation to save sinners from the second death and in the end, the Father will exalt Him as an equal!

At the end of the 1,000 years, Paul's prediction will be fulfilled: **"Then the end will come, when he** [Jesus] **hands over the kingdom to God the Father after he has destroyed all dominion, authority and power. For he** [Jesus] **must reign until he has put all his enemies under his feet. The last enemy to be destroyed is death. For he** [the Father] **'has put everything under his feet.'** **Now when it says that 'everything' has been put under him, it is clear that this does not include God himself, who put everything under Christ. When he** [Jesus has destroyed the works of sin] **has done this, then the Son himself will** [surrender His sovereign power and] **be made subject to him who put everything under him, so that God** [the Father] **may be all in all** [the greatest of all].**"**[33]

The Rules of Interpretation

Please consider how the Four Rules of Interpretation (discussed in the Introduction) are observed in this prophecy:

Rule One says an apocalyptic prophecy has a beginning point and ending point in time and the events within the prophecy occur in the order given. This prophecy begins with a lion (Babylon) rising from the sea and it ends with the beasts being burned in the fire (Second Coming).   The events in this vision occur in chronological order:

a. Lion rises from the sea
b. Bear rises from the sea
c. Leopard rises from the sea
d. Monster beast with ten horns rises from the sea
e. A little horn appears and uproots three horns
f. Eighth horn speaks boastfully and persecutes the saints for 1,260 years
g. Thrones are arranged in Heaven and the Ancient of Days takes His seat
h. Books opened
i. Little horn returns to power, speaks boastfully
j. Beasts burned in the fire

This vision covers the same time span as the vision of Daniel 2 (Prophecy 1), but this vision adds several important details to the time period represented by the feet of iron and clay.

Rule Two says a fulfillment only occurs when all of the specifications are met, and this includes the order stated in the prophecy. This vision has not been fulfilled. It is still underway. The four beasts have come and are almost gone, the power of the eighth horn was broken in 1798, and Jesus has been exalted, but we are waiting for the eighth horn to return to power and speak boastfully! When the religious and political powers of this world are destroyed at the Second Coming, this vision will be fulfilled.

Rule Three says apocalyptic language can be literal, analogous, or symbolic. There are symbolic elements in this prophecy because *relevant* Scripture defines the symbols. The angel told Daniel, **"The four great beasts are four kingdoms that will rise from the earth."**[34] Notice the clarity when God defines a symbol: **"The fourth beast is a fourth kingdom that will appear on Earth. It will be different from all the other kingdoms and will devour the whole earth, trampling it down and crushing it. The ten horns are ten kings who will come from this kingdom. After them another king will arise, different from the**

the earlier ones; he will subdue three kings."[35] History leaves no doubt concerning the identity of the fourth beast or the little horn that uprooted three horns. When God creates a symbol, He clearly defines the meaning of that symbol. This simple process eliminates personal bias, confusion, and theological putty. The Bible will speak plainly and clearly; if it is permitted to do so.

Rule Four says the presence or absence of the Jubilee Calendar determines how God measures time. **"He** [the little horn] **will speak against the Most High and oppress his saints and try to change the set times and the laws. The saints will be handed over to him for a time, times and half a time."**[36] A short presentation on God's Jubilee Calendar is offered in Appendix A. For now, please consider this: The ancients believed planet Earth stood still and the Sun orbited around the Earth. One complete cycle of the Sun (a solar year) was called a year or "a time." The Hebrew word used in Daniel 7:25 for "a time" is *'hiddan'* and it means a defined period of time – such as a solar year. For purposes of calculation, the Jews divided a year into 360 degrees of arc. This technique was most likely derived from observing the number of "sun widths" in a solar year. Each day, when the Sun rises, it appears to move through the twelve constellations by approximately one "sun width." Thus, a solar year consists of four seasons and each season is counted as 90 "Sun widths." For planting purposes, a solar calendar is very useful and even today, many people plant crops according to a solar calendar. Furthermore, a solar calendar was useful to Israel because God's year can be anywhere from 355 to 384 days in length depending on the cycles of the moon. Therefore, the Jews regarded a *calculated* year or solar year to be 360 days because the Sun *appears* to move about 1 degree of arc per day. This forces the absolute distance between two Spring Equinoxes to be 360 degrees. Comparing Revelation 12:6 with 12:14 we find that 1,260 days equals a time, times, and half a time. The math becomes easy to understand because 360 degrees + 720 degrees + 180 degrees equals 1,260 degrees/days.

Rule Four requires all time periods to be translated according to a day for a year if God's Jubilee Calendar is in operation. (1437 B.C. to 1994) Therefore, the time, times, and half a time in Daniel 7:25 equals 1,260 days which must be translated as a day for a year. History easily confirms the validity of this calculation.

Additional Note

When Justinian I (A.D. 483-565) became the ruler of what remained of the Roman Empire in A.D. 527, he aspired to rebuild and restore the empire to its former glory. At the time, Europe and northern Africa had splintered into tribal nations and the city of Rome had been pillaged and burned just fifty years earlier. Western civilization had been fragmented by religion, ethnicity, culture, and language. Justinian knew that he could not directly impose Roman authority on the tribal nations that had pulled the empire apart. He did not have the military might to force them into submission. However, Justinian believed there was an *indirect* way to unify and rebuild the Roman Empire. About A.D. 533, he created this law: *Everyone under the jurisdiction of the empire is required to be a Christian.*

Justinian thought that Christianity would help unify the Roman Empire. As religions go, Christianity was a good thing. Christianity exalted honesty and integrity, and it had one Supreme God (unlike the polytheistic religion of the Romans). When Justinian imposed his demand that everyone under the jurisdiction of the empire must be a Christian, he gave authority to the head of the Christian Church *at Rome* (the pope) to determine who was a Christian and who was not. (This was a political solution that would later prove disastrous for more than twelve centuries.) The pope could not implement Justinian's law in A.D. 533 because three tribal nations (the Ostrogoths, Heruli, and Vandals) were waging war against his authority. (These tribal nations were opposed to certain religious views which the pope had endorsed and they wanted to kill the pope for corrupting the Christian faith.) To make matters worse, Justinian's law and his deference to the pope made them furious.

A series of deadly battles occurred between 534 and 537 and eventually, the Heruli and the Vandals were subdued. In A.D. 537, the Ostrogoths set siege to the city of Rome hoping they could starve the city and capture the pope (who was inside), but Justinian's general, Belesarius, arrived at Rome and broke the siege. Pope Silverius escaped without harm. After the rescue, Belesarius discovered some correspondence indicating that Pope Silverius had been secretly negotiating with the Ostrogoths to end the siege and Belesarius was outraged. Belesairus removed Silverius from his position as pope and demoted him to the position of monk. This happened in March, A.D. 537.

After he removed Silverius from office, Belesarius appointed Vigilius to be the next pope. About a year later, in A.D. 538, Pope Vigilius began to exercise authority that previous popes did not have. As you might understand, this enormous power was abused and over time, the Roman Catholic Church dominated all of Europe! *Justinian created a law that had unintended consequences for 1,260 years!* The devil made a hand puppet out of the Church. He took control of the Church and through it, found a way to persecute God's people. **"When the dragon** [the devil] **saw that he had been hurled to the Earth** [cast out of Heaven on Resurrection Sunday]**, he pursued the woman** [the people of God] **who had given birth to the male child** [in 4 B.C.]**. The woman was given the two wings of a great eagle, so that she might** [escape] **fly to the place prepared for her in the desert, where she would be taken care of for a time, times and half a time,** [1,260 years] **out of the serpent's reach."**[37]

The 1,260 years ended when General Berthier, obeying orders from Napoleon, entered Vatican City and arrested the pope on February 20, 1798 on the grounds that the pope refused to renounce temporal (civil) authority over Europe. On March 7, 1798, Napoleon's Army entered Rome and established the Roman Republic. The civil power of the papacy over Europe was finally broken. So, calculating 1,260 years backward from 1798, we can see that Lucifer begin chasing God's people in A.D. 538. Using the Church as a hand puppet, John saw the devil chase the woman into the wilderness for 1,260 years and history affirms that "the persecuted" eventually became "the persecutors" of the woman.

References

1. Daniel 4
2. Daniel 8:3,20
3. For an end time parallel, see Revelation 13:5,6.
4. Revelation 4:4; 5:11
5. Revelation 5
6. Ecclesiastes 12:14; 2 Corinthians 5:10
7. Revelation 13:5
8. Revelation 19:20; 20:10
9. Ephesians 1:7-10,22
10. Isaiah 45:22-24
11. Revelation 17:15
12. Ezekiel 14:12-21; Revelation 6:8
13. Exodus 20:8-11
14. Compare the current Second Edition English Translation of the Catechism of the Catholic Church with Exodus 20:3-17.
15. Leviticus 25, 26; Revelation 12:6,14; Ezekiel 4:5,6; Numbers 14:34
16. Revelation 13:3
17. Revelation 13:4,5
18. Revelation 6:9
19. Genesis 2:17
20. See Prophecy 6 for a discussion on God's foreknowledge. See also pages 29-37 in my book, *A Study on the Seven Seals and the 144,000*.
21. Revelation 13:8
22. John 14:10,24; 17:8
23. Psalm 2:7-12
24. John 10:17,18; Acts 2:32; 1 Corinthians 6:14
25. Ephesians 1:22; Matthew 28:18
26. John 17:6
27. John 5:22; Revelation 14:7; 11:17; Philippians 2:6-11
28. Psalm 2:7-12; Hebrews 1:5; 5:5

29. Hebrews 8:1

30. Genesis 14:18-20; Hebrews 7:12-17 Note: When writing to the Hebrews, Paul used Melchizedek, to emphasize a few key points about Jesus. The Jews understood that "father Abraham" regarded Melchizedek as a servant of the Most High God because Abraham gave his tithe to him. Abraham's action demonstrated two things. First, Abraham regarded Melchizedek as a priest of the *same* God that he worshiped. Second, Abraham realized that the Most High God had placed someone on Earth in a higher position (as priest and king) than himself. Paul also pointed out that there is no record of Melchizedek's birth or death. To the Jewish mind, this was a huge puzzle because lineage separated the Jews from the Gentiles, the clean from the unclean! Paul used these facts to demonstrate that Jesus is to the Jews what Melchizedek was to Abraham – that is, in matters pertaining to God, superior. Melchizedek and Jesus were divinely appointed. Melchizedek was not a descendant of Abraham and Jesus was not a descendant of Levi. Finally, Melchizedek died and nothing else is known about him. This is unlike Jesus who died, but God raised Him from the dead and took Him to Heaven where He serves as High Priest on the basis of His perfect sacrifice and indestructible life!

31. See Revelation 5:12,13 and 11:17 Note: For a detailed discussion on the linkage between Daniel 7:9,10 and Revelation 5, please see pages 66-72 in my book, *Daniel: Unlocked For the Final Generation* and pages 56-65 in my book, *A Study on the Seven Seals and the 144,000.*

32. Revelation 20

33. 1 Corinthians 15:24-28, insertions mine

34. Daniel 7:17

35. Daniel 7:23,24

36. Daniel 7:25

37. Revelation 12:13,14, insertions mine

Prophecy 3

The Antichrist

Daniel 8:1-12

Beginning Point in Time: About 538 B.C.

Ending Point in Time: The Second Coming

Summary: The essence of this prophecy can be summarized in three sentences: When the 2,300 days expire (1844), Jesus will begin to cleanse Heaven's temple of guilt. Later, Lucifer (the horn power) will physically appear and eventually lead all of the wicked to commit the unpardonable sin. The work of Jesus in the temple (the daily) will end when Lucifer completes his work. By that point in time, every sinner will have reached the point of no return and there is nothing further Jesus can do to save them.

Introduction: We saw how God used the technique of "repetition and enlargement" in Daniel 7 to expand our understanding of Daniel 2. In the same way, this prophecy uses repetition and enlargement to expand our understanding of Daniel 7. As we proceed through the seventeen prophecies, you will see how they work together to tell one harmonious story. The information provided in each prophecy is additive in nature, which means you need to understand the entire prophetic story before you completely understand any part of it! From the beginning, God designed the seventeen prophecies in Daniel and Revelation to work together so that when the time came for the book of Daniel to be unsealed at the time of the end, the mystery and ambiguity encasing apocalyptic prophecy over the past twenty-six centuries would disappear.

Look at figure 3.1. You will see how the prophecies in Daniel 2, 7, and 8 align. Notice the list under 457 B.C. The ram, bear, and silver align. This alignment is important to the final generation because these three prophecies provide a historical setting for two prophetic time periods that are very important. Knowing that most people have little interest in matters of antiquity, God moves our understanding of His plans in very large steps in the book of Daniel. For example, in Figure 3.1, one prophetic time period

Prophecy 3 - The Antichrist

moves us forward in time 2,300 years and another moves us forward 1,260 years.

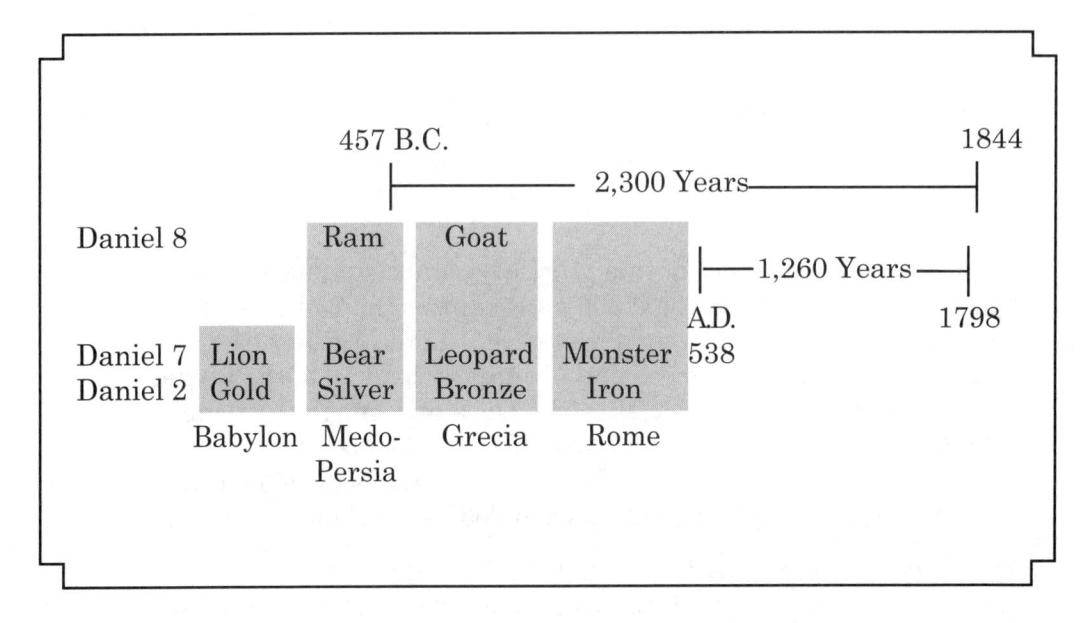

```
                            457 B.C.                                    1844
                            |————————— 2,300 Years —————————|
              Daniel 8        Ram    Goat
                                              |— 1,260 Years —|
                                              A.D.            1798
              Daniel 7  Lion   Bear  Leopard  Monster 538
              Daniel 2  Gold   Silver Bronze  Iron
                      Babylon  Medo-  Grecia  Rome
                               Persia
```

Figure 3.1

The alignment of these three prophecies is important to the final generation because there is an intimate relationship between 1798 and 1844. We learned in Prophecy 2 that the courtroom scene in Daniel 7:9,10 occurred in 1798. We will see in this prophecy that the opening of the books of record occurred in 1844. Daniel 7:10 says: **"The court was seated, and the books were opened."** Because Prophecy 3 overlays Prophecy 2, and Prophecy 2 overlays Prophecy 1, God is building a stack of prophecies to help us understand that even though the plan of redemption is huge, His timing is perfect, always on track. God may seem to be slow, but He is moving with deliberate haste. The problem of sin will not last one day longer than absolutely necessary.

The longest prophetic time period given in the Bible is found in this prophecy. It lasts for 2,300 years. In terms of chronological progression, this is one huge step forward! In fact, it is more than twice the length of the 1,000 year prophecy in Revelation 20. To make sure that people understand when this time period ends, God placed the origin of this time period within a well documented historical setting. By clearly establishing the beginning date of the 2,300 years there can be no mistake about the ending date. Moreover, the ending date is directly linked to a very important event in Heaven's temple. This event is "Judgment Day." The court was seated in 1798, and in 1844 Jesus began to judge the dead so that He might determine the eternal destiny of each person who has lived.

One final point. As we progress through these prophecies (more so in the prophecies of Revelation), we will discover that God sometimes inserts an odd element within a prophecy. For example, this prophecy concerns a ram, a goat, and a horn power. Since all three elements are in the same prophecy, the horn power must have something to do with the ram and goat. At first glance, there also appears to be some "disconnected discussion" in this prophecy about Heaven's temple. For example, verse 14 appears to have nothing to do with the ram, goat, or horn power! Verse 14 says, **"It will take 2,300 evenings and mornings; then the sanctuary will be reconsecrated."** This verse has created all kinds of problems in the past. However, if we understand the essential doctrine of parallel temples[1] and the use of valid rules of interpretation, we can make sense of this vision. It aligns perfectly with the timing in Prophecies 8 and 11.

The Sequence

{1} In the third year of King Belshazzar's reign, I received a vision. {2} I was in the city of Susa, located in the province of Elam. I was standing beside the beautiful Ulai Canal. {3} I looked up into the sky and I saw a powerful ram with two great horns growing out of its head. One horn was longer than the other and the longer horn grew out last. {4} I watched as the ram came from the east. He charged toward the west, the north, and the south. No one could stand against him, and none could escape his awesome power. He did as he pleased and he became great.

Dan. 8:1-4
In the third year of the reign of king Belshazzar a vision appeared unto me, even unto me Daniel, after that which appeared unto me at the first. And I saw in a vision; and it came to pass, when I saw, that I was at Shushan in the palace, which is

Prophecy 3 - The Antichrist

in the province of Elam; and I saw in a vision, and I was by the river of Ulai. Then I lifted up mine eyes, and saw, and, behold, there stood before the river a ram which had two horns: and the two horns were high; but one was higher than the other, and the higher came up last. I saw the ram pushing westward, and northward, and southward; so that no beasts might stand before him, neither was there any that could deliver out of his hand; but he did according to his will, and became great.

Dan. 8:5-8

And as I was considering, behold, an he goat came from the west on the face of the whole earth, and touched not the ground: and the goat had a notable horn between his eyes. And he came to the ram that

{5} While watching this powerful beast, suddenly a goat with a big horn between his eyes came out of the west. He was traveling so fast that he did not appear to touch the ground. {6} He charged the two-horned ram with enormous fury. {7} The goat struck the ram and shattered its two horns. The ram was hurled to the ground and trampled. No one could rescue the ram from the goat's attack. {8} The goat became a great kingdom, but something unusual happened. At the height of its power, the goat's mighty horn was broken off and in its place four substantial horns grew – one toward the north, the south, the east, and the west.

The Antichrist - Prophecy 3

{9} As I watched, I saw another scene. Out of the north I saw a horn approaching. This horn did not have an animal host.[2] It was not related to the ram or the goat or any earthly kingdom.[3] As I watched, it started small, but it quickly grew in power and popularity toward the south, east, and the west (my homeland, the Beautiful Land).

had two horns, which I had seen standing before the river, and ran unto him in the fury of his power. And I saw him come close unto the ram, and he was moved with choler against him, and smote the ram, and brake his two horns: and there was no power in the ram to stand before him, but he cast him down to the ground, and stamped upon him: and there was none that could deliver the ram out of his hand. Therefore the he goat waxed very great: and when he was strong, the great horn was broken; and for it came up four notable ones toward the four winds of heaven.

Dan. 8:9
And out of one of them came forth a little horn, which waxed exceeding great, toward the south, and toward the east, and toward the pleasant land.

Prophecy 3 - The Antichrist

Dan. 8:10
And it waxed great, even to the host of heaven; and it cast down some of the host and of the stars to the ground, and stamped upon them.

{10} This horn grew until his fame was known and honored all over the world. When he became able, he threw down the starry host (various gods that mankind worships) and trampled on them.[4]

Many people make the mistake of thinking the horn in Daniel 8 and the little horn in Daniel 7 are one and the same. There are several reasons why this is not possible. First, this prophecy completely "leapfrogs" the time periods of the fourth beast (168 B.C. - A.D. 476) and the little horn (538 -1798). The fourth empire in Daniel 7 (Rome) is not mentioned in this prophecy because the horn in Daniel 8 is not attached to *any* beast. This horn does not rise out of a world empire. It appears from out of nowhere, "out of the four winds," specifically, out of the north. The north is prophetically important because it is often said in Scripture that divine wrath comes out of the north.[5] Second, within the context of this vision, a beast is a symbol of an empire and a horn is a symbol of a king. The mighty horn on the goat (verse 21) represents the first king of Greecia (Alexander the Great). Similarly, the horn that just appears out of the north represents "a stern-faced king" that will appear and overtake the world "when rebels have become completely wicked" (verse 23). Third, Gabriel told Daniel (verses 17 and 19) that this vision concerns the *appointed* time of the end which occurs *after* the 2,300 day/years expire in 1844. In other words, the horn in this vision will appear on Earth after 1844 – at the appointed time of the end. Prophecies 8 and 11 will further explain why this horn represents the physical appearing of Lucifer, the dreaded Antichrist.

Jesus will permit Lucifer to physically appear before the people of Earth during the Great Tribulation. Jesus will release the devil from the Abyss at an appointed time to lead the world into destruction.[6] Lucifer will deceive the wicked and his followers will be like the sand on the seashore. Lucifer will astonish Earth's inhabitants with his miracles, boldness, and assumed authority. At the sixth trumpet, the devil will abolish all of the religions of the world and trample on them. He will claim to be Almighty God[7] and as such, he will demand that religious diversity be eliminated.[8] He is The Master of Deception. He will deceive Moslems, Jews, Catholics, Atheists, Protestants, Eastern Mystics, and the Heathen by performing great signs and miracles – even calling fire down from Heaven.[9] He will eliminate the starry hosts – an ancient term used for various "gods" or whatever is worshiped as "God"[10] and he will demand that everyone honor and worship him as God Almighty.[11]

{11} Lucifer will masquerade as Almighty God. He will bring to an end the daily ministry Jesus does on behalf of sinners by forcing everyone into a decision. Near the end of the Great Tribulation, everyone on Earth will have either the seal of God or the mark of the beast. With lies and deceit, Lucifer will trample on the honor and respect that belongs to man's Creator.

> The 144,000 will lead many millions of people to receive Jesus as their Savior (see Prophecy 7), but the work of the 144,000 will eventually stall. At the appointed time, Jesus will release the devil from the Abyss and his horrific actions will cause many of the undecided wicked to repent and embrace the gospel. Lucifer will lead the defiant wicked into rebellion[12] against the gospel of Jesus Christ and those who embrace it. The wicked will ridicule and reject the ministry and intercession that Jesus offers for individuals at Heaven's Altar of Burnt Offering. Lucifer will lead the world into rebellion because he knows that *no sinner can be saved on his own merits.* Lucifer knows why Jesus died and he knows that salvation comes only through faith in the atoning sacrifice of Jesus. Masquerading as Almighty God, Lucifer will demand that everyone on Earth obey him or be killed.[13] The choice will be simple: Submit to the laws of our Creator/Redeemer and face death, or submit to the laws of Lucifer and live a few months longer. (See Prophecy 12.) When every person has made a firm decision, Jesus' daily intercession on behalf of individuals will close and God's generous offer of salvation will end.

{12} The horn power cannot appear physically on Earth until Jesus permits him to escape the Abyss. This event (see the fifth trumpet in Prophecy 8) will occur about two and a half years into the Great Tribulation. Because the carnal heart is naturally rebellious toward God and His authority,[14] the devil will find it easy to deceive those who stubbornly rebel against the demands of the gospel of Jesus. Lucifer will lead the wicked to think that God's saints are evil and rebellious, and soon after, the wicked will kill and destroy the saints thinking they are doing God a service.[15] God's people will be defeated. God will remove the power He gave to the 144,000 and the devil's minions will kill them.[16] The wicked will commit the unpardonable sin. They will reject the clearest evidences of truth and defy the ministry of the Holy Spirit. Evil will temporarily triumph because truth will be thrown to the ground as if it were garbage.[17]

Dan. 8:11

Yea, he magnified himself even to the prince of the host, and by him the daily sacrifice was taken away, and the place of his sanctuary was cast down.

Dan. 8:12

And an host was given him against the daily sacrifice by reason of transgression, and it cast down the truth to the ground; and it practiced, and prospered.

> **Dan. 8:13**
> *Then I heard one saint speaking, and another saint said unto that certain saint which spake, How long shall be the vision concerning the daily sacrifice, and the transgression of desolation, to give both the sanctuary and the host to be trodden under foot?*
>
> **Dan. 8:14**
> *And he said unto me, Unto two thousand and three hundred days; then shall the sanctuary be cleansed.*

The devil's demons will use painful torture to subdue rebellious people into worshiping Lucifer as Almighty God during the fifth trumpet.[18] The devil's demons will also lead the wicked to murder millions of saints during the sixth trumpet because they refused to obey the devil's demands.[19] The devil will prosper in everything that he does. He will cause his followers to despise truth. Worse, he will cause billions of wicked people to despise Jesus and His generous gift of salvation.

Discussion

{13} I overheard two angels talking. The first angel asked some clarifying questions: "How long will it take for this vision to be fulfilled? When will the daily intercession of Christ at the Altar of Burnt Offering end? When will this great rebellion that causes desolation occur? When will God's efforts to save man and the saints be trampled underfoot?"

{14} The second angel said to me, "All of these questions are important, but only the first one will be answered in this vision. The rest of the questions will be answered in subsequent visions.

Daniel, this vision concerns the horn power who will come from the north. He is a coming king,[20] but not from an earthly nation. He and his angels will appear in the sky.[21] He is the destroyer in Revelation 9:11 named Abaddon (Hebrew) or Apollyon (Greek), a stern-faced king who will appear at the end of the world. Lucifer cannot physically appear until Jesus allows him to come out of the Abyss[22] and he will not be released from the Abyss until the cleansing (or restoration) of Heaven's temple is about to end."

> The cleansing of Heaven's temple is intimately connected with Lucifer's appearing because Lucifer's bold actions will force undecided people into making a firm decision. When everyone on Earth has chosen whom he will worship and obey, the cleansing of the temple will be completed and salvation's offer will end.
>
> Many people do not understand why Heaven's temple has to be cleansed. Please consider three matters: First, God does not forgive a sin, but God does free sinners of sin's guilt. Earthly temple services teach us that the guilt of repentant sinners was transferred (via the blood of a perfect sacrifice) to the horns of the Altar of Burnt Offering.[23] Of course, once a sinner's guilt is transferred to the altar, the sinner is free of guilt, but his guilt remains upon the altar. Second, the earthly temple ser-

vice teaches us that the Altar of Burnt Offering became defiled because the guilt of sinners was transferred to it daily. (Services at the Altar of Burnt Offering were conducted each day.) Third, the earthly temple was cleansed once a year, on the Day of Atonement. On this day, all of the accumulated guilt was transferred (via the sacrifice of a perfect animal) to a scapegoat. Then, the scapegoat was taken into the wilderness to die a protracted death.[24]

The process of cleansing Heaven's temple is important in this vision because God has set a date (1844), near the end of the world, when Jesus will open the books of record and begin cleansing Heaven's temple. The cleansing process in Heaven works like this: Each person's life is recorded in realtime (as it happens) in a book. Every word, thought, and action is faithfully written down. When a person dies, the recording ends because a dead person has no thoughts, actions, words, or deeds. At the appointed time (1844), Jesus reviews the record of each dead person. For example, let us assume that Jesus started with the record of Abel's life, the first man to die. After thoroughly investigating the life of Abel, Jesus made a decision about Abel's eternal destiny. If Jesus condemns Abel, Jesus will then transfer Abel's guilt from the temple to Abel's head. If Abel is saved, Jesus will transfer Abel's guilt from the temple to the head of the scapegoat (Lucifer).[25] When this investigative process ends, Heaven's temple will be completely *cleansed* of guilt because the guilt that previously contaminated Heaven's Altar of Burnt Offering will be assigned to its rightful owner.

Jesus will reward His saints at the Second Coming.[26] Jesus will "reward" the wicked at the end of the 1,000 years.[27] This information is important because Jesus will permit Lucifer, the horn power from the north, to appear on Earth when Jesus is about to complete the cleansing of Heaven's temple. Lucifer and his demons will bring the cleansing work of Jesus to an end because they will force the living into a firm decision regarding whom they will worship and obey.

{14-Continued} The angel said, "When 2,300 evenings and mornings expire, then shall (future indicative tense) the cleansing work of Jesus in Heaven's temple begin. Later, the horn from the north will appear on Earth and bring Jesus' cleansing work to a close."

(**Note:** God has declared that an evening and a morning constitute one day.[28] Therefore, 2,300 evenings and mornings are

Prophecy 3 - The Antichrist

Dan. 8:14

2,300 days. This time period must be translated as 2,300 day/years because the Jubilee Calendar is in operation. See Appendix A.)

The explanation for the beginning point of the 2,300 years will be revealed in the next vision. For now, here is a brief summary that may be helpful. During the empire represented by the ram, a noble and generous king will come to power. God will move upon this king's heart to help His people rebuild and restore Jerusalem. King Artaxerxes, a future king in Persia, will issue a decree to rebuild and restore Jerusalem in 457 B.C.[29] and 2,300 years later, Jesus will open the books in Heaven's courtroom. Jesus will begin cleansing Heaven's temple in 1844. (**Note:** The breaking of the third seal in Revelation 6 aligns with 1844. See Prophecy 6.)

To summarize, God put a ram, a goat, a 2,300 year time period, and a horn power in this vision. The ram and goat are well documented ancient empires. After the 2,300 years expire, the horn power will appear out of nowhere at the appointed time of the end. The connecting link between these ancient empires and the appearing of the horn power is a prophetic time period of 2,300 years. When the 2,300 years end, Jesus will open the books of record and carefully investigate the life record of each person who sleeps in the grave. When this process draws near its conclusion, Jesus will release the horn power (the devil) from the Abyss so that he can appear physically before mankind. The devil and his angels will take actions that force everyone into a firm decision regarding whom they will worship and obey. Once every decision has been made, there is nothing further that Jesus can do to save anyone. Salvation's offer will then terminate and Jesus' cleansing work will end.

Dan. 8:15-16

And it came to pass, when I, even I Daniel, had seen the vision, and sought for the meaning, then, behold, there stood before me as the appearance of a man. And I heard a man's voice between the banks of Ulai, which called, and said, Gabriel, make this man to understand the vision.

{15} While I, Daniel, was watching this vision and trying to understand it, a glorious being stood in front of me who looked like a man. {16} He was so bright that I had to avert my eyes. I heard Him say, "Gabriel, tell Daniel the meaning of this vision."

Dan. 8:17-19

So he came near where I stood: and when he came, I was afraid, and fell upon my face: but

{17} As Gabriel approached me, I was terrified by his size and brilliance and I fell prostrate on the ground. "Daniel," he said to me, "You must understand that this vision concerns the distant future and it points to 'the time of the end.'" {18} While he was speaking to me, I felt as though my life evaporated. I was in a deep sleep with my face in the dirt. Then he touched me and helped me to my feet. {19} Gabriel said again, "I have come to tell you what will happen in the distant future. The end of the world will be marked by a time of *wrath*. The end of the world will surely come. God has set the date by His own authority. Prior to the Second Coming of Jesus, a great tribulation will overtake Earth and last 1,335 days. God will send a series of devastating judgments upon Earth and everyone will see and experience His wrath. This is why *the appointed time of the end* is also called 'a time of wrath.'

{20} "The empire of Babylon will soon fall. The two-horned ram you saw represents the coming kingdom of the Medes and Persians. The horn on the ram that came up last and reached out farther than the first horn represents the Persian side of this empire. The Persians will dominate the Medes. {21} "Later, the Medes and Persians will be overrun by the Greeks. The shaggy goat represents the kingdom of Grecia. The large horn you saw between the eyes of the goat represents a man, its first king, Alexander the Great. Alexander will die an untimely death at the peak of his power. {22} The four horns on the goat represent four generals who will replace Alexander. These generals will be Cassander, Lysimachus, Ptolemy, and Seleucus. None of these generals will be as powerful as Alexander. They will divide Grecia into four sectors and each will rule over his sector."

> Notice again this important point: A horn in this vision represents a king. The great horn on the goat represents Alexander the Great. The four horns that took Alexander's place represent the four kings who succeeded him. Notice again this distinction: The goat represents the *kingdom* of Grecia, but the horns represent its kings. This distinction is important in this prophecy because the horn that will come from the north will be a king without an earthly empire.[30] He will conquer the whole world.

Dan. 8:17-19

he said unto me, Understand, O son of man: for at the time of the end shall be the vision. Now as he was speaking with me, I was in a deep sleep on my face toward the ground: but he touched me, and set me upright. And he said, Behold, I will make thee know what shall be in the last end of the indignation: for at the time appointed the end shall be.

Dan. 8:20-22

The ram which thou sawest having two horns are the kings of Media and Persia. And the rough goat is the king of Grecia: and the great horn that is between his eyes is the first king. Now that being broken, whereas four stood up for it, four kingdoms shall stand up out of the nation, but not in his power.

Prophecy 3 - The Antichrist

> **Dan. 8:23**
> And in the latter time of their kingdom, when the transgressors are come to the full, a king of fierce countenance, and understanding dark sentences, shall stand up.

The devil will be a "stern-faced king" and he will physically appear out of nowhere when Jesus is almost finished with cleansing Heaven's temple. Paul refers to the appearing of the devil as the man of sin, the man of lawlessness.[31] Isaiah calls him a man[32] and so does Ezekiel.[33]

{23} Gabriel continued, "During the final days of Earth's history, when a majority of people have rejected the gospel and become completely rebellious toward God, this stern-faced king, a master of manipulation (deceit and intrigue), will be permitted to appear. Satan will physically appear as a glorious man and masquerade as Almighty God."

The devil is represented as a horn coming out of the north because divine disaster comes from the north.[34] The fifth trumpet will be a divine curse.[35] Lucifer will only be released from the Abyss when the gospel stalls and a majority of people have rebelled against the clearest evidences of truth.[36]

> **Dan. 8:24**
> And his power shall be mighty, but not by his own power: and he shall destroy wonderfully, and shall prosper, and practice, and shall destroy the mighty and the holy people.

{24} "When Lucifer is released from the Abyss, he will not rest. He and his angels will travel the world constantly. He will become very popular. He will gain control of the world, but not through his own power. The Most High God has granted the devil the authority to lead the wicked astray.[37] Lucifer will perform dazzling miracles.[38] Billions of wicked people will embrace him, give him glory, and obey him as though he were God. The devil will cause astounding devastation and he will succeed in whatever he does. He will kill most, if not all, of God's servants, the 144,000.[39] He will also kill millions of God's saints.[40] The devil will masquerade as God for about a year and the saints will be overrun and conquered.

> **Dan. 8:25**
> And through his policy also he shall cause craft to prosper in his hand; and he shall magnify himself in his heart, and by peace shall destroy many: he shall also stand up against the Prince of princes; but he shall be broken without hand.

{25} "Lucifer will cause deceit to prosper and he will consider himself to be God. After five months of counterfeit signs, torture for the non-religious, and great signs and wonders, the sixth trumpet will sound and the devil will be permitted to kill people. Suddenly his character will change and he will demand that a global church-state, a counterfeit theocracy, be set up. He will rule as King of kings and Lord of lords. To eliminate his opposition, he will kill a third of Earth's population.[41] The remaining two-thirds of the world will worship him and wear a tattoo on their right hand; the mark of the beast. Just before Jesus returns, the devil and his ten puppet kings will take their stand against Jesus, the Prince of princes. The devil and his forces will be utterly destroyed, but not by human power."

> Jesus will destroy the physical body which the devil has occupied at the time of the Second Coming. Jesus will return Lucifer and his demons to the Abyss (the spirit realm) and imprison them on this planet for 1,000 years (while the saints are in Heaven). At the end of the 1,000 years when the Holy City descends from Heaven, Jesus will resurrect the wicked. At that time, Lucifer and his demons will be released from the Abyss for a few days before they are annihilated with fire.[42]

{26} Finally, Gabriel stated, "Daniel, this vision consists of three parts and all of them are true. First, the kingdoms of the ram and the goat will become well known in history. This will help God's people, who will live in the distant future, to determine when King Artaxerxes will issue a very important decree. Second, when the 2,300 years have expired, Jesus will open the books of record and begin judging the dead. Third, during the appointed time of the end, when Jesus is almost finished with cleansing Heaven's temple, the devil will be released from the Abyss. This stern-faced king is the horn from the north. He will appear out of nowhere and cause enormous devastation. He will cause the undecided to make a firm decision regarding whom they will worship and obey. This will bring the intercession of Jesus to an end. Because this information will be pertinent to those who live at the end of the world, this vision will remain sealed up until the final generation arrives.

Dan. 8:26
And the vision of the evening and the morning which was told is true: wherefore shut thou up the vision; for it shall be for many days.

{27} I was exhausted and lay ill for several days. I could not explain what I had seen, but I knew it was horrible. Eventually, I got up and went about the king's business. I was appalled by the vision and I could not understand it. So, I began to pray for understanding.

Dan. 8:27
And I Daniel fainted, and was sick certain days; afterward I rose up, and did the king's business; and I was astonished at the vision, but none understood it.

The Rules of Interpretation

Please consider how the Rules of Interpretation (which are discussed in the Introduction) are observed in this prophecy:

Rule One says an apocalyptic prophecy has a beginning point and ending point in time and the events within the prophecy occur in the order given. This prophecy contains three elements that occur in chronological order. First, the ram represents the Medo-Persian Empire. Second, the goat that follows the ram represents the Grecian Empire. Centuries later, the horn power from the north appears. Notice that there is a large gap of time between the goat and the horn power. This is not uncommon in apocalyptic prophecy. For example, there is a gap of 1,000 years between the sixth seal (the Second Coming) and the breaking of the seventh seal at the end of the millennium. Nevertheless, this prophecy has a beginning point and an ending point in time and the events occur in the order given.

Rule Two says a fulfillment only occurs when all of the specifications are met, and this includes the order stated in the prophecy. History confirms that the Medo-Persian Empire fell to the Grecians. History also confirms that Artaxerxes issued a decree to restore and rebuild Jerusalem in 457 B.C. Even though nothing is written in this prophecy about the starting point of the 2,300 years, the next vision (Daniel 9) will address this topic. Hopefully, you can see how the prophecies interlock with each other – one prophecy cannot say everything that needs to be said. This interdependency between the prophecies means the student needs to understand almost everything before he can understand anything! The Bible reveals much more about the stern-faced king (the Antichrist) and we will learn more about him in subsequent prophecies.

Rule Three states that apocalyptic language can be literal, analogous, or symbolic. We know there are symbolic elements in this prophecy because *the symbols are defined with relevant* Scripture. Gabriel told Daniel the ram represented the Medo-Persian Empire and the goat represented the Grecian Empire.[43] History confirms this sequence! The angel also told Daniel who the horns on the ram and goat represented. Gabriel's words become important because the horn that "just appears" out of the north will be a man.[44] He is defined as "a stern-faced king" who will appear at the appointed time of the end.[45] Remember, when a symbol is used, God always defines the symbol with a relevant text. If this is not the case, prophetic interpretation becomes a cornucopia of confusion.

Rule Four says the presence or absence of the Jubilee Calendar determines how God measures time.. (See Appendix A and Prophecy 4 to learn how the Jubilee Calendar and the seventy week prophecy define Rule Four.) Since we have not examined Prophecy 4 yet, please consider two points: First, weekly cycles of seven years **did not** end when Jesus died on the cross in A.D. 30, because Jesus died in the **middle** of the seventieth week (a Wednesday year). Second, we will find in the next prophecy that the 2,300 days and the seventy weeks have the same starting date. This date is 457 B.C. This means the seventy weeks ended in A.D. 33 and the 2,300 days ended in 1844. Both time periods must be translated because they occur during the operation of the Jubilee Calendar (1437 B.C. - 1994).

Some people teach the 2,300 evenings and mornings in Daniel 8:14 represent 1,150 days. They reach this conclusion by dividing the number 2,300 into 1,150 mornings and 1,150 evenings. This approach will not work for five reasons.

First, six times in Genesis 1,[46] God declared that an evening-morning cycle constitutes one day. Who can usurp what God has defined? The 2,300 evenings and mornings in Daniel 8:14 amount to 2,300 days.

Second, in Genesis 1, one day contains one cycle of *ereb-boqer*. (These are Hebrew words for evening and morning). There is no conjunction between *ereb-boqer* (such as ereb and boqer) and there is no precedent in Scripture for dividing 2,300 *ereb-boqer* into 1,150 days.

Third, God could have said "2,300 *yowm*" in Daniel 8:14. The Hebrew word *yowm* is used more than 2,200 times in the Old Testament and is usually translated "days," but God did not say "2,300 *yowm*." He chose to say 2,300 "*ereb-boqer*." This word choice is important because Daniel 8 refers to services in Heaven's temple. For example, the cleansing of the temple is mentioned, the end of daily services is mentioned, and the place (or the importance) of God's sanctuary is mentioned. Cycles of *ereb-boqer* have a distinct association with services in the temple. Services at the Altar of Incense were conducted daily – *ereb-boqer*.[47] The annual cleansing of the Earthly sanctuary occurred on a specific day which was determined by the arrival of a specific evening and morning – *ereb-boqer*.[48] Services at the Altar of Incense in Heaven will continue (*ereb-boqer*) until corporate intercession is terminated and the censer is cast down.[49]

Fourth, there is a symbiotic relationship between 1798 and 1844. These two dates support each other. The cleansing of Heaven's temple in 1844 could not begin until Jesus was found worthy to receive sovereign power in 1798. The Bible is clear on this point: The court was seated and the books of record were opened *after* the Ancient of Days took His seat. Chronologically, 1844 follows 1798.

Fifth, when we examine Prophecy 6, we will find that 1798 and 1844 work very closely together. The harmony that comes from the sum of these parts is truly amazing! Only God could have created such a tapestry that involves redemption and timing.

When these five issues are considered, there is no possibility that 2,300 cycles of *ereb-boqer* can represent 1,150 days. This is the longest prophetic time period in the Bible and it securely stands upon a historical footing provided by the Medo-Persian and Grecian Empires. During the days of Persian King Artaxerxes, the 2,300 year clock began ticking. Then, Jesus came to Earth and confirmed the accuracy of this clock with His death. This fact will be addressed in the next vision.

References:

1. See Chapters 11 and 12 in my book, *Jesus: The Alpha and The Omega* or freely download these chapters at http://www.wake-up.org/Alpha/Subjindex.htm.
2. Horns do not necessarily have animal hosts: 2 Samuel 22:3; Luke 1:69; Zechariah 1:19-21.
3. 2 Thessalonians 2; Revelation 17:8; Daniel 11:36; Luke 1:69; Ezekiel 29:21; 1 Samuel 2:1,10
4. Deuteronomy 4:19
5. Isaiah 41:25; Jeremiah 1:14; 6:1; Ezekiel 1:4
6. Revelation 9:1-11 Note: The names Abaddon and Apollyon mean the same thing in both languages: Destroyer.
7. Daniel 11:36,37; 2 Thessalonians 2:4
8. Revelation 13:14,15
9. Revelation 13:13
10. 2 Kings 17:16; 21:3-5; 2 Chronicles 33:3-5
11. 2 Thessalonians 2:4
12. 2 Thessalonians 2:3-12
13. Revelation 13:15
14. Romans 8:5-8
15. John 16:1-3
16. Daniel 12:7; Revelation 11:7
17. See this parallel: Isaiah 59:12-15.
18. Revelation 9:1-11
19. Revelation 6:9-11
20. Revelation 9:11
21. Revelation 9:2,3
22. Revelation 9:1
23. Exodus 29:10-14
24. For further study on these matters, please see Chapters 11 and 12 in my book, *Jesus: The Alpha and The Omega* or freely download these chapters at http://www.wake-up.org/Alpha/Subjindex.htm.

25. For sins placed on the scapegoat see Leviticus 16:1-31, for sins placed on the heads of sinners see Leviticus 20:9; 2 Chronicles 6:23; Ezekiel 18:13.
26. Revelation 22:12
27. Revelation 20:15
28. Genesis 1:5
29. Ezra 7:7,8,11-28
30. Revelation 9:11
31. 2 Thessalonians 2:3
32. Isaiah 14:16,17
33. Ezekiel 28:2
34. Jeremiah 4:5,6; 6:1,22; 50:3,41
35. See Revelation 9:12 in Prophecy 8.
36. 2 Thessalonians 2:9-12
37. 2 Thessalonians 2:9-12
38. Revelation 13:13,14; 17:13-17
39. See Revelation 16:4-7 in Prophecy 14 and Revelation 18:24 in Prophecy 15.
40. Psalm 79; Revelation 9:15; 13:7
41. Revelation 9:15
42. Revelation 20
43. Daniel 8:20,21
44. Isaiah 14:16,17
45. Daniel 8:19,23
46. Genesis 1:5,8,13,19,23,31
47. Exodus 29:38-42; Leviticus 24:3
48. Leviticus 23:27-32
49. Revelation 8:2-6

Prophecy 4

The Seventy Weeks

Daniel 8:1-12

Beginning Point in Time: 457 B.C.

Ending Point in Time: Second Coming of Jesus

Summary: The essence of this prophecy can be summarized in a few sentences. While they were exiles in Babylon, God offered the trustees of His covenant (the nation of Israel) a second chance. He granted them 490 years (seventy weeks) to overcome their rebellion and fulfill the terms and conditions of His covenant. If Israel cooperated, the prophecies given in the book of Daniel (Plan B) would be sealed up forever (remain unknown) and the promises and prophecies given to Isaiah, Jeremiah, Ezekiel, and other Old Testament prophets (Plan A) would be fulfilled. On the other hand, if Israel failed, Israel would be destroyed.

Introduction: Many scholars and pastors have separated this prophecy from the previous three prophecies in Daniel and the result is a huge disaster. Millions of people anticipate several events that will not occur. For example, it is commonly taught that the sixty-nine weeks in Daniel 9 are in the distant past, but the seventieth week is in the future! This is impossible! Time is an unbroken continuum. When one second ends, a new second begins. There is no room for additional time between two seconds, minutes, hours, months, days, years, or weeks of years! The seventieth week began when the sixty-ninth week ended. There cannot be a gap of indefinite time between the sixty-ninth and the seventieth week. If additional time can be inserted into a prophetic time period, no one can know the length of that prophetic time period. If a yardstick does not have definite length, it cannot be used for measurement. If the seventieth week did not follow the sixty-ninth week, we cannot assign a number to the week in history that immediately followed the sixty-ninth week.

Prophecy 4 - The Seventy Weeks

Thus far in this book, we have observed that (a) apocalyptic prophecy is additive in nature; each prophecy builds upon another, and (b) God uses a technique called "repetition and enlargement" to create a matrix that expands our understanding of His Word and plans. We will discover in this study that Prophecy 4 builds upon Prophecies 1 through 3 because these four prophecies depend upon each other to tell the whole story. Look at Figure 4.1 (not drawn to scale) and notice four elements. First, at the top, notice that the chart indicates that Jesus died in A.D. 30,[1] which is the middle year of the seventieth week. Second, notice that 457 B.C. as the starting date for the seventy weeks (seven plus sixty-two plus one week) . Third, notice the line from 457 B.C. ending at 1844. Last, notice that 1844 (the end of the 2,300 years) and 1798 (the end of the little horn's persecution for 1,260 years) have close proximity to each other even though these dates are derived from totally different prophecies.

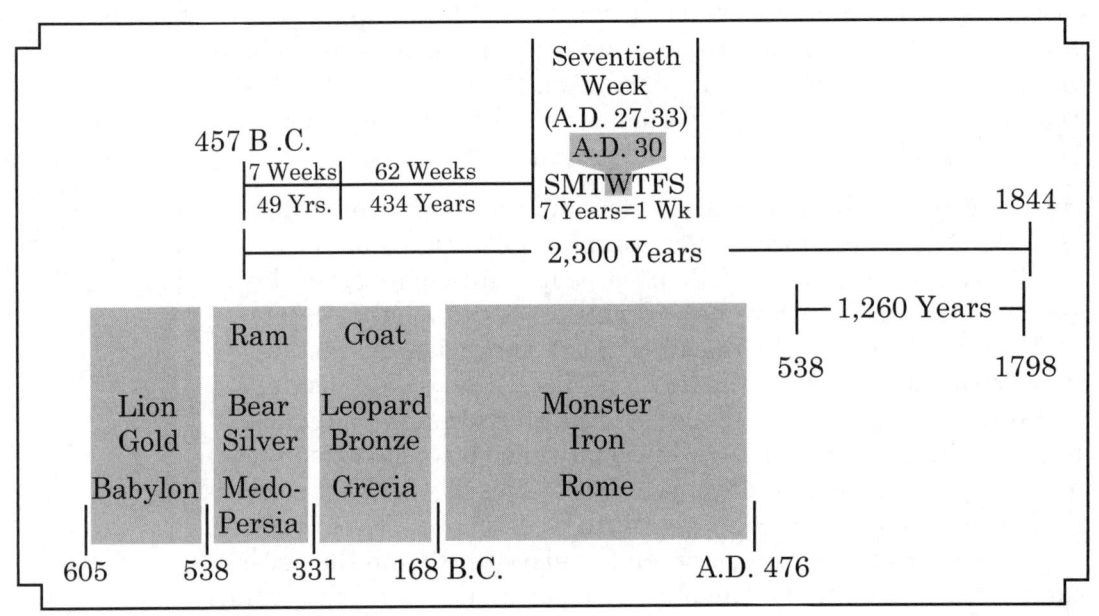

Figure 4.1

God's Weekly Cycle

Since Jesus created the world, the *first day* of each week has aligned with the first day of Creation and the *seventh day* of each week has aligned with God's Sabbath rest. (Genesis 2:1-3) Even though human beings may define a week as any period of seven days, God defines a week as a period of seven days that aligns with Creation's week. (Exodus 20:8-11) God's weekly cycle is important because the middle day of every week is Wednesday. Look again at Figure 4.1. You will see that the middle year of the seventieth week is a Wednesday year. Since Jesus died in the middle of the week, and since Jesus died in A.D. 30,[2] we must align A.D. 30 with a Wednesday year. This alignment forces the first year of the seventieth week (A.D. 27) to be a Sunday year and the Sabbath year of the seventieth week becomes A.D. 33. This information about the seventy weeks is important for two reasons:

First, the seventy weeks in Daniel 9 can be precisely identified because of God's weekly cycle of years. I understand that God created a new calendar for Israel at the time of the Exodus. (Exodus 12:2) This calendar is often called the Jubilee Calendar and it is based on God's weekly cycle. God established a cycle of seven years so that each day of the week represented a year. To ensure the integrity of this cycle, God declared every seventh year dating from the Exodus was to be a Sabbath year of rest for the land. Of course, Israel did not observe Sabbath years in the desert. However, Israel entered Canaan in a Friday year (the 41st year since the Exodus) and their first full year in the Promised Land was a Sabbath year; much like Adam and Eve's first full day of life was a Sabbath day. The Jubilee Calendar measures time in units of forty-nine year cycles (seven weeks of years). When a forty-nine year cycle expired, the following year was declared a year of Jubilee. The year of Jubilee was a special year because debts were cancelled, slaves were set free, and all of the land was returned to the original owners *for free*. The year of Jubilee always fell on a Sunday year. It was counted as the fiftieth year of the outgoing Jubilee cycle and simultaneously, it was counted as the first year of the new incoming Jubilee cycle.

These facts about the Jubilee Calendar are important because the seventy weeks in Daniel 9 did not suddenly appear with a decree to restore and rebuild Jerusalem. Actually, the seventy weeks mentioned in Daniel 9 align with ongoing weekly cycles of years that began at the time of the Exodus. God did not grant 490 random years to Israel, but instead, God defined the 490 years as seventy weeks so that He could draw Israel's attention back to the weekly cycles of years that Israel had long ignored. When Gabriel said to Daniel, "Seventy sevens are decreed for your people" his language was designed to redirect Israel's attention to the Jubilee Calendar which included the release of slaves, Sabbath years of rest for the land every seventh year, and the restoration of the land to its original owners *at no charge!*

Consider the way that Gabriel broke down the seventy weeks in Daniel 9:25:

$$7 \text{ weeks} + 62 \text{ weeks} + 1 \text{ week} = 70 \text{ weeks}$$
$$49 \text{ years} + 434 \text{ years} + 7 \text{ years} = 490 \text{ years}$$

Gabriel expressed the seventy weeks as three segments of time because the first segment of seven sevens is a Jubilee cycle. This was a huge clue for the nation of Israel. The all important decree to rebuild and restore Jerusalem would occur during a year of Jubilee! God wanted His people to anticipate that the land would be returned to the Jews at no charge and the decree to rebuild and restore Jerusalem would occur during a year of Jubilee. This alignment with the Jubilee Calendar was not a casual coincidence.[3] God had exiled Israel to Babylon for seventy years because it had refused to observe the Jubilee Calendar![4]

Gabriel also told Daniel that Messiah would appear and begin His ministry exactly seven weeks plus sixty-two weeks (483 years) after the decree was issued. Then, in the middle of the following week of seven years (the seventieth week), Messiah would be "cut off" (disinherited), but not for Himself (Jesus would be cut off for sinners). When this information is properly assembled, perfect harmony springs from the sum of all of the parts! History says the all-important decree was issued in a year of Jubilee (457 B.C.) and exactly sixty-nine weeks later (A.D. 27), Jesus showed up on the banks of the Jordan River and John baptized Him. Jesus began his ministry in the fall of A.D. 27 (a Sunday year) and was crucified in the spring of A.D. 30, (a Wednesday year, in the middle of the seventieth week.)

Four decrees were issued to rebuild and restore Jerusalem and 457 B.C. is the only one that occurred in a year of Jubilee.[5] Working backwards from the seventieth week and the year of Christ's death, we find that Spring, 457 B.C. ties in with the decree to restore and rebuild Jerusalem. Do not forget, this decree was issued during the time of the ram (see Prophecy 3). King Artaxerxes, a Persian king, issued the all-important decree about Nisan 1 and Ezra departed for Jerusalem with decree in hand on the 12th day of Nisan.[6] Because 457 B.C. is an unimpeachable date, the Thursday year of 1844 becomes unimpeachable as well (see prophecy 3). In this study, we will discover that the seventy weeks prophecy and the 2,300 days prophecy share the same starting date.

There is a second reason for properly positioning the seventy weeks. We learned in Prophecy 2 that the Ancient of Days took His seat in 1798. We also learned that in 1798, the Father issued a restraining order in Heaven and the result on Earth was the termination of 1,260 years of papal power over Europe. The pope was taken prisoner during the French Revolution (February 1798), and he died in exile.

As we review the important dates of 1798 and 1844, consider Daniel 7:10: **"the court was seated and the books were opened."** In Prophecy 3 we learned about 1844. We discovered that Jesus opened the books of record and began to cleanse Heaven's temple of sin's guilt when the 2,300 years ended. We also learned in Prophecy 3 that near the end of Christ's judgment of mankind,[7] a horn from the north (Lucifer, the stern-faced king) will appear out of nowhere and this horn will eventually bring Jesus' intercession in Heaven's temple to a close. There is perfect harmony coming from the sum of all of these prophetic parts!

Prophecy 4 - The Seventy Weeks

> **Dan. 9:1-3**
>
> *In the first year of Darius the son of Ahasuerus, of the seed of the Medes, which was made king over the realm of the Chaldeans; In the first year of his reign I Daniel understood by books the number of the years, whereof the word of the LORD came to Jeremiah the prophet, that he would accomplish seventy years in the desolations of Jerusalem. And I set my face unto the Lord God, to seek by prayer and supplications, with fasting, and sackcloth, and ashes:*
>
> **Dan. 9:20-23**
>
> *And whiles I was speaking, and praying, and confessing my sin and the sin of my people Israel, and presenting my supplication before the LORD my God for the holy mountain of my God; Yea, whiles I was speaking in prayer, even*

The Setting

{1} During the first year of King Darius (the Mede), who became ruler over the province of Babylon after it fell to the Medes and Persians, {2} I understood from Jeremiah the prophet, that the desolation of Jerusalem would last seventy years because my people had violated seventy Sabbatical years.[8] Knowing the seventy years would soon end, {3} I turned to my God and with fasting, prayer, sackcloth, and ashes, pleaded with Him to keep His promise and set my people free.

The Sequence

{20} While I was praying, confessing my sins and the sins of my people, Israel, and making my request to the Lord, my God, for the restoration of my people to Mt. Zion, His holy mountain {21} while still in prayer, Gabriel, the man I had seen in the earlier vision concerning the 2,300 days, came to me in swift flight about the time of the evening sacrifice. {22} He said, "Daniel, I have come to give you insight and understanding about the previous vision containing the 2,300 days. {23} As soon as you began to pray, your prayer was heard, and I have been sent to help you, for you are highly esteemed in Heaven. Therefore, consider my words and understand how your people and the 2,300 days in Prophecy 3 are intimately connected.

    Bible history indicates that Abraham's descendants did not make good trustees. Israel was a rebellious and obstinate nation in spite of God's many efforts to reform His people. Finally, God did what He had promised to do in the covenant.[9] He punished His trustees for their rebellion. He removed Israel from His land and sent them to Babylon as captives of Nebuchadnezzar. During Israel's captivity, God spoke to three prophets: Jeremiah, Ezekiel, and Daniel. God gave Jeremiah and Ezekiel wonderful insight into His future plans for Israel. (Plan A) God wanted Israel to listen to His prophets and understand what wonderful plans He had for His people if they would cooperate with Him. At the same time, God also spoke to Daniel, but He gave Daniel a very different prophetic schematic which is called "Plan B." Plan B is a prophetic schematic built on the premise that if Israel failed to fulfill their covenant with God, God would abandon Israel as His trustees and Jerusalem would be totally destroyed. *God gave conflicting views of the future to these three prophets for a reason; the future of the world would be determined by Israel's behavior during the seventy weeks.* If Israel cooperated with God during the seventy weeks by meeting the terms and conditions set before them, Plan B would not occur. Daniel's visions and prophecies would be forever sealed up (remain meaningless). On the other hand, if Israel continued to rebel against His covenant during the seventy weeks, God would abandon them. He would start over by redefining the offspring of Abraham[10] as believers in Christ and Plan B would proceed unconditionally.[11]

As we study this prophecy, please keep three matters in mind: First, Plan A (the seventy weeks) and Plan B (the 2,300 days) start with the *same* date to rebuild and restore Jerusalem. This was necessary because only one plan would be implemented. Gabriel told Daniel, "Seventy weeks are determined or decreed for your people . . ." The Hebrew word for determined or decreed is *chathak* and it means to cut off; as in cutting off a piece of ribbon or cloth from a larger piece. In other words, the seventy weeks, which equals 490 years, are cut off of a larger time period – the 2,300 days. We know that Gabriel is talking about the 2,300 days because Gabriel said to Daniel in verse 23, **"As soon as you began to pray, an answer was given, which I have come to tell you, for you are highly esteemed. Therefore, consider the message and understand the vision."** Gabriel is talking about the vision previously given to Daniel recorded in Daniel 8.

Second, nothing is written in Prophecy 3 indicating *when* the 2,300 days would begin or end because God was not finished with the vision in Prophecy 3. The vision in Prophecy 3 was deliberately left incomplete for about eleven years! Just before the seventy years in Babylon ended, God wanted to reveal a very important message to His people through Daniel. He wanted to

the man Gabriel, whom I had seen in the vision at the beginning, being caused to fly swiftly, touched me about the time of the evening oblation. And he informed me, and talked with me, and said, O Daniel, I am now come forth to give thee skill and understanding. At the beginning of thy supplications the commandment came forth, and I am come to show thee; for thou art greatly beloved: therefore understand the matter, and consider the vision.

> Dan. 9:23

give them hope. So, Gabriel was sent to Daniel with some very important words.

Daniel learned that Jerusalem would be restored and rebuilt. Seventy weeks after a decree to restore and rebuild Jerusalem, Messiah would appear. Of course, there was a caveat. By starting two different prophetic time periods with the same decree, God hung the destiny of the world on Israel's behavior. If Israel cooperated, Plan A would be fulfilled and the book of Daniel would have remained forever sealed. If Israel rebelled, Plan B would be initiated and after 2,300 years expired, the horn, which is Lucifer, would physically appear out of nowhere at the appointed time of the end.

Third, excluding the book of Daniel, most people fail to realize that the entire Old Testament (Plan A) says nothing about a Second Coming. There would not have been any need for a Second Coming if Israel had met the terms and conditions set before them in Plan A. According to Plan A, Jesus would have come to Earth and begun establishing the kingdom of God on Earth in A.D. 27. In anticipation of the fulfillment of Plan A, God sent John the Baptist[12] ahead of Jesus to announce this marvelous truth! If Plan A had been fulfilled, all of the Old Testament prophecies would make perfect sense just as they read! The history of mankind after the seventieth week would have been entirely different if only Israel had welcomed Messiah.[13]

When Daniel humbled himself according to the conditions presented in the covenant and interceded on behalf of his people,[14] God was pleased to honor Daniel and He remembered His covenant with Israel. God returned Israel to *His* land.[15] God granted the nation of Israel a final opportunity to repent and fulfill the trusteeship for which He called them out of Egypt.[16]

> Dan. 9:24
>
> Seventy weeks are determined upon thy people and upon thy holy city, to finish the transgression, and to make an end of sins, and to make reconciliation for iniquity, and to bring in

{24} Gabriel said to Daniel, "Seventy weeks are 'cut off' of the 2,300 days for the benefit of your people. During this time, God will do everything possible to help Israel fulfill their trusteeship. In return, they must cooperate with the Holy Spirit and be transformed into a people who love God supremely and their neighbors as themselves. Gabriel warned, "Israel must stop rebelling against God's ways (finish transgression), your people must live righteously (put an end to deliberate and defiant sin), your people must provide atonement (restitution) for wickedness as God requires (atone for your wrong doing), your people must purify their hearts and minds to bring in everlasting righteousness, and if they do, they will have the joy of anointing the Holy One of Israel. If your people will do these things, the visions and prophecies found in this book (containing Plan B) will be sealed up and never come to pass."

{25} "About eighty years from now, a Persian king, having the name Artaxerxes, will issue a decree in the seventh year of his reign[17] to restore and rebuild Jerusalem. God will move on the king's heart and make it possible for Israel to return to their homeland in a year of Jubilee.[18] His decree will be issued on or about Nisan 1 during the Sunday year, 457 B.C. Ezra, a priest of God, will leave Babylon to go to Jerusalem on Nisan 12.[19] Even though four decrees will be given to restore and rebuild Jerusalem, only one decree will be given in a Jubilee year.[20] Watch for it because this decree will start the seventy weeks and the 2,300 days. After King Artaxerxes issues the decree in 457 B.C., one complete Jubilee cycle of seven weeks (49 years) will pass, then another sixty-two weeks (434 years) will pass, and finally, the seventieth week will arrive. The seventieth week will begin on Nisan 1, A.D. 27, a Sunday year in God's calendar. During the fall of the year in A.D. 27, John will baptize Messiah and His ministry will begin.[21]

"Your beloved city, Jerusalem, will be reconstructed, but during troublous times. The Lord will use a high priest named Joshua and a king named Zerubbabel to rebuild the city.[22] During Israel's exile in Babylon, warlords have occupied the land of Judah and naturally, they will do everything possible to keep Israel from rebuilding, but the city and the temple will be rebuilt – not by human prowess, but through God's enabling Holy Spirit.[23]

{26} "Regrettably, your people, Daniel, will not comply with God's covenant. When Messiah arrives, they will ridicule Him and reject His teaching. He will speak the words which the Father gives Him and the leaders of your people will be unwilling to listen to the Word of God. Messiah will be murdered. He will be cut down by His own people. Because of stubborn and persistent rebellion, Israel will bring down God's wrath upon their own heads. According to the terms and conditions set forth in His covenant with Israel,[24] God will send the Romans against Jerusalem and they will destroy His temple. Rome will utterly destroy the nation of Israel in A.D. 70. No one will be able to prevent it. Destruction will come upon your people like a mighty flood. Wars and desolation will trouble the city of Jerusalem until the end of the world, and from time to time, the city will be reduced to ruins. This has been decreed.

---

everlasting righteousness, and to seal up the vision and prophecy, and to anoint the most Holy.

Dan. 9:25

Know therefore and understand, that from the going forth of the commandment to restore and to build Jerusalem unto the Messiah the Prince shall be seven weeks, and threescore and two weeks: the street shall be built again, and the wall, even in troublous times.

Dan. 9:26

And after threescore and two weeks shall Messiah be cut off, but not for himself: and the people of the prince that shall come shall destroy the city and the sanctuary; and the end thereof shall be with a flood, and unto the end of the war desolations are determined.

Prophecy 4 - The Seventy Weeks

Dan. 9:27

And he shall confirm the covenant with many for one week: and in the midst of the week he shall cause the sacrifice and the oblation to cease, and for the overspreading of abominations he shall make it desolate, even until the consummation, and that determined shall be poured upon the desolate.

{27} "Messiah will appear, right on time.[25] As the Lamb of God, He will reconcile the world to God[26] and confirm the covenant of salvation first given to Adam and Eve.[27] Messiah will die in the middle year of the seventieth week, which is a Wednesday year, A.D. 30. Jesus will bring the Levitical laws and the sacrificial system with its obligations and animal sacrifices to an end.[28] A few years before Messiah begins His ministry, King Herod will lavish great wealth on the temple in Jerusalem to win the favor of the Jews. But the Romans will burn the temple and destroy the city in A.D. 70. They will pull every stone in the temple apart to remove the melted gold.[29] God has decreed that the second temple shall not stand and a third temple will never be rebuilt on Mt. Zion."

The year of Messiah's death is important for several reasons: First, the death of Jesus aligns A.D. 30 with a Wednesday year. Because this alignment is beyond dispute, 457 B.C. becomes a Sunday year. The year 457 B.C. also aligns with the year of Jubilee in Hezekiah's day (702 B.C.), again emphasizing 457 B.C. as a Jubilee year. Second, the year of Messiah's baptism is beyond dispute. A.D. 27 is a Sunday year, the first year of the seventieth week. Finally, the decree issued by Artaxerxes was issued on or about Nisan 1, 457 B.C. Because the seventy weeks are cut off of the 2,300 days, the books of record were opened and the cleansing of Heaven's temple began on or about Nisan 1, A.D. 1844.

Bible history reveals that Israel did not reform during the seventy weeks granted to them. Thus, God abandoned Plan A and Plan B was implemented. Plan B is based on a new covenant and the books of Daniel and Revelation contain prophecies and promises for Plan B. Merging Plan A prophecies with Plan B prophecies produces insurmountable confusion because both plans are separate and distinct. Soon, the Great Tribulation will begin, and when it does, the judgment of the living will begin.[30]

The Rules of Interpretation

Please consider how the Rules of Interpretation (which are discussed in the introduction to this book) are observed in this prophecy:

Rule One says an apocalyptic prophecy has a beginning point and ending point in time and the events within the prophecy occur in the order given. This vision contains a starting and ending point in time and there is a sequence of events. Notice:

1. The decree to restore and rebuild Jerusalem and the temple begins (457 B.C.).
2. Seven weeks of years will follow (49 years).
3. Sixty-two weeks of years will follow (434 years).
4. Messiah will appear (484th year or A.D. 27).
5. Messiah will be cut off in the middle of the seventieth week causing sacrifices to end (A.D. 30).
6. The city and the temple will be destroyed (A.D. 70).
7. Wars and desolations will continue throughout Israel and Jerusalem until the end of time.

We can be 100% sure that Gabriel's visit in Daniel 9 is related to the vision recorded in Daniel 8. Daniel wrote, **"While I was still in prayer, Gabriel, the man I had seen in the *earlier* vision, came to me in swift flight about the time of the evening sacrifice. . .'Daniel, I have now come to give you insight and understanding. As soon as you began to pray, an answer was given, which I have come to tell you, for you are highly esteemed. Therefore, consider the message and understand the vision** [that was previously given to you – Daniel 8:26,27].' "[31]

Daniel 8 is intimately connected to Daniel 9 for another reason: Gabriel said, **"Seventy 'sevens' are *decreed* for your people."**[32] The Hebrew word for decreed is *chathak* and it means to cut off, to measure from, to determine size or value. Therefore, in this context, *chathak* means the seventy weeks must be *cut off* from a larger time period. Only one time period is given in the previous vision. The shorter time period (490 years) is *cut off* from the longer time period (2,300 years). Both time periods share the same starting date.

Ultimately, the only people who really need to understand 1798, 1844 and the appearing of the stern-faced king from the north is the final generation. The idea that the seventieth week is still future is fiction. Plan A, with its promises and prophecies, was abandoned when Jesus was on Earth.[33] This is true because Jesus initiated a new covenant that contains better promises and prophecies. Plan B is always better than Plan A. Unlike Plan A, Plan B is unconditional. In other words, God's timing in Plan B is not dependent upon the behavior of His trustees.

Love Versus Foreknowledge

Some people become confused when hearing about the concept of Plan A and Plan B for the first time. The confusion often stems from this argument: If God perfectly foreknows the future, there cannot be two plans! Let us carry this argument to its logical conclusion. If God foreknew that Lucifer would sin and He created Him anyway, who is responsible for sin? Why did God create a third of the angels foreknowing that they would participate in Lucifer's rebellion? God also foreknew that Adam and Eve would sin. Did He create them so that Jesus would have to die? Not at all. These are important questions and God has answered them.[34] God declares that He keeps His foreknowledge separate from His love for His subjects. We will examine this topic in depth when we study Prophecy 6.

For now, please consider this: God foreknew the flood in Noah's day would be necessary long before it happened. God foreknew Israel's rebellion long before He led Israel out of Egypt. He foreknew that Israel would have to wander in the desert for forty years. God foreknew that Israel would have to be sent into Babylonian exile. God foreknew that Israel would reject and crucify Christ, and God foreknew that Jerusalem would be totally destroyed in A.D. 70.

Even though He foreknew all of these events, God's foreknowledge did not alter His love or behavior. God does not deal with any created being on the basis of His foreknowledge because *His love is not influenced by His foreknowledge*. God is love. His actions are always consistent with the principles of love. God already knows whether I will be saved or lost, but His foreknowledge does not affect His efforts to win over my heart. God's love will not permit Him to use His foreknowledge to manipulate His children for His own benefit. God created Lucifer foreknowing the damage that

Lucifer would cause. God chose Israel foreknowing the damage His choice would cause. God showered every gift and grace on Israel. He gave Israel many wonderful promises, and most of all, He sent His own Son to Israel because *His love is not influenced by His foreknowledge.*

God loved Israel with all His heart. He wanted Plan A to work out. He went so far as to reveal wonderful things to Jeremiah, Isaiah, Ezekiel, and other Old Testament prophets about the contents of Plan A. The key point that so many people miss is that Plan A was a marriage contract. The fulfillment of Plan A was <u>conditional</u> on Israel's participation.[35] God's perfect foreknowledge allowed Him to outline a portion of Plan B to Daniel even though, at the same time, He was illuminating Plan A to Jeremiah and Ezekiel. This explains why God hid Plan B from human understanding (sealed up the book of Daniel) until Plan A was dead.

The concept of Plan A and Plan B is essential when understanding Bible prophecy. Plan A was based on man's cooperation with God. Plan B is not. If Israel had cooperated with God during the seventy weeks, the New Testament portion of the Bible would not have been necessary. Israel would have been prepared to receive the Messiah and the sin problem would have been resolved as the Old Testament declares. Jesus would have remained on Earth after His resurrection and the kingdom of God would have been established on Earth long ago. If all this had happened as first planned, Plan B would have remained unknown. But Plan A was terminated and God appointed new trustees to be the heirs of Abraham.[36]

Rule Two says a fulfillment only occurs when all of the specifications are met, and this includes the order stated in the prophecy. This vision has a starting point in time. Artaxerxes issued the decree on or about Nisan 1, 457 B.C. When it comes to pinpointing the death of Jesus in the middle of the seventieth week, there is no room for debate on this date when all the facts are presented. The only year that can meet all of the details provided in Scripture and at the same time, align with the Sun and Moon, is A.D. 30. The Sun and Moon are important because their celestial positions eliminate speculation on the timing of Nisan 1 in A.D. 30. Their positions have been carefully researched and the results can be examined at the official website of the U.S. Naval Observatory.[37]

Rule Three says that apocalyptic language can be literal, analogous, or symbolic. We know there are no symbolic elements in this prophecy because *symbols are defined with relevant* Scripture. The language used in this vision is either literal or analogous. No symbols are offered or defined.

Rule Four is heavily used in this prophecy. It says the presence or absence of the Jubilee Calendar determines how God measures time. Both the seventy weeks prophecy and the 2,300 day prophecy fall within the operation of the Jubilee Calendar. Therefore, both of these time periods must be translated – a day equals a year. Moreover, it is important to notice that the weekly cycle of years did not end with the death of Jesus in A.D. 30 because Jesus died in the middle of the week. In fact, the weekly cycle of years did not end in the Thursday year of 1844. The weekly cycle of years ended in 1994, at the end of seventy Jubilee cycles. See Appendix A.

References:

1. See Chapter 6 in my book, *Daniel: Unlocked for the Final Generation*.
2. Ibid., pages 176-209
3. Leviticus 25:13
4. Ezekiel 4:5,6; 2 Chronicles 36:20-22
5. Four decrees were issued to restore and rebuild Jerusalem: Cyrus: 536 B.C.; Darius I Hystaspes: 519 B.C; Artaxerxes: 457 B.C.; Artaxerxes: 444 B.C. Only one decree, 457 B.C., occurs in a Sunday year which also happens to be a Jubilee year. Identifying Jubilee years is important because Daniel 9:25 specifies the decree to restore and rebuild Jerusalem must occur at the beginning of "seven sevens" which is a Jubilee cycle. For further discussion on the patterns of Jubilee cycles, please see Appendix A.
6. Ezra 8:31
7. 2 Corinthians 5:10; Ecclesiastes 12:14
8. Jeremiah 25:11; 2 Chronicles 6:36-39; 36:21
9. Leviticus 26
10. Galatians 3:27-29; Romans 2:28,29; Ephesians 2:1-14
11. For a discussion on the important differences between God's unilateral and bilateral covenants, please see Chapter 8 in my book, *Jesus: The Alpha and The Omega* or freely download at http://www.wake-up.org/Alpha/Chapter8.htm.
12. Mark 1:15
13. John 1:11
14. Leviticus 26:40-44
15. Leviticus 25:23, 55; Leviticus 26:41-45; 2 Chronicles 7:20
16. Exodus 19:4-6; Isaiah 42:6; 49:6
17. Ezra 7:9-13
18. Leviticus 25:10
19. Ezra 8:31

20. Cyrus, 536 B.C. – Ezra 5:13
    Darius I Hystaspes, 519 B.C. – Ezra 6:12
    Artaxerxes, 457 B.C. – Ezra 7:11-13
    Artaxerxes, 444 B.C. – Nehemiah 2:1-8
21. Luke 3:1-3, 15, 23
22. Zechariah 3 and 4
23. Zechariah 4:6-9; Ezra 4
24. Leviticus 26:13-39; Deuteronomy 28:15-29:1
25. Romans 5:6; Galatians 4:4,5
26. Romans 5:10
27. Genesis 3:15 The terms and conditions for salvation were given to Adam and Eve by Jesus. Adam and Eve were covered with the skin of the first animal sacrifice. Genesis 3:21 Abel's offering indicates that he also knew the terms and conditions for salvation. Genesis 4:4
    See Hebrews 11:4.
28. Hebrews 9:26 through 10:14
29. Matthew 24:2
30. See Prophecies 9 and 12.
31. Daniel 9:20-23, italics and insertion mine
32. Daniel 9:24, italics mine
33. Matthew 23; Jeremiah 31:31; Luke 22:20
34. Please see Chapter 10 in my book, *A Study on the Seven Seals and the 144,000*.
35. Please see Chapters 5 and 8 in my book, *Jesus: The Alpha and The Omega*.
36. Ephesians 2; Galatians 3:28,29; Romans 2:28,29 See also Appendix B.
37. Go to http://www.usno.navy.mil and search for the topic "Spring Phenomenon." For a comprehensive presentation on the dating of Christ's death, please also see pages 189-209 in my book, *Daniel, Unlocked for the Final Generation* or download the chapter here: http://www.wake-up.org/Daniel/DanChap6.htm

Prophecy 5 & Epilogue

Wars Between the North & South

Daniel 10:1-12:13

Beginning Point in Time: 538 B.C.

Ending Point in Time: Second Coming

Summary: This vision contains two stories. The first story describes a series of battles that conclude with the destruction of Jerusalem in A.D. 70 and the second story describes a battle that concludes with the destruction of the world at the Second Coming. Two stories are told in this vision because there are important parallels between them.

Using repetition and enlargement, the second story amplifies the appearing of the horn described in Daniel 8. Remember the horn in Daniel 8 appears out of nowhere. We will discover in Prophecies 8 and 11 that Lucifer will be released from the Abyss (spirit realm). He will physically appear and establish a worldwide kingdom on Earth. To do this, he must destroy the religions and governments of the world. Jesus will permit the devil to do this for a minimum of two reasons. First, Jesus wants the universe to witness the nature of government that *any sinner* would establish if given the opportunity and absolute power to acomplish it. Second, Jesus enables the devil to destroy the religions and governments of Earth so that religious heritage and patriotism will not hinder any person from accepting salvation. In other words, when Satan is allowed to abolish patriotism and religious heritage, he will eliminate the two cherished refuges of all mankind. Suddenly, each person will find himself in a very difficult "no-man's land." Each wicked person will have to rethink the basis for his rebellion against the gospel of Christ. Whom will he now worship and obey – the visible despot who gloriously masquerades as God or the unseen Creator of Heaven and Earth that dwells in Heaven?

Prophecy 5 & Epilogue - Wars Between the North and the South

Introduction: The last vision in the book of Daniel is important to two groups of Christians. The first group lived around A.D. 70 and the second group will live at the time of the end. This vision contains two stories because both groups of Christians face the same dilemma, that is, both groups are caught in the middle; trapped between hostile forces.

During the final days of Christ's ministry on Earth, Jesus directed His followers to the first part of this vision because it foretold the upcoming destruction of Jerusalem.[1] Vespesian set siege to Jerusalem in A.D. 66 and the siege was temporarily lifted in A.D. 68 when Nero committed suicide. Vespesian returned to Rome and became the next Caesar. Later, Vespasian's son, Titus, resumed the siege of Jerusalem. It has been said that no Christians remained in Jerusalem when Titus resumed the siege in April, A.D. 70. If this is true, it would be the result of early Christians understanding the first segment of this prophecy because once the siege was set, no one escaped. Titus and his army totally destroyed the city and the temple in September.

The second part of this vision begins with Daniel 11:36. The King of the North is Lucifer. He will physically appear during the fifth trumpet and will be successful until the time of wrath (the Great Tribulation) is completed.[2] Lucifer will conquer the world and destroy everyone who stands in his way. God has given this information to the final generation because He does not want His people to give up or lose faith in Him. During the Great Tribulation, God will permit the forces of evil to kill most of His saints. This is not as horrible as it may sound because God will give His people the grace and strength to die a martyr's death when grace is needed. Even more, sleeping in Christ while the remainder of the Great Tribulation plays out will be a merciful release from suffering and deprivation.

When Lucifer physically appears, he will masquerade as Almighty God, demand an end to religious and political diversity, and order that a one world theocracy be established. He will demand, "There cannot be any religious or political diversity when God lives among men!" Many people on Earth will resist the devil's attempt to establish his theocracy because they do not want to obey him. The devil and his forces (represented in the second portion of this prophecy as the King of the North) will destroy the opposition[3] (represented in this prophecy as the King of the South). God's saints will be trapped in the middle of this war because, like the opposition, they will refuse to worship the devil, but for different reasons.

Even though the first portion of this vision has been fulfilled, it is good to study it and understand it. The first story reveals a salient fact: God overrules. He manages the nations of the world. He sets up kings and takes them down when their cup of sin is filled. As you follow the back and forth wars described in the first segment of this prophecy, remember that Israel was trapped in the middle of what must have seemed like endless fighting.

Prophecy 5 & Epilogue - Wars Between the North and the South

> **Dan. 10:1**
> *In the third year of Cyrus king of Persia a thing was revealed unto Daniel, whose name was called Belteshazzar; and the thing was true, but the time appointed was long: and he understood the thing, and had understanding of the vision.*

> **Dan. 10:2-3**
> *In those days I Daniel was mourning three full weeks. I ate no pleasant bread, neither came flesh nor wine in my mouth, neither did I anoint myself at all, till three whole weeks were fulfilled.*

> **Dan. 10:4-6**
> *And in the four and twentieth day of the first month, as I was by the side of the great river, which is Hiddekel; Then I lifted up mine eyes, and looked, and behold a certain man clothed in linen, whose loins were girded*

The Vision Begins

{1} When Babylon fell to the Medes and Persians, the Medes took control of the province of Babylon. Even though I was about 85 years of age, King Darius appointed me to serve in his court as an advisor. Like myself, the king was an elderly man and he died shortly after God rescued me from the lion's den. After he died, the province of Babylon was given over to Cyrus, king of Persia. During Cyrus' third year as king over Babylon, I received another vision. I knew the message was true because it came from God, but even so, it made me sick. I was shown a great war that seemed to have no end. Two great opponents struggled for supremacy and power, but there was no apparent winner.

{2} After watching the vision, I was depressed for three weeks because I suspected that my people would likely squander the seventy weeks of grace extended to them. I wondered about my people because Gabriel had said that wars and desolations were decreed upon Jerusalem until the end of the world.[4] I did not want to believe that my people would violate God's covenant again, but I knew that my people had a long history of rebellion. Many times, we had refused to honor the God of our forefathers, Abraham, Isaac, and Jacob. As a result, God used King Nebuchadnezzar to drive us out of the Beautiful Land.[5] {3} I petitioned the Most High God for an understanding of this vision, hoping that my worries were misdirected. To show God my sincerity and desire for understanding, I did not eat delicious food; no meat or wine touched my lips; and I used no cologne until the three weeks were over.

Discussion

{4} On the twenty-fourth day of Nisan, I received a follow-up vision. In this vision, I was standing on the bank of the Tigris. {5} I looked up and saw a glorious man dressed in brilliant linen, wearing a belt of finest gold around his waist. {6} His body was as bright as the Sun shining on polished gold, His face was brilliant like lightning, his eyes like flaming torches, His arms and legs like gleaming polished bronze, and His voice sounded like the roar of a great multitude because it could be heard for miles around.

{7} I was the only one who saw Him; the men with me did not see the glorious man, but when the vision began they were terrified and fled for safety. {8} I was left alone, gazing at this glorious being, my body had no strength and my face turned deathly pale. {9} Then I heard Him speak, and as I listened, I fell unconscious falling face first into the dirt. {10} An angel touched me and helped me get up on my hands and knees. I was trembling and had no strength. {11} The angel reassured me saying, "Daniel, you are highly esteemed; carefully consider the words I am about to speak to you. Stand up, for Michael/Jesus, the brilliant man you just saw, has sent me." After the angel said this, my strength returned enough to stand up, even though I was trembling and shaking. {12} Then the angel continued, "Do not be afraid, Daniel. Since the day you received the vision about the great war and began humbling yourself with fasting and prayer for understanding, God heard your words, and He sent me to you.

---

with fine gold of Uphaz: His body also was like the beryl, and his face as the appearance of lightning, and his eyes as lamps of fire, and his arms and his feet like in colour to polished brass, and the voice of his words like the voice of a multitude.

Dan. 10:7-12

And I Daniel alone saw the vision: for the men that were with me saw not the vision; but a great quaking fell upon them, so that they fled to hide themselves. Therefore I was left alone, and saw this great vision, and there remained no strength in me: for my comeliness was turned in me into corruption, and I retained no strength. Yet heard I the voice of his words: and when I heard the voice of his words, then was I in a deep sleep on my face, and my face toward the ground.

Prophecy 5 & Epilogue - Wars Between the North and the South

And, behold, an hand touched me, which set me upon my knees and upon the palms of my hands. And he said unto me, O Daniel, a man greatly beloved, understand the words that I speak unto thee, and stand upright: for unto thee am I now sent. And when he had spoken this word unto me, I stood trembling. Then said he unto me, Fear not, Daniel: for from the first day that thou didst set thine heart to understand, and to chasten thyself before thy God, thy words were heard, and I am come for thy words.

Dan. 10:13-14
But the prince of the kingdom of Persia withstood me one and twenty days: but, lo, Michael, one of the chief princes, came to help me; and I remained there with the kings of Persia. Now I am come to

{13} "But, the prince of this world, the devil, thwarted my efforts for the past twenty-one days. Warlords from Judea have been trying to turn the heart of Cyrus against your people. The squatters around Jerusalem do not want your people to rebuild Jerusalem or the temple. As the devil was strongly urging Cyrus to stop the rebuilding process, Michael/Jesus, the Archangel, the glorious man you saw in the sky above the river, came to my aid. {14} Now that Michael has overcome Lucifer, rebuilding will continue.[6] So listen carefully, for I have come to explain what will happen to your people in the future, for this vision reveals what will happen during and after the seventy weeks. . . ."

Wars Between the North and the South - Prophecy 5 & Epilogue

The Sequence

{20} "Soon, the kingdom of Persia will fill up its cup of iniquity. The kingdom of Grecia will overtake Persia and rise to power. {21} Michael, the Prince of Heaven, manages the rise and fall of earthly kingdoms. {1} For example, during the first year of Darius the Mede, I was assigned to protect him according to the plans of the Most High. Now that Darius has died, the Most High has determined that his territory shall be given to the Persian king, Cyrus. This transition will resolve two difficult problems. First, as king of Babylon, Cyrus can set your people free from Babylon. Second, as king of the Trans-Euphrates territory, Cyrus can give the land of Judea back to your people.

{2} "Three more kings after Cyrus will rule over Persia: Cambyses, Darius I Hystaspes, and False Smerdis (also called Bardiya). Then, a fourth king, Xerxes (also called Ahasuerus, the husband of the future Queen Esther) will come to power. Xerxes will be far richer than the other three. When Xerxes has gained much power by his wealth, he will irritate the newly developing kingdom of Grecia with his conquests. This will later prove to be the undoing of Persia.

---

make thee understand what shall befall thy people in the latter days: for yet the vision is for many days.

Dan. 10:20-11:1

Then said he, Knowest thou wherefore I come unto thee? and now will I return to fight with the prince of Persia: and when I am gone forth, lo, the prince of Grecia shall come. But I will show thee that which is noted in the scripture of truth: and there is none that holdeth with me in these things, but Michael your prince. 11:1 Also I in the first year of Darius the Mede, even I, stood to confirm and to strengthen him.

Dan. 11:2

And now will I show thee the truth. Behold, there shall stand up yet three kings in Persia; and the fourth shall be far richer than they all: and by his strength through his

> riches he shall stir up all against the realm of Grecia.
>
> **Dan. 11:3-4**
> And a mighty king shall stand up, that shall rule with great dominion, and do according to his will. And when he shall stand up, his kingdom shall be broken, and shall be divided toward the four winds of heaven; and not to his posterity, nor according to his dominion which he ruled: for his kingdom shall be plucked up, even for others beside those.

{3} "About one hundred years after the reign of Xerxes, another mighty king, Alexander the Great, will rise to power in Grecia. The four wings on the leopard beast in Daniel 7 represent the amazing speed of his conquest. The great horn on the goat in Daniel 8 represents this unstoppable king. He will rule with impunity and do as he pleases. {4} He will conquer western civilization in a period of ten years and die an untimely death. Remember how the great horn on the goat was broken off at the height of its power. Alexander will die when he is strongest and his empire will not go to his descendants. His empire will be divided toward the north, south, east and west. His generals will not have the military might that Alexander exercised. Years later, the Grecian Empire will fall into the hands of the Romans. They will rise up and rule a large territory with an iron hand."

To appreciate the contents of this vision, three matters must be kept in mind:

First, after Noah died, God called Abraham out of Ur (which was near Babylon) and directed him to relocate to Canaan. God did this because in the future, He planned to put the descendants of Abraham in a highly strategic location.

Second, because Abraham loved God to the point of sacrificing his own son, God chose the descendants of Abraham to be the trustees of His gospel. God wanted the world to learn about His laws of love, His mercy and kindness, and His promise of redemption from sin. God did not *steal* the land of Canaan from the Canaanites and give it to the Jews. He waited until the Cananites filled up their cup of sin,[7] then He gave the land of Canaan to Abraham's descendants.[8] Incidentally, the "full cup principle" also explains why Canaan was taken from the Jews in A.D. 70.[9]

Third, God placed Israel in the geographical center of many nations[10] because trade caravans and armies often passed through Canaan while on their way to other destinations. This natural exposure enabled people living in other parts of the world to hear about the marvelous God who actually lived in a temple in Israel. In fact, the queen of Sheba heard about the fame and riches of Solomon and she went to see him for herself.[11] God did these things because He wanted the world to learn about Him and His character of love. This is why He lavishly blessed the Jews. In turn, He wanted the Jews to lavishly distribute the riches of His graces, taking the light of truth to the Gentiles,[12] showing them the quality of life that comes from serving an infinite God who loves righteousness and hates evil.

> Dan. 11:3-4

The land of Canaan lies between two natural barriers. The great sea (the Mediterranean Sea) lies to the west and the great desert (the Arabian Desert) lies to the east. For thousands of years, these natural barriers forced northbound and southbound travel through the corridor of Canaan. When the tiny nation of Israel crossed over the Jordan and entered Canaan in 1397 B.C., it unwittingly became a nation living between two giants. These giants are described in this prophecy as the "King of the North" and the "King of the South." These titles make perfect sense when viewed from Israel's geographical location.

Because the book of Daniel contains Plan B, God traced many well-known battles between the north and the south during the seventy weeks of Daniel 9. He did this so that if Plan B should become necessary, His people could escape the destruction of Jerusalem. Therefore, the first part of this vision contains information which early Christians could easily decipher. In fact, shortly before His death, Jesus directed His followers to this prophecy![13]

Evidently, early Christians understood Daniel 10:1 through Daniel 11:31 and they fled Jerusalem before it was destroyed in A.D. 70. Historians have indicated that few, if any, Christians perished. The good news is that early Christians foreknew the outcome of the Roman siege which began in A.D. 66 and they were able to escape in A.D. 68 when the siege was unexpectedly lifted. (Nero died.) Of course, the Jews were relieved when the siege was lifted, but to their peril, they did not accept Jesus' words. They would not believe God would allow Rome to destroy *His* city and *His* temple and history reveals that their beliefs had no effect on realities that followed. The Roman army resumed its siege in April and the city fell in September, A.D. 70. The historian, Josephus, wrote that 1.1 million people were killed and 97,000 were taken as slaves.[14]

This vision also contains a segment for people living at the appointed time of the end. God wants His saints to know and understand that they are going to be caught between the devil (the King of the North) and secular forces (the King of the

Prophecy 5 & Epilogue - Wars Between the North and the South

> Dan. 11:3-4

South) opposed to the devil's demands. The devil and his forces will view God's people as part of the opposition and millions of saints will die in the process. (See fifth seal in Prophecy 6.) God has revealed this information in advance so that His people will not abandon their hope or their faith in Him. It is a great shame that a vast majority of Christians today do not know that the saints will be totally defeated during the Great Tribulation.[15] There will be a few believers living when Jesus comes,[16] but externally, the situation will appear hopeless for Christians during the sixth trumpet.

Now that we have briefly discussed the parallel between early Christians and Christians during the Great Tribulation, we will return to the vision. Remember, this first segment belongs to those who lived during the destruction of Jerusalem.

> Dan. 11:5-6
>
> *And the king of the south shall be strong, and one of his princes; and he shall be strong above him, and have dominion; his dominion shall be a great dominion. And in the end of years they shall join themselves together; for the king's daughter of the south shall come to the king of the north to make an agreement: but she shall not retain the power of the arm; neither shall he stand, nor his arm: but she shall be given up, and they that brought her, and he that begat her, and he that strengthened her in these times.*

{5} "One of Alexander's generals, Ptolemy I Soter, will become the king of Egypt. As the King of the South, he will become strong, but a second general from Alexander's empire, Seleucus I Nicator, will become even greater than Ptolemy. Seleucus will extend his domain so that he will rule over the north with great power. {6} After a few years, these two kings will die, and their descendants will become allies through marriage. Bernice, the daughter of Ptolemy II, the King of the South, will go to Antiochus II, the King of the North, to make an alliance. Antiochus II will divorce his wife, Laodice, to marry Bernice and they will produce an heir. However, this alliance will not last long. The vacillating Antiochus II will divorce Bernice and reconcile with his former wife, Laodice. After Antiochus II and Laodice reconcile, Laodice will kill Bernice, her royal escort, and her son by Antiochus II. Laodice will then kill Antiochus II because he left her to support an alliance with Bernice.

{7} "Later on, Bernice's brother in Egypt, Ptolemy III, will become King of the South and take her place. To revenge Bernice's death, he will attack the army of Seleucus II, the new King of the North. Ptolemy III will fight against Seleucus II's army and be victorious. He will plunder their fortresses. {8} He will seize their gods, their metal images and their valuable articles of silver and gold and take them to Egypt. For a few years, Ptolemy III will leave the King of the North alone. {9} After several years pass, Seleucus II will then invade the domain of the King of the South to retrieve the gold and silver that Ptolemy III took from him, but Seleucus II will be defeated and he will return to his own country empty-handed. {10} To avenge the defeat of their father, Seleucus III and Antiochus III, the two sons of Seleucus II, will prepare for war and assemble a great army. They will sweep through the land of the King of the South like the damage that comes from an irresistible flood. The two sons will carry the battle as far as the area of Transjordan, which is to be the fortress of the next King of the South, Ptolemy IV.

> **Dan. 11:7-10**
> *But out of a branch of her roots shall one stand up in his estate, which shall come with an army, and shall enter into the fortress of the king of the north, and shall deal against them, and shall prevail: And shall also carry captives into Egypt their gods, with their princes, and with their precious vessels of silver and of gold; and he shall continue more years than the king of the north. So the king of the south shall come into his kingdom, and shall return into his own land. But his sons shall be stirred up, and shall assemble a multitude of great forces: and one shall certainly come, and overflow, and pass through: then shall he return, and be stirred up, even to his fortress.*

Prophecy 5 & Epilogue - Wars Between the North and the South

Dan. 11:11-13

And the king of the south shall be moved with choler, and shall come forth and fight with him, even with the king of the north: and he shall set forth a great multitude; but the multitude shall be given into his hand. And when he hath taken away the multitude, his heart shall be lifted up; and he shall cast down many ten thousands: but he shall not be strengthened by it. For the king of the north shall return, and shall set forth a multitude greater than the former, and shall certainly come after certain years with a great army and with much riches.

{11} "Later, Ptolemy IV will march out in a rage and fight against Antiochus III, the King of the North, at Raphia, and the large army of Antiochus III will be defeated. {12} When Antiochus III is shamed with defeat, Ptolemy IV, the King of the South, will become full of arrogance and will continue with conquests. He will slaughter thousands as his army moves as far as the border of India, yet he will not remain triumphant. Both he and his wife will die mysteriously. In their place, Ptolemy V Epiphanes, their five-year-old son, will ascend to the throne of the south. {13} Meanwhile, Antiochus III, the King of the North, will muster another army, larger than the first. After several years, his forces will plunder Jerusalem and advance toward Egypt with a huge, well-equipped army.

Dan. 11:14-15

And in those times there shall many stand up against the king of the south: also the robbers of thy people shall exalt themselves to establish the

{14} "During the reign of Ptolemy IV, many people will rebel against this arrogant King of the South. Zealots and violent men from among your own people will rebel against him in fulfillment of this vision, but they will not succeed. {15} However Antiochus III, the King of the North, will come and build siege ramps and will capture the fortified city of Sidon. The forces of the King of the South will not be able to resist; even their best troops will not have the strength to resist.

Wars Between the North and the South - Prophecy 5 & Epilogue

{16} "Years later, a new group of invaders from the north will appear and they will do as they please and no one will be able to resist them. They will eventually establish a huge empire, engulfing the Beautiful Land of Canaan. They will have power to destroy anyone who rebels against them. {17} These invaders from the north will be called Romans. The ruler, Julius Caesar, will come with the might of many legions of soldiers and he will make an alliance with Ptolemy XI, the King of the South, in an effort to keep peace. The two children of Ptolemy XI, Cleopatra and Ptolemy XII, will be placed under the guardianship of Rome. In the years to come, Cleopatra and Ptolemy XII, heirs of the throne in the south, will try to eliminate Roman control over Egypt. Cleopatra will seduce Julius Caesar and Mark Antony into illicit love affairs to gain power. But later, Julius Caesar will be assassinated and Mark Antony will be killed in battle. Therefore, Cleopatra's plans will not succeed or help Egypt.

{18} "When an alliance is made with Ptolemy XI, Julius Caesar will subdue the people living on the islands of the coastlands of Africa. In doing so, Julius Caesar will end the rebellion of Scipio and turn his rebellion into defeat. {19} Julius Caesar will then return home and receive many honors and titles, but remember, he is a mortal man and not a god. An assassin will kill him and he will be seen no more. {20} Caesar's successor, Octavius – later named

vision; but they shall fall. So the king of the north shall come, and cast up a mount, and take the most fenced cities: and the arms of the south shall not withstand, neither his chosen people, neither shall there be any strength to withstand.

`Dan. 11:16-17`

But he that cometh against him shall do according to his own will, and none shall stand before him: and he shall stand in the glorious land, which by his hand shall be consumed. He shall also set his face to enter with the strength of his whole kingdom, and upright ones with him; thus shall he do: and he shall give him the daughter of women, corrupting her: but she shall not stand on his side, neither be for him.

`Dan. 11:18-20`

After this shall he turn his face unto the isles, and

> *shall take many: but a prince for his own behalf shall cause the reproach offered by him to cease; without his own reproach he shall cause it to turn upon him. Then he shall turn his face toward the fort of his own land: but he shall stumble and fall, and not be found. Then shall stand up in his estate a raiser of taxes in the glory of the kingdom: but within few days he shall be destroyed, neither in anger, nor in battle.*
>
> **Dan. 11:21-22**
>
> *And in his estate shall stand up a vile person, to whom they shall not give the honour of the kingdom: but he shall come in peaceably, and obtain the kingdom by flatteries. And with the arms of a flood shall they be overflown from before him, and shall be broken; yea, also the prince of the covenant.*

Augustus – will send tax collectors all over the kingdom to maintain his royal splendor. After reigning 40 years, he will die, not in anger or in battle, but of natural causes.

{21} "Tiberius, a contemptible person who will not come through the royal line, will succeed Augustus Caesar. Augustus will adopt Tiberius and thus, he will become the legal heir to the throne. Tiberius Caesar will take the throne of the kingdom without conflict. In fact, he will seize it through intrigue and the help of his manipulating mother, Livia. {22} Tiberius will prove to be a brilliant general. He will succeed against powerful armies that oppose him in Germany, Armenia, and Parthia. During the fifteenth year of his reign, the Holy One of Israel, the Messiah, will begin His ministry, but your people will reject the Holy One. He will be cut off from His inheritance as a criminal is cut off from his inheritance. The great Prince of God's everlasting covenant, the Messiah, will be put to death by His own people.

{23} "The rise of the Roman Empire will mean the destruction of Israel later on. During its rise to power, Rome will offer mutual assistance pacts to various kingdoms. After these kingdoms have reached a friendly agreement with Rome, Rome will act deceitfully and betray them. With only a few people controlling its great army, Roman leaders will grasp great power and no one will be able to defend themselves against them. {24} When the richest provinces feel secure, Rome will invade and completely dominate them. Rome's authority will extend far beyond that of earlier empires. Rome will finance its conquests by distributing the spoils of war to mercenary soldiers. Consequently, Rome's army will become large and its menacing power will be unstoppable. Rome will plot the overthrow of kingdoms everywhere – but only for a time. According to God's Word, secular Rome will come to an end in due time.

{25} "Consider the following information about Augustus Caesar and his reign. This information will eventually help the saints who live in Jerusalem about A.D. 70. Augustus Caesar will raise up a large army with strength and courage to attack Antony, the King of the South. At the Battle of Actium (31 B.C.), Antony will wage war with a large and very powerful army, but he will not endure because of the plots devised against him. {26} Some who are very close to Antony, even those who eat with him, will try to destroy him. Antony's army will be destroyed and many will fall in battle. However, Antony will remain powerful for a little longer. {27} Augustus and Antony, with evil in each of their hearts, will sit at the same table and lie to each other, to no avail. Both men will want to control the world, but neither of them can possibly dominate the world.

Dan. 11:23-24

And after the league made with him he shall work deceitfully: for he shall come up, and shall become strong with a small people. He shall enter peaceably even upon the fattest places of the province; and he shall do that which his fathers have not done, nor his fathers' fathers; he shall scatter among them the prey, and spoil, and riches: yea, and he shall forecast his devices against the strong holds, even for a time.

Dan. 11:25-27

And he shall stir up his power and his courage against the king of the south with a great army; and the king of the south shall be stirred up to battle with a very great and mighty army; but he shall not stand: for they shall forecast devices against him. Yea, they that

Prophecy 5 & Epilogue - Wars Between the North and the South

feed of the portion of his meat shall destroy him, and his army shall overflow: and many shall fall down slain. And both these kings' hearts shall be to do mischief, and they shall speak lies at one table; but it shall not prosper: for yet the end shall be at the time appointed.

Dan. 11:28

Then shall he return into his land with great riches; and his heart shall be against the holy covenant; and he shall do exploits, and return to his own land.

Dan. 11:29-31

At the time appointed he shall return, and come toward the south; but it shall not be as the former, or as the latter. For the ships of Chittim shall come against him: therefore he shall be grieved, and return, and have indignation against the holy covenant: so shall

{28} "Augustus will return to his own country after the Battle of Actium with great wealth from Egypt. Years later (A.D. 66), your people, those who are trustees of God's holy covenant, will revolt against the emperor, Nero. Nero will send his trusted general, Vespasian, to attack many rebellious cities, including Jerusalem. Nero will commit suicide in June A.D. 68 and Vespasian will suddenly lift the siege around Jerusalem and return to his own country to take Nero's throne.

{29} "During April, A.D. 70, Titus, the inexperienced son of Vespasian, will invade the south. This time the result will be different than before. {30} Countries with many ships from the western coastlands of Africa and Egypt will fight against him, and he will lose his desire to fight them. Instead of returning home, Titus will turn his frustration and fury towards the rebellious city of Jerusalem. Titus will need to win a battle in order to avoid shame and derision when returning to Rome. The Romans will harbor a special hatred for the Jews and Titus will set siege against Jerusalem. He will only spare the lives of Jews who renounce their religion. {31} Titus will conquer the city. He will burn the city and the Romans will completely destroy the temple complex which the Jews will think is impregnable. Daily services will never be conducted in the temple again. Titus will bring Jerusalem and those people who live there to an end. All of Israel's genealogical records will be destroyed in the fire. God declares this future account before it happens so the saints will know that His Word will not fail. The wrath that was promised in His covenant [17] with Israel will surely come to pass.[18] Rome will destroy Israel. Jerusalem will be overrun with wars and desolations until Jesus returns because Israel will violate the grace that was granted them for seventy weeks."[19]

> This concludes the first portion of this vision – the portion that belonged to those who experienced the destruction of Jerusalem. The following four verses pertain to the Dark Ages, the 1,260 years granted to the little horn power in Daniel 7.

{32} The angel continued, "About five hundred years after Christ is born, the Roman Empire will undergo a transition. The centralized government of the caesars will be destroyed in A.D. 476, but future emperors will arise and attempt to rebuild the kingdom. These emperors will appear to embrace Christianity. Their motive will be religious and political unification. Thus, the old Roman Empire (a secular empire) will morph into the Holy Roman Empire (a religious empire) and this explains how the little horn in Daniel 7 will become powerful. With flattery and false doctrines, the Church of Rome will corrupt Christianity and consequently, false religion will enslave Europe for 1,260 years. Yet, there will be a small number of faithful people in the Christian faith who will resist the errors introduced by the Church of Rome.

{33} "As centuries pass, people filled with the Holy Spirit and a deep love for God's Word will hold to the truth and keep it alive at great personal sacrifice. Men and women of God will instruct and encourage the scattered people of God for 1,260 years. The little horn in Daniel 7 will capture and torture many of God's saints during the Dark Ages and millions of God's saints will die. {34} Even though many people will die for the sake of truth, God's truth will not perish. The saints will receive strength from God to keep the torch of truth burning. Eventually, Protestantism will arise and new light shining from the Bible will separate many Christians from the errors of the Catholic Church. Protestantism will become respected in some parts of the world. Unfortunately, many insincere people will become a part of Protestantism and with time, Protestantism will eventually become as corrupt as the Catholic Church. {35} Some of God's people will stumble because they lack faith, but every failure refines and purifies people who are willing

he do; he shall even return, and have intelligence with them that forsake the holy covenant. And arms shall stand on his part, and they shall pollute the sanctuary of strength, and shall take away the daily sacrifice, and they shall place the abomination that maketh desolate.

Dan. 11:32

And such as do wickedly against the covenant shall he corrupt by flatteries: but the people that do know their God shall be strong, and do exploits.

Dan. 11:33-35

And they that understand among the people shall instruct many: yet they shall fall by the sword, and by flame, by captivity, and by spoil, many days. Now when they shall fall, they shall be holpen with a little help: but many shall cleave to them with flatteries. And some of them

> *of understanding shall fall, to try them, and to purge, and to make them white, even to the time of the end: because it is yet for a time appointed.*

to grow and learn from their mistakes. This calls for patience and endurance on the part of the saints because the end is not yet. The appointed time of the end may seem indefinite, but it will surely arrive."

The Time of the End

The final segment of this vision pertains to those who will live at the time of the end. God has provided this information because the final generation needs to understand certain things about the time of wrath. The most amazing event prior to the Second Coming will be the physical appearing of the devil. The appearing and work of Lucifer is described twice in the book of Daniel. God uses repetition and enlargement to inform His children about the future activities of the devil.

Dan. 11:36
> *And the king shall do according to his will; and he shall exalt himself, and magnify himself above every god, and shall speak marvellous things against the God of gods, and shall prosper till the indignation be accomplished: for that that is determined shall be done.*

{36} "Two-thirds of the way through the Great Tribulation,[20] the forward advancement of the gospel of Jesus Christ will come to a stand still. At that point in time, almost everyone will have heard the gospel and will have made their decision to embrace it or reject it.

> Jesus became a man to save the world from sin. Lucifer will become a man to lead the world into destruction. God is fair. Jesus physically appeared and the devil will be permitted to physically appear. God allows the devil to physically appear so that sincere people can compare God's way of love with Lucifer's use of force, lies and manipulation.[21] God will permit the devil to masquerade and exalt himself as Almighty God. God "sends this delusion" to complete the tyranny of evil that began thousands of years ago. The devil will make all kinds of outrageous claims and he will do as he pleases because no one can stop him. When he first appears, he will appear to be generous and benevolent.[22] He will feed the multitudes, just as Jesus did, and perform incredible healing miracles with signs and wonders. All this will be done for one malevolent purpose; Lucifer seeks the worship and honor that belongs to Jesus. Meanwhile, the saints will be trapped in "no-man's land." They cannot unite with those who believe that the devil is God (the religious wicked) and they cannot unite with the non-religious wicked who want nothing to do with Lucifer. The devil will exalt and magnify himself above every god known to mankind and he will say unheard of things against the Most High God. Lucifer will eventually gain control of the whole world. However, his true

identity will be exposed during the fifth bowl, for what has been predetermined by the Most High God will surely take place.

{37} "When the devil appears, he will show no respect for any of the traditional gods (false gods) which the people of the world honor and worship.[23] The devil will show no respect for the Holy One of Israel, the Messiah, the male child which every woman in Israel desires to have as a Son. The devil will exalt himself above them all.

{38} "Instead of respecting the gods that the world's different religions have known and trusted, he will denounce them all and trample them into the dirt. When the sixth trumpet sounds, the devil will abolish the religions and governments of the world and in their place, he will establish a false theocracy (a one world church-state).[24] Everyone will be carefully monitored because promotions and extra rations of food will be given to snitches. Everyone will be required to worship according to the laws that Lucifer establishes. The world will become as one city, and the devil's fortress will be his government. He will turn brother against brother and neighbor against neighbor. Those who worship Lucifer will be fearful because there will be secret police everywhere. No one will be able to trust anyone. Lucifer will rule the world as 'Lord of lords and King of kings through terror.[25] Everyone on Earth will be required to obey his laws or be killed. The devil will finance his theocracy with gold and silver, precious stones, and costly gifts.

{39} "At the time of the sixth trumpet, Jesus will give the devil authority to forcibly take over the world. Lucifer will lead a fierce attack against the political powers that oppose him (the non-religious wicked) and the devil's theocracy will be set up. The devil and his followers will destroy a third of mankind.[26] He will greatly honor those leaders who acknowledge that he is "God." The devil will abolish the nations and religions of the world, he will dissolve all national boundaries and divide the world into ten sectors.[27] He will appoint ten puppet-kings to rule as taskmasters over his slaves, the people of the world.[28] The devil will claim ownership over all real estate and he will redistribute the land to the highest bidders. He will be heartless, ruthless, and lawless. This explains to some extent why the devil must be permitted to physically appear. Jesus wants everyone in the universe to observe what *any sinner* would do if given sovereign authority.

Dan. 11:37

Neither shall he regard the God of his fathers, nor the desire of women, nor regard any god: for he shall magnify himself above all.

Dan. 11:38

But in his estate shall he honour the God of forces: and a god whom his fathers knew not shall he honour with gold, and silver, and with precious stones, and pleasant things.

Dan. 11:39

Thus shall he do in the most strong holds with a strange god, whom he shall acknowledge and increase with glory: and he shall cause them to rule over many, and shall divide the land for gain.

Prophecy 5 & Epilogue - Wars Between the North and the South

Dan. 11:40

And at the time of the end shall the king of the south push at him: and the king of the north shall come against him like a whirlwind, with chariots, and with horsemen, and with many ships; and he shall enter into the countries, and shall overflow and pass over.

Dan. 11:41

He shall enter also into the glorious land, and many countries shall be overthrown: but these shall escape out of his hand, even Edom, and Moab, and the chief of the children of Ammon.

Dan. 11:42-43

He shall stretch forth his hand also upon the countries: and the land of Egypt shall not escape. But he shall have power over the treasures of gold and of silver, and over all the precious things of Egypt: and the

{40} "During the sixth trumpet, a few sincere people will come to their senses. When they observe Lucifer's true character and his evil ways, they will repent of their rebellion and embrace Jesus and His gospel. A few people will finally see that in serving Jesus Christ, there is genuine freedom, but this truth will not become evident until they discover that Lucifer rules through slavery and bondage. Many non-religious people will refuse to embrace the gospel of Jesus and they will also hate the devil's great authority. These people will unite (under the direction of a rebel king) and in a desperate effort to overthrow the devil, they will seal their own fate. The devil will respond with overwhelming force. He and his followers will attack his adversaries by land, air, and a great fleet of ships. He will invade and destroy many countries, and sweep through them like a tsunami, an unstoppable wall of water."[29]

{41} "During the sixth trumpet, Lucifer's army will invade many countries, including Israel. His enemies will fall, but the Most High God will keep his success within bounds. Some of the Israelites escaped the destruction of Nebuchadnezzar by fleeing to the remote areas of Edom and Moab. In a similar way, God will sustain some of His people during the end of days. People like the leaders of Ammon, who kindly protected your people when Nebuchadnezzar destroyed Jerusalem, will also be delivered from Lucifer's hand."[30]

{42} "Ultimately, the devil will impose his government on the world. Egypt will not escape his dominion. {43} The devil will also control the wealth of the world. Even those who hate him and those who hate the Most High God will have *no choice* but to submit to him, for no person will be able to buy or sell unless he submits to Lucifer's laws and wears his approval (a tattoo called the mark of the beast)."[31]

{44} "During the sixth trumpet, the 144,000 will announce three messages to the world: (a) the approaching end of salvation's offer, (b) that everyone who worships the devil will be punished during the seven bowls, and (c) that Jesus' return is imminent. These announcements will make the devil very angry. In a rage, he will attempt to kill everyone he can find who worships the Creator of Heaven and Earth.

{45} "Lucifer will establish his throne 'in the middle of mankind' and he will rule over human beings as Almighty God. His achievement will be short lived because the seven bowls will immediately begin. During the fifth bowl, the devil will be unmasked and the wicked will clearly see that the glorious being they have been worshiping is the devil himself. During the seventh bowl, the devil and his angels will be returned to the Abyss. His defeat will surely come, but not by human hands.

{12:1} "When the devil finally sits down to rule the world from his throne, a sovereign Jesus (Michael), who rules from God's throne in Heaven, will stand up. When Jesus stands up, 6,000 years of intercession for sinners will come to an end. On that day, Jesus will pronounce condemnation upon all who refused His offer of salvation and received the mark of the beast. The wicked will be doomed to receive the wrath of God (the seven bowls) which will be poured out without mercy. The pain and suffering inflicted on the wicked cannot be described, but everyone who has faith like Daniel, everyone whose name is found written in The Book of Life, will be delivered from the suffering which the seven bowls contain. When Jesus stands up, the persecution of the saints will cease and there will never be another Christian martyr, ever!

Libyans and the Ethiopians shall be at his steps.

Dan. 11:44

But tidings out of the east and out of the north shall trouble him: therefore he shall go forth with great fury to destroy, and utterly to make away many.

Dan. 11:45

And he shall plant the tabernacles of his palace between the seas in the glorious holy mountain; yet he shall come to his end, and none shall help him.

Dan. 12:1

And at that time shall Michael stand up, the great prince which standeth for the children of thy people: and there shall be a time of trouble, such as never was since there was a nation even to that same time: and at that time thy people shall be delivered, every one that shall be found written in the book.

Prophecy 5 & Epilogue - Wars Between the North and the South

Dan. 12:2-3
And many of them that sleep in the dust of the earth shall awake, some to everlasting life, and some to shame and everlasting contempt. And they that be wise shall shine as the brightness of the firmament; and they that turn many to righteousness as the stars for ever and ever.

Dan. 12:4
But thou, O Daniel, shut up the words, and seal the book, even to the time of the end: many shall run to and fro, and knowledge shall be increased.

Dan. 12:5-6
Then I Daniel looked, and, behold, there stood other two, the one on this side of the bank of the river, and the other on that side of the bank of the river. And one said to the man clothed in linen, which was upon the waters of the river,

{2} "A few days *before* the Second Coming, all of the martyrs who died during the fifth seal will be resurrected to everlasting life. Those who crucified Jesus will also be resurrected so that they can see the Son of Man coming in clouds of glory.[32] Their shame will never end and they will perish with the wicked who will be destroyed a few days later when Jesus appears in clouds of glory. {3} "Those who love righteousness will shine with the radiant glory of God. In fact, the 144,000 will shine like stars forever and ever."

Epilogue

{4} "But you, Daniel, close up and seal the words of this book. This information is reserved for the final generation. There will be enormous advances in travel and knowledge, but the Most High God has sealed up this book until the final generation arrives."

{5} Then I looked and saw two glorious angels, one stood on this side of the river and the other stood on the opposite bank. {6} One of the angels said to Jesus, the glorious man clothed in bright linen who I saw earlier standing above the waters of the Tigris, "How long will it be before the astonishing events in these visions are fulfilled?"

{7} Jesus lifted His right and left hand toward Heaven, and I heard him say, I swear by myself, who lives forever and ever,³³ "This gospel of the kingdom shall be preached throughout the whole world during the 1,260 days granted to my Two Witnesses.³⁴ After my 144,000 servants have been killed, all of these things will be completed."³⁵

{8} I heard these words, but I could not understand why God's servants will be killed. So I asked the angel, "My lord, what will be the outcome of these events?"

{9} He replied, "Do not worry about these matters, Daniel, because the words of this prophecy are closed up and sealed until the time just before the end. The saints living at the time of the end will understand this vision as it pertains to them, just like the saints living at the destruction of Jerusalem will understand the portion of this vision that pertains to them.

{10} "Many years will come and go. God's people will be purified, made spotless and refined, and the wicked will continue to be wicked. None of the wicked will understand these things because spiritual things are spiritually understood. At the appointed time

---

How long shall it be to the end of these wonders?

Dan. 12:7

And I heard the man clothed in linen, which was upon the waters of the river, when he held up his right hand and his left hand unto heaven, and sware by him that liveth for ever that it shall be for a time, times, and an half; and when he shall have accomplished to scatter the power of the holy people, all these things shall be finished.

Dan. 12:8

And I heard, but I understood not: then said I, O my Lord, what shall be the end of these things?

Dan. 12:9

And he said, Go thy way, Daniel: for the words are closed up and sealed till the time of the end.

Dan. 12:10

Many shall be purified, and made white, and tried; but the wicked

> *shall do wickedly: and none of the wicked shall understand; but the wise shall understand.*
>
> **Dan. 12:11-12**
>
> *And from the time that the daily sacrifice shall be taken away, and the abomination that maketh desolate set up, there shall be a thousand two hundred and ninety days. Blessed is he that waiteth, and cometh to the thousand three hundred and five and thirty days.*
>
> **Dan. 12:13**
>
> *But go thou thy way till the end be: for thou shalt rest, and stand in thy lot at the end of the days.*

of the end, people who are spiritually awake will be able to understand the importance of these things.

{11} "Daniel, write down everything that you have seen and heard because God's people will need to know these things during the Great Tribulation. A time is coming when the corporate intercession of Jesus on behalf of the world will end. On that day, Jesus will cease from His daily intercession on behalf of individuals. He will no longer stand between the wrath of God and sinners. The end of the daily, that is, His corporate ministry in Heaven's temple, will be marked by peals of thunder, rumblings, flashes of lightning, and a great worldwide earthquake.[36] These events will announce the beginning of the Great Tribulation. From this somber worldwide event, the saints will count down the days to the return of Jesus. From the day the daily service at the Altar of Incense in Heaven ends until the devil establishes a universal death decree for all of God's people (an abomination that causes desolation), there will be 1,290 days. {12} Blessed is the person who waits for and reaches the 1,335th day, for he shall see Jesus and hear His voice saying, 'My grace is sufficient for you!'[37]

{13} "As for you Daniel, go on with your business until the end of your life. You will rest in sleep, and then at the end of the 1,335 days you will rise to receive your allotted inheritance with all the other saints. You will be rewarded beyond your wildest imagination for your faithfulness."

The Rules of Interpretation

Please consider how the Rules of Interpretation are observed in this prophecy:

Rule One says an apocalyptic prophecy has a beginning point and ending point in time and the events within the prophecy occur in the order given. Daniel 10:1 through 12:3 contains two visions. Other than seeing a great war, Daniel says nothing further about the first vision. Three weeks later, Gabriel visits Daniel to explain the vision. From Gabriel's visit we learn the original vision spans approximately two and a half millenniums! The events flow in chronological order and this feature proved to be very beneficial for the Christians who lived in Jerusalem just before its destruction in A.D. 70. We can be sure this vision will prove to be beneficial to Christians who live during the Great Tribulation because it offers hope on two fronts. First, the Lord and His truth will prevail over Lucifer. The Lord will deliver His people. "All Israel will be saved!"[38] Many saints will experience death, but death is not the end of life for God's people. Death will be a temporary release from suffering and deprivation. Second, God put several time periods at the end of this vision to encourage the saints. For example, the Great Tribulation will last 1,335 days. The gospel commission will be completed by the 1,260th day (a time, times and half a time) and most, if not all, of God's prophets will be killed. Then, a universal death decree for all saints (which will not be carried out) will be set up on the 1,290th day.[39] During the darkest moments of Earth's history, this vision will offer a ray of hope. God is very much in control of the evil chaos that will sweep over planet Earth.

Rule Two says a fulfillment only occurs when all of the specifications are met, and this includes the order stated in the prophecy. This vision is still underway. We are waiting for the fulfillment of verse 36 which describes the physical appearing of Lucifer (the King of the North). Once Lucifer appears, the remainder of this prophecy will take about one year to unfold.

Rule Three says that apocalyptic language can be literal, analogous, or symbolic. No symbols, *per se*, are offered in this vision. The wars are literal and it is very clear that God's people will once again be caught between two huge armies in the last days, but the outcome will be different than before. Early Christians escaped the destruction of Jerusalem. Most of the final generation will not escape Lucifer's destruction. Most of God's people will perish during the Great Tribulation. However, death is not defeat in God's sight. Look at Jesus! He was resurrected and He lives forever. The same will be true for God's saints.

Rule Four says the presence or absence of the Jubilee Calendar determines how God measures time. The time periods mentioned in the commentary are not to be translated as a day for a year because they occur after the Jubilee Calendar comes to an end (1994). For further discussion on the operation of the Jubilee Calendar, see Appendix A.

References:

1. Matthew 24:15-20; Luke 21:20-24
2. The horn power in Daniel 8 appears during the appointed time of the end which is a time of wrath. Compare Daniel 8:17-25; Daniel 11:35,36 with Revelation 15:1,2.
3. Revelation 9:15,16
4. Daniel 9:26
5. Daniel 9:7-15
6. Ezra 4
7. Genesis 15:16-18
8. Leviticus 18:24-28
9. For a discussion on the full cup principle, please see Chapter 2 in my book, *Warning! Revelation is about to be fulfilled*. This item can be freely downloaded on the internet: http://www.wake-up.org/warnbook/WarnBook.htm.
10. Ezekiel 5:5
11. 1 Kings 10:1-10
12. Isaiah 42:6; 49:6; Leviticus 25:55
13. Matthew 24:15-20; Luke 21:20-24
14. *Josephus*, The Wars of the Jews VI.9.3
15. Daniel 12:7; Revelation 13:7
16. 1 Thessalonians 4:17
17. Leviticus 26:38; Deuteronomy 4:26,27
18. Luke 21:23; Deuteronomy 31:16-18
19. Matthew 23:38; John 1:11
20. This assertion is based on the premise that God keeps the devil in the Abyss for two-thirds of the 1,335 days allotted for the Great Tribulation. For a discussion on God's use of one-third and two-thirds, please see pages 29 and 30 in my book titled, *The Seven Trumpets in my book, Seven Trumpets, Two Witnesses, and Four Beasts*. This item can be freely downloaded on the internet: http://www.wake-up.org/Revelation/RevTrumpets.pdf.
21. 2 Thessalonians 2:3-12

22. 2 Thessalonians 2:4; 2 Corinthians 11:14; Matthew 24:23-26
23. Revelation 13:14; Daniel 8:10; Deuteronomy 4:19; 17:3
24. Revelation 13:14,15
25. 2 Thessalonians 2:1-12; Isaiah 14:16,17; Ezekiel 28:1-19
26. Revelation 9:15
27. Revelation 9:13-21; 17:12-17
28. Daniel 2:42; Revelation 6:15; 17:12
29. Jeremiah 47:1,2; Hosea 5:10; Isaiah 8:6-8
30. Jeremiah 40:11,12; Joshua 6:17
31. Revelation 13:16 See also Prophecy 11.
32. Revelation 1:7
33. Revelation 10:6; Genesis 22;16; Isaiah 45:23; Jeremiah 49:13; Revelation 1:18
34. Revelation 10:5,6; 11:3
35. Revelation 11:2; 13:5-7
36. Revelation 8:3-5
37. Matthew 25:31-36; 2 Corinthians 12:9
38. Romans 11:26
39. Notes on Daniel 11:31: The abomination that causes desolation in Daniel 11:31 is not to be confused with the abomination that causes desolation in Daniel 12:11. The first abomination pertains to the destruction of Jerusalem and the second pertains to the destruction of the saints just before Jesus comes. In both cases, this Hebrew phrase describes the same thing which is' the destruction of God's people.   For further discussion on this topic, please see pages 228-233 in my book, *Daniel Unlocked for the Final Generation* or you can freely download the chapter at http://www.wake-up.org/Daniel/DanChap7.htm.

Introduction to Revelation

Even though the books of Daniel and Revelation were written about 600 years apart, they tell one story, use the same architecture, and overlap each other. Many people do not realize that the prophecies in Revelation are based on facts established in the book of Daniel. This oversight has produced confusion because the four rules that govern apocalyptic interpretation in the book of Revelation are found in the book of Daniel.

Before you examine Prophecies 6 through 17, please consider three things:

1. The book of Daniel provides a chronological foundation upon which the book of Revelation builds. The book of Daniel contains five prophetic "yard sticks." Each yard stick measures a span of time. When these "five yard sticks" are properly aligned, they produce a chronological road map which begins with the Babylonian Empire (605 B.C.) and ends when Jesus destroys Earth at His Second Coming.

2. The books of Daniel and Revelation contain many prophetic elements that have been fulfilled over the past twenty-six centuries. If these two books did not overlap and identify the same prophetic fulfillments, the book of Revelation would be very difficult to interpret. This overlap reveals how the book of Revelation is solidly built on the historical foundation provided in Daniel. When we properly align and understand this simple feature, we eliminate many of the false claims and endless manipulation that often surround the prophecies of Revelation.

3. The book of Daniel was sealed up until the appointed time of the end. The unsealing of Daniel reveals four rules that govern apocalyptic interpretation. These self-evident rules will produce the intended meaning of apocalyptic prophecy when they are properly applied. The rules found in Daniel also apply to the book of Revelation because the architecture is the same in both books. (See Appendix A.) I hope you will review the chart on pages 4 and 5 of this book and refer to it often as you read this commentary. You can also download a free chart titled, "Seventeen Apocalyptic Prophecies" from our website. A visual picture of how various

prophecies relate to each other should be helpful. Sometimes, a picture can be worth several thousand words. To download the free copy of the chart, go to: http://www.wake-up.org/Charts/18prop02.pdf.

Summary

An experienced Bible student knows that the Bible speaks without regard for what we may believe or disbelieve. The Bible speaks the truth and students of the Bible are obligated to harmonize the facts to the best of our ability; whether the facts agree or disagree with what we may currently believe to be true. After all, there is one God, one truth, and one correct explanation. Our job is to discover it.

Seekers of truth constantly stumble into *apparent* conflicts because our knowledge of God and His Word is incomplete. We know that our beliefs have no effect on God. God will do all that He has promised whether we believe or disbelieve His Word. We also know that truth stands on its own two feet, with or without endorsement or human support. Therefore, as seekers of truth it is important to ask ourselves whether we will only accept those truths that agree with our present understanding of God's Word or let go of imperfect knowledge so that we can embrace larger truths that spring from His Word.

It is impossible to be "a defender of the faith" and "a seeker of truth" at the same time because these are two different seasons in life. Therefore, our frame of mind and our attitude toward God and His Word determines to a great extent, our ability to arrive at truth. I often pray for the Holy Spirit to cut through my bias and opinion. I sincerely want to see truth more clearly, because after forty years of Bible study, I have become settled on many of the issues regarding various aspects of truth. Nevertheless, I must still approach Bible study with the same humility as a novice Bible student, prayerfully putting line upon line and precept upon precept. If we follow this approach, the Holy Spirit will reveal perfect harmony because truth is based on the harmony that comes from the sum of its parts. Truth constantly unfolds because God is infinite. Therefore, our knowledge of truth at any given time is always partial and needs improving. Twenty years from now, I hope I will understand twice as much about God's truth as I do now because this life is just the beginning of an eternal study that focuses on God, His character and plans.

Finally, notice that Prophecy 6 (the first apocalyptic prophecy in Revelation) begins with Revelation 4. Please see Appendix C for the reasons the messages to the seven churches are not apocalyptic prophecies. Therefore, they are not included in the seventeen prophecies found in Daniel and Revelation.

Prophecy 6

The Six Seals

Revelation 4:1-6:17

Beginning point in time: 1798

Ending point in time: Second Coming

Summary: This prophecy focuses on a very important book. Before Jesus created any life, the Father wrote a book and He sealed it up with seven seals so that no one, not even the Son or the Holy Spirit, could see what He had written. This book contains a complete history of life. The life of each angel and human being was written down in careful detail before angels and human beings were created! According to His infinite wisdom, the Father decided that the contents of His history book would not be exposed until the drama caused by sin is completed and the seventh seal on the book is broken. When the seventh seal is broken, the universe will be permitted to see everything that the Father foreknew. The reason the Father chose to write the history book may surprise you. In fact, once you understand why the Father wrote The Book of Life and then sealed it with seven seals, you will begin to understand how an all-knowing God of love could create a wonderful angel who would later become the devil.

Note: Because this commentary is as succinct as possible, you may want to examine a more comprehensive analysis of this prophecy. If so, please see Chapter 10 in my book, *A Study on the Seven Seals and The 144,000* or you can freely download this material at: http://www.wake-up.org/Revelation/RevSeg1.htm.

Introduction: It is ironic that many Christians give more attention to the seven seals than the contents of the sealed book! After all, the objective of breaking open the seven seals is to expose the contents of this book!

Each apocalyptic prophecy has a starting point in time and Prophecy 6 has a starting point in time, but the starting point is not described in Revelation 4. The starting point is determined by linking Daniel 7:9-14 with Revelation 4 and 5.[1] Let me explain. Daniel was zoomed forward in Daniel 7 to see the Father, the Ancient of Days, convene a special meeting in 1798. John was also zoomed forward to 1798 to observe the same meeting, but from a different perspective. Both prophets saw the exaltation of Jesus.

Prophecy 6 unfolds in chronological order. John was taken "in the spirit" to visit Heaven's temple. An important item he saw in the Father's right hand was a book sealed with seven seals. John saw the Father search for someone who was worthy to take the book and break the seven seals. Eventually, Jesus was found worthy to receive the book and He began the process of breaking the seals.

The Father wrote The Book of Life to resolve a contradictory problem before a contradictory problem even existed! The Father foreknew that a day would come when His children would question His integrity and He knew the best way to resolve this coming problem was to create a "time capsule." The Father wrote The Book of Life to prove to the universe, at an appointed time, that His foreknowledge has no effect on His actions. Even though the Father knows the outcome of all things before they occur, He does not use this foreknowledge to control future events. God knew that people would claim that God uses His foreknowledge to direct the outcome of future events. This problem explains why He wrote the book and why certain angels have been recording life ever since life began. At the end of the 1,000 years in Revelation 20, the recordings of life made by angels in real time will be compared with the contents of The Book of Life.

When the seventh seal is broken, the Father will demonstrate that His "time capsule" is identical with the recordings made by angels. This will prove to the universe that He perfectly foreknew that sin would occur, as well as who would be saved and who would be condemned long before they were born, and even though He perfectly foreknew the end from the beginning for every angel and person, He loved each one the same. He did not predetermine who would be saved and who would be lost. The Father will prove that He treated each angel and person as though they would live eternally. The Father wants to prove that His love for His children is not affected by His foreknowledge. This is a huge concept to process and we will see this amazing concept unfold in our study on Revelation.

When the Father wrote The Book of Life, He planned that as each seal is broken, there would be a new revelation about Jesus. Therefore, at the appointed time, seven new revelations will be made about Jesus. When the seventh seal is broken at the end of the 1,000 years, both Jesus and the contents of His book will be completely exposed!

Three important goals will be accomplished when the seventh seal is broken open. First, it will reveal that Jesus is a separate and distinct God, a co-eternal equal of the Father. The Father wants the universe to know that Jesus has the same powers, prerogatives, and substance as Himself. Second, the Father will prove to the universe that He will not, under any circumstances, use His foreknowledge to protect Himself or His government from harm or rebellion. In fact, even though the Father foreknows the future, He will not allow His knowledge to alter or influence His love or treatment of any person. Last, the Father will prove to the universe that one of His strangest laws is completely harmonious with principles of love. In my opinion, this prophecy contains one of the most fascinating stories found in the book of Revelation.

The Sequence

{1} After I wrote out the directives of Jesus to the seven churches, I saw Heaven open before me and a great temple came into view. It was an awesome structure, far greater than the temple complex in Jerusalem which had been destroyed in A.D. 70. A doorway leading into this enormous temple was open and a voice from inside the temple said, "Come up here John and I will show you what must take place in the future."[2]

{2} Immediately, I found myself standing in Heaven's temple. When I saw the magnificence of the temple and the glory surrounding those who were present, I was completely overwhelmed. I felt like a speck of sand. The size and scale of everything was huge and beyond my calculation. As I stood there, I realized that Earth itself was a minuscule, insignificant part of God's infinite universe. The temple was at least a thousand times larger than any building I had ever seen. A spectacular and dazzling throne was located in the center of the room. It was huge, several stories high. I could see that someone was sitting on the throne, but the light around Him was so brilliant that I could not see any details. Millions and millions of angels were sitting in the temple, far more than I could count.

{3} Words cannot describe the glory of the Father and His exalted throne. The Father's presence emitted a brilliant light that sparkled like quartz crystal, mixed with bright red flashes of fire.

Rev. 4:1
After this I looked, and, behold, a door was opened in heaven: and the first voice which I heard was as it were of a trumpet talking with me; which said, Come up hither, and I will show thee things which must be hereafter.

Rev. 4:2
And immediately I was in the spirit; and, behold, a throne was set in heaven, and one sat on the throne.

Rev. 4:3
And he that sat was to look upon like a jasper and a sardine stone: and there was a rainbow round about the throne, in sight like unto an emerald.

Prophecy 6 - The Six Seals

A rainbow of many colors encircled His throne. This rainbow appeared to have three dimensions, like rainbows of light that dance on polished emeralds.

Rev. 4:4
And round about the throne were four and twenty seats: and upon the seats I saw four and twenty elders sitting, clothed in white raiment; and they had on their heads crowns of gold.

{4} Twenty-four thrones surrounded the Father's throne, and twenty-four elders redeemed from Earth were seated on these thrones. They wore white clothing and had gold crowns on their heads.

> It is my understanding that the twenty-four elders are people who the Father resurrected along with Jesus. They were taken to Heaven to serve as human observers.[3] The Bible indicates that two witnesses are needed whenever judgment is involved. Therefore, it seems likely that two people were taken from each of the twelve tribes to observe Jesus as He cleanses Heaven's temple, that is, judges each person prior to the Second Coming.[4] The presence of twenty-four human observers around the throne of God speaks volumes about the transparent nature of God's government. It is wonderful to realize that twenty-four witnesses will be able to address any concerns that any saint might have about God's decision on any individual!

Rev. 4:5
And out of the throne proceeded lightnings and thunderings and voices: and there were seven lamps of fire burning before the throne, which are the seven Spirits of God.

{5} Flashes of lightning, heavy rumblings, and peals of rolling thunder emanated from the Father's throne. The floor of the temple trembled with unseen energy and His glory was indescribable. The atmosphere was charged with energy. Seven dazzling angels stood close to the throne. They were so bright that they looked like seven glowing lampstands. They stood around the throne, ready to do whatever the Father might command. These seven angels are the same seven angels that serve the seven churches, receive the seven trumpets, and pour out the seven bowls.[5]

Rev. 4:6
And before the throne there was a sea of glass like unto crystal: and in the midst of the throne, and round about the throne, were four beasts full of eyes before and behind.

{6} The Father's throne rested on a large expanse that looked like pure glass, clear as crystal. In the center of this expanse, closest to the Father, were four strange looking, but highly exalted creatures.[6] Each of the four creatures had six wings. These four creatures did not look like the seven angels. They stood close to the Father, surrounding Him at the four points of a compass: north, south, east and west. The four creatures were identical. It was clear that they had enormous authority and power because they were close to the Father.

> These four living creatures are a representation of the Holy Spirit who cannot be seen. The Holy Spirit has a name because he is a separate and distinct, co-eternal member of the God-

head.⁷ The Holy Spirit is omnipresent, that is, He can be everywhere at once – north, south, east, and west – and this is why John saw him represented as *four clones of the same being*.⁸ The four living creatures were covered with eyes indicating the Holy Spirit is omniscient, that is, He is all-seeing and all-knowing.⁹ Ezekiel saw the same four living creatures (cherubim) that John saw.¹⁰ There are a few differences because God often uses repetition and enlargement to enhance our understanding of complex subjects. This invisible member of the Godhead was visibly represented to John as four clones because the Father wanted John to identify and see the actions of the Holy Spirit. There is nothing in the universe like the Holy Spirit. In substance, He is fully God. His unique person, presence, power, and abilities are visibly caricatured in this vision because God wants us to better understand His ministry on behalf of mankind.

{7} Because of my location, I could see that each living creature had four faces. However, only one face on each creature was shown to me. I saw the face of a lion, an ox, a man, and an eagle in flight. I remembered Ezekiel's description: **"Their faces looked like this: Each of the four had the face of a man, and on the right side each had the face of a lion, and on the left the face of an ox; each also had the face of an eagle."**¹¹ Later on, I discovered that one face on each creature was exposed to me so that I could identify and keep separate the four special tasks which the Holy Spirit would be commanded to carry out.

{8} Each of the four living creatures had six wings – a total of twenty-four wings. This large number of wings indicates instantaneous flight. The Holy Spirit is instantly everywhere or anywhere He wants to be. The four living creatures were covered with eyes, even under their wings. He never stops saying: "Holy, holy, holy is the Lord God Almighty, who was present before anything existed, who lives today and who will eternally exist."

> The eyes covering the four living creatures represent a prerogative that belongs only to deity. The Holy Spirit is omniscient. He sees and comprehends everything occurring in God's vast universe. He can read the minds and thoughts of created beings and He can read the mind and thoughts of the Father because He is a member of the Godhead. Generally speaking, the Holy Spirit serves as a divine conduit. Information flows instantaneously between God's children and the Godhead through the Holy Spirit.¹² He also serves as an infallible reporter to the

Rev. 4:7

And the first beast was like a lion, and the second beast like a calf, and the third beast had a face as a man, and the fourth beast was like a flying eagle.

Rev. 4:8

And the four beasts had each of them six wings about him; and they were full of eyes within: and they rest not day and night, saying, Holy, holy, holy, Lord God Almighty, which was, and is, and is to come.

Father and the Son. He instantly sees and understands the state and condition of every being in the universe and He relays this information to them.[13] The Holy Spirit observes every sparrow that falls on Earth and instantly reports it to the Father. On the other hand, the Holy Spirit is an infallible messenger sent from the Father to all of His children. The Holy Spirit relays blessings and gifts of grace, courage, strength, wisdom, and truth as the Father determines. The Holy Spirit does not speak to God's subjects from His own wisdom. He speaks only what He hears from the throne of the Father.[14] Day and night, the Holy Spirit constantly brings glory and honor to the Father because He loves and worships (submits to) the Father as Jesus submits to the will of the Father.[15]

It is impossible for humans to understand how the Holy Spirit can be in innumerable places at the same time. It is also impossible to understand how He can see everything going on in the universe at the same instant. The Holy Spirit is the only member of the Godhead who exercises the power of omnipresence. This explains why rejecting the Holy Spirit is the only sin that is an unpardonable sin.[16] He is the only means through which angels and human beings can connect with the Father and the Son. The Holy Spirit brings truth, peace, and joy to every willing soul and in turn, He presents our petitions and prayers to the Father with expressions that we cannot understand.[17] The Holy Spirit enables the Father and the Son to be in constant touch with their children wherever they are. As a member of the Godhead, the Holy Spirit understands the mind and thoughts of the Father. Therefore, His greatest joy is to lead God's subjects into endless discoveries about God's truth and love. The Holy Spirit wants everyone in the universe to appreciate and radiate God's love and character. The members of the Godhead love each other more deeply than we can possibly understand and the Holy Spirit never stops giving glory and honor to the Father and the Son.[18]

{9} The Father does incredible things throughout His expanding universe every day. Whenever the Holy Spirit reports another one of the Father's wonderful acts, {10} the twenty-four elders fall down before the Father, amazed and humbled by His infinite goodness. The elders remove their golden crowns and prostrate themselves on their faces before the Father saying, {11} "You are worthy, our Lord and God, to receive glory and honor and power,

> **Rev. 4:9-11**
> *And when those beasts give glory and honour and thanks to him that sat on the throne, who liveth for ever and ever, The four and twenty elders fall down before him that sat on the throne, and worship him that liveth for ever and ever, and cast their crowns before the throne, saying, Thou art worthy, O Lord, to receive glory and honour and power: for thou hast created all things, and for thy pleasure they are and were created.*

for You created all things and only through your sustaining power do they exist."

{5:1} While I was studying the four living creatures, there was a transition in the temple. The thrones of the twenty-four elders were rearranged for a special convocation.[19] A trumpet blast sounded and a hush fell over the vast assembly. One of the seven angels who stand before God spoke in a loud voice. He called a meeting to order. Billions of angels stood reverently as the Ancient of Days took His seat. The host was seated and the meeting began.[20] I was nearly blinded by the dazzling presence of the Father. I could barely see His right hand extending out of incredible glory. In his hand was a book sealed with seven seals.

> The book sealed with seven seals is also called "The Lamb's Book of Life."[21] The Father wrote this book before the creation of the universe, even before the angels were created. The book is sealed with seven seals because the Father does not want anyone to see what He has written until the appropriate time arrives. The Book of Life has been securely stored ever since it was written. Everyone in Heaven knows about the existence of this book, but no one knows the details that are written in it.
>
> The Book of Life contains a complete history of life. Everyone (angels and human beings) involved in the drama of sin is included – past, present, and future. Using His perfect foreknowledge, the Father wrote the book and sealed it for at least two reasons applicable to this study. First, at the appointed time, the contents of this book will be revealed to everyone who has ever lived. The Father wants to prove to the universe that even though He has perfect foreknowledge, He loves everyone without reservation. He will not use His foreknowledge to manipulate His subjects or protect Himself from sin and rebellion. In other words, the Father will prove that even though He foreknew the enormous cost of sin, even though He foreknew that Lucifer would become His greatest adversary and cause great harm in His house, He created and loved him anyway. The Father also used this same foreknowledge and love on Adam and Eve and their descendants.
>
> The Father does not deal with His children on the basis of His foreknowledge. Instead, He deals with us on the basis of His love. Even though He knows every future decision that every being will make, He allows each being to exercise his power of choice. He will not force anyone into performing any action for

Rev. 5:1
And I saw in the right hand of him that sat on the throne a book written within and on the backside, sealed with seven seals.

Rev. 5:1

personal advantage. The Father sealed up the book because, at the appointed time, He wants the universe to see that His foreknowledge does not affect or alter His love for His subjects. He respects the free will of His children to the point that He would rather die than violate our will.

The Father had a second reason for writing The Book of Life. At the appointed time, He will prove to the universe that one of Heaven's most intriguing laws is righteous and it is thoughtfully based on infinite love and wisdom.

The Bible indicates that Bible writers knew about the existence of the book which the Father had written,[22] but again, only the Father knows the details written in it. The Son and the Holy Spirit do not know what is in the book.[23] The Godhead planned it this way because if the Son and the Holy Spirit knew what was written in The Book of Life, the Godhead could be accused of conspiracy once the book is opened. To keep the charge of conspiracy from having any validity, special angels have recorded the history of sin's drama in real time, that is, as life transpires. Recording angels chronicle every thought, word, and action. Their record books are used to judge mankind[24] because the contents of The Book of Life are not exposed until sin's drama is completed. At the end of the 1,000 years, the seventh seal will be broken and everyone will see that the Books of Record (made by angels) are identical with The Book of Life.

Because the Books of Record were recorded in real time and a record of each person's choices is faithfully recorded, there can be no charge that the Godhead conspired to save some people and destroy others. Actually, just the opposite will prove true. The Books of Record will prove that each child of God freely made his or her choices. The record will clearly prove that He loved everyone the same regardless of their choices and their eternal destiny!

Rev. 5:2

And I saw a strong angel proclaiming with a loud voice, Who is worthy to open the book, and to loose the seals thereof?

{2} The angel who called the meeting to order spoke in a loud voice. "Who is worthy to break the seven seals and open The Book of Life?"

This question has no introduction or explanation. Suddenly, John learns that the Father is looking for someone who is worthy to break open the seven seals and expose the contents of The Book of Life. Although the qualifications necessary to break open the seals are not stated at this point, this announcement does indicate that the time has come to begin breaking open the seven seals. We will learn later in this study that the seven seals contain seven secrets about the Lamb. These secrets are revealed as each seal is broken. Therefore, whoever exposes these seven secrets must meet certain qualifications to insure that the seven secrets are properly revealed and understood.

{3} Curiosity settled like a cloud over the vast assembly. Everyone was focused on the book sealed with seven seals. The angels knew this was an unusual meeting and certainly not a routine question or offer. As I watched the process, no one in Heaven, on Earth or even under the Earth (that is, among the dead), was found worthy to open The Book of Life and look inside it.

> Rev. 5:3
>
> *And no man in heaven, nor in earth, neither under the earth, was able to open the book, neither to look thereon.*

The question of worthiness is paramount to breaking the seals because each broken seal launches a new campaign on Earth. When He wrote the book, the Father predetermined that seven campaigns would be necessary to explain who Jesus really is and all that He represents. This exposure is necessary because Jesus, the Creator, so closely identifies with His creation that no one can tell who He really is unless there is a revelation. The Father wants the universe to know that Jesus, in substance, is His equal. The Father wants everyone to know that man's redeemer is a co-eternal, Almighty member of the Godhead just like Himself. Even though they are distinct and separate beings, they are like twins, having no difference in substance, powers, or prerogatives. The seven campaigns will be completed when the seventh seal is broken at the end of the 1,000 years. Then, the revelation of Jesus Christ will be completed at the end of sin's drama. Everyone will then know His full identity. After everyone knows who He is, Jesus will do an amazing thing:

"Then the end will come, when he [Jesus] hands over the kingdom to God the Father after he has destroyed all dominion, authority and power. For he must reign until he has put all his enemies under his feet. The last enemy to be destroyed is death. For he 'has put everything under his feet.' Now when it says that 'everything' has been put under him, it is clear that this does not include God himself, who put everything under Christ. When he has done this, then the Son himself will be made subject to him who put everything under him, so that God may be all in all."[25]

When The Book of Life is opened and the information inside is exposed, the Father will be exonerated. Lucifer's lies and

> Rev. 5:3

sophisticated logic will be proven false and no argument can be made against God's love for His creation. John did not know at the beginning of this vision what the seven seals represented, but he evidently understood that the contents of the book had to do with freeing the Father from a cloud of doubts and suspicions. This is why he wept when no one was found worthy to break the seven seals. What is more grievous and heartbreaking than to see someone you love falsely accused?

God has given His children reasoning powers and the Father is looking forward to a day when everyone in His universe will understand the foundations and operation of His government. When the contents of His book are revealed, everyone in the universe will know that God is love. The Father does not require submission because He is Almighty God. Instead, the Father wants everyone to understand that He is the "servant leader" of the universe. He has every divine power necessary to provide for the welfare of His children and there is no better way through the corridors of eternity than trusting in His infinite wisdom. The Father wants His children to know that He does not use divine power to manipulate His children, instead He uses His divine power to ensure that the laws of love will be forever exalted and enforced. God is called a God of love because His actions are always consistent with love. God is called Almighty God because He insures that nothing will overrule the two laws of love that govern the universe (love God first and your neighbor as yourself). His actions are in perfect harmony with the laws of love because He never steps outside the laws of love!

The Father is a cheerful giver and He loves a cheerful giver.[26] He will accept nothing less than a cheerful decision to trust Him, love Him, and obey Him. Even though He is Almighty God and has incredible powers, He will prove at the appointed time that He has not and will not ever use these powers to control the choices of His children.

Why Is The Book of Life Necessary?

Before we proceed further into this prophecy, a brief explanation about the origin of sin is necessary because The Book of Life will solve several problems created by sin. (A more comprehensive presentation on this topic is found in Prophecy 12.)

Long before Jesus created Earth, a crisis occurred in Heaven. It all started when Lucifer, the highest created being in the universe, became unhappy with the Father because Lucifer wanted more honor and authority than the Father permitted him to have. When Lucifer realized that he could not have the honor and worship that was given to Michael (Jesus Christ), the archangel,[27] Lucifer became anti-Christ. Motivated by jealousy and sustained by endless bitterness, Lucifer began a secret campaign of sedition against God's government. Ultimately, he led one-third of the angels into open rebellion against the Father.

Rev. 5:3

Prior to His life on Earth, Jesus lived among the angels as one of them. As the archangel, Michael,[28] Jesus looked like them and talked like them. Later, when Jesus became a man, Jesus looked like a man and talked like a man. However, Jesus is far more than an angel or a man. Jesus is a member of the Godhead, the Creator of everything that exists.[29] As God, He has lived as an angel and a human. Our Creator is willing to live as one of His creation so that He might reveal the wonderful ways and character of the Father to His creation!

Lucifer had a serious problem with Christ. Lucifer wanted to be exalted among the angels like the archangel. After all, Lucifer was *the other* covering cherub. He cloaked his envy and bitterness with self-righteousness. He began to create doubts about God's integrity by twisting topics that God had not yet clarified. Lucifer discovered that holy angels could be alienated from God if he put the Father and Michael (Jesus) in a suspicious light. For example, everyone in Heaven knew that the Father had foreknowledge. Lucifer argued that since the Father already knew what each angel would think and do, the Father could not be outwitted or overthrown. The Father was a dictator and it was "His way or the highway." Lucifer claimed there could be no freedom or democracy in Heaven because the Father was an all-knowing dictator. The Father would prevent any angel from improving and gaining a higher place in His government. Lucifer insinuated this was grossly unfair. He used his own situation as proof. Why should he be treated as a lesser angel throughout eternity? Why should one covering cherub be more highly honored and worshiped? Lucifer preyed on the other angels' naive sympathy and some of the angels empathized with Lucifer's "unfair" situation. Lucifer also told sympathetic angels that the Father did not give angels the power of choice because any choice that was contrary to God's way would

> Rev. 5:3

be considered rebellion. Further, Lucifer asserted that the angels were just eternal "slaves" and the Father was nothing more than an omnipotent control freak!

To ensure that the angels took his arguments seriously, Lucifer taunted the angels with a law that no one understood at the time. When He created the angels, Michael declared to the angels a "strange law." This law defined the penalty for sin which is *sudden death by execution*. Jesus also explained this law to Adam and Eve at their creation. Simply stated, this strange law says, "You will be killed on the day that you sin."[30]

Using arguments that were skillfully and logically framed to put the government of God in the poorest possible light, Lucifer convinced one-third of the angels that the Father could not possibly be a God of love because "the sudden death law" was inescapable. Lucifer charged that if someone should happen to exercise their power of choice in a way that God did not like, the result would be sudden death! Lucifer's arguments were so sophisticated and convincing that one-third of the angels lost their respect, and finally, their love for the Father and Michael, the archangel.

Lucifer's political propaganda made the Father *appear* to be a tyrant. Lucifer positioned God's strange law in such a way that many of the holy angels became angry with God. Lucifer argued that God's sudden death law and God's foreknowledge are inseparable. Therefore, God *is* a God of control; not love. Lucifer induced animosity and prejudice toward the Father and he taunted the angels who *chose* to remain loyal to the Father and Michael. Ridicule can be intimidating, so Lucifer may have added ridicule to his arguments to further obscure the truth. Using devious subterfuge against the Father, Lucifer created two false options: Either obey God and be His eternal slave or exercise the power of choice and immediately die. These options, he claimed, do not represent a God of love. Lucifer justified his hatred for the Father and Michael with this logic: The Father already knows what we are going to do and He has a law that justifies our death should we step out of line. With God, there is no choice. So, Lucifer invited the angels to join with him and together they form a "better government." They would not be the eternal slaves of a powerful tyrant who claimed to be a God of love.

Remember, rebellion did not exist in the universe before Lucifer began campaigning against the Father and even more, the angels had not observed a single instance of the "sudden death" law. They had no knowledge of good and evil and because no one had seen evil before, Lucifer could make a compelling case against God that *appeared* solid and logical. Eventually, Lucifer's envy led him to commit conspiracy. Lucifer convinced one-third of the holy angels that the Holy Father was unfair and unloving. Strange as this may sound, the Father did not have a *legitimate way* at that time to prove Lucifer wrong. Of course, the Father could have presented logical arguments that would have silenced Lucifer or He could have snuffed out Lucifer's life, but that would prove nothing. God wisely allowed Lucifer to spread sedition throughout Heaven to test the angels' faith. Would they obey God's first commandment? When tempted, would they love God with all their heart, mind, and soul? God permitted the love and faith of His angels to be tested in the same way that He has allowed the love and faith of human beings to be tested. Love and faith in God cannot be validated until it is tested and demonstrated. When Lucifer's rebellion reached critical mass (one-third of Heaven's angels infected with disaffection), God stepped into the fray and ultimately, Lucifer and his angels were cast out of Heaven.

Rev. 5:3

When the Father wrote The Book of Life, He foreknew Lucifer would rebel, He foreknew how Adam and Eve would fall and He foresaw Jesus dying on the cross. The Father foreknew all of these things before any life was created and He wrote them down. Because God is eternally committed to the principles of love, from the beginning His primary concern was not Lucifer's rebellion or Adam and Eve's fall. Looking through the corridor of eternity, the Father planned a way for resolving the sin problem so that the future likelihood of sin would be extremely remote. God does not want sin to occur a third time. This explains why God allowed Lucifer to exercise his freedom for a period of time. He allowed Lucifer's willful rebellion to test the faith and loyalty of His angels.

Each angel carefully considered Lucifer's arguments, and two-thirds of the angels *chose* to remain loyal to the Father even though they could not answer Lucifer's arguments. Two-thirds of the angels chose to remain faithful to God because they were convinced that God is love. Everyone understood that God had given them the gift of life and He had faithfully met every need. Before Lucifer became evil minded, Heaven had been a joyful place to live, but Lucifer's actions changed everything. The angels that chose to remain loyal did so because they believed there was sufficient

Rev. 5:3

evidence to justify their faith and loyalty to God. For them, the evidences of God's love outweighed Lucifer's skillful complaints.

Lucifer's defiance led to war and Lucifer and one-third of the angels disappeared.[31] Suddenly, there was an eerie silence in Heaven. As the full impact of Lucifer's rebellion began to dawn on the remaining angels, I am sure that many hearts were broken. Close friends had parted ways and loving relationships were terminated. I am sure that human words cannot describe the sadness that the Father and Michael, the Creator, felt that dark day.

After the Father cast Lucifer out of Heaven, Lucifer sought a place where he could rule as lord and king. He was determined to show the universe that his ideas for government were superior to God's government. Lucifer saw an opportunity to gain control of a new creation when Jesus created Earth. Maybe Lucifer reasoned that it would be easier to start with a new creation than to destroy an existing government on some planet and rebuild it. I am also sure that Lucifer was fascinated with the ability that God had given to Adam and Eve to procreate. Again, Lucifer saw an opportunity. If he could get Adam and Eve to disobey God's law,[32] he could grow an ever expanding kingdom of subjects. What Lucifer did not know, however, was that God had a plan to redeem sinners should sin occur *without defiance*. Satan did not know that a plan of redemption was prepared if it should become necessary.

Bible students know the story. Lucifer *lied* to Eve, and Adam *willfully* sinned because he loved Eve more than God. (He violated the first law of love.) Ever since that awful day, endless cycles of sorrow, suffering, and death have occurred on Earth. Of course, the Father foreknew all these things and before any of them occurred, He wrote a complete history of life before any life was created. The Father perfectly sealed His book with seven seals to keep the details of His foreknowledge a secret. If the information in The Book of Life was prematurely released, it would be very difficult for the Father to overcome any accusation. For example, consider this often repeated argument: Since the Father knows who will be saved and who will be lost, He has predetermined who will be saved and lost. When The Book of Life is opened, this argument (and others) will be proven false. So, the Father wisely sealed up The Book of Life and the contents will not be exposed until the thousand years have ended.[33]

For the greater good of the universe, the Father did not execute Lucifer and the angels, or Adam and Eve on the day they sinned. He temporarily and wisely stayed their execution to allow sin and rebellion to fully mature. Remember, God's primary objective is preventing a third episode of sin. *Therefore, the Father wants everyone in the universe to clearly understand the properties of sin before He annihilates any sinner.*

Who is Worthy?

Now that we have considered some background information on The Book of Life, let us return to the story of the courtroom scene and the angel's question, "Who is worthy?" The Father is obviously looking for someone who is capable of resolving the sin problem so that His government and policies can be exonerated. The Father is planning ahead. He is looking forward, billions of years in the future. When thousands of new worlds exist and an infinite number of inhabitants have been created, He wants everyone to know that even though He has perfect foreknowledge, He did not and He will never use this divine power to protect Himself from rebellion or sin. He wants everyone to understand that His "sudden death" law is based on divine wisdom and love for oncoming generations. Looking back on sin's drama, all future creations will see that the Father allowed Lucifer and sin to exist for a few thousand years because He wants all current and future beings to understand the horrific consequences of sin. Personally, I believe the Father will dramatically expand the number of children living in His universe after the knowledge of good and evil has been fully defined and understood.

After the truth about good and evil is exposed to the universe, the "sudden death" law will be viewed very differently than before. Unlike human governments that create laws on an "as needed" basis, God does not create moral laws on an "as needed" basis. Consider this scenario: At the end of the 1,000 years, God will resurrect all of the wicked so that Jesus can review their life's record with them. Jesus wants each wicked person to review his or her life and realize that His judgment of them was careful, righteous, and fair. The information in the Books of Record, as recorded by angels, will be presented. Each wicked person will be forced by the evidence presented that his choices were accurately recorded and that Jesus judged righteously. (Every knee will bow.[34])

> Rev. 5:3

After the admission of the wicked takes place, the seventh seal will be broken and The Book of Life will be opened and compared with the Books of Record. Everyone will see that the contents are identical. They will also see that the names of the wicked were blotted out of The Book of Life. This feature makes the event very interesting. Everyone will then be forced by the evidence to admit that God did not use His foreknowledge to protect Himself from rebellion and He did not use His foreknowledge to determine the eternal destiny of any being!

Later, when the wicked advance on the Holy City to destroy it, the saints will also see the wisdom of the Father's "sudden death" law. Going forward into eternity, the beauty of this law is simple. It limits the cancer of sin to one sinner.* By destroying a sinner on the day that he sins, the virus of sin cannot be passed to another person. During the drama of sin, the truth about good and evil was completely revealed. Once the universe properly understands the curse of sin, everyone will agree that God's love and His sudden death law are not in opposition. Furthermore, everyone will know that Jesus will not die again to redeem sinners. Consequently, anyone who deliberately defies the laws of love will be executed on the day he exhibits defiance. There will be no excuse or tolerance for rebellion. Because God's children will always have the power of choice, there will always be a possibility of sin erupting in the universe, but God has allowed sin to run its evil course in Heaven and on Earth one time and this drama will not happen again. If defiance should rise again, it will last one day.

> * **Note:** When the saints are taken to Heaven, none will have a carnal nature. There will be no predisposition toward sin or rebellion toward God.[35] When the carnal nature is removed, committing sin will be more difficult than sinners overcoming temptation. This may be difficult to comprehend, but throughout eternity, sinning will not come naturally or easily. However, rebellion and defiance will always be possible because God grants His children the power of choice.

I have alluded to this point previously, but I believe after the current drama of sin is finished, Jesus will endlessly create new planets and He will fill them with new people. Suppose a billion years from now a newly created person is tempted to sin. I believe the Father will, if necessary, send all of the redeemed from planet

Earth to visit with that newly created being. Ex-sinners will try to reason with that being about the horrible consequences of sin. However, if God's newly created being chooses to defy God and continue to rebel (as Lucifer did), then God will act to protect the universe from sin by annihilating the sinner on the day that he commits sin. If this should occur, all of the watching universe will agree that God's action was appropriate.

These substantive issues have been discussed because breaking the seven seals and revealing the contents of The Book of Life is an extremely important part of apocalyptic prophecy. Even though the Father is Almighty God and is omnipotent, He needs two infallible witnesses who can prove that He is love. The Book of Life will serve as one witness and the other witness must be a worthy person who can break open the seven seals and carry out the requirements ordained in each seal.

The Sequence Continues

{4} Looking at the service taking place in Heaven's temple, it broke my heart to think that the Father needed a savior! The realization that no one was found worthy to exonerate Him cut like a knife into my heart and I began to weep. Was there no one who could clear His holy name?

> This scene is paradoxical in a way. John saw an omnipotent God sitting on a glorious throne. Even with all His might and power, Almighty God needs someone to exonerate Him and His government from Lucifer's lies. The interplay between God's power and wisdom, His vulnerability, and His love is astonishing. The Father has more than enough power to destroy and recreate the whole universe in a split second, but His incredible love for His children prevents Him from violating the will of the weakest being. He never controls us for His personal benefit. What an amazing God! *In Revelation 5, we learn the Father needs a savior to prove that His foreknowledge and the "sudden death" law are governed by love instead of tyranny.* What the Father needs is someone who can successfully lead the universe into the light of this profound truth.
>
> Sin has created a basic problem between man and God. Sinners naturally distrust God and even born again Christians find it difficult to trust in God at all times and in all circumstances! God's infinite ways are vastly superior and often seem mysterious because His ways are not our ways. This makes God espe-

---

Rev. 5:3

Rev. 5:4

And I wept much, because no man was found worthy to open and to read the book, neither to look thereon.

cially vulnerable to suspicion and distrust if anyone *chooses* to be suspicious and distrusting. This vulnerability explains why faith and love are the essential building blocks of God's kingdom. How does a person worship, adore, obey, and live *in the present* with an infinite God whose actions and ways will not be completely understood for several thousand years? Until understanding arrives, faith and love are required. This is why Lucifer was able to make headway against God and one-third of the holy angels made a big mistake. *Faith in God, when seen in reverse, always makes perfect sense.*

When the angel asked, "**. . . . Who is worthy to break the seals and open the scroll?**"[36] the question really contains three parts. Who is qualified to open the book and prove that the Father will not use His foreknowledge and His "sudden death" law to protect Himself and His throne? Who can prove to the universe that the Father is selfless and righteous? Who can prove that His actions and laws are based on love? The four living creatures, the twenty-four elders, or the seven angels who stand before God were not qualified and no one was found on Earth, dead or alive.

Rev. 5:5
And one of the elders saith unto me, Weep not: behold, the Lion of the tribe of Juda, the Root of David, hath prevailed to open the book, and to loose the seven seals thereof.

I wept and wept because I, too, was unworthy to help the Father. I could not exonerate the character and government of my God and Father, even though I would count it an honor to die for Him.

{5} One of the twenty-four elders noticed my weeping. He came over to me and said, "John, do not weep anymore! Look, the Lion from the tribe of Judah, the Root of David, has been found worthy! He is qualified to break open the seven seals and reveal the contents of the book." I immediately thought, how wonderful is this? Jesus will save the Father! And why not? He is my Savior, too!

Rev. 5:6
And I beheld, and, lo, in the midst of the throne and of the four beasts, and in the midst of the elders, stood a Lamb as it had been slain, having seven horns and seven eyes,

{6} I had been so absorbed with the angel's explanations and my own grief that I did not see Jesus come forward and offer Himself to the Father. As I looked through my tears I saw a Lamb, looking as if it had been slain, standing in the center of the throne. He was surrounded by the four living creatures and the twenty-four elders.

In Heaven's economy, supreme acts of love are given highest honor and recognition. Actions speak louder than words in Heaven's currency. Jesus is represented in this scene as an innocent lamb "looking as though it had been slain" because this caricature highlights a profound truth: No one in all of the universe has demonstrated the height, width and depth of love more than Jesus. In Heaven, the worthiest is the loveliest, not according to appearance, but according to action. Jesus was willing to forever cease to exist to redeem sinners. There is no act or sacrifice in the universe that equals what Jesus did. Jesus was willing to forfeit His eternal life so that it could be given to sinners. On the basis of demonstrated love for sinners and perfect love and submission to the Father under the most distressing circumstances possible, Jesus was found worthy to receive the book sealed with seven seals. The Father needed someone who had fully demonstrated the dimensions of love to exonerate His government of love. This is why the Lamb is described as "looking as though it had been slain." The reciprocity between the Father and Jesus is interesting. Jesus totally surrendered Himself to the will of the Father to save mankind and now, the Father will totally surrender His throne to Jesus to exonerate His government! Because Jesus provided the greatest example of love ever witnessed, Heaven's court agreed, only Jesus was worthy to receive the book with seven seals.

When Jesus was declared worthy, a great coronation celebration followed. The Father stepped aside and gave the Lamb sovereign power over the whole universe (represented by the seven horns).[37] The seven angels who stand before God bowed down before Jesus. From this time forward, they will serve as servants of Jesus/Almighty God and do all that He commands.[38]

{7} Jesus approached the Father and received the book from His right hand. From this point on in the book of Revelation, the book with seven seals is called, "The Lamb's Book of Life."

{8} The four living creatures and the twenty-four elders fell down before Jesus and gave Him praise and every honor. As representatives of the human race and beneficiaries of Christ's salvation, each elder was given a harp and a golden bowl full of incense. The harps are used for singing praises and the bowls for burning incense. When the twenty-four elders put special incense on the live coals that were in the bowls, a wonderful fragrance filled the courtroom.

Imagine being there, enveloped in the glory of God and hearing the inexpressible music of Heaven's choir jubilantly singing with gratitude and joy. This glorious assault on the senses must evoke visual, auditory, olfactory, intellectual, and emotion-

which are the seven Spirits of God sent forth into all the earth.

Rev. 5:7

And he came and took the book out of the right hand of him that sat upon the throne.

Rev. 5:8

And when he had taken the book, the four beasts and four and twenty elders fell down before the Lamb, having every one of them harps, and golden vials full of odours, which are the prayers of saints.

Rev. 5:9
And they sung a new song, saying, Thou art worthy to take the book, and to open the seals thereof: for thou wast slain, and hast redeemed us to God by thy blood out of every kindred, and tongue, and people, and nation;

Rev. 5:10
And hast made us unto our God kings and priests: and we shall reign on the earth.

Rev. 5:11-12
And I beheld, and I heard the voice of many angels round about the throne and the beasts and the elders: and the number of them was ten thousand times ten thousand, and thousands of thousands; Saying with a loud voice, Worthy is the Lamb that was slain to receive power, and riches, and wisdom, and strength, and

al overload, all at once! Words cannot describe this magnificent state of heightened awareness and joy.

{9} Then the elders and the four living creatures sang a *new* song. New songs occur in Heaven whenever a new experience occurs. I was amazed that everyone already knew the words of the new song as they sang! It was so inspiring to realize that the Holy Spirit gave everyone the new words to sing at the same time! Words cannot describe the thrill of watching the elders and the living creatures play their harps and sing to the Lamb: "You are worthy to take the scroll and to open its seals, because *You* were slain, and with *Your* own blood *You* have redeemed people for God from every tribe and language and people and nation. *You* have proven that you love others more than you love Your own life.

{10} Even more, *You* will soon receive those on Earth who love you and obey you. *You* have ordained them to be priests to serve our God forever so that sin will never happen again." Amen!

{11} As I looked around the huge room, I heard the voices of that vast throng, numbering thousands upon thousands, and ten thousand times ten thousand. They encircled the throne along with the living creatures and the elders. {12} And in a loud voice they sang: "Worthy is the Lamb, who was slain. He has been exalted above every name.[39] He is worthy to receive the seven attributes of divine sovereignty: Power, wealth, wisdom, strength, honor, glory, and praise!"

{13} Then Heaven seemed to explode again with singing and rejoicing as every creature in Heaven was singing and praising God. In unison they sang: "To God be the glory, to the Father who sits on the throne, and to His Lamb be praise and honor and glory and power, forever and ever! We honor the humility of the Father to be openly examined. We honor the sacrifice and victory of Jesus over sin and we agree that He alone is worthy to break open the seven seals and exonerate the Father." {14} The four living creatures ended the song by saying, "Amen," and again, the twenty-four elders fell down on their faces and worshiped the Lamb and the Father.

A Short Summary of The Seven Seals

Sometimes, it is good to have a bird's eye view of a topic that is quite involved. Therefore, a short summary of my understanding of the seven seals might be helpful before we proceed. The first seal was broken in 1798. This seal is a campaign that promotes salvation through faith in Jesus Christ *alone*. This campaign is controversial because it is in conflict with all of the religions of the world. In fact, millions of Christians have been led to believe that salvation comes through rituals, sacraments, or church affiliation. None of this is true. Salvation comes through faith, obediently surrendering our will (go-be-do) to the will of Christ. The campaign begun with the first seal will continue until the time when the seventh trumpet is about to sound. The second seal was broken in 1800. This seal concerns the translation, publication, and distribution of the Bible – the only book on Earth that speaks authoritatively for God. This campaign will become very controversial during the Great Tribulation because Bible truth is opposed to the desires of the carnal nature. The third seal was broken in 1844. This seal reveals the concept of a pre-advent judgment. Jesus began judging the dead in 1844 and He will judge the living during the Great Tribulation. This campaign has been controversial, in part, because it rejects the idea that a person is judged at death and sent immediately to Heaven or hell. The fourth seal will be a campaign that reveals the sovereign authority of Jesus. This campaign has not begun yet, but when it does, a great controversy will erupt as to what constitutes the will of God. The breaking of the fourth seal will mark the beginning of the Great Tribulation.

honour, and glory, and blessing.

Rev. 5:13

And every creature which is in heaven, and on the earth, and under the earth, and such as are in the sea, and all that are in them, heard I saying, Blessing, and honour, and glory, and power, be unto him that sitteth upon the throne, and unto the Lamb for ever and ever. And the four beasts said, Amen. And the four and twenty elders fell down and worshipped him that liveth for ever and ever.

> Rev. 5:13

Billions of people will learn after the fourth seal is broken that everyone on Earth is required to worship Jesus as Creator and Redeemer. Of course, this will be controversial. The fifth seal will be a campaign that reveals the faith of Jesus. There will be millions of martyrs for Christ when the fifth seal is broken. These martyrs will demonstrate the peace and resolve that only comes through faith in Jesus. The sixth seal will be a campaign revealing Christ's authority as Almighty God. When the sixth seal is broken, Jesus will appear in clouds of glory at the Second Coming. He will return to Earth to destroy the wicked and rescue the righteous. Finally, the seventh seal will be a campaign that reveals the eternal deity of Jesus. The whole universe will learn that Jesus is equal to the Father in every way. After Jesus destroys the wicked and the Earth with fire, He will create a new Heaven and a new Earth. The saints will then watch as Jesus humbles Himself again. Jesus will return the power and authority which the Father gave Him. Once again, Jesus will become submissive to the Father's will. Jesus will do this because of His great love for the Father and His creation.

The seven seals reveal Jesus:

- Seal 1: The salvation of Jesus
- Seal 2: The teachings of Jesus
- Seal 3: The judgment of Jesus
- Seal 4: The sovereign authority of Jesus
- Seal 5: The faith of Jesus
- Seal 6: The glory of Jesus
- Seal 7: The deity of Jesus

When Jesus is revealed for all that He is at the end of the 1,000 years, the universe will see that the three members of the Godhead are inseparably united. They are submissive to each other. They are one in purpose, plan, and action and they love their children with as much love as they love one another. They are mirrors of each other.[40] When Jesus came to Earth at His First Advent, most of the world was unaware of His arrival. When Jesus comes to Earth the second time, the result will be much different. Every eye will see Him.[41] The whole world will know who He is. The saints will rejoice and the wicked will perish.

The Sequence Continues

Seal One – The Salvation of Jesus

{6:1} After the songs of praise came to an end, everyone was seated and silence fell upon the throne room. A sovereign Jesus sat beside the Father on the throne.[42] I watched closely as the Lamb broke open the first seal.

> The seven seals represent a seven step process that will, at the end of the 1,000 years, reveal everything about the love and full identity of Jesus Christ. The Father has ordained that everyone in the universe should know that Jesus Christ is Almighty God, just like Himself. Jesus is made of the same eternal substance as the Father and He has the same powers and prerogatives as the Father. Jesus is a separate, distinct, co-eternal member of the Godhead. Yet, Jesus was willing to lay aside His powers and prerogatives and surrender Himself to the will of the Father in order to save mankind. The humility of Jesus is also seen in the Father. After Jesus received the book sealed with seven seals, the Father took "a back seat." The Father gave Jesus sovereign authority so that the drama of sin and the exoneration of God's government of love could be brought to a successful conclusion. Jesus still continues to carry this enormous responsibility today.
>
> The seven seals can be compared to seven political campaigns in the sense that the purpose of a political campaign is the exposure of a candidate with his or her ideas on "the way government should run." The purpose of the seven seals is a seven-step exposure of Jesus as the savior of sinners, Almighty God, Prince of Peace, King of kings, and Lord of lords.

{6:1 - continued} After Jesus broke the first seal, He spoke for a few moments to the first living creature that had a face which looked like a lion. Then the first living creature spoke to everyone seated in the courtroom. His voice boomed with great authority. It sounded like thunder as he said, "Come and see the assignment the Lamb has given me."

{2} As I watched, the first living creature transformed Himself into a rider on a white horse. I was astonished until I remembered that Zechariah also saw the work of the Holy Spirit represented by four horses.[43]

Rev. 6:1
And I saw when the Lamb opened one of the seals, and I heard, as it were the noise of thunder, one of the four beasts saying, Come and see.

Rev. 6:2
And I saw, and behold a white horse: and he that sat on him had a bow; and a crown was given unto him; and he went forth conquering, and to conquer.

Rev. 6:2

In his vision, Zechariah saw white, red, brown, and gray horses pulling chariots. When Zechariah asked his attending angel what the horses and chariots represented, the angel said, **"These are the four spirits** [the four living creatures] **of Heaven, going out from standing in the presence of the Lord of the whole world."**[44] The colors of the horses are associated with a specific direction in Zechariah's vision. The white horses went toward the west. The red horses went toward the east. The black horses went toward the north and the dappled (gray) horses went toward the south. When viewed in their entirety, the color and identity of the horses in Zechariah's vision and the horses in John's vision are identical. The difference is that in Zechariah's day the horses were pulling chariots. In John's vision there are no chariots. There is only a rider on a horse. I believe this indicates the Holy Spirit must travel faster and farther, because there is less time. In both visions the four living creatures go throughout the Earth toward the four points of a compass.

After the first living creature was transformed into a rider on a horse, He left the throne room in a hurry. He departed on a mission that will not end until the door to salvation is closed.[45]

The four horsemen in Revelation 5 represent four campaigns which the four living creatures (the Holy Spirit) conduct. Each mission is associated with one of the four faces that John saw. Each campaign builds upon the accomplishments of the previous campaign and when the final campaign is completed, the whole world will not only know about Jesus, but it will also know who Jesus really is. Currently, even though three seals have been initiated, most of the world still does not understand who Jesus is. When the fourth seal is broken, progress will abruptly improve. At that time, the groundwork laid by the first three campaigns will prove to be very effective. Jesus will soon shatter the religious paradigms of the world. He will break the fourth seal and a display of divine wrath will turn the whole world upside down. (Note: The first four trumpets in Revelation 8 delineate these horrific events. This topic is examined in Prophecy 8.) When God's wrath is unleashed on Earth, billions of people will hear the message given by God's servants (the 144,000) and thoughtfully consider a gospel that is unlike anything ever heard!

Rev. 6:2

Daniel 7:9-14 aligns with Revelation 5. Daniel saw Jesus exalted to the throne (in 1798) and given sovereign power. John also saw Jesus receive the book sealed with seven seals (in 1798) and given sovereign power.[46] These two scenes align for several reasons, but primarily because sovereign power is bestowed upon Jesus in both visions. When Jesus broke open the first seal, the Holy Spirit (the first living creature with the face of a lion) began a campaign in Europe and the New World (the United States). The Holy Spirit opened up the hearts and minds of people to their great need of salvation *through faith in Jesus.* This was a difficult, but an important transition. For more than twelve hundred years, the Roman Catholic Church had claimed that salvation came through obedience to the traditions and sacraments of the Church. When papal power was broken in 1798, the time had come for the world to hear the truth about salvation. The Bible teaches that salvation comes through faith in Jesus Christ alone. No ritual, clergy, or church can save a sinner. A person's connection to Christ does not come through a priest, preacher, rabbi, or cleric. Rather, a connection with Jesus is available to every person through the work of the Holy Spirit. Jesus speaks to us through the Holy Spirit and Jesus offers salvation to any person willing to obey His teachings and voice.[47]

After the power of the papacy was wounded in 1798, the Holy Spirit put a compelling desire within Protestants to broadcast salvation through faith in Christ around the world. When it comes to revealing all that Jesus Christ is, the doctrine of salvation through faith in Christ (justification and sanctification) is the first and greatest teaching of Christ. The bow carried in the rider's hand is not a weapon of war as artists commonly portray it. The Greek word *toxon* indicates the bow is made of fabric which indicates the bow carried in the rider's hand is a winner's ribbon. This bow indicates the victory that is *given* to everyone who abides in Christ. (See Appendix B.) In fact, victory over the carnal nature is only possible through the indwelling power of the Holy Spirit. A believer can overcome the power of sin through the power that Jesus will send him through the Holy Spirit! The gospel of Jesus always produces division and conflict when it is proclaimed with clarity and power. Lucifer and his demons will be sure of that!

The opening of the first seal initiated a sevenfold process revealing who Jesus really is. The first living creature (the one having a face like a lion) went throughout the Earth searching for souls. The Holy Spirit caused a great awakening in the United States and Europe and many people rejoiced to learn that salvation comes through faith in Christ alone. After breaking the first seal, the work of the Holy Spirit took off and the gospel of Jesus began to grow. This work will continue until the seventh trumpet occurs.

Seal Two – The Teachings of Jesus

{3} The Lamb spoke to the second living creature, the one who had the face like an ox. (Oxen are known for their great strength.) The Holy Spirit spoke in a loud voice, "Come and see the assignment the Lamb has given me!"

{4} With this, the Holy Spirit transformed Himself into a rider on a red horse. He left Heaven's throne room on a mission to empower and expand the spiritual revival that had just begun on Earth. The Holy Spirit carried with Him a great sword which represents the Word of God.[48] This campaign centered on the translation, printing and distribution of God's great sword, the Bible.

In the early 1800s, the Holy Spirit began prompting Protestants to establish Bible societies in Europe and the United States. The result has been impressive: The British and Foreign Bible Society (1804), the Basel Bible Society (1804), the Berlin (later Prussian) Bible Society (1805), the Pennsylvania Bible Society (1808), the Connecticut Bible Society (1809), the Massachusetts Bible Society (1809), the International Bible Society (1809), the Bible Society of India (1811), the Russian Bible Society (1812), the Swedish Bible Society (1814), the Netherlands Bible Society (1814), the Icelandic Bible Society (1815), the Norwegian Bible Society (1816), the American Bible Society (1816), the Bible Society in Australia (1817), and the Protestant Biblical Society of Paris (1818). When viewed as a whole, the task has been laborious and expensive and many people have given sacrificially to this cause. The Bible (or portions of it) now exists in more than 2,572 languages and dialects. Since 1908, Gideons International has distributed about 1.7 billion Bibles. Since 1942, Wycliff Bible translators have helped to complete more than 700 translations. This enormous project, spanning the globe, could not have been possible if it were not through the persistent ministry of the Holy Spirit. No book has outsold the Bible and no other book comes close in terms of exposure and distribution.

Rev. 6:3
And when he had opened the second seal, I heard the second beast say, Come and see.

Rev. 6:4
And there went out another horse that was red: and power was given to him that sat thereon to take peace from the earth, and that they should kill one another: and there was given unto him a great sword.

The relationship between the first two seals is important to notice. First, the Holy Spirit searched for people who were eager to understand the truth about salvation through Christ. Then He moved upon these people to share their knowledge by reproducing and distributing the Word of God. The teachings of Jesus are transforming. First, there is good news that God Himself has provided atonement for our sins through Christ (the doctrine of justification). Second, there is good news that justification is accompanied with a miraculous refining experience (the doctrine of sanctification). People who are willing to overcome the power of sin through Christ's strength will receive a winner's ribbon and a golden crown. The Bible societies have done (and are doing) their appointed work. They have printed and distributed millions of Bibles around the world! This has been strenuous work, but the Holy Spirit *plowed* ahead. He gave dedicated men and women the ability and strength to do the impossible.

Note: The sword of truth always brings conflict. When Jesus lived on Earth, He made people angry by speaking the truth. Jesus said the problem is that men love darkness and they are afraid of the light of truth. The Jews killed Jesus because they did not want the light of truth to expose their evil ways. Evil people will do whatever it takes to keep the truth from being known. During the Great Tribulation, a time will come when speaking Bible truth will be very inflammatory. Evil men will persecute and kill those who love God's Word thinking they can eliminate the light of truth that shines from God's Word,[49] but God's truth cannot be stopped. God will endure forever and so will His truth. The campaign of the second seal will end when Lucifer sets up his theocracy (sixth trumpet).

Seal Three – The Judgment of Jesus

{5} The third living creature said to the assembled host, "Come and see the assignment the Lamb has given me!" I watched as the Holy Spirit transformed Himself into a rider on a black horse! He left Heaven with a pair of balancing scales in His hand. The Holy Spirit carried a solemn message to the people on Earth that Jesus had begun to cleanse Heaven's temple.

Because the third seal indicates judgment and the third seal follows the formation of Bible societies in the second seal, the third seal had to have been broken after the formation of the Bible

Rev. 6:5

And when he had opened the third seal, I heard the third beast say, Come and see. And I beheld, and lo a black horse; and he that sat on him had a pair of balances in his hand.

Rev. 6:5

societies. I believe the third seal was broken in 1844. This seal perfectly aligns with the scene in Daniel 7:9,10 where the court was seated and "the books were opened." The third seal aligns with the cleansing of Heaven's temple mentioned in Daniel 8:14. Consider this: We know from the earthly temple services that the cleansing of the temple was a judicial process. The earthly temple became defiled by the record of sin and this necessitated an annual cleaning on the Day of Atonement. Similarly, Heaven's temple has been defiled by the record of our sins and the assignment of guilt is determined during judgment. When all of the guilt is removed from Heaven's temple and placed on the heads of sinners or the scapegoat, this will leave Heaven's temple cleansed. Furthermore, Revelation 5:5 aligns with the *exaltation* of Jesus in Daniel 7:13,14. Jesus received the book sealed with seven seals and was given sovereign power in 1798 to conclude the sin problem and to exonerate the Father's government. As each seal is broken, the events associated with it provide us a brighter revelation of all that Jesus.

The pre-advent judgment illuminates the ministry of Jesus as the Judge of mankind.[50] After Jesus broke open the third seal in 1844, He opened the Books of Record in Heaven and began to investigate the lives and deeds of men and women who have died throughout Earth's history. The Holy Spirit led people into this timely understanding of truth around 1844. Unfortunately, the nature and importance of 1844 remains largely misunderstood by most Christians today. This darkness will evaporate when the next seal is broken because the judgment of the living begins with the fourth seal.

Rev. 6:6

And I heard a voice in the midst of the four beasts say, A measure of wheat for a penny, and three measures of barley for a penny; and see thou hurt not the oil and the wine.

{6} I heard a voice calling for laborers. The Holy Spirit called many people saying, "God needs you to be His missionary. To finish His work on Earth, Jesus needs Bible teachers to help the world understand the everlasting gospel. Who will go and teach this message? Be assured that each teacher will receive a quart of wheat for a day's wages. Later, when the barley crop is ripe for harvest, he will be paid three quarts of barley for a day's wages. On top of this, fresh oil and new wine will be included!"

The purpose of this calling is both a solicitation and a promise. Jesus needs a continual supply of born-again trustees who will teach His gospel. Everyone who labors for the Lord will be paid a respectable wage for their effort. Interestingly, the currency used in Solomon's day to pay the laborers who built God's temple was wheat, barley, oil, and wine![51]

Now that we have investigated the first three campaigns, notice that the first three seals are additive in nature. This means that the activity generated by each campaign builds on the accomplishments of the preceding seal. The first three seals were carefully designed to prepare the world for the horrific events that will occur when the fourth seal is broken.

Seal Four – The Sovereign Authority of Jesus

{7} When the Lamb broke open the fourth seal, He spoke to the fourth living creature who had the face of a flying eagle and said, "Come and see the assignment the Lamb has given me!" Instinctively, I knew this campaign would be awful. The face of a flying eagle is fierce, focused, and deadly. Like the eagle that silently swoops down on its prey, the events of the fourth seal will come unexpectedly and the results will be deadly.

{8} As I watched, the fourth living creature (the one with the face of an eagle) transformed Himself into a rider on a pale, gray horse. The rider's name was death and the grave followed close behind. The Holy Spirit was sent on a mission of death and destruction. The scope of destruction was greater than words can describe. I shuddered when I saw one-fourth of Earth's population perish. God's wrath is as overwhelming as His grace. God has four deadly judgments. They are sword, famine, plague, and wild beasts.[52]

> The fourth seal will be broken soon and God's pent-up wrath will be released. The scale of death and destruction that follows the breaking of the fourth seal defies description. (See Prophecy 8.) The breaking of the fourth seal marks the beginning of the Great Tribulation and the judgment of the living. (See Prophecy 12.) A topic of worldwide interest when God's destruction begins will be the question of what constitutes God's will. Many people will repent and recognize their accountability to God. Of course, many others will not. One thing is certain. When the fourth seal is broken, life on Earth as we currently know it will end. The whole world will soon experience our Creator's displeasure with our decadent and degenerate ways.

> This may seem strange at first, but the Holy Spirit (in the form of the fourth living creature) will be sent on a mission to kill 1.75 billion people. Christians do not usually attribute such actions to the Holy Spirit. However, we need to remember three clarifying points: First, the Lamb sends the four riders on horses from the throne room. In other words, Jesus sends the fourth

Rev. 6:7

And when he had opened the fourth seal, I heard the voice of the fourth beast say, Come and see.

Rev. 6:8

And I looked, and behold a pale horse: and his name that sat on him was Death, and Hell followed with him. And power was given unto them over the fourth part of the earth, to kill with sword, and with hunger, and with death, and with the beasts of the earth.

> Rev. 6:8

rider from Heaven to Earth to do a deadly work.[53] Second, the rider on the horse is the fourth living creature. For reasons already discussed, we know the four living creatures represent the Holy Spirit. Third, as an example of the Holy Spirit taking action, the Bible states that Ananias and Sapphira lied to the Holy Spirit and He killed them.[54] The Holy Spirit is also God. He has the power to give life and when the Father spoke the word, the Holy Spirit restored Jesus to life.[55] The Holy Spirit is deity and He is more than capable of carrying out the directives of the fourth seal. There is no need for confusion over this. Even though the Father, Son, and Holy Spirit are separate and distinct beings, they are one in purpose, plan and action. Therefore, it does not matter ultimately who causes the destruction for they are united about it.

You may be wondering about the relationship between the Great Tribulation, the fourth seal, and The Book of Life. Remember, the Father wants everyone to know that like Himself, Jesus is a sovereign God. To demonstrate the sovereign authority of Jesus to a religiously diverse world, God must use divine action. For 2,000 years, Christians have been trying to tell the world who Jesus is, and today, 75% of the world has no knowledge or interest in Jesus. Jesus will implement the wrath of God and God's actions will force everyone to consider who Jesus really is. Remember, Jesus is worthy of worship. He is an equal of the Father.[56] During the Great Tribulation, many people will lament, "Why is God punishing everyone? He already knows who will be saved and who will be lost! Why doesn't He save the righteous and destroy the wicked and be done with this?" Of course, the Father foreknew who would be saved and who would not before the world was created, but He will not allow anyone to see what He foreknew until the seventh seal is broken at the end of the 1,000 years. Let me be clear. *Jesus does not know who will be saved and who will not!*[57] This is why Jesus began judging the dead in 1844 and He will judge the living in real time. Jesus can only pass judgment on what is seen and heard. This is why the Books of Record are necessary. Jesus judges the dead according to their deeds.[58] Jesus will judge the living according to their deeds, but He will only do so after we have been tested. (See Prophecy 9.)

Seal Five – The Faith of Jesus

{9} As I continued to watch, the Lamb broke open the fifth seal on The Book of Life and there was an enormous slaughter of God's saints. I saw that Jesus had a twofold purpose for the martyrdom of His people. First, the strongest testimony that a Christian can give in defense of righteousness and truth is his willingness to lay down his life for Jesus. (Remember Stephen, the first Christian martyr?[59]) Second, Jesus is willing to sacrifice several million Christians in order to save a few non-Christians. In other words, Jesus knows that a few non-Christians will repent and become Christians when non-Christians see the faithful testimony and death of Christians. You may think it strange that Jesus would sacrifice millions of Christians to save a few non-Christians, but remember, Jesus, who is worth more than a million worlds, was sacrificed to save us.

> When temple services were conducted in Jerusalem, it was customary for priests to pour the blood of animal sacrifices into a large container at the base of the Altar of Burnt Offering.[60] John saw the Altar of Burnt Offering in Heaven's temple. Beneath this altar was a large container holding the blood of the saints who had been martyred because of their steadfast love for Jesus and His Word.[61]

{10} When Cain murdered Abel, the Bible says that Abel's blood called out to God for justice.[62] Abel's blood is personified in Genesis because a great injustice had been inflicted on Abel. In a similar way, the blood of the martyrs will call out to Jesus from the container beneath the altar. I heard the cry, "How long, Sovereign Lord, holy and true, must this martyrdom go on? How long, O God, until You avenge our wrongful death?"

{11} Then, all of the martyrs were given a white robe (given the assurance of Christ's righteousness, the wedding garment) and told to be patient. The saints were told that they were being used by Jesus as living sacrifices so that Jesus might save to the utmost. Martyrdom would continue until a predetermined number of martyrs were killed.[63] In other words, after the number of believers to be killed are killed, martyrdom will serve no further purpose in saving non-Christians.

> There is an interesting connection between the sword of truth (the Bible) in the second seal and the martyrdom of the saints

---

Rev. 6:9
And when he had opened the fifth seal, I saw under the altar the souls of them that were slain for the word of God, and for the testimony which they held:

Rev. 6:10
And they cried with a loud voice, saying, How long, O Lord, holy and true, dost thou not judge and avenge our blood on them that dwell on the earth?

Rev. 6:11
And white robes were given unto every one of them; and it was said unto them, that they should rest yet for a little season, until their fellowservants also and their brethren, that should be killed as they were, should be fulfilled.

Prophecy 6 - The Six Seals

during the fifth seal! When the second seal was broken, the Holy Spirit started a Bible campaign. The Bible was translated, printed, and widely distributed around the world. When the fifth seal is broken, many people will be martyred because the distribution of Bibles had exposed them to God's truth and they stand firmly for the truth proclaimed in the Word of God.

A predetermined number of saints and most, if not all, of the 144,000 will be killed during the fifth seal.[64] The blood of martyrs is a powerful testimony and it cannot be easily ignored or silenced. It is comforting to know that Jesus has only to speak the word and millions who now sleep in the dust will come forth from the grave to life immortal![65] The first death is like a temporary sleep, but the second death is forever.[66]

To be honest, sleeping through the remainder of the Great Tribulation will prove to be a sweet blessing.[67] The blood of martyrs will cry out for justice, but some of the wicked, after observing the sacrifices of innocent saints, will repent and be saved. Be assured that each martyr will be given a martyr's faith. The Holy Spirit will comfort and empower each martyr to stand firm. Each one will have perfect peace knowing that Jesus will remember him when He calls the dead in Christ to life!

Seal Six – The Glory of Jesus

Rev. 6:12-14

And I beheld when he had opened the sixth seal, and, lo, there was a great earthquake; and the sun became black as sackcloth of hair, and the moon became as blood; And the stars of heaven fell unto the earth, even as a fig tree casteth her untimely figs, when she is shaken of a mighty wind. And the heaven departed as a scroll when it is rolled together; and every mountain and island were moved out of their places.

Rev. 6:15-17

And the kings of the earth, and the great men,

{12} I continued to watch as the Lamb broke open the sixth seal. I saw a great commotion. Earth began to tremble and everyone was filled with fear. The Sun became an eerie black disk in the heavens, the moon turned blood red in color, {13} thousands and thousands of fiery meteors fell from the sky, like late figs drop from a fig tree when it is shaken by a strong wind. {14} The sky became violent, rolling up like a scroll, and *every* mountain and island was removed from their places.

{15} Then the kings of the Earth, the princes, the generals, the rich, the mighty, even the slaves, and free men, hid in caves and among the rocks of the mountains. {16} They called to the fiery hailstones,[68] saying, "Fall on us and hide us from the face of the Father who sits on His throne and from the wrath of the Lamb who sits at His right hand! {17} For the great day of their wrath is here, and who can stand?"

The sixth seal describes the physical appearing of Jesus at the Second Coming. The wicked will be horrified when they see Jesus sitting at the right hand of the Father.[69] As we think about this dramatic scene, two elements are important to consider. First, remember that the Book of Life is not opened at the Second Coming. The Book of Life remains sealed until the seventh seal is broken at the end of the 1,000 years.[70] It is not until the end of the one thousand years that the Father is vindicated. Second, remember that the seven seals are additive in nature. As each seal is broken, a brighter and clearer understanding of who Jesus really is unfolds. Consider the following:

1. The first seal reveals the truth, salvation comes through faith in Jesus alone

2. The second seal reveals the teachings of Jesus, found only in the Bible

3. The third seal reveals the judgment seat of Jesus, He is our judge

4. The fourth seal reveals the sovereign authority of Jesus, His deadly judgments

5. The fifth seal reveals the faith of Jesus through His martyrs

6. The sixth seal reveals Jesus as King of kings and Lord of lords

7. The seventh seal reveals that Jesus is Almighty God, identical to the FatherNotice that the first six seals relate to each other in pairs. The first three seals are *causes*, and the following three seals are their *effects*.

and the rich men, and the chief captains, and the mighty men, and every bondman, and every free man, hid themselves in the dens and in the rocks of the mountains; And said to the mountains and rocks, Fall on us, and hide us from the face of him that sitteth on the throne, and from the wrath of the Lamb: For the great day of his wrath is come; and who shall be able to stand?

Relationships in the Six Seals

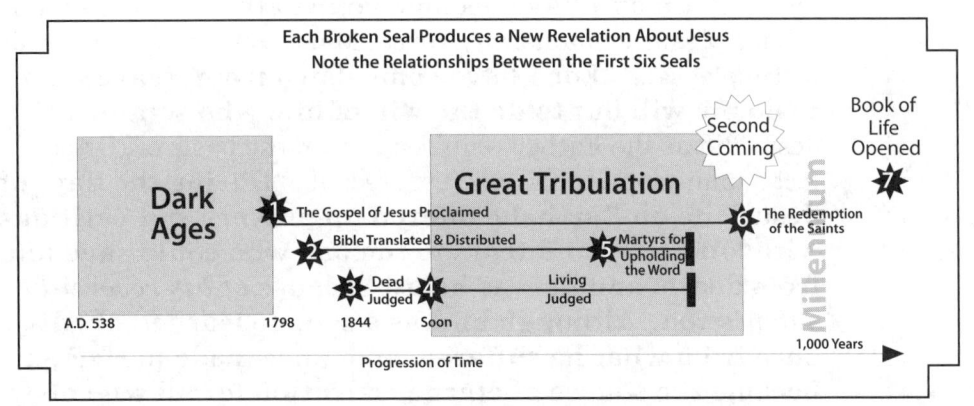

Figure 6.1

The *first* seal describes the first work of the Holy Spirit. He impresses sinners with their need of a Savior and the solution is a gospel of salvation through faith in Jesus. The work begun in the first seal ends with the *sixth* seal because eternal life is imparted to the saints at the sixth seal, that is, at the Second Coming.[71] Notice how the *second* seal pairs with the fifth seal. The second seal concerns the distribution of the Bible around the world and the *fifth* seal concerns martyrdom that will come when people firmly stand on Bible truth (the Word of God). Finally, the *third* seal concerns the doctrine of a pre-Advent judgment (the judgment of the dead) which connects to the fourth seal that deals with the judgments of God and the judgment of the living. When the fourth seal is broken, the seven trumpets will begin. God's wrath will awaken the living to hear that the hour of God's judgment has come.[72]

Evidence That Supports Prophecy 6 Beginning in 1798

The weight of evidence indicates Prophecy 6 began in 1798.

1. Many Christians do not understand the humiliation of Jesus, therefore the exaltation of Jesus as Almighty God in Daniel 7:13,14 and Revelation 5 does not seem important. (This topic is examined in greater detail in Prophecy 12.) The basic idea underlying the humiliation of Jesus is that to save mankind from death, Jesus, a co-eternal member of the Godhead who is equal with the Father in every way, had to completely surrender Himself to the Father's will. This event is described in Psalm 2: **"I will proclaim the decree of the Lord** [the Father]**: He said to me** [Jesus]**, 'You are my Son** [subject]**; today I have become your Father."**[73] The humiliation of Jesus explains why He could not come to Earth and do as He pleased. **"For I have come down from Heaven not to do my will but to do the will of him who sent me."**[74] Jesus did as the Father required and on the basis of His perfect submission, Jesus was resurrected. **"During the days of Jesus' life on Earth, he offered up prayers and petitions with loud cries and tears to the one who could save him from death, and he was heard because *of his reverent submission*. Although he was a son, he learned obedience from what he suffered and, once made perfect, he became the source of eternal salvation for all who obey him and was designated by God to be high priest in the order of Melchizedek."**[75]

2. When Jesus returned to Heaven, He served as man's high priest until the time came for the sin problem to be concluded.[76] Centuries later, a great convocation was called in Heaven. For reasons discussed in Prophecy 2 (Daniel 7), I believe the Ancient of Days took His seat in Heaven's courtroom in 1798. The Father issued a restraining order against the little horn power and 1,260 years of papal persecution ended. Then, Jesus went before the Ancient of Days and was given *sovereign* power and a kingdom.[77] We know that Jesus was given "all authority" over His church before He ascended from Earth,[78] but His authority over the church is not to be confused with *sovereign power* over Heaven and Earth.[79] After Jesus was found worthy on the basis of demonstrated love, the Father stepped aside. He gave Jesus sovereign power in 1798 to conclude the sin problem. Daniel and John both saw this event because it exposes an extremely relevant part of who and what Jesus is all about.

   Using repetition and enlargement, Prophecy 6 adds some vital information to Daniel 7. Jesus was found "worthy" to receive a book sealed with seven seals *when He was given* sovereign power (represented by the seven horns on the Lamb's head). John also heard Heaven joyfully singing that Jesus was worthy to receive seven attributes of worship reserved only for deity: **"Power and wealth and wisdom and strength and honor and glory and praise!"**[80] Therefore, Christ's appearance (having seven horns), His worthiness declared to receive the book sealed with seven seals, and the joyful singing in Revelation 5 perfectly aligns with the exaltation of Jesus described in Daniel 7:13,14. The year is 1798 because the convocation assembled that year.

3. The second seal adds historical fulfillment to the prophecy. The sudden formation of Bible Societies around the world after 1798 is a historical phenomenon that cannot be overlooked. Given the limitations of communication between the continents in the early 1800's and the rise of various denominations, what could have caused Christians to suddenly embrace the same spiritual objective and mission (the translation, printing and distribution of the Bible) if not the Holy Spirit?

4. Finally, the breaking of the third seal perfectly aligns with the cleansing of Heaven's temple.[81] In other words, when the 2,300 days ended in 1844, Jesus began to judge the dead from the books in Heaven.[82] When the third seal is broken, the rider

leaves the throne room holding a pair of scales in his hand. This imagery perfectly aligns with the pre-Advent judgment of mankind. Scales have been used for centuries to convey the idea that justice requires weighing the claims and actions of people. Do you remember the words of Daniel to Belshazzar the night the king was killed? "[O King,] **This is what these words** [the handwriting on the wall] **mean:** *Mene* **: God has numbered the days of your reign and brought it to an end.** *Tekel* **: You have been weighed on the scales and found wanting."**[83]

The Rules of Interpretation

Consider how the Rules of Interpretation are observed in this prophecy:

Rule One says an apocalyptic prophecy has a beginning point and ending point in time and the events within the prophecy occur in the order given. This prophecy conforms to Rule One because chronological order is self-evident. Additionally, the ordinal numbers given to the seals one through six, affirm chronological order. It is relatively easy to determine that this prophecy ends with the Second Coming (comparing Revelation 6:14-16 with 16:17-21), but when does it begin? I believe the evidence points to 1798. Here is how:

1. Jesus completely abased Himself to provide salvation for sinners.
2. Revelation 5 and Daniel 7:13,14 describe the exaltation of Jesus in 1798.
2. Bible societies on different continents began to translate, print, and distribute the Bible just after 1798 (the second seal).
3. The 2,300 years in Daniel 8:14 ended in 1844. Jesus began cleansing Heaven's temple (this is the third seal). Jesus opens the books and cleanses Heaven's temple by assigning guilt and judging the dead. Christ's pre-Advent judgment perfectly aligns with the rider sent to Earth carrying a pair of scales.

Rule Two says a fulfillment only occurs when all of the specifications are met, and this includes the order stated in the prophecy. I believe this prophecy began in 1798 and ends at the Second

Coming. This prophecy is underway, but it has not been fulfilled. There are elements within this prophecy that have been fulfilled, but seals four, five and six are yet to be opened. The fourth seal is the next seal to be broken and when this occurs, the world will experience God's wrath. Death and destruction on an apocalyptic scale will unfold. Twenty-five percent of the world's population will die. Soon, everyone will see and feel the sovereign power of Jesus Christ, even though it will be grossly misunderstood for a while.

Rule Three says that apocalyptic language can be literal, analogous, or symbolic. To reach the intended meaning of a prophecy, the reader must consider (a) the context, (b) the use of parallel language in the Bible, and (c) if an element is thought to be symbolic, the Bible must interpret the symbol with a *relevant* text. The language used in this prophecy is not symbolic because there are no relevant texts defining symbols. On the other hand, we do find the extensive use of analogous, literal, and parallel language. For example, the four living creatures described in Ezekiel 1 and 10 are the same four living creatures described in Revelation 4. The four horses described in Zechariah 6 parallel the four horses in Revelation 4.

Rule Four is not used in this prophecy.

References:

1. For further discussion on this topic, please see pages 58-65 in my book, *A Study on the Seven Seals and The 144,000*. You can freely download the article at: http://www.wake-up.org/Revelation/RevSeg3.htm.
2. Like Paul in 2 Corinthians 12:2, John was taken in the spirit to Heaven to see certain things.
3. Compare Psalm 68:17,18 and Matthew 27:52,53 with Ephesians 4:8. When Jesus ascended, He led, as first-fruits of the dead, a small group of people who had been resurrected with Him. Evidently, two human witnesses were taken from each of the twelve tribes to witness Christ's future actions, specifically, His judgment of mankind and termination of sin's drama. These twenty-four elders will be able to answer any question which the saints may have about the judgment of any individual. They were present during the judgment and their observation (as human beings) of Jesus makes them reliable witnesses.
4. 2 Corinthians 5:10; Daniel 7:9,10; Revelation 22:12
5. Revelation 1:20; 8:2; 15:1
6. See descriptions in Ezekiel 1 and 10.
7. Matthew 28:19
8. Compare with Ezekiel 1:4-26.
9. See also Ezekiel 10:12.
10. Compare Ezekiel 1 and 10 with Revelation 4 and 5.
11. Ezekiel 1:10
12. John 16:13-15
13. Acts 5:3
14. John 16:13-15
15. John 6:38
16. Matthew 12:31,32
17. Romans 8:26
18. John 16:14,15
19. Daniel 7:9
20. Daniel 7:10

21. Revelation 13:8; 21:27 (Note: After the Lamb receives the book from the Father, John calls the book the Lamb's Book of Life.)
22. Exodus 32:32; Psalm 139:16-19; Luke 10:20
23. See Matthew 24:36 (NIV) for evidence that Jesus does not know everything the Father knows.
24. Daniel 7:9,10
25. 1 Corinthians 15:24-28
26. 2 Corinthians 9:7
27. For a discussion on why Jesus is Michael the archangel, please see Chapter 2 in my book, *Jesus: The Alpha and The Omega.* or download the article at: http://www.wake-up.org/Alpha/Chapter2.htm.
28. Jude 1:9; 1 Thessalonians 4:16
29. Colossians 1:16
30. Genesis 2:17
31. Isaiah 14:12-17; Ezekiel 28:14-19; Revelation 12:3,4
32. Genesis 2:16,17
33. Revelation 20:12
34. Romans 14:10-12
35. Hebrews 8:10
36. Revelation 5:2
37. Daniel 7:13,14; Luke 1:32; Hebrews 2:8; Ephesians 1:9,10
38. Zechariah 4:10; Psalm 34:15; Proverbs 15:3
39. Philippians 2:9-11; Isaiah 45:23,24
40. John 14:9-11; Hebrews 1:3
41. Revelation 1:7
42. Hebrews 8:1; 9:12
43. See Zechariah 1:8-11; 4:6; 6:1-8. Special horses were bred for long distance endurance in ancient times so that they might quickly carry a king's edict throughout his kingdom. The four horses in Revelation 6 reflect this imagery. John saw the Holy Spirit sent out into the world on four horses in the same way that King Xerxes sent horses and riders throughout his empire in Esther's day. See also Esther 8:8-10.

44. Zechariah 6:5, insertion mine
45. Revelation 14:14-16
46. See my book, *A Study on The Seven Seals and The 144,000*, pages 58-65 or go here to download: http://www.wake-up.org/Revelation/RevSeg3.htm.
47. John 14:15; Matthew 7:21,22; 1 John 2:4-6; James 2:24
48. Hebrews 4:12; Ephesians 6:17
49. Revelation 12:11; 20:4
50. John 5:22; 2 Corinthians 5:10
51. 2 Chronicles 2:8-10
52. Ezekiel 14:12-21
53. See Esther 8:8-10 for a parallel. In Bible times, it was customary for riders to be sent from the king's throne on especially bred horses so that the king's bulletins might be quickly proclaimed and implemented.
54. Acts 5:3-10
55. Galatians 1:1; 1 Peter 3:18
56. John 5:22,23; Philippians 2:6
57. John 5:30
58. Ecclesiastes 12:13,14; 2 Corinthians 5:10
59. Acts 7:54-8:5
60. Exodus 29:12
61. Revelation 12:11; 20:4
62. Genesis 4:10
63. Revelation 6:11
64. Revelation 16:6; 18:24
65. 1 Corinthians 15:51-53; 1 Thessalonians 4:16
66. John 11:11-14; Revelation 20:14,15
67. Revelation 14:13
68. Revelation 16:21
69. Mark 14:62; Revelation 6:16
70. Revelation 20:3-15
71. John 6:40
72. Revelation 14:6,7

73. Psalm 2:7, insertions mine
74. John 6:38
75. Hebrews 5:7-10, italics mine
76. Hebrews 7:16,17
77. Daniel 7:13,14
78. Matthew 28:18
79. Ephesians 1:9,10
80. Revelation 5:11,12
81. Daniel 8:14
82. 2 Corinthians 5:10
83. Daniel 5:26,27, insertion mine

Prophecy 7

The 144,000

Revelation 7:1-8:1

Beginning point in time: 1994
  (See Appendix A for a discussion on 1994.)

Ending point in time: End of the 1,000 years

Summary: This prophecy introduces the selection and empowerment of 144,000 prophets. Jesus will speak to the world through the lips of His servants during the Great Tribulation. Empowered by the Holy Spirit and validated with Bible truth, the 144,000 will proclaim four profound messages that will separate sheep from goats. A numberless multitude, coming from every nation, kindred, tongue, and people, will embrace the gospel proclaimed by the 144,000 and gather around God's throne after the Second Coming. A thousand years later, Jesus will break the seventh seal on the Book of Life and the revelation of Jesus will be complete. At that time, the contents of The Book of Life will also be exposed.

Introduction: This prophecy consists of three chronological events even though there are gaps of time between the three events. The first event occurs just before the Great Tribulation begins.[1] The second event occurs after the Second Coming,[2] and the third event occurs at the end of the 1,000 years.[3] These events may appear to be disconnected, but they are intimately related.

The selection and ministry of the 144,000 (12,000 from each of the tribes) produces the numberless multitude (who come from every nation, tribe, language, and people) that are gathered around God's throne. Notice that the numberless multitude described in Revelation 7 is limited to those who "came out of" the Great Tribulation.[4] Going forward, the numberless multitude who gather around God's throne contributes to our understanding of the seventh seal in an interesting way. Rule One forces the seventh seal to be broken *after* the sixth seal (the Second Coming). So, the seventh seal must be broken *after* the numberless multitude are taken to Heaven. This fact is affirmed in Revelation 20:12 because according to Scripture, The Book of Life is opened after the one thousand years have ended.

Jesus' Final Victory

Prophecy 7 - The 144,000

This prophecy begins with four angels standing at the four corners of Earth (east, west, north, and south). These angels had been given power to hurt the Earth. Before the angels can begin their destruction another angel comes from the east. He tells the four angels to wait until the 144,000 are selected and sealed. After the 144,000 are selected and sealed, the four angels then proceed to hurt the Earth. This destruction (the first four trumpets described in the next prophecy) will initiate the Great Tribulation. More than 1.75 billion people will perish. *The breaking of the fourth seal on The Book of Life aligns with the release of these four angels.* Needless to say, apocalyptic upheaval is approaching and God's coming judgments will overwhelm and subdue the whole world.

God's wrath will change life on Earth for everyone in a single day. Shock and awe will subdue the arrogance of mankind and enable the 144,000 to proclaim a gospel that would be declared outrageous today. Jesus has a gospel which the world will hear and currently, religious diversity prevents His gospel from being heard. For example, if God chooses a Muslim to speak for Him, what Christian would listen? Conversely, if God chooses a Christian to speak for Him, what Muslim would listen? Religious paradigms are deeply intertwined with some of the most powerful emotions known to man. (A paradigm is a series of intricate concepts that seem to be right and true to the owner of the paradigm. A religious paradigm is a particular view of God and His will.) Religious paradigms are so powerful that one religious body cannot convince another religious body that it has superior knowledge about God and His will. God understands the gridlock and He has a solution. Jesus will humble the world with shock and awe so the world will listen to His servants and the Bible declares that a numberless multitude will embrace the gospel presented by the 144,000. Honest-hearted people in every religious body will abandon their religious paradigms when the time comes because honest-hearted people love truth, no matter what truth may be.

God has linked certain events in Heaven with identifiable events on Earth. I like to call this linkage the "Heaven-Earth-Linkage-Law." This law is very useful. For example, when the fourth seal is broken in Heaven, great harm will occur on Earth. When twenty-five percent of Earth's population is suddenly destroyed, people can know by events on Earth that the fourth seal has been broken on The Book of Life in Heaven.

To make sense of Revelation 7, a little background information may be helpful. For now, please consider the following explanation which will be presented in much more detail in Prophecy 8. The Bible tells us that seven high ranking angels stand before God. These mighty angels are His servants, sent on errands and missions as He directs. In 1994 (see Appendix A), each of these angels was given a trumpet and four of them were told to wait for the appointed time. Prophecy 8 is an excellent example of the Heaven-Earth-Linkage-Law. When each of the seven trumpets sound, a divine judgment will occur on Earth. The seven trumpets will produce an unbelievable amount of death and destruction. The seven trumpets will begin when the fourth seal is broken. (Please examine this alignment on the chart at pages 4 and 5.)

During the past six thousand years, God has used His four deadly judgments when necessary. Sword, famine, plague, and wild beasts are judgments which God uses to punish evil doers.[5] When a majority of people in any nation becomes wicked and violent, God sends warnings and redemptive judgments so that if possible, people might repent and future generations can flourish. If a nation refuses to repent of greed, idolatry, and sexual immorality, God ultimately sends total destruction.[6] God uses sword, famine, plague, and wild beasts in two different ways – redemptive and destructive.

Soon, Jesus will punish the world with His four deadly judgments. The seven trumpets will produce sword, famine, plague, and wild beasts. These judgments will be redemptive in the sense that the doorway to redemption will remain open. Everyone willing to put their faith in Jesus will be saved. When the seven trumpets are finished, seven bowls will be poured out on the wicked. These judgments will be totally destructive. Jesus will deal with the defiance of the wicked and avenge the suffering which the wicked unjustly imposed on His saints during the Great Tribulation.

When the fourth seal on The Book of Life is broken, the seven trumpets will begin. I believe God's forbearance with Earth (corporately speaking) ended in 1994. (See Appendix A.) At that time, the seven angels who stand before God were given seven trumpets. Four of the seven angels were sent to Earth on a mission to deliver God's devastating judgments. Before God gave the signal for the four angels to proceed with their assigned judgments, He told them to wait until the 144,000 were sealed.

Prophecy 7 - The 144,000

The Sequence

Rev. 7:1

And after these things I saw four angels standing on the four corners of the earth, holding the four winds of the earth, that the wind should not blow on the earth, nor on the sea, nor on any tree.

{1} I saw Earth laid out like a giant map and four angels, having four trumpets, took their place at each corner of the world. These angels had been given power to hurt the land, the sea, and the trees, but they were commanded to wait for Jesus to break the fourth seal on The Book of Life.

When the fourth seal is broken, God's wrath begins. God's wrath will be horrible, but it will accomplish a wonderful objective. God's wrath will shatter the religious paradigms of seven billion people. The honest in heart will thoughtfully and intelligently consider the testimony of Jesus which will come through the mouths of the 144,000. Currently, there are billions of honest-hearted people who cannot hear the gospel of Jesus because of their religious paradigms and culture, but God's judgments will tear down these walls and a numberless multitude will hear and embrace the gospel of Jesus.

Rev. 7:2,3

And I saw another angel ascending from the east, having the seal of the living God: and he cried with a loud voice to the four angels, to whom it was given to hurt the earth and the sea, Saying, Hurt not the earth, neither the sea, nor the trees, till we have sealed the servants of our God in their foreheads.

{2} I saw a mighty angel approach from the east. He was carrying the seal of the living God. He shouted to the four angels who had been given authority and power to harm the land and the sea saying: {3} "Do not harm the land or the sea or the trees until I seal the servants of our God."

Shortly before God's wrath is released, Jesus will select 12,000 people from each of the twelve tribes of Israel. The "Israel" of God today is not a biological Israel. (See Appendix B.) According to the New Covenant, the Israel of God consists of people who love Him with all their heart, mind, soul, and their neighbor as themselves.[7] God redefined Abraham's heirs,[8] a new Israel of God, at the cross.[9] The Bible indicates that God will select 12,000 *from* each tribe[10] to be part of the 144,000. This means that each tribe is larger than 12,000 people. In other words, God will only use a portion of each tribe.

Rev. 7:4

And I heard the number of them which were sealed: and there were sealed an hundred and forty and four

{4} I heard the number, 144,000 people were selected, sealed, and empowered by the Holy Spirit.[11]

There are no symbolic numbers in apocalyptic prophecy. According to Rule Three, a symbol requires a relevant text to define the symbol. The math in Revelation 7 is literal and straightforward – 12,000 people are taken from twelve tribes and the total equals 144,000 people. The 144,000 (a definite number of people) are not to be confused with the numberless multitude (an indefinite number of people). The 144,000 are called firstfruits[12] because they will be sealed first. The 144,000 will have their carnal natures removed and Christ will seal them against the corruptive power of sin. During the Great Tribulation, everyone who embraces the gospel of Jesus and passes the test of faith will also be sealed. The 144,000 are described as belonging to the twelve tribes of Israel because believers in Christ are counted as the heirs of the promises given to Abraham. Like Abraham, the 144,000 know how to live by faith. The 144,000 will also demonstrate the gift of sanctification that comes through faith (see Appendix B). Jesus wants the world to see living examples of what any sinner can become. So, the gospel of Jesus will come with a demonstration as well as a proclamation of God's truth and love!

{5} Jesus selected and sealed 12,000 from the tribe of Judah, Reuben 12,000, Gad 12,000, {6} Asher 12,000, Naphtali 12,000, Manasseh 12,000, {7} Simeon 12,000, Levi 12,000, Issachar 12,000, {8} Zebulun 12,000, Joseph 12,000, and from the tribe of Benjamin 12,000.

> The 144,000 will be people who have shown exemplary love, loyalty, and determination to serve God, regardless of personal circumstances or distress. Jesus will appear to each of the 144,000 as He did to the Apostle Paul on the road to Damascus. When Jesus appears to them, they will be astonished. Jesus will inform each person that he or she has been selected to serve as His mouthpiece. Jesus, through the ministry of the Holy Spirit, will give each person the words that Jesus will speak through them.[13] The 144,000 will not speak on their own. To keep His servants from failure, Jesus will remove their carnal nature in a single day.[14] They will be the first people (firstfruits) set free from sin's power and temptation since the fall of Adam and Eve. They will be examples to everyone that any sinner can be set free of sin's power through faith in Christ. A seal will be placed *in* their foreheads. This seal will not be a visible mark like the mark of the beast (which will be a tattoo), but a seal of ownership which God alone can see.[15]
>
> For 1,260 days the 144,000 will prophesy in sackcloth (fierce persecution and anguish). Their words will oppose the religious paradigms of the world. Their words will inflame the religious and political leaders of Earth. The 144,000 will experience the same suffering that Jesus had to endure when He was upon Earth – threats, hate, rejection, ridicule, bodily injury, and

thousand of all the tribes of the children of Israel.

Rev. 7:5-8

Of the tribe of Juda were sealed twelve thousand. Of the tribe of Reuben were sealed twelve thousand. Of the tribe of Gad were sealed twelve thousand. Of the tribe of Aser were sealed twelve thousand. Of the tribe of Nephthalim were sealed twelve thousand. Of the tribe of Manasses were sealed twelve thousand. Of the tribe of Simeon were sealed twelve thousand. Of the tribe of Levi were sealed twelve thousand. Of the tribe of Issachar were sealed twelve thousand. Of the tribe of Zabulon were sealed twelve thousand. Of the tribe of Joseph were sealed twelve thousand. Of the tribe of Benjamin were sealed twelve thousand.

Prophecy 7 - The 144,000

> **Rev. 7:9-10**
>
> *After this I beheld, and, lo, a great multitude, which no man could number, of all nations, and kindreds, and people, and tongues, stood before the throne, and before the Lamb, clothed with white robes, and palms in their hands; And cried with a loud voice, saying, Salvation to our God which sitteth upon the throne, and unto the Lamb.*
>
> **Rev. 7:11-12**
>
> *And all the angels stood round about the throne, and about the elders and the four beasts, and fell before the throne on their faces, and worshipped God, Saying, Amen: Blessing, and glory, and wisdom, and thanksgiving, and honour, and power, and might, be unto our God for ever and ever. Amen.*

death. Eventually, most, if not all, of the 144,000 will be killed in the line of duty for the sake of God's truth.

Note: Most likely, the tribe of Dan is not mentioned as one of the twelve tribes because this tribe was destroyed during the rebellion of the ten tribes.[16] If this conclusion is true, it explains how the tribe of Levi, which was not originally counted as one of the twelve tribes, takes the place of Dan. It is also interesting to note that the tribe of Levi is not identified as "the priests of Israel" or elevated above the other tribes in this list. Remember, after Jesus died on the cross, God redefined Israel. The priesthood of the Levites was eliminated and transferred to all believers.[17] There is no spiritual distinction between Levites or Benjamites under the New Covenant. Also notice that the tribe of Joseph is used as another name for the tribe of Ephraim. For further discussion on the "Israel of God," please see Appendix B.

{9} I looked again toward Heaven and saw a numberless multitude standing around God's throne. This multitude included people from every nation, tribe, and language. They stood in front of the Lamb, wearing white robes and holding palm branches in their hands. {10} They cried out in a loud voice: "Salvation belongs to our God, who sits on the throne, and to the Lamb."

This multitude consists of people who have embraced the gospel of Jesus during the Great Tribulation. Consequently, they have received God's gift of righteousness during the last hours of Earth's history. Christ's righteousness and eternal life are theirs because they surrendered to Christ's authority and His gospel. No wonder they sing, "Salvation belongs to our God who sits on the throne and to the Lamb!" Their experience mirrors that of the thief on the cross. They are absolutely astonished at God's incredible mercy and His gift of salvation because they chose to place their faith in Him!

{11} Millions of angels gathered around the numberless multitude and around the twenty-four elders and the four living creatures. Altogether, the vast throng fell down on their faces and worshiped God {12} saying: "Amen! Praise and glory and wisdom and thanks and honor and power and strength be to our God forever and ever. Amen!"

This scene is emotionally overwhelming because the angels, the twenty-four elders, and the four living creatures know and understand the incredible value of eternal life. The song of the redeemed will be one of the most touching songs ever sung in the universe. A numberless multitude will stand before the Father and the Lamb. They will wear white robes and hold palm branches in their hands. They had been sinners in a degenerate world, without hope or purpose, but they heard the gospel and put their faith in Christ during those last, horrible, dark days of the Great Tribulation. As a result, their fortunes changed! When the redeemed grasp the magnitude of God's love and generosity, when they see the golden streets of the Holy City for themselves, and when they grasp the value of eternal life with Jesus, certainly they will fall on their faces and say, "God is love – God is love! Having hearts filled with gratitude, they will sing, "Redeemed! How I love to proclaim it. Redeemed by the blood of the Lamb!"

{13} As I watched, one of the twenty-four elders approached me and asked, "These people in the white robes; who are they, and where did they come from?" {14} I answered, "Sir, you know." And he said, "Yes, I know who they are and I want you to tell everyone that the numberless multitude will be made up of people who come out of the Great Tribulation. They are the harvest which were gathered by the 144,000. These are the people who abandoned their families and religious heritage. They placed their faith in Jesus by obeying His Word. They washed their robes in His blood by patiently enduring persecution and their faith in Christ has been purified and refined through intense suffering for the sake of truth.

{15} "Because their faith in God was thoroughly tested, they will be given high positions in His government. They will serve God as priests and kings, day and night in His temple; and God will provide everything they need. {16} Never again will they hunger as they did during the Great Tribulation; they will never thirst as they did during the days of God's wrath. The Sun's scorching heat will not beat down on them again. {17} For the Lamb will be their Shepherd; He will lead them to springs of living water. God will wipe away every tear from their eyes. He will grant them joy and happiness beyond understanding – forever and ever and ever."

Rev. 7:13-14
And one of the elders answered, saying unto me, What are these which are arrayed in white robes? and whence came they? And I said unto him, Sir, thou knowest. And he said to me, These are they which came out of great tribulation, and have washed their robes, and made them white in the blood of the Lamb.

Rev. 7:15-17
Therefore are they before the throne of God, and serve him day and night in his temple: and he that sitteth on the throne shall dwell among them. They shall hunger no more, neither thirst any more; neither shall the sun light on them, nor any heat. For the Lamb which is in the midst of the throne shall feed them, and shall lead them unto living fountains

One Thousand Years Later

> Rev. 7:15-17
>
> *of waters: and God shall wipe away all tears from their eyes.*

One thousand years after the Second Coming, the holy city, New Jerusalem, will descend from Heaven to Earth. The wicked (who are resurrected at the end of the 1,000 years) will meet Jesus face to face. Everyone who has ever lived on Earth will be alive and present for this occasion. The saints will be safe within the Holy City and the wicked of all ages will stand outside the city. Everyone will see each other and Jesus as well. The physical contrast between the wicked and the saints will be stunning. The saints, possessing glorious bodies and radiant countenances, will stand along the walls of the New Jerusalem. The wicked will stand before God in the *same* degenerate bodies that they had during their life on Earth. The physical, mental, and spiritual toll that sin imposed on mankind will be shocking and obvious.

Perhaps the scenario continues like this: Jesus will raise His arms and silence will settle over the vast crowd. He will point upward and everyone will look into the sky and watch a compelling scene. The clouds will be pulled back like a giant curtain to form a huge screen. Each person will then watch a flawless replay of his own life. The details will be clear and truthful. Faithful angels recorded every word and action in real time and now, each person will be permitted to see his life as God saw it.[18] In addition to his own life, each person will be shown scenes of Christ's life. Everyone will watch His birth, suffering, and death at Calvary. In fact, everyone will see the Plan of Redemption and the enormity of God's grace and love as the movie unfolds. At the end, Jesus will speak *to each wicked person, explaining why* He could not save them. On that day, every person will see that his choices during this life determined his eternal fate. When this phase of the Great White Throne Judgment ends, every knee will bow.[19] The wicked will admit that Jesus is a righteous judge, He has carefully taken everything into consideration, and His decision is just and fair. Meanwhile, the saints inside the city will say that the Lord's forgiveness, mercy, and grace are undeserved. After the wicked and saints acknowledge the righteousness of Christ as the judge of mankind, Jesus will draw everyone's attention to The Book of Life. There is one remaining seal left to be broken. Jesus will break open the seventh seal and the contents of The Book of Life will be exposed!

The Sequence Continues

{8:1} When the Lamb broke the seventh seal, He opened The Book of Life and everyone saw a second "movie" in the sky. The wicked and the saints stood in silence for about a half-hour as they watched a phenomenal story.

> **Rev. 8:1**
> *And when he had opened the seventh seal, there was silence in heaven about the space of half an hour.*

When Jesus breaks the final seal on The Book of Life, everyone will see what the Father foreknew before any life was created. Everyone will see that the Father knew who would *choose* salvation and who would not; even before any life was created. Everyone will realize that the contents of The Book of Life are identical to the Books of Record which the angels recorded in real time.[20] The Father's foreknowledge concerning the life and details of each person will be stunning!

The contents of The Book of Life will prove to the universe that the Father did not use His foreknowledge to manipulate the behavior or destiny of anyone. God did not prevent anyone from choosing to sin. He did not prevent Lucifer, the angels, or Adam and Eve from rebelling against His authority. The Books of Record (recorded in real time) and The Book of Life (written before any life was created) are identical in every way, which proves that every being had been given *the privilege* of choice, and that every creature had been given *the power* that comes with choice. The difference between privilege and power is important. The "privilege" of choice means that we are free to choose. The "power" of choice means that we are free to act on our choices and direct ourselves. Consequently, each person is responsible and accountable to God for his or her actions.

The discovery of the power and privilege of choice reveals a new aspect of God's love for everyone. God permits His children to love Him or hate Him. God permits His children to surrender to His authority or rebel against it. God allows this because He has given us the privilege and power of choice! Suddenly, the controversy over God's sudden death law will make sense. Even though He created that law before life began, God does not implement this law until everyone has a complete knowledge of good and evil. God has wisely permitted a few thousand years of sorrow, suffering, and death to transpire so that sin would not have to be tolerated again; not even for one single day. I cannot think of anything more wonderful than this!

The Books of Record will be identical with The Book of Life with one exception – the names of those individuals who rejected the

Rev. 8:1

Holy Spirit were blotted out when the Father originally wrote The Book of Life and sealed it. In other words, the Father foreknew, before each person was created, who would commit the unpardonable sin, but His foreknowledge did not stop Him from giving that person the privilege and power of choice! Remember, The Book of Life is not used when Christ judges mankind. The Book of Life is opened only at the end of the 1,000 years. Only the Books of Record, recorded in real time by the angels, are used when Jesus judges the dead. The wicked must die because they were defiant – they blasphemed the Holy Spirit. The remaining names in The Book of Life will go on living; they will never cease to enjoy eternal life because they chose submission!

The Rules of Interpretation

Consider how the Rules of Interpretation are observed in this prophecy:

Rule One says an apocalyptic prophecy has a beginning point and ending point in time and the events within the prophecy occur in the order given. This prophecy conforms to Rule One because chronological order is self evident in this prophecy. The sealing of the 144,000 is followed by the numberless multitude gathered around God's throne which is followed by the breaking of the seventh seal.

Rule Two says a fulfillment only occurs when all of the specifications are met, and this includes the order stated in the prophecy. Currently, I do not see any evidence that the 144,000 have been selected and sealed. However, I do believe this could happen at any time.

We noticed earlier that the four angels were told to wait until 144,000 people were selected and sealed. Why does God tell us about this delay? Why do we need to know that four angels were sent to harm the Earth in 1994? (See Appendix A.) What role does this delay play in Revelation's story?

1. This delay indicates that God is waiting for an appointed time to arrive.[21] In other words, the selection and empowerment of the 144,000 is based on the arrival of an appointed time that the Father has predetermined. I believe that since 1994, God has been waiting to synchronize the end of sin with the arrival of the 6,000[th] year. If so, this in part, explains the delay.

2. This delay is included in Revelation's story because God wants us to understand that His wrath is overdue. When His wrath does begin, He wants us to understand that His wrath is not arbitrary or an emotional outburst.

3. This delay reveals that God is longsuffering, not willing that any should perish,[22] but, as in the days of Noah, divine patience has a limit.[23]

Rule Three says that apocalyptic language can be literal, analogous, or symbolic. To reach the intended meaning of a prophecy, the reader must consider (a) the context, (b) the use of parallel language in the Bible, and (c) if an element is thought to be symbolic, the Bible must interpret the symbol with a *relevant* text.

The language used in this prophecy is not symbolic because there are no relevant texts defining a symbol. On the other hand, we do find an extensive use of analogous, parallel, and literal language. For example, the four angels are four angels. The four winds describe God's four deadly judgments: Sword, famine, plague, and wild beast.

Rule Four is not used in this prophecy.

References:

1. Revelation 8:2
2. Revelation 7:9
3. Revelation 20:3,12
4. Revelation 7:14
5. Ezekiel 14:12-23
6. Colossians 3:5,6; Revelation 6:7,8
7. Matthew 22:37-40
8. James 1:1; 2:1
9. Romans 2:28,29; Ephesians 2:18-21; Galatians 3:28,29; 5:6 (See also Appendix B.)
10. Revelation 7:5-8
11. Compare Ezekiel's appointment as a prophet in Ezekiel 2:8-3:4 with John's appointment in Revelation 10:8-11. I see John's experience as representing the selection and sealing of the 144,000. See Joel 2:28-31.
12. Revelation 14:4; compare with 1 Corinthians 15:20.
13. Compare Ezekiel 2:8-3:4; Luke 12:11,12
14. Hebrews 8:8-13
15. 2 Corinthians 1:21,22 See also Ezekiel 9 for parallel language. Keep in mind that the vision given to Ezekiel was figurative. No one at any time actually went through the city of Jerusalem with a marker to indicate who would be killed or saved. Ezekiel was in Babylon and the Lord gave this vision to the prophet so that he could inform the elders of Israel that God clearly saw Israel's evil ways, even the behavior of each individual.
16. Deuteronomy 4:26,27; 2 Kings 17.
17. Hebrews 7:12
18. Ecclesiastes 12:13,14; 2 Corinthians 5:10
19. Isaiah 45:23,24
20. Daniel 7:9,10; Revelation 20:12; Malachi 3:16
21. Daniel 8:19; Daniel 11:35
22. 2 Peter 3:9
23. Genesis 6:3; Ezekiel 23

Prophecy 8

The Six Trumpets

Revelation 8:2-9:21

Beginning point in time: 1994

Ending point in time: The 1,260th day of the Great Tribulation

Summary: This prophecy begins with seven angels receiving seven trumpets. Afterwards, a special service takes place in Heaven. This service marks the end of God's patience with mankind. Because many events in Heaven are linked to events on Earth, we can easily determine when this special service will occur. When the service ends, God will initiate seven judgments against mankind. The sounding of a trumpet in Heaven preceeds each judgment. These judgments will awaken the whole world to the reality of a sovereign Jesus Christ. Ultimately, these judgments separate the sheep from the goats.

Introduction: A series of punitive judgments will soon impact Earth. At first glance, it may seem out of character that a "meek and lowly" Jesus would punish Earth with these judgments, but remember that Jesus is as much committed to justice, as He is to mercy. The devastation that will be caused by the seven trumpets (and the seven bowls that follow the seven trumpets), can be compared to Noah's flood.[1] When the 1,335 days of the Great Tribulation have ended, no life will remain on Earth. God exercises His wrath when extended mercy has no further redemptive effect on sinners. God's wrath is aroused when the sins of the fathers multiply and rob oncoming generations of the quality of life that God created for mankind. Seven judgments are linked with the sounding of trumpets in Heaven's court. In Bible times, trumpet blasts were used as signals[2] and the seven trumpets in the book of Revelation have the same purpose. Each trumpet blast signals another step towards Jesus Christ's second coming. While the first six judgments are mixed with mercy, they will still be terrible. Earth's population will be reduced by more than 50% before the seventh trumpet sounds.[3]

I anticipate the first four trumpet judgments will occur during a period of about sixty days. These trumpet judgments will in-

Jesus' Final Victory

flict a fatal blow on the ecological infrastructures of Earth, causing damage that cannot be repaired. These judgments include a meteoric firestorm of burning hail, two asteroid impacts, and the eruptions of many volcanos. About two years and three months after the fourth judgment, a fifth judgment will occur. This judgment will be the physical appearing of Lucifer and his fallen angels (demons). Although many people do not realize it today, Lucifer is *the* dreaded Antichrist. He will physically appear before mankind, masquerading as Almighty God. He will produce all kinds of counterfeit signs and wonders and deceive everyone who rejects the gospel of Jesus. Five months after the devil appears, a sixth trumpet will sound in Heaven and a great war will break out on Earth. During the sixth trumpet, Jesus will permit Lucifer to kill a third of mankind, set up a counterfeit theocracy and take control of Earth. The devil will rule as king of kings and lord of lords for about nine months. The wicked will depend on him for leadership, rations, and direction. Of course, the saints will refuse the mark of the beast (a tattoo which Lucifer will require) and they will not be able to buy or sell.

The first six judgments will be redemptive in nature. Jesus will use these events to awaken the people of the world to their need of His salvation. When Jesus tears the world apart, He will prove to laymen in every religious system that their clergy do not know the truth about God or His Word. Currently, strong religious paradigms prevent most of the world's population from hearing or considering the gospel. For example, Muslims cannot listen to Christians and Christians cannot listen to Muslims. God understands the gridlock and His deadly judgments will humble the arrogance of all mankind so that the message of the 144,000 will be heard. The Holy Spirit will empower 144,000 people to speak for Jesus. They will proclaim the eternal gospel. People will hear the gospel of Jesus in their own language and culture. Millions who presently do not know Jesus will embrace Him and receive His salvation. This will be possible because the first six trumpet events will shatter the religious paradigms of the honest in heart.

Architecture

The seven trumpets are organized in an architecture that is similar to the seven seals. Remember that six seals are described in Prophecy 6, but the seventh seal is located in Prophecy 7. Likewise, six trumpets are described in Prophecy 8, but the seventh trumpet is found in Prophecy 9. I believe God deliberately created this architecture for the following reasons:

1. Rule One forces the seventh seal to follow the sixth seal. Since the Second Coming occurs during the sixth seal, the seventh seal must occur *after* the Second Coming. So, the question rises, "When will Jesus break open the seventh seal?" Revelation 20:12 states the seventh seal will be broken at the end of the 1,000 years by declaring that "another book was opened, which is The Book of Life." Since the book having seven seals is The Book of Life, the opening of The Book of Life indicates the seventh seal is broken at the end of the 1,000 years. By de-linking the seventh seal from the first six seals, God accomplishes two purposes. First, He has been able to hide a great deal of information "in plain sight" for two thousand years because the architecture makes no sense until the four rules of interpretation are understood. Second, by putting the seventh seal in a prophecy after the numberless multitude is in Heaven, we discover the seventh seal has to be broken open when The Book of Life is opened at the end of the thousand years.

   Consider for a moment the beauty of separating the seventh trumpet from the other six. We know that chronologically, the seventh trumpet has to occur *after* the sixth trumpet. We also know that the seventh trumpet occurs after the Two Witnesses are resurrected and taken to Heaven.[4] Therefore, the facts combine to tell us that Jesus will do everything possible to save sinners before the seventh trumpet sounds. In other words, when extended mercy has no further redemptive effect on the wicked, the seventh trumpet will sound. This trumpet will announce the end of God's generous offer of redemption. No one will be lost because he was undecided.

2. God disconnected the seventh seal and the seventh trumpet from their six counterparts to emphasize their importance. The seventh seal brings "the revelation of Jesus" process to a grand finale by highlighting the eternal deity of Jesus and the seventh trumpet brings the generous salvation of Jesus to a grand finale by highlighting His extended efforts to save every sinner. Consider this amazing point again: God's mercy for sinners only ends *after* every sinner has made his or her decision. This is crucial. Just before

the seventh trumpet sounds, the population of the world will be sharply divided into two camps: The sheep will obey Jesus and the demands of the eternal gospel and the goats will obey Lucifer and the dictates of his theocracy. To obey Lucifer and the dictates of his government, every wicked person has to defy the Two Witnesses and commit the unpardonable sin. *Therefore, the seventh trumpet signals the end of grace and mercy because there is no further purpose for grace and mercy!*

God is the source of love and He is the perfect example of how love functions in all circumstances. Jesus wants mankind to understand His intricate process for resolving the sin problem because this drama reveals how true love actually functions. God's approach to resolving the sin problem is complex. God is not shallow or careless. His ways are magnificent, reasonable, and generous. Throughout eternity, the redeemed will study God and His actions. They will see that God used justice and mercy to redeem the greatest number of people possible. They will also see that He is not self-seeking, manipulative, or impure. No one in all the universe is purer in heart than the Godhead. They are more selfless and humble than words can express.

Have You Wondered?

Many people open their Bible to Revelation 8:1 and conclude that the seventh seal occurs just before the trumpets sound because after the seventh seal was opened, there was silence in Heaven for about half an hour.

Centuries ago, when translators added chapter and verse numbers to the Bible (for purposes of quick reference), they broke up sentences into verses and chapters according to their "best guess." The original manuscripts of the Bible do not have chapter and verse designations. Nevertheless, this innocent endeavor has caused much confusion in the book of Revelation. Revelation 8:1 is the last verse in Prophecy 7 and Revelation 8:2 is the first verse in Prophecy 8. Remember, each prophetic sequence has a beginning point in time and an ending point in time and the events within each prophecy occurs in the order stated. Since Revelation 8:2 does not chronologically follow Revelation 8:1 (Revelation 8:1 occurs at the end of the 1,000 years), a new prophecy begins with Revelation 8:2 (Prophecy 8).

The Sequence

{2} As I looked toward Heaven, I saw the seven angels who stand before God. Each angel was given a golden trumpet.

> Seven highly exalted angels stand before God. They are "on call" to carry out God's will at a moment's notice. These angels were given seven trumpets (in 1994 – see Appendix A) and are waiting for the signal to sound their trumpets. When Jesus gives the signal, each angel will sound his trumpet and a dreadful judgment will impact Earth. I believe the first four judgments will occur over a period of approximately sixty days and they will fall on notably wicked places. The last three trumpet judgments will fall on wicked people. The first four angels have been standing ready to do what the Lord asks of them since 1994. They are waiting for the 144,000 to be selected and sealed. This delay will end soon and when it does, God's wrath will be released. The first four judgments will kill twenty-five percent of the world's population. This means that one out of every four people will die.[5] Words cannot describe the death, destruction, and chaos the first four trumpets will produce.

{3} My attention was directed toward the golden Altar of Incense located before God's throne. I saw a highly exalted angel serving at the Altar of Incense. He had a golden censer in his hand.

> Before we discuss the importance of this scene, some background information about temple services is required. Two different altars were used in the earthly temples built by Moses and Solomon. Services conducted at these two altars teach us that God does not forgive sin, instead He transfers the guilt of a repentant sinner to the horns of the Altar of Burnt Offering. This may be a new thought, so please consider the following illustration: When a sinner commits a sin, the penalty for sin (death) rests on the sinner's head. The only way a sinner can escape this penalty is through faith in God's grace.

> Before Jesus died on the cross, repentant sinners in Israel had to go through a certain process to be set free of their guilt (condemnation). A sinner had to present a perfect lamb to a priest at the Altar of Burnt Offering. Standing at that altar, the sinner confessed his sins by putting his hands on the lamb's head and declaring his sinful actions. After confession, the sacrificial lamb was placed on the altar and the sinner took its life by cutting the jugular vein. The priest captured some of the lamb's blood in a cup and sprinkled the blood on the horns of the Altar

---

Rev. 8:2

And I saw the seven angels which stood before God; and to them were given seven trumpets.

Rev. 8:3

And another angel came and stood at the altar, having a golden censer; and there was given unto him much incense, that he should offer it with the prayers of all saints upon the golden altar which was before the throne.

of Burnt Offering as a record of this transaction. The sinner's guilt was *transferred* to the horns of the altar via "sinless blood," and the sinner came away from the altar free of condemnation (forgiven).

At the end of the religious year, the High Priest cleansed the Altar of Burnt Offering on the Day of Atonement. The accumulated guilt was transferred from the altar to the head of a scapegoat and the scapegoat was then taken out into the wilderness by a very strong man. The man was instructed to take the goat to a desolate place so it might die a protracted death. Two points stand out in this process. First, sin itself cannot be forgiven, but guilt can be transferred from the sinner to the temple's altar via the blood of a perfect lamb. Second, a scapegoat was required to cleanse the temple of accumulated guilt. On the Day of Atonement, the guilt which had accumulated on the horns of the altars was placed on the scapegoat's head and the scapegoat was led away to die.

The Old Testament ceremonial system demonstrates two truths. First, the blood of a perfect lamb (representing Jesus) was required to release a sinner from the penalty of sin. Second, the guilt of sin was put on the scapegoat. This point confuses many people. Jesus lived a perfect life so that He could provide the sinless blood required to transfer our guilt to the author of sin. Because sin cannot be forgiven, the author of sin must die for creating sin. Lucifer will die a protracted death. He must suffer and die for his own sins as well as the guilt of those who received Christ as their Savior.

Now that we have considered the daily service conducted at the bronze Altar of Burnt Offering, we need to turn our attention to the golden Altar of Incense and its daily service. Try to keep this thought in mind as you proceed: *Daily* services at the golden Altar of Incense provided "corporate atonement," whereas *daily* services at the bronze Altar of Burnt Offering provided "individual atonement."

Two levels of atonement (two altars) were required in the earthly temple because of timing. When God initiated temple services in the wilderness, the population of Israel exceeded two million people (and the nation became much larger later on). Therefore, an Israelite could not bring a sacrificial lamb to the Altar of Burnt Offering each time he sinned or at any time he desired. He had to wait for his turn. The Talmud indicates that the twelve tribes were assigned specific time periods when they could come to the temple for services at the Altar of Burnt Offering.[6] For example, suppose the tribe of Judah was scheduled for services at the Altar of Burnt Offering during the month of Tishri (the seventh month of the year). Suppose also that during the year, all of the people belonging to the tribe of Judah sinned a few times each month. Because sinners cannot live in God's presence, the Lord provided a way for the tribe of Judah to be "covered" from guilt until their turn came for the Altar of Burnt Offering. The grace extended through the whole year to the tribe of Judah came through *daily* services at the Altar of Incense. Here's how:

A priest conducted a special service at the golden Altar of Incense each evening and morning. He took a perfect one year old lamb[7] *from the temple's herd* and sacrificed it on the Altar of Burnt Offering. Then, he carried the blood into the Holy Place of the temple and applied the lamb's blood to the horns of the golden Altar of Incense. This process was conducted to benefit the whole camp. The guilt of the whole camp of Israel (not the guilt of a particular individual) was transferred to the horns of the Altar of Incense twice a day.[8] This daily atonement allowed an all-consuming God to live among sinners without destroying them. The blood applied to the horns of the Altar of Incense kept God's wrath away from the camp.

We know from Scripture that ceremonial services in the earthly temple are shadows of services that are conducted in Heaven's temple.[9] Because this parallel exists, we can determine the meaning of the service that John describes in Revelation 8:3-5. Here is a brief explanation:

Jesus began interceding for *all mankind* (corporate intercession) at the Altar of Incense on the day that Adam and Eve sinned. Jesus stood between the sudden death law[10] and the guilty pair. Jesus explained His intercession to Adam and Eve when He covered them with animal skins.[11] For 6,000 years, Jesus has protected the whole world from the sudden death law because He interceded for us daily at the Altar of Incense. Prior to the cross, God required individuals to show their faith in God's plan of redemption by offering a perfect lamb on an altar of burnt offering. Abel showed His faith through obedience, Cain did not. After the cross, burnt offerings were terminated, but living by faith remains unchanged. God still requires each person to surrender his will to God's will. He calls us to offer ourselves as living sacrifices.[12]

Prophecy 8 - The Six Trumpets

The corporate intercession that began when Adam and Eve sinned will soon end. When it does, the censer at Heaven's Altar of Incense will be cast down and God's wrath (the seven trumpets) will break out. God will release the four angels at the four corners of Earth and His four deadly judgments will punish the world. His four deadly judgments are sword, famine, plague, and wild beasts.[13] The seven trumpets contain these deadly judgments.

> **Rev. 8:4**
>
> *And the smoke of the incense, which came with the prayers of the saints, ascended up before God out of the angel's hand.*

{4} I saw a brilliant angel standing at the Altar of Incense. He served the Lord as a priest. Then, I saw all of God's saints on Earth kneeling in prayer. They were fasting and praying, imploring God to do something quickly because it seemed that everyone on Earth was about to perish. World leaders were crying out for peace and safety.[14] While the saints were earnestly praying, the angel was given much incense. He put the incense on the altar's live coals and a cloud of sweet fragrance filled the temple. The sweet scent, along with the petition of the saints, was presented to Jesus. He saw the entirety of the situation on Earth and was moved. There was war on Earth, the saints were very anxious, and the timing was perfect. Jesus sat in deep thought for a few moments. I could see deep agony reflected on His face. Then, He spoke to the angel ministering at the altar. He said, "Stop the corporate atonement service, there will be no more delay."[15]

Since this scene occurs after 1798, Jesus is seated on the throne. He is not the priest at the Altar of Incense. It should not be surprising that angels serve God as priests because human beings will also serve God as priests.[16] The angel-priest casts down the censer because Jesus gave Him the command to do so.

Why are *all* of the saints praying? What is the relationship between casting down the censer and the prayers of all the saints? The casting down of the censer and the termination of corporate intercession is the answer to the prayers of the saints. I assume one event which would move all of God's saints to pray the same prayer at the same time would be a nuclear exchange. Paul makes it clear in 1 Thessalonians 5:3 that when people are saying "peace and safety," God will send sudden destruction. When Revelation 8:3-5 occurs, the world will be on the edge of self-destruction and the saints will be praying for the Lord to intervene. World leaders will be demanding peace and safety and Jesus will respond. He will tell the angel who ministers at the Altar of Incense, "It is finished. The delay (that began in 1994) is over." Corporate intercession for Earth will be terminated. The angel will respond by removing the fire from the altar and throwing it down on the Earth. This dramatic action indicates indignation. Corporate mercy has ended, the fourth seal will be broken open, and the appointed time of the end will now begin.

{5} The angel serving at the Altar of Incense removed the live coals on the altar and put them in a censer. Then he threw the censer to Earth. There came peals of deafening thunder that caused people to panic. There were voices coming out of the ground and huge bolts of angry lightning filled the sky. Then a great earthquake violently shook the whole world for several minutes[17] and then the whole world came to a standstill.

> When the censer is cast down, Jesus will immediately empower His servants who have been selected and sealed. The 1,260 days allotted for the Two Witnesses will begin. The 1,335 days allotted for the Great Tribulation will begin. The "end of days" begins when *daily services* conducted at the Altar of Incense cease.[18] The appointed time of the end is a well-defined period of time.[19] Everyone will see and feel God's wrath. The Great Day of the Lord will be terrible.
>
> It is my understanding that since 1994, four angels have been holding back God's deadly judgments. There have been huge disasters on Earth, including earthquakes, tsunamis, tornados, and fires, but these have not been God's deadly judgments. They have been prophetic samples of events to come. The difference between a random act of violent nature and God's wrath is a message of redemption. There are several instances recorded in the Old Testament where God's wrath broke out and thousands perished.[20] When these instances occurred, there was always a divine message. As we approach the day when the censer will be cast down, remember that perfect love drives out fear.[21] If we abide in Jesus, there is nothing to fear. He has promised to be with us until the end of the world.[22] Given the scope and scale of destruction presented in the book of Revelation, it seems almost impossible that anyone will survive God's wrath. In fact, less than fifty percent of Earth's present population will live to see the Second Coming; yet, amid all the coming devastation, remember that God is love. He has carefully and deliberately designed the Great Tribulation to save the largest number of people possible and the Bible says a numberless multitude will be redeemed! God has several objectives for the seven trumpets, and as we have discussed, one objective will be

Rev. 8:5

And the angel took the censer, and filled it with fire of the altar, and cast it into the earth: and there were voices, and thunderings, and lightnings, and an earthquake.

> **Rev. 8:6**
>
> *And the seven angels which had the seven trumpets prepared themselves to sound.*

> **Rev. 8:7**
>
> *The first angel sounded, and there followed hail and fire mingled with blood, and they were cast upon the earth: and the third part of trees was burnt up, and all green grass was burnt up.*

to shatter the religious beliefs of mankind. When religious people discover that their religious beliefs are false, the honest in heart will discard their worthless paradigms and embrace God's truth as proclaimed by the 144,000 and they will be saved.

{6} The seven angels took their position and prepared to sound their trumpets.

When the censer is cast down, the seven angels will prepare to sound their trumpets. I believe the first four trumpets will sound over a period of about 60 days.

First Four Trumpets

{7} Jesus gave the signal and the first angel blew his trumpet. Everyone in Heaven was watching, closely focused on this tiny planet. There came a meteoric hailstorm from the sky that was composed of burning rocks. The white-hot rocks were unquenchable, like burning sulphur. One-third of the land was burned up, one-third of the trees were burned up, and all of the green grass was burned up; men were powerless. They could not stop the falling rocks or quench the great fires. Millions lost their lives in the fires.

The first four trumpets will serve as "a surgical strike." Jesus will destroy thousands of notably wicked places, like Sodom and Gomorrah, with precision. The Bible does not explicitly indicate this. I make this assertion for four reasons:

First, God's judgments are always deliberate. They are not random acts of violent nature. When the censer is cast down, God's response to rebellion and degeneracy will be plainly seen and felt. The 144,000 will direct everyone to the book of Revelation so that everyone will see that God's wrath was clearly predicted.

Second, Jesus wants everyone on Earth to listen to His servants, the 144,000. There is no better way to open the ears of people than to destroy thousands of places around the world that are widely known for their wickedness. Jesus will use the destruction of wicked places to arrest mankind's attention. He wants everyone to listen to His servants instead of their religious leaders. Getting people to listen to the 144,000 instead of their clergy will not be easy. To make this happen, Jesus will expose the ignorance of the clergy. Honest-hearted people will catch on quickly. They will soon realize that their religious leaders did not warn them of God's coming wrath because they do not know God's Word or His plans.

Third, Prophecy 11 states that Babylon (a coming global government) will form during the fourth trumpet because the leadership of the world will be convinced (when they see thousands of notably wicked places have been destroyed) that Almighty God is very angry. God's wrath against wickedness will be unmistakable, based on the evidence of destruction. Notably wicked places will become non-existent. When world leaders see that 1.75 billion people have been obliterated, they will set aside their religious and political differences, and unite in an effort to appease God's wrath.

Finally, the first four trumpets affect the land, sea, and trees (physical things and places). The last three trumpets are called woes (or curses) because they will directly impact wicked rebels. In other words, if destroying thousands of wicked places does not produce repentance and reformation, destroying defiant rebels is all that remains.

One-Third / Two-Thirds

It is important to understand that God's judgments will be mixed with mercy during the seven trumpets. This point is highlighted by the repetitive use of one-third; a third of the trees will be burned up, a third of the ships will sink, and a third of the day will be without light. In fact, "one-third" is mentioned twelve times in the seven trumpets! Jesus assures us a dozen times that even though His wrath is great, He is more than generous. Instead of destroying two-thirds of everything, Jesus spares two-thirds of everything! To appreciate this point, we have to examine a few passages from the Old Testament to understand the ancient practice of sparing one-third and destroying two-thirds.

During Old Testament times, a conquering king might feel that some grace might be merited or politically expedient. If so, he would typically spare one-third of his enemies. Notice this text: **"David also defeated the Moabites. He made them lie down on the ground and measured them off with a length of cord. Every two lengths of them were put to death, and the third length was allowed to live. So the Moabites became subject to David and brought tribute** [paid their taxes]."[23]

King David was as generous as he was wise. He spared one-third of the Moabites for two *redemptive* reasons. First, he felt the surviving Moabites might have a change of heart and gladly pay their tribute [taxes] if he spared their lives. (It is amazing what people

Rev. 8:7 can do when motivated by gratitude!) Second, David did not want to eliminate a significant portion of his tax base. David knew that the Moabites would recover from this war and repopulate their tribal nation. Future taxes would mean additional future income for Israel's treasury! So, David spared one-third of the Moabites.

Now notice how Jesus applied the one-third / two-thirds principle when He destroyed Jerusalem during the days of Nebuchadnezzar: **"Therefore as surely as I live, declares the Sovereign Lord, because you have defiled my sanctuary with all your vile images and detestable practices, I myself will withdraw my favor; I will not look on you with pity or spare you.** *A third* **of your people will die of the plague or perish by famine inside you;** *a third* **will fall by the sword outside your walls; and** *a third* **I will scatter to the winds and pursue with drawn sword."**[24]

This last text is another confirmation of the ancient custom of sparing one-third and destroying two-thirds: **" 'In the whole land,' declares the Lord, 'two-thirds will be struck down and perish; yet one-third will be left in it.' "**[25]

In light of typically destroying two-thirds, the repetitive destruction of one-third in Revelation makes sense. This language reveals to us that the seven trumpets are *redemptive* in nature. The seven trumpets will be mixed with mercy. Instead of *justifiably* destroying two-thirds of everything, the Lord will restrain His wrath by only destroying one-third. Jesus is "double generous!" Of course, when God's wrath breaks out, very few people will think that Jesus is generous at all, but man's ignorance has no bearing on God's actions. If God destroyed two-thirds of everything during the seven trumpets, His actions would be justified in the eyes of watching angels because, corporately speaking, the world today is very similar to the world in Noah's day; beyond redemption.

The first trumpet judgment will be fiery hail *mixed* with blood, that is, wrath *mixed* with the interceding blood of the Lamb. This mixture also indicates redemptive mercy and it stands in contrast to God's wrath during the seven bowls where there is no mixture of mercy.[26] Mercifully, Jesus spares two-thirds of the world from fire during the first trumpet. The survivors will quickly conclude that the destruction of notably wicked places was not a random event of nature. Many evil people will turn from their ways and seek the Lord with repentance and a contrite heart.

The Six Trumpets - Prophecy 8

The Sequence Continues

{8} Jesus gave a signal and the second angel blew his trumpet. Immediately, a large asteroid came out of the sky at a terrific rate of speed and impacted an ocean. One-third of the ships were destroyed by the resulting impact, but the heaviest damage was caused by a towering wall of water that raced outward from the impact zone. It was several hundred feet high. The tsunami soon reached all of the coastal cities on the ocean's rim within which resulted in total devastation. Huge waves of water raced back and forth across the ocean and thousands of coastal cities around the ocean were totally destroyed.[27] Because of atmospheric friction, the asteroid was very hot at the time of the impact; so hot that it boiled the oxygen out of the water. {9} As a result, one-third of the creatures living in the ocean either died from the shockwave, boiling water, or the loss of oxygen. Soon after the impact, the water turned red, like blood.

> Red algae thrives in oxygen deficient water. When this toxic algae blooms, it causes water to look like blood. When sea creatures eat the blooms, a toxin in the algae kills the creatures. When birds and other creatures eat fish killed by the toxin, they also die.

> Think about the consequences of this judgment: *Thousands* of cities, formerly located around the rim of the ocean, will be washed away. International trading will cease, shipping ports will no longer exist and the economies of the world will collapse.

> The world will be in shock. First, there was a global earthquake. Then came unquenchable fire from Heaven and now, huge walls of destructive water. The 144,000 will tell the world that God's wrath is proportionate to the wickedness that plagues Earth and that more judgments are coming. The next judgment will be poisoned drinking water. Many people will curse God, others will cry out that God is hateful and cruel. "How can a God of love do such things?"

> The Bible declares that God is love.[28] This means that God's actions *are always and forever consistent* with principles of love. If we closely examine God's behavior, we will find that the God who died on the cross for our sins is the same God who destroyed the world in Noah's day and killed the firstborn in Egypt! Jesus willingly died on the cross because He "so loved the world"[29] and because He loved us before we knew Him.[30]

Rev. 8:8-9

And the second angel sounded, and as it were a great mountain burning with fire was cast into the sea: and the third part of the sea became blood; 9 And the third part of the creatures which were in the sea, and had life, died; and the third part of the ships were destroyed.

Jesus' Final Victory

Rev. 8:8-9

With a little effort, we can properly understand God's love. Love is more than an emotion of good will and kindness. Love is the balance between justice and mercy. When we say that God is love, we are saying that God is committed to principles of righteousness, fairness, and selflessness. When we say that God has wrath, we are saying that God executes justice when righteousness, fairness, and selflessness are threatened. Consider the flood in Noah's day. A "God of love" destroyed the whole world (men, women, and children) when a majority of the people became wicked, defiant, and violent.[31]

God hates to see individuals and nations self-destruct through degeneracy, rebellion, and sexual immorality.[32] God is patient and longsuffering, not willing that anyone should perish.[33] We sometimes forget that God loves oncoming generations just as much as He loves the present generation. At times, God has destroyed decadent generations so that future generations can be free of the heavy yoke of suffering that sin imposes on subsequent generations. Remember, the burden of sin grows more extreme with each generation. The sins of the fathers are passed down to the third and fourth generation![34] Over time, the consequences of decadent behavior becomes exponential. Sin is like gravity. It creates a downward vortex that pulls everyone (including the innocent) into its grip of sorrow, suffering, sickness, and death. To stop the vicious vortex, God steps in with destruction. He cauterizes the cancer of sin so that future generations can have a chance to live without the accumulated baggage (addiction, ignorance, idolatry, poverty, and cruelty) passed down from the previous generation. When a majority of people become sexually immoral, defiant, and violent, a God of love notices and responds accordingly.

God's people are sometimes destroyed along with degenerate people. His wrath against wickedness is not discriminating. For example, when God sent King Nebuchadnezzar against Jerusalem,[35] the pagan king killed many of God's people and he took some young men, like Ezekiel and Daniel, to Babylon as captives. When God destroyed the world in Noah's day, thousands of innocent children perished. God's wrath is like the indiscriminate destruction of an atomic bomb. This does not mean that everyone destroyed by God's wrath is condemned forever! The cause of death is not important to God. What matters to Him is how well we conform to His two commandments: Love God with all your heart, mind and soul and your neighbor as yourself.[36] Whether a person dies of illness, crime, accident, or during an expression of God's wrath, the cause of death has nothing to do with one's eternal destiny. In every situation, God will carefully and thoughtfully judge all people according to their actions.[37]

The 144,000 will tell the world that God's wrath is consistent with His love because in God's heart, there is a perfect balance between justice and mercy. Most of the world will respond with ridicule and hatred. The 144,000 will also tell the world that God has witnessed our corporate behavior and His actions are commensurate with our wickedness and rebellion. This will shock many people! They will retort, "Are we really all that evil in God's sight?" The 144,000 will encourage people to repent of their evil ways and to make peace with God. They will explain that Jesus demands worship because He is the Creator of life and our Redeemer. The 144,000 will declare that God is sovereign and He requires everyone to obey His commands. Unfortunately, the testimony of the 144,000 will offend many people and they will refuse God's offer of salvation.

{10} Jesus gave a third signal and the third angel blew his trumpet. A great star, having a long tail like a comet, fell from the sky and impacted a continent. This asteroid impact released an amount of energy that exceeded ten million atomic bombs! It seemed that Earth itself would break into pieces because the impact was so great. Huge tectonic plates broke loose. Ground waves and huge aftershocks radiated from the impact zone at very high rates of speed. The ground waves broke underground aquifers, sheared water-wells, septic systems, and sewage leaching fields. Toxic waste, which was thought to be safely buried deep within the Earth, spilled from containers, seeped into the aquifers, and one-third of the rivers and springs of water became poisonous. Within a week, tens of thousands of people died from drinking bitter water.

> Because the first four trumpets are surgical strikes directed at notably wicked places, I believe this asteroid will strike a continent or nation that God finds particularly offensive.

{11} People called this asteroid, "The star of death." The name of the star is "Wormwood." The word means poisonous water.[38] Millions of people, facing an agonizing death because of dehydration, drank the water and died.

Rev. 8:8-9

Rev. 8:10
And the third angel sounded, and there fell a great star from heaven, burning as it were a lamp, and it fell upon the third part of the rivers, and upon the fountains of waters;

Rev. 8:11
And the name of the star is called Wormwood: and the third part of the waters became wormwood; and many men died of the waters, because they were made bitter.

> **Rev. 8:12**
>
> And the fourth angel sounded, and the third part of the sun was smitten, and the third part of the moon, and the third part of the stars; so as the third part of them was darkened, and the day shone not for a third part of it, and the night likewise.
>
> **Rev. 8:12**
>
> And I beheld, and heard an angel flying through the midst of heaven, saying with a loud voice, Woe, woe, woe, to the inhabiters of the earth by reason of the other voices of the trumpet of the three angels, which are yet to sound!
>
> **Rev. 9:1**
>
> And the fifth angel sounded, and I saw a star fall from heaven unto the earth: and to him was given the key of the bottomless pit.

{12} Jesus gave a fourth signal and the fourth angel blew his trumpet. It seemed that every volcano surrounding the Pacific Rim erupted. This ring of fire spewed hundreds of millions of tons of ejecta and soot into the atmosphere. The amount of ash and soot was so great that sunlight could not penetrate the clouds. High speed winds (the jet stream) carried ash and soot all over the world. As a result, the middle one-third of Earth did not receive any light from the sun, moon, and stars. At first, the darkness was silent, eerie, and surreal. As the weeks went by, the survivors began to understand that crops would soon fail. Fears about what to eat became paramount as people realized that global famine had begun.

{13} As I watched these horrifying scenes, I heard the fourth living creature who had the face of the flying eagle cry out. He shouted in a loud voice: "Woe! Woe! Woe! The remaining three judgments will be worse than the first four!" I became sick to my stomach. I could not bear to watch this any longer.

> John heard the Holy Spirit announce three more woes. The last three trumpets are curses that are worse than the first four trumpets. The last three trumpets are curses directed at wicked people because Jesus steps up His efforts to get wicked people to repent of their evil ways. He wants everyone to embrace the testimony of the 144,000, honor and worship their Creator and receive eternal life!

{9:1} About twenty-seven months after the fourth trumpet, Jesus gave the signal and the fifth angel, who was located in Heaven's temple, sounded his trumpet.

> According to Daniel 12:12, the Great Tribulation will last 1,335 days. This number can be divided into three segments of 445 days. If Jesus spares mankind by keeping Lucifer in the abyss for two-thirds of the time allotted for the Great Tribulation, the devil would appear on the 891st day. Although the Bible does not indicate when the fifth trumpet will sound, we do know that one-third is used twelve times during the seven trumpets to indicate God's mercy. Because the last three trumpets are curses (woes) on defiant rebels, it is reasonable to assume that the last three trumpets might be limited to the last third of the time allotted for the Great Tribulation. If so, the length of time between trumpets four and five would be approximately twenty seven months.

To appreciate the fifth trumpet judgment, some background information is necessary. When Jesus created the angels, Lucifer was the first, highest, and brightest angel created. He was a glorious being; very happy and content before he sinned. Over time, Lucifer became jealous of Michael/Jesus and he turned away from God's love and authority. Lucifer coveted the prerogatives that belonged only to Michael/Jesus. (We will carefully examine this matter in Prophecy 12.) When it became clear that the Father would not grant Lucifer's desires, Lucifer became bitter. As Lucifer's anger and jealousy grew, he sought out sympathizers. One-third of the angels joined Lucifer and a revolt occurred in Heaven. This revolt caused God to cast Lucifer and his followers out of Heaven.[39]

After God cast Lucifer out of Heaven, Jesus created Adam and Eve. Lucifer preyed on Eve in the Garden of Eden at the Tree of Knowledge of Good and Evil and he cleverly led her into sin. Adam loved Eve and he purposely sinned because he did not want to be separated from Eve. Later, Cain, the firstborn son of Adam and Eve, killed his brother Abel because of jealousy. This sequence of events reveals a profound truth. Sinners become predators when they cannot have what they want. Lucifer preyed on innocent angels. Lucifer preyed on innocent Eve. Cain preyed on innocent Abel. In fact, the predatory nature of sin grew to be so horrible that God had to destroy the whole world in Noah's day. Sin is only controlled through death. This is why the penalty for sin is death. There is no other way to stop the predatory nature of sin. It is like a spreading cancer.

About 4,000 years after the world was created, Jesus was born and took human form. Lucifer's hatred toward Jesus had not changed. This is why Lucifer did everything within his power to destroy baby Jesus at birth.[40] Consider the sequence: Lucifer worked through King Herod in an attempt to destroy Jesus as an infant. When this failed, Lucifer worked through Jewish leaders to crucify Jesus and the devil did everything within his power to keep Jesus in the tomb. When Jesus ascended to the Father on Resurrection Sunday, Lucifer refused to yield his position to Jesus as prince of this world.[41] There was another war in Heaven, and Lucifer and his angels were cast out of Heaven forever[42] and thrown into Earth's Abyss. (Note: In Bible times, the Abyss was thought to be the realm of spirits, a fiery region located under a flat Earth, the source of fire-breathing dragons and volcanos.) Since Resurrection Sunday, the devil and his demons have not been allowed to show themselves in Heaven

Rev. 9:1

Prophecy 8 - The Six Trumpets

Rev. 9:1

or on Earth. Even though the devil and his demons have been confined to the spirit realm (the Abyss), they are free to go about their demonic mischief. Now and then, demons have been able to escape the Abyss by gaining control of a human being (demonic possession),[43] but they cannot physically appear. The devil and his angels know how to gain control over a human being. They typically use mind-altering things as tools (alcohol, drugs, music, pornography, gluttony, sexual immorality, greed, or the love of money) with great success. These and other temptations are a doorway to demonic possession.

John saw an angel fly from Heaven to Earth when the fifth trumpet sounded. The angel went to the doorway of the Abyss and he gave Lucifer the key to his prison. The devil and his demons will be ecstatic when the fifth trumpet occurs, because they can escape the confinement of the spirit realm and *physically appear* before human beings. Jesus will release the devil and his angels from the Abyss for at least two reasons. First, Jesus wants the people of Earth to actually see the enemy of God and man.[44] Second, Jesus wants the universe to experience a government created by a supernatural sinner who will exercise absolute authority and power. The enormous differences between Lucifer's government and God's government will be studied throughout eternity.

Rev. 9:2-3

And he opened the bottomless pit; and there arose a smoke out of the pit, as the smoke of a great furnace; and the sun and the air were darkened by reason of the smoke of the pit. And there came out of the smoke locusts upon the earth: and unto them was given power, as the scorpions of the earth have power.

{2} When the devil unlocked the door to the Abyss, I saw a cloud rising from the Abyss that looked like smoke from a gigantic furnace. The devil and his demons were so numerous that from a distance, they {3} looked like a giant swarm of locusts and they darkened the sky! Even though they had been physically released from the Abyss, Jesus limited their activities. For example, they could only torture people who had not received the seal of God.

The fifth trumpet will occur about two and a half years (891st day?) after the Great Tribulation begins. Prior to the fifth trumpet, the 144,000 will present the gospel of Jesus to the whole world. The gospel will polarize the people of Earth into three distinct groups of people: The saints, the religious wicked, and the non-religious wicked. Of course, the saints are people who will embrace the gospel of Christ. The religious wicked are people who will insist on remaining loyal to their religious heritage. The third group, the non-religious wicked, are people who will refuse to worship God or have any religious connection at all (atheists, agnostics, etc.).

When the devil physically appears before mankind, his eloquent masquerade and miracle working powers will easily deceive the religious wicked. Needing a Savior, but hating the gospel of Jesus, many of the religious wicked will embrace the devil as though He were Almighty God. To gain the respect of religious people, Lucifer will display all kinds of supernatural powers, doing things that only Almighty God can do! For example, he will call fire down from Heaven at will.[45] On the basis of his glorious appearance and marvelous miracles, millions of religious wicked people will be deceived. They will embrace the devil as Almighty God and put their faith in him because "seeing is believing."

Lucifer is not permitted to torture anyone having the seal of God (the 144,000 and the saints) during the fifth trumpet. Of course, he will not torture those who believe he is God (the religious wicked). The devil will target non-religious people because he wants to eliminate his opposition. Lucifer's goal is global dominion within five months and this endeavor requires that he rapidly eliminate his opponents. Jesus will limit Lucifer's assault for five months; he will not be allowed to kill anyone. However, Jesus will permit Lucifer's demons to inflict indescribable pain on the non-religious wicked and this will force them (and their families) into making a decision. Some of the non-religious wicked will embrace the gospel, worship Jesus and be saved. Most, however, will capitulate and worship the devil as Almighty God.

{4} During the fifth trumpet, the devil and his demons were not allowed to harm the physical elements of Earth such as crops, plants, or trees. Otherwise, the devil would destroy all means of survival before the Second Coming.   Further, the demons are not allowed to harm the 144,000 or anyone else who had received the seal of God. {5} Lucifer's demons were not allowed to kill anyone. They could torture people for five months, but they could not kill them. I watched as people suffered in agony from the torture. The pain can be compared to the searing pain of a scorpion's sting when it strikes a man.   {6} Their agony was unbearable. Men longed to die, but death eluded them. They remained trapped in their agony until they made a decision.

This torment in the fifth trumpet is similar to the time when God released poisonous serpents upon a rebellious Israel in the wilderness. Healing came when dying people acknowledged

Rev. 9:2-3

Rev. 9:4-6
And it was commanded them that they should not hurt the grass of the earth, neither any green thing, neither any tree; but only those men which have not the seal of God in their foreheads. And to them it was given that they should not kill them, but that they should be tormented five months: and their torment was as the torment of a scorpion, when he striketh a man.

> **Rev. 9:4-6**
> *And in those days shall men seek death, and shall not find it; and shall desire to die, and death shall flee from them.*

their need of a Savior. By faith, when they gazed on the bronze serpent which Moses had put on the pole, they were cured of the venom that was killing them.[46]

When the fifth trumpet occurs, almost everyone on Earth will have reached a decision (yes, no, or ignore) on the gospel of Jesus. To challenge the decision of the wicked, Jesus releases the devil from the abyss. The physical appearing of Lucifer will be a very strong and convincing delusion for those who said "no" to the gospel the 144,000 presented. Paul predicted "a strong delusion" would be sent to the wicked because they refused to love the truth and be saved.[47] Because the wicked love darkness and lies, Jesus will release the king of darkness and lies and they will have to worship him.

Jesus will permit the devil to torture the non-religious wicked so that this group can be pushed into a final decision. At the Second Coming, there will be only two groups of people: Sheep and goats. Therefore, the non-religious group must be dissolved. Consider how demonic torment will put a non-religious person in the valley of decision. Whenever a demon "stings" a non-religious person, the pain will be excruciating. The demon will say, "Worship "God" (Lucifer) and your pain will be gone!" One of the 144,000 will say to the victim, "Repent of your rebellion and surrender your life to Jesus. Worship your Creator and your pain will be gone because Lucifer cannot hurt those who have the seal of God!" Pain will push the non-religious group into a decision for or against the gospel of Jesus Christ.

God is deliberate and purposeful in everything He does and the seven trumpets are no exception. Jesus will inform every person on Earth through the ministry of 144,000 servants that God's two laws of love are not optional. Each person wishing to participate in His coming kingdom must love God with all his heart, mind, and soul and his neighbor as himself. When God informs a human being of His will and if that human being rejects the enlightenment, God can do nothing further for that person. For two and a half years, the 144,000 will faithfully present the gospel of Jesus (enlightenment from God). At the fifth trumpet, Lucifer and his demons will be released from the Abyss. The comparison between the ministry of the 144,000 and the efforts of the devil and his followers will be striking. Circumstances will force each human being into a decision. Each person will either choose to submit to the authority of his Creator or he will choose to submit to Lucifer. By the end of the seven trumpets, everyone will serve one of two masters.

{7} When Lucifer and his angels were released from the Abyss, they looked like a giant swarm of locusts coming down on the Earth. As they drew near, they looked like riders on horses prepared for battle. The devil appeared to be a great king, surrounded by a powerful angelic host. The look on their faces was intense, they were on a mission to take control of Earth. On their heads, the demons wore something that looked like crowns of gold. These crowns indicated they were superior to human beings, they had authority over mankind. Their faces resembled human faces and they were somewhat beautiful, but also fearful in appearance. {8} Their hair was lovely – long and flowing like women's hair but their teeth were shaped like lions' teeth. When put together, this caricature means that Lucifer's demons will be attractive, but deadly. {9} They had breastplates that resembled the breastplates of iron, and the sound of their wings was powerful, like the thundering of many horses and chariots rushing into battle.

> These descriptions are telling. The devil and his angels have intelligence and powers far superior to mankind. Bullets cannot kill demons. Suicide bombers cannot stop them. The world will be helpless and vulnerable to the superior authority of Lucifer and his angels. The saints know their only hope of survival rests in Jesus.

{10} The demons that accompanied Lucifer were given power to hurt non-religious people. The demons had tails and stings like scorpions. This caricature indicated they had the power to inflict great pain on human beings. Of course, fallen angels do not actually have long tails like scorpions, but they were represented in this way so that I could understand their ability to inflict unbearable agony on a person. For five months, Lucifer's demons went throughout the Earth subduing nations of non-religious people. Wishing to avoid further torture, most of the non-religious people acquiesced and worshiped the devil as though he was Almighty God.

> Even though the devil's demons will torture the non-religious wicked, the demons cannot hurt the 144,000 or those who have been sealed.

Rev. 9:7-9

And the shapes of the locusts were like unto horses prepared unto battle; and on their heads were as it were crowns like gold, and their faces were as the faces of men. And they had hair as the hair of women, and their teeth were as the teeth of lions. And they had breastplates, as it were breastplates of iron; and the sound of their wings was as the sound of chariots of many horses running to battle.

Rev. 9:10

And they had tails like unto scorpions, and there were stings in their tails: and their power was to hurt men five months.

> **Rev. 9:11**
> And they had a king over them, which is the angel of the bottomless pit, whose name in the Hebrew tongue is Abaddon, but in the Greek tongue hath his name Apollyon.

{11} During the five months allotted to the fifth trumpet, Lucifer gained control over the people of Earth. It was an appalling scene to watch. The angel king from the Abyss masqueraded as Almighty God and he conquered the world through deceit. In Hebrew, the devil's title is Abaddon, and in Greek, Apollyon. Both titles mean the same thing: Lucifer is the ultimate destroyer. His title is stated in Hebrew and Greek so that the saints (like the Jews in the inner court) and the wicked (like the Gentiles in the outer court) both can understand who he truly is.

The Bible declares that God does not change.[48] For six thousand years God has consistently followed a policy that limits the growth and malignancy of sin. I call this policy, "The Full Cup Principle." When God sets up a nation,[49] He gives that nation a measure of freedom and resources necessary to prosper. If the nation turns away from righteous principles, God's love for the innocent and oncoming generations is aroused. He sends messengers and warning judgments. If these efforts fail to turn the nation around, God sends destruction. Sometimes, God Himself is the destroyer; God destroyed Pharaoh and the Egyptian army in the Red Sea. Sometimes, God sends an angel as a destroyer; an angel from God killed 185,000 Assyrians.[50] Sometimes, God sends a man as a destroyer; God sent King Nebuchadnezzar to destroy Jerusalem[51] and Titus to destroy Jerusalem again in A.D. 70. When a nation fills its cup of iniquity, destruction comes.[52] This explains why the title "Destroyer" is given to Lucifer. Jesus will release Lucifer from the Abyss to be a destroyer. Jesus will permit Lucifer to do something that Lucifer wants to do! Jesus will allow Lucifer to destroy the world because the whole world has filled up its cup of iniquity and a majority of people will have refused to embrace righteousness (the gospel of Christ). Remember, the apostle Paul predicted that God will send a great delusion on the Earth during "a great rebellion" because the wicked refused to love the truth and be saved.[53] This delusion will be Lucifer, masquerading as Almighty God.

During the fifth trumpet, the devil and his angels will rush around the world to conduct their deceptive work. Three telling characteristics about Lucifer's carnal nature will unfold. First, the devil loves adulation and fame. He wants to be worshiped and exalted as God, but he is the epitome of self-centeredness and selfishness. He will use great miracle-working powers to advance his lies and evil schemes. He will appear to be gracious and benevolent because he will be on a mission to deceive people for five months, but he is evil incarnate, thoroughly cruel, and hateful. He is a demon having no compassion. Second, when Lucifer implements control over Earth (sixth trumpet), there will be no law or order except his own. The devil is petty, arbitrary, and manipulative. He can go into a fearful rage at the slightest provocation. The devil rules through manipulation, intimidation, and fear. He enjoys torturing people. He has no reservation about inflicting pain and suffering on his own followers when necessary! The devil remembers everything and forgives nothing. When it comes to committing shameful atrocities, he will make the actions of Hitler appear insignificant. Third, the devil will be a master at making right appear wrong. He will grossly distort the testimony of Jesus and the work of the 144,000. He will distort Bible truth so that righteousness appears evil. Remember, he is a highly intelligent being, a master at manipulation and deceit. No one will be able to stop him or overpower him. When a majority of people believe that he is God (by the close of the fifth trumpet), the devil will suddenly change character. He will impose himself on mankind and no one will be permitted to challenge or question his sovereign authority. It is no wonder that Paul called him, "The man of lawlessness (or man of sin, KJV)."[54]

> Rev. 9:11

{12} When the five months allotted for the fifth trumpet ended, I heard a voice from Heaven say, "The first curse has past; two greater curses are coming!" I wondered, "How can things get worse?" {13} Jesus gave the signal and the sixth angel blew his trumpet. I heard the voice of the mighty angel who stood at the golden Altar of Incense that is before God. {14} He said to the sixth angel who had the trumpet, "Release the four demons bound at the great river Euphrates."

> Rev. 9:12-14
>
> *One woe is past; and, behold, there come two woes more hereafter. And the sixth angel sounded, and I heard a voice from the four horns of the golden altar which is before God, Saying to the sixth angel which had the trumpet, Loose the four angels which are bound in the great river Euphrates.*

The fifth, sixth, and seventh trumpets are progressive in nature. They can be described as Phase 1, 2 and 3. Phase 1 (the fifth trumpet) describes the physical appearing of the devil with his demons. During this phase, Lucifer will put on a glorious show to deceive most of the world into believing that he is Almighty God. During this time, Jesus will allow Lucifer and his demons to torture non-religious people for five months. This torture will cause some people to embrace the gospel of Jesus and it will also go a long way toward eliminating all non-religious people from Earth. Remember, by the seventh trumpet, the people of Earth will either be sheep (worshiping Jesus) or goats (worshiping Lucifer).

> Rev. 9:12-14

Phase 2 (sixth trumpet) describes the establishment of Lucifer's world government; a counterfeit theocracy. The devil will be permitted to eliminate all religions, all governments and his forces will kill a third of mankind (those who oppose him). For a short time, Lucifer will reign over the world as king of kings and lord of lords.

Phase 3 (seventh trumpet) marks the end of Christ's intercession for mankind and His wrath on those who defied the two laws of love. The door to redemption closes just before the seventh trumpet sounds because everyone will have reached a firm decision regarding whom they will worship (Jesus or Lucifer). The seventh trumpet also marks the end of redemptive wrath and the beginning of destructive wrath.

The three "woes" (trumpets 5,6, and 7) are intimately connected to one another. The sixth trumpet builds upon developments that occurred during the fifth trumpet and the seventh trumpet builds on developments that occurred during the sixth trumpet.

The command to release the four angels that are bound at the great river Euphrates follows an important parallel. Remember in Revelation 7 that God's four angels (having the first four trumpets) were told to wait until the 144,000 were sealed. Similarly, Lucifer's four demons must wait until the appointed hour, day, month, and year arrives. Remember that when Jesus breaks open the fourth seal, twenty-five percent of the world's population will be killed (twenty-five percent of seven billion equals 1.75 billion people). Similarly, when the sixth trumpet sounds, Lucifer will cause one-third of the world's population to be killed (one-third of the remaining 5.25 billion also equals 1.75 billion people). The Lord and Lucifer will kill the *same* number of people. When both totals are added together, it is sobering to realize that half of the world's population (3.5 billion) will die *before* the seventh trumpet occurs!

During Bible times, the Euphrates River was the northern boundary of Israel. The river was a natural barrier that protected Israel from the marauding kings of the north. In ancient times, predator kings would pounce on weaker nations each spring and take what possessions and loot they could carry off. However, Spring thaws in the mountains caused the great river Euphrates to flood each spring and this flooding kept the kings of the north from invading Israel. Sometimes, the Euphrates would flood excessively and this caused *overwhelming* destruction within Israel. Bible writers have compared the devastation caused by floods (a type of tsunami) with the devastation caused by war[55] because the outcome looks very similar. When the sixth trumpet sounds, Jesus will remove the barrier that He imposed on Lucifer and his demons during the fifth trumpet. During the fifth trumpet, the devil and his demons are not permitted to kill anyone; however, this limitation will be removed in the sixth trumpet. The devil and his troops will be allowed to kill one-third of mankind.

The language used in the sixth trumpet uses Israel's geography to illustrate a larger, but parallel concept. In Bible times, the ancients believed that divine destruction came out of the north.[56] Because the Euphrates River was a natural barrier on Israel's *northern* boundary, the release of the four demons bound at the river indicates the river will no longer be a barrier of protection. When released, Lucifer's four demons will raise up an army of two hundred million troops to kill a third of mankind. This slaughter is associated with the Euphrates River because excessive flooding was totally destructive and in Bible times, divine judgment always came out of the north.[57] These two features align with the fact that the devil's title in Greek and Hebrew means "destroyer." Lucifer is represented as the horn power out of the north in Daniel 8 and also the King of the North in Daniel 11[58] for an important reason. Lucifer will be released from the Abyss to destroy. The torture of the non-religious during the fifth trumpet, the imposition of the mark of the beast, and the wholesale slaughter of saints and rebels during the sixth trumpet will produce a profound result. By the time the sixth trumpet is finished, all survivors will have made *a firm decision* regarding whom they *will* worship.

{15} Long ago, the Father predetermined the very hour, day, month, and year appointed for the sixth trumpet. When the sixth trumpet sounded, Lucifer abruptly changed character because the devil and his forces were allowed to kill one-third of mankind.

After five months of convincing people that he is Almighty God, Lucifer will move in to make "the kill" when the sixth trumpet sounds. Perhaps the sixth trumpet will sound on the 1,039th day of the Great Tribulation.[59] Lucifer will make outrageous demands and his forces will kill whoever stands in opposition. Remember, there is a definite limit to the number of saints that Lucifer can kill.[60] To purify the world and establish his so-called "kingdom of God," Lucifer *will demand* that everyone abandon his former religion and government and participate in his ev-

Rev. 9:12-14

Rev. 9:15

And the four angels were loosed, which were prepared for an hour, and a day, and a month, and a year, for to slay the third part of men.

> **Rev. 9:16**
>
> And the number of the army of the horsemen were two hundred thousand thousand: and I heard the number of them.

erlasting government, a new one-world-order, the devil's one-world-church-state (theocracy). This demand will create confusion and a great deal of opposition. Therefore, killing a third of mankind will be necessary.

{16} Four of Lucifer's mighty demons went throughout the world and raised an army of two hundred million troops to conduct holy *jihad* against all unbelievers.*

Remember, Lucifer will appear to be a wonderful, benevolent, and gracious God during the fifth trumpet. Billions of people will see him and marvel at his signs and wonders. He will imitate Jesus' miracles and it is reasonable to assume that millions of starving people will eat "loaves and fishes" from his hands.[61] When the sixth trumpet sounds, Lucifer will suddenly assert authority as Almighty God. He will suddenly speak as a ruthless dictator. The devil will make painful demands that people cannot escape. For example, Lucifer will declare that the time has come to establish the kingdom of God on Earth. There has to be one God, one faith, and one church on Earth – all others will be deemed false and forbidden. Think about Lucifer's clever logic. If "God" dwells among men, religious diversity is impossible. When "God" lives among mankind, every religious system must be abandoned because there is no room for divergent opinions on or about God's will or laws. Lucifer, masquerading as Almighty God, will impose himself on all mankind. He will declare his laws to be "the laws of Almighty God" and everyone will either obey them or be killed. (This will be an interesting implementation of "the sudden death law" which Lucifer originally used to mislead a third of God's angels. See Prophecy 12.)

Lucifer will abolish the governments of the world and declare that all governments other than his will be considered adversaries to "the kingdom of God." Think about this: When "God" (e.g., Lucifer masquerading as God) establishes his kingdom on Earth, he will establish a new order on Earth. The devil will create a counterfeit theocracy and consolidate the religious powers and civil powers of Earth into this theocracy. (Lucifer's theocracy is described as "the image to the beast" in Revelation 13 and

---

* **Note:** For the sake of comparison, in 2006 (the most recent year records were available), the number of active military personnel for all nations was about thirteen million.

"the great whore" in Revelation 17.) Lucifer will rule over the whole world as king of kings (the state) and lord of lords (the church). After he has abolished the religions and governments of the world, the devil will divide the world into ten sectors and appoint ten "puppet kings" to oversee the purification of these sectors. These ten kings will report directly to Lucifer. Anyone caught refusing to obey his laws will be killed immediately.[62]

Jesus will permit the devil to torment the non-religious wicked during the fifth trumpet so that He can save those few people who will repent and be saved. Jesus has the same objective during the sixth trumpet. He will allow the devil to abolish the religions and governments of the world during the sixth trumpet to save a few more people. Take a moment to consider the problem and the solution. Religion always exerts compelling power over people. Because of this fact, very few people (less than 5% of the world's population) actually transition from one religious system to another. (This transition is not Christians changing churches. The transition refers to people moving from one religious system to another, such as a Muslim becoming a Catholic or a Catholic becoming a Hindu. Can you imagine a Jew becoming a Muslim or vice versa?) Many of the *religious wicked* will reject the true gospel of Jesus because they simply cannot bring themselves to abandon their religious heritage (the religious system into which they were born). It will come as a tremendous shock when the religious wicked are forced to abandon their religious heritage during the sixth trumpet. Jesus permits Lucifer to eliminate the religious systems of the world so that *all people have to abandon their religious system prior to the Second Coming!*

When confronted with Lucifer's demand that everyone worship and join his theocracy and when forced to abandon their lifelong religious system, heritage and training, the religious wicked will have a critical decision to make. Will they grudgingly obey the laws of the devil and receive his mark to save themselves or will they embrace the two laws of love, embrace the gospel of Jesus and be saved from the curse of sin? Hopefully, more than a few of the religious wicked will come to their senses and embrace the gospel of Jesus during the sixth trumpet! Of course, there will be a great deal of opposition to Lucifer's outrageous demands, but for now, can you imagine the impact on loyal Catholics when the Catholic faith is declared illegal? Can you imagine the impact on loyal Muslims when the Muslim faith is declared illegal? Can you imagine the impact on Jews, Hindus,

Rev. 9:16

Rev. 9:16

Protestants, and Atheists when their faith is declared illegal? The devil knows that his demands will create strong opposition. The devil also knows that the only way to eliminate opposition is to kill everyone who will not obey his demands.

During the sixth trumpet, the devil will assert himself over all that is called God or that is worshiped as God.[63] I believe the devil will declare that the kingdom of God is among men and Lucifer will impose, for logistical purposes, the ancient practice of dividing and organizing large numbers of people into groups of a thousand.[64] By the time the sixth trumpet occurs, life on Earth will be primitive. Electricity, communication, banking, transportation, and healthcare will be largely non-existent. After the first four trumpets, the world will be in survival mode (extreme problems demand extreme solutions), and taking advantage of this desperate situation, the devil and his demons will quickly reorganize the whole world. He will use the justification that food rations and the necessities of life are best distributed when there is a high level of organization and control.

Working through his ten kings, the devil will follow Moses' example and appoint one captain over each group of 1,000 people.[65] This will leave 999 people in each group. When the devil announces the demise of all religions and governments, people and nations will rebel against Lucifer's authority, but he will be prepared. The devil will issue a death decree that will put everyone in shock.[66] The devil will demand that the "kingdom of God" must be purified. Therefore, one-third of each group of 1,000 people must be put to death.[67] The ten kings will praise the devil for generously sparing two-thirds of mankind![68]

I believe Lucifer's sixth trumpet death decree will include this announcement: The *first* 666 people in each group who are willing to receive a tattoo on the right hand showing the number, 666, will live. The remaining one-third, 333 people, must be killed, even if they are willing to wear the mark! This announcement will cause the wicked to move quickly to receive the mark of the beast. The devil will claim his decree is justified because there will be insufficient rations for everyone. Therefore, it is better to feed two-thirds of the people than have everyone die from starvation. By limiting survival to the *first* 666 people willing to receive the tattoo, the devil will eliminate the weak, the old, the sick, and all of the rebellious (including the saints and anyone else opposed to his authority). I am sure the devil will promise that the world will be a better place once all of the rebels are killed.

When 666 people in each group receive the mark of the beast, Lucifer's demons will motivate many people within each group of 666 to hunt down the remaining 333 people who remain in opposition. Lucifer will be able to create a great army of two hundred million troops and only those people who wear the number 666 on their right hand will be spared from death. Everyone wearing the number 666 on their right hand will be permitted to buy and sell (to survive), but the rest of mankind (1.75 billion people) will be hunted and slaughtered like animals.

The sixth trumpet war will not be a war of one country against another. This war will occur *within* each group of 1,000 people. Since 333 people within each group must be destroyed, the race to be among the first 666 will mean the difference between life and death. The wicked will be caught in a struggle against each other. The devil will be delighted because he knows that wicked people are selfish and they will do whatever it takes to survive. The saints, on the other hand, will be caught in a very different struggle. Their struggle will be to maintain patient endurance and faithfulness[69] to the very end. The wicked will be focused on the "here and now," but the saints will be focused on the hereafter; endless joy and eternal life with Jesus. The devil is cruel and heartless and his character will be clearly revealed during the sixth trumpet. He would kill 100% of the world's population in an instant (even his own followers) if Jesus permitted it. However, Jesus limits the powers of the devil and his angels to 33% of the world's population because there are several object lessons in the concluding drama of sin which the universe will observe and study throughout eternity.

When Lucifer issues his first death decree (there will be two death decrees, one during the sixth trumpet and one directed at the saints on the 1,290th day), he will boast that this holy war (*jihad*) will be the war that ends all wars. Of course, he will be lying because this war will neither be "holy" nor will it end all wars, for Armageddon still remains to be fought. Those who join with Lucifer in killing a third of mankind will think they are doing "God" a service.[70] Murderers will be promised high positions in Lucifer's government and the carnage that follows this death decree will be like the carnage that occurred in 1994 when Hutu militia in Rwanda slaughtered 800,000 Tutsies during a period of one hundred days. There was no compassion or

Rev. 9:16

justice – only the madness and insanity of demonic possession. Similarly, during the sixth trumpet, individuals possessed by demons will slaughter 333 people in their own group! However, Jesus will not allow the devil or his angels to directly murder a single human being. Instead, demon possessed people (like King Herod and Hitler) will carry out these atrocities. This scenario will prove that given enough time and power, all sinners will eventually mirror Lucifer's behavior.

> **Rev. 9:17-19**
> And thus I saw the horses in the vision, and them that sat on them, having breastplates of fire, and of jacinth, and brimstone: and the heads of the horses were as the heads of lions; and out of their mouths issued fire and smoke and brimstone. By these three was the third part of men killed, by the fire, and by the smoke, and by the brimstone, which issued out of their mouths. For their power is in their mouth, and in their tails: for their tails were like unto serpents, and had heads, and with them they do hurt.

{17} The horses and riders in the sixth trumpet were different from the creatures that I saw in the fifth trumpet. The locusts described in the fifth trumpet consisted of demons released from the Abyss, but the army in the sixth trumpet is made up of human beings armed with weapons of war. This army wore colored breastplates which indicated their particular division. The colors were fiery red, dark blue, and yellow like sulfur.[71] The heads of their horses (war machines) resembled the heads of lions, and out of their mouths came fire, smoke, and sulfur. {18} A third of mankind was killed by the plagues of fire, smoke, and sulfur that came out of their war machines. {19} The riders could shoot from the front or from the tails of their war horses. This was the bloodiest war ever fought on Earth. The cruelty that people inflicted on each other was unbelievable.

John's report is not a description of modern weapons, it is a caricature of modern devices that will be used to kill a third of mankind. The wicked will use explosives to shoot each other (fire and smoke) and poisonous gas (clouds of sulfur) to kill millions of people. Lucifer will exalt these murderers. Everyone found not having the tattoo on his right hand is to be killed. This is the tragic end of a story that began 6,000 years ago, a story of one brother killing his brother over the issue of worship. This civil war will last several months.[72] During this war, Jesus will send 144,000 prophets to the front lines. They will boldly deliver the fourth angel's message without dilution.[73] The 144,000 will proclaim the gospel of Jesus Christ. This will infuriate the wicked and they will kill most, if not all, of the 144,000.[74] Jesus said His gospel will go to every nation, kindred, tongue, and people *and then* the end would come.[75] During the sixth trumpet, Lucifer intends to kill his opposition and be worshiped and revered as Almighty God. To achieve this goal, he will subjugate the wicked to his evil desires. When Lucifer's objective is reached, Jesus will close the door to redemption because by this time, everyone will have finalized their choice and the seven bowls will begin.

{20} I was amazed at the behavior of those who received the mark of the beast. Lucifer's actions were disgusting and vile, but his followers would not repent of the work of their hands; they would not stop worshiping demons and idols of gold, silver, bronze, stone, and wood that could not see, hear, or walk. {21} The devil's followers would not repent of their murders, magic arts, sexual immorality, or thievery. They were a defiant and incorrigible body of people. They hated the 144,000, the saints, and the gospel of Christ!

> The curse of sin is a dominating power that few people understand. It causes rational people to do stupid and irrational things. The curse of sin can be defined as "passion overpowering wisdom." This explains why God will not allow sin to ever flourish again. During the sixth trumpet, all of the wicked will pass the point of return and commit the unpardonable sin.[76] Every wicked person will become demon possessed. Passion will overpower wisdom and the wicked will behave much like the pigs that rushed into the water and drowned.[77] When a person commits the unpardonable sin, he cannot change himself or be transformed into a better person because he has shut the door on the Holy Spirit. So, the wicked must be destroyed to remove the vestiges of sin.
>
> In review, the first two woes will accomplish two great objectives: First, the non-religious wicked group will disappear and the religious wicked group will be purged when all people will have to abandon their religious heritage. Second, the gospel will be preached to every person on Earth. The people of Earth will be squeezed by circumstances to make a choice. At the end of the sixth trumpet, each person will have either the seal of God (and his carnal nature removed) or he will have committed the unpardonable sin and received the mark of the beast.

The Rules of Interpretation

Consider how the Rules of Interpretation are observed in this prophecy:

Rule One says an apocalyptic prophecy has a beginning point and ending point in time and the events within the prophecy occur in the order given. This prophecy conforms to Rule One because chronological order is self evident:

Rev. 9:20-21

And the rest of the men which were not killed by these plagues yet repented not of the works of their hands, that they should not worship devils, and idols of gold, and silver, and brass, and stone, and of wood: which neither can see, nor hear, nor walk: Neither repented they of their murders, nor of their sorceries, nor of their fornication, nor of their thefts.

1. The seven angels stand before God and are given seven trumpets
2. The angel ministering at the golden Altar of Incense presents a petition to the Lord that comes from all of the saints
3. The Lord answers the petition of His saints and the censer is cast down, terminating the services at the Altar of Incense
4. The angels prepare to sound their trumpets
5. The trumpets sound in chronological order

For reasons presented in Appendix A, I believe this prophecy began in 1994. For reasons that will be discussed in the next prophecy, this prophecy ends on the 1,265th day of the Great Tribulation.

Rule Two says a fulfillment only occurs when all of the specifications are met, and this includes the order stated in the prophecy. At this time, one element in this prophecy has been fulfilled. The seven angels have received the seven trumpets. According to the previous prophecy (Prophecy 7), these angels are waiting for the selection and sealing of the 144,000. Once the 144,000 have been sealed, Jesus will announce that there will be no more delay and God's wrath will begin.

Rule Three says that apocalyptic language can be literal, analogous, or symbolic. To reach the intended meaning of a prophecy, the reader must consider (a) the context, (b) the use of parallel language in the Bible, and (c) if an element is thought to be symbolic, the Bible must interpret the symbol with a *relevant* text. The language used in this prophecy is not symbolic because there are no relevant texts defining a symbol. On the other hand, we do find an extensive use of analogous and literal language. The language used in the first four trumpets should be taken literally, although some analogous language is mixed in. For example, the Bible says, **"there came hail and fire mixed with blood, and it was hurled down upon the earth."**[78] If the first trumpet is a meteoric firestorm of burning hail that burns up a third of the Earth and all of the green grass, then the phrase "fire mixed with blood" must be explained. The first trumpet judgment is an expression of God's wrath. He will burn up a third of the Earth in the same way that He burned up Sodom and Gomorrah; by raining down a hailstorm of burning meteors. There is a mixture of blood mentioned in this judgment which means there is a mixture of mercy. (This mixture stands in contrast to the seven bowls which have no mixture of mercy. Revelation 14:10) Instead of destroying two-thirds of the world, Jesus destroys one-third. The parallels between wrath and mercy, fire and blood are obvious. God began offering mercy to mankind through the promise of Christ's atoning blood the day that sin came to Earth.

I maintain that trumpets five and six also use literal and analogous language. Remember, if an element is thought to be symbolic, the Bible must interpret the symbol with a relevant text that specifically addresses the symbol. The difficulty with these two trumpet judgments is that there are biblical concepts involved which are difficult to describe within the limitations of language. The devil and his demons are literal beings, yet they currently live in a realm that human beings cannot smell, taste, hear, touch, or see. Our physical senses cannot detect Lucifer and his followers. So, God used some ideas that were common in John's day to illustrate concepts that human beings cannot explain. For example, the Bible says, **"They** [the locusts described in verse 7] **had as king over them the angel of the Abyss, whose name in Hebrew is Abaddon, and in Greek, Apollyon."**[79] Who is the angel of the Abyss? Who is king over a great cloud of locusts that have faces that resemble human faces, wear gold crowns on their heads, have long hair and lion's teeth? The Bible uses literal language to describe spiritual details and this misleads people into thinking the book of Revelation is full of mysterious symbols. Instead, God describes spiritual things with literal language so that we can properly grasp concepts that go beyond human reality. God has stayed within the limits of language to explain what a visible Lucifer and visible demons will do once they are permitted to physically appear on Earth! If Rule Three is carefully observed, the Bible will make sense, "just as it reads."

Rule Four says the presence or absence of the Jubilee Calendar determines how God measures time. The fifth trumpet has a time period of five months. The Jubilee Calendar expired in 1994 and time is not translated a day for a year after 1994. This allows two interesting issues to unfold. First, if we assume that Jesus keeps the devil and his angels in the Abyss for two-thirds of the 1,335 days allotted for the Great Tribulation, the fifth trumpet should occur around the 891[sh] day of the Great Tribulation. The five months allotted for the fifth trumpet (remember, a month in God's calendar is one new moon to another new moon – or 29.53 days) would end around the 1,039th day of the Great Tribulation. (890 days + 148 days = 1,038 days) If this calculation is correct, then the sixth trumpet will occur approximately two years and ten months after the Great Tribulation begins. Perhaps "Day 1039" will be the "very hour, day, month and year" predicted. **"And the four angels who had been kept ready for this very hour and day and month and year were released to kill a third of mankind."**[80]

The second interesting issue that unfolds from God's use of literal time is that the sixth trumpet appears to span 226 days. This number is determined as follows:

    1,265 days (the seventh trumpet sounds)
   - 1,039 days (the end of the fifth trumpet)
  equals 226 days or about seven and a half months.

These calculations enable us to put some perspective on the time allowed for Lucifer's physical presence on Earth. Given the limitations of travel and communication that will exist during the time of the fifth trumpet, and given the fact that there are approximately 220 nations on Earth, five months (148 days) is a very short period of time for Lucifer to deceive the whole world. Then, if we allow 226 days for the sixth trumpet, Lucifer has to work fast to accomplish the following:

1. The abolition of the world's religions and governments
2. The slaughter of a third of mankind and establishment of a worldwide government
3. The enforcement of the mark of the beast
4. Secure his position as king of kings and lord of lords

Clearly, the last 445 days of the Great Tribulation will be awful. This span of time covers the last three woes.

Rule Four is very helpful in this prophecy because it produces perfect harmony from the sum of its parts. The Great Tribulation is 1,335 days in length, so everything described above *easily* fits together with respect to timing and accomplishment!

References

1. Matthew 24:37
2. Leviticus 25:9; Joel 2:1
3. Revelation 6:8 and Revelation 9:15 Note: Suppose world population is 7 billion and 25% die when the fourth seal is broken. This means that 1.75 billion people will perish. 7 billion people minus 1.75 people leave 5.25 billion people remaining. Then, one-third of the world's population is killed during the sixth trumpet. One-third of 5.25 billion people is 1.75 billion people. Therefore, 1.75 billion deaths plus 1.75 billion deaths equals 3.5 billion people or 50% of the world's population.
4. Revelation 11:7-19
5. Revelation 6:7,8
6. See http://www.wake-up.org/links/soferim.htm. Even the priests served in a rotation of 24 groups. See also Luke 1:8,9.
7. Exodus 29:38-43
8. The Bible indicates the blood for corporate sins was applied to the horns of the Altar of Incense, whereas blood shed for individual sins was applied to the horns of the Altar of Burnt Offering. Compare Leviticus 4:7,18 with Leviticus 4:25,30. Furthermore, on the Day of Atonement, the horns on the Altar of Incense required cleansing just like the horns on the Altar of Burnt Offering. (Leviticus 16:18,19) Therefore, the Altar of Incense was contaminated by corporate sin in the same way that the Altar of Burnt Offering was contaminated by the sins of individuals.
9. Hebrews 8:1-5
10. Genesis 2:17
11. Genesis 3:21
12. Romans 12:1,2
13. Revelation 6:7,8
14. 1 Thessalonians 5:3
15. Revelation 10:6
16. Revelation 1:6; 5:10; Hebrews 5:1

17. See Hebrews 12:27 and compare physical signs and wonders in Revelation 8:5 with Revelation 11:19 and 16:18-20.
18. Daniel 12:11,12
19. Daniel 8:19
20. Numbers 16:46-50; 2 Samuel 24:15,16; 2 Kings 19:35; 2 Chronicles 28:6; 1 Corinthians 10:8
21. 1 John 4:18
22. Matthew 28:20
23. 2 Samuel 8:2, insertion mine
24. Ezekiel 5:11,12, italics mine
25. Zechariah 13:8
26. Revelation 14:10; 15:1
27. Luke 21:25,26
28. 1 John 4:8
29. John 3:16
30. Romans 5:8
31. Genesis 6:5-7
32. Genesis 13:13
33. 2 Peter 3:9
34. Exodus 20:5
35. Jeremiah 25:8,9
36. Matthew 22:37-39
37. Ecclesiastes 12:13,14; 2 Corinthians 5:10
38. Jeremiah 9:15 (KJV)
39. Isaiah 14:12-16; Ezekiel 28:12-19
40. Matthew 2:13-20; Revelation 12:4,5
41. John 12:31,32
42. Revelation 12:7-9 Note: Prior to Resurrection Sunday, Lucifer and his angels had limited access to Heaven. (Job 1:6,7) Evidently, God recognized Lucifer as the prince of this world after Adam and Eve fell. (John 12:31) As the prince of Earth, Lucifer had a seat in God's government. When Jesus paid the price for sin with His own blood,

Jesus redeemed the world (that is, He bought the world back). Jesus was appointed the prince of this world on Resurrection Sunday, but Lucifer would not relinquish his position and this explains the war described in Revelation 12:7-9.

43. Mark 5:7-15
44. Isaiah 14:16,17; Revelation 17:8
45. Revelation 13:13,14
46. 2 Thessalonians 2:9-12; John 8:44
47. Numbers 21:4-9
48. Malachi 3:6
49. Daniel 2:21
50. 2 Kings 19:35
51. Jeremiah 25:8,9
52. Compare Leviticus 18:26-30 with Leviticus 26:14-39.
53. 2 Thessalonians 2:9-12
54. 2 Thessalonians 2:1-12
55. Daniel 9:26; Hosea 5:10; Revelation 12:15; Jeremiah 47:1-4
56. Jeremiah 6:22,23; 25:9; 31:8; 51:48; Ezekiel 9:2
57. Jeremiah 1:14; Ezekiel 26:7; Job 37:22
58. Daniel 8:9,23; 11:36 Note: The horn that comes out of the north in Daniel 8 is called a stern-faced king implying the stern-faced king comes out of the north.
59. This date is based on the assumption that the fifth trumpet will begin on a new moon, the 891st day of the Great Tribulation. Five lunar months will expire (148 days) and then, the sixth trumpet will sound (the 1,039th day of the Great Tribulation).
60. Revelation 6:11
61. See Mark 6:36-44 for a parallel.
62. Revelation 13:15
63. 2 Thessalonians 2:4
64. Exodus 18:19-26; Numbers 31:14; Deuteronomy 1:15; 1 Samuel 8:10-20
65. Exodus 18:23-25

66. Revelation 13:15
67. Consider these references, including these where God and King David spared one-third and killed two-thirds: Revelation 9:15; 13:15; Zechariah 13:8; Ezekiel 5:11-13; 2 Samuel 8:2
68. Revelation 17:15-17
69. Revelation 13:10 (NIV)
70. John 16:1-3
71. Ezekiel 23:6,14
72. The sixth trumpet appears to be 226 days in length. The seventh trumpet occurs on the 1,265th day of the Great Tribulation, so 1,265 days minus 1,039 days equals 226 days.
73. Revelation 18:1-7
74. Revelation 6:11; 16:4-7; 18:24
75. Matthew 24:14
76. Matthew 12:31-32
77. Matthew 8:28-34
78. Revelation 8:7
79. Revelation 9:11, insertion mine
80. Revelation 9:15

Prophecy 9

The Two Witnesses

Revelation 10:1-11:19

Beginning point in time: A few days before the censer in Revelation 8:5 is cast down

Ending point in time: The 1,265th day of the Great Tribulation

Summary: God will empower His Two Witnesses for 1,260 days at the end of Earth's history. Their work is vital during the Great Tribulation because the people who will be alive then (the living) cannot be judged without the input of His Two Witnesses. God told Moses that no one could be put to death on the testimony of one witness because condemnation had to be validated by two or more witnesses.[1] God uses two witnesses in the book of Revelation to indicate the living will be judged and two infallible witnesses will exonerate or condemn each person. According to Matthew 24:14, the gospel of Jesus will be proclaimed throughout the world as a *testimony* to all nations before the end will come. The 144,000 will deliver the gospel and Jesus will pass judgment on each person according to the testimony of His Two Witnesses. Shortly after His pre-Advent judgment is completed, Jesus will return to Earth to deal with humanity.

Introduction: If the previous prophecy on the seven trumpets reveals the severity of God's redemptive wrath, this prophecy reveals the amazing reach of God's redemptive grace. The Bible declares that God is love.[2] This means that God's actions are eternally consistent with principles of love. In other words, if you want to see what love does in any given situation, study God's actions. Because God has infinite wisdom, He knows how and when to impose justice and when to extend mercy.

Although it is not obvious at first, this prophecy aligns with the selection and empowerment of the 144,000 and it ends with a powerful display of physical phenomena at the seventh trumpet. The Two Witnesses and the 144,000 are inseparably linked because the Two Witnesses will validate the testimony of God's prophets. As

Jesus' Final Victory

you examine this prophecy, keep this crucial fact in mind: The Bible teaches that validation requires two or more witnesses. Jesus said to the Pharisees, **"If I testify about myself** [claiming that I am the promised Messiah]**, my testimony is not valid. There is another who testifies in my favor** [you have heard John the Baptist testify about me]**, and I know that his testimony about me is valid. You have sent** [a delegation of priests] **to** [question and investigate] **John and he has testified to the truth. . . . And the Father who sent me has himself** [also] **testified concerning me.** [But the testimony of the Father means nothing to you because] **You have never heard his voice nor seen his form, nor does his word dwell in you, for you do not believe the one he sent."**[3]

Jesus came to Earth to reveal the truth about God. Jesus spoke the words which the Father gave Him and His testimony was true, but His words created a firestorm of conflict because light is incompatible with darkness. We know that anyone can claim to speak for God. Anyone can claim to be born again. People often make outrageous claims, but self-made claims of legitimacy are not valid. Two or more witnesses are required for validation. This is why Jesus offered the testimony of John the Baptist and His Father's voice as two witnesses that validated His Messianic identity. The issue of legitimacy explains why the 144,000 will need two witnesses to validate their testimony!

The Bible declares that God loves everyone on Earth the same.[4] Therefore, it is reasonable to conclude that the 144,000 will be dispersed among the inhabitants of Earth on the basis of population. This assertion is made on the basis that God will ensure everyone on Earth *will have an equal opportunity to hear and consider* the eternal gospel concerning Jesus Christ before the Second Coming. Jesus said, **"And this gospel of the kingdom will be preached in the whole world as a testimony to all nations, and then the end will come."**[5] The 144,000 will present a gospel that stands in conflict with almost everything people believe to be true. God knows this will be the case, so He will not ask anyone to believe His servants on the basis of their testimony or miracles. Instead, God's Two Witnesses will validate the gospel of Jesus and each person will determine his eternal destiny by his response to God's two witnesses!

If the 144,000 are distributed by population, then the United States will have approximately 6,200 of the 144,000 prophets. China and India will each have about 24,000 prophets and Mexico City's ten million people will have about 200 prophets. When the censer is cast down and the first four trumpets sound, life as we know it will dramatically change. Television, radio, telephone, banking, travel, and other infrastructures that we now depend on will become very limited or nonexistent. This means the 144,000 will work alone as did Elijah, who thought for a while that he was the only person left in Israel who had refused to worship Baal.[6] As time passes though, honest-hearted people will listen to the 144,000 and these people will embrace the gospel because God's Two Witnesses will confirm and convict them that this gospel is true. These converts will join with the 144,000 during the Great Tribulation and encourage others to receive Christ and be saved. However, compared to the opposition, the number of people aligned with God's prophets will be a small minority. This is always the case. Remember how Elijah faced down 450 prophets of Baal on Mt. Carmel.[7]

When we contrast the singularity of God's prophets with the many clergy employed by the religious systems of the world (which are opposed to the gospel of Jesus), and add the number of people who have no interest in God or His gospel, a serious problem emerges for the 144,000. Who or what will validate their testimony? *What will prove to the diverse people of the world that one lone voice speaks for Almighty God?* This is the same situation that Jesus faced when He came to Earth to reveal the Father to the nation of Israel. Jesus fed multitudes, healed the sick, cast out demons, restored eyesight to the blind, and raised at least two dead people. These miracles did not affect the leaders or the majority of Israel at all. This brings us to a very important point: Miracles do not change hearts. *Miracles affirm what the heart wants to believe.* This explains why Lucifer's counterfeit miracles[8] will be such a powerful delusion. He will call fire down out of the sky at will simply to affirm a false gospel which the wicked want to believe. Jesus knew that any self-made claims about His identity would be worthless and the same conclusion will be true for the 144,000.

Once we grasp the idea that the 144,000 will be geographically distributed all over the world, we can see why each prophet of God will require two witnesses. Something has to validate their testimony. Even more, God's Two Witnesses will observe each person's response to the gospel and report back to Jesus. Their testimony will enable Jesus to pass judgment on the living.

From Observer to Participant

John's role changes in this prophecy. Earlier in the book of Revelation, John writes from the perspective of an observer, but in this prophecy, he becomes a participant. John is transformed into a participant so he can describe the experience of the 144,000 to us. I think God made John a participant because false prophets are found everywhere. People all over the world prophesy out of their own imagination every day. They claim that God has shown them certain things when in reality, God has shown them nothing. People who do this are offensive in God's sight and He will punish them at the appointed time.[9] God made John a participant in this prophecy so that ordinary people will have the ability to determine who is a member of the 144,000. Each person who is one of the 144,000 will have a personal encounter with Jesus similar to John's experience. Each person will be given words to speak (represented by the little book given to John) and like John, they will be commissioned to prophesy and measure the inner court in the temple. As an example for the final generation, God put John through the same experience that each last day prophet will have to endure. If a person claims to speak for God during the Great Tribulation and he or she has not had the experience recorded by John in this prophecy, and if his or her testimony is not validated by God's Two Witnesses, then he or she is a false prophet.

Many people, who do not realize what they are saying, express their desire to be one of the 144,000. If Jesus should call you to be among that group, then you must accept His calling. You can be sure He will enable and sustain those He calls. On the other hand, no human should desire the experience the 144,000 will face. There will be 1,260 days of strenuous effort, torture, rejection, imprisonment, and death. The 144,000 will suffer as Jesus suffered and there will be no relief from their burden until death. God gave John a participant's experience so that we can understand the sacrifice, the distress, and the victory of God's servants. Ordinary people will not know when the 144,000 are called and sealed. Unless one of the 144,000 happens to be a close friend who shares his experience of meeting the Lord and eating the little book, I do not think we will know who the 144,000 are until the censer is cast down on Day One of the Great Tribulation.

Personification

Personification is described as giving "life" to something that is inanimate. For example, after months of wrangling, in 2010, the House and Senate of the United States passed a health care bill that dramatically changed the health care system. Prior to the final vote, some protesters carried signs on Capitol Hill that read, "Kill the Bill." Of course, no one can "kill" a piece of paper, but people treat House Bills as living things because once a bill is signed into law, it takes on a life of its own. Therefore, killing a bill (voting down some concepts written on a piece of paper) before it is signed into law is the only way to stop a bill from coming to "life."

God also uses personification in the Bible. For example, God personified the behavior of a divided Israel (ten tribes and two tribes) as two adulterous sisters in Ezekiel 23. Personification is effective because it says so much with so few words. By personifying Himself as Israel's faithful husband and Israel and Judah as two adulterous sisters, God wanted His people to understand His breaking heart. What better way could He reveal His sorrow than to portray His people as two adulterous women? This background information about the use of personification has been presented because in this prophecy, God personifies the work of His Two Witnesses. This literary technique has misled many people to reach conclusions that are not valid, but we will see in this prophecy that God also speaks of His Two Witnesses as two lampstands and two olive trees as well as two prophets.

Consider this: When Moses raised his staff and stretched out his hand over the Red Sea, the Red Sea parted, but we know that Moses did not make the Red Sea part.[10] We know that an ordinary man does not have this kind of power. When Peter commanded the lame beggar to walk, Peter did not make the beggar walk, even though the beggar jumped up and began running around! Peter addressed the astonished crowd who had gathered saying, "... **Men of Israel, why does this surprise you? Why do you stare at us as if by our own power or godliness we had made this man walk?**"[11] God's power rested on Peter and it was God's power that healed the man; not Peter's power.

Metaphorically, Moses and Peter were "the arms and legs" through which the Holy Spirit's power was manifested. Keep in mind that even though Holy Spirit power rested upon them, Moses did not enter the Promised Land and Peter was martyred for his faith. In other words, Holy Spirit power did not keep Moses from sinning or Peter from death. Moses and Peter were ordinary mortals like you and me, but when God's power came upon them – His "power" enabled them to do signs and wonders.

We learned in Prophecy 6 that the Holy Spirit is an unseen member of the Godhead that works through people when directed by Jesus or the Father to do so. The Holy Spirit will not be one of the 144,000, but instead, the Holy Spirit will work through the 144,000 in the same way that He worked *through* Moses and Peter. We will discover in this study that one of the Two Witnesses is the Holy Spirit and the other witness is two great laws of love that govern the whole universe. God's Two Witnesses are personified in this prophecy because they are invisible. Keeping the Two Witnesses separate and distinct from the 144,000 makes their work and mission easier to understand. The 144,000 will proclaim the gospel of Jesus and they will *appear* to perform many signs and wonders, but the signs and wonders will actually come through Holy Spirit power and their words will come from the little book that Jesus will give them. And like Moses and Peter, Revelation 16:4-7 and other texts indicate that most, if not all of God's last day prophets, will die in the line of duty.

One more point must be refreshed before we begin with this prophecy. The 144,000 will receive the seal of the living God *prior* to the beginning of their ministry for three reasons: First, there will be no hint of sin (dishonesty, greed, or immorality) in God's servants. Given the amazing powers that will rest upon them, the removal of the sinful nature will prove to be very important. God's holy name will not be profaned by some foolish choice of words or impetuous act. Second, the 144,000 will be living examples of what human beings can become when the sinful nature is removed. When a repentant sinner finally understands the incredible power that sin has over him, he wants to be set free of this curse. Therefore, Jesus will start the Great Tribulation with 144,000 living examples of what it really means to have freedom from sin's curse! This demonstration will be very encouraging to those who love truth because the gospel of Jesus includes the promise that anyone can be sealed – if only he will surrender to the demands of the gospel and live by faith! Finally, the 144,000 could not accomplish the task before them if they had sinful natures. The ridicule, rejection, persecution, and torment which they will endure would be too great for man's fallen nature. Remember how Moses met with God on several occasions and that Moses performed many signs and wonders, but God did not permit Moses to enter the Promised Land because his carnal nature rose up on one rebellious occasion and indignation caused him to sin.[12]

The Sequence

{1} I was standing on Earth when I saw a mighty angel[13] descend from Heaven. He came alone. This was not the Second Coming. Jesus was robed with a dark cloud and no one on Earth could see Him but me.[14] He had a rainbow above His head[15] and the brilliance of His face was like the Sun. His legs glowed like fiery pillars of molten metal. {2} He held a little book in His hand that was open. As I watched, Jesus planted His right foot on the sea and His left foot on the land. His posture and position indicated sovereign authority over land and sea. There was a bold confidence about Him, like that of a military general. It appeared that Jesus had come to Earth to conduct specific business. {3} He gave a loud command, like the roar of a lion and seven thunderous voices spoke. {4} I clearly heard and understood the seven thunders and I was about to write down their testimony, but a voice from Heaven said, "John, do not write down the words that you have heard."

> It may seem strange that John was forbidden to write down the testimony that he heard, but there is a simple reason for this. John, as one of the 144,000, heard Jesus speak seven times. During the Great Tribulation those who have been sealed along with the 144,000 will hear and understand Jesus' words as they roll like thunder throughout the Earth. Jesus will speak seven times and those who understand His words will know for themselves that they have been sealed! The saints will be greatly encouraged by each thunder to patiently endure. To the rest of the world, these seven events will be frightening, sounding like a deep rumbling in the Earth or peals of rolling thunder,[16] but they will not hear Jesus' voice.

{5} Then Jesus raised His right hand toward Heaven. {6} With a loud voice He swore an oath in His own name,[17] as the Creator of Heaven and everything that is in it, the Earth and all that is in it, and the sea and all that is in it,[18] He said, "There will be no more

---

Rev. 10:1-4

And I saw another mighty angel come down from heaven, clothed with a cloud: and a rainbow was upon his head, and his face was as it were the sun, and his feet as pillars of fire: And he had in his hand a little book open: and he set his right foot upon the sea, and his left foot on the earth, And cried with a loud voice, as when a lion roareth: and when he had cried, seven thunders uttered their voices. And when the seven thunders had uttered their voices, I was about to write: and I heard a voice from heaven saying unto me, Seal up those things which the seven thunders uttered, and write them not.

Rev. 10:5

And the angel which I saw stand upon the sea and upon the earth lifted up his hand to heaven,

Rev. 10:6-7

And sware by him that liveth for ever and ever, who created heaven, and the things that therein are, and the earth, and the things that therein are, and the sea, and the things which are therein, that there should be time no longer: But in the days of the voice of the seventh angel, when he shall begin to sound, the mystery of God should be finished, as he hath declared to his servants the prophets.

delay![19] {7} But in the days when the seventh angel is about to sound his trumpet, the mystery of God will be completed, just as he announced to His servants the prophets, the 144,000."

This scene will occur shortly before the censer in Revelation 8:5 is cast down. When this event occurs, Jesus will declare the end of God's patience with mankind. Then, the fourth seal will be broken and the censer at the Altar of Incense will be cast down. The four angels who have been waiting (since 1994) will be released to hurt the Earth. God's redemptive wrath will begin.[20] Wicked places all over the world will be punished for degenerate and decadent behavior.[21] The 144,000 will begin proclaiming the eternal gospel on Day One of the Great Tribulation and all who repent of their sins and embrace Jesus as their Creator and Savior will be tested, sealed, and saved.[22]

The "mystery of God" that will be completed just before the seventh trumpet sounds is the sealing (removal of the carnal nature). Prior to the Great Tribulation, all born-again believers received the Holy Spirit as "a deposit, guaranteeing what is to come."[23] In other words, the righteousness of Christ has been imputed to God's children ever since sin began. During the Great Tribulation, the righteousness of Christ will be imparted to God's children. "The seal of the living God" described in Revelation 7:2,3 is the outpouring of the fullness of the Holy Spirit given to everyone who faithfully worships Jesus, the Creator.

This seal of God will be given *first* to the 144,000. The seal of God will not be a visible stamp. This seal is like a lock that keeps the sinless nature in and the carnal nature out. Remember how the tomb of Jesus was securely sealed so that His disciples could not steal His body.[24] The seal of God is similar. When the curse of sin is removed from each saint, the door will be sealed. The seal of God can be compared to a king putting a wax seal on an important scroll. Once the scroll is written and sealed, the document cannot be changed. Similarly, during the Great Tribulation, God will test each living person to see who loves Him with all their heart, mind and soul, and his neighbor as himself. After the sinner is tested and found faithful, God will perform a miracle. He will remove the carnal nature from that sinner and put a seal on his forehead. This action indicates that sin will have no further influence on that person.

The sealing described in Revelation is the final step in sanctification. When Jesus removes the carnal nature and applies the seal of God to a sinner, this indicates a *complete transformation*[25] has occurred. The 144,000 will be the first to experience this final step. Consider how this process works: Step one begins when a sinner surrenders his will to Jesus (to go-be-do as the Holy Spirit directs) and receives Christ as his Savior. Jesus immediately covers the sinner with His righteousness (this process is called "justification through faith"). Step two quickly follows. God requires that we turn from wickedness and walk in righteousness with Him! If a sinner is willing to undergo the sanctifying process, fights the good fight of faith and is an overcomer, Jesus keeps the sinner covered with His righteousness so that in God's sight, the sinner *appears* to be a saint. (This process is called "sanctification through faith" – see Appendix A.) God's willingness to cover sinners with Christ's righteousness is called "imputed righteousness." Ever since Adam and Eve sinned, God has been imputing righteousness to sinners.[26]

Rev. 10:6-7

The judgment of the living will occur during the first 1,260 days of the Great Tribulation. Since the 144,000 are the firstfruits of the harvest, they will be the first people to be judged, purified, and sealed. Currently, when we surrender our will to Jesus and receive Christ as our Savior, our surrender is less than perfect because the carnal nature is present. Paul, after being a Christian for about thirty years, reminds us in Romans 7 that it is impossible for anyone having a carnal nature to perfectly keep it subdued. The power of sin is greater than our best intentions and efforts. Even worse, it is possible to sin and not even know it! This explains why sanctification on Earth is an endless process. As we learn and overcome, we grow in Christ. We are cursed by the power of sin from within and the minute that we overcome one sin, another one pops up! God understands the problem and He has a profound remedy.

When a person dies, there is nothing further to worry about because a dead person cannot sin again. When the dead in Christ are resurrected to enjoy eternal life, they will receive a nature that has no proclivity toward sin. I highlight this point because the judgment of the *living* (which takes place during the Great Tribulation) poses a problem. Everyone having a carnal nature will sin if given enough time. God's solution to this problem is unbelievably generous and dramatic. During the Great Tribulation, God will test each of us to see if we love Him with all our heart, mind, and soul and if we love our neighbors as ourselves. If we pass the test, Jesus will remove our carnal nature (that pesky attraction for sin that lives inside us) so that we can be

> Rev. 10:6-7

set free of sin's power and attraction. The righteousness of Christ will be *imparted* (actually put within us). Then, Jesus will put His seal on us so that His righteousness within us does not change. I am sure one of the favorite songs of the saints during the sealing will be that old gospel song written by Fanny Crosby, "Redeemed how I love to proclaim it! Redeemed by the blood of the Lamb. Redeemed through His infinite mercy, His child and forever I am!" The sealing is "the mystery of God" that He will accomplish just prior to the seventh trumpet.

When their sinful natures are removed, the 144,000 will be a perfect reflection of Christ's character and so will everyone else who receives the seal of God. God's saints will be free of sin's power. They will be living examples of what God will do for any sinner, no matter how degenerate or evil a person may be or may have been. He will give righteousness to those who pass the test of faith and will completely transform him or her into a new person! Addicts, prostitutes, liars, thieves, murderers, and sinners of all kinds will see a living example of what they too can become through Christ. *The really-really-really good news during the Great Tribulation is that God is willing to give the gift of sanctification to anyone putting their faith in Christ!*

Prior to the 1,260 days allotted to the Two Witnesses, God's gift to mankind has been described as "justification." When the judgment of the living begins, God increases His gift to the faithful by *imparting* the righteousness of Jesus to each sinner. This is the gift of "sanctification." Words cannot describe the joy that "eleventh hour" sinners will experience when they receive the riches of God's grace and are set free from sin's power. The seal of God will keep every sanctified sinner safe from falling back into the clutches of sin. Revelation 7:1-4 indicates that the first people to receive the seal of God will be the 144,000. Revelation 14:4 reveals that the 144,000 will be the firstfruits of the end time harvest. Therefore, people who choose Christ as their Savior throughout the Great Tribulation will be sealed like the 144,000 because the harvest and its firstfruits are always identical. (For example, if the harvest is barley, the firstfruits are also barley.) The sealing process will remain operational until the 1,260th day ends. Five days later, the seventh trumpet will sound.

A person who has a sinful nature cannot enter Heaven. Many Christians have just assumed that the redeemed will receive sinless natures at the Second Coming and this assumption is true, but only for the righteous dead. However, for the living, their carnal nature has to be removed prior to the seven last plagues because the intercession of Jesus will end on the 1,260th day of the Great Tribulation (see Prophecy 12) and the Second Coming occurs on the 1,335th day. Ever since the day that sin began, there has been an intercessor in Heaven for sinners![27] For six thousand years the righteousness of Christ has been *imputed* to everyone who lives by faith[28] and when the righteous dead are resurrected at the Second Coming, each will be given a sinless nature and a new body. However, a day is coming when the offer of redemption will end and there will be no further intercession in Heaven, because an intercessor will no longer be needed. All of God's saints will be sealed!

{8} While I was thinking about the mystery of God, I heard a voice from Heaven speak to me. It said, "John, take the little book from Jesus' hand." {9} I went over to where Jesus was standing and asked for the little book. He said, "Take it and eat it. It will taste as sweet as honey in your mouth, but it will turn your stomach sour." I asked Jesus what was written in the little book. He said, "This little book contains my words. You will speak my words during the Great Tribulation."[29]

{10} So, I ate the little book. There came a rush, a heightened experience unlike anything I had ever known. There was an explosion of truth and knowledge in my mind. It was as though I saw and understood many new things. Words cannot describe the elation and joy that I felt. God's love, character, ways, and plans were as sweet as honey in my mouth, but I soon discovered that proclaiming the words of Jesus produced great bitterness.[30] Few people wanted to hear them. In fact, almost everyone seemed hostile toward me. I felt like wearing sackcloth and sitting in ashes, my grief became so great.[31] {11} Jesus spoke to me as though I was one of the 144,000,[32] "You *must prophesy again* before[33] many peoples, nations, languages, and kings."

> The phrase, "must prophesy again" indicates the gospel of Jesus – in its present form – has become contaminated. Therefore, a purified gospel[34] must be proclaimed *again* to the whole world. The little book Jesus gave John contains the words which the 144,000 *will speak*. God's servants will not dilute or deviate from these words.[35] They will clearly present the truth about Jesus and His salvation with no ambiguity. The unvarnished truth will be told and sin will be called by its right name. The

Rev. 10:8-9

And the voice which I heard from heaven spake unto me again, and said, Go and take the little book which is open in the hand of the angel which standeth upon the sea and upon the earth. And I went unto the angel, and said unto him, Give me the little book. And he said unto me, Take it, and eat it up; and it shall make thy belly bitter, but it shall be in thy mouth sweet as honey.

Rev. 10:10-11

And I took the little book out of the angel's hand, and ate it up; and it was in my mouth sweet as honey: and as soon as I had eaten it, my belly was bitter.

And he said unto me, Thou must prophesy again before many peoples, and nations, and tongues, and kings.

Prophecy 9 - The Two Witnesses

> Rev. 10:10-11

gospel of Jesus is powerful, like a double edged sword. It separates people from each other (it separates honest-in-heart sheep from darkness-loving goats). The kingdom of God is like a great magnet. The pure in heart are attracted to it, but people with hearts of stone are unaffected. God's children are people who love and exalt righteousness and truth as He does.[36]

Each member of the 144,000 will eat the same little book that John ate. Even though they will not know each other, the 144,000 will proclaim the same gospel; a gospel that is pure and undefiled by men's opinions. The Holy Spirit will anoint their lips with coals of fire, just as the Lord anointed the prophet Isaiah's lips.[37] The 144,000 will speak with power and penetrating clarity to every nation, kindred, tongue, and people as the first four trumpets devastate the Earth. The effects of the trumpets will traumatize and overwhelm the remaining inhabitants of the world. People will truly fear God for a short time. This fear will silence nations and people so that everyone can hear and consider a gospel that is unlike anything they have heard before. During the Great Tribulation, a numberless multitude of honest-hearted people will abandon their religious heritage and do whatever He asks once they know that God is truly speaking. God's Two Witnesses will validate the testimony of the 144,000 and a numberless multitude will be sealed. God's love for sinners is beyond understanding. He *really* loves us!

> Rev. 11:1-3
>
> given me a reed like unto a rod: and the angel stood, saying, Rise, and measure the temple of God, and the altar, and them that worship therein. But the court which is without the temple leave out, and measure it not; for it is given unto the Gentiles: and the holy city shall they tread under foot forty and two months. And I will give power unto my two witnesses, and they shall prophesy a thousand two hundred and threescore days, clothed in sackcloth.

{11:1} My first experience as one of the 144,000 was painful and difficult. Jesus handed a measuring stick to me and said, "Go measure my temple. Go into the inner court and see who 'measures up' to the terms and conditions of the eternal gospel because I want to know who loves me. Billions of people attend religious services each week, but in truth, I do not know them.[38] Present the gospel to the inner court and if they refuse to measure up, drive them out. {2} Exclude the outer court because it will be used to collect the Gentiles. They will trample on my holy people[39] for forty-two months." {3} Jesus spoke again to John. "To validate your testimony, I will give power to my Two Witnesses, and they will prophesy for 1,260 days, clothed in sackcloth."

Before Jerusalem was destroyed in A.D.70, the temple in Jerusalem had two courts. Gentile converts to Judaism worshiped in the outer court.[40] The inner court was reserved for Jews and those converts who had achieved a "purified" ancestry. Using this imagery, John was sent to measure the inner court because it contains worshipers who say they know God. Before the temple was destroyed in A.D. 70, the outer court contained people who God loved, but they did not have the same privileges and opportunities given to those in the inner court. God designed this separation to give Gentile converts time to assimilate into His ways before He gave them full rights as members of Israel.

The two courts in this prophecy represent Christianity (the inner court – sheep) and all non-Christians (the outer court – goats). Currently, Jesus has sheep in both courts and the devil has goats in both courts. During the Great Tribulation, Jesus will purify the inner court through the testimony presented by the 144,000. Those people who accept the testimony of the 144,000 will be persecuted. Persecution will cause the goats to run out of the inner court. Meanwhile, the gospel will attract God's sheep who live in the outer court. At the end of the 1,260 days, all of the Lord's sheep will be found in the inner court and all of the goats will be found in the outer court.

The book that John ate contains the gospel of Christ, words that must be spoken throughout the world as a testimony to all nations. John was given a measuring stick and sent to the inner court to measure the temple and count the worshipers. The measuring stick indicates judgment. The 144,000 will prophesy (preach the gospel) and the honest in heart will embrace it and "measure up." Honest-hearted people will also hear the gospel and join with the worshipers in the inner court.[41] This migration between the two courts is an important concept to understand. *At the end of the Great Tribulation, all of the saints will be gathered in the inner court and all of the wicked will be gathered in the outer court.* This separation process will produce much sorrow and bitterness. Families will be broken apart and many close relationships will end because of the sword of Christ's gospel. Those in the outer court will hate those in the inner court and will persecute them.[42] The outer court occupants will trample on God's holy people for forty-two months, thinking that they are doing God a service.[43] This painful process made John's stomach turn sour during the vision.

The phrase, "clothed in sackcloth" means the 1,260 days will be a time of anguish, mourning, and discouragement.[44] Please study this text: **"The man clothed in linen, who was above the waters of the river, lifted his right hand and his left hand toward heaven, and I heard him swear by him who lives forever, saying, 'It will be for a time, times and half a time. When the power of the holy people has been**

Rev. 11:1-3

> Rev. 11:1-3

finally broken, all these things will be completed.' "[45]
When we examine Prophecy 11 we will discover that 1,260 days equals "a time, time and half a time." We will also discover that there are two separate and distinct time periods of 1,260 days. One period occurred between 538 and 1798 and the other is in the future. Because of Rule Four, one time period is translated a day for a year and the other is not. When these two time periods are added together, God's people are persecuted for a total of seven times (periods of time). According to Daniel 12:7, the 1,260 days granted to the Two Witnesses will end "when the power of the holy people (the 144,000) has been finally broken."

God's Two Witnesses are eternal and omnipresent. They have always been and they will always be. They serve several purposes. One purpose is to detect sin and rebellion. The Two Witnesses report to the Father everything they *see* and this is why they are called "witnesses." God's first witness is two perfect laws; represented by the two lampstands. The highest laws in the universe are: You shall **"Love the Lord your God with all your heart and with all your soul and with all your mind. This is the first and greatest commandment and the second is like it: Love your neighbor as yourself."**[46]

The following concept may surprise you, but a law is a witness.[47] A law defines the will of the lawmaker and using personification; the law measures the actions of those who live under its obligation. If a person fulfills the intent of the law, he measures up to the law. The law also testifies to the lawmaker whether a person is with or without fault. If a person fails to fulfill the intent of the law, the law testifies the person does not measure up to its requirements. He falls short because he has done evil.[48] The Bible is clear on this point, God's laws are His witnesses.[49]

The two laws of love are not hard to understand, but they are impossible to obey consistently because our carnal nature stands in opposition to them. Our thoughts and actions *naturally* spring from love for self. If we try to obey the law because it is the law, compliance will not necessarily fulfill the intent of the law. Paul wrote, "If I give all that I possess to the poor and surrender my body to the flames, but have not love, I gain nothing."[50] It is possible to show piety and generosity without having love. Everyone is capable of deception and history teaches that religious leaders are among the worst. Because everyone has a carnal nature, we do not naturally love God with all of our heart, mind, and soul. Further, it is not natural to love our neighbors as ourselves. Those in power usually love power more than they love others. To fulfill the two laws of love that God has imposed on mankind, we must receive a new heart and a new mind each day. This daily transformation is compared to being "born again" and our need of this transformation brings us to the ministry of the Holy Spirit.

The Holy Spirit is God's second witness. The Holy Spirit reads our minds. He knows our thoughts, affections, and motives. Nothing is hidden from the Holy Spirit. (Remember, the four living creatures in Revelation 4 and 5 are covered with eyes!) The Holy Spirit faithfully reports to God everything that He hears and sees. He is a living witness! If a person hears the gospel of Jesus and sincerely wants a new heart and mind, the Holy Spirit makes it happen. Through the transforming ministry of the Spirit, things the sinner used to hate, he will love and things he used to love, he will hate![51] Each time a sinner petitions the Lord for a pure heart, the Lord sends the Holy Spirit with another dose of transforming power. The Bible describes the daily process as crucifying the carnal nature so that God's love can reign supreme in the "born again" life.[52]

The only act which God cannot forgive is blaspheming (insulting) the Holy Spirit.[53] When a person knows to do right, but does not do it, the law testifies without prejudice or deviation that the rebel is a sinner. If a person refuses to obey the Holy Spirit's "prompting from within," or if a person refuses to do what the Holy Spirit says is holy and right, the Holy Spirit testifies to Jesus that the sinner is defiant. The Spirit knows a defiant rebel when He sees him because He reads each sinner's heart![54] So, a defiant rebel is condemned by the testimony of two witnesses.[55] If a person knowingly and persistently defies the laws of God, eventually the Holy Spirit will abandon that person because the Holy Spirit is not permitted to overrule defiance. When the Holy Spirit abandons a person because of defiance, the sinner has committed the unpardonable sin.[56] When the Holy Spirit finally abandons a defiant rebel, that person will have no further interest in doing what is right. That person may think that he is free to do whatever he wants, but instead he has been given over to destruction. His carnal nature will lead him deeper into sin and his degenerate behavior will eventually lead to demonic bondage.[57] A person abandoned by the Holy Spirit is selfish, cruel, narcissistic, and a predator. Such a person has no feelings or compassion for others. He has no peace or happiness. When the heart of a rebel becomes hard

> Rev. 11:1-3

as stone, it cannot be transformed, even by Almighty God, unless the rebel repents. Without the ministry of the Holy Spirit, repentance is impossible!

To appreciate the eternal role of God's Two Witnesses throughout His universe, we must understand that in God's economy, no one is condemned on the testimony of one witness. In other words, God's laws of love and the testimony of the Holy Spirit must be in perfect agreement. God's two laws of love measure behavior, defining righteousness and unrighteousness, and the Spirit reads our hearts and knows our motives. God requires the law and the Holy Spirit to perfectly agree about a person before a defiant rebel can be condemned to death. If a person does something wrong (violates God's law), but the Spirit (who reads the heart) testifies that the deed was done in ignorance, that person is not condemned in God's sight![58] God is so good! His generosity never ends! God does not condemn anyone who is ignorant of sin; however, God will condemn a person if he refuses to do the good that he knows he should do.[59]

During the time of Moses, two or more witnesses were required to condemn a person to death.[60] During the Great Tribulation, the same holds true. Here is the process: God will ensure that everyone hears His demands. The 144,000, through their ministry, will proclaim God's two laws of love. The Holy Spirit will deeply impress every person that obeying these two laws is God's will. The 144,000 will perform signs and wonders to affirm that God's two laws are holy and true. After the clearest evidences of God's will have been set before the people, and after the Holy Spirit has done everything possible to convict people that God's laws are righteous and true, God's Two Witnesses will condemn everyone rejecting the gospel of Jesus. Ultimately, defiant rebels will be put to death. They must die because of rebellion.

Once God's Two Witnesses agree that a person should be condemned, there is no higher court for further appeal. Down through the centuries, various judicial systems on Earth have offered defendants the right to appeal their case to a higher court. A defendant might hope for a better outcome if he can show that the first trial was not conducted properly or perhaps he can bring new or better facts to a second trial. However, in God's judicial system, there is no higher court. There are no appeals because *God's Two Witnesses never make a mistake.* They cannot be fooled with lies or clever arguments. If a person is clearly informed about God's will and he chooses to rebel against it, that is his privilege. However, the law will testify that his actions were evil and the Holy Spirit will testify that his heart was defiant. When a person rebels against the Holy Spirit's inner push to obey God's will, the Holy Spirit detects the resistance. If a person insists on defiance day after day, a time will come when the Holy Spirit will report to Jesus that there is nothing further that can be done. Defiance produces a sin that is unpardonable. During the Great Tribulation, God's Ten Commandments will measure our actions. The Holy Spirit will see our motives. Together, they will report to Jesus and He will pass judgment on each person. Everyone who surrenders to the will and love of God will be given the gift of sanctification and sealed. The sinful nature will be removed. Everyone else will end up hopelessly selfish and totally defiant. All of the wicked will end up at the same place – committing the unpardonable sin. All rebels will be destroyed at the Second Coming.[61]

{4} Jesus said to me, "To help you better understand the role and purpose of my Two Witnesses, they are the two olive trees and the two lampstands that stand before my throne."

> To understand these symbols (the two olive trees and the two lampstands), we need first to examine a vision given to Zechariah.[62] Zechariah was a Levite who received a vision from God shortly after Israel's Babylonian captivity ended. In his vision, Zechariah saw a golden lampstand located in Heaven. He saw a bowl sitting on top of the lampstand and seven lamps were located around the edge of this fixture. He also saw seven golden pipes coming from two olive trees that were located on each side of the lampstand. The seven pipes carried fresh olive oil to each lamp so that the seven lights never went out. As a priest, Zechariah should have had some understanding of what he saw, but he could not figure out the meaning. Finally, an angel explained the vision to Zechariah.

> The lampstand represented the nation of Israel. God had chosen the descendants of Abraham to be a nation of priests, a light to the Gentiles. Israel had been set apart from the other nations to be trustees of His gospel, but over the years, Israel became unfaithful to God and the Benefactor sent His trustees into Babylonian captivity for seventy years. Now that Israel's captivity was nearly over, a new beginning was underway for Israel. God wanted Zechariah to understand why Israel had previously failed. He also wanted to make sure that Israel

Rev. 11:1-3

Rev. 11:4

These are the two olive trees, and the two candlesticks standing before the God of the earth.

Rev. 11:4

understood His purpose for choosing it as a nation of trustees/priests.[63]

In the vision, Zechariah saw two olive trees on each side of a golden lampstand. The olive trees were alive and they produced an endless supply of fuel oil. (The two olive trees represent the never ending energy and power of the Holy Spirit.) As long as the candlestick remained connected to the two olive trees, the lamps would burn forever. The seven lights on the lampstand represented God's love. God wanted Israel to radiate His two laws of love throughout the world and He wanted Israel to teach others about the Lord's perfect ways and laws.[64] The candlestick with its seven lamps and the two olive trees beautifully portrayed God's connection and purposes for Israel.[65] This imagery also contained a warning. If Israel did not remain connected to the two olive trees (the Holy Spirit), Israel could not be a light to the Gentiles and Israel's trusteeship would end.

About 500 years later after Zechariah's vision, Israel rejected the Son of God when He came to Earth as the Messiah. God responded by abandoning the nation of Israel. Using a new covenant, God redefined the offspring of Abraham because He had made several promises to Abraham. All believers in Christ are now the heirs of Abraham.[66] God gave the trusteeship of His gospel to Christians. The transition from one lampstand in Zechariah's vision to seven lampstands in John's vision reveals that the seven churches replaced Israel as the trustees of the gospel.[67]

Unfortunately, church history confirms that the seven churches in Revelation mirrored Israel's behavior. Like Israel, Christianity has gone through endless cycles of apostasy and revival and God will soon turn the trusteeship of His gospel over to 144,000 servants. Just before the Great Tribulation begins, God will raise up a diverse group of honest-hearted people from every language, religion, and culture. These people will be the final trustees of the gospel of Jesus Christ. Like Gideon's tiny army of three hundred soldiers,[68] this tiny group of diverse people will accomplish all that God wants done. Not by might or human power, but by God's Spirit the gospel will go quickly throughout the world. Jesus will give the 144,000 the words to speak and Jesus will validate their testimony through His Two Witnesses.

The Holy Spirit (represented by the two olive trees) will bear witness that the 144,000 speak for God by enabling the 144,000 to speak about subjects which they could not otherwise know.

I believe the 144,000 will be able, as needed, to read people's thoughts, just as Jesus read the thoughts of the Pharisees and Sadducees in Matthew 12:25-37. They will also work signs and wonders just like Jesus.[69] The 144,000 will proclaim God's will; specifically the demands of His two laws of love (represented by the two lampstands). The demands of the Ten Commandments will test the heart and faith of each person.[70] Currently, few people will listen to the gospel of Jesus, but God will shake up the world with an overwhelming display of wrath. He will bring the world to a standstill so that everyone can hear His servants, the 144,000. God's Two Witnesses will validate the testimony of the 144,000.[71] The Ten Commandments will declare their gospel is true. The Holy Spirit will impress every sinner's heart with their need of a Savior. Persecution will intensify and everyone will be tested.

The two olive trees represent the two functions of the Holy Spirit. These functions are sometimes described in the Bible as two rains such as the early rain and the latter rain.[72] To appreciate the importance and function of these two rains, please consider the setting. In Bible times, Israel's economy was based on agriculture. Farmers planted crops in the autumn and in the spring. The autumn crop matured in early spring and the spring crop matured in the autumn. Both crops were nourished by two rains, the early and the latter rain. The early rain softened the soil to receive the seeds and weeks later, the latter rain brought the crops to maturity. So it is with the work of the Holy Spirit. His first work is to soften the soil of the human heart so that seeds of truth might take root and grow. His second work is to bring people to spiritual maturity in preparation for the harvest.[73] For 1,260 days, during a period of great distress (sackcloth and ashes), the Holy Spirit will "rain" on everyone.[74] Millions of people will hear and thoughtfully consider the gospel of Jesus for the first time in their lives (the early rain experience) and a numberless multitude will embrace the gospel of Jesus. They will be tested and after passing the test of faith, given a sinless nature. Jesus will impart His righteousness to the sinner and place a seal on his forehead; indicating that he will not fall back into sin.

Remember, two lampstands plus two olive trees equals Two Witnesses. Together, the Ten Commandments (two tablets defining the two laws of love) and the ministry of the Holy Spirit make up the Two Witnesses. As you know, God's two laws are very simple to understand, but they are exceedingly difficult to

> **Rev. 11:4**

fulfill because of our sinful natures. The carnal nature inherently loves self above everything else and it will do whatever it takes to honor, exalt, defend, and fulfill itself. The carnal nature is self seeking, selfish, arrogant, competitive, and subtle. The carnal nature is naturally hostile toward God's two laws of love. Paul wrote, "Those who live according to the sinful nature have their minds set on what that nature desires; but those who live in accordance with the Spirit have their minds set on what the Spirit desires. The sinful mind is hostile to God. It does not submit to God's law, nor can it do so. Those controlled by the sinful nature cannot please God."[75] Man's biggest problem is his carnal nature and the removal of the carnal nature (the sealing process) is the most wonderful gift that God can bestow upon those who live during the judgment of the living! When the carnal nature is removed, ex-sinners will have no further conflict with God's two laws of love! **"I will put my laws in their minds and write them on their hearts. I will be their God, and they will be my people."**[76]

> **Rev. 11:5**
> *And if any man will hurt them, fire proceedeth out of their mouth, and devoureth their enemies: and if any man will hurt them, he must in this manner be killed.*

{5} If anyone tries to harm my Two Witnesses, fire comes from their mouths and devours them. This is how anyone who wants to harm them must die.

The Two Witnesses are described as fire-breathing witnesses because in John's day, fire-breathing dragons were the most invincible objects that John knew about. For example, in the fifth trumpet John saw an angel come down from Heaven with the key to the Abyss and after the Abyss was opened, he saw a great swarm of locusts come out. God used language and concepts which John understood, using mythical objects to describe spiritual concepts. Of course, we know there is no literal key to the Abyss because the Abyss that John saw does not exist physically. The devil's angels are not an actual swarm of locusts and fire-breathing lampstands and olive trees do not exist. Metaphors and personification are literary tools that can be used to describe things when language is insufficient.

Jesus used a metaphor to describe the Two Witnesses when he told John they will be fire-breathing witnesses. I believe John understood that no one can thwart their mission and everyone who rejects their testimony will be destroyed by fire – eventually. Jesus frequently silenced the arguments and sophistry of the Pharisees and Sadducees with a few well chosen words[77] and the same will hold true for the 144,000. Their testimony will be invincible. The leaders of the world will not be able to trap the 144,000 with clever arguments because Jesus Himself will be speaking through the lips of His servants. Thus, the whole world will hear "the testimony of Jesus" because the Holy Spirit will take words from Jesus and put them in the mouths of the 144,000.[78]

{6} These ~~men~~ [witnesses] have power to shut up the sky so that it will not rain during the time they are prophesying; and they have power to turn the waters into blood and to strike the earth with every kind of plague as often as they want.

> The word "men" is not found in the Greek text. It has been supplied by well-meaning translators. The antecedent of the pronoun "These" refers to "the Two Witnesses" mentioned in the previous verse. The KJV correctly translates this phrase saying, "These have power to shut heaven, that it rain not in the days of their prophecy. . ."
>
> We learned in Prophecy 7 that the 144,000 will be ordinary people like Moses and Peter. When Moses was filled with Holy Spirit power, he could call down plagues on Egypt at will. Peter healed the lame man at will because Holy Spirit power had been given to him. Remember, the 144,000 will be sealed and empowered before the Great Tribulation begins. Once empowered, God will work signs and miracles through them. This power will be safe in the hands of the 144,000 because their carnal natures have been removed. Like Elijah, they will ask God to withhold the rain[79] so that multitudes of disbelieving people will witness that they truly speak for Almighty God. Months and months without rain can be a powerful validation! This end time display of divine power parallels the showdown that took place on Mount Carmel long ago when Elijah triumphed over Jezebel's 450 prophets of Baal.

{7} When the Two Witnesses have finished their testimony (at the end of their 1,260 days of empowerment), the beast that comes up from the Abyss will attack them, overpower them, and kill them.

> Three passages of Scripture are required to identify the beast that comes up from the Abyss. First, we know that an *angel king* is released from the Abyss in Revelation 9:1-11. Second, we know that *a beast* will come up out of the Earth in Revelation 13:11-18. Third, Revelation 17:8 says the wicked will be astonished when they actually *see* the beast that comes up from the Abyss (comes up out of the Earth) because he once was *visible*, he is not *visible* today, but he will come out of the Abyss

Rev. 11:6
These have power to shut heaven, that it rain not in the days of their prophecy: and have power over waters to turn them to blood, and to smite the earth with all plagues, as often as they will.

Rev. 11:7
And when they shall have finished their testimony, the beast that ascendeth out of the bottomless pit shall make war against them, and shall overcome them, and kill them.

> Rev. 11:7

and be *visible*! When these specifications are aligned, it is obvious that Lucifer, the angel king of the Abyss, is "the lamblike-dragon-speaking" beast that will kill the influence and testimony of God's Two Witnesses at the end of their 1,260 days.

The story of Lucifer is described in different places and different ways in the Bible[80] because God wants His people to be prepared for the physical appearing of this incredible enemy. *The world has never seen anything that can compare with the appearing of Lucifer.* It is ironic that millions of Christians anticipate a coming Antichrist, but their expectations are far too low for the Antichrist who is coming. What man on Earth can descend from the sky with millions of angels in attendance? What man on Earth can call down fire from Heaven at will? What man on Earth can abolish the religions and governments of the world? Earth has never seen an equivalent to the appearing of Lucifer. To make this matter clear, God uses repetition and enlargement to give mankind an encompassing view of Lucifer and his purposes, ambition, and ultimate destruction. There is so much more to Lucifer's physical appearing than one prophecy can convey. The devil's signs and wonders will be so deceptive that if possible, the very elect (the 144,000) would be deceived.[81]

The Bible declares the beast from the Abyss will kill God's Two Witnesses. This one specification has misled millions of people into believing the Two Witnesses have to be two people. When people hear me say that the Two Witnesses are not two people, they often ask: "If the Two Witnesses are the Ten Commandments and the Holy Spirit, how can Lucifer kill them?" Actually, this question has to be restated. "If the Two Witnesses are two lampstands and two olive trees, how can Lucifer kill them?" The solution is found in personification.

To understand God's use of personification, we need to review some basic facts. We know that the *influence* of the Holy Spirit is terminated in a person's heart when that person commits the unpardonable sin. When God's Spirit cannot live in a person's heart, it becomes impossible for that sinner to submit to God's two laws of love. Of course, no one can kill the Holy Spirit, but a sinner can kill the *influence* of the Holy Spirit through defiance. In Zechariah 4, Zechariah saw a lampstand and two olive trees that were *in Heaven*. In Revelation 1, John also saw seven lampstands that were *in Heaven*. Obviously, the devil cannot touch these objects and neither can mankind, but Lucifer can kill the *influence* of the Ten Commandments and the Holy Spirit by leading people into defiance against the eternal gospel. (See Prophecy 12.)

Rev. 11:7

When Lucifer sets life and death choices before everyone on Earth during the sixth trumpet, millions of people will attempt to save themselves from death. People will acquiesce to the devil's demands – knowing that what they are doing is evil. Everyone who rushes to be among the first to receive the mark of the beast willingly and willfully "kills" whatever *influence* the Two Witnesses may have had in his heart.[82] When a person commits the unpardonable sin, there is no motive to repent! The following passage describes the actions of those people who grieved away the Holy Spirit: **"And the rest of mankind that were not killed** [during the sixth trumpet] **still did not repent of the work of their hands; they did not stop worshiping demons, and idols of gold, silver, bronze, stone and wood – idols that cannot see or hear or walk. Nor did they repent of their murders, their magic arts, their sexual immorality or their thefts."**[83]

The Two Lampstands Cannot Represent a Human Agency

Some Bible students conclude that if the lampstand in Zechariah's day represented the nation of Israel and the seven lampstands in John's day represented the seven churches, the two lampstands in Revelation 11:4 should also represent some form of a human agency. While this argument seems logical, my response to this conclusion consists of four steps:

1. In round numbers, God has invested 6,000 years in human agents (the Patriarchs, Israel, and Christianity). These groups failed because the carnal nature of man overtook them. This explains why the last group of trustees (the 144,000) will be *sealed before* they begin their work! The 144,000 must be sealed so that the carnal nature will not interfere and ruin God's final efforts to redeem mankind!

2. The two olive trees in Revelation 11:4 and Zechariah 4:3 are identical. The two trees represent the renewing and endless energy of the Holy Spirit.[84] His work comes in two phases; the early rain and the latter rain.[85] There is no question that the Holy Spirit reports to God. He is the living witness who sees[86] and hears everything.[87] (Remember, the four living creatures are covered with eyes. The phrase, "the eyes of the Lord" is used more than eighty-five times in the Bible.)

> Rev. 11:7

3. The two lampstands in Revelation 11:4 represent one of the Two Witnesses. I believe the two lampstands represent God's two immutable laws of love because laws can be witnesses and these two laws are infallible. They define righteousness and wickedness. God's laws of love testify about the behavior of God, the angels, and human beings. The Bible declares that God is love because His actions are always consistent with His two laws of love. God's two laws testify without prejudice or fear and their testimony is righteous and perfect.[88] Consider the words of Moses: **"After Moses finished writing in a book the words of this law from beginning to end, he gave this command to the Levites who carried the ark of the covenant of the Lord: 'Take this Book of the Law and place it beside the ark of the covenant of the Lord your God. There it will remain as a witness against you.' "**[89]

4. The Ten Commandments are not to be confused with the laws that Moses wrote. This is a very important point! Moses' laws were temporary and written on parchment by a man. The principles underlying the Ten Commandments are eternal. God spoke them on Mount Sinai before He wrote them with His own finger on two tablets of stone. This may come as a surprise, but the Ten Commandments are also called "the two tablets of the Testimony." Look at this text: **"When the Lord finished speaking to Moses on Mount Sinai, he gave him *the two tablets of the Testimony*, the tablets of stone inscribed by the finger of God."**[90] The golden box that contained the two tablets of the Testimony (the Ten Commandments) is called, "the Ark of the Testimony" thirteen times in the Bible, because the Ten Commandments testify. The Ten Commandments are an infallible witness. They declare what pure love is and is not, what pure love will do and will not do. These two tablets measure every action and the Holy Spirit measures every motive.

The story of the Two Witnesses significantly increases our understanding of end time events. Consider what we have learned regarding the Two Witnesses:

1. The testimony of the 144,000 must be validated with two witnesses.

2. Two witnesses are needed to exonerate or condemn each living person.

3. The two olive trees represent the ministry of the Holy Spirit.

4. The two lampstands represent God's two eternal laws of love.

When we consider that the Two Witnesses will be empowered during the judgment of the living, there is perfect harmony rising from the sum of all of the parts.

People often ask this question: "If the Two Witnesses are two eternal laws of love and the Holy Spirit, why is their power limited to 1,260 days?" God's Two Witnesses are eternal and in a limited way, they have been effective on Earth during the past 6,000 years. However, their empowerment is required for the judgment of the living, a one-time process that will occur near the end of the world. This process will take 1,260 days.

Soul Sleep and Pre-advent Judgment

Contrary to what many Christians believe, a person's soul does not go to Heaven or hell at the time of death. The Bible says **"The soul who sins is the one who will die."**[91] At death, the soul ceases to exist with no consciousness. Even though some Bible texts seem to support the idea that souls are alive in Heaven or hell, a dead person does not have any knowledge or awareness of what is happening.[92] All people go into a grave of silence at death.[93] It is as though the dead are in a deep sleep caused by anesthesia. The Bible teaches there are two deaths.[94] Like sleep, the first death is temporary."[95] Jesus referred to the death of Lazarus as though he was asleep.[96] The only difference between the first death and the second death is duration. The second death will be a state of eternal non-existence like Sodom and Gomorrah.[97] At the Second Coming, only the righteous dead will be awakened out of their "sleep." Those judged to be unfit for eternal life will be awakened out of their sleep at the end of the 1,000 years.

The righteous and the unrighteous are tested and separated prior to the Second Coming.[98] *This explains why a pre-Advent judgment is necessary.* Most Christians have not considered the implications of a pre-Advent judgment because they assume that a person is judged at the time of death and sent immediately to his eternal reward in Heaven or hell. Catholics believe that judgment occurs at death and the wicked are immediately sent to hell, but "good people" are sent to "Purgatory" where they must suffer through a purification process before being pure enough to enter Heaven.

Apocalyptic prophecy informs us that the judgment of the dead has been occurring since 1844. When Jesus appears in clouds of glory,

Rev. 11:7 He will resurrect the righteous because He determined earlier who was righteous during His pre-Advent judgment.[99] On the other hand, the wicked who are alive at the Second Coming will be slain by the sword that comes out of His mouth.[100] This outcome is only possible because Jesus will determine each person's reward before He appears in clouds of glory.[101] (Further information about the state of man in death and the pre-Advent judgment is available in Chapter 13 of my book, *Jesus: The Alpha and The Omega*.[102])

The judgment of the dead requires the testimony of three witnesses. The first witness is the actual record of the dead person's actions. The second witness is a record revealing the knowledge base of the dead person. (Each person on Earth has a unique set of beliefs about right and wrong and I call this set of beliefs a knowledge base of good and evil.) The third witness is the Holy Spirit. When Jesus investigates the life record of a dead person, He compares the dead person's actions, his knowledge of good and evil, and He listens to the testimony of the Holy Spirit. For example, if the dead person's actions align with his knowledge base and his actions demonstrate that he lived up to all that he knew to be right and true, and if the Holy Spirit testifies that this person was open to His guidance, then Jesus has sufficient evidence to determine the dead person was honest in heart. On the basis of the dead man's honesty and fidelity to what he knew to be right, Jesus imparts His righteousness to the dead man and he will be saved.

When Jesus judges mankind (both the dead and the living), He *consistently follows one principle*: **"Anyone, then, who knows the good he ought to do and doesn't do it, sins."**[103] The phrase, "the good he knows he ought to do" is a reference to our knowledge of good and evil or our conscience. Man's conscience is an interesting governor. Unless the conscience is dead,[104] it contains our sense of right and wrong (acquired through parental training, cultural influence, education, etc.) and it is the doorway for the Holy Spirit. The "still small voice" of the Holy Spirit is a gift from God to every person. Those who nurture the still small voice of the Holy Spirit please God because spirit-led people love honesty and truth. An honest heart means more to God than anything else. When we honestly know that something is right and good and we do not do it, God considers our action(s) to be sinful because we have violated our knowledge base of good and evil and we have violated the voice of the Holy Spirit.

From a larger perspective, billions of people lived on Earth before Jesus was born to Mary. After He returned to Heaven, billions more have lived and died without any knowledge of His redemption. To make this matter even more complicated, millions of Christians have lived and died believing erroneous concepts about God and His redemption. These facts are not a problem for God because God does not condemn people for being ignorant! Salvation is not based on knowledge (perfect or imperfect). Salvation is based on faith and doing what is right regardless of the cost. The honest in heart live by faith and their actions prove it! They do the good they know they ought to do. "Anyone who knows the good he ought to do and does not do it, sins." This is not to say that a person will be saved for doing good acts. We cannot save ourselves with good works, but we can show God our love for truth and honesty. Jesus bases His judgment of mankind (both the dead and the living) on our faith. *Our faith is revealed when we do the good that we know we ought to do regardless of the consequences.*

Rev. 11:7

The judgment of the living will occur during the Great Tribulation and this process will begin with global enlightenment. The 144,000 will proclaim the eternal gospel and they will proclaim to everyone living on Earth "the good he ought to do" (the two laws of love). Naturally, the devil will move quickly to make it very difficult to do the good we ought to do! Torture and persecution will intimidate millions of people, but the honest in heart will put their faith in Christ and embrace His eternal gospel. For 1,260 days, *every living soul will have an opportunity to hear and thoughtfully consider God's will.* Because everyone will be informed on good and evil, Jesus can judge the living and base His judgment on each individual's response to God's two laws of love. To help us submit to the two laws of love, the Holy Spirit will do everything possible to convict us of God's will.

Each person will be tested as though he was the only person on Earth. If a person chooses to defy the two laws of love, if he defies the Holy Spirit's attempt to bring conviction that this is God's will, the Two Witnesses will condemn that person. They will declare that the person does not love God with all his heart, mind, and soul and does not love his neighbor as he should. Of course, this person should not be given eternal life! At the end of the sixth trumpet, Jesus will bring the judgment of the living to a close because every decision will be made. The living will either have the seal of God or the mark of the beast. At the end of 1,260 days, the

Rev. 11:7 — work of the Two Witnesses will be finished and their influence on the wicked will vanish.

Theological Vacuum

The Bible is clear that God will separate the sheep from the goats at the end of the world. Today the world is full of antagonistic religions and competing gospels. This is not a problem for God. The Father decided long ago to demolish the religious gridlock that would exist at the end of the world with seven "justifiable" judgments on mankind. These judgments are designed to accomplish several objectives at the same time. For example, they will shatter billions of false paradigms, humble everyone, prove the reality of God, and will reveal man's need of a Savior.

When the censer is cast down and the seven trumpets begin, Jesus will create a theological vacuum. This vacuum will suddenly form because the world's clergy do not properly understand the Bible, especially the books of Daniel and Revelation. They do not anticipate the seven trumpets and seven bowls. Consequently, they do not understand God's end time plans or purposes. The clergy of the world will be caught by total surprise when the censer is cast down. Jesus will use the seven trumpets to discredit the clergy because He wants laymen to consider a gospel they have not heard before. Jesus will use overwhelming destruction and the temporary vacuum that follows to propel the eternal gospel throughout the world with a minimum of resistance.

The 144,000 will have an opportunity to present a gospel that is contrary to what most people currently believe. The 144,000 will proclaim:

1. The Creator of Heaven and Earth and everything in them is Jesus Christ. (This will be a hard pill for Atheists, Hindus, Jews, and Muslims to swallow.)
2. Jesus Christ is Sovereign God and He is angry with man's degenerate behavior. He is responsible for the judgments that are striking the Earth. (This will be a very hard pill for many Christians to swallow.)
3. After creating the world in six days, Jesus rested on the seventh day of the week[105] and declared it holy and he commands all mankind to rest from labor on His holy day, Saturday, the seventh day of the week. (This will be a very hard pill for

Catholics, Protestants, Muslims, Hindus, Buddhists and Atheists to swallow.)

4. All have sinned and everyone is condemned to death because of his sins. There is only one way to escape the second death and that is to worship Jesus and do as He commands. (This will be a hard pill for billions of religious people to swallow.)
5. Jesus has paid the price for every repentant sinner with His own blood. There is no other means to salvation.
6. Jesus will gather His followers on the 1,335th day of the Great Tribulation. (Billions of people will scorn this information.)

Rev. 11:7

The religious and political leaders of the world will respond to the testimony of the 144,000 with hatred and blasphemy. They will claim to have a better idea, a better solution. They will create a global government (called Babylon in the book of Revelation) which (they think) will appease God's wrath. They will demand uniformity and will eventually persecute everyone who rests on Sabbath, the seventh day of the week!

Demonstrating a Profound Point

Remember, Jesus consistently judges the dead and the living according to this principle: **"Anyone, then, who knows the good he ought to do and doesn't do it, sins."**[106] While this principle sounds very simple, it is profoundly wise! Please consider two points:

1. The religious and cultural diversity of mankind is infinite. Suppose fifty billion people have lived on Earth during the past 6,000 years and most of these people lived and died without even hearing the eternal gospel. This is not a problem for God because Jesus came to Earth and paid the penalty for sin for every honest-hearted person. **"For God so loved *the world* that He gave . . . ."**[107] Many Christians do not understand that Jesus paid the penalty for sin for everyone – including those who died without hearing about Jesus and His redemption! As we just discussed, Jesus fairly and justly uses three witnesses to judge the dead and two witnesses to judge the living.
2. Knowledge expands over time. Have you marveled at the explosion of knowledge over the past two hundred years? For thousands of years, man could travel no faster than a horse could run and today we think nothing of commercial jets flying from city to city at 350+ mph. Knowledge has radically

Rev. 11:7

transformed life on Earth during the past two centuries, but some people still live in very primitive conditions. The gulf between people flying in jets and those people living in primitive conditions has been highlighted to make an important point. Suppose that at any given time in Earth's history, the gulf in man's knowledge of eternal truth ranges between 1% and 10%. (No one is totally ignorant of the laws of love and no one but God has 100% perfect knowledge.) When Jesus judges a dead person who has a knowledge base that contains 1% truth, He judges that person according to what he knew to be right and true. When Jesus judges a living person during the Great Tribulation who has heard ten times more truth, He will judge that person in the same way He judges a dead person, according to what that person knew to be right and true. Since Jesus judges according to this principle, everyone is judged in the same way.

God's policy for judging people illuminates a profound fact: Anyone who conscientiously does the good that he knows he should do is honest-hearted. Each time our knowledge expands, God challenges our honesty all over again. *God constantly challenges us to see if we will be happy in an environment where advancing knowledge of eternal truth never ends.* An honest-hearted person will embrace truth (regardless of the consequences) because he loves truth. Such a person, even if he died having only 1% truth, would be eternally happy in the company of God and the holy angels because his knowledge of God's truth will forever expand. Jesus said, **"But whoever lives by the truth comes** [continues coming] **into the light, so that it may be seen plainly that what he has** [learned and] **done has been done through God."**[108] The 144,000 will proclaim the eternal gospel throughout the whole world with great power and authority for 1,260 days. To make sure that the living know that the 144,000's testimony is true, the Holy Spirit will torment every heart and convict the world of sin, righteousness, and judgment![109] The honest in heart will respond to this enlightenment just like steel responds to the pull of a magnet. A love for truth will separate the sheep from the goats!

Long ago, the Father predetermined that the living would be tested with enlightenment at the end of the age. Because the Kingdom of God is built upon the two laws of love, God wants to test mankind to see who will embrace His two laws of love *after* the 144,000 proclaim them and after they are fully proclaimed and validated. The amazing thing about this coming test is that two self-selecting groups of people will form. In other words, the sheep (the honest in heart) and the goats (those who disdain honesty) will voluntarily separate themselves from each other by exercising their power of choice! The Father foreknew the whole process could be accomplished in 1,260 days. Actually, every human being will make his decision before the 1,260th day ends, but God will hold the door open a little longer to make sure that everyone is settled in his or her decision. This is why Jesus will empower the Two Witnesses for 1,260 days at the end of the world. The living must be tested and separated. The influence of the Two Witnesses cannot be killed until this mission is accomplished.

The Sequence Continues

{8} The bodies of the Two Witnesses will lie in the street of the great city, figuratively called Sodom and Egypt, where also their Lord was crucified. {9} For three and a half days men from every people, tribe, language, and nation will look at their bodies and refuse to bury them.

> Remember, God is using personification to describe the experience of the 144,000 and His Two Witnesses. John's experience in this prophecy represents the experience of the 144,000. The Two Witnesses are personified as two prophets because they testify – they confirm the testimony of the 144,000. The death of the Two Witnesses personifies the death of the 144,000 (who serve as the arms and legs of the Two Witnesses). One-third of mankind will be killed during the sixth trumpet.[110] Many of God's people, and most, if not all of the 144,000, will be killed. These are the martyrs described in the fifth seal.[111] Because of their contempt and hatred for the saints, Satan's forces will refuse to bury God's saints and prophets when they are slaughtered. Throughout history, armies have left their enemies to rot in the street as a display of utter contempt for their foes. Scenes of dead people rotting in the street; providing food for vultures and vermin sent a repulsive message to anyone who might want to rebel.[112]

> It is interesting to notice that the language used in verses 8 and 9 parallels the language used in Revelation 19:19-21. When Jesus destroys His enemies at the Second Coming, He too, will not bury His defiant foes. They will be left to rot in the street and vultures will gorge themselves on their flesh![113]

Rev. 11:7

Rev. 11:8-9

And their dead bodies shall lie in the street of the great city, which spiritually is called Sodom and Egypt, where also our Lord was crucified. And they of the people and kindreds and tongues and nations shall see their dead bodies three days and an half, and shall not suffer their dead bodies to be put in graves.

> Rev. 11:8-9

The phrase "the great city that is figuratively called Sodom and Egypt, where also their Lord was crucified" is symbolic and the Bible defines this symbol with a relevant text. The Bible says **"the woman is *the great city* that rules over the kings of the Earth."**[114] The book of Revelation contrasts two women. One is pure and gives birth to the Savior of the world.[115] The other woman is a wealthy whore.[116] The pure woman represents the people of God (His holy city). The whore represents the wicked (a great city containing people who worship Lucifer). The pure woman is called "the bride of Christ." The corrupt woman is called "Mystery, Babylon the Great, the Mother of Prostitutes and of the Abominations of the Earth." The whore has no conscience. She sits on a beast having seven heads and ten horns (Babylon), drinking the blood of God's prophets and saints.[117] Corporately speaking, the wicked who join Lucifer's theocracy will make up "the great city." When the Bible says the bodies of the Two Witnesses will lie in the street of *the great city* (the whore), the Bible is not talking about a geographical location. It is talking about a worldwide group of defiant people described as Sodom (sexual perverts), Egypt (hard hearts) and Jerusalem (people who rejected the clearest evidences of truth).

God uses repetition and enlargement in the book of Revelation to help us understand the counterfeit theocracy that Lucifer will establish. Lucifer's whore (Lucifer's theocracy) is given another name in Revelation 13. She is also called "an image to the beast."[118] Lucifer's theocracy will *be a mirror image* of the crisis government that man created during the first four trumpets. The essential difference between the formation of the crisis government (Babylon – Phase I) and the formation of the whore/image (Babylon – Phase II) is consolidation. When the seven trumpets begin, world leaders will create Babylon (a crisis government – Phase I) and the governments of the world will obey the instructions of the seven heads (the seven religious systems on Earth). When the sixth trumpet sounds, Lucifer will assert his authority and abolish the religions and governments of the world so that he can set up a counterfeit theocracy (Babylon – Phase II). He will rule over the world as king of kings and lord of lords. The devil will create a one-world-church-state religion and ten puppet kings (the ten horns on the composite beast) will report to him. During the time of the whore/image, (Babylon – Phase II), Lucifer will do his best to kill the opposition. He will kill a third of mankind. Babylon – Phase II, is described as a prostitute because everyone participating in Lucifer's theocracy knowingly does wrong. The wicked will prostitute themselves to do whatever Lucifer demands in exchange for survival.

Rev. 11:8-9

Now that we have identified the prostitute (the great city, Lucifer's theocracy) which will be established during the sixth trumpet, let us return to the phrase in verse 8 that says, "their bodies will lie in the street of *the great city*." Lucifer's theocracy (his great city) will encompass the whole world. Therefore, the street of the great city cannot be a geographical spot or street. When the 144,000 [the arms and legs of the two witnesses] are slain, their dead bodies will be found all over the world. The wicked, because of defiance and hatred of God's servants, will refuse to bury them. Later on, however, the table will turn and Jesus will resurrect the 144,000, vindicate them in the presence of their enemies and take them to Heaven. During the seven bowls, Jesus will prove to the wicked that Lucifer and his great whore have nothing to do with the God of Heaven. The ten kings will discover Lucifer's deception during the fifth bowl and they will turn on him and burn his prostitute (theocracy) with fire.[119]

Lucifer's whore is described as "a great city" because in Bible times certain cities were fortified as cities of refuge.[120] No one dared to live very far from a city in Bible times because there was no other means of protection. Marauding tribal kings looted and plundered everything they could steal and they made slaves of everyone who could be captured. It is interesting that Cain feared for his life after killing Abel and he was the first person to build a city.[121] During the Great Tribulation, the saints will put their faith in Jesus. They will obey the gospel of Jesus and depend upon the Lord as their city of refuge.[122] On the other hand, the wicked will trust in Lucifer and they will depend on him as their great city of refuge.[123]

Revelation's story personifies the people of Earth as a tale of two women and two cities. During the Great Tribulation, the inhabitants of Earth will be required to make an informed choice between two different forms of government. *Choice will determine citizenship.* One government, directed by Jesus, will be based on God's two laws of love. The other government will have an arbitrary dictator. Those willing to put their faith in Christ will be eagerly accepted into the city of God (personified). Those defying God's demands will be "herded" out of fear of death or persecution into a great city (personified) that offers *temporary* refuge, but there is no safety in the arms of a whore.

Prophecy 9 - The Two Witnesses

Rev. 11:8-9

She cannot be trusted. She is immoral. She always sells out to the highest bidder.

Trampling on the Holy City 42 Months

Revelation 11:2 indicates Gentiles will trample on the *holy* city for 42 months. What does this mean? New Jerusalem is a city in Heaven. It is holy because God dwells there.[124] The language in verse 2 does not point to New Jerusalem or the ancient city of Jerusalem located in the Middle East. (At one time, ancient Jerusalem was said to be a holy city because God dwelled there, but Israel's rejection of Messiah caused God to destroy the city.) The phrase, "holy city" in Revelation 11:2 must be compared to "the great city," the whore, in Revelation 17. The wicked at the end of the world are called "the great city" and the saints are called "the holy city." The reason for dividing the people of Earth into two cities is "refuge." Every believer in Jesus is granted citizenship in God's kingdom when he surrenders to the authority of Jesus.[125] His refuge is in Christ and even though he may die, he knows he will not perish.[126] The Bible is clear. The holy city in Revelation 11:2 and the saints in Revelation 13:5 will be trampled on for 42 months.[127] Repetition and enlargement clarify the meaning of this phrase.

Sodom, Egypt and Jerusalem

Figuratively speaking, the prostitute (Lucifer's counterfeit theocracy) is called Sodom, Egypt and Jerusalem (the city where our Lord was crucified) and for good reason. Sodom was notorious for sexual perversion and immorality[128] and Egypt was notorious for hardness of heart. Pharaoh was given the clearest evidences of God's will, yet he hardened his heart ten times![129] Those who rush to join Lucifer's counterfeit theocracy and receive his tattoo "666" will have the same attitude toward God as did Pharaoh (in Egypt) and the perverts in Sodom who insisted on having sex with the angels who had come to rescue Lot. Think about this: *Defiance toward God's laws of love requires the death of God or the death of those in defiance.* There can be no compromise. The leaders of Israel appeared to be very righteous in the eyes of ordinary people, but when Jesus came to Earth, He revealed that they were hypocrites.[130] Even though the Pharisees put on a great show of piety, many of Israel's religious leaders were totally corrupt, sexually immoral, and hardhearted.[131] For fear of humiliation, loss of power, wealth and position, Jewish leaders crucified Jesus.[132] If

He had been allowed to live, Jesus would have exposed their sinful actions to the people and the people would have destroyed them.[133] Jesus said, "Everyone who does evil hates the light, and will not come into the light for fear that his deeds will be exposed."[134] The same will be true at the end of the 1,260 days. The attitudes of the wicked during the Great Tribulation will mirror Egypt (hardness of heart), Sodom (unrestrained evil), and Jerusalem (where Jesus (the Truth) was crucified).

The Sequence Continues

{10} The inhabitants of the earth will gloat over the death of the Two Witnesses. They will celebrate by sending each other gifts, because *these two prophets* had tormented those who live on the earth.

> At the close of the 1,260th day most, if not all, of the 144,000 will be dead – their testimony silenced. Many of God's saints will also be dead. At the 1,260th day, the population of the world will be half of what it was when the Great Tribulation began. The whole world will be in shambles, but instead of shuddering with fear for what is about to happen (the third woe), the wicked will be elated! They will rejoice and be jubilant because the Holy Spirit no longer torments them.[135] The annoying prophets (the 144,000) who continually stirred up controversy and condemned their evil ways will be gone. At last, the conflict for souls between Christ and Satan will be over. God's Two Witnesses have reported everything to Jesus and each person has been judged. To celebrate their Pyrrhic* victory over truth and righteousness, Lucifer will declare a great global holiday. Four days will be dedicated to rejoicing and celebration. The wicked will interpret the slaughter of one-third of mankind and the establishment

> ***Note:** The phrase "Pyrrhic victory" is named after King Pyrrhus of Epirus, whose army suffered irreplaceable casualties in defeating the Romans at Heraclea in 280 B.C. and Asculum in 279 B.C. After these wars, Plutarch quotes King Pyrrhus as saying, "If we are victorious in one more battle with the Romans, we shall be utterly ruined." Even though King Pyrrhus won two battles against the Romans, he did not make a dent in the number of soldiers that belonged to Rome's army. Ultimately, he lost his kingdom because the price of victory robbed him of the soldiers necessary to defend his territory. Hence the ironic term, "Pyrrhic victory."

Rev. 11:10

And they that dwell upon the earth shall rejoice over them, and make merry, and shall send gifts one to another; because these two prophets tormented them that dwelt on the earth.

> Rev. 11:10

of Lucifer's counterfeit theocracy as a glorious development because there will be no more opposition. Other than small numbers of saints hiding in caves and remote places around the world, only those having the tattoo on their right hand will be alive at this time in Earth's history. Resources (food, energy, and the necessities of life) will last longer now that the population of Earth has been greatly reduced. During the celebration, Lucifer's grandest lie will be presented to cheering crowds. The devil will triumphantly announce the beginning of a thousand years of peace and happiness. The wicked will rejoice and "God's" millennial reign will be declared. The crowds will roar with approval and excitement.

Verse 10 describes the Two Witnesses as "two prophets" and if it were not for the larger context of personification (the two lampstands and two olive trees), the context in verse 10 could indicate the Two Witnesses are two human beings. This oversight has lead many Bible students to erroneously conclude that the Two Witnesses are two people. There are two reasons why this conclusion cannot be true!

First, let us suppose that at the 1,260th day, the Two Witnesses are two people living in Washington D.C. What impact would the deaths of these two people have in Russia, Australia, and Germany given the fact that Lucifer and his forces just killed 1.75 billion people for refusing to receive the mark of the beast? (Remember, the infrastructures of travel and communication will be practically non-existent at the time. How long will it take for news of their death to travel around the entire world?) We know that the wicked will celebrate for 3.5 days when the 1,260 days end, but why should the wicked rejoice over the death of two prophets when there are 144,000 prophets? Actually, the wicked will not celebrate the death of two prophets, they will celebrate their freedom from the Holy Spirit's torment! This is a key point that many Christians do not understand.

Do you remember the note that Pilate's wife sent to her husband when he was about to condemn Jesus to death? She wrote, **"Don't have anything to do with that innocent man, for I have suffered a great deal today in a dream because of him."**[136] The Holy Spirit tormented Pilate's wife by revealing the identity of Jesus to her and I am sure that her unsolicited note haunted Pilate for the rest of his life. During the Great Tribulation, the Holy Spirit will torment the wicked as He tormented Pilate's wife. The Bible says, **"There is no rest day or night for those who worship the beast and his image, or for anyone who receives the mark of his name."**[137] During the sixth trumpet, the Holy Spirit will cause every wicked person to suffer enormous guilt. The torment will be awful. The Holy Spirit will do everything short of violating a person's will to save that person from the penalty of sin. While this torment is occurring, the 144,000 will proclaim a fourth and final message from Jesus, **"Come out of her, my people, so that you will not share in her sins, so that you will not receive any of her plagues; for her sins are piled up to heaven, and God has remembered her crimes"**[138] and in spite of these divine endeavors, millions of people will rush forward to be among the first to receive the tattoo on their right hand (the mark of the beast). When a person receives the tattoo, the Holy Spirit gives up and departs. There is nothing further that He can do to save that soul. As the Holy Spirit withdraws from the wicked, any desire or conviction within them to do right also leaves. Lucifer will seize this opportunity and beginning on the 1,261st day of the Great Tribulation, he will lead the wicked into a victory festival! This uninhibited celebration will parallel, in a perverse way, the exuberance which the Jews experienced after destroying their enemies in the days of Queen Esther. In fact, many Jews still celebrate Purim by giving gifts to each other to mark their nation's victory over their enemies![139]

Second, the Bible calls the Two Witnesses "two prophets." We need to consider the Greek word *prophetes*. The word is usually translated "prophets," but the word includes a broader meaning, such as "an inspired speaker" or "one who speaks for God." Abraham is the first man in the Bible to be called a prophet,[140] but Noah could also be called a prophet because he was an inspired speaker.[141] The Two Witnesses are called two *prophetes* because they will be inspired speakers. They will speak for God. When ordinary men and women are enabled by the Holy Spirit to speak words they could not say on their own, these people are called *prophetes*.[142] In fact, the 144,000 are called *prophetes* in Revelation 10:7 and they are separately identified from the saints in the book of Revelation[143] in several places. We have already learned in this study that God wrote His two laws of love on two tablets of stone. These two stones are called "the Testimony" and they reside in "the Ark of the Testimony" because the Ten Commandments testify. They declare what pure love will do and will not do. The Ten Commandments have a divine

Prophecy 9 - The Two Witnesses

Rev. 11:10

origin and they speak for God, therefore the Ten Commandments (the two lampstands) are one witness and this witness can be called a *prophete*.

The two olive trees represent the Holy Spirit. The Holy Spirit is a *prophete* because it speaks for God. The Holy Spirit will impress God's two laws on the hearts of people. Their common objective is conviction – a moment of truth which requires a pivotal decision. Empowered by the Holy Spirit, the 144,000 will speak with authority as did Jesus and John the Baptist.[144] God's Two Witnesses will work through 144,000 *prophetes* and Jesus will pass judgment on the living according to their response. Even if the Two Witnesses were two people sent from Heaven, their deaths at the end of the 1,260 days would have no more impact on the whole world than did Jesus' death. When we consider the population of the whole world in A.D. 30, very, very few people rejoiced at the death of Jesus.

{11} But after the three and a half days a breath of life from God entered them, they stood on their feet, and the people celebrating their death were struck with terror.

Rev. 11:11

And after three days and an half the Spirit of life from God entered into them, and they stood upon their feet; and great fear fell upon them which saw them.

The Two Witnesses will remain dead for 3.5 days. Jesus will resurrect them in the presence of their enemies and He will take them to Heaven. There is evidence indicating the 144,000 could be taken to Heaven on a Sunday because first fruits were presented to God on the first day of the week.[145] For example, in Numbers 28:26, a presentation of firstfruits took place at the feast of Pentecost which always fell on a Sunday.[146] We know that Jesus was resurrected on Sunday, and He ascended to the Father that morning as the first fruits of the dead.[147] If the 144,000 are resurrected, taken to Heaven, and presented to God and the Lamb on a Sunday, this is consistent with first fruits being offered on a Sunday. The Bible does declare the 144,000 will be the first fruits of the coming harvest.[148]

The three and a half days can be easily demonstrated using an example with actual dates. Suppose, for sake of discussion, that the 1,260[th] day of the Great Tribulation ends on Wednesday, sundown, February 4, 2015, in New York City. Remember, that with God, a day begins and ends at sundown – local time.[149] Suppose the wicked in New York City gaze upon the dead bodies of God's prophets for three full days – Thursday, Friday, and Sabbath. Also, suppose the 144,000 are resurrected at dawn on Sunday morning, February 8, 2015. The elapsed time would be three and a half days. Although *the actual date of their resurrection is unknown* at this time, we do know that the 144,000 are the firstfruits of the coming harvest and it is possible they could be taken to Heaven and presented to God and the Lamb on a Sunday, the first day of the week.

Imagine the anxiety that will overwhelm murderous revelers when they actually see the resurrection of God's prophets. Words cannot possibly describe their terror when they see the dead awaken and stand up. The 144,000 will shine with the same glory that radiated from Moses when He descended Mt. Sinai. The courage and bravado of the wicked will melt. Fearing for their lives, the wicked will run for cover like cockroaches when exposed to light.

{12} Then, a loud voice spoke from Heaven to the 144,000: "Come up here." And immediately, the 144,000 ascended to Heaven in a cloud while their enemies looked on.[150] {13} At that very hour, there was a severe earthquake and a tenth of the great city (that is, a tenth of Lucifer's government) was destroyed by the earthquake. The ground swallowed up the highest ranking administrators within Lucifer's government (all seven thousand of them).[151]

> This text may indicate that Lucifer's government will consist of 70,000 officials. If so, each king (there will be ten kings) may rule over 7,000 officials. When the 144,000 are resurrected and taken to Heaven, 7,000 of Lucifer's highest officials will perish. I believe this divine event declares, "Game Over." Maybe Jesus will destroy 7,000 demon possessed officials who were known and feared for their inhumane cruelty. Regardless, Lucifer and his officials used their power to destroy God's people and now Jesus will use higher power to destroy them. The earthquake will terrify the surviving saints, but they will rejoice and give glory to Jesus because they know He is about to end their misery and suffering! Lucifer's government will be badly damaged by the loss of this leadership, but Lucifer will not care. The celebration will end abruptly and a cloud of heavy worry will fall on the wicked.

{14} Then a loud thunder came from Heaven. A voice said: "The second woe has passed; the third woe is coming soon."

Rev. 11:11

Rev. 11:12

And they heard a great voice from heaven saying unto them, Come up hither. And they ascended up to heaven in a cloud; and their enemies beheld them. And the same hour was there a great earthquake, and the tenth part of the city fell, and in the earthquake were slain of men seven thousand: and the remnant were affrighted, and gave glory to the God of heaven.

> **Rev. 11:14**
>
> *The second woe is past; and, behold, the third woe cometh quickly.*

Prior to the seventh trumpet, the gospel of Jesus Christ will reach every nation, kindred, tongue, and people. When the 1,260th day arrives, everyone on Earth either has the seal of God or the mark of the beast. The saints will have their carnal natures removed and the wicked will have committed the unpardonable sin. What a contrast! After 3.5 days of celebration, the seventh trumpet will sound on the 1,265th day, perhaps a Sunday. Jesus will resurrect the 144,000 and take them to Heaven. The seventh trumpet will sound in Heaven shortly after the 144,000 arrive in Heaven and an earthquake will swallow up 7,000 of Lucifer's officials. The seventh trumpet marks a very important transition in Earth's history. All that remains is the execution of justice. Remember, *during the Great Tribulation there will be no justice for God's people. Therefore, Jesus avenges their suffering and death.* Over a period of seventy days, the wicked and ultimately, planet Earth itself, will be totally destroyed.

Jesus has several purposes for the seven bowls and we will examine them when we study Prophecy 14:

1. Jesus will use the first five bowls to incrementally undo Lucifer's deception. Jesus will unmask the devil because He wants every wicked person to recognize and acknowledge that the glorious being masquerading as Almighty God is the devil himself. As you can imagine, forcing defiant people into this position will take a great deal of pain.

2. Jesus will use the seven last plagues to punish the wicked for defiance. No sovereign can tolerate open and defiant contempt within his kingdom. The wicked must be punished because they deliberately insulted and willfully defied the commandments of the Creator of the Universe who is King of kings and Lord of lords. For 1,260 days the clearest evidences of God's will and truth were set before all mankind, but the wicked refused to hear God's servants and they blasphemed the Holy Spirit. They willingly and knowingly refused to obey Almighty God. Not only this, they tortured and killed God's saints knowing that what they were doing was wrong! Now, the table turns. Almighty God will deal with these rebels. For seventy days, they will suffer in the extreme and there will be NO mercy! The defiant cannot escape drinking the bitter dregs of God's wrath.[152]

3. Finally, Jesus will repay the wicked for the suffering which they heaped upon His people. Justice demands that the

golden rule be applied. This rule declares: "As you did unto others, the same will be done unto you."¹⁵³ The pain and suffering, sorrow and death imposed upon God's saints during the Great Tribulation will be the equivalent of war crimes in God's sight. Therefore, Jesus will punish the wicked for crimes against humanity. Remember that the punishment inflicted on the wicked during the seven bowls does not affect or eliminate the restitution which will be extracted from the wicked at the end of the 1,000 years.

> Rev. 11:14

The second thing that must be discussed before considering the horrors of the third woe is that God's anger with the wicked is limited by His two laws of love. God does not extract revenge beyond the demands of justice.¹⁵⁴ God faithfully adheres to His two laws of love. Righteousness and justice are the foundation of His throne.¹⁵⁵ Restitution is a cornerstone of God's government of love. This is why God said in the Old Testament, **"But if there is serious injury, you are to take life for life, eye for eye, tooth for tooth, hand for hand, foot for foot, burn for burn, wound for wound, bruise for bruise."**¹⁵⁶ By closely studying God's actions, we see what pure love is and what pure love does and how pure love behaves – under all circumstances. God is righteous and pure; He demands the highest standards of conduct for Himself and from His creation.

Seventh Trumpet Sounds

{15} I heard the seventh trumpet sound and I heard loud voices in Heaven say, "The kingdom of the world has become the kingdom of our Lord and of his Christ, and he will reign for ever and ever."

> Rev. 11:15
>
> *And the seventh angel sounded; and there were great voices in heaven, saying, The kingdoms of this world are become the kingdoms of our Lord, and of his Christ; and he shall reign for ever and ever.*

Some Christians believe that Jesus received the kingdom of this world when He ascended to the Father after His resurrection. There is some confusion on this topic, so please consider the following:

In the beginning, Jesus created everything in the universe for the Father.¹⁵⁷ Jesus is the creative agent of the Godhead, but everything He created belonged to the Father. When Adam and Eve sinned, they were to be immediately executed because the Father has "a sudden death law."¹⁵⁸ The wages of sin is death by execution, but Jesus went to the Father and offered to be executed in man's place. The Father told Jesus that His plan for man's redemption required a perfect substitute. In other words, if Jesus perfectly carried out the Father's will, sinners could be saved if they put their faith in Christ's atonement and did their

Prophecy 9 - The Two Witnesses

Rev. 11:15

best to carry out the teachings of Jesus. (see Appendix C.) The Father also promised to give the world to Jesus if He successfully carried out His plans.

On the day that Adam and Eve sinned, Jesus relinquished His rights and privileges as a co-eternal member of the Godhead to the Father. Jesus subjected Himself to the Father's will and Jesus became known as the Son [the subject] of God.[159] The title, "Son of God" does not mean that the Father created Jesus or that Jesus is not equal to the Father. Jesus is fully God just like the Father. The Hebrew word *ben* (son) means subject – as a child is subject to the will of his parents or a citizen is subject to his nation's constitution or the will of His king. Jesus humiliated Himself [subjected Himself] to the Father's will for man's redemption and this is why the title, 'the Son of God' means, 'the Subject of God.' Four thousand years after sin began, Jesus came to Earth to carry out the will of the Father in His flesh[160] and just before going to the cross, Jesus prayed these words:

"Father, the time has come. Glorify your Son, that your Son may glorify you. For you granted him authority over all people that he might give eternal life to all those *you have given him*. . . . I have brought you glory on earth by completing the work you gave me to do. And now, Father, glorify me in your presence with the glory I had with you before the world began. I have revealed you to those whom you gave me out of the world. *They were yours*; *you gave them to me* and they have obeyed your word. . . . For I gave them the words you gave me and they accepted them. They knew with certainty that I came from you, and they believed that you sent me. . . . All I have is yours, and all you have is mine. And glory has come to me through them."[161]

When Jesus ascended to Heaven on Resurrection Sunday, the Father did not give the kingdom of the world to Jesus as many people think. Instead, He made Jesus the head of the church. Paul wrote, **"And God placed all things under his feet and appointed him to be head over everything for the church."**[162] During the first century following the ascension of Jesus, the disciples believed that Jesus had been given sovereign power over everything and they also believed that Jesus would shortly return to Earth. This understanding was not harmful, but it was not fact. Just before Jesus ascended to Heaven, He spoke to His disciples: **"Then Jesus came to** them and said, 'All authority in Heaven and on Earth has been given to me. Therefore go and make disciples of all nations, baptizing them in the name of the Father and of the Son and of the Holy Spirit."[163] The disciples heard these words, but they did not understand that the authority given to Jesus was limited to His church. The apostle Paul also thought that Jesus had received all authority after returning to Heaven. Paul did not understand the timing of apocalyptic prophecy when He wrote, **"And he [the Father] made known to us the mystery of his will according to his good pleasure, which he purposed in Christ, to be put into effect when the times will have reached their fulfillment– to bring all things in heaven and on earth together under one head, even Christ."**[164] (See commentary on Prophecy 2 for further discussion of the time when Christ is given sovereign power.)

Rev. 11:15

These and other Bible texts have given many people the idea that Jesus received the kingdom of this world when He ascended, but apocalyptic prophecy indicates this is not the case. The book of Daniel teaches that Jesus was found worthy to receive sovereign power in 1798.[165] Because the book of Daniel was sealed up until the time of the end,[166] the disciples and the apostle Paul could not possibly know certain things about the future. However, the disciples did understand that Jesus would be given all authority and the kingdom of this world, but no one could know the truth on this matter until the book of Daniel was unsealed.

All Bible writers have one flaw in common. They try to put everything shown to them in vision within the context of their knowledge or life span. Of course, an infinite God is not limited by time or our knowledge. So, the limitations of Bible writers are not a problem once we understand the four rules that govern the interpretation of apocalyptic prophecy. For example, Peter, John, Paul, and James had no idea that 2,000 years would pass before Jesus returned to Earth. Look at their thoughts: Paul wrote, **"What I mean, brothers, is that the time is short. From now on those who have wives should live as if they had none."**[167] John wrote, **"Dear children, this is the last hour; and as you have heard that the antichrist is coming, even now many antichrists have come. This is how we know it is the last hour."**[168] Peter wrote, **"The end of all things is near. Therefore be clear minded and self-controlled so that you can pray."**[169] James wrote, **"You too, be patient and stand firm, because the Lord's coming is**

Prophecy 9 - The Two Witnesses

> Rev. 11:15

> Rev. 11:16-18
>
> *And the four and twenty elders, which sat before God on their seats, fell upon their faces, and worshipped God, Saying, We give thee thanks, O Lord God Almighty, which art, and wast, and art to come; because thou hast taken to thee thy great power, and hast reigned. And the nations were angry, and thy wrath is come, and the time of the dead, that they should be judged, and that thou shouldest give reward unto thy servants the prophets, and to the saints, and them that fear thy name, small and great; and shouldest destroy them which destroy the earth.*

near."[170] Obviously, these godly men would not have written such things if they had known that Jesus' return would be 2,000 years in the future.

Earlier in this book, we examined Revelation 5. We found that Jesus was found worthy to receive the book sealed with seven seals in 1798 for several reasons. Jesus also began breaking the seven seals on The Book of Life in 1798. We have examined the alignment of the third seal with 1844, the alignment of the fourth seal and the commencement of the seven trumpets, and the alignment of the fifth seal with the sixth trumpet. After the Two Witnesses complete their work, the 144,000 will be taken to Heaven and then the seventh trumpet will sound. What a privilege and honor for *the 144,000 to be there and see Jesus receive the kingdom which the Father will give Him.* This is why the angels and the elders rejoice! **"The kingdom of the world has become the kingdom of our Lord and of his Christ, and he will reign for ever and ever."**[171]

{16} The twenty-four elders, who were seated on their thrones before God, fell on their faces and worshiped Him, {17} saying: "We give thanks to you, Lord God Almighty, the One who is and who was, because you have exercised your great authority and have *now begun* to reign [as King of kings and Lord of lords].

{18} I also heard the elders sing a passage from Isaiah: **"Come near, you nations, and listen; pay attention, you peoples! Let the Earth hear, and all that is in it, the world, and all that comes out of it! The Lord is angry with all nations; his wrath is upon all their armies. He will totally destroy them, he will give them over to slaughter. Their slain will be thrown out, their dead bodies will send up a stench; the mountains will be soaked with their blood. All the stars of the heavens will be dissolved and the sky rolled up like a scroll; all the starry host will fall like withered leaves from the vine, like shriveled figs from the fig tree. My sword has drunk its fill in the heavens; see, it descends in judgment on Edom** [my enemies]**, the people I have totally destroyed."**[172]

The elders continued, "Oh Lord God, we give thanks to you, the time has come for avenging the sacrificial blood of your martyrs. The number permitted to die during the fifth seal has been completed. The time has come to reward your servants, the 144,000, who stand before your throne. The time has come to reward your waiting saints on Earth and all who reverence your holy name; both small and great. Mercy has ended and justice has come. Destroy the whore and all who belong to her, destroy those who ruined the Earth with violence, hostility, murder, sexual immorality and every evil known to mankind."

{19} When the elders finished, I looked up into the sky and saw a marvelous sight. I was not alone as everyone on Earth could see God's temple in Heaven. Words cannot describe the dazzling glory that radiated from His temple. Inside the temple, in full view of everyone, was a golden box. Our eyes were drawn to that box because brilliant beams of light flashed from it. A loud voice said to the inhabitants of Earth, "Look at the Ark of God's covenant!"

> Rev. 11:19
> *And the temple of God was opened in heaven, and there was seen in his temple the ark of his testament: and there were lightnings, and voices, and thunderings, and an earthquake, and great hail.*

There has been considerable debate through the centuries on the whereabouts of the Ark of the Covenant. The Bible indicates the temple veil in Jerusalem was torn from top to bottom when Jesus was crucified,[173] but the Ark of the Covenant was not found in the Most Holy Place in Jerusalem's temple! God evidently took the Ark of the Covenant to Heaven for safe keeping after Israel rejected Messiah. For reasons why I believe that the Ark of Moses has been taken to Heaven for everyone to see at the seventh trumpet see this reference.[174]

The Ark of the Covenant was a small box overlaid with gold. God had it built shortly after Israel was delivered from Egypt. God had this special box made so that Israel would have a resting place for the two tablets of His Testimony, His covenant with mankind. When the Ark of the Covenant was on Earth, no one saw it other than Israel's high priests – and only then, once a year on the Day of Atonement. God prevented Israel from seeing the Ark of the Covenant because He did not want Israel worshiping a golden box or the two tablets of stone. Because the Ten Commandments are based on two laws of love, God's law is not effective unless it is written in the hearts of His subjects.[175]

Jesus will reveal the Ark of the Covenant to everyone on Earth at the seventh trumpet (1,265th day of the Great Tribulation). God's two laws of love are called a covenant (a promise) because they declare what pure love will do and will not do. When God's two laws are written in a person's heart, that person naturally lives in harmony with everything the law declares![176] The first four commandments reveal what pure love for God will produce and the last six reveal what pure love for your neighbor will produce. In other words, at Mount Sinai, God wrote a promise

> Rev. 11:19

on two tablets of stone. He declared what pure love will produce within man if man will follow the prompting of the Holy Spirit.

Many people claim to love God, but who determines what pure love will do? Love for God is not pure unless it produces results that conform to the first four commandments. Love for our neighbor is not pure unless it produces results that conform to the last six commandments. This is why the Ten Commandments are called a covenant. God *promises* that pure love will produce everything that is written in the Ten Commandments. When the carnal nature is removed, God's children will *naturally* do what is written in the Ten Commandments! This is why Paul wrote, **"Love is the fulfillment of the law!"**[177] Until the carnal nature is removed, God's children cannot consistently do what is written in the Ten Commandments, even though it is their greatest desire. This is why the sealing process is so important. During the Great Tribulation, everyone will be tested. Jesus wants to see who loves God and his neighbor with a pure heart. God will generously reward everyone who passes the two tests of love. Their carnal nature will be removed. God will then put a seal on that person and he will be free from falling back into the power of sin!

Consider this: A person can obey the Ten Commandments without *fulfilling* the Ten Commandments. For example, a person may not commit murder because the law says that murder is forbidden. Of course, avoiding murder (even if the action is not out of love) is beneficial for society, but avoiding murder is not the full intent of the law. The promise in God's covenant is this: If you love your neighbor as God loves you, you will never have a desire to commit murder. You would rather die for your neighbor than take his life. Thus, pure love fulfills the intent of the law and as a covenant, the Ten Commandments predict how pure love will be expressed in the human heart!

According to God, love is not a loosely defined sentiment that everyone defines to his own satisfaction. God governs the universe according to two eternal rules of love that are clearly defined. The world has all kinds of ideas about love, but God's definition of love is all that matters. God is love. This means that the actions of the Godhead are a demonstration of what love is and is not. Three co-eternal members of the Godhead live within these two laws and on the basis of their combined powers, they guarantee these two laws will never be amended and they will never cease to exist. The Father's goal is to bring fallen man back into harmony with these two laws so that our union and communion with the Godhead might be perfect!

God's two laws of love are so important that Jesus Himself descended to Mount Sinai to speak the Ten Commandments. To keep "the Testimony" from being altered by fallen man, Jesus wrote the two laws of love on two tablets of stone with His own finger. Moses knew the Ten Commandments were a covenant. Moses understood that if Israel surrendered to the ministry of the Holy Spirit, He would fill them with God's love and the outcome would be a nation reflecting God's two great commandments. When pure love is present, the obligation of law goes unnoticed! Think about this: Adam and Eve did not have a single conflict with God's laws of love before they fell, because God's laws were written in their hearts and minds. After Adam and Eve fell, they immediately came into conflict with God's laws of love at every turn because the carnal nature is hostile toward pure love. **"The sinful mind is hostile to God. It does not submit to God's law, nor can it do so. Those controlled by the sinful nature cannot please God."**[178]

God Shows the Ark of the Covenant to the World

Revelation 11:19 says, "Then God's temple in Heaven was opened and within His temple was seen the Ark of His Covenant. . . ." When we consider the timing and setting of this event, we have to ask what is the purpose and significance of showing the Ark of His covenant to the world? Before we proceed into this explanation, please review the sequence of events surrounding this amazing revelation:

1. The Two Witnesses are killed on the 1,260th day.

2. The wicked will celebrate for 3.5 days.

3. All of the wicked will be wearing the mark of the beast.

4. The 144,000 will be resurrected and taken to Heaven.

5. Seven thousand of Lucifer's officials will be killed by an earthquake.

6. The Ark of the Covenant will be seen and. . . .

7. The seven bowls will begin immediately.

Jesus will show the Ark of the Covenant to the world at the appointed time because it contains His two laws of love, the Ten

> Rev. 11:19

Commandments, written on two stone tablets with His own finger. In other words, Jesus will show the wicked "the Testimony" that condemned them. God wants the wicked to see "the two highest laws of the universe," the laws they rejected, despised and defied. Like King Belshazzar, the wicked will clearly understand that their actions have been examined and they did not measure up.[179] The seventh trumpet marks the end of the judgment of the living. It also marks the commencement of the third and final woe: The seven last plagues.

To put this event in a better perspective, we need to examine the origin and God's purpose for the Ark of the Covenant. Notice what Moses said to the Israelites before entering Canaan, **"The Lord gave me *two stone tablets inscribed by the finger of God.* On them were all the commandments *the Lord proclaimed to you* on the mountain out of the fire, on the day of the assembly. At the end of the forty days and forty nights, the Lord gave me *the two stone tablets, the tablets of the covenant.*"**[180]

When Moses came down from the mountain, **"He [Moses] took *the Testimony* [the Ten Commandments] and placed it in *the ark,* attached the poles to the ark and put the atonement cover over it. Then he brought *the ark* into the tabernacle and hung the shielding curtain and shielded *the ark of the Testimony* [from view], as the Lord commanded him."**[181] The Ark of the Covenant was "holy" because "God's presence" protected the Ark. Whenever the Israelite priests carried the ark from one location to another, the rest of the camp had to keep a distance of a thousand yards between themselves and the Ark of the Covenant.[182]

Millions of Christians have been led to believe the Ten Commandments were nailed to the cross with Jesus. They believe the Ten Commandments were part of "the old covenant" which was abolished when Jesus died. But ironically, most Christians believe that nine of the Ten Commandments should be obeyed! So here is the question: *If the Ten Commandments were abolished at the cross, why does God show the golden box containing the Ten Commandments to the world at the seventh trumpet?*

The answer is simple. There will be a great controversy during the Great Tribulation over the topic of worship. The Holy Spirit will demand (through the preaching of the 144,000) that everyone must obey God's two laws of love and this includes observing God's seventh-day rest (the fourth commandment).

Of course, obeying the Ten Commandments cannot produce salvation. However, when persecution and/or death is promised to everyone obeying God's Ten Commandments, faith and love for God will be tested and we know that it is through faith that we are saved! This is a critical point: When worship requires a sacrifice, when obeying God means the loss of family, friends, and possessions, faith is severely tested and those who pass the test of love and faith will be sealed and saved!

Rev. 11:19

The religious leaders of the world will also demand worship, but the worship which Babylon demands will be contrary to the worship that God demands. This is how the issue of worship will become a hotly debated topic during the Great Tribulation. Revelation 13:5-8 indicates that all who honor and observe God's Sabbath rest will suffer persecution. When the judgment of the living ends, God will open the temple in Heaven and show the wicked why they are evil in His sight. Wickedness occurs when God's two laws of love are violated. This is the testimony of His law and its conclusion is beyond impeachment or appeal.

When the surviving saints see the Ark of the Covenant beaming from Heaven's temple, they will rejoice because they will know that God's two laws of love are sealed within their hearts. The saints will know from personal experience why the Ten Commandments are called a covenant. They have been transformed, literally, by God's pure love. Their sinful natures have been removed and they find themselves in perfect harmony with God and His two laws of love. God's laws of love are noble, wise, honorable, and everlasting. **" 'This is the covenant I will make with the house of Israel after that time,' declares the Lord. *I will put my laws in their minds and write them on their hearts.* I will be their God, and they will be my people.' "**[183]

The wicked will not be able to hide themselves from the glory of this event. They will gaze at the Ark of the Covenant. This spectacle in the sky will leave them speechless and dumbfounded. They will be awestruck by the somber reality and importance of God's eternal laws. Mortals will remember their defiance against Almighty God, the King of kings and Lord of lords and will sense their impending doom. The wicked will realize that they rejected every opportunity to repent and that they rejected every overture made by the Holy Spirit who was prompting them to submit to God's two laws of love. The tattoos on their right hands (the mark of the beast) confirms they willingly

> Rev. 11:19

and knowingly chose to worship and obey a demon. This will be a horrible moment of truth for the wicked. During the seventy days of the seven bowls, the wicked will not forget the Ark of the Covenant. God has predetermined that those who rebel against Him will remember the law that testifies against them as they suffer the seven bowls of His wrath.[184]

{19 - Continued} After everyone on Earth saw the Ark of His Covenant, there came flashes of lightning, rumblings, peals of thunder, an earthquake, and a great hailstorm of burning meteors. Once again, fire from Heaven fell on particularly evil places and they were incinerated like Sodom and Gomorrah. The saints heard a loud voice. (One of the seven thunders?) It was Jesus. He said, **"Let him who does wrong, continue to do wrong; let him who is vile, continue to be vile; let him who does right, continue to do right; and let him who is holy, continue to be holy."**[185]

The Rules of Interpretation

Consider how the Rules of Interpretation (discussed in the Introduction of this book) are observed in this prophecy:

Rule One says an apocalyptic prophecy has a beginning point and ending point in time and the events within the prophecy occur in the order given. This prophecy has a beginning point in time, but the date cannot be precisely known. However, we do know from Revelation 7 and 8 that the 144,000 will be selected and sealed shortly before the commencement of the first four trumpets. We also know that the Two Witnesses will be empowered for 1,260 days and we know from Daniel 12:11,12 that the Great Tribulation will last 1,335 days. Therefore, it appears that Revelation 10:1 occurs a few days before the censer is cast down and the 144,000 are empowered.

Rule Two says a fulfillment only occurs when all of the specifications are met, and this includes the order stated in the prophecy. Of course, this prophecy has not yet begun, therefore it has not been fulfilled. On the other hand, we clearly see a chronological flow within this prophecy:

1. John saw Jesus come to Earth, he was told to eat the little book (the selection of the 144,000)

2. John was told to prophesy again (the 144,000 will proclaim an undefiled gospel)

3. John was given a measuring rod (the 144,000 will deliver a message that measures people)
4. God's Two Witnesses empowered for 1,260 days (the 144,000 are empowered by the Holy Spirit to proclaim God's two laws of love)
5. The Two Witnesses are killed (the ministry of the 144,000 ends)
6. The Two Witnesses are resurrected (the 144,000 will be resurrected and taken to Heaven)
7. The seventh trumpet sounds (the judgment of the living concludes)
8. Ark of the Covenant is shown (the wicked are condemned)
9. Physical phenomenon occur (lightning, rumblings, thunder, earthquake, hail)

Rule Three says apocalyptic language can be literal, analogous, or symbolic. To reach the intended meaning of a prophecy, the reader must consider (a) the context, (b) the use of parallel language in the Bible, and (c) if an element is thought to be symbolic, the Bible must interpret the symbol with a *relevant* text.

This prophecy uses all three types of language. For example, the two lampstands and the two olive trees are symbolic. There are relevant texts in the Bible to define these symbols. The great harlot symbolizes a great city (of refuge), but the Ark of the Covenant in God's temple is literal. This prophecy also uses parallel Scripture. Ezekiel and John ate books that were given to them. The message was sweet in their mouths (the truth is wonderful), but bitter in their stomachs (telling those who do not want to hear is very difficult). John's experience in this vision personifies the experience of the 144,000. The two lampstands and two olive trees personify the two laws of love and the Holy Spirit.

Rule Four says the presence or absence of the Jubilee Calendar determines how God measures time. The 1,260 days allotted for the empowerment of the two witnesses does not require translation because the 1,260 days occur *after* the Jubilee Calendar ended in 1994. (See Appendix A.)

References

1. Numbers 35:30; Hebrews 10:28; Matthew 18:15-17
2. 1 John 4:8,16
3. John 5:31-33,37,38
4. Acts 10:34,35
5. Matthew 24:14
6. 1 Kings 19:14-18
7. 1 Kings 18
8. 2 Thessalonians 2:9-11; Revelation 13:13,14
9. Ezekiel 13
10. Exodus 14:16-21
11. Acts 3:2-12
12. Numbers 20:11,12; Deuteronomy 31:2; Romans 7:14-23
13. Jesus is described as a mighty angel because He is the Archangel. 1 Thessalonian 4:16; John 5:25-28 (See also Chapter 2 in my book, *Jesus: The Alpha and The Omega*. You can freely download this chapter at: http://www.wake-up.org/Alpha/Chapter1.htm.)
14. Compare Daniel 10:7 with Acts 9:7.
15. The rainbow suggests the presence of divinity, see Revelation 4:3. (See also pages 108-114 in my book, *A study on the Seven Trumpets, Two Witnesses and Four Beasts*. You can freely download this chapter at: http://www.wake-up.org/Revelation/RevWitnesses.pdf.)
16. John 12:28-30
17. Genesis 22:16; Jeremiah 22:5
18. John 1:1-14; Hebrews 1:2; Colossians 1:13-17; Ephesians 1:9-11
19. This delay began in Revelation 7:2,3. Please compare with Daniel 12:7. The 1,335 days mentioned in Daniel 12:11,12 begin with this declaration.
20. Daniel 8:17,19; Luke 21:23. Please compare with Isaiah 24:1-6.
21. Luke 21:22; Colossians 3:5,6; Ephesians 5:6
22. For parallel texts, see Acts 2:17-21 and Joel 2:28-32.

23. 2 Corinthians 5:1-5
24. Matthew 27:66
25. Hebrews 8:10,11; 1 John 3:2,3
26. Genesis 3:21; 15:6
27. Hebrews 7:25
28. Genesis 15:6
29. See a parallel in Ezekiel 2 and 3. See also Deuteronomy 18:18-22.
30. See parallel experience in Ezekiel 3:14,15.
31. Daniel 9:3
32. See Zechariah 3:7,8 for a parallel. God spoke to Joshua and those with him as though they were people that would later appear on Earth.
33. The Greek preposition *epi* can be and should be translated 'before' instead of 'about' in this passage. (See also the KJV translation and Revelation 10:11.)
34. Revelation 14:6,7
35. Revelation 14:5
36. Hebrews 4:12,13; Matthew 5:3-11; Revelation 22:11
37. Isaiah 6:5-12
38. Revelation 2:9; Matthew 7:16-23
39. For a discussion on the holy city representing God's people, see commentary following Revelation 11:8 in this prophecy. (See also Revelation 13:5 for confirmation on the 42 months.)
40. Deuteronomy 23:2-8
41. John 10:14-16; 14:21-27
42. Revelation 13:5-7; Daniel 12:7.
43. John 16:1-3
44. Genesis 37:34; 1 Kings 21:27; Psalm 69:7-13
45. Daniel 12:7
46. Matthew 22:37-39
47. Deuteronomy 31:26
48. Daniel 9:11-13; 1 John 3:4; Romans 7:7-12
49. Genesis 31:44-48; Deuteronomy 31:19,26; Isaiah 8:20

50. 1 Corinthians 13:3
51. 2 Corinthians 5:17
52. 1 Peter 1:22-2:2
53. Matthew 12:31,32
54. Romans 8:26,27
55. See Numbers 35:30.
56. Matthew 12:31,32, 43-45; Hebrews 10:26
57. Romans 1:18-32
58. Leviticus 4:13,14,20; Romans 2:14,15; James 4:17
59. James 4:17
60. Deuteronomy 17:6; 19:15; 2 Corinthians 13:1
61. Revelation 9:20,21; 19:19-21
62. Zechariah 4:1-14
63. Exodus 19:4-6; Isaiah 42:6,7; Matthew 5:14
64. Psalm 19:7
65. Isaiah 42:6; 49:6
66. Galatians 3:28,29
67. Matthew 23:37,38; Ephesians 2:10-22; Galatians 3:28,29; Revelation 2:5
68. Judges 7
69. Acts 14:3
70. Revelation 3:10
71. John 8:13-18
72. See KJV Deuteronomy 11:14; Joel 2:23; James 5:7
73. Ephesians 4:11-16
74. Joel 2:27-29
75. Romans 8:5-8
76. Hebrews 8:10
77. Matthew 22:34
78. Revelation 14:5
79. James 5:17,18
80. Isaiah 14:12-17; Ezekiel 28:12-19; Daniel 8:9-13; 11:36-45; 2 Thessalonians 2:2-12; Revelation 9:1-11; 13:11-18; 17:11-17; 20:2

81. Matthew 24:24-26
82. Mark 8:35; Revelation 13:15
83. Revelation 9:20,21, insertion mine
84. Zechariah 4:6
85. KJV Deuteronomy 11:14; Joel 2:23; James 5:7
86. 2 Chronicles 16:9
87. Acts 5:32; Romans 8:16
88. Psalm 19:7,8
89. Deuteronomy 31:24-26
90. Exodus 31:18, italics mine
91. Ezekiel 18:4
92. Ecclesiastes 9:5,6
93. Psalm 115:17
94. Revelation 2:11; 20:14
95. John 11:11-15; 1 Corinthians 15:50-55; John 5:25-29; 2 Peter 3:4; Revelation 20:5
96. John 11:11
97. Malachi 4:3; 2 Peter 2:6
98. 2 Corinthains 5:10
99. 1 Thessalonians 4:13-18
100. Revelation 19:21
101. Revelation 22:12
102. You can freely download this chapter at: http://www.wake-up.org/Alpha/Chapter13.htm.
103. James 4:17
104. 1 Timothy 4:2
105. Genesis 2:1-3
106. James 4:17
107. John 3:16
108. John 3:21, insertion mine
109. John 16:8
110. Revelation 9:15
111. Revelation 6:9-11; 16:4-7; 18:24, 20:4

112. Deuteronomy 28:15-28; Psalm 79:1-3; Jeremiah 19:7; Ezekiel 29:5
113. Revelation 19:17-21
114. Revelation 17:18
115. Revelation 12:1-6
116. Revelation 17:3-6
117. Revelation 17:3-6
118. Revelation 13:14
119. Revelation 17:16
120. See Numbers 35.
121. Genesis 4:14-17
122. Psalm 48:8; 14 and 91.
123. For a parallel passage, see Isaiah 1:21-26.
124. Revelation 21:2,10
125. Ephesians 2:19,20
126. John 11:25,26
127. Compare Revelation 11:2,3 with Revelation 13:5-7. See also Daniel 12:7.
128. Genesis 18:16 - 19:13
129. See chapters 8-11 and 14 in Exodus.
130. Matthew 5:20; 6:1-4
131. John 8:3-11; Matthew 19:7,8; Matthew 23
132. John 3:19-21; 19:5-7; Acts 3:13-15
133. John 11:50
134. John 3:20
135. Compare Revelation 11:10 with 14:11.
136. Matthew 27:19
137. Revelation 14:11
138. Revelation 18:4,5
139. Esther 9:17-32
140. Genesis 20:7
141. Genesis 6:8-22
142. 2 Peter 1:20,21; Joel 2:27-30

143. Revelation 10:7; 11:18; 16:6; 18:24
144. Matthew 7:28,29; 11:7-14
145. Leviticus 23:10,11; Numbers 28:26
146. Leviticus 23:16
147. 1 Corinthians 15:20
148. Revelation 14:4
149. Genesis 1:5
150. Compare the timing in Revelation 14:1-5 with 19:1-8 for evidence showing the 144,000 are in Heaven prior to the Second Coming.
151. For a parallel event, see Numbers 16:24-34.
152. Revelation 14:9,10; 15:1,4
153. Matthew 7:12
154. Romans 12:19
155. Psalm 89:14
156. Exodus 21:23-25; Luke 12:2-9
157. Hebrews 1:1,2
158. Genesis 2:17
159. Psalm 2:7-12; Hebrews 5:5
160. John 6:38
161. John 17:1-10, italics mine
162. Ephesians 1:22
163. Matthew 28:18,19
164. Ephesians 1:9,10
165. Daniel 7:13,14
166. Daniel 12:4,9
167. 1 Corinthians 7:29
168. 1 John 2:18
169. 1 Peter 4:7
170. James 5:8
171. Revelation 11:15

172. Isaiah 34:1-5 Note: The title Edom is another name for Easu and it is sometimes used in the Old Testament to identify those who despise God's covenant. See Genesis 25:34.

173. Mark 15:38

174. The Bible does not explicitly say that the Ark of the Covenant was taken to Heaven after Jeremiah hid it from the approaching Babylonians. Contrary to the claims of many, here are nine reasons why this author is convinced the Ark of the Covenant was taken to Heaven after Israel rejected Messiah and it awaits a glorious display before the whole world at the appointed time.

    1. During the Great Tribulation, travel and communication for ordinary people will be basically nonexistent. There would be no value of finding the Ark in or near Jerusalem during the Great Tribulation if only a few thousand people in the Middle East will hear about it and only a few thousand get to see it. Other than local interest, there would be no global impact.

    2. If, prior to the Great Tribulation, the Ark of the Covenant was found in a cave and put on display in a museum in Jerusalem, it would gain worldwide attention, but for the wrong reason. It would be regarded as a historical relic. As a religious relic, the Ark of the Covenant would have no authority. Its end time value would not be understood. Therefore, in terms of defining rebellion or producing guilt on the wicked, the global impact would be zero if the Ark of the Covenant was found on Earth prior to the Great Tribulation.

    3. If the Ark of the Covenant is found prior to the Great Tribulation, the Jews would immediately lay claim to the Ark and they would do whatever is necessary to take possession of it. They would likely keep it in a place that had limited access. The result would be the same as it is now – the Ark would essentially remain hidden from view and worse, the religious property of the Jews. I say "worse" because most Christians think the Ten Commandments are Jewish laws anyway. In terms of defining rebellion or producing guilt, there would be no impact on the world in this scenario.

4. If the Ark of the Covenant was found prior to the Great Tribulation and no one was killed after touching it (as was Uzzah - see 1 Chronicles 13:10), this would prove that God's power did not rest on the Ark. This would also prove that the Ark is nothing more than a religious relic. This would give many Christians the proof they need that the Ten Commandments are null and void, because millions believe the Ten Commandments were nailed to the cross. Again, in terms of defining rebellion or producing guilt, there would be no global impact in this scenario.

5. The only people permitted to touch the Ark were the descendants of Kohath. (Numbers 4:15) Even an ordinary Levite could not touch the Ark. So, if the Ark were found on Earth prior to the Great Tribulation, who could move it or handle it if God's power still rests upon it? If God's power does not rest upon the laws which He wrote with His own finger, the Ten Commandments are interesting stone tablets and nothing more. In this scenario, we are back to the issue of a religious relic or the worship of a religious object.

6. I believe God took the Ark to Heaven because He plans to show it to the whole world at the appointed time. We know that God took Enoch and Elijah to Heaven, so surely He can take a small golden box to Heaven. It seems obvious from Revelation's context that when the Ark is unveiled and shown to the world from Heaven's temple, it will not be regarded as a relic by any scoffer at that time. It will be a divine display from the Lawmaker Himself condemning all who refused to submit to the terms and conditions of His two laws of love.

7. Imagine a brilliant Ark with its two stone tablets surrounded with blazing light in the sky. The scene would be an impressive and awesome sight. A display of the Ark will confirm the faith of the obedient – there is the law they accepted by faith. On the other hand, this display will condemn the wicked who willingly defied the sovereign authority of Jesus. The wicked will shiver with guilt. Showing the Ark of the Covenant to everyone on Earth is designed to be an ominous event

that marks the close of salvation. The global impact will be huge! A museum piece hidden under a blanket can not achieve this.

8. Another point to consider is that Jesus Himself delivered the Ten Commandments from Mt. Sinai with such power and majesty that the Israelites thought they were going to die. (Exodus 20:18,19) Another Mt. Sinai experience is coming again. The same thing will happen when the Law Maker of the Universe shows the Ark of His Covenant from Heaven's temple.

9. Finally, Jesus wrote the two tablets of stone placed in the Ark of the Covenant. (Deuteronomy 10:4) This makes the Ten Commandments in the Ark of the Covenant originals, not copies. I conclude that the Ark of the Covenant in Heaven is the original Ark built by Moses and it will be unveiled and shown to the whole world at the appointed time. God Himself will show mankind what He thinks of His two laws of love. This is why I believe the Ark of the Covenant is not on Earth.

175. Hebrews 8:10
176. Hebrews 8:10,11
177. Romans 13:10
178. Romans 8:7,8
179. Daniel 5:27-30
180. Deuteronomy 9:10,11 See also Exodus 31:18.
181. Exodus 40:20,21
182. Joshua 3:3,4,11-17
183. Hebrews 8:10
184. See Leviticus 26:14-43 and Ezekiel 18:20-28 for God's thoughts on defiance.
185. Revelation 22:11

Prophecy 10

The Baby Jesus
Revelation 12:1-6

Beginning point in time: Just before Jesus was born

Ending point in time: 1798

Summary: This is a story about Lucifer (the dragon), Christ (the male child), and the people of God (the woman). Although it is not explicitly said in this story, Lucifer hated Christ long before Jesus was born. This prophecy begins with Lucifer attempting to kill Jesus at birth, but he fails. Lucifer then focuses his hatred for Jesus on the bride of Christ, but she flees into the wilderness to a place prepared for her. For 1,260 years, God's people overcame persecution and difficult circumstances through faith in Jesus.

Introduction: Prophecy 10 provides a foundation for Prophecy 11 in the same way that Prophecy 1 (Daniel 2) provides a foundation for Prophecy 2 (Daniel 7). We have seen, in this book, how repetition and enlargement allows God to review many important concepts with the fewest possible words. This technique is important to remember because in John's day, every copy of Scripture was made by hand. Therefore, shorter books meant less work and repetition and enlargement required fewer words. On the surface, this prophecy appears to be short and simple, but its depth may surprise you.

This prophecy reveals two essential facts in a mere six verses. First, in broad strokes, it chronicles the passage of eighteen centuries, from the birth of Jesus in 4 B.C. down to 1798.[1] Second, it speaks volumes about the actions of Lucifer. Most Christians believe in a devil, but few have carefully studied his clever and determined efforts. Some Christians unintentionally derail the purpose of this prophecy by forcing Lucifer's "agents" into the spotlight. In other words, they put King Herod and papal Rome at center stage, but this should not be done. Jesus and Lucifer are the central characters in this prophecy. The agents involved are secondary to the story. Keep in mind that before the world was created, Jesus and Lucifer became protagonists. They have been engaged in a deadly conflict for a very long time.

Lucifer is a fallen angel, a demon that human beings cannot see with the naked eye. Of course, God clearly sees the devil and He wants the final generation to understand Lucifer's prowess before he is released from the Abyss (the spirit realm) to physically appear on Earth. As you already know, during the first four trumpets, a crisis government (a beast called Babylon) will rise to power. When this occurs, the devil will take over. He will give Babylon its great power, authority, and throne.[2] He will accomplish this by using leaders who are controlled by their carnal nature. The carnal nature loves sexual immorality, money, power, and fame and Lucifer knows it.

Jesus will permit the devil to exercise great influence over Babylon during the Great Tribulation because the Holy Spirit will exercise great influence over all people. Lucifer will empower Babylon while Jesus empowers the 144,000 and this will sharpen the contrast between right and wrong. Jesus will not allow either party to override anyone's power of choice. The devil will have one objective for Babylon. He intends to destroy God's people, the remnant of the woman.[3] Through his agents, (the leaders of Babylon and those who obey them), the devil will wage a war against God's people for 42 miserable months.[4]

God placed Prophecy 10 in the Bible so that Christians can look behind a curtain and see what really occurred when Jesus was born. Lucifer is a predator and a heartless thug. He will do whatever it takes to destroy God's purposes and people. One interesting part of this story is that the devil is able to get agents to unwittingly carry out his wishes.[5] Therefore, God wants everyone to know and understand that there is a determined and intelligent demon at work who cannot be seen (at the present time). Events transpiring before our eyes are not always what they appear to be. Every day, we see and hear about horrible crimes and the secular mind interprets these atrocities as evil people doing evil things, but there is far more to evil behavior than this. Remember how King Herod decreed that all of the baby boys in Bethlehem under the age of two were to be killed.[6] Secular historians claim that Herod was a wicked man who committed this atrocity to protect his throne from a messianic baby, but the Bible pulls back the veil and reveals something far more sinister. Lucifer controlled Herod. Herod actually carried out Lucifer's desire to kill Baby Jesus. *Herod did not act on his own.* Over time, the king had come under Lucifer's demonic control and Herod's predatory behavior reveals the depth of his demon possession. *The clearest evidence of demonic possession is predatory violence.* Think about this: If the 144,000 will be the "arms and legs" of the Two Witnesses, it stands to reason that demon possessed people will serve as Lucifer's "arms and legs" during the Great Tribulation.

The Sequence

{1} I looked up into the sky and an awesome drama occurred. Although I did not see the origin of this drama, the story implied there was an ongoing conflict between Christ and Lucifer long before Mary gave birth to Jesus. As I watched, I saw a beautiful woman dressed as a bride. She was wearing white linen that was as bright as the Sun. She stood with the moon under her feet and on her head she wore a golden *stephanos* (Greek: a winner's crown, a crown of victory) containing twelve stars. {2} She was pregnant, and cried out in pain because she was about to give birth.

{3} Then another character appeared in the sky. I saw an enormous red dragon with seven heads and ten horns wearing seven *diadema* (Greek: the crown of a sovereign or a king, seven crowns indicating sovereign authority) on his seven heads. {4} The great red dragon had astonishing ability and power. In fact, before Jesus created the world, his mighty tail caused a third of God's angels to be cast out of Heaven and flung to the Earth. The dragon knew that the woman was about to give birth to his archenemy and he was prepared. He stood in front of the woman who was about to give birth so that he might devour her child the moment it was born.

> **Rev. 12:1-2**
> *And there appeared a great wonder in heaven; a woman clothed with the sun, and the moon under her feet, and upon her head a crown of twelve stars: And she being with child cried, travailing in birth, and pained to be delivered.*
>
> **Rev. 12:3-4**
> *And there appeared another wonder in heaven; and behold a great red dragon, having seven heads and ten horns, and seven crowns upon his heads. And his tail drew the third part of the stars of heaven, and did cast them to the earth: and the dragon stood before the woman which was ready to be delivered, for to devour her child as soon as it was born.*

> **Rev. 12:5-6**
>
> *And she brought forth a man child, who was to rule all nations with a rod of iron: and her child was caught up unto God, and to his throne. And the woman fled into the wilderness, where she hath a place prepared of God, that they should feed her there a thousand two hundred and threescore days.*

{5} The woman gave birth to a male child who will someday rule all nations with an iron scepter.[7] After living on Earth for a few years, God snatched the woman's child from Earth and put Him on His throne.[8] {6} When the dragon saw that he could not destroy Jesus, the dragon focused his wrath on the woman. To escape the dragon's fury, the woman fled to the wilderness, to a desolate place that God had prepared for her. Against all odds, the woman survived because God sustained her for 1,260 years (A.D. 538-1798).[9]

The woman standing on the moon represents the people of God, the bride of Christ.[10] This is a cosmic drama, the woman is not on Earth. Contrary to what many people believe, she does not represent Mary, the mother of Jesus. She represents God's people from Eden lost to Eden restored. According to God's promise, Jesus came through the offspring of faithful Abraham at the appointed time.[11] At the appointed time, Jesus will return to Earth and all of God's people will be united with the Lamb at a great wedding banquet in Heaven.[12] The wedding of the Lamb and His church will occur at the Second Coming. The bride's brilliant dress represents Christ's righteousness. Jesus Himself provides the prerequisite wedding garment to each person who reverently surrenders to the authority of the Holy Spirit.[13] The moon under the bride's feet is a faithful witness of God's promise.[14] The woman stands on a promise that has no end: *If you will be my people, I will be your God.*[15] Her *stephanos* (golden crown) signifies the victory that comes through faith in Christ and the twelve stars represent the twelve tribes of Israel.[16] The 1,260 day/years in the wilderness represent the Dark Ages – a period of time during which God permitted His people to be scattered and persecuted. This time period is the same period granted to the little horn in Daniel 7:25.[17]

Before we can appreciate the contents of this vision, we need to understand two important foundational points.

1. Before Earth was created, a rebellion occurred in Heaven. Lucifer caused this rebellion. He became jealous of Jesus and through clever lies and insinuations, he led one-third of the angels to have contempt toward God. (The tail (tale) of the great red dragon swept many innocent angels into his mutiny.) Lucifer's followers were cast out of Heaven because of their defiance and some time later, Earth was created. (See Prophecy 12 for a discussion on this subject.)

2. After Jesus created Adam and Eve, Lucifer preyed on Eve and led her to sin. Then, Eve led Adam into sin. Because Adam and Eve sinned without defiance, the Father and Jesus immediately initiated the "Plan of Redemption." The Father had devised this plan long before sin began because He foreknew sin would occur. Jesus volunteered to die in man's place and the Father accepted Jesus' offer provided that Jesus agreed to do exactly as the Father decreed. If Jesus deviated from any part of the plan, humanity would have no further opportunity for salvation. Jesus willingly subjected Himself to whatever the Father required. In return, the Father promised to give all of the redeemed and even the planet to Jesus if He successfully carried out the Plan of Redemption.[18]

Rev. 12:5-6

Now that these foundational points have been presented, certain elements of this prophecy will become obvious. It is easy to see why Lucifer desperately wanted to kill Jesus as soon as He was born. Lucifer hated Jesus long before He was born on Earth and Lucifer wanted to terminate the plan of redemption before it could be carried out![19]

The Plan of Redemption is far more involved than the earthly ministry of Jesus and His death on the cross. Jesus became the Lamb of God on the day that Adam and Eve sinned.[20] Prior to His birth, Jesus managed the affairs of mankind from Heaven. Many significant events show that Jesus was working toward fulfilling the Plan of Salvation. For example, Jesus sent the flood in Noah's day, He spoke from Mt. Sinai, and He came to Earth to live as a man. After Jesus returned to Heaven, His service continued. Jesus destroyed Jerusalem in A.D. 70 and Jesus limited the efforts of the little horn to destroy His people for 1,260 years. Then, in 1798, Jesus was found worthy to receive sovereign power and the book sealed with seven seals. In 1844, Jesus opened the Books of Record and began judging the dead. We learned in Prophecy 8 that the seven angels who stand before Jesus were given seven trumpets in 1994. (See Appendix A.) Soon, the fourth seal will be broken and everyone will see the sovereign power of Jesus. Jesus has been working for the redemption of mankind for 6,000 years!

The Plan of Redemption's scope is huge and it has many objectives and dimensions. For example, the plan includes the exoneration of God's character and government; a topic we examined in Prophecy 6. The Plan of Salvation involves the test-

> Rev. 12:5-6

ing of mankind; a topic we examined in Prophecy 7. The plan of salvation involves passing eternal judgment on mankind; a topic we examined in Prophecy 9. The plan of salvation calls for the faithful to be redeemed and the defiant to be destroyed, but these objectives must be completed in such a way that everyone finally agrees that God is love. The plan also calls for a new Heaven and a new Earth to be created and each step in the plan of redemption must be perfectly "full-filled" before the entire plan can be declared "finished."[21]

The Rules of Interpretation

Consider how the Rules of Interpretation (discussed in the Introduction of this book) are observed in this prophecy:

Rule One says an apocalyptic prophecy has a beginning point and ending point in time and the events within the prophecy occur in the order given. This prophecy begins with the birth of Christ and ends in 1798. The events described within this prophecy occur in chronological order.

Rule Two says a fulfillment only occurs when all of the specifications are met, and this includes the order stated in the prophecy. Because all of the elements given in this prophecy are in the past, we can say this prophecy has been fulfilled.

Rule Three says apocalyptic language can be literal, analogous or symbolic. To reach the intended meaning of a prophecy, the reader must consider (a) the context, (b) the use of parallel language in the Bible, and (c) if an element is thought to be symbolic, the Bible must interpret the symbol with a *relevant* text. This prophecy uses all three types of language: symbolic, analogous and literal.

For example, the woman and the dragon are symbols. The woman represents the bride of Christ[22] and the great red dragon represents Lucifer.[23] The Sun and the moon are used in this prophecy as cosmic props because this scene contains *concepts that have their origin in Heaven*. The woman in this prophecy is not Mary, the mother of Jesus. According to Rule Four, it is impossible for Mary, herself, to be chased into the desert for 1,260 years. The woman is clothed with brilliance as bright as the Sun, indicating her wedding garment represents the righteousness and purity of Jesus.[24] She wears a crown of victory having twelve stars. These stars represent the twelve tribes and from them, 144,000 people will shine like the stars![25] The woman stands on the moon,[26] a witness of God's faithful promise of redemption. Her Son is Jesus – who was caught up to God's throne and will one day, rule all nations with a rod of iron[27] (meaning unbreakable rulership).

Consider this: Revelation's story concerns a lamb and a dragon. The great red dragon is Lucifer. Even though King Herod was involved in Lucifer's efforts to kill baby Jesus, Herod is not identified in this vision and neither is the Holy Roman Empire (the agency that Lucifer used to chase the woman into the wilderness for 1,260 years). It is a violation of Rule Three to force the identity of the great red dragon beyond the definition given in Scripture. (See Revelation 12:9.) Do not confuse the Lamb of God with His church. The Lamb is Jesus. The woman represents His people. The male child is Jesus, whom God snatched up to His throne to serve as our High Priest. This vision tells an amazing story in six verses! It is a story that illuminates an ongoing conflict between Christ and Satan. It is a story of an angry dragon that attempts to destroy baby Jesus the moment He is born and it is a story of God in the form of a human being taken to Heaven and God's throne. Ultimately, the story ends with Jesus ruling with an iron scepter (an endless and unbreakable rule). When properly understood, the story is amazing and beautiful.

Rule Four says the presence or absence of the Jubilee Calendar determines how God measures time. The 1,260 days mentioned in verse 6 require translation because they occur prior to 1994 while the Jubilee Calendar is operating. Therefore, 1,260 days must equal 1,260 years. These 1,260 years perfectly align with the time, times, and half a time mentioned in Daniel 7:25 and Revelation 12:14. The woman fled to the wilderness to escape the dragon's persecution in Revelation 12:6 and the saints were handed over to the little horn in Daniel 7:25.

References

1. See Prophecies 2 and 6 for information on the importance of 1798.
2. Revelation 13:2
3. Revelation 12:17
4. Revelation 13:5-7
5. Ephesians 6:12
6. Matthew 2:16
7. Revelation 19:15
8. Hebrews 8:1
9. Daniel 7:25; Revelation 12:14
10. Revelation 22:17; Genesis 3:15.
11. Galatians 3:16; 4:4
12. Revelation 19:6-8
13. Malachi 4:2; Romans 1:17; Genesis 15:6; Romans 5:10
14. Psalm 89:34-37
15. Jeremiah 7:23; 30:22; Revelation 21:7
16. Galatains 3:28,29; James 1:1,2;1; Daniel 12:3; Philippians 2:14-16
17. See also Revelation 12:14.
18. Psalm 2:7-12; John 17:3-10
19. The Plan of Redemption required Jesus to experience and suffer far more than God's people would ever face on Earth. It also required Jesus to experience *the penalty* that the wicked would experience. Remember, there is a difference between the penalty for sin and the consequences of sin. Jesus was not required to suffer the consequences of sin because He is not the author of sin. The author of sin (Lucifer, the scapegoat) will receive this judgment when the sins of the saints are put upon his head at the end of sin's drama. Jesus was required to face and overcome extreme temptation, suffer the harshest persecution, live a perfect sinless life and die the second death. (See Luke 4:1,2; Hebrews 2:18; 5:7,8; 2 Corinthians 5:21; Romans 1:17; 5:10; 6:23 and Revelation 21:8.)
20. Psalm 2:7-12; Revelation 13:8

21. Revelation 21:6
22. Revelation 19:7; 21:2; 21:9; 22:17
23. Revelation 12:9
24. Revelation 19:8; Matthew 13:43; 22:13
25. Daniel 12:3; Revelation 7:4-8; Philippians 2:14-16
26. Psalm 89:35-37
27. Revelation 19:15

Prophecy 11

The Rise of Babylon

Revelation 12:7-14:5

Beginning point in time: Resurrection Sunday, A.D. 30

Ending point in time: 1,265th day of the Great Tribulation

Summary: This apocalyptic prophecy describes three types of kingdoms: Political, religious, and demonic. The first type lasted approximately 1,000 years (605 B.C.- 538 A.D.). During this time, *political* leaders governed world empires (represented by the four beasts in Daniel 7). The second type lasted 1,260 years (538-1798). During this time, *religious* leaders dominated the nations of Europe (the little horn in Daniel 7). The third and final type of kingdom will last 42 months and a *demon* will dominate it. This progression speaks volumes.

The final kingdom will have two phases. During Phase I, Lucifer will achieve an important objective through the world's religious and political leaders. After the first four trumpets demolish the infrastructures of Earth and 1.75 billion people have been killed, the whole world will be in a state of panic and trauma. The devil will seize the moment to bring the whole world under the jurisdiction of one government. The book of Revelation calls this government Babylon. To appease God's wrath, the leaders of the world will unite in a common effort to eliminate the sinful behaviors they believe made God angry. Once this union becomes functional, the devil will inspire the leaders of Babylon to create and implement "sin-less" laws to appease God's wrath. Because the world will be very fearful of God, these laws will seem "reasonable and appropriate," but they will quickly put God's saints in a dire situation. The leaders of Babylon will not realize, at first, the unintended consequences of their laws. The laws of Babylon will stand in direct opposition to the laws of God. *Lucifer's objective during Phase I is to identify and punish all who choose to obey the eternal gospel.* Civil authorities, like police officers or militia in each locality, will enforce the laws of Babylon. They will do as they are commanded (even after many within their ranks realize that what they are do-

Jesus' Final Victory

ing is wrong) for fear of losing their job and/or being punished by their commanders.

Phase II will begin when Lucifer physically appears on Earth with his angels. John describes the physical appearing of the devil in three different places throughout the book of Revelation[1] and each reference reveals a new dimension about this wily foe. Masquerading as Almighty God, Lucifer will betray the leadership of Babylon so he can establish a counterfeit theocracy during the sixth trumpet. The devil will abolish all the religions and governments of the world. During Phase II, there will be one lord, one faith, and one baptism; a one-world-church-state. For a short time, the devil will rule over the world as king of kings and lord of lords. Everyone will do as he says or die.

Prophecy 11 describes the transition of Lucifer from an invisible state to a visible state. The devil will appear physically as a majestic being wearing a glorious garment of brilliant light![2] Jesus permits the devil to appear so that mankind can observe his words and actions. Because Lucifer is evil incarnate, even a wicked person will learn for himself that Lucifer is a grossly evil super power.

This prophecy begins on Resurrection Sunday and it reaches to the time when the 144,000 ascend on the 1,265th day of the Great Tribulation. God has given us this prophecy because He wants us to study and anticipate Lucifer's actions even though he is currently invisible. The devil is extremely clever and powerful. The world has not seen anything that even remotely compares with the physical appearing of Lucifer. He will come down from the sky, attended by millions of demons (fallen angels). They will be very large in stature, perhaps fifteen feet tall.[3] They will physically dwarf the people of Earth and worse, guns and artillery cannot kill them.[4] The whole world will find out that human beings are no match for fallen angels. Lucifer will take over the world and no one can thwart him.

Introduction: This prophecy consists of five events that occur in chronological order.

1. The devil is cast out of Heaven (verses 7-12)
2. The devil persecutes the woman for 1,260 years (verses 13-16)

3. The devil wages war on the remnant of the woman (verses 12:17-13:10)
4. The devil physically appears, sets up his theocracy and implements the mark of the beast (verses 13:11-18)
5. The 144,000 celebrate in a victory ceremony in Heaven (verses 14:1-14:5)

At first, it might seem strange that the victory celebration of the 144,000 is part of this prophecy because the first four events in this prophecy focus on Lucifer's actions. God often embeds an event within a prophecy to provide additional information that we could not otherwise know. For example, if you recall, the seventh trumpet is embedded in Prophecy 10 instead of Prophecy 9 where the other six trumpets are located. Similarly, the seventh seal is embedded in Prophecy 7 instead of Prophecy 6 which contains the six seals. When God inserts a "strange" event in a prophecy, He is actually highlighting the timing and importance of the strange event. I believe the victory celebration of the 144,000 is included in this prophecy because the 144,000 will be victorious over Lucifer's demonic efforts to stop them! With God's help, ordinary human beings will not only prevail against Lucifer and his demons, they will win the war!

The coming victory celebration of the 144,000 may not seem to be "all that important" today, but a day is coming when their victory celebration will serve as a powerful beacon during a very depressing time. During the sixth trumpet, Lucifer will appear to meet his objectives. He will abolish the religions and governments of the world, kill a third of mankind, and set up a counterfeit theocracy. Even more distressing, many of the remnant of the woman (the saints) will be killed and most, if not all, of the 144,000 will also be martyrs. Thankfully, this dismal situation is not the end of this story! Victory day will surely come. When the remaining saints see the 144,000 resurrected and taken to Heaven, the saints will be overjoyed! When wicked murderers see the 144,000 taken to Heaven, they will become terrified and panic stricken. The resurrection and ascension of the 144,000 is pivotal in this story because it marks the end of Lucifer's success. After he gathers the "first fruits" to Heaven, Jesus will methodically destroy Babylon and the wicked with the seven bowls of justice. Jesus will avenge the suffering of His saints.[5]

Structurally, this prophecy is similar to Prophecy 7. If you remember, Prophecy 7 contained three elements which seemed at first, to have no connection:

1. The sealing of the 144,000
2. A numberless multitude standing around God's throne
3. The breaking of the seventh seal

We discovered in Prophecy 7 (the selection and sealing of the 144,000) that these three elements are intimately connected. For example, the breaking of the seventh seal has to occur *after* the numberless multitude are taken to Heaven. This is true because John saw the numberless multitude stand around God's throne *before* the seventh seal is broken![6] Chronological order within Prophecy 7 requires this progression.

In Prophecy 9 (the story of the Two Witnesses), we found that Jesus will resurrect the 144,000 and take them to Heaven on the 1,265th day of the Great Tribulation. Remember, this happens just *before* the seventh trumpet sounds later that day. Therefore, if the 144,000 are taken to Heaven on the 1,265th day in Prophecy 9, it appears that the victory celebration of the 144,000 in Revelation 14:1-5 aligns with the 1,265th day for two reasons: First, we know that firstfruits are always presented to God *before* the harvest is actually gathered. Therefore, taking the 144,000 to Heaven (they are the firstfruits of the coming harvest) before the Second Coming is in perfect harmony with the 1,265th day. Second, Revelation 15:2-4 and 19:1-8 places the 144,000 in Heaven before the Second Coming occurs. They praise God that He has condemned the great whore who corrupted the Earth and killed them.[7] No one can sing the song of Moses and the Lamb[8] but the 144,000, so the 144,000 must be in Heaven prior to the Second Coming! The 144,000 can sing the song of Moses and the Lamb because the 144,000 led God's people out of slavery (bondage to sin) as did Moses and they overcame the world (victory through death) as Jesus did.[9]

Consider a parallel for a moment. From the disciples' point of view, the torture and death of Jesus on the cross was a great disappointment. Their hopes and dreams of seeing the kingdom of God established on Earth ended with the arrest and crucifixion of Jesus. However, from the Father's point of view, the torture and death of Jesus was a tremendous success! God's justice was fulfilled by Jesus' death, because Jesus died in our place, and through

His perfect sacrifice, God's mercy has been lavishly extended so any sinner could be pardoned from his sins! During the Great Tribulation, the wicked will consider the slaughter of the 144,000 and millions of God's saints during the fifth seal a tremendous success. They will gloat in victory and celebrate the occasion as they send congratulatory gifts to each other.[10] But from God's point of view, this vile celebration only confirms that the wicked are defiant, hopelessly incorrigible and beyond the possibility of redemption.

Because the life, ministry, and death of Jesus was a perfect success, the Father raised Jesus to life on Resurrection Sunday. He called Jesus to Heaven and gave Lucifer's position as prince of this world to Jesus. There was a war that morning because Lucifer would not yield his position. Similarly, the ministry and death of the 144,000 will be a perfect success. Jesus will raise them to life (on another Resurrection Sunday?) and take them to Heaven. When they arrive in New Jerusalem, Jesus will bestow the highest positions possible on them and all of the angels will rejoice.

The Devil's Identity

A few words of caution are needed. Many people distort Revelation 12 and 13 by switching the identity of Lucifer with one of his agents. Let me be clear. No agent or prophet of Jesus is Jesus and no prophet or agent of Lucifer is Lucifer. It is important that we keep the devil's identity separate and distinct from that of his agents. For example, in Revelation 12:7-9, Lucifer *himself* is cast out of Heaven with his angels. In Revelation 12:13,14 the great red dragon *himself* pursues the woman for a time, times, and half a time. This is a story about the devil. Lucifer is not Herod in Revelation 12 and Lucifer is not the little horn power in Daniel 7, even though Lucifer controlled Herod and the little horn.

I am belaboring this point because God wants mankind to know there is a determined and highly intelligent being at work who can see and hear us, even though we cannot directly see or hear him. (Lucifer or a demon sometimes speaks through spiritists or mediums,[11] but again, we cannot directly see or hear him.) The devil is evil incarnate and he *himself* intends to destroy the remnant of the woman. Lucifer will have agents working for him during the Great Tribulation, however these agents will have no idea (at first) that they are under Lucifer's control.

Unfortunately, God's people will soon find themselves caught up in a deadly conflict that has been ongoing for thousands of years. Since 1798, the devil has been preparing for his final assault on God's people and most Christians do not have a clue. When the first four trumpets occur, the devil will take advantage of the situation and initiate his first assault on those who stand for truth and righteousness. The devil's agent will be a government called Babylon. This global government will spring to life in a worldwide crisis and be energized by demonic power. God has generously given us this warning so that everyone can understand Lucifer's diabolical plan. Do not be discouraged. Jesus has a greater plan! Even though Jesus will permit millions of His saints to perish during the fifth seal, the death of His saints will not be in vain. Some of the wicked will turn from their defiance when they witness the calm and peaceful presence of the Holy Spirit within God's people, when they are martyred solely for loving Jesus with all their heart, mind, and soul and their neighbors as themselves.

Sunday, April 9, A.D. 30[12] was an incredibly glorious day in history. According to my calculation, Jesus came from the tomb on this date! Very early on Sunday morning, about the time of first light, the Father resurrected Jesus.[13] After He came out of the tomb, Jesus waited nearby for Mary Magdalene and the other Mary (His mother) to arrive[14] so that they could see Him and serve as two witnesses. He wanted them to go and encourage His scattered disciples with the fact that He was truly alive! Jesus was in a hurry to get to Heaven, but knowing that His disciples were terribly discouraged and disoriented, He patiently waited by the tomb. What a thoughtful God! When the women arrived at the tomb, they were dumbfounded. They had just witnessed His crucifixion on Friday, but that morning an angel told them that Jesus was alive! Filled with joy, the women ran off to tell the disciples, but they did not go far before encountering Jesus. They fell at His feet and worshiped Him.[15] They did not want to let him out of their sight! But Jesus told Mary Magdalene, **"Do not hold on to me, for I have not yet returned to the Father. . . ."**[16]

A few minutes later, as Jesus ascended toward the gates of the Holy City, a chorus of angels sang out: **"Lift up your heads, O you gates; be lifted up, you ancient doors, that the King of glory may come in. Who is this King of glory? The Lord strong and mighty, the Lord mighty in battle. Lift up your heads, O you gates; lift them up, you ancient doors, that the**

King of glory may come in. Who is he, this King of glory? The Lord Almighty – he [Jesus Christ] **is the King of glory."**[17] What a glorious and happy morning!

Many people do not understand why Jesus ascended to Heaven on Resurrection Sunday.[18] Please consider the following: First, Jesus was called up to Heaven and presented to the Father as the firstfruits of the dead,[19] because Jesus was the first person to experience the penalty for sin, which is the second death. Consider this: Because of sin, there are two deaths. The first death comes as a *consequence* of sin. The second death comes as a *penalty* for sin. Everyone currently in the grave has experienced the first death. The first death is sometimes called "sleep" in the Bible because it is temporary, like sleep. Sooner or later, every dead person will be resurrected from the first death! The second death is very different. Those who die the second death will have **no** hope of resurrection. When Jesus died on the cross, He experienced the second death which is the penalty for sin. Jesus willingly died the death of a wicked person. He laid down His life without any hope of resurrection. The Father abandoned Jesus on the cross. He is the first person to experience the penalty for sin.

Jesus predicted His resurrection,[20] but His statement was a matter of prophetic faith (believing the Father would restore Him to life if the Father was pleased with His sacrifice). However, when Jesus hung on the cross, the Father abandoned Jesus as though He had committed the unpardonable sin[21] and this separation caught Jesus by surprise. Jesus cried out, **"My God, My God, Why have you forsaken me?"**[22] Jesus died with the impression that He would not be resurrected because the Father abandoned Him. The amazing thing about this excruciating moment is that Jesus could have exercised a last-minute option. Before He came to Earth, the Father gave Jesus an exit. At any time while on Earth, Jesus could exercise divine power and terminate the redemption of mankind.[23] Jesus knew that mankind could not be saved unless He paid the price for sin and died the second death. Jesus also knew that the Father would resurrect Jesus only if the Father was pleased with Jesus' sacrifice. Amazingly, for no reason other than love, Jesus chose to remain on the cross and cease to exist. Even after the Father abandoned Him, Jesus still chose to forfeit His eternal life so that sinners could have it. Thus, Jesus went to His death without any hope of resurrection. What a title – "Firstfruits of the dead." It brings tears to my eyes because there will never be a greater display of love than this.[24] What can mere mortals do to honor such a magnificent Creator/Redeemer? What title or words can describe the price He paid for our salvation?

A second reason why Jesus ascended on Resurrection Sunday. During Old Testament times, firstfruits were presented to God on the first day of the week.[25] Therefore, it was fitting that Jesus be presented to the Father that morning as the firstfruits of the dead.

Finally, Jesus was called to Heaven on Sunday morning to receive a very special gift. When Adam and Eve sinned, Jesus volunteered to die in their place. In return, if Jesus successfully redeemed mankind, the Father promised to give the world over to Jesus.[26] After resting in the tomb, the Father called Jesus to Heaven to restore His rightful position as the "prince of this world." What Lucifer stole through deceit, Jesus purchased with His blood.

The Bible indicates that Lucifer would not relinquish his position. There was war in Heaven that morning and after Jesus forcibly expelled Lucifer from Heaven for the last time,[27] He returned to Earth Sunday afternoon.[28] Jesus spent the next forty days with His disciples. He did this for two important reasons: First, Jesus needed to provide undisputed evidence that He had been resurrected.[29] Second, Jesus needed to prepare His disciples for His departure and the mission that loomed before them.[30]

Positions Change

To appreciate why the war occurred in Heaven on Sunday morning, some additional information is necessary. God is love and He only rules over those who love Him and want Him to rule over them. When Adam and Eve sinned, Jesus lost His position as "the prince of mankind" because the carnal nature of sinners keeps them from wanting God to rule over them. Sinners want self-rule and self-determination. Immediately after the guilty pair sinned, they became rebellious toward Jesus because the sinful nature is naturally hostile toward God.[31] Think about this: The sinless natures of Adam and Eve immediately changed after they sinned. They became *immature miniatures* of Lucifer. Thus, they became less like Jesus and more like Lucifer. This is how sin (and the originator of sin) became lord and master over them.

When Adam and Eve sinned, the Father granted the devil certain authority over Earth. This recognition explains how Lucifer became known as "the prince of this world."[32] Before Jesus died on the cross, the Father permitted Lucifer to attend administrative meetings in Heaven as a representative of Earth.[33] After Jesus paid the penalty for sin on the cross, the Father resurrected Jesus and called Him to Heaven so that the Father could bestow on Him the title "The Prince of this World." Evidently, it was the Father's plan that Jesus would serve as "The Prince of this World" until He was found worthy to conclude the sin problem in 1798. At that time, Jesus was given sovereign power [34] and the title, "King of kings and Lord of lords."[35]

On Resurrection Sunday, a Heavenly confrontation took place that possibly went something like this: The Father summoned Lucifer and all of his angels to Heaven. When Jesus arrived as a triumphant conqueror, the holy angels fell at His feet. Naturally, Lucifer and his angels refused to show any sign of worship or adoration. The contrast between Jesus and His angels with the sulking and hateful Lucifer and his angels could not have been more obvious. Before their fall, Lucifer and his followers had been physically beautiful.[36] In fact, Lucifer had stood beside God's glorious throne as an anointed cherub. But now, things were vastly different. His evil and tortured mind had disfigured his beautiful countenance. His face was malevolent and hatred glowed in his eyes. Lucifer's angels also exhibited the horrifying effects of sin.

Jesus and Lucifer stood before the awesome brilliance that enshrouds God's throne. The contrast was shocking. Lucifer had incited the Jews to murder Jesus just three days earlier without considering that he would have to face the Son of God on this morning. Since Jesus had perfectly complied with the Father's plan to redeem mankind, the Father had legitimately and righteously resurrected Jesus. The tension was obvious. Everyone standing in that assembly knew that Jesus had faced and overcome every temptation Lucifer had put before Him.[37] Everyone also knew the Father had promised to give Earth to Jesus if He perfectly carried out His will.[38] It was obvious to everyone in the Heavenly court that Lucifer was not going to yield to his mortal enemy without a fight. Arrogance would rather die than accept defeat. Lucifer would rather die as "a hero in battle" than to surrender to the authority of Jesus. The Father presented the facts about the ministry of Jesus and how He overcame every temptation, even the temptation to avoid the second death. The Father then asked Lucifer to surrender his position and step down as the prince of

Earth. Lucifer responded bitterly and swore that he would never surrender.

The Sequence Begins

{7} There was a war in Heaven. Michael (the name which Jesus used before coming to Earth as a human)[39] and His angels fought against the great red dragon and his angels.

> A few hours before His death, Jesus made the following statement: " **'Father, glorify your name!' Then a voice came from Heaven, 'I have glorified it, and will glorify it again.' The crowd that was there and heard it said it had thundered; others said an angel had spoken to him. Jesus said, 'This voice was for your benefit, not mine. Now is the time for judgment on this world;** *now the prince of this world will be driven out.*' "[40] Jesus knew that Lucifer would be permanently cast out of Heaven if the Father approved His sacrifice. When Jesus said, "Now is the time for judgment on this world. . . ," He meant that the time had come for the Father to determine who should be the rightful prince of this world. When Jesus said, "now the prince of this world will be driven out," Jesus predicted the war described in verse 7. This war occurred on Resurrection Sunday.

{8} But the devil and his demons were thrown out of Heaven, never to enter again.

> God did not destroy the devil and his angels on Resurrection Sunday because His purpose for them was not finished. God permitted open warfare in Heaven between Lucifer and his angels and Jesus and his angels for a significant reason. The Father wanted to make sure that among the holy angels, no sympathy for the once adored and highly exalted Lucifer remained. This war was not a test of faith as the first war had been.[41] This war produced a revelation. The Father allowed the battle to last long enough to see where each angel firmly stood. After 4,000 years, there was no change. Those loyal to Lucifer defended their evil leader and remained unchanged. Those loyal to Michael also remained unchanged.

{9} Once the loyalty of the angels was confirmed, the devil and his angels were once again thrown out of Heaven, at the speed of lightning.[42] The Father threw the devil and his angels into an earthly abyss and confined them there.

Rev. 12:7
And there was war in heaven: Michael and his angels fought against the dragon; and the dragon fought and his angels,

Rev. 12:8
And prevailed not; neither was their place found any more in heaven.

Rev. 12:9
And the great dragon was cast out, that old serpent, called the Devil, and Satan, which deceiveth the whole world: he was cast out into the earth, and his angels were cast out with him.

Ever since Resurrection Sunday, the devil and his angels have been bound to this planet, limited to the dimensions of the spirit realm (represented to John as the abyss). Originally, the great red dragon and his angels were hurled out of Heaven because of defiance. Four thousand years later, their defiance remains unchanged. The great red dragon is that ancient serpent called the devil, or Satan, who leads the whole world astray. He was hurled *into* the Earth, and his angels with him.*

{10} After the war in Heaven ended, I heard a loud voice in Heaven say: "Now that salvation has been paid in full and the devil has been defeated, the gospel of Jesus Christ and His coming kingdom will advance with clarity and power throughout the Earth. Lucifer's position as "the prince of Earth" has been honorably overthrown by the perfect life, ministry, death, and resurrection of Jesus Christ. The accuser of our human brothers, who accuses them before God day and night, has been hurled down and his endless arguments and accusations in Heaven against repentant sinners have been silenced."[45]

{11} The voice continued: "Even though our brothers on Earth are sinners, they are not hopeless or defeated. Lucifer's claim that God cannot legally justify sinners has been silenced because Jesus paid the price for every sinner who surrenders to the directives of the Holy Spirit and the gospel of Jesus Christ. Through faith in Christ, repentant sinners are covered with Christ's righteousness (justified as though they never sinned) in God's sight."[46]

> When a person surrenders to the directives of the Holy Spirit, he honors and upholds the Word of God at all costs, and the word of his testimony proves that he is loyal to God, even willing to die for Him if necessary.

{12} "Therefore, rejoice holy angels, all of you who live in Heaven because atonement for sinners has been paid in full, but woe to God's people on Earth for the devil's wrath is upon you! He is filled with fury, because he now knows that he will fail miserably.

---

* **Note** - At the fifth trumpet, the devil and his angels will be permitted to exit the abyss. Therefore, a time is coming when the devil and his angels will physically appear before the people of Earth.[43] At the Second Coming, Jesus will destroy the bodies used by the devil and his angels and Jesus will return them to the abyss (spirit realm).[44]

Rev. 12:10
And I heard a loud voice saying in heaven, Now is come salvation, and strength, and the kingdom of our God, and the power of his Christ: for the accuser of our brethren is cast down, which accused them before our God day and night.

Rev. 12:11
And they overcame him by the blood of the Lamb, and by the word of their testimony; and they loved not their lives unto the death.

Rev. 12:12
Therefore rejoice, ye heavens, and ye that dwell in them. Woe to the inhabiters of the earth and of the sea! for the devil is come down unto you, having great wrath, because he knoweth that he hath but a short time.

Lucifer and his angels know they have no further standing in God's courtroom or in the court of public appeal. They are doomed, condemned to die the second death. The demons know their days are numbered and the countdown cannot be stopped."

The Dragon Pursues the Woman for 1,260 Years

{13} When the dragon saw that he had been forever locked out of Heaven, when he saw there was no further point in accusing sinners before God (hoping to find sympathy among the holy angels), he focused his rage on the woman who had given birth to Jesus. He and his demons agreed they would not let her rest until she was totally destroyed.

{14} However, God gave the woman two wings of a great eagle so that she could flee to remote places that He had prepared for her. God's people were sustained for a time, times, and half a time. Later, this time period would become known as, "The Dark Ages."

> The Bible declares the dragon chased the woman for "a time, times, and half a time." This time period is defined in verse 6 as 1,260 days. Two different expressions for the same time period enables us to nail down this period of time. When translated according to Rule Four, we find that 1,260 days equals 1,260 years.[47] History indicates this time period ended in 1798 when the power of the little horn (the papacy) was broken. Counting backward 1,260 years, this prophetic time period began in A.D. 538. The language used in Revelation 12:14 is identical with Daniel 7:25 and they easily align and identify the same time period.

Why Did God Say "A Time, Times, and Half a Time?"

God is deliberate and purposeful in everything He does. There is an important reason for everything that God does and discovering some of the reasons behind His ways is very exciting and inspiring. For example, in Daniel 9:24, God did not say that 490 years were allotted to Israel, instead, He said "seventy weeks." He used the expression "seventy weeks" when He could have said "490 years" because the expression, "seventy weeks" indicates that as far as God is concerned, weekly cycles of seven years are ongoing. In fact, weekly cycles of seven years began with the year of the Exodus.[48] Therefore, God used the expression "seventy weeks" in Daniel 9:24 because there is far more to this 490 years than a random period of 490 years.

Rev. 12:13
And when the dragon saw that he was cast unto the earth, he persecuted the woman which brought forth the man child.

Rev. 12:14
And to the woman were given two wings of a great eagle, that she might fly into the wilderness, into her place, where she is nourished for a time, and times, and half a time, from the face of the serpent.

When God used the phrase, "seventy weeks," He gave Israel a very big clue about the appearing of Jesus that would help them identify Him as the Messiah.[49] In God's calendar, a week of years always begins with a Sunday year. God wanted Israel to watch for a decree to rebuild and restore Jerusalem that would be issued during a *Sunday* year. History records four decrees that were issued to restore and rebuild Jerusalem, but only one (457 B.C.) occurred during a Sunday year. If God had said "490 years" instead of "seventy weeks," it would have been much more difficult for Israel to determine the beginning of this time period. God chose the term "seventy weeks" because He wanted His people to be prepared for Messiah's arrival. By choosing the term "seventy weeks," God identified 490 years that align with the weekly cycles of seven years that began at the Exodus. God provided this calendar so Israel could determine the exact year when Messiah would begin His ministry and the exact year when Jesus would die on the cross (the Wednesday year of the seventieth week)![50]

An interesting question we need to consider is, "Why did God say the dragon would chase the woman to the wilderness for "a time, times, and half a time" in verse 14, but in verse 6, He says the dragon would chase the woman into the wilderness for 1,260 days?" Please consider the following issues:

1. God described the same prophetic time period in two different ways to tell us that "a time, times, and half a time" equals 1,260 days. Additionally, the 1,260 days allotted to the Two Witnesses in Revelation 11:3 equals "a time, times, and half a time."

2. God declares "a time, times, and half a time" equals 1,260 days in Revelation 12, but there must be a method to calculate this relationship mathematically. Please take a few moments to consider the following concepts:

    It is widely known that ancient nations often observed two or more calendars at the same time. (We do the same thing today. For example, we have a calendar that defines a year as January through December, a calendar that defines a school year as August through May, and we may have a calendar that defines a fiscal year at our place of business as July through June.) The ancients also used different calendars to meet different needs just like we do today. History indicates that ancient nations used solar calendars (based

> Rev. 12:14

on the orbit of the Sun), lunar calendars (based on lunar cycles of the moon), as well as religious, civil, and other types of calendars. Calendars are important and necessary in any society because they enable people to plant crops, make and meet appointments with each other and to establish specific dates for business contracts. Ultimately, the purpose of any calendar is to measure time, both forward and backward.

It appears that a solar calendar of 360 days (twelve months of thirty days) was in use at the time of Noah's flood. When Moses wrote the book of Genesis, he wrote that the waters flooded the Earth for 150 days.[51] Moses also says that the flood began on the seventeenth day of the second month[52] and that Noah's ark came to rest on the seventeenth day of the seventh month.[53] I believe five months amounts to 150 days because Moses used a solar calendar based on twelve months of thirty days. If Moses had used a lunar calendar, he would have said 148 days because five lunar months contain 147.65 days.

The ancient use of a solar calendar should not be surprising. Although history does not explicitly reveal why the ancients correlated 360 degrees of arc with a solar year of 365.24 days, I believe there is a simple explanation for this correlation: *The ancients studied the Sun.* When looking at the stars each morning, they noticed that the rising sun *appears* to advance through the twelve constellations about "one Sun width" per day. From Spring Equinox to Spring Equinox, there are approximately 360 "sun widths." From this observation, the ancients may have created a complete cycle of the Sun called "one time" or "one solar year." This may also explain how a circle came to have 360 degrees of arc. For purposes of calculation, the solar year may have been defined as twelve months of thirty days or 360 days. Moreover, the orbit of the Sun naturally divides a year into four seasons and each season contains approximately ninety "sun widths." Because the ancients relied upon their observation of the Sun to determine the timing for planting crops, it is possible that many ancient nations defined a solar year as having approximately 360 days."[54]

For purposes of calculation, the nation of Israel needed a fixed solar year because Israel's religious year was based on a solar/lunar calendar that contained 354 or 384 days. Because of this variance, when calculating time periods forward or backward, it was very difficult for the Jews to determine the exact number of days in a given year because each year varies in length. A solar calendar resolves this complexity. It simply has 360 days, or 12 months of 30 days.[55]

When God exiled Israel to Babylon in 605 B.C., there is biblical evidence showing that the Jews and the Babylonians were acquainted with a solar year of 360 days.[56] History records that Nebuchadnezzar's lengthy conquest of Tyre and Egypt ended in 570 B.C.[57] Evidently, the king became delusional with his success and he began to think more highly of himself than God thought he should. Twelve months after conquering Tyre and Egypt, (569 B.C.), God imposed seven times (seven solar years) of punishment on Nebuchadnezzar and the king ate grass like an animal from 569 to 563 B.C. The Bible indicates that Nebuchadnezzar finally returned to his senses and to his throne after the seven years ended and historians believe that he died about two years later, in 561 B.C.

3. The Aramaic word, *'iddan* is used in Daniel 7:25. **"The saints will be handed over to him** [the little horn power] **for a time, times and half a time."** The word *'iddan* means a definite period of time, such as one solar year. Literally speaking, three and a half solar years contain 1,278.34 days, but the ancients did not count actual days. Instead, they counted 360 "sun widths" per solar year which evidently became the basis for a circle of 360 degrees. God affirms this method of counting solar years in Revelation 12:6,14 by defining "a time, times and half a time" as 1,260 days.

4. Rule Four of prophetic interpretation defines how God measures time; therefore, the "time, times, and half a time" in Daniel 7:25 and Revelation 12:14 must be translated into 1,260 years.[58] So, to calculate when the dragon chased the woman for 1,260 years, we have to determine a starting point (to count forward) or an ending point (to count backward). I understand the little horn power in Daniel 7 represents the dominion and power of the Roman Catholic Church over the nations of Europe which ended in 1798.

Rev. 12:14

Prophecy 11 - The Rise of Babylon

Rev. 12:14

Obeying orders from Napoleon, General Berthier entered Vatican City and arrested the pope on February 20, 1798 on the grounds that the pope refused to renounce temporal (civil) authority over Europe. On March 7, 1798, Napoleon's army entered Rome and established the Roman Republic. On this date, the power of the papacy was broken.

To find the beginning date for "the time, times and half a time," we subtract 1,260 years from 1798 which results in the year A.D. 538. The dragon began chasing the saints in A.D. 538. Here is a short version of the story: When Justinian I (A.D. 483-565) became the ruler of the Roman Empire, he aspired to reunite a fractured empire. He created and issued various laws between A.D. 529-534 that formed the basis of his government. "The very first law in his Codex required all persons under the jurisdiction of the [Holy Roman] Empire to belong to the Christian faith."[59] Justinian made this law a priority because like Constantine, he thought Christianity (a religion having one Lord, one faith, and one baptism) could solve many problems that plagued the empire. When Justinian issued this law, the head of the Christian Church at Rome (the pope) did not have sufficient power to implement and enforce the law because three tribal nations (the Ostrogoths, Heruli, and Vandals) were at war with the church. They were determined to kill the pope.

A series of battles took place between A.D. 534 and 537 and eventually, the Heruli and the Vandals were defeated. In A.D. 537, the Ostrogoths set siege to the city of Rome in hopes of capturing the pope (who was inside the city), but Justinian's general, Belesarius broke the siege and Pope Silverius escaped without harm. After the rescue, Belesarius discovered correspondence indicating that Pope Silverius had been secretly negotiating with the Ostrogoths to end the siege and Belesarius was outraged. Belesairus deposed Pope Silverius in March 537. (This event happened exactly 1,261 years, to the month, before Napoleon established the Roman Republic in March 1798.)

After Belesarius removed Silverius from office and demoted him to the position of monk, Belesarius appointed Vigilius to be the next pope. About a year later, in A.D. 538, Pope Vigilius began to exercise temporal (civil) authority that no previous pope had been able to exercise because the distracting enemies of the papacy had been uprooted or rendered powerless. At last, the pope was able to make the first law of Justinian's codex effective. When these historical events are aligned with the time frame A.D. 538 to 1798, two conclusions become apparent. First, according to Daniel 7, there is no question about the identity of the little horn power. The little horn that grew up out of the fourth beast (Rome) was the papacy and as it grew to power, it uprooted three of the original ten horns (the Ostrogoths, Heruli, and Vandals). Second, the fall of the little horn in 1798 is the terminus of the 1,260 years mentioned in Revelation 12. The details and specifications given in Prophecies 2, 6, 10, and 11 firmly align with world history. Even though the Bible does not offer a specific event to mark when the 1,260 years began, it does limit the dragon's persecution to 1,260 years. John saw the devil chase the woman to the wilderness for 1,260 years and history records the papacy fell (received "a deadly wound") in 1798.

Rev. 12:14

A review of what we have learned regarding the 1,260 years may be helpful. First, Revelation 12 indicates that "a time, times, and half a time" equals 1,260 days. Second, God is deliberate and purposeful. His ways of measuring time are unlike man's ways. Therefore, when studying apocalyptic prophecy, we have to carefully consider the God given name of each time period. Evidently, "a time, times and half a time" is based upon a solar year of 360 "sun widths." During a solar year, the Sun completes a circle of 360 degrees with respect to the stars. Third, the Aramaic word *'hiddan* (used in Daniel 7:25) refers to a definite period of time – such as a solar year (this stands in contrast to God's solar/lunar calendar where a year is 354 or 384 days). Fourth, history confirms the rise and fall of the papacy (538-1798). All of this information perfectly aligns with the dragon chasing and persecuting the woman in Daniel 7:25 and Revelation 12:6,14.

There is a reason God called this time period, "a time, times, and half a time." God wants the *final generation* to understand that *a second period* of persecution is coming upon His people – a second period of "a time, times, and half a time" is coming!

Consider this: God's perfect number is seven – a number denoting totality, fullness, and completion. For example:

> Rev. 12:14

- God created the world in six days and rested on the seventh day. Unlike the other six days, He made the seventh day holy.
- God brought seven clean animals into Noah's ark, but only two of the unclean.
- God promised to punish Israel seven times over if they violated His covenant.
- The high priest sprinkled blood before the atonement cover on the Day of Atonement seven times.
- The people marched around Jericho seven times on the seventh day.
- God imposed seven times on King Nebuchadnezzar.
- Jesus told us to forgive our brother seven times seventy.
- There are seven churches in Revelation.
- The Lamb in Revelation has seven horns.
- There are seven angels that stand before God.
- John heard seven thunders.
- There are seven seals, seven trumpets, and seven bowls.
- There are seven heads on the great red dragon and the composite beast.
- There are seven lampstands.

Many other examples in the Bible show that God uses seven to denote fulness and completion, but these suffice to make the point that seven is God's perfect number.

Time, Times, and Half a Time is Half of the Story!

Because God often uses the number seven to show completion and fullness, it appears that the phrase "a time, times and half a time" is God's way of dividing seven years of persecution into two segments. A time (one solar year), times (two solar years), and half a time (half a solar year) totals 3.5 years and *3.5 years is half of seven years*. There are two periods of persecution in Daniel and Revelation that last "a time, times, and half a time." When added together, they produce seven years of persecution. The first 3.5 years of persecution occurred during the Dark Ages. The "time, times, and half a time" mentioned in Daniel 7:25 must be translated into 1,260 years because of Rule Four. The second period of 3.5 years will occur during the Great Tribulation.

Because Revelation 12 proves that 1,260 days is equivalent to a time, times, and half a time, the 1,260 days allotted to the Two Witnesses in Revelation 11:3 are equivalent to a time, times and half a time. Daniel 12 confirms this: **"The man clothed in linen, who was above the waters of the river, lifted his right hand and his left hand toward heaven, and I heard him swear by him who lives forever, saying, 'It will be for *a time, times and half a time.* When the power of the holy people** [the 144,000] **has been finally broken, all these things will be completed.'"**[60] Compare Daniel's prediction with John's prediction: **"And I will give power to my two witnesses, and they will prophesy for *1,260 days*** [a time, times and half a time], **clothed in sackcloth. . . . Now when they have finished their testimony, the beast that comes up from the Abyss will attack them, and overpower and kill them."**[61]

Rev. 12:14

The Bible indicates there are two separate periods of persecution for the saints. Each period will last 3.5 years. (See Figure 11.1.) Currently, we are living between these two time periods. Here are three suggestions why God permits His people to be persecuted for a period of seven times:

First, persecution keeps the church (the body of Christ) pure. Nominal Christians cannot endure persecution. They will either flee or dilute the gospel through compromise. James wrote, **"Consider it pure joy, my brothers, whenever you face trials of many kinds, because you know that the testing of your faith develops perseverance. Perseverance must finish its work so that you may be mature and complete, not lacking anything."**[62]

Second, persecution matures our faith and love for God and our love for those who also suffer for His sake. Faithless people go around in endless circles whining, murmuring, and complaining, but faithful people live by faith (and do so happily!). Faithfull people anticipate God's sustaining grace each day and their love and admiration for those who suffer as they suffer produces a bond of fellowship and comradery that words cannot express. Peter wrote, **"These** [trials and suffering] **have come so that your faith – of greater worth than gold, which perishes even though refined by fire – may be proved genuine and may result in praise, glory and honor when Jesus Christ is revealed. Though you have not seen him, you love him;**

> Rev. 12:14

and even though you do not see him now, you believe in him and are filled with an inexpressible and glorious joy, for you are receiving the goal of your faith, the salvation of your souls."[63]

Third, persecution causes God's children to "hunger and thirst" after the Word of God. No martyr ever went to the stake questioning the reasons for his faith. When a person is threatened with suffering and death because of his determination to uphold God's Word, the Word of God becomes his bread and water. John wrote, **"When he opened the fifth seal, I saw under the altar the souls of those who had been slain *because of the Word of God and the testimony they had maintained.*"**[64]

Summary

Corporately speaking, God's people are persecuted for a period of "seven times" before they are taken to Heaven. The first 3.5 years (1,260 years) occurred between 538 and 1798. The second 3.5 years (literally 1,260 days) will occur during the Great Tribulation. We are living during the intermission.

God's People Persecuted Seven Times

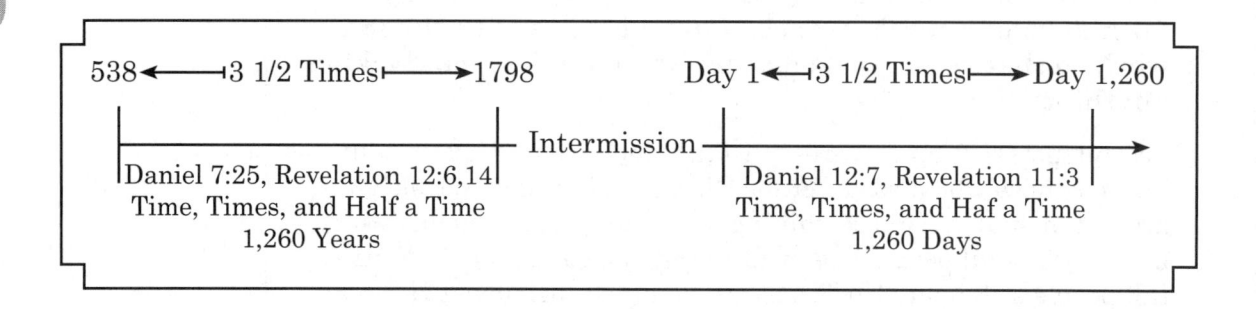

```
538 ←—3 1/2 Times—→ 1798        Day 1 ←—3 1/2 Times—→ Day 1,260
       |                  |— Intermission —|                    |
   Daniel 7:25, Revelation 12:6,14       Daniel 12:7, Revelation 11:3
   Time, Times, and Half a Time          Time, Times, and Haf a Time
          1,260 Years                           1,260 Days
```

Figure 11.1

Jesus said to His disciples, **"Remember the words I spoke to you: 'No servant is greater than his master.' If they persecuted me, they will persecute you also. If they obeyed my** teaching, they will obey yours also. They will treat you this way because of my name, for they do not know the One who sent me."⁶⁵ To prepare His disciples for the suffering that lay ahead, Jesus gave them the most wonderful gift known to mankind. **"Peace I leave with you; my peace I give you. I do not give to you as the world gives. Do not let your hearts be troubled and do not be afraid."**⁶⁶ God gave us the books of Daniel and Revelation because He wants us to know His plans in advance. God permitted His people to be purified for 1,260 years and we anticipate that He will allow His people to be purified again.⁶⁷ However, the woman was not and will not be tested beyond what she can bear.⁶⁸ Make no mistake about this, a numberless multitude will come out of the Great Tribulation because there are millions and millions of honest-hearted people on Earth!

Rev. 12:14

Finally, here is an interesting thought. You may recall that the Bible predicts the wicked will rejoice over the death of the Two Witnesses for 3.5 days. This period of time (which is half of seven days) suggests that there may be another 3.5 days to consider. I am speculating, but if God grants the wicked 3.5 days to celebrate their shameful victory over the death of the Two Witnesses, it seems fair that God would also grant the redeemed 3.5 days to celebrate their victory over the beast and his image. Personally, I like the idea of the numberless multitude rejoicing around God's throne in Heaven for 3.5 days.⁶⁹ I hope to meet you there!

The Sequence Continues

{15} About two hundred fifty years before the 1,260 years⁷⁰ ended, the devil observed the rise and influence of the Protestant Reformation in Europe. The dragon could see that if God's truth was not stopped, light would triumph over darkness. Being the devil that he is, he attempted to destroy advancing truth with a tsunami of persecution.

Rev. 12:15

And the serpent cast out of his mouth water as a flood after the woman, that he might cause her to be carried away of the flood.

> John saw the devil's endeavor to destroy the woman as a dragon spewing a great flood of water out of his mouth.⁷¹ This caricature is full of irony because people in John's day believed that dragons spewed fire, not water, from their mouths. This unusual illustration indicates that God would not allow the devil to completely stop the Protestant reformation. The devil tried to sweep the woman away in a torrent of persecution that culminated with the French Revolution (1789-1799), but try as he might, the devil could not destroy the woman.

> **Rev. 12:16**
> And the earth helped the woman, and the earth opened her mouth, and swallowed up the flood which the dragon cast out of his mouth.

{16} God opened up a place on Earth for the battered woman. The Earth swallowed up the river that the dragon spewed out of his mouth.

Twenty-two years before the papacy fell, God established a new nation in a largely uninhabited part of the world. God led the founding fathers of this new nation to create a constitution that separated the powers of church from the powers of the state. This new nation was built on principles of religious liberty and the equality of human beings (although it would take about a century after becoming a nation to end slavery and give equal rights to women). Geographically speaking, the earth *helped* the Protestant Reformation by offering the woman a place where she might flee and worship God according to the dictates of conscience. The poor, the tired, the homeless, and those persecuted for their faith found civil and religious freedom in the United States of America.

Dragon Prepares for War on the Remnant of the Woman

> **Rev. 12:17**
> And the dragon was wroth with the woman, and went to make war with the remnant of her seed, which keep the commandments of God, and have the testimony of Jesus Christ.

{17} When the dragon saw the outcome of the French Revolution and the downfall of the Catholic Church in 1798, he knew the Ancient of Days had issued a restraining order against him.[72] The devil was forced to cease and desist in his war against the woman, but this is not the end of the story. He retreated from his assault on the woman to lay plans for his final war against the last of her offspring, those who love and obey the Ten Commandments and live by faith according to the testimony of Jesus, which His 144,000 prophets will speak.

The devil understands the story contained in the book of Revelation. Like us, he knows the outcome. For centuries, He has known that during "the appointed time of the end," God will permit him to make one final war against *the remnant* of the woman for 42 months. He knows that he and his demons will be permitted to physically appear during the fifth trumpet. He also knows that God will allow him to establish a counterfeit theocracy during the sixth trumpet. Knowing these facts in advance, the devil has laid careful plans to utterly destroy *the remnant* of the woman. Keep in mind, that even though the devil and his angels understand that they will be destroyed in hell at the end of the thousand years, their hatred for the Father and the Lamb knows no bounds. Hatred motivates them to do whatever they can to ruin God's endeavors to save mankind from sin. Lucifer and his demons are relentless predators. They were at

Calvary and witnessed the love that Jesus has for sinners. They are full of hatred and they plan to do everything possible to lead people away from Christ and His salvation so that as many people as possible will be destroyed. Lucifer and his demons are insatiable predators who are without love or sympathy. Lucifer and his demons are like beasts that have rabies. They are mad; there is no reasoning.

Rev. 12:17

Lucifer's behavior will be studied throughout eternity. His life is sin personified and this explains why God has permitted the devil to live for several thousand years after his initial rebellion. God wants everyone to see the gruesome power and consequences of sin. *Lucifer's life and actions mirror the actions of any sinner and given enough time and power every sinner would follow in Lucifer's footsteps.* The drama that unfolds on Earth during the Great Tribulation will prove this fact. The sinful nature is everything that the sinless nature is not. When the sinful nature is opposed or its demands are denied, hatred and resentment erupt. This inevitable process explains why sin and sinners must be eliminated from the universe. Hatred and loathing produces a predator. Hatred often leads to murder.[73] A sinless nature is not capable of hatred or predatory violence. Individuals with a sanctified nature understand good and evil and they are capable of carrying out the demands of justice, but they have no hatred, meanness, or maliciousness within their hearts.

As previously stated, the Father restrained the devil from making war on the woman in 1798. For more than two hundred years, the devil has been preparing for his final assault on *the remnant* of the woman. The devil is extremely intelligent and he understands sinful nature very well. Knowing that he would be permitted to make war on the last of the saints, the devil and his demons have conducted four clever campaigns over the past two centuries that will come to fruition during the Great Tribulation. These campaigns are Bible illiteracy, sexual misconduct, love for power, money, pleasure, and materialism, and the use of addictive substances. The devil and his demons have been operating in stealth mode, dumbing down each generation by removing the importance of God and His Word from society. Today, the world is full of people who do not know God or His will (Bible illiteracy). The devil has glamorized sex, money, power, pleasure, and materialism. Consequently, billions of people are sexually immoral. They lie, cheat, and steal without concern. We live in a world where people are lovers of money and plea-

> Rev. 12:17

sure and even more, billions are hopelessly trapped in an addiction of some kind. If you step back and study the path to degeneration over the past two hundred years, it becomes obvious that Lucifer's four campaigns have been very successful.

Why Does God Permit Suffering?

Many Christians believe that it is inconsistent to say that a God of love will permit His saints to be tortured and killed during the Great Tribulation. However, a quick review of Scripture and church history reveals that God does permit His saints to be tortured and killed, even His own Son! We know that God permitted the little horn to chase the woman into the desert for 1,260 years and we know that He will permit the remnant of the woman to be persecuted during the Great Tribulation![74] Thankfully, no matter how grievous the situation may be, *God always gives sufficient grace and peace to His children. He will never abandon them under any circumstances.*

We may not want to admit it, but persecution benefits God's people in several ways. Persecution enables the saints to see and depend on God's gracious providence (which is obscured during prosperity). Persecution causes the saints to exalt the value and importance of God's Word (which is neglected during prosperity). Persecution requires the saints to be vigilant, constantly sorting through Lucifer's efforts to make wrong appear right (which is not detected during prosperity). Finally, suffering brings the saints into close communion with Jesus (which is barely negligible during prosperity).[75] Suffering for Christ's sake causes a saint to endure each day according to the strength that Jesus gives him each day. Total dependency on God creates perfect peace and happiness! Persecution reveals a God who is intimately acquainted with the needs of each soul. Those who suffer for Christ would not have it any other way. This is so ironic. Nominal Christians are annoyed by persecution while genuine Christians are refined. Genuine Christians realize that in Christ, persecution brings out the best of times, when it is the worst of times, all at the same time.[76]

The Beast from the Sea

{13:1} I saw the great red dragon standing on the shore of the sea, waiting for the day to arrive when he could once again, make war upon the remnant of the woman. As I watched, I saw a strange beast come up out of the sea. This beast looked similar to the great red dragon because it had the same seven heads and ten horns, but this beast had different body parts. This beast was a composite beast made up of three predators: A leopard, a bear, and a lion.

> John does not attempt to explain how or why this beast appears. It just appears. John's silence is not a problem because valid rules of interpretation reveal the purpose, origin, and identity of this beast. This beast represents a one-world-government that will form during the first four trumpets. Of course, today such a government is unthinkable, not even possible, but a crisis of apocalyptic proportion is coming upon the whole world and this crisis has no comparison since Noah's flood. God's coming judgments will catch the world by complete surprise. When the censer is cast down and the first four trumpets sound, God's judgments will reduce the whole world and its infrastructures to shambles. Twenty five percent of the world will perish and the ruins of *thousands* of cities will force world leaders to respond to a new reality. There is an Almighty God and He is very angry with the behavior of all mankind. Rising out of a "sea of humanity," this composite beast represents mankind's unified response to God's wrath. The religious and political leaders of the world will unite out of fear and together they will create this monster-beast as the best possible solution to stop God's wrath.
>
> The first four trumpets will turn life on Earth upside down. Every nation will be overwhelmed with shock and awe. Political leaders will be filled with panic, and fearing more judgments will soon fall, they will turn to their clergy for a solution to appease God's wrath. Religious leaders will conclude that given the universal scope of God's anger, the best possible option will be to form one worldwide authority that can dictate to the nations what is "acceptable and unacceptable behavior" in God's sight. Because the world is religiously diverse, solutions will be determined on a nation-by-nation basis. The religious leaders of the world will reason that if sinful behavior caused God's wrath to occur, then corrective behavior should appease God and cause His wrath to cease.

Rev. 13:1

And I stood upon the sand of the sea, and saw a beast rise up out of the sea, having seven heads and ten horns, and upon his horns ten crowns, and upon his heads the name of blasphemy.

> Rev. 13:1

Martial Law Will Terminate Individual Rights

The first four trumpets will devastate the infrastructures of all nations and political leaders will be forced to implement martial law in their respective nations. The constitutional rights of citizens will have to be suspended "until the crisis is over." Historically, governments have enacted martial law to control chaos. Martial law is a tool that suspends individual rights, concentrates executive power, expedites decisions, and implements whatever laws are thought to be necessary to preserve government. Anarchy erupts (gangs rule) when there is no government and martial law is often justified as a necessity to maintain some semblance of order. The composite beast will not dissolve the governments of the world, instead, each nation will implement martial law and the leaders of each nation will submit to the dictates of the composite beast. Throughout the world, political leaders and civil authorities in each nation will carry out the beast's demands. Survivors will be very motivated to appease Almighty God so that His judgments will stop.

Man will create the composite beast (the global crisis authority overseeing man's attempt to appease God). The political and religious leaders of the world will have good intentions, but unwittingly, the composite beast will quickly become a tool of the devil. The Bible says that Lucifer will give the composite beast its extraordinary power, throne, and great authority. The behavior and power of the composite beast will be stunning. Working through carnal-minded political and religious leaders (who are more concerned with expediency than morality), Lucifer will insert his hand into this puppet government so that he can use it to persecute and destroy the remnant of the woman.

When it comes to controlling conduct that is offensive to God, *the only tool* which religious and political leaders have is legislation. After observing the overwhelming destruction caused by the first four trumpets, the religious and political leaders will reason that God's judgments might end if everyone repents and ceases behavior that offends God. Therefore, the composite beast will create "sin-less" laws which political leaders (wielding martial law) will implement and enforce. Civil authorities in every nation will arrest and impose severe penalties on anyone who breaks the laws of the composite beast. The composite beast will gain control of the world without firing a single bullet because the civil powers of Earth will humbly submit (out of fear for God's wrath) to the demands of the world's religious leaders hoping to end God's judgments. Incidently, the book of Revelation calls the composite beast Babylon (which means confusion) because Babylon's laws will create an enormous amount of confusion, hostility, and persecution.

{13:1 - Continued} The composite beast had ten horns and seven heads. Each of the seven heads had a blasphemous name written on it and there were ten crowns on the ten horns.

For reasons presented in our study on Revelation 17,[77] the seven heads on the composite beast represent the seven religious systems of the world: Atheism, Heathenism, Judaism, Eastern Mysticism, Islam, Catholicism, and Protestantism.[78] The blasphemous name associated with each head indicates that each head (each religious system) is anti-Christ. This means that each religious system is opposed to the sovereign authority and demands of Jesus Christ. This opposition will be demonstrated during the 1,260 days allotted to the Two Witnesses. The 144,000 will proclaim the gospel of Jesus (the demands of Jesus Christ) and each religious system on Earth will oppose it. The problem is that each head of Babylon claims to know God and speak His truth, but the seven religions of the world are in fact, an insult to Almighty God. They do not know Him, speak for Him, obey Him, or represent His interests. In fact, if the seven religious systems of the world knew Jesus and had some understanding of the Bible, they would listen to His servants, the 144,000. The seven religious systems of the world will fiercely oppose the efforts and testimony of the 144,000 and they will also persecute those who embrace and obey the gospel of Jesus.

You may recall in Revelation 12:3 that seven diadems (crowns of authority) rested on the seven heads, but in this prophecy the diadems rest on the ten horns. This transition means there is a change in persecuting authority. For 1,260 years, *religious authorities* persecuted the woman. During the Great Tribulation, *civil authorities* will persecute the remnant of the woman. Babylon will operate as a church state. The seven heads represent the church side of Babylon and the ten horns represent the state side of Babylon. When Babylon is created, the composite beast will function as a global church state. The religious leaders of Babylon will make demands and the civil authorities in each nation will carry them out.

> **Rev. 13:2**
>
> *And the beast which I saw was like unto a leopard, and his feet were as the feet of a bear, and his mouth as the mouth of a lion: and the dragon gave him his power, and his seat, and great authority.*

{2} I noticed that the body of the composite beast resembled a leopard, but it had feet and claws like a bear and a mouth like a lion. I also saw that the source of Babylon's awesome power was Lucifer. The devil gave this government beast its power, its throne, and great authority. The power within this puppet beast was "supernatural."

This beast from the sea is called a 'composite beast' because it has features borrowed from three awesome predators. This combination of features exposes the predatory nature of Babylon. The composite beast will be swift like a leopard, ferocious like a bear and deadly like a lion. Currently, the world does not anticipate the first four trumpets or the creation of the composite beast. Millions of Christians are totally unaware of what the Bible predicts. They have no idea that the devil has been preparing for more than two hundred years to ambush everyone who follows Jesus. Lucifer is crouched like a lion, waiting to pounce on the remnant of the woman with the ferocity of a grizzly bear and no one can outrun a leopard. When millions of Christians are forced by circumstances to admit that there will not be a pretribulation rapture, when millions of other Christians are forced to admit that the seven trumpets were not fulfilled in past history, a devastating tsunami of bitterness will flood through Christianity and wash many away.

> **Rev. 13:3**
>
> *And I saw one of his heads as it were wounded to death; and his deadly wound was healed: and all the world wondered after the beast.*

{3} One of the seven heads seemed to have had a fatal wound, but when the composite beast rose from the sea, the fatal wound *had been healed* (notice the past-perfect tense). Because the first four trumpets had destroyed much of the world and its population, the survivors sought to appease God's wrath by following the instructions of the composite beast.

The seven heads on the composite beast represent the seven religious systems of the world: Atheism, Heathenism, Judaism, Islam, Eastern Mysticism, Catholicism, and Protestantism. In terms of political clout and religious prowess, the Roman Catholic Church (having approximately one billion members and one leader) is the preeminent religion of the world. The Roman Catholic Church today has diplomatic relations with heads of state in 179 nations. History and Bible prophecy indicate the sixth head[79] of the composite beast (the Roman Catholic Church) received a fatal wound in 1798, but the Bible also indicates the fatal wound *will be healed* when Babylon forms. The healing of the wounded head points forward to a time when a pope will be restored to a position that has persecuting power. In fact, the pope will lead a coalition of religious leaders into persecuting the remnant of the woman.

During the first four trumpets, the religious leaders of the world will unite in an effort to appease God's wrath. They will create a global authority (Babylon) that will be responsible for "helping" the nations of the world appease God. World leaders will select the pope to oversee this authority. This does not mean that the pope will be able to impose Catholic beliefs on non-Catholics (approximately 85% of the world is non-Catholic). Instead, the pope will be appointed to lead a coalition of religious leaders in a united endeavor to appease God on a nation by nation basis so that His wrath will cease. At first, almost everyone will accept the pope as the leader because they realize that something must be done quickly. Millions of people will be traumatized and religiously disoriented (humbled and confused) by the evidences of God's wrath. The Catholic Church has an existing network already established among the nations, so the pope will be the obvious choice to lead Babylon, but he will not serve alone. Religious and political leaders of the world will also serve on Babylon's board of directors and this unity will enable Babylon to move quickly, as the leopard portion of this composite beast reminds us.

> Rev. 13:3

{4} People worshiped the devil when they obeyed the laws of Babylon without realizing at first, that they were actually worshiping the devil. Out of fear for God, most people cooperated with the demands of Babylon, the composite beast. No one wanted to do anything that might further offend Almighty God.

> Rev. 13:4
>
> *And they worshipped the dragon which gave power unto the beast: and they worshipped the beast, saying, Who is like unto the beast? who is able to make war with him?*

This verse teaches a profound truth: A person worships the devil when he *knowingly* obeys a law that has a requirement contrary to the law of God. The composite beast (Babylon) will create many laws regarding worship and moral conduct. Civil authorities will implement these laws as though they were the will of God, when actually, these laws will be the handiwork of Lucifer. *Any law regarding worship that stands in conflict with the Ten Commandments, including the fourth commandment, is blasphemy.* The religious leaders of Babylon will prove that their religious system is blasphemous (insulting to God) when they make laws that oppose the laws of God. Jesus is man's Creator and during creation week, He set aside the seventh day as a memorial to Creation by declaring it holy. The 144,000 will faithfully and clearly present God's demand that everyone rest

> Rev. 13:4

from their work on the Creator's seventh day Sabbath. (This topic will be examined in Prophecy 12.)

The 144,000 will inform the world that Babylon's laws are blasphemous in God's sight. Furthermore, Babylon's efforts to appease God's wrath will have no effect on God's wrath! Corporate atonement for Earth ended forever when the censer was cast down. The first four trumpets have sounded and the fifth trumpet will occur on time! Life as it was known is over! There will be no further judgments from God until the fifth trumpet sounds.

Of course, the testimony of the 144,000 will inflame and insult the arrogance of Babylon's leaders. Babylon's leaders will become furious when the 144,000 explain that Babylon is merely a hand puppet of Lucifer that is designed to destroy the remnant of the woman, those who love Jesus and keep His commandments. The testimony given by the 144,000 will cause a great uproar. Many wicked people will attempt to harm and kill the 144,000, but they cannot be silenced until they have completed their work. Severe penalties will be imposed on anyone who defies the laws of Babylon. God permits this so that faith can be tested. God wants to reveal who will worship as Babylon demands and who will trust in God and do as He requires (live by faith).

Many people will complain to the 144,000, "Why should we resist the laws of Babylon and be punished? We have seen the wrath of God. We know that God is angry with the world's degenerate behavior. If all of us do not repent and worship God, we will offend Him further and bring more disaster upon ourselves. What difference does it matter if we worship God on Tuesday, Friday, Saturday, or Sunday? *As long as we worship God, which day we worship should not matter."* The 144,000 will respond that God's law has higher authority than any law made by man. Surprisingly, Babylon will maintain that it does not matter which day a person keeps holy and it will then establish a day it wants people to observe as a holy day. However, the fourth commandment clearly indicates that a person cannot honor the Creator and treat His seventh day Sabbath as a secular day.

The Bible identifies the remnant of the woman as those who obey the commandments of God.[80] Currently, this distinction is not apparent, but this will change when the remnant defy the commandments of men.[81] Even though most people do not consider the topic of worship to be essential, it will become a topic of heated debate during the Great Tribulation. Worshiping God as He commands will produce a great deal of conflict, persecution and suffering for God's people. It is ironic that the worship experience of Cain and Abel illustrates this problem. Abel offered the required lamb. Cain ignored God's command to sacrifice a lamb and he presumptuously offered fruit from his garden. God honored Abel's offering and rejected Cain's offering. When Cain saw that God had rejected his worship, Cain was insulted and embarrassed. He became jealous of his younger brother, thinking that Abel might take his place as the first-born of mankind. In a rage of jealousy and hatred, Cain killed Abel. Think very carefully about this point. If we presume to tell God how and when He is to be worshiped, we are like Cain. When we defy God's authority by telling God how and when we will worship Him, we attempt to supplant God.

Rev. 13:4

{5} Babylon (the composite beast) created many laws which usurped God's authority.[82] Babylon insulted the Creator of Heaven and Earth with insults and blasphemies and it exercised authority for forty-two months (42 lunar months times 29.53 days per month equals 1,241 days).

Rev. 13:5

And there was given unto him a mouth speaking great things and blasphemies; and power was given unto him to continue forty and two months.

> Contrary to what many private interpretations claim, Rule One proves the composite beast does not yet exist even though all of the elements that will make up the beast are present. (A building full of car parts does not mean that a car is in the building.*)

> The composite beast will be granted power for forty-two months. The forty-two months in verse 5 are not to be confused with 1,260 days granted to the Two Witnesses.

Note: Rule One requires the composite beast to rise out of the sea *after* 1798 because the Bible states that when the composite beast rises from the sea, the deadly wound had been healed (past perfect tense). If the papacy received a deadly wound in 1798, then it stands to reason that the healing of the deadly wound must occur *after* 1798. Therefore, the composite beast has to appear on Earth after 1798 and we know this has not occurred because a one world crisis government does not yet exist.

Jesus' Final Victory   321

1,260 Days Are Not 42 Months

Rev. 13:6

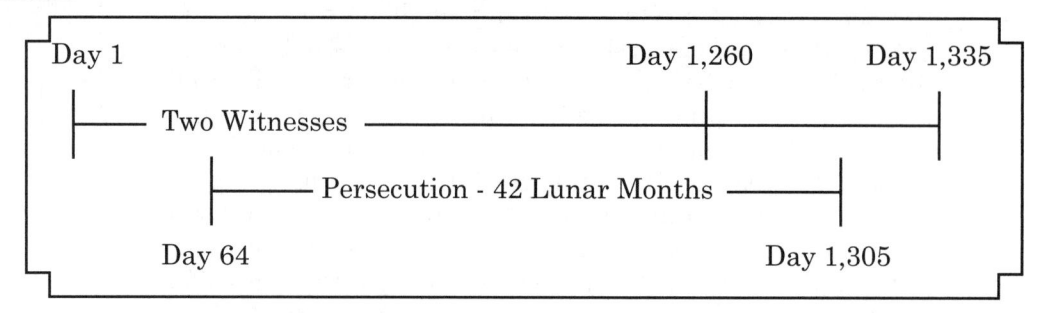

```
Day 1                          Day 1,260      Day 1,335
|———— Two Witnesses ——————————|              |
        |——— Persecution - 42 Lunar Months ———|
        Day 64                         Day 1,305
```

Figure 11.2

The Two Witnesses will begin their work on Day 1 of the Great Tribulation and their work will end on the 1,260th day of the Great Tribulation. As I calculate it, the forty-two months given to the composite beast will begin on Day 64 and end on Day 1305 when the fifth bowl begins. Remember, 42 lunar months equals 1,241 days, whereas 1,260 days equals a time, times, and half a time.

Because the world is religiously diverse (having seven religious systems), the leaders of Babylon will have to adjust their demands on a nation by nation basis. In countries where Christians are a majority, Babylon will require worship on Sunday. In countries where Islam is dominant, Babylon will require worship on Friday, and in countries where Judaism is dominant, Babylon will require worship on Saturday. In nations where Atheists and Eastern Mysticism (Hinduism, Buddhism, etc.) is dominant, a day for worship will be selected and announced as circumstances permit. Babylon will create worldwide confusion over the issue of worship, because its policies will be so diverse. This is ironic when you consider that from man's point of view, Babylon was created to appease God's wrath. However, from Lucifer's larger point of view, Babylon was created to persecute God's people.

Rev. 13:6
And he opened his mouth in blasphemy against God, to blaspheme his name, and his tabernacle, and them that dwell in heaven.

{6} As the Great Tribulation progressed, the leadership of Babylon became more bold in their blasphemy. Persecution intensified. When the fifth trumpet occurred, the devil appeared physically and Babylon's leaders slandered God's holy name by claiming that God and his angels dwelled among men! They proclaimed, "Let the world and everyone in it worship him!" The saints on Earth and the angels in Heaven abhorred this degrading insult.

Blasphemy occurs whenever man usurps God's prerogative or authority. God commands everyone to rest from labor on Saturday, the seventh day of the week.[83] When Babylon forms, it will require the nations to worship God according to the religious majority in each nation. Babylon's religious leaders will make many declarations about God that are insulting and blasphemous. For a while, it will seem like God's wrath has stopped and Babylon will take credit for causing God's wrath to cease. What the leader's of Babylon do not know is that God does not send devastating judgments during the fourth and fifth trumpets. Babylon will demand that all people worship God or be severely punished. Ironically, when men presume to tell the Creator of the universe when He is to be worshiped, they presume to have God's authority! Blasphemy is the logical end of the fallen nature. When confronted with the clearest evidences of God's will, the carnal nature will naturally defy God's authority. This is why the unpardonable sin is blasphemy against the Holy Spirit.[84] If we deliberately continue to make sinful choices, eventually God will be unable to save us.

Babylon's blasphemy will continue to escalate because Lucifer is the hand inside the puppet. Babylon's persecution will be intense, intimidating many Christians. For fear of punishment and lack of food, many Christians will give in to Babylon's demands and refuse to put their faith in Jesus. The remnant of the woman will be imprisoned, beaten, tortured, and many saints will be put to death. Like the Pharisees and Sadducees in Christ's time, religious leaders will angrily reject the testimony of Jesus, faithfully spoken through the lips of the 144,000.

{7} Babylon made war against the remnant of the woman for forty-two (lunar) months. By the end of the forty-two months, it appeared as though the saints had been eliminated from Earth. The power of the holy people (the 144,000) was broken.[85]

During the Great Tribulation, God will speak forcibly and clearly through His servants, the 144,000. In addition to this, the Holy Spirit will be poured out on all flesh[86] so that everyone will be stirred to hear and thoughtfully consider the testimony of the 144,000.[87] The gospel presented by the 144,000 cannot be defeated because Jesus Himself will speak through their lips. Most, if not all of the 144,000 will be killed on or before the 1,260th day of the Great Tribulation[88] and Babylon will exercise authority over *every* tribe, people, language, and nation on Earth (including the United States). God's sheep (the honest in

> **Rev. 13:6**

> **Rev. 13:7**
> *And it was given unto him to make war with the saints, and to overcome them: and power was given him over all kindreds, and tongues, and nations.*

heart) will hear Jesus' voice[89] and they will embrace and obey His two laws of love.[90] It is interesting to note that in God's sight, the difference between sheep and goats is the direction of love. Sheep love outwardly, goats love inwardly.

> **Rev. 13:8**
>
> *And all that dwell upon the earth shall worship him, whose names are not written in the book of life of the Lamb slain from the foundation of the world.*

{8} *All* inhabitants of Earth will worship and obey the laws of the composite beast (Babylon); all whose names have not been written in The Book of Life that was written before the creation of the world. The Book of Life is the book sealed with seven seals and is the book belonging to the Lamb that was slain.[91]

The second word in verse 8 speaks volumes. With the exception of the saints, the whole world will worship and obey Babylon's laws. Lucifer brings this specification to fulfillment during the fifth and sixth trumpets. John defines the wicked in verse 8 in an interesting way. He describes them as **"all whose names have not been written in the Book of Life that was written before the creation of the world."** This phrase is used for good reason. The Father, having perfect foreknowledge, foreknew the names of those who would rebel against His kindness and grace, but everything possible was done to save each person. Jesus will send out the 144,000 so that God's will might be clearly set before all mankind. Jesus will pour out the Holy Spirit on every person so that everyone will intelligently and thoughtfully consider God's will. Jesus has leveled the playing field by offering salvation to everyone who puts their faith in Him and obeys the eternal gospel. Even though the Father foreknew the choices that everyone would make, He has done everything possible to save *all* mankind.

In a sense, Jesus was slain from the creation of the world, because before Adam and Eve were created, a plan for redemption existed. Jesus volunteered to die in their place the day they sinned.[92] Of course, Jesus did not actually die until 4,000 years later, but when Jesus promised to die, His promise was as good as done because God always fulfills His promises![93]

Jesus will permit the composite beast to rule over the world (Babylon - Phase I) until the sixth trumpet occurs and then Jesus will allow Lucifer to overtake the world and reign as king of kings and lord of lords (Babylon - Phase II). Prior to the sixth trumpet, millions of saints will support the ministry of the 144,000. Their love for one another, and their testimony and loyalty to Jesus will impress many of the wicked to repent and be saved. Consequently, the saints will nurture millions of new converts who put their faith in Jesus. Prior to the fifth trumpet, the number of people sealed will increase daily. When the gospel fails to transform additional people, the fifth trumpet will sound. When the devil and his angels arrive, they will eliminate most of the non-religious wicked through torture. Then, during the sixth trumpet (Babylon - Phase II), Jesus will bestow a martyr's faith on millions of His saints so that they can be *sacrificed* as martyrs. (This is the fifth seal). Jesus needs sacrificial martyrs because there is no greater testimony that a person can give than that of a martyr who willingly lays down his life for what is true. Jesus will permit many Christians to die during the sixth trumpet in an attempt to convert those few souls in Babylon who are still open to the prompting of the Holy Spirit. If the Father so loved the world that He gave His only begotten Son to redeem one sinner, it is easy to see why Jesus would be willing to sacrifice a few million people to save a dozen sinners. The value of one sinner in God's sight can only be measured by the enormous price He was willing to pay for our redemption.

Rev. 13:8

Do we really need to understand this prophecy at the present time? Jesus said to His disciples, **"All this I have told you so that you will not go astray."**[94] Jesus knows the value of foreknowledge. By giving His followers a schematic of His plans and purposes, they will not go astray. They will not be discouraged or caught off guard when this crisis occurs. Paul knew that many Christians would not want to hear from God's Word. He warned Timothy, **"For the time will come when men will not put up with sound doctrine. Instead, to suit their own desires, they will gather around them a great number of teachers to say what their itching ears want to hear. They will turn their ears away from the truth and turn aside to myths."**[95]

{9} If a person has an ear for the things of God, the Holy Spirit will make sure that he hears and understands this prophecy. Jesus said, **"Do not worry about tomorrow, for tomorrow will worry about itself. . ."**[96]

Rev. 13:9

If any man have an ear, let him hear.

> Jesus said, **"I have told you these things, so that in me you may have peace. In this world you will have trouble. But take heart! I have overcome the world."**[97]

Jesus' Final Victory

> **Rev. 13:10**
>
> *He that leadeth into captivity shall go into captivity: he that killeth with the sword must be killed with the sword. Here is the patience and the faith of the saints.*

{10} Jesus knows who will go into captivity and who will die. (See NIV translation.) Therefore, He says, "Do not worry about the future or your personal situation. I will never leave you or forsake you." We need to learn all that we can from God's Word. We need to practice standing firm for what is right and true each day by allowing Jesus to take care of the consequences. This is the essence of living by faith. Trust in God! Be assured that when Jesus requires the death of a saint, He will bestow a martyr's faith on that saint. The words, grace, and courage needed for the moment will be provided and on top of this, that saint will receive eternal life. So, even though these matters may be unsettling, we need to know and understand God's plans and purposes without worrying about tomorrow. If we abide in Jesus, we can do everything He commands. A great reward awaits the faithful, those who patiently endure to the end or their end.

The Beast from the Abyss

> **Rev. 13:11**
>
> *And I beheld another beast coming up out of the earth; and he had two horns like a lamb, and he spake as a dragon.*

{11} At the beginning of the fifth trumpet, the 891st day of the Great Tribulation, I saw another scene. I saw a beast come up from the Abyss,[98] out of a hole in the Earth. This beast looked very similar to the Lamb that had been slain in Revelation 5, but it had only *two* horns instead of seven.[99] Even though this beast looked like the Lamb, it spoke like the dragon.

> The "lamb-like" beast is the great red dragon wearing sheep's clothing. Lucifer will personate Jesus. Lucifer will appear on Earth about two years after the composite beast appears. The devil and his angels will be released from the Abyss at the fifth trumpet. Meanwhile, the 144,000 will deliver a third message (discussed in detail in Prophecy 12) warning everyone to have nothing to do with this beast for his appearing is the greatest deception ever created.[100] Because the saints understand Bible prophecy, they will anticipate the arrival of this deception and they will not even go out to see Lucifer and his angels when he arrives at their locale.[101]
>
> The devil knows that "seeing is believing," and in his situation, this phrase will be particularly true. During the five months of the fifth trumpet, Lucifer and his angels will travel the world nonstop from one heavily populated area to another. Wherever he goes, millions of people will go out to see him. He will claim to be God. He will claim that he

sent the first four trumpet judgments upon Earth because of man's degenerate and decadent behavior. His brilliant glory and awesome powers will appear to back up his blasphemous assertions. Physically, he will be larger than life. He will be a glorious being surrounded by thousands of dazzling angels (demons in disguise). Every day, the devil will put on a great show of signs and wonders to bedazzle his spectators. He will speak kind words and heal the sick. He will even appear to raise some dead people from their graves! His demeanor will seem genuine and generous. He will show sympathy for the suffering of mankind. He will miraculously feed millions who have been impacted by the severity of the famine in the land.[102] When people consider this glorious being with all his generous actions, billions of people will easily accept his claims of divinity.

{12} To make this deception all encompassing, Jesus gave the lamblike beast greater miracle working powers than He had given to the 144,000. To obtain loyal support from Babylon's leaders, the devil performed an assortment of miracles on their behalf. When he appeared in different world locations, he honored the leaders of Babylon by telling the people that they must obey (worship) God as Babylon's leaders dictate. This flattery, of course, made the leaders of Babylon very happy to think that God himself would endorse their legislative efforts to appease His wrath!

> God empowers Lucifer (the man of lawlessness) to come as "a strong delusion" because the wicked refused to believe the truth and be saved. **"The coming of the lawless one will** [appear to be the work of God, but it will] **be in accordance with the work of Satan displayed in all kinds of counterfeit miracles, signs and wonders, and in every sort of evil that deceives those who are perishing. They** [those refusing the eternal gospel must] **perish because they refused to love the truth and so be saved. For this reason God sends them a powerful delusion so that they will believe the lie and so that all will be condemned who have not believed the truth but have delighted in wickedness."**[103]

{13} At various times and in different places, the devil called fire down from Heaven in full view of men. This miracle was his most overpowering deception and the devil reminded everyone that even in Elijah's day, *only* the true God could send down fire from Heaven.[104]

Rev. 13:11

Rev. 13:12
And he exerciseth all the power of the first beast before him, and causeth the earth and them which dwell therein to worship the first beast, whose deadly wound was healed.

Rev. 13:13
And he doeth great wonders, so that he maketh fire come down from heaven on the earth in the sight of men,

Day 1,039 – Everything Changes

> **Rev. 13:14**
> *And deceiveth them that dwell on the earth by the means of those miracles which he had power to do in the sight of the beast; saying to them that dwell on the earth, that they should make an image to the beast, which had the wound by a sword, and did live.*

{14} The devil's miracle working powers eclipsed and silenced the miracles performed by the 144,000. As a result, millions of wicked people were deceived. They embraced Lucifer, believing that God Himself had come to Earth to dwell among men. The wicked were ensnared by what they saw. Of course, the wicked did not realize that Jesus permitted the devil to put on this show of deception because they refused to love the truth and be saved.[105] Since the wicked had refused to believe the truth and be saved, they would be compelled to believe a lie and be condemned.

For five months the lamblike beast will produce miracles *on behalf* of Babylon's leadership. The devil will quickly subdue nonreligious people and gain the confidence, allegiance, and adoration of most of the world, but on day 1,039 of the Great Tribulation, everything will change. The sixth trumpet will sound in Heaven's temple and the angel standing at Heaven's Altar of Incense will say, "Release the four angels who are bound at the great river Euphrates."[106] When these words are spoken, the devil and his demons will *abruptly* change character. This phrase sets the devil free to forcibly take control of the world.[107] During the fifth trumpet, the devil will not be allowed to kill anyone. When the sixth trumpet sounds, the devil's "benevolent" character will immediately change and he will be permitted to kill one-third of mankind. Suddenly, he will begin speaking as a dictator, for without a doubt, the great red dragon is a narcissistic dictator. He will immediately **dissolve** the religions of the world because when "God" dwells among men there is no room for religious diversity. There will be one lord, one faith, and one baptism for everyone on Earth. The devil will also move to **dissolve** the governments of the world because as "God," he owns the whole world. He will distribute the land to his wealthy followers.[108] He will appoint ten puppet-kings to rule under him. Their purpose will be to oversee the day to day administration of an evil and brutal theocracy.[109]

By dissolving the religions and governments of the world, the devil effectively consolidates Babylon into a one world church state. He will declare that Phase I was necessary because of man's diversity, but now that "God (referring to himself) lives among men," there has to be one faith, one lord, and one baptism. He will tell the world that he has come to establish a thousand years of peace on Earth. Therefore, the religious and political diversity of the world has to be eliminated. There must be one government and one religious body and no one other than God himself can rule as king of kings and lord of lords.

Because God's Sabbath day will be an inflammatory issue, it seems likely that the devil will change the weekly cycle from seven days to ten days to insult the Creator and His Sabbath rest. By establishing a day for worship which the whole world will accept as a holy day,[110] the devil will expose those who rest from working on the seventh day If the devil makes this transition, his action would end the argument that it does not matter which day a person sets aside to worship God.

{15} After the sixth trumpet sounded, everyone refusing to worship Lucifer and obey the laws of his counterfeit theocracy was killed (if captured). {16} Everyone wishing to survive, including the small and great, rich and poor, free and slave, received a mark, a *tattoo* (Greek: *charagma* means an etching) on his right hand or on his forehead.[111]

> It is likely that to manage the logistical needs of Earth's population, the lamblike beast will **command** the people of Earth to be divided into groups of one thousand.[112] One person from each group will be chosen to serve as the captain of the group. Each captain will be told that the first 666 people to receive a tattoo on their right hand showing the number "666" can live, while all others must be put to death. This gruesome tactic will work very well. It will quickly eliminate those in opposition or hesitant to go along with Lucifer's counterfeit theocracy.[113]

{17} No one was permitted to buy or sell (that is, able to survive) unless he had the tattoo. The captains of each group also received an additional tattoo on their foreheads. This tattoo showed their high rank in Lucifer's government and the tattoo was the name by which Lucifer was called.[114]

> Many people overlook the fact that the mark of the beast is more than a number tattooed on the right hand. This mark of the beast actually includes the name of the beast, that is, the name that Lucifer will be called. Lucifer's name will be tattooed on the foreheads of his captains so that everyone can tell from a distance that one of Lucifer's captains is approaching or present. Lucifer will have their foreheads tattooed to mock Jesus because after the 144,000 are taken to Heaven, they will wear the name of the Father and the Lamb on their foreheads (signifying their exalted rank).[115] Of course, the name of the Father and the Son

---

Rev. 13:14

Rev. 13:15-16
And he had power to give life unto the image of the beast, that the image of the beast should both speak, and cause that as many as would not worship the image of the beast should be killed. And he causeth all, both small and great, rich and poor, free and bond, to receive a mark in their right hand, or in their foreheads:

Rev. 13:17
And that no man might buy or sell, save he that had the mark, or the name of the beast, or the number of his name.

will not be an ugly defacing patch of ink. Instead, I believe the names of the Father and Son will have an eternal electro-luminescent glow, a beautiful insignia of light that never fades.

{18} Understanding how the mark of the beast becomes the number 666 is a simple calculation for those who are perceptive.

> **Rev. 13:18**
> *Here is wisdom. Let him that hath understanding count the number of the beast: for it is the number of a man; and his number is Six hundred threescore and six.*

After a captain is selected from each group of a thousand, this leaves 999 people in each group. After one-third of the group is killed, this leaves 666 survivors in each group.[116] The tattoo showing "666" on the right hand will serve as a non-transferrable passport (physical evidence) showing that the wearer is loyal to the devil's counterfeit theocracy and that he is eligible to buy or sell rations, the necessities required to remain alive. A simple tattoo will be a very efficient identification method because it does not require accounting, electricity, computers, or paper work. Those who wear the tattoo on their right hand will belong to the devil. They defied the gospel of Jesus. They rejected the clearest evidences of God's will and they blasphemed the Holy Spirit. Receiving the tattoo means they committed the unpardonable sin. Therefore, they become Satan's servants. They prostituted their souls to the devil for the sake of survival. Conversely, God's people will be totally shut off from all earthly support, but Jesus will not abandon His children. He will provide for them because, "The just shall live by faith."[117]

Jesus loves children and also those who are not mentally capable of making these kinds of choices. In His sight, a person is not considered guilty of blasphemy or defiance when he is not qualified to make an intelligent and informed decision to do so. Jesus paid the price for sinners long ago, so do not worry about minors or those who are not capable of making the decisions that are forthcoming. Jesus understands their situation, and long ago He generously provided atonement for them."[118]

After Lucifer destroys a third of mankind and the 144,000, open opposition to his demands will no longer exist. This will prove to be a mixed blessing because the wicked will then turn to Lucifer to fulfill his promises. They will expect him to use his miracle working powers to create a new Heaven and a new Earth as he so often promised. The wicked will not anticipate the seven bowls that God is about to pour upon them on the 1,265th day. Early on the morning of the 1,265th day, the 144,000 will be resurrected.[119] The people who murdered the 144,000 will see their victims come to life right before their eyes. They will hear a voice say to the 144,000, "Come up here," and the 144,000 will ascend to Heaven. Fear and uneasiness will overtake the wicked. They will begin asking, "If God is here on Earth, who called the 144,000 to Heaven? Is this a divine vindication of the 144,000 and their testimony?" Then, the seventh trumpet will sound.

Rev. 13:18

{14:1} I looked into Heaven and saw the 144,000 standing on Mount Zion with the Lamb. Everyone was filled with inexpressible happiness. I saw Jesus welcoming the 144,000 with open arms. The 144,000 had the names of Jesus and of the Father written on their foreheads.

Rev. 14:1

And I looked, and, lo, a Lamb stood on the mount Sion, and with him an hundred forty and four thousand, having his Father's name written in their foreheads.

John saw the 144,000 standing on "Mount Zion" with the Lamb. I believe this scene takes place on the 1,265th day of the Great Tribulation and it underscores a very interesting point. When the 144,000 reach Heaven they will stand *on Mount Zion* with Jesus. Contrary to what millions of Christians believe, Mount Zion on Earth is no longer important to God! In fact, Mount Zion on Earth is insignificant since He abandoned Plan A. God has created a *new* Mount Zion to accomdate *a new* Jerusalem!

Mount Zion (also called Mount Moriah) is significant because God directed Abraham to Mount Zion to offer up his son, Isaac. God sent Abraham to a specific spot on Mount Moriah because it was God's plan that Jesus would be offered as the sacrificial lamb on the *same spot* where Abraham's faith had been tested, but this did not occur. Jesus died among two criminals *outside* the city of Jerusalem.

When the Israelites were in Egypt building pyramids for Pharaoh, the Jebusites were building a fortress on top of Mount Zion. Centuries after the Exodus, David captured the fortress that was sitting on top of Zion.[120] After David began reigning from the city, he changed the name from Jebus to Jerusalem.[121] Through the years, Mount Moriah, Mount Zion, Jebus, the City of David, and Jerusalem are names given to the *same* geographical place. The city has several names because each name says something unique about this special place on Earth.

After David died, God directed Solomon to build His temple over the very spot where Abraham had offered up Isaac.[122] At the dedication of the temple, God's presence filled the temple and Jerusalem became the seventh and final city of refuge.[123] Under Plan A, God intended that Jerusalem would endure forever.[124] However, when Jesus came to Earth, He found Jerusalem

> Rev. 14:1

to be a city of apostasy and blasphemy. Jesus did not die on the Altar of Burnt Offering as originally planned.[125] Jesus did not die where Abraham offered up Isaac. Plan A was abandoned because of Israel's apostasy and according to the terms of His covenant with Israel,[126] God sent the Romans to utterly destroy Jerusalem in A.D. 70. Centuries later, God eliminated any possibility that the Jews would build another temple on Mount Moriah by allowing Moslems to build a mosque (The Dome of the Rock) there.

When Israel failed to receive Messiah, God did not give up on humanity. Instead, Jesus implemented Plan B which is based on a New Covenant.[127] Forty days after His resurrection, Jesus returned to Heaven to prepare a *new* city of refuge there. This city is called *new* Jerusalem because it will replace the original Jerusalem. A new Jerusalem became necessary because God had made a promise to Abraham.[128] God told Abraham that He would someday build a new city and Abraham and his descendants would live there forever. This promise explains why the patriarch looked forward "to a city whose builder and maker is God."[129] The significance of the 144,000 standing on Mount Zion *in Heaven* is a picture worth ten thousand words. They are victorious over Babylon and the great red dragon. Their presence on Mount Zion in Heaven validates the certainty of Plan B. There is redemption and refuge on Mount Zion! God's promise to Abraham will be fulfilled and together with his descendants and the 144,000, they will worship the Father and the Lamb in the *eighth* city of refuge. New Jerusalem is a reality and it will endure forever! Nothing impure or that defiles[130] will enter this city and its High Priest will be Jesus Christ Himself.[131]

John also saw another interesting feature about the 144,000. He saw the 144,000 wearing the names of the Father and Jesus on their foreheads. I am sure the effect will be radiant and very beautiful; very different from the ugly tattoo which the devil will place on the foreheads of his servants. I believe the names of Jesus and the Father will be highly visible throughout eternity, because the 144,000 will serve as administrative assistants to Jesus. They will make up His personal entourage and follow Him wherever He goes. The honor that will rest upon these people is the highest that God can bestow. Everyone will recognize Christ's personal assistants from a distance by looking upon their lovely faces. No one else in the universe will wear anything like the names of the Father and Jesus on their foreheads.

{2} Then I heard a sound from Heaven like rushing waters and roaring like loud peals of thunder. I continued to listen and the awesome sound I heard was like harpists playing a song on their harps. {3} The 144,000 sang a new song before the throne and before the four living creatures and the elders. This was an amazing event. A brand new, unheard song was perfectly performed before Jesus and the Father! I looked around Heaven and everyone other than the 144,000 was silent. No one could sing the song except the 144,000 who had been redeemed from Earth.

> The 144,000 will sing a new song when they get to Heaven. It will be a song of experience and faithful endurance and no one else in Heaven can sing this exact song. In Heaven, a song is a unique testimony describing a personal experience that tells of trouble, perplexity, suffering, and victory through God's sustaining power and His infinite love. Only those who have endured that experience can sing a song that has never been heard!

{4} The 144,000 are God's priests forever. They will accompany the Lamb wherever He goes, for they were purchased from among men and offered as firstfruits to God and the Lamb.[132] The 144,000 are men and women who came out of the Great Tribulation.[133] They will come from every nation, tongue, and people and special honor was given to them because of their faithful service and endurance. {5} Most, if not all of the 144,000 will die as martyrs because they spoke the words given to them without regard for personal consequences. In God's sight, they are blameless. They stood firmly for God's truth and they proclaimed everything that He wanted the wicked to hear.

> When we see their service, faithfulness, and courage, when we see the abuse they will suffer for Christ's sake, when we observe their rejection, sorrows, and the endurance required, we too, will appreciate and honor their faithful and determined efforts to carry the eternal gospel to every nation.[134]

The Rules of Interpretation

Consider how the Rules of Interpretation (discussed in the Introduction of this book) are observed in this prophecy:

Rule One says an apocalyptic prophecy has a beginning point and ending point in time and the events within the prophecy occur in the order given. This prophecy begins with war in Heaven on Resurrection Sunday and it ends with the 144,000 rejoicing with

---

Rev. 14:2-3

And I heard a voice from heaven, as the voice of many waters, and as the voice of a great thunder: and I heard the voice of harpers harping with their harps: And they sung as it were a new song before the throne, and before the four beasts, and the elders: and no man could learn that song but the hundred and forty and four thousand, which were redeemed from the earth.

Rev. 14:4-5

These are they which were not defiled with women; for they are virgins. These are they which follow the Lamb whithersoever he goeth. These were redeemed from among men, being the firstfruits unto God and to the Lamb. And in their mouth was found no guile: for they are without fault before the throne of God.

Jesus on Mount Zion (Day 1,265 of the Great Tribulation). Notice the chronological order in Prophecy 11:

1. Revelation 12:7-12 (A.D. 30)

    There was war in Heaven on Resurrection Sunday. Lucifer and his angels were cast out of Heaven a second, final time.

2. Revelation 12:13-14 (A.D. 538-1798)

    The dragon chased the woman to the desert for 1,260 years (a time, times and half a time). According to Rule Four, this time period must be translated using a day for a year because the Jubilee Calendar is in operation.

3. Revelation 12:15,16 (1798 to the present)

    The Earth helped the woman. God provided a safe place (the United States of America) where she could escape religious persecution.

4. Revelation 12:17 (1798 to the present)

    When the 1,260 years ended, the devil went off to make plans for war on the remnant of the woman. This assault will occur during the Great Tribulation.

5. Revelation 13:1 (future)

    When God's wrath reduces the world to ruins (the first four trumpets), a composite beast having seven heads and ten horns will rise. This beast will be a *global* government. Religious and political leaders will create this government to appease God so that His wrath will cease. The seven heads represent the seven religious systems of the world.[135] The head on the beast that was wounded in 1798 is the Roman Catholic Church. When the composite beast (also called Babylon) forms, the pope will be selected as its leader. This is how the head that received the deadly wound in 1798 will become completely healed.

6. Revelation 13:2-6 (future)

    Babylon (the composite beast) will become a hand puppet of the devil. The devil will use Babylon to persecute *the remnant of the woman* for forty-two lunar months. Rule Four requires that this time period not be translated because the Jubilee Calendar is not in operation. Therefore, forty-two lunar months in Revelation 13:5 represent 1241 literal days ($42 \times 29.53 = 1240.26$ days).

7. Revelation 13:7-10 (future)

    God's people will be conquered and defeated. Most of them will be killed or put in prison and *all* inhabitants of the Earth will obey the laws of Babylon, *all* that is, except the saints.

8. Revelation 13:11-18 (future)

    About two years after the composite beast is created, the devil and his angels will be released from the Abyss to physically appear before the people of Earth during the fifth trumpet. (See Revelation 9:1-11.) Lucifer is the "lamblike" beast in Revelation 13:11 that comes up out of the Earth. During the sixth trumpet, the devil's forces will kill a third of mankind (most, if not all of the 144,000 will be killed). The lamblike beast will set up a worldwide counterfeit theocracy (the image to the composite beast) and implement his mark, a tattoo showing the number, 666.

9. Revelation 14:1-5 (future)

    Jesus will resurrect the 144,000 at the seventh trumpet and take them to Heaven on the 1,265th day of the Great Tribulation. They will be presented to God as the first fruits of the coming harvest.

Rule Two says a fulfillment only occurs when all of the specifications are met, and this includes the order stated in the prophecy. Because some of the elements in this prophecy are in the future, we can say that this prophecy has not been fulfilled even though certain elements have been fulfilled in the past.

For example, the dragon chased the woman to the wilderness for 1,260 years (538-1798). This has been fulfilled. However, the dragon's efforts to destroy the remnant of the woman during the Great Tribulation will last forty-two months. This has not been fulfilled.

Rule Three says apocalyptic language can be literal, analogous, or symbolic. To reach the intended meaning of a prophecy, the reader must consider the context, the use of parallel language in the Bible, and if an element is thought to be symbolic, the Bible must interpret the symbol with a *relevant* text.

This prophecy uses all three types of language: symbolic, analogous, and literal. Consider these examples: The great red dragon is a symbol representing **"that ancient serpent called the devil."**[136] The Earth literally helped the woman.[137] Geographically speaking, a new territory on Earth (the United States of America) was discovered to become a place to receive those who had been persecuted for their faith. Analogous language is also used when describing the beast from the sea: "The beast I saw resembled a leopard, but had feet like those of a bear. . . ."[138]

Rule Four says the presence or absence of the Jubilee Calendar determines how God measures time. The time, times, and half a time (1,260 days) mentioned in verses 6 and 14 require translation because they occur while the Jubilee Calendar (1437 B.C.-1994) is operating. The 1,260 years mentioned in this prophecy perfectly align with the time, times, and half a time mentioned in Daniel 7:25. However, the forty-two months mentioned in Revelation 13:5 should not be translated because this time period occurs after 1994 (after the Jubilee Calendar expired).[139]

Avoiding Internal Conflict

There are time periods in Daniel and Revelation where a day should be translated as a year (for example, the seventy weeks of Daniel 9 are translated into 490 years), but there are other time periods where translation is not permitted. Because some time periods in prophecy are translated a day for a year and others are not, a valid rule is required to tell us when time periods should be translated and when they should not.

Faulty rules produce faulty conclusions. There is no valid rule that requires *every* time period in Daniel and Revelation to be literal or translated as a day for a year. Faulty rules always put the Bible *in a position of internal conflict (inconsistency)*. In other words, the Bible cannot speak for itself when its chronological order is put in conflict with its timing! A valid rule of interpretation cannot have an exception, for if it does, no one but God has the authority to tell the world when an exception is permitted. Moreover, *a valid rule will not force the Bible into a position where it cancels something it declares*. This point is emphasized because valid rules and valid conclusions are always in harmony with all that God has said.

References

1. See Revelation 9:1-11; 13:11-18 and 17:8. Compare also with 2 Thessalonians 2.
2. 2 Corinthians 11:14
3. 1 Kings 6:25 (A cubit is approximately 18 inches.)
4. Daniel 8:25 (Lucifer cannot be killed by human power.)
5. Revelation 18:5,6
6. Revelation 7:9 occurs before Revelation 8:1. Further, the seventh seal is not broken and The Book of Life opened until the one thousand years have ended. See Revelation 20:12.
7. Revelation 19:2
8. Revelation 15:2,3
9. John 16:33 Overcoming the world is defined as overcoming the temptations of the world. "For everything in the world – the cravings of sinful man, the lust of his eyes, and the boasting of what he has and does – comes not from the Father but from the world." (1 John 2:16) Like Jesus, the 144,000 will be resurrected and presented as first fruits of a coming harvest. See 1 Corinthians 15:20.
10. Revelation 11:10
11. 1 Samuel 28
12. For a discussion on the dating of the crucifixion and resurrection of Jesus, please see pages 185-207 in my book, *Daniel: Unlocked for the Final Generation* or you can freely download this chapter at: http://www.wake-up.org/Daniel/DanChap6.htm.
13. Luke 24:1; Acts 10:40; 13:30-37; Revelation 1:18
14. Matthew 28:1
15. Matthew 28:9
16. John 20:17
17. Psalm 24:7-10, insertion mine
18. Luke 24:13-34
19. 1 Corinthians 15:20
20. Mark 10:32-34
21. 2 Corinthians 5:21

22. Matthew 27:46
23. John 10:18
24. John 15:13
25. Leviticus 23:15-17.
26. Psalm 2:8; John 17:6; Hebrews 1:2
27. Revelation 12:7-9
28. Luke 24:13-35
29. Matthew 28:11-15
30. Matthew 28:18-20
31. Romans 8:5-8
32. John 12:31; 14:30; 16:11
33. Job 1:6-12
34. Daniel 7:13,14
35. Revelation 19:16
36. Ezekiel 28:12-15
37. Hebrews 4:15
38. Psalm 2:7-9; Acts 13:34; Hebrews 5:5-9
39. Please see Chapter 2 in my book, *Jesus: The Alpha and The Omega* or you can freely download the chapter at: http://www.wake-up.org/Alpha/Chapter2.htm.
40. John 12:28-31, italics mine
41. Ezekiel 28:12-17
42. Luke 10:18
43. See Prophecy 8.
44. See Prophecy 15.
45. Compare with Zechariah 3:1-7.
46. Ephesians 2:8,9; Galatians 2:15-17; James 2:23, 24
47. See Appendix A and comments under Revelation 12:14.
48. See Leviticus 25:1-18. Even though weekly cycles of seven years began at the time of the Exodus, Israel did not observe Sabbath years in the desert. Just as Adam and Eve's first full day was God's seventh day Sabbath, so Israel's first full year in Canaan was God's seventh year Sabbath. For a detailed discussion showing that God began counting Jubilee cycles at the time of the Exodus and

not from Israel's entrance into Canaan, please download this free article: http://www.wake-up.org/daystar/ds2000/Great%20Clocks.htm.

49. There is evidence in the Bible showing that some people understood the proper location of the seventy weeks. See Mark 1:15 and Luke 3:15; 10:11.

50. For a discussion on this topic, please see pages 185-212 in my book, *Daniel: Unlocked for the Final Generation* or you can freely download this article at: http://www.wake-up.org/Daniel/DanChap6.htm.

51. Genesis 7:24
52. Genesis 7:11,12
53. Genesis 8:3,4
54. Genesis 1:14 For further information about the Sun appearing to travel 360 degrees of arc over the course of a solar year, go to http://www.wake-up.org/links/astronotes.htm.
55. Isaiah 16:14
56. Daniel 4:29-32
57. Ezekiel 29:18,19
58. See Appendix A.
59. See Book 1-1 at http://www.wake-up.org/links/codex.htm.
60. Daniel 12:7, insertion and italics mine
61. Revelation 11:3,7, insertion mine
62. James 1:2-4
63. 1 Peter 1:7-9, insertion mine
64. Revelation 6:9, italics mine
65. John 15:20,21
66. John 14:27
67. Daniel 12:7
68. 1 Corinthians 10:13; 2 Corinthians 1:8,9; Hebrews 11:17
69. Revelation 7:9-17
70. Revelation 12:6
71. See Hosea 5:10; Isaiah 8:6-8; 59:18,19; Daniel 9:26
72. Daniel 7:20,21

73. John 8:44
74. Revelation 13:5-7
75. Deuteronomy 8:11-19; 28:63
76. Philippians 1:20-29; 4:11,12; Hebrews 13:5
77. See The Angel Explains - Part I.
78. For a discussion on the identity of the seven heads, please see pages 165-177 in my book, *A Study on the Seven Trumpets, Two Witnesses and Four Beasts* or you can freely download the article at: http://www.wake-up.org/Revelation/724Book.pdf
79. Ibid. See also commentary in this book on Revelation 12:14.
80. Revelation 12:17
81. Mark 7:8,9; Acts 5:29-32
82. Revelation 17:12
83. Exodus 20:9-11
84. Matthew 12:31,32
85. Daniel 12:7
86. Joel 2:28-31; Revelation 11:3
87. Revelation 11:3; 14:11
88. Revelation 11:7-9
89. John 10:14-16
90. Matthew 22:36-40
91. Revelation 5:6-9 See also pages 38-44 in my book, *A Study on the Seven Seals and the 144,000* or you can freely download the article at http://www.wake-up.org/Revelation/RevSeg2.htm.
92. Psalm 2:7-12
93. Compare Genesis 15:13-18 with Exodus 12:40-42.
94. John 16:1
95. 2 Timothy 4:3,4
96. Matthew 6:34
97. John 16:33
98. Revelation 9:1-11; 11:7; 17:8; 20:1-3
99. Revelation 5:6

100. Revelation 14:9-11; 2 Thessalonians 2:3-12; Matthew 24:23-27
101. Matthew 24:26
102. Revelation 6:8
103. 2 Thessalonians 2:9-12
104. 1 Kings 18
105. 2 Thessalonians 2:3-12
106. Revelation 9:14
107. For a discussion on this matter, please see pages 55-63 in my book, *A Study on the Seven Trumpets, Two Witnesses and Four Beasts* or you can freely download the article at http://www.wake-up.org/Revelation/724Book.pdf .
108. Daniel 11:39
109. Revelation 17:12-14
110. This claim is based on five underlying presuppositions.
    1. The Bible says the devil will not honor one particular religious body. He will oppose all of them. (2 Thessalonians 2:4) Therefore, he would need a universal holy day that does not favor Muslims, Jews, Catholics, or Protestants who worship on either Friday, Saturday, or Sunday.
    2. The Bible teaches the core conflict during the Great Tribulation will be over worship. (Revelation 13:15) Therefore, when Lucifer establishes his one world church state (a counterfeit theocracy), he will have to create a holy day for worship which everyone must observe.
    3. The Bible reveals that God will show the Ark of the Covenant at the close of the seventh trumpet. (Revelation 11:19) One of the underlying reasons for this exposure is God's fourth commandment. The fourth commandment establishes a week of seven days, with the seventh day of the week (Saturday) being God's holy Sabbath. A weekly cycle of ten days with a different holy day will clearly stand in opposition to the higher law of God. Thus, the condemnation resting upon the wicked will be clear cut and inescapable.

4. If the devil changes the weekly cycle to ten days, those worshiping on God's seventh day will be easily detected because God's true Sabbath will land on different "work days." In fact, there would be several ten day weeks that would have two, seventh day Sabbaths in them! Thus, a ten day week will flush out the remnant of the woman; those who love and obey God's fourth commandment.

5. The seven last plagues are seventy days in length; this could mean that ten days are allotted to each plague. God's clocks are based on the number seven. (Seven days per week, seven months in the religious year, seven years in a week of years and seven weeks of years in a Jubilee cycle and seventy weeks in one "Great Day.") On the other hand, man's numbering system is based on ten. We count in terms of tens, hundreds, thousands, ten years per decade, ten decades per century, and ten centuries in a millennium. Ancient civilizations in Egypt and China followed ten day weekly cycles for centuries. After the French Revolution, France enacted a ten day week for a few years (1793-1805) in an effort to overthrow the influence and power of religion. God's clocks are unlike man's clocks. In an effort to confuse people and show contempt for God's Sabbath, I believe the devil will install a weekly cycle that will appeal to man's "base ten" numbering system.

In summary, it seems reasonable to assume that a ten day weekly cycle will be part of Satan's plan at the time of the sixth trumpet because a new day for worship does not favor any religious system on Earth. The purpose is to defy God's seventh day Sabbath and clearly expose those who keep it. Of course, time will tell if my conclusions are correct.

111. For further discussion on this topic, please see my commentary on Revelation 9:16.

112. For a discussion on this topic, please see pages 220-227 in my book, *A Study on The Seven Trumpets, Two Witnesses and Four Beasts* or you can freely download the article at: http://www.wake-up.org/Revelation/724Book.pdf.

113. Revelation 9:15
114. Compare with Revelation 17:5. Lucifer's title is unknown at the present time.
115. Revelation 14:1; 22:4
116. For further discussion on this topic, please see pages 220-227 in my book, *A Study on the Seven Trumpets, Two Witnesses and Four Beasts* or you can freely download the article at http://www.wake-up.org/Revelation/724Book.pdf.
117. Romans 1:17
118. For a discussion on this topic, please see the *Wake Up Report,* October 2008, "Are Children Born Saved or Lost?" at http://www.wake-up.org/daystar/ds2008/Oct.htm.
119. Revelation 11:11,12 From the time the censer is cast down until the Two Witnesses have completed their work is 1,260 days. (Revelation 11:3) Then the bodies of the Two Witnesses will lie in the street for 3.5 days which is counted as four days when counting inclusively. On Sunday, the 1,265th day, the 144,000 are resurrected. See Prophecy 9.
120. 2 Samuel 5:7
121. Judges 19:10; 1 Chronicles 11:4-8
122. 2 Samuel 24:16-25; 1 Chronicles 21:22-22:1; 2 Chronicles 3:1; Genesis 22:2-9
123. Numbers 35:1-14; Isaiah 14:32; Joel 3:16
124. 1 Kings 2:2-4
125. Zechariah 12:10-13:1, 6
126. Leviticus 26; Deuteronomy 28
127. Luke 22:20
128. John 14:1-3; Galatians 3:28,29
129. Hebrews 11:10
130. Revelation 21:27
131. Hebrews 6:20
132. Exodus 23:19; Leviticus 23:20; Numbers 18:12,13
133. Joel 2:29
134. Matthew 24:14

135. See commentary on Revelation 17.
136. Revelation 12:9
137. Revelation 12:16
138. Revelation 13:2
139. See Appendix A.

Prophecy 12

The Eternal Gospel

Revelation 14:6-15:6

Beginning point in time: When the Censer is Cast Down (Revelation 8:5)

Ending point in time: 1,265th day of the Great Tribulation

Summary: The essence of this prophecy can be summarized in a few sentences. For 1,260 days, God will empower His Two Witnesses to speak through His 144,000 prophets. The 144,000 will proclaim three messages* to everyone on Earth. The first message will contain a demand, the second will contain an inflammatory declaration, and the third will contain an ultimatum. Circumstances will force everyone to respond to these messages and our response will determine our eternal destiny.

Introduction: This prophecy contains five elements which occur in chronological order. They are:

1. God sends an outright demand
2. God sends an inflammatory declaration
3. God sends an ultimatum
4. God's offer of salvation comes to an end
5. The victory celebration of the 144,000

Jesus will not expect human beings to embrace the testimony of the 144,000 on the basis of the miracle working powers which they will exhibit.[1] Instead, the testimony of the 144,000 will be vali-

---

*Note: Actually, the 144,000 will present four messages from God during the Great Tribulation. Three messages are found in this prophecy and the fourth message is found in Prophecy 14. These four messages are easily understood. When the time comes for their delivery, those knowing very little or nothing about the Bible will be able to *validate* the testimony of the 144,000 from the Bible for themselves.

dated by God's Two Witnesses. If a person defies the testimony of God's Two Witnesses, that person commits the unpardonable sin. The issue of validation is important because the devil and his prophets will also work amazing miracles during the Great Tribulation. Miracle working powers will gain attention, but miracles do not necessarily validate the testimony of a person claiming to speak for God. By putting four messages in a plain, "thus saith the Lord" format in the book of Revelation, the essential elements for salvation will be easy for everyone to understand when the time comes. In addition to these plainly worded messages in Scripture, the Holy Spirit will strongly impress each heart with their importance and validity. The gospel of Jesus will be clear, unmistakable, simple, and obvious. If a person chooses to reject the clearest evidences of truth and the strongest influence that the Holy Spirit can exercise in that person's heart, God can do nothing else to save that person.

Redemption through Faith or Survival through Works?

The four messages presented by the 144,000 will add a dimension to the Great Tribulation that few people anticipate. Currently, millions of Christians believe a Great Tribulation is coming, but few understand the coming contest for souls; a contest between salvation through faith and survival through works. After the first four trumpets occur, everyone will question the possibility of survival. God's deadly judgments will turn the world upside down. Out of Earth's smoldering ruins, Babylon will arise with a foolish plan to appease God's wrath. Its solution will unwittingly defy the authority of Jesus and the testimony of the 144,000. The conflict between Babylon and the 144,000 forces everyone into making a decision. If a person obeys God's truth, he will be severely punished by the authorities of Babylon. If a person obeys the laws of Babylon, Jesus will destroy him during the seven last plagues. This will be a "no win" situation that catches most Christians by surprise. Regardless of familial ties, language, culture, education, religion, or race, four simple messages from God will separate mankind into two groups of people; the sheep and the goats.

The Great Tribulation Begins

The first message that comes from Jesus will be shocking. It will come as an outright demand and billions of people will immediately find it offensive. The 144,000 will declare that everyone is required to worship Jesus Christ, the Creator of Heaven and Earth. This message will begin on Day One of the Great Tribulation, when the censer is cast down.[2] This demand will be proclaimed and heard until the 1,260th day of the Great Tribulation. A second message will join with the first message when the composite beast, Babylon, rises from the sea. The second message will be highly inflammatory. This message from Jesus will declare that Babylon's endeavor is false, its demands are an insult to Jesus and its ways are blasphemous. Of course, the second message will make the leaders of Babylon furious with the 144,000 and all who embrace it. Later, a third message will come from Jesus as an ultimatum. After the devil physically appears on Earth (during the fifth trumpet), the 144,000 will warn, "If anyone worships and obeys the 'lamblike beast,' Jesus will destroy that person at the Second Coming."[3] Finally, a fourth message will be given when the sixth trumpet sounds (when Lucifer sets up a counterfeit theocracy). This message will be God's last call to mankind.[4] This final message will push the undecided into a firm decision. Those who refuse to worship Jesus and obey His commandments will reject the Holy Spirit. They will worship the beast and commit the unpardonable sin.[5] Once every decision has been made, Jesus will conduct a special service in Heaven.[6] He will terminate God's generous offer of redemption with this declaration: **"Let him who does wrong continue to do wrong; let him who is vile continue to be vile; let him who does right continue to do right; and let him who is holy continue to be holy."**[7]

Victory Celebration

The final event recorded in this prophecy is a victory celebration in Heaven. This ceremony will take place on the 1,265th day of the Great Tribulation. On this day, the 144,000 will be resurrected and taken to Heaven. They will gather around the throne of God and sing a song of deliverance and vindication just before the seven last plagues begin. The scene described in this prophecy (Revelation 15:2-4) is a repetition and enlargement of the scene presented in the previous prophecy (Revelation 14:1-5).

It may seem strange that God would "tack on" the victory celebration of the 144,000 to a prophecy that contains three messages and a scene that describes the close of salvation. Do you recall that we found this phenomenon in Prophecies 7, 9, and 11? God sometimes embeds an "odd" element in an apocalyptic prophecy to reveal something that could be misunderstood or easily overlooked. Because each element in an apocalyptic prophecy occurs in chronological order and is related to the other elements in that prophecy, we need to look for the relationship that exists between the odd element and the rest of the elements! This process always produces a wonderful discovery. In this case, this prophecy concludes with the victory celebration of the 144,000 because *they* overcame the beast. They successfully presented three difficult messages to a very hostile world! In other words, their celebration is included in this prophecy because they accomplished the impossible task (humanly speaking) of delivering the gospel of Jesus to every nation, kindred, tongue, and people on Earth!

Consider, for a moment, the daunting challenge of being a prophet. When it comes to enduring physical, emotional, and spiritual suffering, speaking for God is one of the most difficult tasks on Earth. Bible history reveals that God's prophets often have a short life span because the carnal nature is always hostile to the will and ways of God. God often requires prophets to deliver inflammatory words even though proclaiming them may be difficult! Bible history clearly reveals how God's prophets have been scorned, rejected, exiled, put in dungeons, tortured, and put to death because the carnal nature hates God's authority.[8] Jesus warned His disciples that they would be persecuted just as He had been persecuted.[9] In fact, the apostle John was exiled to the Isle of Patmos because he spoke the words which God gave Him to speak![10] Like the prophet John, the 144,000 will faithfully deliver the Word of God during the Great Tribulation, day after day, without regard for the consequences and their suffering will be extreme. Most of the world will oppose the 144,000, but suffering and persecution will not intimidate them or stop them. They do not let up, put up, or shut up until death silences them.[11] Therefore, God has planned a great celebration for them and this event is found at the end of this prophecy!

Who Will Deliver the Three Angel's Messages?

The Bible indicates that *only* the 144,000 will speak for God during the Great Tribulation. Please consider the following six items:

1. We learned in Prophecy 7 that 144,000 people will be selected and sealed (carnal natures removed) before God's wrath (the first four trumpets) occur.

2. We learned in Prophecy 9 that John, representing the experience of the 144,000, was given a little book to eat. This book contains the words which the 144,000 will speak during the Great Tribulation. When the appointed time arrives, Jesus will make this declaration from Heaven: **"There will be no more delay."** The censer will be cast down and Day One of the Great Tribulation will begin. The 144,000 will immediately go to work, proclaiming the gospel of Jesus for 1,260 miserable days. Eventually, the devil and his forces will kill most, if not all of the 144,000. On the 1,265th day of the Great Tribulation, the 144,000 will be resurrected and taken to Heaven.

3. The Bible says the 144,000 will be presented to God as firstfruits of the coming harvest. They are called firstfruits because they are the first to be sealed and the first of the final harvest to be taken to Heaven. They will be God's mouthpieces during the Great Tribulation. The Bible says, **"No lie was found in their mouths."** This means they faithfully spoke the words which God gave them to speak without compromise or deviation. They will faithfully deliver everything that Jesus tells them to say without diluting His words to avoid personal injury or rejection.

4. In this prophecy (Prophecy 12), we will discover that these three messages are sent to mankind from God's throne. Only the 144,000, *those selected, sealed, and empowered to speak for God* can deliver these messages. Only the 144,000 people *free of the carnal nature*, can present the testimony of Jesus to the human race without deviation or compromise.

5. At the end of this prophecy (Prophecy 12), we will find the 144,000 in Heaven singing the song of Moses and the song of the Lamb. Only the 144,000 can sing the song of Moses and the Lamb because they lived through a similar experience to Moses and the Lamb! God selected Moses to lead His people out of slavery. It took forty frustrating years for Israel to arrive at Canaan's door, but Moses accomplished the work which the Lord gave Him to do. In a similar way, the 144,000 will lead God's people, under extreme circumstances, out of sin's slavery and into the sealing experience. The song of the Lamb is a song sung by Jesus. The Father sent Jesus to Earth as the Lamb of God. Jesus

came to a hostile world so that the Father could speak His truth through Him.[12] Jesus did not deviate from the words that the Father gave him and the Jews killed Jesus. This same "truth" will cause the devil and his forces to kill the 144,000. Therefore, only the 144,000 can sing the songs of experience which Moses and the Lamb sing. The numberless multitude will sing a different song.

6. Finally, this prophecy (Prophecy 12) indicates there will be a victorious celebration over the beast and his image and the number of his name *prior to* the commencement of the seven last plagues.[13] Consider the following specification closely: **"And I saw what looked like a sea of glass mixed with fire and standing beside the sea, *those who had been victorious over the beast and his image and over the number of his name. . . .*"**[14] This text indicates the celebrants were on Earth *when* the image of the beast was set up and the mark of the beast imposed. There is only one group of people who can meet these specifications and be in Heaven *before* the seven plagues begin – the 144,000. Once we have examined the story found in this prophecy, the inclusion of a great victory celebration at the end will make perfect sense!

The Sequence Begins

This prophecy begins with Day One of the Great Tribulation, the day when services at the Altar of Incense will be terminated.[15] When Day One arrives, I believe the whole world will be involved with a horrible war that includes a nuclear exchange.[16] When the angel serving at the Altar of Incense casts down the censer, a great display of divine power will impact Earth. The sky will suddenly become dark, angry clouds will appear, and there will be an awesome display of electrical power. The sky will explode into huge sheets of rapid-fire lightning. Deafening and intimidating peals of thunder will seem to pile upon each other and the noise will be so great that everyone on Earth will tremble. Meanwhile, groans and voices will be heard coming out of the Earth. It will seem as though Earth itself is trying to speak. Then, a *global* earthquake will break the whole world into geographic cells. (Maybe there will be 144,000 cells, one cell for each of the 144,000.) There will be no place of safety, no escape from these phenomena. This earthquake will destroy thousands of buildings, power grids, dams, highways, bridges, antennas, trestles, runways, and overpasses. Suddenly, without warning, in the middle of a nuclear war, the Great Tribulation begins. The infrastructures of the world are ruined. Within minutes, the inhabitants of Earth will discover that communication and travel are next to impossible. The impact of these phenomena will be so great that the nuclear war will end. The nations will stop fighting each other and Earth will fall strangely silent. Everyone will be scared to death. Many religious people will correctly guess that Almighty God has signaled His displeasure with the degenerate behavior of mankind.[17] As a result of these horrific events, a global crisis of apocalyptic proportion will begin to unfold. Eventually, nations will discover that other nations have also been ravaged and no one will be in a position to help another. Everyone will have to do his best to survive.

The First Angel's Message: An Outright Demand

{6} I looked into the sky and I saw a brilliant angel descend from God's throne. He came to Earth and orbited the planet for 1,260 days. He carried a demand from Jesus – a timeless truth – a gospel that is everlasting, having no beginning or end. He spoke to the people below, to every nation, tribe, language, and people. Everyone understood his words in his or her own tongue.

{7} He said in a loud voice, "Fear God Almighty. His name is Jesus Christ. Be afraid of Him. Give Him the honor and glory that He is due. Submit to His authority because the time has come for Him to pass judgment upon the living. You must worship Him by resting from your labors on His holy day, His seventh day Sabbath. His Sabbath remains a memorial to His creative work. He created the heavens, the Earth, the sea, and the springs of water in six days and rested on the seventh."

The Eternal Gospel

A display of divine power on Day One of the Great Tribulation will stop the world in its tracks. Jesus will put mankind on notice that the previous order of life has been terminated. Jesus will take matters into His capable hands and He will ensure that everyone hears and intelligently considers His gospel. The casting down of the censer and the physical phenomena (including a global earthquake) that follow will serve as a signal which no one can deny. These events will tell the informed that Day One of the Great Tribulation has begun. For 1,260 days God's prophets will proclaim the eternal gospel to every nation, kindred, tongue, and people.

> **Rev. 14:6**
> *And I saw another angel fly in the midst of heaven, having the everlasting gospel to preach unto them that dwell on the earth, and to every nation, and kindred, and tongue, and people,*
>
> **Rev. 14:7**
> *Saying with a loud voice, Fear God, and give glory to him; for the hour of his judgment is come: and worship him that made heaven, and earth, and the sea, and the fountains of waters.*

Prophecy 12 - The Eternal Gospel

Rev. 14:7

The eternal gospel is a timeless, non-negotiable demand that has no beginning and no end. Therefore, it would be a contradiction in terms to say that the *eternal* gospel is limited to the 1,335 days allotted for the Great Tribulation. Before time began and anything was created, the Father ordained the eternal gospel. This gospel is that throughout eternity, all creation must worship Jesus Christ, the Creator, just as they worship the Father.[18] This is the reason for the term, the "eternal" or "everlasting" gospel. When Lucifer tempted Jesus in the wilderness, Jesus reminded Lucifer of the eternal gospel.[19] Jesus is the Creator of everything that exists.[20] Therefore, every being in Heaven and on Earth is commanded to fear, honor, and worship Jesus the Creator. During the Great Tribulation, every human being will hear the 144,000 proclaim the eternal gospel and everyone will be required to submit to its demand or be destroyed. This is the Father's will. Each person's eternal destiny will be determined by his response to the eternal gospel."[21]

As you might expect, when the eternal gospel is proclaimed to the world with power and authority, it will offend billions of people for two reasons. First, most of the world opposes the idea that Jesus Christ is Almighty God (an equal with the Father in every way) and second, billions of people (including millions of Christians) reject the idea that Jesus is the Creator of Heaven and Earth[22] by rejecting His claim that He made the Earth in six days and rested on the seventh. Most Christians also believe that it is not necessary to obey the Creator's Ten Commandments, especially His fourth commandment which declares the seventh day of the week to be holy. Therefore, when Catholics, Protestants, Jews, Muslims, Hindus, Buddhists and all other religious groups are told to worship Jesus Christ by resting from their labor on His seventh day Sabbath, a huge majority of the world will immediately become hostile toward the 144,000!

The eternal gospel will upset most everyone in one way or another, but the Father determined long ago that it must be presented to the world *as a testing truth* before the end can come.[23] To subdue the hearts and minds of people so that they can hear the eternal gospel, Jesus will send a series of divine judgments. An awesome display of divine authority will bring the whole world to a stand still on Day One of the Great Tribulation. Then, a few days later, the first four trumpets will begin. In other words, overwhelming and overpowering wrath will subdue and humble the world. Nuclear war will cease and mankind will hear what Jesus has to say. The 144,000 will be selected and sealed just before Day One occurs. Then, on Day One, they will be empowered by the Holy Spirit to fearlessly present the eternal gospel. The 144,000 will perform great signs and wonders, the Holy Spirit will deeply trouble every listener's heart with the validity of the eternal gospel and the Bible will plainly validate the testimony of the 144,000. What could be more fair?

Rev. 14:7

The ministry of the 144,000 during the Great Tribulation is represented in this prophecy as three glorious angels orbiting Earth because the eternal gospel will be presented to everyone in the clearest of terms. The orbiting angels (flying in the sky) indicate global coverage. Because the 144,000 will be located in every quadrant (or geographic cell) of the world on Day One, the delivery of the eternal gospel will be quickly heard throughout the world. Additionally, the arrival of three angels from Heaven indicates there will be three messages that come straight from God's throne. To level the playing field, the eternal gospel will not be presented by a religious body or organization. The 144,000 will consist of honest-hearted people coming from all walks, cultures and religious systems.[24] Once they meet with Jesus (as Paul did on the road to Damascus and as John did when he received the little book), they will become believers in Christ and they will be given the words that God wants them to speak to their own people. Because Jesus intends to save as many people as possible during the Great Tribulation, Jesus will have "brothers" speaking to "brothers." What could be more effective than having an honest-hearted Moslem who has met with Jesus and believes in Jesus delivering the words that Jesus gave him to speak? This converted Moslem knows the language, culture, and religious beliefs of his brothers. What could be more effective at winning Moslems over to the eternal gospel of Jesus? What could be more effective than an honest-hearted Catholic speaking the words that Jesus gave him to speak to fellow Catholics? What could be more effective than a converted Hindu speaking the words that Jesus gave him? In terms of saving the highest number of people, what could be more effective than 144,000 brothers and sisters speaking to *their own* brothers and sisters?

The Great Tribulation will begin like a thief in the night. It will be an overwhelming surprise, even to those of us who anticipate it. People will be traumatized, confused and disoriented for awhile,

Rev. 14:7 but the demands of the eternal gospel will not abate. The eternal gospel existed before life was created and this gospel of God's kingdom will endure throughout eternity. This eternal truth will be declared: Jesus Christ is Almighty God just like the Father. Jesus is an equal of the Father.[25] He is the Creator of everything that exists and on the basis of Jesus' divinity, the Father has determined that Jesus will receive the same honor and worship given to the Father, whom no one has seen or can see."[26]

Fear Jesus?

Why does the eternal gospel begin with the phrase, "Fear God?" Why should we be afraid of our Creator, Jesus Christ? The Greek word, *phobeo* (English: phobia) literally means what it says, "be afraid!" Within the context of the eternal gospel, *phobeo* means that all created beings are to fear the Creator (Jesus) with the same fear, honor, and respect that we give to God the Father.[27] You have heard the expression, "Like father, like son," and in this case, this phrase is an eternal truth. Although Jesus is a separate and distinct co-eternal God, He has every power and substance that the Father has![28] This means that the redemption of mankind is far more expensive than most people realize. To redeem sinners, our Creator, a coeternal member of the Godhead who is equal with the Father,[29] gave up everything He possessed, even His eternal life so that we might have it.

Before Jesus came to Earth as "the Son of man," He set aside His divine powers and subjected Himself to whatever the Father required for man's salvation.[30] The Father predetermined that Jesus should be presented to the human race as a poor man, a man without education, good looks, or wealth. The Father decided that Jesus had to live among the poorest of people. Jesus was not given a handsome appearance. There was nothing physically appealing about Him.[31] Socially speaking, Jesus was an outcast.[32] In terms of human behavior, He was strange, unlike His peers. Even as a teenager, He never sinned.[33] If it had not been for the words and miracles that the Father performed through Him, the leaders of Israel would not have given Jesus two minutes of their time. Even His disciples abandoned Him when He stood before Pilate and went to the cross.

When the first message is presented to mankind, fearing Jesus will be a new thought for most people because currently, the full identity of Jesus is poorly understood. You might be interested to know that a similar thing happened to the angels! Please consider the following story.

The Revealing of Jesus Christ in Heaven

> [**Note:** This explanation on the origin of sin is to be understood as my "best guess." I have merged many Bible facts and a few parallels from Christ's ministry on Earth to tell a story about Lucifer's eviction from Heaven. The purpose of this explanation on the origin of sin is to demonstrate how the *eternal* gospel could have been used to separate the angels in Heaven and of course, how it will also be used to separate the people of Earth during the Great Tribulation.]

There was a time in Heaven when the angels poorly understood the fullness of all that Jesus is. The angels called (and they still call) Jesus by the name, Michael. He was Michael, the archangel, long before mankind called Him Jesus.[34] The angels were delighted to worship Michael whenever and wherever they saw Him. Physically speaking, Michael looked like an ordinary angel. Even though He was the archangel, there was nothing special about His appearance. He mingled among the angels in Heaven with the same humility that He later displayed among men on Earth. In both cases, one could not tell by His physical appearance that He was in fact, the Creator of the universe.

Even though the name Michael means "One who is like God," the angels did not question the origin of Michael or the natural order of their wonderful life. They were happy and safe. Heaven was harmonious and the angels were completely engaged with learning and doing new things every day. God's universe is huge and full of ceaseless wonders. To make matters even better, Michael conducted classes in different parts of Heaven from time to time and sitting at His feet was a very special treat for the angels. Michael was their favorite teacher although Lucifer was deeply loved and respected as a substitute teacher. Lucifer served as the leader of the angels when Michael was elsewhere, but Lucifer was not the archangel. For a long time, Lucifer was very close to Michael and they spent much time together. Lucifer had many natural gifts and responsibilities. Lucifer was Heaven's most extraordinary angel.

> **Rev. 14:7**

Lucifer held the highest position given to any created being. As the second covering cherub, he stood on the left side of God's throne whenever convocations with the Father were held,[35] whereas Michael stood at the right hand of the Father. The angels worshiped the Father on a regular basis and they also worshiped Michael wherever and whenever they saw Him. The angels always looked forward to worshiping in the presence of the Father who lives in unapproachable light.[36]

The angels knew the Father was the Supreme Ruler, the Most High God of the universe. His gifts to the angels constantly renewed their love and adoration for Him. The angels also worshiped Michael whenever they saw Him because they understood *by faith* that He was their Creator. They also understood *by faith* that Michael was the source and sustainer of life within each angel. In Him, the angels moved and had their being.[37] Even though the angels believed these things about Michael, they had no idea how His creative powers worked.

Adam and Eve did not see Michael create the Earth because they were created last, on the sixth day of the week. In fact, Adam did not see Jesus create Eve because Jesus put Adam into a deep sleep![38] Similarly, the angels did not watch Jesus create the universe. Jesus created them *after* He created the universe. This is important to the story because the angels did not witness Michael exercising His awesome creative powers *before* Lucifer fell. The angels knew that Michael created them, but they embraced this truth and worshiped Michael on the basis of *faith alone*. The angels did not see the creative powers of Michael demonstrated in much the same way that all of Creation Week was hidden from human view.

Over time, Lucifer became jealous of Michael. His jealousy began when he coveted 'the higher position' of *the other covering cherub*. The angels worshiped Michael, but they did not worship Lucifer. Michael could enter into the unapproachable light that surrounds the Father[39] and Lucifer could not. It was also odd that Michael looked like an ordinary angel and Lucifer did not. Lucifer was created as a model of perfection; he was more beautiful than any of the other angels. Lucifer eventually became jealous of Michael because he allowed passion to overrule self-control. Lucifer's jealousy began with vanity and a desire for higher entitlement. He came to think more of himself than he did of Michael and he coveted the worship and adoration that was given to Michael. Lucifer nursed his envy for a long time before he made a fatal choice.

Lucifer's Vanity

One day, Lucifer found a clever way to put himself on par with Michael. Lucifer began by using his perfect beauty and exalted position as a covering cherub[40] to elevate himself *into equality with* Michael among his closest friends. Over time, Lucifer argued that to be fair, the angels "really should" worship *both* covering cherubs. Lucifer's friends did not suspect an evil intent. They had sinless natures and they loved Lucifer and deeply respected his leadership. As a result, some angels did not see anything logically wrong with worshiping 'the other covering cherub.' However, there was something about this that did not seem right to most of the angels. As time went by, Lucifer gained sympathizers because he promoted those who worshiped him to higher positions and with this maneuver, the concept of politics began in Heaven. Suddenly, two parties existed in Heaven; angels loyal to Lucifer and angels loyal to Michael. Happiness and innocence began to evaporate. Tension displaced happiness. Attitudes and allegiances began to go in different directions and this was very unsettling.

Lucifer was careful to avoid open conflict with Michael. Instead, Lucifer preferred to present his arguments in secret meetings, using the excuse that his hushed endeavor was all about fairness. One of his favorite arguments went like this: "How can it be fair of God to permit the angels to worship one covering cherub and not the other?" Unfortunately, many angels sided with Lucifer and concluded that in fact, God was unfair! Angels loyal to Lucifer defended him saying that he was just as worthy and important as Michael because he was a covering cherub, the *other* chief prince![41] As disaffection for the Father and Michael grew, the devil twisted everything that Michael did and said. Lucifer put righteousness in the worst possible light. He made Michael's actions appear self-serving and harmful to the angels' welfare, although nothing harmful had ever happened. Lucifer raised many questions and doubts about God's government which God had not specifically addressed. Lucifer presented clever arguments which ultimately caused one-third of the angels to doubt that the Father was fair and Michael was the Creator of the universe. Remember, no angel had seen Michael create anything at that time, so Lucifer's arguments gained some traction with sympathizers.

Rev. 14:7

Prophecy 12 - The Eternal Gospel

Rev. 14:7

Lucifer's campaign against Michael went on for a long time. He undermined the joy of Heaven and over time, Lucifer's controversy with Michael became widely known. Lucifer's rebellion matured when he recruited enough followers and he began to secure their loyalty with promises of higher positions and freedom from the Father's tyranny. Of course, the Father knew everything that was going on. Time after time, the Holy Spirit tried to convict Lucifer of wrong doing, but Lucifer would not listen. The Father and Michael spent time with Lucifer and addressed his concerns, but Lucifer would not relent. He could not be embarrassed before his followers. Lucifer and his followers were warned repeatedly that their disaffection would bring about their destruction,* but they mistook the Father's patience as indecisiveness and the threat of destruction as evidence of tyranny.

Lucifer told his followers, "God cannot tolerate the possibility of competition. He is not a God of love. You have heard Him say that it is His way or sudden death." Lucifer used such propaganda to accelerate his wicked agenda and his followers eventually became bold in their rebellion. The sweet and softening influence of the Holy Spirit was totally shut out. The Holy Spirit could not change the growing bitterness within Lucifer or his followers.

The Demand

Lucifer's controversy with Christ came to a head at a regularly scheduled convocation. As usual, Lucifer called the meeting to

---

*__Note:__ Before the angels were created, the Father implemented a law that requires the immediate death for anyone who sins. This law was *also* imposed on Adam and Eve in the Garden of Eden,[42] but the Father has suspended this law until the knowledge of good and evil has matured.[43] After the drama of sin is completed, this law will be enforced. In the future, if someone should willfully ignore the testimony of ex-sinners and the urging of the Holy Spirit, that defiant sinner will be destroyed on the day that he sins. If God's sudden death law should be implemented at any time in the future, God's children will not question the righteousness of this law because everyone in the future will understand all that sin does. Sin and its curse will not permeate God's universe again. There will be no salvation for any future sinner after the current drama with sin ends.

order. The angels gathered around God's awesome throne and typically, before the Father's glorious presence filled the temple, Michael arrived and took His position on the right side of the throne. When Michael took His position on that day, one-third of Heaven's angels refused to bow down before Him. This had never happened before. Suddenly, the Father's glorious presence came into the temple. His presence was unusually brilliant. Of course, the service abruptly stopped.

Rev. 14:7

The Father spoke. He commanded everyone to stand up and carefully consider His words. He acknowledged the conflict between Lucifer and Michael. He described Lucifer's jealousy and his subsequent campaign to gain the adoration and worship of the angels. His report was presented with embarrassing clarity. He reviewed incidents and conversations that were not common knowledge. He also exposed many lies which Lucifer had made up. In short, the Father laid bare the jealousy of Lucifer and his hatred for Michael. Then, the Father said, "Let everyone hear and understand this eternal truth: Fear Michael who, like myself, is Almighty God. Give Michael the honor and glory that you give me. Worship Michael your Creator as you worship me, because He made you and the Heavens and all that is in them. In Him, you move and have your being. The hour of your judgment has come. Bow down and worship Him right now or you will be destroyed!"

Every angel was caught by surprise. A clear line had been drawn, a decisive moment of truth confronted them. Their faith in Michael was put to a test. Was Michael the Creator of the angels and the universe or was He not? Each angel was forced to make a decision that would affect his eternal destiny. There was a sound of movement as two-thirds of the angels bowed down before Michael, but Lucifer, sensing this would be his last defense, broke the awkward silence with his commanding voice. He spoke adamantly and with authority, "I will not worship Michael." Then, he pointed to his many followers who were still standing. He said, "We do not think the Father is fair. You claim to be a God of love, but you give us no choice! Your law says "obey and live, disobey and die!" How loving is this? Is it fair that the Father requires us to worship and honor Michael while ignoring the exalted position of *the other covering cherub?* You say that Michael is the Creator, but we have not seen any evidence of His creative powers! Many of us think that your government is based on arbitrary whim and it is secured through your mighty powers. You and your Tattletale, Michael, have con-

> Rev. 14:7

spired to keep us as your slaves and if we rebel, you threaten to destroy us. This is not right, this is not fair, this is not love and we will not bow down and worship Michael."

Lucifer's defiant response to the Father was shocking. The silence that followed was unbearable. Heaven had never experienced any tension like this! Lucifer and his followers remained standing. One-third of the angels had disobeyed a direct order! They had been warned of the consequences of rebellion and still, they openly defied the clearest evidences of the Father's will. They refused to bow down before Michael. They refused to worship a God who lived in the form of an angel. Suddenly there was a frightening sound like the sizzle and searing crackle of nearby lightning. A tremendous burst of light blinded the angels' eyes and a deafening crash of thunder fell upon the assembly. The ground trembled and a great crevice opened up. Lucifer and his angels were swept into the crevice and in a matter of seconds, it closed up. Lucifer and his angels were cast out of Heaven at the speed of lightning.[44] The drama was so overwhelming and it happened so fast that the remaining angels remained prostrate on their faces until the Father spoke again. He said kindly, "My children, today *your faith in Christ* has saved you. Stand up and behold your Creator!"

This dramatic event defined Michael in a new way that the angels had not considered. Prior to Lucifer's expulsion, they were innocent and naive. They lived in a sinless universe and had sinless natures. The angels naturally loved one another and serving the Father, the Archangel and Lucifer was a special delight. Angels had not seen sin or rebellion, so they could not understand the malignant effects that sin produces, but their naivete vanished. The knowledge of good *and evil* began to unfold that day.

Creation Observed

After Lucifer and his followers were expelled from Heaven, the angels witnessed for the first time, the awesome creative power of Michael. They watched in awe as He created the Earth and all that is in it.[45] **"For he spoke, and it came to be; he commanded, and it stood firm."**[46] After watching the creation of Earth and the creation of millions of life forms that would occupy Earth in six, twenty-four hour days, the angels worshiped Michael as though He was a new deity in Heaven! It was so exciting. Suddenly, the Michael they had known for thousands of years was so much more than the archangel. He was so humble in appearance, yet His creative powers were awesome and divine! Later on, when the heavenly angels saw Jesus die on Calvary, they gained another perspective on the depth of Michael's love that words cannot convey. It became clear to them that Michael/Jesus is not an angel. In fact, He is not a man. Jesus is The Alpha and The Omega, the beginning and the end, the first and the last, He is Almighty God, just like the Father. Prior to coming to Earth, Jesus lived as an angel so that He could show the angels how God would live if He were an angel. Jesus also lived as an angel so that He could tell the Father about the angel's experiences from their perspective. What amazing love!

Rev. 14:7

One last point. The angels did not see Michael create the Earth and all that is in it until their faith in Him as Creator had been tested. In other words, *after* Lucifer and his angels were cast out of Heaven, the angels saw Michael create for the first time. Similarly, the saints will not see Jesus exercise His creative powers until their faith in Him has been tested. At the end of the 1,000 years, Jesus will destroy Lucifer and all the wicked. After destroying death itself, the saints will watch as Jesus once again exercises His amazing power. Jesus will create a new Heaven and a new Earth! In Heaven and on Earth, the creative powers of Michael/Jesus and other facts about Him have been hidden for a time,[47] because *faith in Jesus Christ* is always and forever the key to eternal life.

Lucifer Permitted to Live

I hope you can see how there was a time when the angels did not fully understand who Michael was. This knowledge was not revealed until their faith in Him could be tested. Similarly, the angels could not know what sin was all about until sin occurred and matured. This also means the angels could not know the fullness of Michael's love and power until they saw Him resolve the sin problem! A bittersweet thing has happened because of sin. The Father permitted Lucifer and his angels to live for a while so that the nature, scope, and complexity of sin might mature and the universe could clearly understand the consequences of sin. The Father's decision to allow sin to mature has produced an enormous amount of questioning, suffering, and death, but this outcome has been offset by two wonderful developments.

First, God wants everyone to know that He has given His subjects the power of choice. In fact, sin and rebellion only exist because

Rev. 14:7

Lucifer and his followers *chose* to sin and rebel. At the end of the 1,000 years, Jesus will destroy Lucifer and his followers – not because He dislikes them or they offended Him. In fact, Jesus loves the wicked angels, but He must destroy Lucifer and his followers because sin turned them into predators. Consider the process: Lucifer became jealous of Jesus; he wanted the adoration and worship that belonged to Michael. Lucifer was moved by his envy and jealousy to seek sympathizers. He preyed upon innocent angels with lies and propaganda. After God banished Lucifer from Heaven, he preyed upon Eve and Adam. Cain was motivated by jealousy to prey upon Abel. Throughout the ages, history has revealed the wicked are predators and they always prey on the innocent and/or the righteous. This is why God destroyed the world with a flood in Noah's day. This is why God burned Sodom and Gomorrah to the ground. *Given enough time and the right circumstances, all sinners will exhibit predatory behavior.* Predatory behavior stems from selfishness. Predatory behavior occurs because it offers the shortest path to fulfilling a selfish desire and this natural orientation within fallen man is inescapable. This is why the removal of the carnal nature, the sealing, is so important. The sinless nature naturally conforms to God's two laws of love. Predatory behavior is the result of sin and this is why those who refuse to repent and forsake their sins must be destroyed. God is willing to give us the strength to subdue our predatory nature if we are willing to receive His strength. Eternal salvation is as much about eternal life as it is freedom *from the predatory tendencies* that comes with sin. Every born again believer can taste the joy and peace of eternal life which will come in due time. Strength and grace from God transforms sinners so that they can overcome passion and the power of sin each day![48]

Second, by allowing Lucifer to live and flourish for a time, God chose to use the curse of sin to reveal the depth of His love for His creation. Because of sin, many aspects about the Father and His government have been revealed that would have otherwise remained obscure for billions of years! The Father wisely permitted sin to exist for a period of time and once it is destroyed, sin will never permeate the universe again. Once the drama of sin is completed, everyone in the universe will have the knowledge of good and evil and all future creations will have the opportunity to study the sin problem and how it developed. No one who has been freed from sin's curse will ever want a repetition of living with sin's curse.

Rev. 14:7

Our Heavenly Father predetermined long ago that the capstone to resolving the sin problem was a full disclosure of our Creator, Jesus Christ! The sin problem started when Lucifer (a created being), wanted to be an equal or better than Jesus (the Creator). Of course, when Lucifer became jealous he did not know everything about Jesus. Lucifer could see that Jesus was not as beautiful as himself. Lucifer did not know that Jesus was "God in angel's feathers" and this led to his assumption that he should be respected with the same adoration and worship. Little did Lucifer realize that the humble archangel was Almighty God who was the Creator of life itself. We know much more about Jesus today than ever before. The Bible declares that Jesus is the Creator of Heaven and Earth.[49] He is Almighty God.[50] He is the only antidote for sin.[51] Our Creator is the Savior of mankind and a mirror of the Father's humble character.[52] It is ironic that Lucifer and his angels were created with sinless natures, yet they chose to rebel. On the other hand, the offspring of Adam and Eve were born with rebellious natures, but many have chosen to surrender to the Holy Spirit and be saved! All who obey the Holy Spirit will be saved and the redeemed of Earth will repopulate Heaven! God will restore Heaven's population to three-thirds again and this time, Heaven will be better than before because one-third of God's house will be conquerors over rebellion! They lived in sin and overcame it through Christ's power.[53]

Pharaoh and Nebuchadnezzar

When the 144,000 present the eternal gospel by telling the world that Jesus is Almighty God the Creator, billions of people will be strongly opposed. We can be sure that the demand to worship Jesus by resting on His Sabbath day will inflame 99.9% of the world, but the evidences of God's wrath will keep people subdued for a short time.

When presented to the world, the eternal gospel will produce an enormous problem. This is to be expected. When the Father declared the eternal gospel in Heaven, He tested each angel. The angels had no doubt about God's will, for they heard the Father's voice with their own ears. Similarly, each person's response to the eternal gospel will reveal the true condition of his heart. Keep in mind, the eternal gospel will be clearly presented, but the demand

Rev. 14:7 will not be based on "ears" alone. The Holy Spirit and the two laws of love will bear witness that the testimony of the 144,000 is faithful and true! Those who love God and are acquainted with the Holy Spirit will obey once they understand. Unfortunately, billions will reject "a plain thus saith the Lord" from Scripture. They will also reject the Holy Spirit.

Jesus understands the cultural and religious diversity of mankind. In fact, Jesus is responsible for the diversity of mankind. It all began at the Tower of Babel when Jesus divided the language of the world.[54] Jesus made the dispersion of mankind permanent when He later divided the Earth into continents.[55] Jesus knew that after mankind was separated, great spiritual darkness would cover each nation. To counteract this darkness, He chose the descendants of Abraham to be a light to the Gentiles. Unfortunately, Israel failed. Then, Jesus raised up the Christian Church and later, a Protestant movement within it, but they failed too. The religious arrogance and ignorance that plagues the world today cannot be overcome by the will of man. One man cannot prove to another the superiority of his religious thinking. Therefore, the presentation of the eternal gospel will require an unusual display of divine power. A very interesting experience awaits the world.

The eternal gospel will produce a confrontation similar to the day that Moses and Aaron went to the palace and presented themselves before the king of Egypt. Pharaoh was going about his usual routines when suddenly, "**. . . Moses and Aaron went to Pharaoh and said, 'This is what the Lord, the God of Israel, says: 'Let my people go, so that they may hold a festival to me in the desert.' Pharaoh said, 'Who is the Lord, that I should obey him and let Israel go? I do not know the Lord and I will not let Israel go.'**"[56]

I am sure that Pharaoh was stunned when he heard two old men present the Lord's demand. Pharaoh spoke the truth when he said that he did not know the God of Israel. Therefore, he *naturally* refused to obey such a command. Jesus respects the reasoning powers that He gave to mankind. Jesus knew that Pharaoh did not know Him. Jesus also knew that from a practical point of view, Pharaoh could not let his slaves go free because they would never come back! Jesus knew from the beginning that Pharaoh would reject His demand[57] because the departure of Israel (cheap labor) would ruin Egypt's economy! Pharaoh knew that if he gave an inch, the Israelites would take a mile. Therefore, he *reasonably* refused to obey God's demand and let Israel go. However, Pharaoh made a huge mistake. After watching ten plagues fall on his kingdom, the king should have realized (as Nebuchadnezzar finally did) that there is a Most High God in Heaven that overrules the will of man.[58] It is ironic that after suffering ten destructive plagues, Pharaoh would not recognize or acknowledge God's higher authority. Therefore, God destroyed him in the Red Sea.

In a sense, sinners are kings like Pharaoh and Nebuchadnezzar! Each person rules over his own heart and mind. When the people of Earth hear the eternal gospel for the first time, they will reject it because it is foreign. Like Pharaoh, most people do not know Jesus. Initially, the eternal gospel will make almost everyone angry. However, the first four trumpets will produce so much destruction that many survivors will begin to listen. This may sound strange, but God's wrath will enable Him to save many people that would not otherwise listen to Him! Moses and Aaron called down plagues on Egypt. God responded with dire judgments to soften Pharaoh's heart, but Pharaoh refused to submit to God's sovereign power even after there was unmistakable evidence of God's will. Pharaoh made the fatal mistake of thinking that his authority was greater than the God of the Hebrews. King Nebuchadnezzar also made the same mistake, but after seven years of eating grass like an animal, he confessed there is a Most High God who rules over the kingdoms of men. Nebuchadnezzar finally submitted to God's authority and gave Him glory!

Jesus understands the rebellious nature of the carnal heart very well and this explains why the seven trumpets will be redemptive judgments. This is why the Two Witnesses will testify for 1,260 days. The 144,000 will present the demand that everyone worship the Creator who made the Heavens, the Earth, the sea, and the fountains of waters. By the way, these four items are included in the eternal gospel because the Creator who made them will destroy one-third of each of them! The scope and sequence of these coming judgments (plainly described in Revelation 8) will prove to the sincere in heart that the eternal gospel is a demand from God. Furthermore, the 144,000 will call down all kinds of plagues on Earth (just like Moses and Aaron did) as often as they want[59] to further demonstrate that their testimony comes from God."

Prophecy 12 - The Eternal Gospel

Rev. 14:7

Faith or Works?

Propaganda is a clever mixture of truth and lies. As a political tool, propaganda is highly effective because most people do not have access to the whole truth. Therefore, propaganda is often used to influence or determine the outcome of a political race. Propaganda is not concerned with "the whole truth and nothing but the truth," so consequently, propaganda enables evil minded people to promote or believe whatever they want. Propaganda is effective because it creates or enhances bias and prejudice. Lucifer is *the* creator and master of propaganda. Lucifer led a third of the angels astray with propaganda and he will use this tool to lead the wicked into destruction. Ironically, during the Great Tribulation Lucifer will promote *the same false gospel* that he once accused God of imposing on the angels. Lucifer will make the eternal gospel appear to say: "Obey and live, disobey and die."

Many people do not properly understand the relationship between faith and works. How does faith in Christ and the eternal gospel mix together? Before Lucifer was expelled from Heaven, he became a liar.[60] He became a master at misrepresenting the actions of the Father and Michael. Using propaganda, he skillfully made the Godhead appear to be evil minded and one-third of Heaven's holy angels believed his lies! (Eve, in her sinless state, also believed Lucifer's lies.) Lucifer's cunning and sophistry is beyond measure. If the demands of the eternal gospel were set before the people of Earth *at any other time* than during the Great Tribulation, one could argue the point that the eternal gospel boils down to, "obey and live, disobey and die!" To eliminate this possibility, a presentation of the eternal gospel *requires a special setting*, a context where God Himself clearly sets the evidence of His will before people and each person is informed in advance about the consequences of his decision. This is the way it happened in Heaven and this is the way it will happen on Earth! Two-thirds of the holy angels were saved by faith when the eternal gospel was set before them and a numberless multitude of saints will be saved because of their faith!

The Special Setting

Sin has physically separated human beings from God's presence, which promotes endless confusion around the world about the identity and will of whatever is worshiped as God. Because each of the world's religious systems are convinced that their knowledge of God is truth and all others are in error, unimpeachable evidence must accompany the eternal gospel to prove that the 144,000 speak truth while the rest of the religious world speak lies. What will prove that worshiping Jesus on His seventh day Sabbath is the will of God? This is a profoundly important question that will confront Muslims, Jews, Hindus, Catholics, Atheists, Protestants, and all others. How can religiously diverse people make an intelligent and informed decision about a gospel that is unlike anything they believe to be true?[61] The solution is rather simple.

Rev. 14:7

Jesus will speak to each religious group through the lips of the 144,000. Their words will be invincible and the 144,000 will perform signs and wonders as often as needed to confirm their testimony.[62] Jesus already knows each person on Earth, He knows what to say to the honest in heart in every nation and religious system.[63] Jesus is no respecter of persons.[64] He loves everyone the same, He is the Creator of *all* mankind.[65] Therefore, to be fair and impartial to people in all religious systems, the eternal gospel will be attended with "a plain thus saith the Lord" from Scripture and on top of this, everyone will feel the internal prompting of the Holy Spirit to do what is right. God's Two Witnesses will validate the testimony of Jesus for 1,260 days.[66]

There is a second element in this special setting for the eternal gospel. The eternal gospel must be presented with *inspired* words. Human argument will not be sufficient. Spiritual things are spiritually understood.[67] Consider the current gridlock on Earth. One religious man cannot prove the superiority of his religious beliefs to another religious man. More people have been killed on Earth because of religion than for any other reason. Therefore, the Holy Spirit will give the testimony of Jesus' penetrating power. Jesus will speak through the lips of the 144,000. The honest in heart will be troubled by the demand of the eternal gospel and they will be moved by the testimony of Jesus to obey His commands.[68] Worshiping the Creator will come with consequences, but don't forget, defiance will also come with consequences. Everyone will be forced by circumstances to take a side because the world will be fully informed.[69] The Holy Spirit will convict the world of *sin, righteousness, and judgment*.[70] The honest in heart will be convicted that defying the eternal gospel is sin. They will worship Jesus as the Creator because it is the righteous thing to do (God's will). Finally, everyone on Earth will be told that their eternal reward will be determined by his response to the eternal gospel. If a person defies

> Rev. 14:7

the conviction of the Holy Spirit after hearing and seeing the clearest evidences of God's will, there is nothing further that God can do. The sinner has chosen defiance and committed the unpardonable sin.[71]

Babylon Unwittingly Serves God's Purpose

Babylon will form when the leaders of the world conclude that a unified response is necessary to appease God's wrath. God will use Babylon's ignorance, arrogance, and blasphemy to set the stage for a huge conflict. Babylon will create a series of "sin-less" laws that will produce unintended consequences. When it becomes clear that the 144,000 stand in opposition to Babylon's laws, Babylon will persecute the 144,000 and all who embrace the eternal gospel. Within the context of persecution, sin, righteousness, and judgment become very distinct and clear to the honest in heart. This is how the eternal gospel will go throughout the Earth as a testing truth. Everyone who puts his faith in Christ will be saved, all others will be destroyed at the Second Coming.[72]

Faith and obedience are brother and sister. Salvation comes through faith and Jesus will *test the faith* of every person on Earth during the Great Tribulation.[73] Jesus said, **"If you love me, you will obey what I command."**[74] Revelation 12:17 identifies the saints as **"those who obey God's commandments and hold to the testimony of Jesus."** *When obeying God comes with a price, obedience quickly becomes a matter of faith and love for God.*

There is a critical difference between salvation through works and salvation through faith. When a person obeys God's command, thinking that his obedience merits God's favor and salvation, salvation has become a matter of works. In God's sight, obedient sinners are just as guilty of sin as rebellious sinners, **"for the wages of sin is death."**[75] On the other hand, when obedience is motivated by love to obey God and the sinner understands that his obedience does not merit God's salvation, this is salvation through faith! Faith means obeying God at all costs. Eternal life is almost immaterial![76] Think about Jesus. Because He loved the Father and sinners, He submitted to the will of the Father and He perished without any hope of resurrection. What a perfect example of salvation through faith!

Faith in God is tested when the price of obedience becomes significant. This is why persecution plays an important role during the

Great Tribulation. When the people of Earth hear the eternal gospel proclaimed and when Babylon imposes punishment on those who obey the eternal gospel, faith will be tested. Who will love the Creator/Redeemer of mankind enough to worship Him on His holy day? Who will love the Creator/Redeemer of mankind enough to suffer persecution for His sake?[77]

Rev. 14:7

Upon hearing the eternal gospel, many Christians will discover like Peter, that they are initially unwilling to suffer for Christ's sake and they will find a way to justify their rebellion. Later on, these people will repent. Other Christians, like Judas, will remain angry and rebellious. They will not repent and will go to their death cursing God. Judas loved the gifts of the Giver instead of the Giver of the gifts. Judas became a predator and he betrayed Jesus for thirty pieces of silver. The eternal gospel will separate the people of Earth. The phrase, "obey and live, disobey and die" does not summarize the eternal gospel. Lucifer used this sound bite in Heaven to slander God's love. If a sound bite can summarize the eternal gospel, it could be, "When worship requires a price, I am willing to pay." Faith and love always submits to the will of God regardless of cost whereas defiance always justifies rebellion.

What Is Worship?

When the word worship is used as a verb, action is involved. For example, John fell at the angel's feet to worship him in Revelation 19:10. John bowed before the angel to show submission and loyalty, but the angel told John, "Do not do it!" When the angels in Heaven were tested with the eternal gospel, the Father required everyone to immediately bow down and worship Michael. Those believing that Michael was their Creator obeyed the Father's command. Doing as commanded is an *act* of worship. Those loyal to Lucifer remained standing; this was an *act* of defiance. Abel's obedience was an act of worship. Abel did as God commanded. He built an altar and offered the required lamb. God was pleased with his worship. Cain, on the other hand, built an altar and presented fruit. He presumed to worship God, but Cain insulted God. *A created being cannot dictate the terms of worship to his Creator!* It must be the other way around. Worshiping Jesus means obeying His commands and remaining loyal to Him.[78]

Consider the creation of the Sabbath day for a moment. Human beings did not see Jesus create the Earth and all that is in it. Therefore, to commemorate His work, Jesus created a memorial to

> Rev. 14:7

Creation Week. This memorial is the seventh day Sabbath.[79] To ensure the perpetuity of this memorial, Jesus declared the seventh day holy.[80] God's Sabbath is unlike the other six days of the week, it is holy (set apart). This memorial was created for the benefit of man.[81] Not only is the Sabbath a day for physical rest and spiritual renewal, but it is also a reminder of our origin. The Sabbath was created to keep mankind from forgetting their Creator and their accountability to Him. It is interesting that from the very beginning, God has required human beings to honor something they did not see. Therefore, properly observing God's Sabbath is *an act that acknowledges the work of our Creator.*

Lucifer has done everything possible to eliminate all traces of God's memorial to creation. He has done this so that all mankind would forget Jesus and our accountability to Him. It is interesting that Muslims worship on Friday, Christians worship on Sunday, and Jews, who deny that Jesus is the Creator, worship on Saturday. The devil knows all about the eternal gospel (he lost his place in Heaven because of it). He knows that our faith in Christ will be tested and that God's Sabbath rest will become the focus of a great controversy all over the world during the Great Tribulation. He has been preparing to make war on the remnant of the woman for more than two hundred years. When Babylon rises to power, this war begins.[82]

The Memorial Protected by Law

Jesus protected the sanctity of His Sabbath memorial with the force of law. He did this so that His memorial to creation would not be forgotten. Adam and Eve knew and observed the holiness of the Sabbath in the Garden of Eden before sin began. This statement is valid because Adam and Eve's first sin was not that of violating the holiness of God's Sabbath. After Adam and Eve were cast out of the garden, the importance of observing God's Sabbath was passed down through the patriarchs. Adam, the first patriarch, lived for approximately 250 years after Methuselah was born and Methuselah died the year of the flood. Therefore, two men, who knew each other well, spanned the time between Creation Week and Noah's flood! The knowledge of God's holy Sabbath was not lost before the flood.

Even though the Garden of Eden remained on Earth until the flood, it would be fair to say that very few people observed God's seventh day Sabbath at the time of the flood.[83] Even though the

Bible does not explicitly say so, I assume that Noah observed God's holy Sabbath because Noah was a righteous man (a law abiding man) and He walked with God![84] If Noah did not know about the holiness surrounding God's seventh day, Jesus would have told him. I am confident that Noah and his employees did not work on the ark on God's Sabbath. The Bible declares that God sent the flood in Noah's day because the world was full of gross degeneracy and endless wickedness.[85] Wickedness is unrighteous and unlawful behavior[86] and the salvation of eight people at the time of the flood indicates that very few people worshiped the Creator by resting from their labors on His holy day.

Prior to the Exodus (and the giving of the law at Mt. Sinai), the Lord tested Israel's faith by imposing His Sabbath rest upon them. (Exodus 5) This made Pharaoh furious! Then again, shortly after the Exodus (but prior to the giving of the law at Mt. Sinai), the Lord tested Israel with His Sabbath rest. (Exodus 16) A few weeks after the Exodus, the Lord Himself descended to Mt. Sinai to pronounce the Ten Commandments because Israel had been chosen to be the light of the world.[87] The holiness of God's seventh day Sabbath did not began at Mt. Sinai. It began at Creation.[88]

The two laws of love underlying the Ten Commandments are eternal. All created beings are required to love God supremely and their neighbors as themselves.[89] These two laws of love are amplified in the Ten Commandments. The first four commandments define love for God and the last six commandments define love for man. Mankind does not have the privilege of defining what love is and is not. God is love, He defines love. The Ten Commandments are called "a covenant"[90] because they contain a promise. The Lord has promised that the Ten Commandments are a reflection of what a born again person will *naturally want to do* when there is no rebellion in his heart.[91]

We know that the Ark of the Covenant will be presented to the world at the end of salvation's offer at the seventh trumpet.[92] We know that Jesus wrote the Ten Commandments with His own finger on two tablets of enduring stone.[93] We know that at the end of the Great Tribulation, there will be two groups of people. One group will worship the Creator on His holy Sabbath, the other group will worship Lucifer on a false sabbath.[94] The Ark of the Covenant will be visibly presented to the people of Earth as physical evidence confirming the Father's will. The test of worship

> Rev. 14:7

will then be over. The saints are rewarded for their faith and the wicked are destroyed because of defiance.

God's Sabbath is far more than a holy day. When the Sabbath is ignored, the Creator is ignored. The devil knows that when a man or woman loses sight of his accountability before God, the result will be horrible. Sinners will lie, cheat, steal, kill, and commit adultery if they think they can get away with it. When people forget God, they behave in the most disgusting and despicable ways. Predators prey on the innocent and the weak. Children are abused and the elderly robbed or abandoned. Spiritual people can see the problem, but fools have no understanding. They say, "There is no God,"[95] but wise men know better. Many years ago the Russian philosopher Aleksandr Solzhenitsyn wrote, "If I were called upon to identify the principal trait of the entire 20th century, I would be unable to find anything more precise than to reflect once again on how we have lost touch with our Creator. . . . Men have forgotten God."[96]

Persecution and the Sabbath Rest Test

Earlier, it was said that Jesus tested the faith of the Israelites before the Exodus. He required His trustees to *rest* from their labors on His Sabbath[97] as a precondition to deliverance from Egypt. He did this to test their faith in Him. When worship requires a price, faith is revealed! The Israelites showed their regard for God's higher authority by resting on His holy day and their cessation from work was considered an act of defiance. Pharaoh severely persecuted his slaves.[98]

This Exodus story has an end time parallel. Before Jesus delivers the saints from the bondage of sin (removes the carnal nature), He will test our faith by requiring us to rest from our labors on His seventh day Sabbath! Resting on God's Sabbath according to His commandment is an act of worship. In an effort to appease God's wrath, Babylon will make laws demanding that God be worshiped, but on days other than the Creator's Sabbath. The leaders of Babylon will become furious with God's saints because they will interpret worshiping the Creator on His holy day as an act of defiance.[99] It is interesting to anticipate how the seventh day Sabbath, an institution as old as Creation week and the divinity of Jesus, as Creator of Heaven and Earth, will become inflammatory topics during the Great Tribulation.

When the eternal gospel is set before mankind as a demand from God, a great controversy will arise and there will be a surprising outcome. The honest in heart will hear the 144,000. They will learn of Christ and His salvation and millions will embrace the eternal gospel and keep God's Sabbath holy even though they will be severely punished for it. A time is coming when the world will see devout Moslems, Jews, Hindus, Atheists, Baptists, Catholics, pagans, and others *worshiping Jesus* by resting on His Sabbath day! This amazing phenomenon will prove to the universe that the honest in heart are worthy of salvation because they are willing to do whatever God asks (once they know His will), regardless of the price or lifelong heritage.

Give Him Glory

The eternal gospel includes this phrase, **'and give Him glory.'** People give glory and praise to those they admire. Giving glory to Jesus is a righteous demand because He is our Creator, Redeemer, and Almighty God. He has done many things for mankind which no one else in the universe can do. He gave us life, but He was willing to cease to exist so that we might have His eternal life. Jesus has promised that sinners can overcome temptation if we will abide in Him and receive His strength. Jesus was tempted in every way as we are and He did not sin.[100] Jesus was tempted in ways that go beyond the human experience (such as turning stones into bread) and He did not fail. On the basis of Christ's perfect life and death, the Father reconciled the world unto Himself.[101] Jesus overcame the world,[102] and His victory assures us that we can have victory through His power. Therefore, "give Him glory" is a righteous demand. When the honest in heart hear and understand who Jesus really is, once they understand the love that He has bestowed on sinners and the victory that He has achieved for sinners, they will joyfully embrace Him and give Him glory! People like Pharaoh will stubbornly refuse. The wicked will submit to the laws of Babylon to avoid punishment. They justify their defiance for fear of punishment or suffering. The delivery of the eternal gospel by the 144,000 will produce many surprises and one of the biggest will be the response of family members and friends!

Babylon Suddenly Forms

Consider Earth's situation after the destruction caused by the first four trumpets. The whole world will look something like a giant ant hill that has been scalped by a lawnmower. People will

Rev. 14:7 be rushing around, confused and bewildered. They will be filled with anxiety, desperately looking for ways to survive. Some will be cursing God and others will be questioning God, trying to make sense of what happened. The leaders of the world will be feverishly working on a global plan to appease God's wrath. Religious diversity will cause great confusion at first, but eventually the leaders of the world will unite, naively creating a beast that will soon become a monster. The leaders of the world will create a one world crisis government. Babylon's stated purpose will be simple and singular: We must quickly appease God's wrath or we will all be destroyed.

During the first four trumpets, God's wrath will burn up (like Sodom and Gomorrah) a third of the Earth and then will destroy thousands of coastal cities. God's wrath will wipe out a continent and the heavens will turn so dark that crops cannot grow. The carnage will be indescribable. When 1.75 billion people die from these judgments and the survival of mankind looms large, the political and religious leaders of the world will get the picture. They will rightly conclude that man's sinful behavior has made Almighty God very angry, but they will wrongfully reason that if mankind's offensive behaviors are eliminated, God will be pleased and His judgments will cease. The political leaders of the world will agree to enforce whatever laws religious leaders might think appropriate and almost everyone will go along with Babylon's reasoning and demands – at first.

Three Enabling Lies

Babylon will justify its origin with three lies. The first lie will be this: Everyone on Earth worships *the same God*. Even though He is called by different names or given different titles, there is one God. This lie may sound reasonable, but nothing is further from the truth. The religions of the world do not know and worship Jesus and He is not to be confused with Allah or any other God. The first lie will enable religious and political leaders to unite on two core principles. First, all religions believe that God's wrath can be aroused by decadent and degenerate behavior. Second, all religions believe that Almighty God is entitled to respect and worship. These two principles will combine with the first lie to produce a second lie. The second lie will be this: God will be pleased when mankind unites and *enforces laws outlawing decadent and degenerate behavior*. They will think that every reduction in sinful behavior will surely please The Almighty. Finally, the third lie supporting Babylon's theological framework will be this: God will be pleased when *one agency on Earth* represents all of the religions of the world. This "divinely appointed agency" can coordinate the worship and appeasement of The Almighty for all nations.

Rev. 14:7

As the dust from the first four trumpets settles, everyone on Earth will be very afraid of God. A dramatic show of divine power on Day One and the overwhelming destruction caused by the first four trumpet events will change everything. Suddenly, mankind will face the reality of an angry God. The smouldering evidences of God's wrath will produce a knee-jerk religious revival. Not surprisingly, the people of the world will suddenly become "religious" after the first four trumpets, but they will be motivated by fear of more wrath to come. Ironically, the people of Earth, including the religious leaders of the world who claim to know the will of God, will not know that it will be more than two years before the fifth trumpet occurs. In other words, almost everyone will be anticipating more judgments to fall right away and even though a great religious awakening will take place, a great religious embarrassment will also unfold.

Millions of Christians who believe in a pretribulation rapture will be shocked to discover that their pastors and scholars have misled them. The deaths of 1.75 billion people will be unmistakable. The pretribulation rapture doctrine will vanish because it is fiction and a religious backlash will follow. On the other hand, millions of other Christians will be forced to admit that the seven trumpets did not occur in the past. These Christians will discover that their historical view of Revelation is fiction and a similar backlash will follow. Catholics will be shocked when they discover that their clergy know nothing about Bible prophecy. In Muslim countries, millions of people will sit in shocked silence. The Koran says nothing about the seven trumpets, nor does it explain God's final plans or the eternal gospel. Muslim clergy will say that Allah is definitely offended, but they have no further information on God's plans or the revealing of Jesus Christ as Almighty God. Meanwhile, the 144,000 will speak boldly. They will tell everyone about the seven trumpets of Revelation. They will explain the eternal gospel and their testimony will lead the honest in heart to conclude that the world's religious leaders know nothing about God, His Word, or His plans. This will be a bitter pill for many religious people to swallow. Like King Nebuchadnezzar, this discovery will make many people angry at first.[103] Meanwhile, Babylon will form and it will issue a decree requiring everyone to worship Almighty God. Of course, Babylon's demand will sound very similar to the eternal gospel, but there will be a number of sharp differences.

The Second Angel's Message: An Inflammatory Message

> Rev. 14:8
> And there followed another angel, saying, Babylon is fallen, is fallen, that great city, because she made all nations drink of the wine of the wrath of her fornication.

{8} I saw a second angel descend from Heaven and orbit the Earth. He carried a message from Jesus that made the leaders of Babylon furious. He said in a loud voice, "Lies! Babylon the Great is promoting falsehood! The leaders of Babylon do not speak for God. Their presuppositions are false. Their endeavors are false. Their doctrines are blasphemy. They do not know God or His plans. Babylon has made all nations drunk with the delusion that men can appease God's wrath. This is a lie. The censer has been cast down. Corporately speaking, there is no return to God's grace. Babylon cannot save anyone or even itself. In fact, the Creator will destroy Babylon and all who obey its laws during the seven bowls."

The second angel's message will unite with the first angel's message and together, they will become an endless source of conflict and contempt for the 144,000. At first, the solution offered by Babylon will seem reasonable to most people on Earth.[104] Communal suffering will unite the religious and political leaders of the world. Local communities will want God's wrath to cease. A spiritual revival will spring up within each religious system on Earth like the world has never seen. People will turn to their religious experts for an explanation but the people will quickly learn that the leaders know nothing about God, His Word, or His plans. Like the 144,000, the leaders of Babylon will demand that everyone must worship God, but one question will be on everyone's heart. Who speaks for God? How does a world of diverse religions appease and worship one angry God?

False religion always exhibits two characteristics: First, it leads laymen to think that God is impressed with ritual, formal piety, and worship services; and second, the last resort of false religion is force. Actually, the opposite is true in both cases! In terms of salvation, rituals and sacraments are meaningless to God. They cannot produce salvation. Jesus is our Judge. He determines our salvation[105] after listening to the testimony of His Two Witnesses. The Holy Spirit tells Him if a person has a humble and contrite spirit.[106] Jesus only accepts the offerings of a cheerful giver.[107] Jesus sees the motives of each heart. The Holy Spirit reads each mind.[108] The Lord loves honesty and integrity.[109]

Jesus hates sexual immorality, impurity, lust, evil desires, and greed.[110] Jesus is pleased when a person admits and confesses his sin[111] and makes restitution when/as necessary.[112] Jesus has promised eternal life to every overcomer because faith and works are inseparable![113] Faith in God means loving God enough to trust and obey Him no matter what the consequences may be.[114]

Rev. 14:8

The first angel's message will demand that everyone worship the Creator. Genuine worship is an act of obedience. As God and Creator, Jesus has the prerogative to command His subjects to obey Him, but we can choose rebellion. If a person is willing to put His faith in Jesus and obediently follow His teachings,[115] Jesus will give that person peace and serenity, not the temporal peace that the world gives.[116] Jesus has the ability to satisfy each soul. He offers a better life and the gift of salvation to every person who will abide in Him.[117]

The second angel's message will be painfully divisive. It will drive a big wedge between relationships. In many cases, mother and father, brother and sister, husband and wife will take opposing stands. People cannot be saved according to church membership. People cannot be saved according to family membership. Each person has to be saved according to his own faith. Remember Jesus' words? **"Anyone who loves his father or mother more than me is not worthy of me; anyone who loves his son or daughter more than me is not worthy of me; and anyone who does not take his cross and follow me is not worthy of me. Whoever finds his life will lose it, and whoever loses his life for my sake will find it."**[118]

The leaders of Babylon will be adamant: Everyone who refuses to obey Babylon's dictates will be caught and severely punished. They will do this because they think that God's wrath against mankind will not cease until all forms of offensive behaviors are eliminated. Ironically, the leaders of Babylon will not realize that their actions are an insult to God! The 144,000 will rebuke the leaders of Babylon. They will speak plainly and with impressive authority. They will speak against the laws created by Babylon and this will put the honest in heart in a very difficult situation. Conflict will be everywhere. Multitudes will find themselves in a valley of decision. The consequences will be real: Obey God and be punished by Babylon or obey Babylon and be punished by God. This contest will require substantial faith in God or submission to Babylon will be inevitable."

Rev. 14:8

Why Does God Permit Persecution?

Contrary to what many Christians believe, Jesus will put the final generation through an intense testing process. *Jesus will permit the final generation to determine its eternal destiny by choosing whom it will obey.* A test of obedience always reveals who has faith in God. Through the ages God has allowed His people to be tested because testing keeps them close to Him. "In fact," Paul wrote, "everyone who wants to live a godly life in Christ Jesus will be persecuted."[119] Why must it be this way? When there are no trials and temptations, the carnal nature will quickly focus on self and wander away from God. Earlier in this book, we learned that God handed the saints over to the little horn for 1,260 years (538-1798).[120] Prior to this, God handed His people over to the Romans who severely persecuted them and even earlier, most of Christ's disciples were martyred for their faith. Ever since Jesus lived on Earth, His followers have been persecuted. Christians living in Europe and the United States over the past two hundred years have been largely free of religious persecution and this explains, to a great extent, the rapid deterioration of Christianity.

Consider the following story of faith: King Nebuchadnezzar received a vision from God indicating that successive kingdoms would follow the kingdom of Babylon. In his vision, the king saw a man made of different metals. After receiving the vision, the king could not recall the vision and he demanded that his religious experts reveal the forgotten vision. They could not help him. Later, Daniel revealed and interpreted Nebuchadnezzar's vision.[121] At that time, Daniel and his three friends, Shadrach, Meshach and Abednego were given high positions over the wise men of Babylon. When word got out that the king had a vision indicating another kingdom would eventually overthrow Babylon, the king faced an enormous problem. He quickly moved to discredit the truth by erecting a giant image made of solid gold. (He wanted everyone to believe that his kingdom, represented by the head of gold, would endure forever.) He called the leaders of his empire together and demanded that everyone bow down and worship the golden image. When the music sounded everyone bowed down except Shadrach, Meshach, and Abednego. (Daniel did not attend the service.) Their refusal to bow down and worship the image delighted the wise men and they immediately approached the king to taunt him with the rebellion of his Jewish officials:

"At this time some astrologers came forward and denounced the Jews. . . . 'But there are some *Jews whom you* have set over the affairs of the province of Babylon– Shadrach, Meshach and Abednego– who pay no attention to you, O king. They neither serve your gods nor worship the image of gold you have set up.' Furious with rage, Nebuchadnezzar summoned Shadrach, Meshach and Abednego. So these men were brought before the king, and Nebuchadnezzar said to them, 'Is it true, Shadrach, Meshach and Abednego, that you do not serve my gods or worship the image of gold I have set up? Now when you hear the sound of the horn, flute, zither, lyre, harp, pipes and all kinds of music, if you are ready to fall down and worship the image I made, very good. But if you do not worship it, you will be thrown immediately into a blazing furnace. Then what god will be able to rescue you from my hand?' Shadrach, Meshach and Abednego replied to the king, 'O Nebuchadnezzar, we do not need to defend ourselves before you in this matter. [You well know that we worship The Creator of Heaven and Earth and He does not permit His subjects to bow down to idols or worship them.[122]] **If we are thrown into the blazing furnace, the God we serve is able to save us from it, and he will rescue us from your hand, O king.** *But even if he does not, we want you to know*, O king, that we will not serve your gods or worship the image of gold you have set up.' Then Nebuchadnezzar was furious with Shadrach, Meshach and Abednego, and his attitude toward them changed. [Because the governors of his empire were witnesses to their defiance, he had no choice but to order their death.] **He ordered the furnace heated seven times hotter than usual and commanded some of the strongest soldiers in his army to tie up Shadrach, Meshach and Abednego and throw them into the blazing furnace.**"[123]

Rev. 14:8

The fire was so hot that it killed the soldiers that cast Shadrach, Meshach, and Abednego into the furnace, but the three men came out of the furnace without even a hint of smoke in their hair or clothing. What an amazing miracle! Although God can do marvelous things, He *does not usually honor* the faith of His faithful children with such a show of supernatural victory. Normally, Jesus is much more modest in dealing with the problems of His saints. He often resolves problems in subtle ways or He may even choose to let His saints perish and honor them later at

Rev. 14:8

the resurrection. His thoughtful and wise approach to each situation eliminates many problems later on. For example, if one desperate believer experiences a miracle and another desperate believer does not, what does this say about God to both believers and those who intimately know the circumstances in both situations? A miracle can have a terrible fallout. The believer without the miracle may conclude that he is unworthy, that God does not love him, or he lacks enough faith. On the other hand, the believer receiving the miracle may erroneously conclude that God answered his prayer because he did something right to gain God's favor or worse, that God loves him more than the one who did not receive a miracle.[124]

By definition, a miracle occurs when the law of "cause and effect" is suspended. If God suspends the law of "cause and effect" too many times, people would be prone to ignore the rules of life and count on a miracle to save them from foolish decisions. This disconnect would create an irrational view of life which would produce a huge set of problems that do not exist. Jesus still produces miracles, but He is very careful about each miracle because He knows the potential for good and bad that each miracle can have. Because God's wisdom and love for His people is infinite and constant, He requires our faith in Him to be complete. He knows our needs before we cry out for help. He numbers the hairs on our head, and He knows our thoughts. If a miracle is needed in a given situation, He will produce it. If there is a better solution, He will produce that also.

God is pure in heart. God is love. His infinite wisdom is beyond comprehension. The remaining angels in Heaven have been studying God's words and actions for a very long time and they will testify to the redeemed someday that He *never* deviates from the best possible solution that a God of love can provide! For thousands of years they have been observing Him. It is their greatest joy to meet with Him and worship Him. There is nothing in the universe more interesting than the Godhead!

During the Great Tribulation, the saints will be surprised and encouraged by the comforting presence of the Holy Spirit. They will find the Great Tribulation to be the worst of times and the best of times all at the same time. For about twenty-seven months, the 144,000 will proclaim the eternal gospel. They will denounce Babylon's doctrines and laws. Persecution will abound, but the suffering inflicted on the honest in heart will not be pointless. The Holy Spirit will do many things through the 144,000. The sick will be healed, the blind will see, and the deaf will hear. The saints will be busy encouraging and helping new converts each day. Most of all, the saints will experience a camaraderie of love with other saints that words cannot express. When the wicked see the love that the saints have for one another, when they see the extent of their losses and suffering for God's truth, when they see the saints take a bold and deliberate stand for Jesus, many of the wicked will be moved to rethink the importance of the testimony of the 144,000. The Holy Spirit will use the persecution of God's people to soften many hearts and the result will be a harvest of a numberless multitude.[125]

Rev. 14:8

When two-thirds of the 1,335 days allotted to the Great Tribulation expire, the world will be in a most desperate condition. Famine and suffering will be everywhere. The misery index will be great. Most of the people on Earth will have heard and made a decision regarding the eternal gospel. Billions of people will have joined up with Babylon to receive rations and avoid persecution. Meanwhile, most of the saints will be in prison or fleeing from place to place to avoid capture. For 890 days, the 144,000 will faithfully present the first two angel's messages, but their endeavor will stall and come to a standstill a few weeks before the 890th day. Day after day, Jesus will continue to speak through the 144,000. The wicked will not listen and decide the price for worshiping Jesus is too great. The proclamation of the eternal gospel and the formation of Babylon will create three distinct groups of people around the world: The saints (those who will obey the commandments of God and believe the testimony of Jesus), the religious wicked (those who will obey the laws of Babylon), and the non-religious wicked (those who will refuse to obey the laws of God and the laws of Babylon).

When the 891st day of the Great Tribulation arrives, the fifth trumpet will sound in Heaven's temple.[126] The devil and his angels will be released from prison. They will rise quickly from the Abyss (the spirit realm)[127] and take flight. Masquerading as Almighty God, the Bible indicates the devil and his attending angels will *descend to Earth* in a great show of brilliance and power.[128] As the devil and his angels travel the world, they will imitate the Second Coming over and over. Lucifer and his angels will be seen approaching Earth for miles away. When they decide to leave a particular area, the devil and his angels will ascend into the sky as Jesus did when He returned to Heaven.

This will be an over powering deception. It is interesting to notice that Lucifer and his angels will not be permitted to hover in the sky over Earth as Jesus will do at the Second Coming.[129] Lucifer's appearing will be a series of local events.[130] In other words, the devil and his entourage can only appear at one place at a time. As time goes by, the devil's fame and news of his appearing will grow.[131] Huge crowds will go out to see him.

After descending from the sky,[132] the devil will perform incredible signs and wonders,[133] even calling fire down out of Heaven,[134] to convince the multitudes that He is Almighty God.[135] God will not allow the 144,000 to perform this miracle and this overpowering delusion[136] will cause many of the non-religious wicked to join Babylon. Everywhere Lucifer goes, he will speak gracious words of hope and promise. He will feed the multitudes and heal the sick. He will be worshiped and adored as "Almighty God." Of course, the saints know the true identity of this glorious being and they will refuse to go out to see him.[137]

The Third Angel's Message: An Ultimatum

Rev. 14:9-10

And the third angel followed them, saying with a loud voice, If any man worship the beast and his image, and receive his mark in his forehead, or in his hand, The same shall drink of the wine of the wrath of God, which is poured out without mixture into the cup of his indignation; and he shall be tormented with fire and brimstone in the presence of the holy angels, and in the presence of the Lamb:

{9} I saw a mighty angel descend from God's throne. As he orbited the Earth, he said in a loud voice, "Listen! Listen! If anyone worships Lucifer, if anyone participates in Lucifer's theocracy, if anyone receives Lucifer's tattoo on the forehead or on their right hand {10} that individual will drink the wine of God's wrath which has been poured full strength into the cup of His fury.

This is a very serious message and it will be presented to the wicked when Lucifer appears at the fifth trumpet. This message contains a promise. Everyone who obeys and worships Lucifer will experience the full fury of God's wrath. Everyone who receives the mark of the beast will be condemned to death. There will be no exception because once a person chooses to swallow the devil's poisonous lies, the victim will have no control over the outcome.[138] All who join up with Lucifer to carry out his evil schemes will be tormented with burning sulfur in the presence of the Lamb and His holy angels.

{11} At the Second Coming, Jesus will ignite a lake of fire[139] and the leaders of Babylon, as well as all who were employed by Babylon. will be thrown alive into it.[140] Of course, everyone thrown into the fire will be consumed just as people are consumed in fires now, but the smoke from this lake of fire will ascend for a thousand years because this lake will burn as 'a memorial flame' for 1,000 years.¹⁴¹ "The rest of the wicked will be slain by a command (the sword) that came out of Jesus' mouth. Their bodies will be left to rot in the streets and the birds will gorge themselves on their flesh."¹⁴²

> Consider a strange paradox: Even though the wicked will go along with Babylon's demands to avoid punishment, they will not have any rest or peace of mind day or night. They will feel anxious and desperate the whole time. The Holy Spirit will do everything, short of violating the human will so that, if possible, the wicked might surrender their hearts to Jesus and be saved. How can there be love, joy, or peace when separated from God who is the Source of love, joy, and peace?"

{12} When the 144,000 deliver the third angel's message, the intensity of persecution will grow and suffering will increase substantially. The 144,000 will outrage and highly offend those who obey and worship the devil as though he was "Almighty God" when the 144,000 say that Lucifer is the devil! This will enrage the wicked and they will persue and persecute the people of God even more. Nevertheless, the 144,000 will be bold and fearless.¹⁴³ Meanwhile, the saints will be sustained by the Holy Spirit and the fulfillment of God's Word. They will be given divine strength and encouraged to be patient and faithful.

{13} When the sixth trumpet sounded in Heaven,¹⁴⁴ the fifth seal on The Book of Life was broken open.¹⁴⁵ There was a great deal of martyrdom for the sake of Christ. Then I heard a voice from Heaven say, "Write this down, John: The Lord will especially bless those saints who die for Him from *now on*." "Yes," says the Holy Spirit, "they will temporarily rest from their labors and suffering, for their deeds will surely follow them."

> This announcement indicates that a time has come for many of God's saints to be put to death. Jesus permits a large number of saints to become martyrs for two reasons. First, their deaths will eventually cause some of the wicked to repent and be saved. Second, Jesus permits many of His saints to sleep through the rest of the Great Tribulation. However, all who die during the fifth seal will be resurrected a few days early to see the Second Coming of Jesus. Those who put Jesus on the cross will also be resurrected at the same time to see Jesus appear in clouds of glory.¹⁴⁶

Rev. 14:11

And the smoke of their torment ascendeth up for ever and ever: and they have no rest day nor night, who worship the beast and his image, and whosoever receiveth the mark of his name.

Rev. 14:12

Here is the patience of the saints: here are they that keep the commandments of God, and the faith of Jesus.

Rev. 14:13

And I heard a voice from heaven saying unto me, Write, Blessed are the dead which die in the Lord from henceforth: Yea, saith the Spirit, that they may rest from their labours; and their works do follow them.

The End of Salvation

Rev. 14:13

Before continuing with verse 14, we need to review a few facts so we can truly appreciate the contents of verse 13. When the devil physically appears at the fifth trumpet, many of the non-religious wicked will convince themselves that Lucifer and his angels are a religious apparition of some kind and they will refuse to honor Lucifer as Almighty God. However, most of the non-religious wicked will have a change of mind when the devil's demons begin to attack them and afflict them with searing pain. The pain that will be inflicted on the non-religious wicked is worse than the sting of a scorpion! The victims will long to die, but they cannot.[147]

Lucifer's demons will freely use torture to force resistant and undecided people into worshiping the devil. The devil's objective will be the elimination of all non-religious people, but the 144,000 will proclaim that the torment inflicted by the demons proves that Lucifer is not God, but the devil! A God of love will never accept forced worship! Many will chose to obey and worship Lucifer to avoid further suffering, but force is always the last resort of false religion. The 144,000 will explain to the non-religious wicked that in Christ, there is freedom.[148] If a person puts his faith in his Creator and obeys the eternal gospel, that person will receive the seal of God and the assurance of eternal life. Of course, the non-religious wicked will also see that the saints are protected from Lucifer's attacks[149] during the fifth trumpet and this will convince many in that group to surrender their hearts to their Creator.[150] At the end of the fifth trumpet, the world will be reduced to two groups of people: The saints, who obey the commandments of Jesus and the testimony of Jesus, and the religious wicked, who obey the commandments of Babylon and the testimony of Lucifer. The persecution of the non-religious wicked during the fifth trumpet will eliminate this entire group.

I believe the sixth trumpet will sound in Heaven on the 1,039th day of the Great Tribulation.[151] At this time, Lucifer will suddenly change character. Overnight, he will set aside His masquerade as a generous and benevolent God to become a ruthless dictator. He will demand the creation of a counterfeit theocracy because there is no room for religious diversity when "God" dwells among men. He will set himself up as king of kings and lord of lords and there is nothing that mankind can do to stop or thwart the actions of the devil.

The devil will suddenly dissolve the religious systems and governments of the world. He will set up a one world church state. He will instruct his forces to divide the population of the world into groups of one thousand and then, after selecting one person from each unit of 1,000, he will demand one-third of each group be killed.[152] The devil will announce that the first 666 people to receive his mark (a tattoo) from each group will be allowed to live. Those who wish to be saved must swear allegiance to him and his government by voluntarily wearing a tattoo on the right hand showing "666." The carnage that follows will be degenerate, disgusting, and sickening. Millions of God's people will be captured and killed.[153] A much larger number of the devil's followers will also be slain to meet the quota. The devil and his demons will be very pleased with their deadly achievement.

When the sixth trumpet ends, the population of Earth will be less than 50% of what it was when the censer was cast down. When the sixth trumpet ends, the 1,260 days allotted to the work of God's Two Witnesses will end. The work and testimony of the 144,000 will be finished. During the sixth trumpet, the 144,000 will faithfully deliver the fourth angel's message. This message calls for everyone to come out of Babylon and defy Lucifer's authority. By the end of the sixth trumpet, circumstances will force everyone into a firm decision. There will be no turning back. Two distinct groups of people will live on Earth, a small group of sheep and a large number of goats.

The results of the third and fourth angel's messages will be encouraging. Many people will reconsider the eternal gospel during the fifth trumpet and they will join with the saints in worshiping the Creator. Then, during the sixth trumpet, the 144,000[154] will present God's final message[155] to the world and even at this late hour, a few more people will favorably respond. They will put their faith in Christ and receive the seal of God. By the time the 1,260 days of the Two Witnesses end, every decision will have been firmly made. Most, if not all of the 144,000 will be dead; their testimony is finished because God's offer of salvation has done all it can do.

{14} In front of me was a white cloud. I saw Jesus sitting on the cloud. He had a crown of gold (Greek: *stephanos,* crown of victory) on His head and a sharp sickle in His hand. {15} An angel came out of the temple bringing a message from the Father. He called to Jesus, "Wave your sickle over the Earth because the harvest is

Rev. 14:13

Rev. 14:14

And I looked, and behold a white cloud, and upon the cloud one sat like unto the Son of man, having on his head a golden crown, and in his hand a sharp sickle.

Prophecy 12 - The Eternal Gospel

Rev. 14:15-16
And another angel came out of the temple, crying with a loud voice to him that sat on the cloud, Thrust in thy sickle, and reap: for the time is come for thee to reap; for the harvest of the earth is ripe. And he that sat on the cloud thrust in his sickle on the earth; and the earth was reaped.

ripe." {16} So Jesus waved His sickle over the Earth and the offer of salvation ended.

This solemn scene marks the close of redemption. Like the door on Noah's ark, the door to eternal life will be shut.[156] Consider two important features: First, at the end of the sixth trumpet, the Holy Spirit will review every heart on Earth and once He determines that every decision is firmly made, He will inform the Father there is nothing further that He can do. The Father will send word to Jesus *when* to terminate the offer of salvation and close the door to eternal life. Second, all possibility of redemption ends *prior* to the seven last plagues *because everyone will either have the seal of God or the mark of the beast. Those having the mark of the beast are incorrigible because they committed the unpardonable sin.*[157]

Rev. 14:17-20
And another angel came out of the temple which is in heaven, he also having a sharp sickle. And another angel came out from the altar, which had power over fire; and cried with a loud cry to him that had the sharp sickle, saying, Thrust in thy sharp sickle, and gather the clusters of the vine of the earth; for her grapes are fully ripe. And the angel thrust in his sickle into the earth, and gathered the vine of the earth, and

{17} Then I saw another mighty angel come out of the Heavenly temple. He also had a sharp sickle in his hand. {18} Then, another angel in charge of the fire at the Altar of Burnt Offering called to the angel who had the sharp sickle, "Take your sharp sickle and gather the clusters of grapes from Earth's vineyard, because the grapes are ripe, ready to be crushed in the winepress of God's wrath." {19} The angel swung his sickle over the Earth and everyone having the mark of the beast was eternally condemned. These people will be crushed in the great winepress of God's wrath during the seven last plagues. {20} I also saw that everyone having the mark of the beast would be crushed in the winepress of God's wrath *outside* the city. The number of wicked people thrown into the winepress of God's wrath was so great that blood flowed out of the press as high as the horses' bridles for a distance as long as the length of the nation of Israel (from top to bottom, about 180 miles).

This phrase, "outside the city" means the wicked will be "cut off" from having any inheritance. There is no safety outside the city of refuge! The wicked will not be allowed to enter the New Earth.

{15:1} I saw seven angels holding seven bowls, these bowls contain seven *last* plagues. These seven judgments will serve as the winepress of God's wrath. These plagues are called "last," because they follow the seven trumpets (seven first plagues) and they will utterly crush the wicked and destroy the planet as well. {2} Then, I saw a great expanse supporting the throne of God. It looked like a sea of glass mixed with sparkling fire.[158] Standing beside the sea of glass were the 144,000. They had been victorious over the beast and his image and over the number of his name. They had faithfully accomplished the mission given to them and they had been taken to Heaven on the 1,265th day of the Great Tribulation. They held harps that God had given to them {3} and they sang the song of Moses, the servant of God, and the song of the Lamb: "Great and marvelous are your deeds, Lord God Almighty. Your ways are just and true, King of the Ages."

---

cast it into the great winepress of the wrath of God. And the winepress was trodden without the city, and blood came out of the winepress, even unto the horse bridles, by the space of a thousand and six hundred furlongs.

Rev. 15:1-3

And I saw another sign in heaven, great and marvellous, seven angels having the seven last plagues; for in them is filled up the wrath of God. And I saw as it were a sea of glass mingled with fire: and them that had gotten the victory over the beast, and over his image, and over his mark, and over the number of his name, stand on the sea of glass, having the harps of God. And they sing the song of Moses the servant of God, and the song of the Lamb, saying, Great and marvellous are thy works, Lord God Almighty;

> *just and true are thy ways, thou King of saints.*
>
> **Rev. 15:4-6**
>
> *Who shall not fear thee, O Lord, and glorify thy name? for thou only art holy: for all nations shall come and worship before thee; for thy judgments are made manifest. And after that I looked, and, behold, the temple of the tabernacle of the testimony in heaven was opened: And the seven angels came out of the temple, having the seven plagues, clothed in pure and white linen, and having their breasts girded with golden girdles.*

{4} Referring to the wicked who were about to be crushed in the winepress of God's wrath, the 144,000 sang, "Who will not fear you, O Lord, and bring glory to your name? For you alone are holy. People from all nations will come and worship you, for your righteous acts of vengeance have been revealed." {5} After the 144,000 finished singing, I looked and the temple, that is, the tabernacle containing the Ark of the Testimony, was opened. {6} Out of the temple came the seven angels who stand before God.[159] They were carrying seven bowls which contain seven plagues. They were dressed in clean, shining linen and wore golden sashes around their chests. Their clothing and golden sashes indicated they were sent from Almighty God, sent on an honorable and righteous mission. They were commissioned by the Creator of Heaven and Earth to avenge the great suffering of His saints." Jesus said, " **'It is mine to avenge; I will repay.'** "The Lord will judge [avenge] **his people.' It is a dreadful thing to fall into the hands of the living God."**[160]

The Rules of Interpretation

Consider how the Rules of Interpretation (discussed in the Introduction) are observed in this prophecy:

Rule One says an apocalyptic prophecy has a beginning point and ending point in time and the events within the prophecy occur in the order given." This prophecy conforms to Rule One because chronological order is self evident.

1. God sends an outright demand (first angel's message)
2. God sends an inflammatory declaration (second angel's message)
3. God sends an ultimatum (third angel's message)
4. God's offer of salvation comes to an end (end of salvation)
5. The victory celebration of the 144,000

Rule Two says a fulfillment only occurs when all of the specifications are met, and this includes the order stated in the prophecy. Even though the three angel's messages have been understood for a while, they have not been set before mankind as a testing truth. The elements described in this prophecy have not begun. The judgment of the living does not begin until the censer is cast down. Babylon does not rise until the Great Tribulation begins and Lucifer does not appear until the fifth trumpet sounds. Finally, the 144,000 have not begun their ministry. Therefore, this prophecy has not been fulfilled.

Rule Three says that apocalyptic language can be literal, analogous or symbolic. To reach the intended meaning of a prophecy, the reader must consider (a) the context, (b) the use of parallel language in the Bible, and (c) if an element is thought to be symbolic, the Bible must interpret the symbol with a *relevant* text. The language used in this prophecy is not symbolic because there are no relevant texts defining a symbol. On the other hand, we do find an extensive use of analogous and literal language. For example, the three angels orbiting the Earth represent three messages from God that will be heard around the world. The three angel's messages are self-explanatory once we understand the setting in which they are delivered. The scene where Jesus waves His sickle over the Earth because the harvest is ripe uses language that is analogous with a harvest. The "winepress of God's wrath" is easy to understand. Grapes are crushed in a winepress and indeed, God's wrath will crush the wicked who live during the seven bowls.

Rule Four is not used in this prophecy.

References:

1. Revelation 11:6
2. Revelation 8:5
3. Revelation 14:9-11; 19:19-21
4. Revelation 18:1-5 See Prophecy 15.
5. Revelation 13:8; Matthew 12:31,32
6. Revelation 14:14-19
7. Revelation 22:11
8. Romans 8:6-8
9. John 16:1-3; 15:20,21
10. Revelation 1:9
11. Revelation 11:7,8; 16:4-6
12. John 14:10,24,31
13. Revelation 15:2-6
14. Revelation 15:2, italics mine
15. Revelation 8:3-5
16. For further discussion on this assertion, please see pages 22-24 in my book, *A Study on the Seven Trumpets, Two Witnesses and Four Beasts* or you may freely download the article at: http://www.wake-up.org/Revelation/724Book.pdf.
17. Ibid. Pages 12-15.
18. John 5:22,23; 6:46; Philippians 2:6; Isaiah 40:25-28; Nehemiah 9:5-7
19. Matthew 4:10
20. Colossians 1:16
21. John 5:22,23; 2 Corinthian 5:10; Ecclesiastes 12:13,14; Matthew 24:14
22. John 1:1-14; Colossians 1:13-19
23. Matthew 24:14; Revelation 3:10
24. See pages 152-174 in my book, *A Study on the Seven Seals and The 144,000*. Or you may freely download this article at: http://www.wake-up.org/Revelation/Rev144.htm
25. Philippians 2:6

26. John 5:22,23; 1 Timothy 6:16
27. John 5:22,23; Nehemiah 9:6; Revelation 14:7
28. John 16:15
29. Philippians 2:6
30. Psalm 2:7-12; John 6:38; 10:18
31. Isaiah 53:2
32. Matthew 8:20
33. Hebrews 4:15
34. For further discussion on the identity of Michael, please see pages 22-29 in my book, *Jesus: The Alpha and The Omega.* http://www.wake-up.org/Alpha/Chapter2.htm
35. Colossians 1:15; John 6:46; 1 Timothy 6:16
36. 1 Timothy 6:16
37. Acts 17:28
38. Genesis 2:21,22
39. John 6:46; 1 Timothy 6:16
40. Ezekiel 28:12-15
41. Ezekiel 28:14; Daniel 10:13 Note: Although the Bible does not state a number, this author concludes there were two chief princes in Heaven, e.g., two guardian cherubs – Michael and Lucifer. After the expulsion of Lucifer, it is understood that Gabriel took his place. See also John 12:31; 14:30; Luke 1:19.
42. Genesis 2:17 (KJV)
43. See comments on Revelation 5:4.
44. Luke 10:18
45. Job 38:4-7
46. Psalm 33:9
47. Exodus 6:3; Romans 16:25
48. 1 John 5:4 See Appendix D.
49. Colossians 1:16
50. Isaiah 44:6; Revelation 1:8, 17,18
51. Acts 4:12
52. John 14:9

53. Romans 8:32-39
54. Genesis 11:1-9
55. Genesis 10:25
56. Exodus 5:1,2
57. Exodus 7:1-5
58. Daniel 4:34-37
59. Revelation 11:6
60. John 8:44
61. Matthew 24:14
62. Revelation 11:5,6; Acts 14:3
63. Romans 9:25,26; 2:28,29; Galatians 3:28,29
64. Acts 10:28-34
65. Acts 17:26,27; Romans 5:12
66. Revelation 11:3
67. 1 Corinthians 2:14
68. Matthew 27:19; John 10:16; Revelation 1:2; 12:17; 14:11,12; Matthew 7:28,29
69. Revelation 14:9,10; 21:7,8; Matthew 24:14,25,26; 5:11,12
70. John 16:1-13
71. Matthew 12:31,32
72. Revelation 19:19-21
73. Revelation 3:10
74. John 14:15
75. Romans 6:23
76. Daniel 3:14-18
77. Matthew 5:11; 19:29
78. Revelation 12:17
79. Genesis 2:1-3; Exodus 20:8-11
80. Genesis 2:1-3; Exodus 16:23-30
81. Mark 2:27,28
82. Revelation 13:5-8

83. We know that Eden is called, "the garden of God." (Ezekiel 28:13) We also know that Eden remained on Earth after Adam and Eve were cast out. See Genesis 3:22-24, 4:16 and compare with Ezekiel 31:16-18. At the flood, this author assumes that God took Eden to Heaven to save it for the Earth made new. Compare Revelation 22:1-3 with Genesis 2:10. It is possible that the *same* Tree of Life that Adam and Eve once enjoyed will be found in the New Earth.
84. Genesis 6:9
85. Genesis 6:5,12
86. 1 John 3:4; Romans 4:15
87. Exodus 20:3-17; Isaiah 42:6; 49:6; Matthew 5:14
88. Genesis 2:1-3; Exodus 20:8-11
89. Matthew 22:36-40
90. Exodus 34:28; Deuteronomy 4:13; Numbers 14:44
91. Hebrews 8:10-12
92. Revelation 11:19; 15:5,6
93. Exodus 31:18
94. Revelation 13:15
95. Psalm 14:1
96. Aleksandr Solzhenitsyn, *National Review,* July 22, 1983
97. See Exodus 5. For a discussion on this topic, please see Chapter 9 "What Happened to the Lord's Day?" in my book, *Jesus: The Alpha and The Omega* or you can freely download this article at: http://www.wake-up.org/Alpha/Chapter9.htm.
98. Exodus 5:14-22
99. Revelation 13:4-8; 18:1-24
100. Hebrews 4:15
101. Romans 5:10
102. John 16:33
103. Daniel 2:9-13
104. Revelation 13:3
105. John 5:22
106. Psalm 51:17

107. 2 Corinthians 9:7
108. 1 Chronicles 28:9; Romans 8:27
109. Leviticus 19:35,36
110. Colossians 3:5,6
111. 1 John 1:9
112. Matthew 5:23,24
113. Revelation 2:7,11,17,26; 3:5,12,21; 21:7,8
114. Hebrews 11
115. John 15:14
116. John 14:27
117. John 15:4-11
118. Matthew 10:37-39
119. 2 Timothy 3:12
120. Daniel 7:25; Revelation 12:6,14
121. Daniel 2
122. Exodus 20:4-6
123. Daniel 3:8,12-20, insertions and italics mine
124. See John 9.
125. Revelation 7:9
126. Revelation 9:1-11
127. Revelation 12:9
128. Revelation 9:3
129. Revelation 1:7
130. Matthew 24:23-28
131. Daniel 8:9
132. Revelation 9:2,3
133. Revelation 13:14; 2 Thessalonians 2:9-12
134. Revelation 13:13
135. 2 Thessalonians 2:4
136. 2 Thessalonians 2:1-12
137. Matthew 24:24-27
138. Jeremiah 25:15-18; John 18:11; Luke 22:42
139. Revelation 19:19-21

140. God holds leaders to a higher standard of accountability. Numbers 25:3-5; Deuteronomy 32:35-43; Revelation 18:8-10; Isaiah 29:15-20
141. Revelation 20:10
142. Revelation 19:15-18
143. Revelation 11:5,6
144. Revelation 9:13
145. Revelation 6:9-11
146. Matthew 26:64; Revelation 1:7.
147. Revelation 9:5,6
148. 2 Corinthians 3:17
149. Revelation 9:4
150. Compare the scene in Revelation 9:6 with the story found in Numbers 21:4-9.
151. This date is calculated. In keeping with God's use of one-third and two-thirds during the seven trumpets, it is assumed that Jesus protects Earth from Lucifer and his angels by keeping them in the Abyss for two-thirds of the 1,335 days. If so, the devil and his angels will appear on the 891st day, a new moon. Five months of torment amounts to 148 days counting inclusively (29.53 days per month x 5 months = 148 days).
152. Revelation 9:15
153. The fourth message will be examined in Prophecy 14.
154. Revelation 6:9-11
155. Revelation 18:1-5
156. Matthew 25:1-13
157. Revelation 14:9,10
158. Ezekiel 1:22-28
159. Revelation 8:2
160. Hebrews 10:30,31

Prophecy 13

The Seven Bowls
Revelation 15:7-16-21

Beginning Point in Time: 1,265th Day of the Great Tribulation

Ending Point in Time: Second Coming

Summary: The book of Revelation indicates there will be two distinct phases of God's wrath during the Great Tribulation. The first phase will be redemptive in nature. The second phase will be totally destructive. The first phase is called the seven trumpets and Jesus extends salvation to everyone who will worship Him. The second phase is called the seven *last* plagues or the seven bowls (or seven vials – KJV). Everyone who receives the mark of the beast will die during the seven bowls. The seven last plagues are represented as seven bowls (or vials) because every wicked person will be forced to drink (that is, experience) God's wrath, a bitter mixture that contains no mercy.

Introduction: According to my calculations, the seven bowls will occur over a period of seventy days. If true, each plague could last ten days.[1] The seven bowls are not discussed very often because most Bible students do not think they are particularly relevant. It is true that they will occur in the future, but they reveal additional information about God's love and character that is helpful right now! Before we examine the seven bowls in detail, please notice they can be divided into two groups:

Plagues on Individuals	**Plagues on Corporate Entities**
1. Ugly and painful sores	5. Painful blindness on Lucifer's officials
2. Oceans turn to blood	6. Kings of the Earth gathered for Armageddon
3. Rivers and springs turn to blood	7. Hailstones weighing 100 pounds each and a sword that comes out of Jesus' mouth
4. Scorching heat	

Jesus' Final Victory

The seven bowls are listed in two columns because the first four bowls serve a different purpose than the last three. All who receive the mark of the beast will be affected by the first four bowls. These judgments will extract restitution from those who preyed on God's saints. The last three bowls are directed at the defiant leaders of the world and those who work for them. Jesus intends to destroy kings and soldiers alike. The fifth bowl will strike down Lucifer's theocracy (his officials and employees). The sixth bowl will unite the kings of the Earth and their armies to make war on Jesus as He appears and the seventh bowl will totally destroy the wicked and make Earth desolate. Jesus will destroy the kings and their armies by casting them into a lake of fire at the Second Coming and the rest of the wicked will drop dead when He commands them to die. (This command is represented as a sword that comes out of Jesus' mouth.) By the end of the seventh bowl, all wicked people will be dead.[2] As the saints meet the Lord in the air, Earth will be left desolate.

The seven last plagues are puzzling to some people. They ask, "Why would a God of love torture people? Isn't torture the invention of the devil?" These questions are reasonable because the Bible says that God is love.[3] However, the phrase, "God is love," means more than many people realize. It means that all of God's actions are consistent with principles of love. Because God's actions are often misunderstood, the principles of love are often misunderstood. I prefer to define God's love as a perfect balance between justice and mercy. According to infinite wisdom and changeless consistency, God knows when mercy is appropriate and when the demands of justice are required. This balance is always perfect because God is love personified! *God's actions demonstrate what love is and what love is not.* Given this eternal truth, the seven bowls have to be understood as an expression of love because God will send them. As incredible as it seems, God's love will be expressed through vengeance, exposure, and discovery. A few words about each element might be helpful.

1. Vengeance

There is an important distinction between vengeance and revenge. Vengeance is a righteous process that lawfully achieves justice. When a *disinterested* party, who has no relationship with either a perpetrator of a crime (predator) or a victim of that crime, imposes a sentence on the predator on behalf of the victim, the disinterested party exercises vengeance. Revenge, on the other hand, is another word for retaliation. When an *interested* party, who has a relationship with the victim of a crime, imposes a sentence on a predator which the party deems appropriate, the interested party exacts revenge. The problem with revenge is that justice is often ignored to satisfy passion. In other words, the person exercising revenge will often go beyond the demands of justice and also become a predator.

When God implements justice, He seeks two objectives. The first objective is the restoration of the victim; the second objective is the punishment of the predator. For example, if a thief is caught, the predator must restore more than he stole. **"If a man steals an ox or a sheep and slaughters it or sells it, he must pay back five head of cattle for the ox and four sheep for the sheep. . . . A thief must certainly make restitution, but if he has nothing, he must be sold to pay for his theft. If the stolen animal is found alive in his possession – whether ox or donkey or sheep – he must pay back double."**[4] God's second objective in justice is punishment. When a person sins against his neighbor, he also sins against God. Therefore, after making restitution, a predator must also offer a sin offering to the Lord before his guilt can be removed.[5]

When the crimes of predators become so great that restitution is not possible, the Lord rises up and punishes the predators without mercy. **"With the coming of dawn, the angels urged Lot, saying, 'Hurry! Take your wife and your two daughters who are here, or you will be swept away when the city is punished.'"**[6] The Bible speaks clearly. God will surely punish those who violate the golden rule and harm others. He sent a flood in Noah's day and destroyed the whole world because a majority of the antediluvians had become predators. God's love for victims of crime requires the exercise of justice. Therefore, God seeks the restitution and punishment of predators.

The seven last plagues must be understood within the context of restitution. The seven bowls contain God's vengeance. Jesus will lawfully extract restitution from the wicked during the seven last plagues because there will be no justice for God's people during the Great Tribulation. The wicked will treat God's saints with contempt and hatred. God's people will have their possessions taken from them, and ultimately, many will die because of their loyalty to Jesus and their determination to obey the eternal gospel. Demons will keep the wicked enraged at God's saints. The wicked will impose an unimaginable level of cruelty and hardship on God's people and there will be no justice for God's despised people. Of course, the watchful eye of Jesus will not miss a single predatory act. Recording angels will capture every thought, word, and deed because Jesus will see that justice is served at the appointed time. At the end of the day, a God of love will repay the wicked with *a double measure* of the suffering they imposed on His saints.[8] The apostle Paul was well acquainted with persecution and He wrote, **"Do not take revenge, my friends, but leave room for God's wrath, for it is written: 'It is mine to avenge; I will repay,' says the Lord."**[9] We should never forget these words: **"I will repay, says the Lord."**[10]

We have examined the difference between vengeance and revenge because the seven bowls contain God's vengeance. During the Great Tribulation, desperate circumstances will separate the people of Earth into two groups. The sheep will embrace the testimony of the 144,000, worship the Creator and love one another. The goats will rebel against God's authority and submit to Babylon's authority out of cowardice. The contest between God's authority and Babylon's authority will be sharp and distinct. At first, the wicked will do whatever it takes to save themselves from suffering, but they will eventually discover that the path of least resistance leads to slavery. Their master will be the devil. There will be no justice for God's saints during the Great Tribulation, so Jesus Himself will execute vengeance on the wicked during the final seventy days of the Great Tribulation. Jesus will repay the wicked for their predatory behavior.

2. Exposure

Another purpose for the seven bowls is exposure. Jesus will expose the devil's masquerade during the fifth bowl. About one year *before* the fifth bowl occurs, the fifth trumpet will occur. Jesus will permit Lucifer to leave the spirit realm and physically appear before mankind. He will lead the wicked into total rebellion against God's authority. The devil will masquerade as Almighty God and he will perform many magnificent miracles, even calling fire down from Heaven! Many people will embrace the devil as though he was "God." When the sixth trumpet sounds, the devil will suddenly change character and demand that everyone on Earth worship as he dictates or be killed. The devil will rule over Earth as king of kings and lord of lords. This pompous and totally corrupt despot will rule over the whole world for about nine months, but during the fifth bowl, Jesus will strip away the devil's masquerade. Jesus will expose the great liar (the false prophet). Every wicked person will discover that he has been worshiping the devil!

Jesus will pour out the fifth bowl on a specific group of people. He will strike down those individuals who have served as officials and employees in Lucifer's government (theocracy). They will be totally debilitated with excruciating pain and blindness. Lucifer's officials and employees will become totally dysfunctional and Lucifer's control of Earth will suddenly end. There is a specific irony in the fifth plague. People who refused to see any light in the gospel of Jesus Christ will no longer be able to see the god of darkness they chose to serve. When the world observes the painful blindness and the administrative devastation imposed on the devil's officials and employees, and that Lucifer cannot undo or cancel the impact of this destructive plague upon his own government, the wicked will have to admit that "a higher power" has punished the one who claimed to be "Almighty God." Thus, the devil will be exposed for who he really is. Then, great fear will overwhelm the kings of Earth and those wearing the mark of the beast causing extreme distress. They will hate the devil and loathe themselves. They will remember the testimony of the 144,000, but it will be too late. The wicked will realize that their destruction is inescapable.

3. Discovery

When the wicked discover that the glorious being who masquerades as Almighty God is the devil, they will also discover that they have no Savior and no refuge from the wrath of the true Almighty God. They will have no one to worship, no spiritual assurance, no divine being in whom to trust, and no hope for the future. The fifth bowl will force the wicked to see their true condition before the Creator of the Universe. When the sixth bowl is poured out, the wicked will realize that their rebellion and efforts to save themselves from God's wrath are nearly over. Lucifer will send three of his most powerful demons to the kings of Earth. These demons will perform amazing miracles before the kings of Earth and then, they will present Lucifer's proposal. They will inform the ten kings that Jesus will soon arrive and destroy the whole world. Therefore, Lucifer invites them to join forces with his angels to make war on Jesus when He appears. The demons will say, "This is your only hope for survival."

Two interesting facts will emerge during the sixth bowl. First, the Bible predicts the ten kings of the Earth will join forces with Lucifer's demons knowing that Lucifer is the devil and that his angels are demons. Consider the ramifications of this union for a moment. To save themselves from death, the ten kings will knowingly and willfully unite with the devil and his demons in an attempt to destroy the Creator of the Universe. Second, the actions of the ten kings prove that sin has the same effect on human beings as angels. All sinners will become predators given enough time and power. Under the right circumstances, all sinners would attempt to destroy a God of love if possible. A sinner's love for self is so unlike the love of a sinless being. Sinless beings exalt righteousness, truth, and the two laws of love, whereas those ruled by the carnal nature exalt wickedness, lies, and selfishness.

The Cross of Calvary proves that the Creator of the Universe, Jesus Christ, was willing to cease to exist so sinners might be saved. This is infinite love in action! Contrast this with the war against Jesus at the Second Coming. *The sixth bowl demonstrates why sin and sinners cannot be tolerated in God's universe ever again.* If given the time, power, and opportunity, every sinner will become a predator. The seven bowls provide a vivid illustration of how the predatory nature of sin works.

During the Great Tribulation, the inhabitants of Earth will be put into a spiral of increasing distress. As circumstances become more desperate, a sharper distinction between sheep and goats will appear. One group will choose the way of divine love. They will worship the Creator and love one another. The other group will grasp at every straw to save themselves from suffering, hardship, and death, only to incur God's wrath, extended suffering and finally death.

Love for God will take the sheep in one direction and love for self will take the goats in a different direction. As the Great Tribulation escalates, the wicked will prey on the saints to survive. The wicked will take the saint's possessions and treat them with shameful contempt. God's saints will be tortured, imprisoned, and killed for rebelling against Babylon's laws. When each person has chosen his spiritual destination, that is, *sealed* as a sheep or *marked* as a goat, God's offer of salvation will end. Then, Jesus will execute vengeance for His helpless saints. He will lawfully punish the wicked with seven last plagues and holy angels will declare that God is righteous in His actions! Justice will be served. Unrepentant predators will suffer according to the suffering they have caused. **"For we know him who said, 'It is mine to avenge; I will repay,' and again, 'The Lord will judge his people.' It is a dreadful thing to fall into the hands of the living God."**[11]

The Sequence

{7} While the wicked on Earth were celebrating the death of the Two Witnesses,[12] one of the four living creatures gave a golden bowl filled with God's wrath to each of the seven angels that stand before God. All Heaven watched with solemn interest, for the angels know that Jesus Christ is the same yesterday, today and forever.[13]

> During the Great Tribulation, the blood of God's saints will cry out for justice in the same way that Abel's blood cried out to the Lord[14] and the seven last plagues will be the Lord's response.

{8} After the seven angels received the seven bowls, Heaven's temple was filled with smoke from the glory of God and from His power. Everyone had to leave the temple for His wrath is a consuming fire.[15] No one could enter the temple until the seven plagues were finished. The empty temple means there is no further intercession or salvation for individuals. God's offer of redemption was finished.

> When the 1,265th day of the Great Tribulation arrives, Jesus will resurrect the 144,000 and take them to Heaven. On that morning, the sky will become violent and threatening. Great sheets of lightning will slice through the darkness and peals of intimidating thunder will boom throughout the Earth. Voices will be heard rumbling deep from within the Earth. People who have the mark of the beast will be paralyzed with terror. When the saints observe these manifestations of divine power, they will know that the time for the seven bowls has come and there is nothing further they can do. They will flee to the wilderness or the mountains to wait for Jesus to appear.

Rev. 15:7
And one of the four beasts gave unto the seven angels seven golden vials full of the wrath of God, who liveth for ever and ever.

Rev. 15:8
And the temple was filled with smoke from the glory of God, and from his power; and no man was able to enter into the temple, till the seven plagues of the seven angels were fulfilled.

PROPHECY 13 - The Seven Bowls

Rev. 16:1
And I heard a great voice out of the temple saying to the seven angels, Go your ways, and pour out the vials of the wrath of God upon the earth.

Rev. 16:2
And the first went, and poured out his vial upon the earth; and there fell a noisome and grievous sore upon the men which had the mark of the beast, and upon them which worshipped his image.

Rev. 16:3
And the second angel poured out his vial upon the sea; and it became as the blood of a dead man; and every living soul died in the sea.

Rev. 16:4-7
And the third angel poured out his vial upon the rivers and fountains of waters; and they became blood. And I heard the angel

{16:1} Then I heard a loud voice in Heaven say to the seven angels, "Go now and make the wicked drink from the cup of God's wrath."

> Jesus said to the first angel, "Lucifer controls the world. He will not permit my people to buy or sell because they will not wear his mark. He intends to starve my people to death. Do to the wicked as they have done to my people. Go and poison their food. Let those who are wearing the mark of the beast eat their cursed food and suffer from the horrible boils that will follow." **"The day of the Lord is near for all nations. As you have done, it will be done to you; your deeds will return upon your own head."**[16]

{2} The first angel poured out his bowl of poison on *the land*, and ugly and painful sores broke out on everyone who had the mark of the beast, but the saints were not affected. When the wicked realized that their food supplies from the land were the source of their boils, they rushed to the ocean to find food.

> Then Jesus said, "Neither shall the sea provide food for the wicked. Poison the oceans of the world!"

{3} The second angel poured out his bowl upon the oceans and the water turned into a thick blood-like fluid, like the blood of a dead man. *Every* living creature in the sea died. The remains of the sea creatures floated to the surface and washed onto the shores. Nothing from the sea could be eaten, but the saints were not affected. God provided food for them.

> Jesus said to the third angel, "Many of the wicked participated in the slaughter of my servants, the 144,000. Since they are bloodthirsty, take away their water and give them blood to drink."

{4} The third angel poured his bowl of poison on the rivers and springs of water, and the springs of water became like blood, just like the ocean. The drinking water became poisonous for everyone who had participated in the murder of God's people. The agony suffered by the murderers was intense. They were hungry, thirsty and the agony they suffered was unbearable. {5} The angel with the third bowl spoke to Jesus: "Eternal God, you are just and fair in these judgments, for you have judged righteously. {6} For these devil worshipers have shed the innocent blood of your saints and prophets, and you have given them blood to drink." {7} Then, the mighty angel who stood at the Altar of Incense also responded:

"Yes, Lord God Almighty, your vengeance is righteous and your actions are justifiable."

> After the third bowl is poured out, the wicked will be in great anguish all over the world. The devil, who pompously masquerades as Almighty God, cannot prevent or cancel the effects of the first three bowls. To keep his deception intact, the devil will stall for time by promising to improve food supplies and provide fresh water, but his promises will not be fulfilled. To further divert the attention of the wicked from his failure to save them from these plauges, Lucifer will direct the wicked to utterly destroy the remaining saints because he will claim they are aligned with "the devil." Lucifer will lead the wicked into thinking that the saints have managed to bring a great curse upon the Earth and if they are eliminated, the curse will end. Immediately, the wicked will agree to kill the saints beginning on a specific day (the 1,290th day of the Great Tribulation). Great rewards will be promised to everyone who captures and kills God's saints, but Jesus will protect His saints. None of His people will perish. Jesus will say to the fourth angel having the fourth bowl, "The wicked intended to kill my people, now let them feel the heat of my wrath."

{8} The fourth angel poured out his bowl on the Sun. The Sun became so hot that it scorched Earth with unbearable heat. The stench rising from dead sea creatures was unbearable. No one could go outside and it was worse indoors. There was no water. There was no electricity. {9} Objects became so hot that people were badly burned by merely touching them. Millions of wicked people, exhausted from their efforts to survive, died from hunger, thirst, and heat exhaustion. Even the devil's highest ranking officials had very little food and water and there was no protection from the searing heat. Nevertheless, the wicked refused to repent of their wickedness and worship the Creator of Heaven and Earth, the only true God. They cursed the saints and their God who had control of these plagues and refused to glorify Him.

> The wicked will call out to Lucifer, "If you are Almighty God as you claim, stop these curses. Ever since you became king of kings and lord of lords (during the sixth trumpet), our condition has become worse and worse. Use your miracle working powers to end our suffering! Show us that you are Almighty God!" These requests will put the devil in a great predicament. He cannot undo the effects caused by the first four bowls.

---

of the waters say, Thou art righteous, O Lord, which art, and wast, and shalt be, because thou hast judged thus. For they have shed the blood of saints and prophets, and thou hast given them blood to drink; for they are worthy. And I heard another out of the altar say, Even so, Lord God Almighty, true and righteous are thy judgments.

Rev. 16:8-9

And the fourth angel poured out his vial upon the sun; and power was given unto him to scorch men with fire And men were scorched with great heat, and blasphemed the name of God, which hath power over these plagues: and they repented not to give him glory.

Prophecy 13 - The Seven Bowls

> **Rev. 16:10-11**
> And the fifth angel poured out his vial upon the seat of the beast; and his kingdom was full of darkness; and they gnawed their tongues for pain, And blasphemed the God of heaven because of their pains and their sores, and repented not of their deeds.

{10} A few days later, the fifth bowl was poured out. Suddenly, a painful plague afflicted everyone who worked for the devil. His officials and employees became dysfunctional because of blindness. These people had willingly closed their eyes to the light of God's truth (presented by the 144,000), therefore Jesus removed their eyesight. Because Lucifer's officials and employees could not function, his theocracy came to a sudden end. The pain was so great that the only thing the devil's officials and employees could do was gnaw their tongues in agony. {11} They cursed the God of Heaven (Jesus) because of the pain, but they refused to repent for what they had done.

The fifth plague will stun the wicked who are not officials and employees of Lucifer's government. Suddenly, they will begin to question the identity of the glorious being who claims to be Almighty God. Why would He send a curse of painful blindness upon his own officials and employees? Why would he destroy his entire work force and kingdom with painful blindness? Why would he treat his loyal followers with such horrifying contempt unless he *really was* an imposter? Could he actually be the devil?

The fifth bowl will force the wicked to admit that the 144,000, who they ridiculed and murdered as "false prophets," are true prophets of Almighty God. The fifth plague will force the wicked to admit that the glorious being masquerading as Almighty God is the devil, the dreaded Antichrist. The wicked will discover that he is *the* "false prophet," just as the 144,000 claimed. The wicked will be crushed by unspeakable disappointment and tormented with fear when they realize, too late, that they were duped. They were duped by a very clever show of power and lies because they refused to love the truth and so be saved.[17] Instead of putting their faith in Jesus and submitting to the authority of a God of love, the wicked temporarily avoided persecution. They placed their loyalty and trust in the father of lies,[18] a cunning devil who told them all kinds of lies and performed endless miracles to win their confidence and loyalty.

> **Rev. 16:12**
> And the sixth angel poured out his vial upon the great river Euphrates; and the water thereof was dried up, that the way of the kings of the east might be prepared.

{12} The sixth angel poured out his bowl on the great river Euphrates so that the water in the river dried up. This event prepared the way for the kings from the East to appear.

A few words of explanation about the drying up of the great river Euphrates are necessary. There is an important connection between the sixth trumpet (day 1,039) and the sixth bowl (day 1,315). When the sixth trumpet sounds in Heaven on day 1,039, God will release the four angels bound at the great river Euphrates to kill a third of mankind.[19] In Bible times, the great river Euphrates was a natural barrier for the northern boundary of Israel. The river was deep and it flowed fast enough in the spring that invading armies *from the north* could not cross the river. Because divine destruction is represented in the Bible as coming out of the north,[20] the language used in the sixth trumpet (the four angels bound at the great river Euphrates) indicates that Jesus allows the devil to kill people. The devil's four angels will be released at an appointed hour, day, month, and year to kill one-third of mankind.

Rev. 16:12

Jesus permits the devil to kill one-third of mankind at the appointed time (beginning with day 1,039) for the following four reasons: First, food and water rations will last longer if fewer people are living on Earth. Jesus wishes to sustain the wicked long enough to fully demonstrate the predatory nature of sin. Second, the devil will find and eliminate almost everyone who stands in opposition to his theocracy. God allows the devil to do this so that everyone can see what a "carnal nature" government looks like. Third, the wicked, knowing that the mark of the beast is evil, nevertheless will commit the unpardonable sin and receive the mark of the beast in an effort to save themselves. This demonstrates how sin deadens a person's conscience and shuts out God's voice to the point that the carnal nature honors self-preservation above principle. Finally, Jesus will permit many of His saints to perish during the sixth trumpet so they can sleep through the rest of the tribulation until the Second Coming.

Now that we have considered the sixth trumpet, let us jump forward to the sixth bowl (about nine months later). When the sixth bowl is poured out, Jesus will *dry up* the great river Euphrates. This analogous language describes the elimination of the natural barrier that protected the northern boundary of Israel. In other words, at the sixth bowl, Jesus will remove all protection from the wicked. Divine destruction will descend out of the north and nothing can prevent the wicked from being totally destroyed. Notice the wording in this NIV text: **"Out of the north He comes in golden splendor; God comes in awesome majesty."**[21] When Jesus arrives, He will kill every wicked person by casting them into a lake of fire or by the sword that comes out of His mouth.[22] The phrase, "the kings from the East," is plural. It refers to the fact that the Father and the

> Rev. 16:12

Son will come together at the Second Coming.[23] Any object approaching this planet appears in the east because of our planet's rotation. (For example, the Sun appears to come up in the east because of rotation.) Therefore, the Second Coming is said to come from the north (the arrival of divine destruction) and from the east (the physical appearing of two kings, Jesus and the Father). The Holy Spirit will already be on Earth, sealed within each saint.

Remember, when the fifth bowl is poured out, Lucifer's employees and officials will be unable to function because of blindness. The devil will be unmasked and his theocracy will collapse. The wicked will be forced to admit that Lucifer is the devil and they will loathe him and his failed government.[24] In a desperate and final attempt to lead the world into total destruction, Satan will employ demonic sophistry one last time and the kings of the Earth will actually believe his last lie!

> Rev. 16:13
>
> *And I saw three unclean spirits like frogs come out of the mouth of the dragon, and out of the mouth of the beast, and out of the mouth of the false prophet.*

{13} I saw three demons that looked like frogs. They came out of the mouth of the great red dragon, out of the mouth of the lamblike beast and out of the mouth of the false prophet.

Three times in the book of Revelation, Lucifer is caricatured. He is the great red dragon that attempted to murder baby Jesus and failing to do so, He persecuted the saints of God for 1,260 years (a period of time also called "The Dark Ages"). As the lamblike beast, he is the Antichrist that leads the world astray and kills a third of mankind. Masquerading as Almighty God, he is the false prophet (the great liar) which leads the wicked into destruction. The devil is described as three entities in the book of Revelation because he uses three disguises to accomplish his evil plans. I believe that the demons in verse 13 are described as frogs, because frogs catch their prey with their tongues.

When the kings of the Earth discover that the glorious being they worship is actually the devil, they will hate him and refuse to have anything to do with him. Therefore, to bring them back into the clutches of his control, the devil will send his most powerful demons to the kings of the Earth with a simple message. They will perform amazing miracles and then tell the ten kings that Jesus will appear in the sky in about ten days. They will warn the kings that their only hope for survival is to unite with Lucifer and his army so that together, everyone can make war against Jesus when He gets close enough to Earth.

{14} Lucifer sends his demons throughout the world to deceive the kings and gather them for battle when the Lord returns.

> Lucifer's miracle working demons will deceive the kings of the world with lying tongues and this will set the stage for a battle that will culminate with the destruction of everyone having the mark of the beast. Ironically, the wicked received the mark in order to survive, but now, the mark dooms them to certain destruction.

{15} While Lucifer's demons were uniting the kings of Earth, Jesus spoke a word of encouragement to His waiting saints. "Behold, I am on my way. Do not be discouraged. You will soon be blessed, therefore, stand firm in your faith and remain alert. Do not fret over Armageddon! I will strip my enemies of their weapons so their nakedness and shame will be exposed."

{16} As they prepared for war, the kings of Earth found themselves in a great predicament called Armageddon in the Hebrew tongue.

> Armageddon is not a geographical location. The term Armageddon consists of two Hebrew words that are joined together to create a colloquialism. This colloquialism basically means, "caught between the devil and the deep blue sea." In other words, there is no solution, no escape, no savior, and no place to go. Literally translated, the words 'ar means mountain and mageddon refers to Megiddo, a plain where Kings Ahaziah and Josiah died.[25]

> During the days of Elijah, a defining contest between Baal and Jehovah took place on the top of Mt. Carmel.[26] When it became clear that the prophets of Baal could not call fire down to consume the sacrifice, Baal was proven to be a false god. When Israel saw that Baal was a worthless god, Elijah legitimately killed Jezebel's 450 prophets. In a similar way, the kings of the Earth will unite with the devil and his demons to destroy Jesus when He appears, but the wicked will find there is no contest on the mountain. There is no other God but Jehovah! Jesus will throw the devil and his demons into a lake of fire and Jesus will destroy the rest of the wicked by a command that comes out of His mouth. Jesus will legitimately kill His enemies. The word Armageddon is a contracted word. The first portion of the word points to a mountain top experience and the second portion points to the plain of Megiddo where kings died. Anyone who fights against an omnipotent God will die.[27]

Rev. 16:14
For they are the spirits of devils, working miracles, which go forth unto the kings of the earth and of the whole world, to gather them to the battle of that great day of God Almighty.

Rev. 16:15
Behold, I come as a thief. Blessed is he that watcheth, and keepeth his garments, lest he walk naked, and they see his shame.

Rev. 16:16
And he gathered them together into a place called in the Hebrew tongue Armageddon.

Rev. 16:16

Before we leave this section, consider the condition of the wicked kings during the sixth bowl. They once were confident and loyal to Lucifer, but now they see that their loyalty was misdirected and their confidence misplaced. They were once part of a powerful world government, but now they are powerless and broken. They were deceived and after their eyes are opened, they will realize that there is no chance of survival other than to knowingly unite with the devil. The wicked will look around on Earth and see that everything is dead or dying. They still suffer from the boils, the oceans are dead, the springs of water are poisoned, the heat is unbearable, and their great savior turns out to be the devil himself. The planet they call home has been ruined. It is as hostile to life as sin is to happiness. The kings wear a crude tatoo imposed on them by their demonic leader, yet they continue to oppose a God of love, who is the Creator of Heaven and Earth. Because their hearts have been hardened by rebellion and hatred, they will voluntarily unite with Lucifer in an effort to destroy Jesus when He appears. This is the delusion and curse of sin.

Rev. 16:17

And the seventh angel poured out his vial into the air; and there came a great voice out of the temple of heaven, from the throne, saying, It is done.

{17} The seventh angel poured out his bowl into the air and from the temple, a loud voice was heard saying: "It – is – finished!"

When these words echo through Heaven, the angels, the elders, and the four living creatures will become jubilant. Finally, the Plan of Redemption is consummated. The knowledge of good and evil is complete. The behavior and nature of sin has been fully disclosed. A God of love has given mankind every possible opportunity for salvation. From now on, no one can intelligently question God's love and righteousness ever again. All that remains on Earth is to destroy the wicked and rescue the saints!

Rev. 16:18-19

And there were voices, and thunders, and lightnings; and there was a great earthquake, such as was not since men were upon the earth, so mighty an earthquake, and so great. And the great city was

{18} As the Father, the Son, the glorious angels and 144,000 servants of God appeared in the distant sky, there came huge flashes of lightning, rumblings, deafening peals of thunder, and a severe earthquake. No earthquake of this magnitude has ever occurred since man lived on Earth. The whole world was leveled. {19} The great city of Babylon split into three parts and all of the cities of the nations collapsed. Jesus remembered each deed committed by the leaders of Babylon and He poured out the wine of the fury of His wrath on them.

Jesus will divide the great empire of Babylon into three segments for punishment. First, Jesus will destroy Lucifer's throne and authority by casting him and his angels into the lake of fire.

(That is, Lucifer and his angels will lose the physical bodies given to them at the fifth trumpet. Jesus will strip them of their physical bodies and return them to the Abyss for 1,000 years.[28]) Second, Jesus will throw Lucifer's government (that is, the employees and officials of his theocracy) into the lake of fire where they will perish. Finally, Jesus will destroy all of the citizens of the world, who wear the tattoo "666," with white-hot meteorites. Babylon is divided into the three parts so that each part can receive appropriate vengeance! The Lord will righteously and completely dispense justice.

{20} The earthquake was so powerful that every island disappeared and all the mountains crumbled. {21} Huge meteorites, weighing a hundred pounds each, fell upon the wicked. As King Jesus appeared in clouds of glory and the wicked cried out for the rocks to "fall on us and hide us from them that sit on the throne."[29] In spite of God's demonstration of power and justice, the wicked continued to curse Him because the plague was so terrible.

The Rules of Interpretation

Consider how the Rules of Interpretation (discussed in the Introduction of this book) are observed in this prophecy:

Rule One says an apocalyptic prophecy has a beginning point and ending point in time and the events within the prophecy occur in the order given. This prophecy easily conforms to Rule One because the chronological order of the seven bowls is self evident.

Rule Two says a fulfillment only occurs when all of the specifications are met, and this includes the order stated in the prophecy. Again, this rule will become self evident when the seven bowls are poured out on the wicked.

Rule Three says that apocalyptic language can be literal, analogous, or symbolic. To reach the intended meaning of a prophecy, the reader must consider (a) the context, (b) the use of parallel language in the Bible, and (c) if an element is thought to be symbolic, the Bible must interpret the symbol with a *relevant* text. The language used in this prophecy is a mixture of literal, analogous, and symbolic. The great river Euphrates is used in an analogous way and the term Babylon is symbolic. Babylon is defined with relevant Scripture in Revelation 17:5,15,18.

Rule Four is not used in this prophecy.

---

divided into three parts, and the cities of the nations fell: and great Babylon came in remembrance before God, to give unto her the cup of the wine of the fierceness of his wrath.

Rev. 16:20-21

And every island fled away, and the mountains were not found. And there fell upon men a great hail out of heaven, every stone about the weight of a talent: and men blasphemed God because of the plague of the hail; for the plague thereof was exceeding great.

References

1. This claim is based on five underlying presuppositions. First, the Bible says the devil will not honor a particular religious body when He physically appears. The devil will not favor one religious system and alienate the others. To be consistent, he will oppose them all. (2 Thessalonians 2:4) In fact, when the devil establishes his one world church state (theocracy) he will eliminate all of the religions of the world including their holy days.

   Second, the Bible says the core conflict during the Great Tribulation will be one of worship. (Revelation 13:15-18; 14:9-12) Lucifer will have to establish a day for worship that does not have anything in common with existing holy days. For this reason, I believe Friday, Saturday, and Sunday will become ordinary days.

   Third, the Bible says that Jesus will open the sky and show the Ark of the Covenant to the inhabitants of Earth at the close of the seventh trumpet. (Revelation 11:19) I believe He will do this for several reasons. One reason is to show the world that literally, there is a *higher* law than any law on Earth! Another reason will be the exposure of the "worship commandment" which the wicked refused to obey. The worship commandment is the fourth commandment. (Exodus 20:8-11) It declares a weekly cycle of seven days beginning with the first day of Creation week. The fourth commandment also declares the seventh day of each week (Saturday) to be God's holy day. When Jesus reveals the Ark of the Covenant, everyone on Earth will plainly see the defiance manifested toward God's higher law. Thus, God's lawful condemnation of the wicked will be clear and inescapable.

   Fourth, the length of the Great Tribulation will be 1,335 days. The Two Witnesses will testify for 1,260 days and after lying in the street for 3.5 days, the 144,000 will be resurrected on the 1265th day of the Great Tribulation. This means the seven last plagues will be seventy days in length, perhaps with ten days allotted to each plague. God's clocks are based on the number seven. (Seven days per week, seven months in the religious year, seven years in a week of years, and seven weeks of years in a Jubilee cycle and seventy weeks in one "Great Day.") On the other hand, man's numbering system is based on ten. We count in terms of tens, hundreds, and thousands of years, or ten years per decade, ten decades per century, and ten centuries in a millennium. Ancient civilizations in Egypt and China followed ten day weeks for centuries. After the French Revolution, France enacted a ten day week for a few years (1793-1805) trying to overthrow the influence and power of Catholicism.

Finally, if the devil does change the weekly cycle to ten days, people who worship on God's seventh day will be easily identified because God's Sabbath rest will land on different work days within a period of ten days. In fact, some ten day weeks will have two seventh day Sabbaths in them! Thus, Satan's establishment of a ten day week will physically flush out the remnant of the woman who keep the fourth commandment of God.

In summary, it seems possible that a ten day weekly cycle may be forthcoming at the time of the sixth trumpet because a new day for worship will not favor any religious system on Earth, it defies God's seventh day Sabbath, and clearly exposes those who keep it. Of course, time will tell.

2. Revelation 16:21; 19:19-21
3. 1 John 4:8,16
4. Exodus 22:1,3,4
5. Leviticus 4:27-29
6. Genesis 19:15
7. Exodus 21:23-25
8. Revelation 18:6 Note: A double portion of restitution is required when malicious intent is premeditated and carried out. Exodus 22:4-9
9. Romans 12:19
10. If a murderer is caught and executed for his crime, the demands of the law (life for life) have been met. However, restitution for the suffering caused by the crime (to the victim and the family of the victim) has not been met. Restitution must also be paid in full. God's law encompasses punitive (punishment) action as well as compensatory damages (restitution). If a murderer should confess

and repent of his sin before his execution, his death will satisfy the punitive requirement of God's law and the compensatory requirements for suffering will be transferred to the scapegoat (Lucifer) at the end of the 1,000 years. On the other hand, if a murderer does not repent of his sin and he dies a natural death, the murderer will suffer in the lake of fire at the end of the 1,000 years according to the amount of compensation required of him. (1 Corinthians 6:2,3) Then, he will die the second death because the penalty for his sin remains upon his own head.

11. Hebrews 10:30,31
12. Revelation 11:10
13. Hebrews 13:8
14. Genesis 4:10; Revelation 11:18; 15:4
15. Exodus 24:17; Deuteronomy 4:24; Psalm 97:3; Hebrews 12:29
16. Obadiah 1:15
17. 2 Thessalonians 2:8-12
18. John 8:44
19. Revelation 9:13-15
20. Isaiah 41:25; Jeremiah 1:14; 46:2-6; Ezekiel 26:7
21. Job 37:22 (NIV)
22. Revelation 19:19-21
23. Matthew 26:64; Revelation 6:15-17
24. Revelation 17:16
25. 2 Kings 9:27; 23:28-30; 2 Chronicles 35:20-24
26. 1 Kings 18
27. Revelation 19:19-21
28. Revelation 20:1-3
29. Revelation 6:14-17

The Angel's First Visit

Revelation 17:1-18

Summary: Twice in the book of Revelation, God sends an angel to John to explain elements in the visions which John had seen. (The same process took place in the book of Daniel. Gabriel was sent to Daniel (see Daniel 9) to further explain what the prophet had previously seen in Daniel 8.) John's first visit from an angel is recorded in Revelation 17 and the second visit begins with Revelation 21:9. After John viewed Prophecies 6 through 13, Jesus sent an angel to provide more information about the devil's physical appearing and efforts. Actually, Jesus sent the angel to John for the benefit of the final generation. When the devil and his angels physically appear, no one will have an excuse for being deceived by the incredible glory and miracle working powers that Lucifer will exercise. To be forewarned is to be forearmed

A Short Review on Trumpets Five and Six

Since Revelation 17 builds on the information provided earlier in this book, and since some people may skip around without reading all of the previous chapters, a short review of trumpets five and six is necessary. If you have read all of the previous chapters in this book, you may want to skip to the section titled, "The Sequence."

We learned in Prophecy 8 that Jesus will release Lucifer and his angels from the Abyss during the fifth trumpet. Lucifer and his angels will physically appear before the people of Earth. For five months, the devil and his angels will travel around the world so that everyone can see for themselves that "God" has come to live among men! The devil will demonstrate supernatural powers and on the basis of marvelous signs and wonders, billions of people will conclude that he is Almighty God. When he is released from the spirit realm, the devil will masquerade as a generous and benevolent God. The devil will imitate Jesus' actions when He was on Earth. The devil will heal the sick, restore sight to the blind, cast out demons, multiply "the loaves and fishes," and encourage suffering people with an inspiring message of hope and restoration. The religious wicked will fall prostrate at his feet. They will honor and

Jesus' Final Victory

worship the devil believing that Almighty God lives among men! His wishes will be their commands.

While the devil is busy deceiving the world, some of his demons will go out on a search and destroy mission. They will look for people who refuse to worship Lucifer as God. These demons are not allowed to harm those who believe that Lucifer is God and they cannot hurt those who have received the seal of God.[1] Instead, these demons will focus on a group of people described previously in this book as the "non-religious wicked," since these people refuse to worship any God. Lucifer focuses on this group and sends out his demons to eliminate them. Jesus permits the devil to torture the non-religious wicked because spiritual indifference is no longer an option for anyone after the fifth trumpet. Every human being will submit to a higher authority or suffer horribly.

When Lucifer's demons find a person who refuses to worship the devil as Almighty God, they will inflict a horrible pain on that person. The Bible says this pain is like the agonizing sting of a scorpion. The victims will long to die, but death will elude them.[2] The non-religious wicked (and their families) will quickly discover a startling fact. All human beings are subject to a higher power. By the fifth trumpet, independence from God or isolation from God will no longer be possible. Millions of non-religious wicked people will be tortured for refusing to worship Lucifer, and soon, the non-religious wicked group disappears. Most of the non-religious wicked will capitulate and worship the devil, but a few will choose to put their faith in Jesus and be saved. They will gratefully obey the demands of the eternal gospel and worship the Creator. By the end of the fifth trumpet, the non-religious group will be almost eliminated.

When the sixth trumpet sounds in Heaven's temple, Lucifer will abruptly change character. Because billions of people will believe that he is Almighty God, Lucifer will make unheard of demands and his followers will have no choice but to obey. For example, Lucifer will *demand* that the governments and religions of the world be destroyed. He will claim there is no room for civil diversity or religious pluralism when God lives among men. Lucifer's solution to the onerous diversity of mankind will be to establish a counterfeit theocracy. This theocracy will be a one world church state government where "God" rules as king of kings (the head of the state) and lord of lords (the head of the church). Lucifer's theocracy is described as "an image to the beast" in Revelation 13 because it will mirror the composite beast (the beast that looked like a leopard, had claws like a bear and a mouth like a lion) in several ways.

We learned in Prophecy 11 that a composite beast (also called Babylon[3] or Babylon - Phase I) will rise from the sea during the first four trumpets.[4] For about two and a half years, Babylon will function as a global government; managing the crisis between God and mankind. The religious and political leaders of the world will unite in a global effort to appease God's wrath so that His judgments will cease. When the survivors learn that 1.75 billion people died because of the first four trumpets, no one will want to offend an angry God any further. Therefore, most of the world will be willing to do whatever Babylon requires because everyone will want to appease God so that His wrath will quickly subside. The development of Babylon (during Phase I) and the implementation of its "sin-less" laws explains how the saints will be persecuted for forty-two months. The laws of Babylon will stand in direct conflict with the laws of God and this conflict will force each person to show his true allegiance. Babylon will persecute people who obey Jesus' demands and people who obey Babylon's laws will experience the seven bowls (the last plagues). Sooner or later, everyone will suffer during the Great Tribulation; it will be a time of wrath for everyone.[5]

The composite beast will rule over the whole world and its government will be composed of seven different religions and many different governments. As a result, Babylon will appear to be a united body having one objective, to appease God's wrath, but the big question will become which is the right way to accomplish this objective. Each religious system views God's will (what is morally right and wrong) in a different way. Similarly, each nation on Earth has its own culture and principles of law. And, for all the good that Babylon vainly hopes to accomplish, it will only make matters worse. Babylon's Phase I will be internally conflicted because of religious and political diversity. Nevertheless, a conflicted composite beast will function for 890 days, it will blaspheme the Creator of Heaven and Earth, and punish His saints. Babylon will insult the sovereign authority of Jesus (blasphemy) by defying the laws of God.

When the devil physically appears, he will order the leaders of Babylon to divide the world into groups of 1,000 people for purposes of logistics and rations. This was also done in ancient times for the same reasons.[6] One person from each group of 1,000 will be selected to serve as captain of the group. This will leave 999 people to a group. When the sixth trumpet sounds, Jesus will permit the devil to kill one-third of mankind. Because the devil knows that God will not stop him, he suddenly changes character and Babylon - Phase II begins. The devil will demand that one-third of each group be put to death. (His demand will be similar to God's decree in Ezekiel 5:8-12.) The first 666 people to receive a tattoo on their right hand showing "666" will be allowed to buy and sell, and ultimately, survive. Those who refuse to worship the devil will be killed. Those who hesitate or show any reluctance for worshiping the devil will also be killed. Of course, millions of saints will be killed, too.[7] When the killing is completed, two-thirds of each group, 666 people will be left alive. No one will be permitted to buy or sell without showing the mark of the beast (the Greek word *charagma* is translated as "mark," but it means an engraving, as in a tattoo).

Jesus will permit Lucifer to kill a third of mankind for at least three reasons. First, the additional death of 1.75 billion people will reduce demands for the world's dwindling food supply by one-third. This allows the remaining food supplies to sustain the wicked while the 144,000 continue to labor for the salvation of souls. Even at this late hour, a few people will accept the offer of the eternal gospel during the sixth trumpet and be saved. Second, when Jesus allows the devil to martyr the saints and slaughter the wicked, this will prove to be a great blessing. By putting a third of mankind to death, millions will escape the last and most horrific ten months of the Great Tribulation. Third, when God allows Lucifer to slaughter one-third of mankind (including the 144,000 and millions of saints), it will place Lucifer in an undisputed position of sovereign authority. Simply put, all of his opposition will be dead or silenced! (The few saints who remain alive during this time will be hiding in remote places and unable to offer any opposition.)

Jesus will give the world over to Lucifer for a short time to demonstrate what the carnal nature (perfectly illustrated by Lucifer) will do to others when given absolute authority. This development will demonstrate a profound truth. The universe would be a very dark and awful place to live if it was not ruled by a God who is love and subject to the laws of love. The wonderful thing about God is that He only uses His mighty powers of omnipotence and omniscience to ensure the eternal rule of the laws of love. His actions are always consistent with the two laws of love. By allowing Lucifer to exercise absolute authority over this planet for a short period of time, an ever expanding universe will have a clear and powerful contrast between governments to study.

Lucifer's theocracy is caricatured in Revelation 17 as a prostitute. Most prostitutes have no morals and are willing to sell sexual favors for money. Prostitution is an abomination in God's eyes because it destroys both parties involved, ruins the lives of the unborn by producing unfit mothers and unwanted children, demeans women, and fosters predatory behavior on women. No matter how glamorous and expensive her services may be, any woman selling sexual favors destroys her self-worth and self-respect and she violates her body and conscience for money. The man who buys sexual favors has no love for the woman or love for the unborn that he may create. Further, the man who buys the services of a prostitute has no concern for the well being of the prostitute. He is only interested in using her body for sexual pleasure. For him, a prostitute is nothing more than an object of temporal gratification. There is nothing wholesome or ennobling that comes from prostitution. It is soulless barter. From the prostitutes point of view, it is money for sexual favor. From the buyer's point of view, it is sexual favors for money. Prostitution and its sister, pornography, denigrate womanhood, manhood, and ruin society. When women are viewed as objects of sexual gratification, they become cheap and disposable in men's eyes.

The most intimate and meaningful relationship that a man and a woman can have is destroyed by fornication and prostitution. Lucifer's theocracy is described in Revelation 17 as "a great prostitute" because the wicked will sell their souls to the devil and wear his dreaded tattoo in order to survive and the wicked will knowingly and willingly do this to save themselves from death. Lucifer will not love those who worship him. In his eyes, they are cheap, disposable tramps who sold their souls for survival. Even though he will appear to be happy and pleased that the remaining two-thirds of the world worship him, he will actually loathe them for he knows that they do not love him. Instead, they have done what they needed to do to stay alive.

The carnal nature loves life more that it loves God – to the point that it will violate itself in order to save itself. On the other hand, the born again nature exalts God and His righteousness to the point that it would rather die than to compromise with evil. The words of Jesus are so true: **"For whoever wants to save his life will lose it, but whoever loses his life for me will find it."**[8]

The Sequence

{1} After watching the seven angels pour out the seven bowls of God's wrath, one of the seven angels having the seven bowls approached me and said, "Come with me and I will show you God's vengeance on the great whore, a global, church state government which Lucifer will establish during the sixth trumpet. Lucifer's theocracy wields control over every tribe, nation, language, and people."

{2} The angel carried me away to see Earth at the time of the sixth trumpet. When the sixth trumpet sounded, the devil was permitted to murder a third of mankind. The devil was very pleased. Having absolute power to kill or spare people, he suddenly changed character and demeanor. He *demanded* a one world church state government be formed (the formation of the prostitute), and by exercising his "divine authority," he abolished the religions and governments of the world. He divided the Earth into ten sectors [9] and appointed ten "puppet" kings to rule over mankind. These kings "committed adultery" with the whore (they did whatever she wanted for her immoral favors). Because of Lucifer's miracle working powers, his eloquence and inspiring words, the wicked drank the devil's lies and became intoxicated with his promise that "a better world is just around the corner."

{3} When the sixth trumpet sounded, Earth was ugly and disheveled, ravaged like a war zone. I saw destruction and death on every side. Then, I saw a seductive woman sitting on a scarlet beast that had seven heads and ten horns. The scarlet colored beast was covered with blasphemous names, indicating this beast was a great insult to the God of Heaven.

> The composite beast in Revelation 13:1-8 and the scarlet beast in this chapter are the *same* beast. If you recall, the composite beast had the speed of a leopard, the ferocious claws of a bear and a powerful mouth like that of a lion. When John sees the woman riding (controlling) the composite beast, there is one

---

Rev. 17:1
And there came one of the seven angels which had the seven vials, and talked with me, saying unto me, Come hither; I will show unto thee the judgment of the great whore that sitteth upon many waters:

Rev. 17:2
With whom the kings of the earth have committed fornication, and the inhabitants of the earth have been made drunk with the wine of her fornication.

Rev. 17:3
So he carried me away in the spirit into the wilderness: and I saw a woman sit upon a scarlet coloured beast, full of names of blasphemy, having seven heads and ten horns.

important change. The composite beast is now scarlet in color because the great *red* dragon is the hand inside the composite beast; much like a red hand in a latex glove. Remember, the devil gives the composite beast its power, throne, and great authority.[10]

{4} The woman sitting on the composite beast was dressed in purple and scarlet. Purple is the color of royalty or kings (the state) and scarlet is the color of clergy (the church). This woman represents Lucifer's theocracy and she controls the composite beast as she rides throughout the Earth. She is wealthy, seductive, and she glitters with gold, precious stones, and pearls. She holds a golden cup in her hand that is full of abominable things, the filth of her adulteries. She is alluring, but demonic. She has everything the world can offer, but she is a whore, an empty shell having no virtue, no value, and no love.

> Remember, the great red dragon had seven diadema (Greek: a *diadema* is a crown of authority) on his seven heads in Revelation 12:3 and the composite beast will have ten crowns on its ten horns when it rises from the sea in Revelation 13:1. The relocation of the diadema from the heads to the crowns indicates a transition in persecuting authority. When Jesus was on Earth, religious leaders persecuted Him for blasphemy. When Babylon rises to power, civil authorities will persecute those who refuse to obey Babylon's laws. Nothing is said in Revelation 17 about the crowns because the whore represents a global consolidation of church and state. In other words, the Bible traces the transition of persecuting authority from religious power (in Christ's day), to civil power (when Babylon rises - Phase I), to the whore (Phase II) who kills people for religious or civil disobedience.

{5} The whore had this title written on her forehead: **MYSTERY, BABYLON THE GREAT, THE MOTHER OF PROSTITUTES AND OF THE ABOMINATIONS OF THE EARTH.**

> This title indicates the whore is the personification of evil. She is the greatest embodiment of evil the world has ever known. There are two great powers on Earth. Religion wields the higher power and civil authority is the lesser power. When God called Israel out of Egypt, He kept these two powers separate. Moses represented civil authority and Aaron represented religious authority. False religion always unifies these two powers because the carnal nature is not satisfied until absolute power has been achieved. Therefore, this woman is described as a

---

Rev. 17:4

And the woman was arrayed in purple and scarlet colour, and decked with gold and precious stones and pearls, having a golden cup in her hand full of abominations and filthiness of her fornication:

Rev. 17:5

And upon her forehead was a name written, MYSTERY, BABYLON THE GREAT, THE MOTHER OF HARLOTS AND ABOMINATIONS OF THE EARTH.

The Angel's First Visit

> **Rev. 17:6**
> *And I saw the woman drunken with the blood of the saints, and with the blood of the martyrs of Jesus: and when I saw her, I wondered with great admiration.*
>
> **Rev. 17:7**
> *And the angel said unto me, Wherefore didst thou marvel? I will tell thee the mystery of the woman, and of the beast that carrieth her, which hath the seven heads and ten horns.*
>
> **Rev. 17:8**
> *The beast that thou sawest was, and is not; and shall ascend out of the bottomless pit, and go into perdition: and they that dwell on the earth shall wonder, whose names were not written in the book of life from the foundation of the world, when they behold the beast that was, and is not, and yet is.*

whore because she is a global consolidation of church and state. She will be a one world church state. She is also described as a great city of wickedness; containing people who have no morals or interest in right doing. She is the devil's whore; a government having no virtue and respecting only power and wealth. The devil will use her to torment mankind. Her name is Babylon the Great. Her lover's name is *Appolyon or Abbadon*[11] which means, "the destroyer."

{6} Empowered by the great red dragon himself, the whore killed millions of God's saints, even the 144,000. She enjoyed killing; even those within her own family. She considered death and persecution to be a sport and she used the blood of the saints to cower the wicked into submission. The wicked acquiesced to her demands to save their miserable lives. I saw the whore drunk and senseless with abuse of power. As I watched her, I became overwhelmed.

{7} The angel said to me: "Why are you overwhelmed? I will explain the mystery of the whore to you and the composite beast she rides, which has seven heads and ten horns. However, before I tell you about her, I need to explain the appearing of the lamblike beast, the beast that will arise out of the Earth. Lucifer will be released from the Abyss and during the sixth trumpet, he will create this woman (Babylon - Phase II) and give her power over the composite beast (Babylon - Phase I).

{8} "The great red dragon which you saw in Revelation 12 was once a covering cherub in Heaven.[12] Because of rebellion, God cast him and his angels out of Heaven.[13] When Lucifer and his angels were cast from Heaven, God made them invisible to mankind. Later on, Adam and Eve sinned and Lucifer became the prince of this world.[14] As a prince, God gave him a seat in Heaven's government as Earth's representative.[15] About four thousand years later, Jesus came to Earth to redeem mankind. When Jesus ascended to Heaven on Resurrection Sunday to take Lucifer's place, Lucifer would not yield his seat (as prince of this world) to Jesus. There was war in Heaven and Jesus cast Lucifer and his angels out of Heaven forever.[16] The devil and his angels have been confined within the Abyss ever since. Human beings cannot see them because God keeps Lucifer and his angels 'locked' in the spirit realm until the fifth trumpet. At the fifth trumpet, Jesus will permit the devil and his angels to exit the spirit realm (the Abyss) and physically appear before mankind. The wicked will be astonished when they actually see the devil. They will be "blown away" by his incredible powers and radiant glory.

Rev. 17:8

Because "seeing is believing," most of the "religious wicked" will quickly fall in line and worship Lucifer, thinking that he is God. When the Great Tribulation is over, God will destroy the physical bodies used by the devil and his angels and return them to the spirit realm (the Abyss).[17]

This text includes a powerful declaration that many people do not appreciate: **"The inhabitants of the Earth whose names have not been written in the Book of Life from the creation of the world will be astonished when they see the beast, because he once was** [visible], **now is not** [visible], **and yet will come** [out of the Abyss and be visible]."[18]

Before any life was created, the Father wrote a complete history of the world. He included the thoughts, words, and actions of each person. The Father then did something that confuses a lot of people. He blotted out *the names* of wicked people, those who would someday live upon the Earth and would refuse His offer of salvation. Keep in mind, the Father did not blot out the record of any life, He only blotted out the names of those who would defy the Holy Spirit and reject eternal life. Then, the Father sealed the book with seven seals so that no one could see or know what He had written. This book bothers many people. They conclude that it proves predestination is true, that is, the Father predetermined who would be saved and who would be lost. Actually, once you know the whole story, the Father's actions prove the opposite.

The Father has perfect foreknowledge. He foreknows who will be saved and who will not, but God wants to prove to the universe that His foreknowledge has no influence over the eternal destiny of any person. (God could say in another way, "I know that you will get hungry if you go without food for two days, but this foreknowledge has no influence on your hunger pains.") God is love. He has given each person the power of choice. He allows each person to determine his eternal destiny. Our destiny is determined by our response to the Holy Spirit. If we reject the Holy Spirit (blaspheme the Holy Spirit), we commit the unpardonable sin and will be destroyed.[19] If we obey the prompting of the Holy Spirit, God will reward our faith with eternal life. Eternal life and eternal death are determined by

> Rev. 17:8

each person's response to the Holy Spirit. Therefore, salvation is a matter of choice and not predestination.

God wrote The Book of Life before the world was created and sealed the book with seven seals because at the appointed time, He will prove that even though He has perfect foreknowledge (He knew who would be saved and who would be lost), He did not use His foreknowledge to predetermine the eternal destiny of anyone.

Very important point: The book sealed with seven seals (The Book of Life) has nothing to do with judging mankind. Jesus determines the eternal destiny of all mankind *prior* to the Second Coming using books of record which angels recorded in real time (as events occurred). The Book of Life *is not opened* until the 1,000 years have ended.[20] Therefore, keeping the books of record separate and distinct from The Book of Life is important because God did not predestined anyone to eternal life or death when He wrote The Book of Life.[21]

When The Book of Life is opened, everyone will learn three astonishing facts. First, the Father foreknew that sin would arise (He knew when and through whom) and He did nothing to protect Himself from it. Second, the Father foreknew the great price that sin would impose upon Jesus and the human race, and yet, He did nothing to prevent it. Finally, the books recorded by the angels will be identical with the contents written in the Book of Life. These three facts will prove that each person was free to determine his eternal destiny. Even though the Father foreknew the outcome, He did nothing to *influence* the outcome except He gave us Jesus and the Holy Spirit to save us from sin. Jesus came to Earth to tell us the truth about God and die in our place, and Jesus sent the Holy Spirit into the world to lead us into all truth so that every sinner might escape the penalty for sin.

The angel's declaration in Revelation 17:8 indicates the wicked will be astonished when they see the devil, but their astonishment and deception will be their own making. The wicked refused to receive the truth and be saved, so God sent them a strong delusion to bring everyone into a firm decision![22] Of course, the saints will not be surprised when the devil appears on Earth because they will already know the true identity of this glorious being. The saints will not go out to see this beast and they certainly will not worship this grand illusion. The devil's appearing will catch the wicked by complete surprise because they refused to listen to the 144,000. Ironically, prior to the fifth trumpet, God will do everything possible to save the wicked from this glorious deception, but choices made by the wicked will set them up for astonishment and destruction.

God permits the devil to appear during the Great Tribulation for two reasons: First, corporately speaking, God releases the devil (the epitome of rebellion) from the Abyss so that wicked people can be gathered together under one banner.[23] God keeps the devil in the Abyss until the gospel has won over as many people as possible (perhaps 890 days). When most of the wicked have taken a position against the gospel, God will send a great delusion so that the wicked will discover a powerful fact. Higher powers exist and all mankind will submit to one power or the other. Second, on an individual level, God permits Lucifer to physically appear and masquerade as Almighty God so that the wicked can observe evil incarnate. Lucifer will say and do horrible things that a righteous God would not say and do.[24] Lucifer will oppose truth, honesty, and love. The devil will malign the truth and tell lies. The devil is all about himself and his hateful ways are extreme. Hopefully, his demonic behavior will awaken even the hardest heart. Every wicked person should be able to see that Lucifer cannot possibly be God and some of the wicked will discover during the fifth and sixth trumpets that man's only refuge is in Jesus.[25]

{9} "When the time comes for fulfillment, Revelation's story will not be hard to understand. However, understanding these matters *beforehand* requires considerable study and diligence. Therefore, John, consider the composite beast which the great whore will control. The seven heads on the composite beast are seven mountains (the Greek word *oros* means hills or mountains)."

> The seven heads can be described as seven mountains because a mountain is changeless, unmovable, and steadfast like God. A religious system can be compared to a mountain because people look *up* to their religious leaders much like ancient travelers looked *up* to the mountains for navigation.[26] People want their religion to be changeless, unmovable and steadfast (that is, infallible, true and towering above all others) like a mountain.
>
> From ancient times, mountains have been intimately involved with religious beliefs. Before Vespasian's army destroyed Jerusalem in A.D. 70, the city was called 'Mount Zion'[27] for an important reason. It was God's dwelling place. King Solomon's

Rev. 17:8

Rev. 17:9
And here is the mind which hath wisdom. The seven heads are seven mountains, on which the woman sitteth.

The Angel's First Visit

Rev. 17:9

temple was located on top of Mount Moriah, God's holy hill.[28] Pagan worshipers frequently ascended to mountain tops and high hills to meet with their gods because they believed their gods lived there.[29] It is interesting that even today, the most important building in the United States is called "Capitol Hill" for in this building, the nation's laws are created.

We already know two facts about the seven heads. First, in Revelation 13:1 we find they have blasphemous names written on them. This indicates they are religious in nature and they are anti-Christ. Second, we know that one head was wounded, but the deadly wound was healed when the composite beast comes up from the sea. The head (or hill) that was wounded is the papacy. There are seven heads, that is, there are seven of the same thing. Because the wounded/healed head represents a religious system (the papacy), the remaining six heads must also represent religious systems.

Rev. 17:10

And there are seven kings: five are fallen, and one is, and the other is not yet come; and when he cometh, he must continue a short space.

{10} "The seven heads are also seven kings. Each religious system is a kingdom having subjects (church members). Each religious system has its own order and authority. When a church member rebels against the system, he may be cast out of the system, excommunicated or killed depending upon the religious system that he belongs to. The seven heads are described as seven mountains and seven kings because these definitions narrow the solution to one right answer. Each blasphemous head/mountain/king is a religious system having its own hierarchy and laws." The angel continued, "Five religious systems have fallen (have been exposed as false) and one religious system exists which has not yet become false. Later on, it will also be exposed as false and another religious system will appear, but it will only exist for a short time."

When Jesus came to Earth, five religious systems fell. In other words, Jesus declared five religious systems were false. These five systems are: Atheism, Heathenism, Judaism, Eastern Mysticism, and Islam.* Atheism says there is no God. Jesus says this is not true.[30] Heathenism says there are many Gods, but Jesus says this is not true.[31] Judaism and Islam teach that salvation comes through obedience to specific rules,[32] but Jesus

---

*Note: The title, Islam, as used here, refers to the ancient religion of Ishmael. Even though Mohammed lived during the sixth century A.D., Moslems hold that Ishmael, the first offspring of Abraham, is the founder of Islam.

says that salvation comes through faith in Him.[33] Eastern Mysticism teaches that the soul is immortal, it lives forever. After enough generations, man can become a divine being, but Jesus says none of this is true.[34] Rather, a divine being became a man to save mankind from the penalty for sin.[35]

The sixth head (Christianity) was just beginning in John's day. Eventually, this head was called the Roman Catholic Church. John was a charter member of this religious system, but it followed in Israel's footsteps. It became a false religion and blasphemous over time. The power of the Roman Catholic Church was severely wounded in 1798,[36] but the deadly wound will be healed[37] during the fourth trumpet. The seventh head appeared on Earth around 1500 A.D. and it is called Protestantism. When we consider that six of the seven religious systems have endured for 2,000 years or more, the life span of Protestantism is short.

{11} "Lucifer is the lamblike beast described in Revelation 13:11. He once was visible and now, he is not visible, but at the fifth trumpet he will become visible. At first, the devil will masquerade as Almighty God. He will be far superior to the seven religious systems of the world and his supernatural powers will eclipse the prowess of all mankind and naturally, he will become "an eighth king."

> The devil is described as an eighth king who belongs to the seven heads for an important reason. In Prophecy 2, a little horn appeared and it grew in power and as it did, it uprooted three of the original ten horns. This made the little horn an eighth king. The eighth horn dominated the seven horns for 1,260 years. Similarly, the devil will start small.[38] He will physically appear and dominate the seven heads. During the sixth trumpet, the devil will establish an eighth religious system (the whore, his great theocracy) and he will rule over the religious systems of the world. Of course, the devil will be destroyed at the end, but not by human power.[39]

{12} "The ten horns on the composite beast represent ten kings (the ten toes in Daniel 2) which Lucifer will appoint as agents of his government. Presuming sovereign authority, the devil will dissolve the governments of the world and direct these ten kings to oversee his one world church state. {13} These ten kings will have one purpose. They will do everything the devil wishes.

Rev. 17:10

Rev. 17:11
And the beast that was, and is not, even he is the eighth, and is of the seven, and goeth into perdition.

Rev. 17:12-13
And the ten horns which thou sawest are ten kings, which have received no kingdom as yet; but receive power as kings one hour with the beast. These have one mind, and shall give their power and strength unto the beast.

The Angel's First Visit

Rev. 17:14
These shall make war with the Lamb, and the Lamb shall overcome them: for he is Lord of lords, and King of kings: and they that are with him are called, and chosen, and faithful.

Rev. 17:15
And he saith unto me, The waters which thou sawest, where the whore sitteth, are peoples, and multitudes, and nations, and tongues.

Rev. 17:16
And the ten horns which thou sawest upon the beast, these shall hate the whore, and shall make her desolate and naked, and shall eat her flesh, and burn her with fire.

{14} "When Jesus appears in clouds of glory, these ten kings will unite with the devil in a violent attack on the Lamb, but the Lamb will destroy them because the Creator is Lord of lords and King of kings. When Jesus returns, the wicked will see Jesus and they will also see His 144,000 prophets who were taken to Heaven at the seventh trumpet."[40]

{15} Then the angel said to me, "The many waters upon which the whore sits represent peoples, multitudes, nations, and languages."

The wicked are described as many waters because water is a fluid. Water has no backbone. Water conforms to whatever shape it is poured into. Water always flows in the path of least resistance; a fitting description of the wicked. When the devil abolishes the religions and governments of the world to set up his theocracy, he will kill a third of mankind and the survivors will be like water conforming to his evil desires. For approximately nine months, the devil will rule over the world and mankind will be powerless to stop him from doing as he pleases. His whore (his government) will sit as a queen and the devil will gleefully rule as a presumed king of kings and lord of lords.

{16} During the seven last plagues, when the fifth bowl is poured out on the officials and employees of the devil's government, the devil's empire will crumble. His servants will suddenly lose their eyesight and become dysfunctional. The rest of the wicked will suddenly figure out who Lucifer really is because reason says that God would not destroy His own servants and government! When this revelation occurs, the religious systems of the world will briefly revive and the ten kings will turn on the devil. They will hate Lucifer's theocracy (the whore). A global rebellion will occur, but the revolt will be for nothing because the wicked are doomed. The wicked will destroy Lucifer's one world church state. The kings of the Earth will be furious with the whore and they will strip her naked, "burn her with fire and eat her flesh."

The phrase, "burn her with fire and eat her flesh" denotes loathing and desperation. This parallels God's promise to ancient Israel. Consider God's warning to Israel if Israel turned their backs on Him: **"The Lord will bring a nation against you from far away, from the ends of the earth, like an eagle swooping down, a nation whose language you will not understand, a fierce-looking nation without respect for the old or pity for the young. They will devour the young of your livestock and the crops of your land until you** are destroyed. They will leave you no grain, new wine or oil, nor any calves of your herds or lambs of your flocks until you are ruined. They will lay siege to all the cities throughout your land until the high fortified walls in which you trust fall down. They will besiege all the cities throughout the land the Lord your God is giving you. Because of the suffering that your enemy will inflict on you during the siege, you will eat the fruit of the womb, the flesh of the sons and daughters the Lord your God has given you. Even the most gentle and sensitive man among you will have no compassion on his own brother or the wife he loves or his surviving children."[41]

> Rev. 17:16

{17} From the sixth trumpet to the fifth bowl (a period of about nine months), the kings of the Earth will do whatever the devil demands because the Holy Spirit will have no influence within them.

> Rev. 17:17
>
> *For God hath put in their hearts to fulfil his will, and to agree, and give their kingdom unto the beast, until the words of God shall be fulfilled.*

After a person commits the unpardonable sin, God turns that person over to Lucifer so that Lucifer's goals might be accomplished. This is a profound point that every Christian should understand: Whenever a person goes beyond the point of redemption by committing the unpardonable sin, that person forfeits God's grace and the power of choice![42] Lucifer is free to use the services of that person as he deems best for that person is a "whitewashed tomb," a member of the living dead.[43]

{18} "Finally, John, the woman you saw will be a great city that will rule over the kings of the Earth. For nine miserable months, Lucifer's theocracy will serve as "a city of refuge" of sorts for the wicked, but she is a tomb, her day of doom will surely come and everyone within her will be destroyed."

> Rev. 17:18
>
> *And the woman which thou sawest is that great city, which reigneth over the kings of the earth.*

The Rules of Interpretation

Consider how the Rules of Interpretation (discussed in the Introduction of this book) are observed in this prophecy:

Rule One is not used in this portion of Scripture. Revelation 17 is not an apocalyptic prophecy. It is a commentary, an explanation of matters previously presented.

Rule Two says a fulfillment only occurs when all of the specifications are met, and this includes the order stated in the prophecy. Since this portion of Scripture contains an explanation about several earlier visions, each element will be fulfilled in its declared order. As fulfillment occurs, the angel's explanation will make perfect sense just as it reads.

Rule Three says that apocalyptic language can be literal, analogous, or symbolic. To reach the intended meaning of a prophecy, the reader must consider (a) the context, (b) the use of parallel language in the Bible, and (c) if an element is thought to be symbolic, the Bible must interpret the symbol with a *relevant* text. All three types of language are used in this prophecy. The beast from the Abyss refers to Lucifer, the lamblike beast, the angel king that will arise from the Earth at the fifth trumpet. The composite beast having seven heads and ten horns represent the seven religious systems of Earth and ten kings which the devil will appoint. The whore represents a global consolidation of church and state authority. Lucifer's theocracy will be a one world church state. To the wicked, the great whore will appear to be a city of refuge at first, but she is a very seductive trap. Jesus will destroy all who unite with her.

"My son, give me your heart and let your eyes keep to my ways, for a prostitute is a deep pit and a wayward wife is a narrow well. Like a bandit she lies in wait, and multiplies the unfaithful among men."[44]

Rule Four is not used in this prophecy.

References:
1. Revelation 9:4
2. Revelation 9:6
3. Revelation 14:8; 18:2-4,10,21
4. Revelation 13:1-8
5. Daniel 8:19; Joel 3:14,15
6. In Bible times, large groups of people were often divided into groups of a thousand. See Exodus 18:21, 25; Numbers 31;14,48,52,54; Deuteronomy 1:15; 1 Samuel 8:12, 22:7; 1 Chronicles 13:1; 26:26; 27:1. For further discussion on this topic, please see pages 220-227 in my book, *A Study on the Seven Trumpets, Two Witnesses and Four Beasts* or download this article: http://www.wake-up.org/Revelation/RevBeasts.pdf .
7. Revelation 6:9-11; 13:7; Daniel 8:24
8. Matthew 16;25
9. Daniel 11:39
10. Revelation 13:2
11. Revelation 9:11
12. Ezekiel 28:12-19
13. Isaiah 14:12-17
14. John 16:11
15. Job 1:6-12
16. John 12:31; Revelation 12:10-13
17. Revelation 20:1-3
18. Revelation 17:8, insertions mine
19. Matthew 12:31,32
20. Revelation 20:7-12
21. Daniel 7:9,10; 2 Corinthians 5:10; Ecclesiastes 12:14; 2 Corinthians 6:2,3
22. 2 Thessalonians 2:9-12
23. Revelation 14:18-20; Daniel 8:23
24. Daniel 11:36-38
25. Revelation 9:4-6; 14:9-12

26. Isaiah 2:2; Daniel 9:16,20; Jeremiah 3:6; Psalm 2:6; 15:1; Hosea 4:13
27. Psalm 2:6; 48:2; 132:13
28. 2 Chronicles 3:1; Daniel 9:16,20; Zechariah 8:3
29. 1 Kings 14:22-24; Jeremiah 2:19,20; Ezekiel 6:13
30. Psalm 14:1,2; Isaiah 45:5,21,22
31. Deuteronomy 6:4; James 2:19; 1 Timothy 2:5
32. Matthew 5:20; 19:25,26; Romans 1:5
33. John 3:16
34. 1 Corinthians 15:51-54
35. Luke 22:70
36. Daniel 7:21-26
37. Revelation 13:3
38. Daniel 8:9
39. Daniel 8:25
40. 1 Thessalonians 4:14 See also Prophecy 9 on the resurrection of the 144,000.
41. Deuteronomy 28:49-54
42. Romans 1:28-2:9
43. Matthew 8:22; 23:27
44. Proverbs 23:26-28

Prophecy 14

The Second Coming

Revelation 18:1-19:10

Beginning Point in Time: The Beginning of the Sixth Trumpet (1,039th day*)

Ending Point in Time: End of Sixth Bowl (1,324th day*)

Summary: This prophecy contains a message which the 144,000 will deliver to the world during the sixth trumpet. I calculate the beginning of the sixth trumpet as follows. If the fifth trumpet sounds and the devil is released from the Abyss on the 891st day (two-thirds of the way through the Great Tribulation) and the fifth trumpet torment lasts for 148 days (five lunar months), the sixth trumpet would begin on the 1,039th day of the Great Tribulation (891 + 148 = 1,039). Next, if 1,039 days are subtracted from the 1,260 days granted to the Two Witnesses, the sixth trumpet will last 221 days (1260 - 1039 = 221 days or a little more than seven months). During the sixth trumpet, the 144,000 will proclaim the message described in this prophecy. When the wicked people consider this message in the environment of Lucifer's atrocities, a few of them will reconsider their evil ways. They will refuse to receive the mark of the beast, repent of their sins, come out of Babylon, and be saved. I believe most, if not all, of the 144,000 will die while delivering this message because of its inflammatory nature. When properly understood, this prophecy reveals a depth of divine love and compassion that is incalculable.

---

* Note: The dates above and astericked on the following pages are not absolute. They are derived from a mathematical matrix that involves several timing factors. For example, when considering the 1,260 days allotted to the Two Witnesses, the resurrection of the Two Witnesses after 3.5 days,[1] the 1,290 and 1,335 days mentioned in Daniel 12, and the forty-two months in Revelation 13:5, there is very little room for data manipulation. Even so, let me say again, these dates are not absolute. Ultimately, these messages will be obvious to everyone on Earth when they occur.

Introduction: The 144,000 will present four distinct messages during the Great Tribulation. Prophecy 12 contains the first three messages and this prophecy contains the fourth and final message. Lucifer will set up a counterfeit theocracy during the sixth trumpet and this message will be Jesus' final call to a rebellious planet. Remember, when the sixth trumpet begins, Lucifer will abruptly change character. Overnight, he will terminate his benevolent and gracious mask and become the cruel dictator that he really is. His forces will kill 1.75 billion people (a third of mankind)[2] under the pretense of divine authority, eliminating those who oppose the establishment of his one world church state (theocracy). To appreciate the fourth message, we need to briefly review the first three messages:

First Message – Day One: When the censer is cast down and the Great Tribulation begins, the first message (containing the eternal gospel) will be given throughout the world. The 144,000 will suddenly begin proclaiming their first message to the inhabitants of Earth and it will be an outright demand. They will say: **"Fear God and give him glory, because the hour of his judgment** [that is, the time for judging the living] **has come. Worship him** [the Creator] **who made the Heavens, the Earth, the sea and the springs of water."**[3]

Second Message – Day 64*: The 144,000 will add a second message when religious and political leaders of the world assemble to find a solution to God's wrath. When Babylon forms and begins to function with authority, world leaders will insist that God's retribution has impacted Earth because *"all* have sinned" and offended Almighty God with decadent behavior. The leaders of Babylon will assert that everyone must worship God and live righteously. "This endeavor," they reason, "will show The Almighty our corporate sorrow and His destructive wrath will cease."

The 144,000 will counter Babylon's leaders with this inflammatory declaration in the second message: **"Fallen! Fallen** [false] **is Babylon the Great, which made all the nations drink the maddening wine** [logic] **of her adulteries."**[4] The 144,000 will maintain that Babylon's presupposition, that God's wrath can be appeased, is false. Therefore, the 144,000 will declare that Babylon's demands, worship and repentance, are blasphemous. Of

---

* Note: See note on page 433.

course, worship and repentance are not blasphemous when a sinner is motivated by sorrow for his sin, but the irony in all this will be profound at this time in Earth's history. Babylon will be demanding worship and repentance and so will the 144,000, but the underlying motives between these two groups will be worlds apart.

The phrase, "the maddening wine of her adulteries" indicates two ideas. First, the leaders of Babylon will unknowingly "drink" many religious lies that will have a numbing effect. The term, maddening wine, is an ancient expression for bad wine that causes otherwise fine people to lose their minds and "go mad." Babylon will produce some "bad wine" and she will make all nations go mad (become incoherent) because they believe its lies. The result will be universal adultery between church and state. The union of church and state is an adulterous affair because Jesus is the head of His church. Until Jesus is the head of Earth's government, any union of church and state is an adulterous union because power corrupts. Man's fallen nature will not allow him to love God and others as himself. Leaders always abuse their power when church and state are united. History has clearly proven that the church cannot be faithful to Jesus and simultaneously exercise civil authority.[5] When the leaders of the world create Babylon, they do not anticipate the blasphemous behavior that Babylon will display. Also, they will not know that Jesus will soon destroy Babylon (and its leaders). Therefore, when the leaders of Babylon hear the second message, they will do their best to silence the 144,000.

Third Message – Day 891*: The 144,000 will present their third message when Lucifer and his angels physically appear. Speaking through His servants, Jesus will send this ultimatum throughout the world: **"If anyone worships the** [lamblike] **beast** [who masquerades as Almighty God] **and** [if anyone participates in] **his image** [theocracy] **and receives his mark** [tattoo] **on the forehead or on the hand, he, too, will drink of the wine of God's fury, which has been poured full strength into the cup of his wrath. He will be tormented with burning sulfur in the presence of the holy angels and of the Lamb."**[6]

Fourth Message – Day 1039*: The 144,000 will add a fourth message to their presentation when the sixth trumpet begins (day 1,039*). The fourth message will come at a time when everyone on

---

* Note: See note on page 433.

Earth is afraid for his life. Lucifer's forces will be in the process of killing a third of mankind and people will be standing in line to receive the mark of the beast on their right hand. The fourth message contains a tender invitation as well as a solemn threat. Jesus will speak through His servants and say, **"Come out of her** [the great whore, Lucifer's theocracy] **my people. . . . For her sins are piled up to Heaven, and God has remembered her crimes.** [He will] **Give back to her as she has given;** [He will] **pay her back double for what she has done."**[7]

When the sixth trumpet begins, I believe Holy Spirit power will rest upon the 144,000 in an unusual way. God's prophets will glow with a radiant light just as Moses did when he came down from Mt. Sinai.[8] This illumination will be so glorious that it will be difficult to look at the 144,000. This manifestation of divine power will produce the highest possible credibility. God's prophets will proclaim a message of truth, grace, and mercy. It seems incredible that even with this dramatic display of power, very few people will repent and be saved, but God's love for sinners knows no bounds. If I am correct and the 144,000 do shine with supernatural glory during the closing days of salvation's offer, this could explain how the whole world is illumined by the splendor of the fourth angel. I cannot think of a more effective way to announce to the world that where sin abounds, grace much more abounds![9]

During the sixth trumpet, Jesus will speak through His glorified servants in the clearest and tenderest of terms, " **'Fallen!** [false and blasphemous] **Fallen is** [the harlot-theocracy of Lucifer,] **Babylon the Great! She has become a home for demons and a haunt for every evil spirit, a haunt for every unclean and detestable bird** [this language refers to the fact that vultures feed on dead flesh without any concern for whose flesh it might have been]. **For all the nations have drunk the maddening wine of her adulteries** [the whole world is intoxicated with the lies and glorious plans promoted by Lucifer]. **The kings of the earth committed adultery with her** [the kings of the Earth have immorally united with Lucifer's whore, they have allowed her religious power to usurp their civil powers], **and the merchants of the earth grew rich from her excessive luxuries** [the merchants are those people who went along with the whore for financial gain. They are like vultures who feed on the poor and become fat and rich through extortion].' **Then I heard another voice from heaven say:** '[Jesus Himself will speak to the whole world:] **Come out of her, *my* people** [though your sins are like scarlet, they shall be as white as snow – if you will repent now of your rebellion. Please come now, come out today]**, so that you will not share in her sins, so that you will not receive any of her plagues.' "**[10]

Obviously, the 144,000 will remain alive until the first four messages are delivered. Everyone on Earth will "see and hear" the fourth message during the sixth trumpet. However, the fourth message will be so inflammatory that most, if not all, of the 144,000 will be killed for delivering it. When this occurs, Jesus will end His offer of grace and mercy for sinners. At the end of 1,260 days, the ministry of the Two Witnesses will be completed. Most, if not all of the 144,000 will be dead. Jesus will wave His sickle over Earth[11] and the people who have the mark of the beast will be condemned to die the second death. Six thousand years of redemption will end on the 1,260th day of the Great Tribulation. Each person on Earth will have made an informed and final choice and Jesus will reward each person accordingly when He appears.[12]

The Sequence

{1} I saw a mighty angel come down from Heaven. He spoke with great authority and the whole world heard his testimony. The angel illuminated the Earth with his glory.

> The fourth message presented by the 144,000 is represented as an angel messenger sent directly from God's throne. This message contains God's final offer of redemption. The fourth message will join with the previous three messages and together they will swell into the clearest and strongest statement of truth that God can present to mortals. Jesus will speak through the 144,000. He will declare the truth because what matters most to God is our response to truth.
>
> The honest in heart always love truth. The indwelling presence and peace of the Holy Spirit is more desirable to the honest in heart than any benefit stemming from compromise with evil. When a person stands firm for the truth, the Holy Spirit confirms God's will and the Bible assures him that he stands on solid ground. When the Holy Spirit and the Word of God are allowed to do their divine work within an individual, that person is filled with peace. To impress the wicked with the importance of this final offer of salvation, the 144,000 will radiate with the glory of God as did Moses when he came down from Mt. Sinai.[13]

Rev. 18:1
And after these things I saw another angel come down from heaven, having great power; and the earth was lightened with his glory.

> Rev. 18:1

Jesus knew that sinners could not provide an atonement for sin. For no other reason than unfailing love, Jesus came to Earth and died a cruel death so that every sinner could be saved. His goal during the Great Tribulation is to save as many sinners as possible. He is not willing that one soul should perish.[14] Conversely, Jesus offers no grace to a defiant sinner. When a person defies the Holy Spirit, he defies the two laws of love. He rejects the wisdom and authority of Almighty God.[15] This is why defying the Holy Spirit is unpardonable. The Bible leaves no question about God's love for sinners, but unfortunately, many sinners do not want to love God or their neighbor.

Jesus will speak through the mouths of the 144,000.[16] To make His words receptive, Jesus will also pour the Holy Spirit out on all flesh.[17] The Holy Spirit will pound hard on the door to each heart enticing each person to surrender to God's two laws of love. God's offer of redemption is extremely generous. He has paid the price for our sins. He is willing to remove our sinful nature[18] if we are willing to worship Him according to the demands of the eternal gospel. Of course, obeying the eternal gospel will require faith. The price of worship will be great. Satan will see to it that Babylon's decrees are in direct conflict with God's laws. The contest between competing laws will force everyone to make a choice and take a stand for or against the eternal gospel.

When the Two Witnesses complete their work (on the 1,260th day of the Great Tribulation), Jesus, our High Priest, can do nothing more to save one more soul. Everyone will have *firmly settled* into their final decision. Two distinct and separate groups of people will exist: Sheep and goats. The sheep cannot change their ways for they have been sealed. The goats cannot change their ways for they have committed the unpardonable sin. The following benediction indicates that Jesus has done everything that can be done and now, He will honor each person's choice: **"Let him who does wrong continue to do wrong; let him who is vile continue to be vile; let him who does right continue to do right; and let him who is holy continue to be holy."**[19]

> Rev. 18:2
>
> *And he cried mightily with a strong voice, saying, Babylon the great is fallen, is fallen, and is become the habitation of devils, and the hold of every foul spirit, and a cage of every unclean and hateful bird.*

{2} When the sixth trumpet begins, Jesus will speak through the 144,000 with a mighty voice. Using the clearest of terms, He will say, " '. . . . Fallen! [false and blasphemous] Fallen is [the harlot, Lucifer's theocracy,] Babylon the Great! She has become a home for demons and a haunt for every evil spirit, a haunt for every unclean and detestable bird [this language refers to the fact that vultures delight to feed on dead flesh without any concern for who it belonged to].

{3} "For all the nations have drunk the maddening wine of her adulteries [the whole world has become intoxicated with her lies and the blasphemous claims of Lucifer]. The kings of Earth committed adultery with her [the kings of Earth have united with the whore, they have surrendered their civil authority to Lucifer to maintain power], and the merchants of Earth grew rich from her excessive luxuries [the merchants are those who will profit from Lucifer's theocracy]."

{4} Then I heard another voice from heaven say: "[Jesus Himself will speak to the whole world through the mouths of the 144,000,] Come out of her, *my* people [even though your sins are like scarlet, they shall be as white as snow[20] if you will repent and honor me as your king. Come out now, come out of Babylon], so that you will not share in her sins, so that you will not receive any of her plagues; {5} "for her sins are piled up to Heaven, and God has faithfully recorded every crime.

{6} "I will pay her back according to the punishment she has imposed on my people; I will punish her *double* for what she has done. She deserves a *double* portion from her own cup, for she has violated my saints and she has rebelled against Me. I am twice the sovereign king of Earth; first by creation and second by redemption. I own the Earth and the fullness thereof. "I will cause the officials and employees of Lucifer's government to suffer punishment and grief in proportion to the glory and luxury she gave herself. {7} They thought they were invincible. His officials thought Lucifer's government was secure, the whore claimed to be the queen of Earth, she claimed to be the kingdom of God, but her boasting is vanity.[21]

> **Rev. 18:3**
> *For all nations have drunk of the wine of the wrath of her fornication, and the kings of the earth have committed fornication with her, and the merchants of the earth are waxed rich through the abundance of her delicacies.*
>
> **Rev. 18:4-5**
> *And I heard another voice from heaven, saying, Come out of her, my people, that ye be not partakers of her sins, and that ye receive not of her plagues. For her sins have reached unto heaven, and God hath remembered her iniquities.*
>
> **Rev. 18:6-7**
> *Reward her even as she rewarded you, and double unto her double according to her works: in the cup which she hath filled fill to her double. How much she hath glorified herself, and lived deliciously, so much torment and*

Rev. 18:7

for she saith in her heart, I sit a queen, and am no widow, and shall see no sorrow.

Rev. 18:8

Therefore shall her plagues come in one day, death, and mourning, and famine; and she shall be utterly burned with fire: for strong is the Lord God who judgeth her.

Rev. 18:9-10

And the kings of the earth, who have committed fornication and lived deliciously with her, shall bewail her, and lament for her, when they shall see the smoke of her burning, Standing afar off for the fear of her torment, saying, Alas, alas that great city Babylon, that mighty city! for in one hour is thy judgment come.

Rev. 18:11-13

And the merchants of the earth shall weep and mourn over her; for no man buyeth their

{8} "Therefore, her plagues will begin on the 1,265th day of the Great Tribulation and I will bring her to total ruin. During the next seventy days, she will be consumed by death, mourning, and famine. She will be consumed by fire, for I, Almighty God, will judge her and bring her to a violent end."

{9} When the kings of the Earth who committed adultery with her and shared her luxury see the smoke of her burning, they will weep and mourn over her. {10} Terrified at her torment, they will stand far off and cry: "Woe! Woe, O great city, O Babylon, city of power! In one hour your doom has come!'

Lucifer's government will implode during the fifth bowl. The kings of the Earth will be sorrowful when they see Lucifer's government collapse because they prospered from the devil's theocracy. The language in this chapter of Revelation can be compared to passages in the book of Job. You may recall how Job's misguided friends used "calamitous prose" and "lofty language" to describe Job's tragic misfortunes. In this case, the kings of the Earth will be wailing and weeping because the very doom they sought to escape is now upon them. To soothe their anxiety, the devil will send three powerful demons to speak to the ten kings during the sixth bowl. These demons will perform many powerful miracles, convincing the kings of the Earth that there is a glimmer of hope, a chance of survival.

{11} The merchants of the earth will weep and mourn over her because no one buys their cargoes any more; {12} cargoes of gold, silver, precious stones and pearls; fine linen, purple, silk and scarlet cloth; every sort of citron wood, and articles of every kind made of ivory, costly wood, bronze, iron and marble; {13} cargoes of cinnamon and spice, of incense, myrrh and frankincense, of wine and olive oil, of fine flour and wheat; cattle and sheep; horses and carriages; and the bodies and souls of men.

merchandise any more: The merchandise of gold, and silver, and precious stones, and of pearls, and fine linen, and purple, and silk, and scarlet, and all thyine wood, and all manner vessels of ivory, and all manner vessels of most precious wood, and of brass, and iron, and marble, And cinnamon, and odours, and ointments, and frankincense, and wine, and oil, and fine flour, and wheat, and beasts, and sheep, and horses, and chariots, and slaves, and souls of men.

Rev. 18:14

{14} The merchants will lament, 'The fruit you longed for is gone from you. All of your riches and splendor have vanished, never to be recovered.'

And the fruits that thy soul lusted after are departed from thee, and all things which were dainty and goodly are departed from thee, and thou shalt find them no more at all.

Rev. 18:15-16

The merchants of these things, which were made rich by her, shall stand afar off for the fear of her torment, weeping and wailing And saying, Alas, alas, that great city, that was clothed in fine linen, and purple, and scarlet, and decked with gold, and precious stones, and pearls!

{15} The merchants who sold these things and gained their wealth from her will stand far off, terrified at her torment. They will weep and mourn {16} and cry out: "Woe! Woe, O great city, dressed in fine linen, purple and scarlet, and glittering with gold, precious stones and pearls!"

Rev. 18:17-19

For in one hour so great riches is come to nought. And every shipmaster, and all the company in ships, and sailors, and as many as trade by sea, stood afar off, And cried when they saw the smoke of her burning, saying, What city is like unto this great city! And they cast dust on their heads, and cried, weeping and wailing, saying, Alas, alas, that great city, wherein were made rich all that had

{17} In one hour such great wealth has been brought to ruin!' Every sea captain, and all who travel by ship, the sailors, and all who earn their living from the sea, will stand far off. {18} When they see the smoke of her burning, they will exclaim, "Was there ever a city like this great city?" {19} They will throw dust on their heads, and with weeping and mourning cry out: "Woe! Woe, O great city, where all who had ships on the sea became rich through her wealth! In one hour she has been brought to ruin!"

{20} Then I heard a loud voice from Heaven say, "Rejoice over her, O heaven! Rejoice, saints and apostles and prophets for God has judged her for the way she treated you! {21} Then a mighty angel picked up a boulder the size of a large millstone and threw it into the sea, and said: "With such violence the great city of Babylon will be thrown down, never to be found again.

{22} The music of harpists and musicians, flute players and trumpeters, will never be heard in you again. No workman of any trade will ever be found in you again. The sound of a millstone will never be heard in you again. {23} The light of a lamp will never shine in you again. The voice of bridegroom and bride will never be heard in you again. *Your merchants were the world's great men, but their greatness and riches have come to nothing.* By your magic spell the nations were led astray."

ships in the sea by reason of her costliness! for in one hour is she made desolate.

Rev. 18:20-21
Rejoice over her, thou heaven, and ye holy apostles and prophets; for God hath avenged you on her. And a mighty angel took up a stone like a great millstone, and cast it into the sea, saying, Thus with violence shall that great city Babylon be thrown down, and shall be found no more at all.

Rev. 18:22-23
And the voice of harpers, and musicians, and of pipers, and trumpeters, shall be heard no more at all in thee; and no craftsman, of whatsoever craft he be, shall be found any more in thee; and the sound of a millstone shall be heard no more at all in thee; And the light of a candle shall shine no more at

Rev. 18:23

all in thee; and the voice of the bridegroom and of the bride shall be heard no more at all in thee: for thy merchants were the great men of the earth; for by thy sorceries were all nations deceived.

Rev. 18:24

And in her was found the blood of prophets, and of saints, and of all that were slain upon the earth.

Rev. 19:1-3

And after these things I heard a great voice of much people in heaven, saying, Alleluia; Salvation, and glory, and honour, and power, unto the Lord our God: For true and righteous are his judgments: for he hath judged the great whore, which did corrupt the earth with her fornication, and hath avenged the blood of his servants at her hand. And again they said, Alleluia. And her

{24} In her was found the blood of prophets and of the saints, and of all who have been killed on the Earth.

At first glance, verse 24 seems out of place in this narrative, however this declaration vindicates the whore's destruction. After the kings of the Earth have their eyes opened (fifth bowl), they will be forced to admit their atrocities against God's innocent saints. Of course, crimes against humanity always come with a death penalty and the kings of the Earth will realize their impending doom. When the "belly of the whore" is cut open (figuratively speaking), the kings of Earth will be forced to see the evidences of their crimes and discover their solemn accountability to God for their abusive use of power.

{19:1} During the sixth bowl, I heard what sounded like the roar of a great multitude in heaven shouting: "Hallelujah! Salvation and glory and power belong to our God, {2} for true and just are his judgments. He has condemned the great prostitute who corrupted the Earth by her adulteries. He has avenged on her the blood of his 144,000 servants." {3} And again they shouted: "Hallelujah! The smoke from her destruction goes up for ever and ever (justice is served)."[22]

{4} The twenty-four elders and the four living creatures fell down and worshiped Jesus, who was seated on the throne. And they cried: "Amen, Hallelujah!" {5} Then a voice came from the throne. It said to the 144,000, "Your turn for praise has come! Praise our God, you servants of Jesus Christ, you who fear him, both small and great!"

{6} Then I heard what sounded like a great multitude, like the roar of rushing waters and like loud peals of thunder. It was 144,000 voices singing: "Hallelujah! For Jesus Christ, our Lord God Almighty reigns. {7} Let us rejoice and be glad and give him glory! For the wedding of the Lamb has come, and his bride (his people) has made herself ready. {8} Fine linen (the righteousness of Jesus), bright and clean (without spot or wrinkle), was given her to wear."

> Jesus will give the saints a wedding garment of fine linen. This garment represents the righteousness of Christ that was freely given to them because of faithful obedience.[23]

> The great multitude in Revelation 19:6 are the 144,000, not the innumerable multitude seen standing around the throne *after* the Second Coming in Revelation 7:9. This distinction can be determined by the chronological timing in Revelation 19:5. The scene in Revelation 19:5 occurs *before* the Second Coming. Notice the directive given to the great multitude. **"Then a voice came from the throne, saying: 'Praise our God, all you his [144,000] servants, you who fear him, both small and great!'** "[24]

> In Revelation 7:3, the 144,000 are called God's "servants." In Revelation 10:7, the 144,000 are identified as "servants the prophets." In Revelation 11:12, God will resurrect the 144,000

---

smoke rose up for ever and ever.
Rev. 19:4-5
And the four and twenty elders and the four beasts fell down and worshipped God that sat on the throne, saying, Amen; Alleluia. And a voice came out of the throne, saying, Praise our God, all ye his servants, and ye that fear him, both small and great.
Rev. 19:6-8
And I heard as it were the voice of a great multitude, and as the voice of many waters, and as the voice of mighty thunderings, saying, Alleluia: for the Lord God omnipotent reigneth. Let us be glad and rejoice, and give honour to him: for the marriage of the Lamb is come, and his wife hath made herself ready. And to her was granted that she should be arrayed in fine linen, clean and white: for the fine linen

is the righteousness of saints.

and take them to Heaven at the seventh trumpet (on the 1,265th day of the Great Tribulation). In Revelation 17:16, the beast (religious leaders) and the ten kings (political leaders) will turn on the great whore (Lucifer's theocracy) and burn her with fire. When these facts are properly assembled, it becomes clear that the great multitude in Heaven prior to the Second Coming consists of 144,000 "servants." After all, they were presented to God on the 1,265th day as the firstfruits of the coming harvest![25]

Using a marriage analogy, the 144,000 will be the equivalent of groomsmen. They will accompany the Groom when He comes to Earth to receive His bride.[26] No wonder they sing, **"Let *us* rejoice and be glad and give him glory! For the wedding of the Lamb has come, and his bride has made herself ready."**[27] The 144,000 will declare that the wedding banquet has arrived at the beginning of the seventh bowl. After this declaration, Jesus and His wedding party (including the 144,000) will depart Heaven to retrieve the saints from Earth. According to the timing matrix used in this book, this glorious procession will approach Earth over a period of ten days.[28]

Rev. 19:9
And he saith unto me, Write, Blessed are they which are called unto the marriage supper of the Lamb. And he saith unto me, These are the true sayings of God.

Rev. 19:10
And I fell at his feet to worship him. And he said unto me, See thou do it not: I am thy fellowservant, and of thy brethren that have the testimony of Jesus: worship God: for the testimony of Jesus is the spirit of prophecy.

{9} After the fourth message was delivered to all the Earth and the whore was destroyed, after the 144,000 have rejoiced and heard the announcement that the time for the wedding banquet had come, the angel said to me, "Write: 'Blessed are those who are invited to the wedding supper of the Lamb!'" And he added, 'All that you have seen and heard is truth, these are the true words of God.'

{10} At this I fell at his feet to worship him. But he said to me, "Do not do it, John! I am not divinity. I am only a mouthpiece, a fellow servant of God like you and your brothers who hold to the testimony of Jesus. Worship God! For the testimony of Jesus is eternally true and infallible. He is the Word of God.[29] When Jesus speaks, the Holy Spirit conveys His words to His servants who have received the gift of prophecy.[30] Even though Jesus may speak through us, we are not divine. Worship God and serve Him."

The Rules of Interpretation

Consider how the Rules of Interpretation (discussed in the Introduction of this book) are observed in this prophecy:

Rule One says an apocalyptic prophecy has a beginning point and ending point in time and the events within the prophecy occur in the order given. This prophecy conforms to Rule One because chronological order is self evident. The fourth angel's message is delivered by the 144,000, the great whore is destroyed, the 144,000 rejoice that the great whore is destroyed, and they announce the arrival of the wedding banquet.

Rule Two says a fulfillment only occurs when all of the specifications are met, and this includes the order stated in the prophecy. The events described in this vision unfold over a period of about 300 days. When these events occur, this prophecy will be fulfilled.

Rule Three says that apocalyptic language can be literal, analogous, or symbolic. To reach the intended meaning of a prophecy, the reader must consider (a) the context, (b) the use of parallel language in the Bible, and (c) if an element is thought to be symbolic, the Bible must interpret the symbol with a *relevant* text. All three types of language are used in this prophecy. For example, the pronoun "she" is used eight times in this prophecy. "She" refers to the great whore which is defined as a symbol of Lucifer's theocracy in Revelation 17. Analogous and literal language are also used in this prophecy. These phrases are self-evident.

Rule Four is not used in this prophecy.

References:

1. Rev 11:3,11,12
2. Revelation 9:15
3. Revelation 14:7, insertion mine
4. Revelation 14:8, insertion mine
5. Revelation 14:8; Matthew 22:21 **Note:** When God delivered Israel from Egypt, He set up a theocracy in Israel. He kept civil authority (the work of Moses) and religious authority (the work of Aaron) separate and distinct from each other. Exodus 28:1-4; 30:17-21; 1 Kings 13; 1 Samuel 15 If the Dark Ages (538-1798) prove anything, they prove that when church authority usurps civil authority, the church becomes immoral and utterly corrupt.
6. Revelation 14:9,10
7. Revelation 18:4-6, insertion mine
8. Exodus 34:29-35
9. Revelation 18:1; Romans 5:20
10. Revelation 18:2-4, insertions and emphasis mine
11. Revelation 14:14-16
12. Revelation 22:12
13. Exodus 34:29-35
14. 2 Peter 3:9
15. Revelation 22:14,15
16. Revelation 10:10,11; 7:3-4
17. Joel 2:28-31
18. Hebrews 8:10-12
19. Revelation 22:11
20. Isaiah 1:18
21. For parallel language between ancient Jerusalem and modern Babylon, see Lamentations 1.

22. Revelation 21:1 indicates the whore will be annihilated. She will not burn throughout eternity because the first Heaven and first Earth will pass away and there will be no sea (no lake of fire). The Greek language uses an ongoing sense for fire at times to convey the idea that justice goes on and on until justice is completed. See also Revelation 14:11 and 20:10.
23. Matthew 22:2-13 speaks of "the sign" of the Son of Man appearing in the sky.
24. Revelation 19:5, insertion mine
25. Revelation 14:4
26. Matthew 25:6
27. Revelation 19:7, italics mine
28. Matthew 24:30,31 Since the seven bowls occur during a period of seventy days, it is assumed that ten days will be allotted to each bowl. Therefore, I conclude that the appearing of Jesus during the seventh bowl will be a ten day period.
29. John 1:1-12
30. 1 Corinthians 12:10,11; John 16:14,15

Prophecy 15

P15

The Day of the Lord

Revelation 19:11-20:10

Beginning Point in Time: The Beginning of the Sixth Bowl (1,315th day*)

Ending Point in Time: The End of the 1,000 Years

Summary

The Great Tribulation will be a culmination between forces of good and evil. A global struggle between righteousness and evil will occur and the struggle will culminate in a horrific war. The kings of Earth and their armies will make war against Jesus and His army as Jesus draws close to Earth. This war will prove that sinners are willing to destroy Almighty God if it means their own survival. In other words, Armageddon will prove that when the carnal nature is confronted with divine authority, it would rather die than

---

*****Note:** This date is not absolute. For reasons presented in Prophecy 11, reference note 105, I believe the seven bowls will occur over a period of seventy days with each plague allotted about ten days. If true, the devil's demons will go to the ten kings of Earth (the sixth bowl) on the 1,315th day. When the kings of the Earth see their impending doom, they will have a few days to mobilize their armies in an attempt to destroy Jesus when He appears. The seventh bowl will begin on the 1,325th day of the Great Tribulation and when Jesus and His entourage are close enough to Earth, Armageddon begins. The armies of Earth will attack Jesus and His approaching entourage. Of course, the combined military might of mankind will do nothing to stop Jesus and He will continue to draw near the earth. Panic will overtake His enemies and they will run for their lives.[1] It appears that Jesus will deal with the wicked on Sabbath, the 1,334th day of the Great Tribulation. On Sunday, the 1,335th day, the saints (both the dead and the living) will rise to meet the Lord in the air. Together with Jesus, a great party of joyful saints will head for New Jerusalem.

Jesus' Final Victory

yield. What a contrast! When divine nature was confronted with sin, the Father was willing to give His Son and Jesus was willing to die in our place so that sinners might be restored to eternal life! Armageddon will be studied throughout eternity for it summarizes the problem with the carnal nature. Armageddon will bring 6,000 years of sin to a close. Jesus will justifiably annihilate the wicked and take the saints to Heaven on the 1,335th day.[2]

Introduction

This prophecy begins with scenes of preparation in Heaven for the Second Coming. During the sixth bowl, the devil will entice the kings of the Earth and their armies to gather together and make war against Jesus.[3] At the appointed time, the Father, Jesus, their entourage of angels, and the 144,000 will leave Heaven and travel to Earth. During the final ten days of the Great Tribulation (the seventh bowl), the kings of the Earth will be anxiously watching as Jesus draws near. They will be armed and prepared to destroy Jesus the moment He draws close enough to Earth. Ironically, Lucifer's great government will be impotent. His loyal officials and dedicated employees will be useless because they were blinded by the judgment poured out during the fifth bowl. Consequently, the kings of Earth and their armies will have to make war against the Lamb on their own. There is a reason for this. Jesus wants the universe to see that even after Lucifer's demonic power is neutralized, the carnal heart is rebellious through and through. Every sinner is a miniature of Lucifer. Stupid mortals will make war against Almighty God thinking they can save themselves. Of course, the devil and his angels already know that inescapable doom will come. They dread Jesus' appearing because they know that Jesus will destroy their bodies and return them to the Abyss for 1,000 years – held there until death can be imposed upon them.

After the seventh bowl is poured out, a "sign" of the Son of Man will appear in the sky.[4] A small object that looks like a cloud will appear in the east and it will grow larger with each passing day until it completely spans the horizon. As the cloud draws near, people on Earth will see flashes of lightning and hear peals of thunder coming from it. People will tremble as this cloud fills the horizon. The kings of Earth will fire missiles and artillery toward the threatening cloud, but man's weapons will have no effect. Finally, on Sabbath*, the 1,334th day of the Great Tribulation, Jesus and His mighty host will break out of the darkness in full glory and brilliance. This glory will illuminate Earth with light brighter than the Sun. Earth will heave and crumble from the pulsating glory of its Creator. Sheets of lightning will blaze from east to west with peals of deafening thunder, voices will cry out, and burning hailstones will fall. A final global earthquake will rip the whole world apart. All of Earth's islands and mountains will be moved out of their places. The geological strata of Earth will convulse. Gases and other flammable substances buried deep in the fiery core of Earth will escape from ocean floors causing the oceans to become a huge lake of fire. Burning hail, each stone weighing about one hundred pounds,[5] will pulverize the Lord's enemies.

When the Great Day of God Almighty arrives, Jesus will throw the devil, his angels, his blind officials, employees, the kings of Earth, and their armies into a lake of fire.[6] Then, Jesus will speak a command and the rest of the wicked, everyone having the mark of the beast, will drop dead. No wicked person will escape the sword that comes out of His mouth[7] and vultures will gorge themselves on the flesh of the wicked.

Sunday, the 1,335th day of the Great Tribulation will be the first day of the seventh millennium. This is the day which the saints have longed for.[8] Suddenly, Jesus will speak with a thunderous voice from the sky.[9] He will call the righteous dead of all ages out of their tombs. People like Abel, Noah, Abraham, King David, and Daniel will appear, rising up from out of the dust. After a few moments, these saints will defy gravity as they ascend to meet Jesus *in the air*.[10] While the righteous dead are ascending toward Jesus, He will call the righteous living to join with them so that together, the saints of all ages will meet the Lord *in the air at the same time*! The Bible teaches there is only one gathering of the saints and please notice that through all of this that Jesus does not touch Earth. He will remain in the air, hovering above Earth until all the saints are gathered to Him. When every saint has been accounted for, He will return to Heaven with them.[11] What an awesome day of joy that will be! An unforgettable day in Earth's history that will have no equal.

The Day of the Lord

A few words about the phrase, "the Day of the Lord" are necessary because the Second Coming will be "the great Day of the Lord." At the first advent, Jesus came in peace and with goodwill, to reveal the truth and love of the Father. However, the second advent will have an entirely different character. Jesus will come with sovereign authority and omnipotent power to execute vengeance upon His enemies. His vengeance will be dreadful and totally destructive. As you consider the following passages, remember that the "Day of the Lord" prophecies, whether in Plan A or Plan B, share the same theme. When the Lord takes matters into His own hands, there is no further recourse. His patience with sin and sinners is exhausted, His devastating actions are righteous, and His objectives are holy. The fear of the Almighty separates the wise from the foolish. King David wrote, **"The fear of the Lord is the beginning of wisdom."**[12] In today's language, this statement would be, "When it comes to acquiring wisdom, an intelligent person will fear God *first*. Everyone and everything else is secondary."[13]

1. **Look, He is coming with the clouds, and every eye will see him,** *even those who pierced him*; **and** *all the peoples of the earth will mourn* **because of him. So shall it be! Amen.**[14]

    The Bible does not indicate when Christ's murderers will be resurrected. I assume Jesus will resurrect them on or about the time of the seventh bowl (1,325th day) to observe and comprehend the majesty, authority, and power of the Holy One who they ridiculed, tortured, and called a blasphemer. Of course, those who crucified Christ will be put to death on the 1,334th day with the rest of the wicked. However, the righteous dead of all ages and the surviving saints (who lived through the Great Tribulation without seeing death) – will meet the Lord *in the air*.[15]

2. **For the day is near, the day of the Lord is near – a day of clouds,** *a time of doom for the nations*.[16]

3. **The Lord thunders at the head of his army; his forces are beyond number, and mighty are those who obey his command. The day of the Lord is great; it is dreadful. Who can endure it?**[17]

4. **Will not the day of the Lord be darkness, not light – pitch-dark, without a ray of brightness?**[18]

5. **The day of the Lord is near for all nations. As you have done, it will be done to you; your deeds will return upon your own head.**[19]

6. The great day of the Lord is near – near and coming quickly. Listen! The cry on the day of the Lord will be bitter, the shouting of the warrior there. That day will be a day of wrath, a day of distress and anguish, a day of trouble and ruin, a day of darkness and gloom, a day of clouds and blackness, a day of trumpet and battle cry against the fortified cities and against the corner towers. I will bring distress on the people and they will walk like blind men, because they have sinned against the Lord. Their blood will be poured out like dust and their entrails like filth. Neither their silver nor their gold will be able to save them on the day of the Lord's wrath. In the fire of his jealousy the whole world will be consumed, for *he will make a sudden end of all who live in the earth.*[20]

7. The sky receded like a scroll, rolling up, and every mountain and island was removed from its place. Then the kings of the earth, the princes, the generals, the rich, the mighty, and every slave and every free man hid in caves and among the rocks of the mountains. They called to the mountains and the rocks, "Fall on us and hide us from the face of him who sits on the throne and from the wrath of the Lamb! For the great day of their wrath has come, and who can stand?"[21]

Notice the distinction between "the face of Him who sits on the throne" and "the wrath of the Lamb." Notice also the plural, "the great day of *their* wrath has come." Compare these facts with Matthew 26:64. The Father will come to Earth with Jesus at the Second Coming.

These few verses (and there are others) declare a profound truth: Jesus' return means the wicked will be annihilated. No one will remain alive on Earth after the 1,335th day.[22] Besides destroying the wicked, Jesus will gather up all of the saints in the air[23] because He intends to fulfill a promise that He made long ago. **"And if I go** [to my Father's house] **and prepare a place for you, I will come back and take you to be with me** [in my Father's house] **that you also may be where I am."**[24]

The Sequence

> Rev. 19:11-12
>
> *And I saw heaven opened, and behold a white horse; and he that sat upon him was called Faithful and True, and in righteousness he doth judge and make war. His eyes were as a flame of fire, and on his head were many crowns; and he had a name written, that no man knew, but he himself.*

{11} I looked toward Heaven and I saw a white horse whose rider is called Faithful and True because He fulfills every promise and never deviates from truth. With justice He judges the thoughts and deeds of mankind[25] and when necessary, He makes war against His enemies. {12} His eyes were like blazing fire. No one can hide from His penetrating gaze. He had many crowns on His head (some were *stephanos* and some were *diadema,* crowns of victory and authority, respectively). He is an experienced warrior. He overcame every temptation to sin and He will overthrow His enemies. He had a name written on Him that no one knows but He Himself.[26]

> Rev. 19:13-14
>
> *And he was clothed with a vesture dipped in blood: and his name is called The Word of God. And the armies which were in heaven followed him upon white horses, clothed in fine linen, white and clean.*

{13} He is acquainted with death. He is dressed in a robe dipped in His own blood. He was wounded for our transgressions, bruised for our iniquities, tortured for our sakes and with His scars, we are healed![27] His name is the Word of God. He is the faithful and true expression of the Father and His will.[28] {14} The armies of Heaven followed Him. They rode on white horses prepared for battle. They were dressed in fine linen, clean and white.

> Rev. 19:15-16
>
> *And out of his mouth goeth a sharp sword, that with it he should smite the nations: and he shall rule them with a rod of iron: and*

{15} When Jesus speaks, a sharp sword comes out of His mouth. With this sword He strikes down the nations. No person can escape the sovereign authority of the Creator of Life. Everything that lives derives its life from Him. He alone has the keys of life and death.[29] When Jesus offered to die in man's place, the Father promised Jesus that a day would come when, "He would rule the nations with an iron scepter."[30] An iron scepter means that His rulership and authority cannot be broken or appealed. There is no higher authority. With justice and righteous indignation, He treads the winepress of the fury of the wrath of God Almighty. {16} On His robe and on His thigh He has this name written: KING OF KINGS AND LORD OF LORDS and no one will be able to diminish this claim when He appears in glory.[31]

{17} I saw a mighty angel (Gabriel?) robed with glory as bright as the sun. He called out in a loud voice to all the birds flying in midair, "Come, gather together for the great supper of God, {18} so that you may eat the flesh of kings, generals, and mighty men, of horses and their riders, and the flesh of all people, free and slave, great and small, for their bodies will lie in the street of the great city."

he treadeth the winepress of the fierceness and wrath of Almighty God. And he hath on his vesture and on his thigh a name written, KING OF KINGS, AND LORD OF LORDS.

Rev. 19:17-18

And I saw an angel standing in the sun; and he cried with a loud voice, saying to all the fowls that fly in the midst of heaven, Come and gather yourselves together unto the supper of the great God; That ye may eat the flesh of kings, and the flesh of captains, and the flesh of mighty men, and the flesh of horses, and of them that sit on them, and the flesh of all men, both free and bond, both small and great.

Prophecy 15 - The Day of the Lord

Rev. 19:19

And I saw the beast, and the kings of the earth, and their armies, gathered together to make war against him that sat on the horse, and against his army.

{19} Then I saw the beast (with seven heads and ten horns) unite with the kings of Earth and their armies to make war against Jesus and His army.

Lucifer's theocracy (the great whore that rides upon the composite beast) will last for approximately nine months. When the fifth bowl (a plague of painful blindness) is poured out on Lucifer's officials and employees, Lucifer's theocracy will cease to function. The wicked of Earth will then realize that Lucifer is the devil and they will revolt against him and abandon his one world church state government. Lucifer will respond to the implosion of his government by sending miracle working demons to the kings of the Earth. These powerful demons will inform the kings of Earth that Jesus will totally destroy them and their only hope for survival is to join with Lucifer attacking the Lamb when He appears. The kings will be forced to join the devil and his forces. They will prepare their armies to destroy Jesus as He draws near Earth.

The beast mentioned in verse 19 is the composite beast, Babylon. After the devil is exposed for who he is and his false theocracy implodes, the remnant of Babylon can be compared to a angry beast. Because Lucifer's officials and employees will be blinded during the fifth bowl,[32] the kings and their armies will war against the Lamb without the devil's administrators. God wants to demonstrate that wicked people will knowingly unite with the devil, when necessary, to save themselves, even if it means the destruction of their Creator.

When Jesus comes close enough to Earth, the armies of Earth will fire weaponry at the magnificent host of angels in the sky, but weapons will have no effect. The efforts of wicked men will be futile and useless. The wicked will be filled with terror when they realize their hopeless situation. They will cry out for the rocks and mountains to fall upon them, calling for sudden death so their terrified torment will end.[33]

Rev. 19:20-21

And the beast was taken, and with him the false prophet that wrought miracles before him, with which

{20} Above the din of war, I heard a great noise, like the sound of a trumpet.[34] Jesus spoke and many brilliant angels suddenly descended from the sky. They captured Lucifer (the false prophet who had performed miraculous signs on behalf of the composite beast[35]) and his angels. They also captured Lucifer's blind officials, his employees, and the kings of the Earth with their armies and the angels threw them alive into a fiery lake of burning sulfur. {21} Suddenly, the rest of the wicked fell dead. Jesus killed them with a command (the sword that came from His mouth) and all the birds gorged themselves on their flesh.

Lucifer is called "the false prophet" in Revelation three times[36] because he will defy and contradict the testimony of God's true prophets (the 144,000) with outrageous blasphemy and awesome miracles. Many people are confused about the false prophet's identity, but the specification given in verse 20 (". . . he performed miraculous signs on behalf of the composite beast. . . and he deceived those who had received the mark of the beast and worshiped his image") perfectly aligns with the lamblike beast's actions described in Revelation 13:11-18.

Remember that during the fourth message the Holy Spirit will give the 144,000 great power. They will physically glow from God's glory resting on them as did Moses when He came down from Mount Sinai and through them, the whole world will be illumined to hear the final call to come out of Babylon. To counteract this glorious manifestation of 144,000 true prophets, Lucifer will take a bold and defiant stand. He will call fire down out of Heaven at will to "prove" to the wicked that he is God and he will perform many counterfeit miracles.[37]

The lake of fire that burns the beast and false prophet is not to be understood as an ongoing hell even though this fire will burn for a thousand years.[38] God will use fire at the end of the age to destroy Babylon in the same way that He destroyed Sodom and Gomorrah. Historians state that the ancient city of Jerusalem burned for months after Rome set it afire in A.D. 70, but realize that after a person is dead, the duration of the fire is immaterial.

The burning lake of sulfur will not destroy Lucifer and his angels. Instead, the physical bodies they occupied will be burned up. The officials and employees of Lucifer's government and the kings of the earth with their armies will all perish by fire, but the devil and his angels will only lose their physical bodies so they can be returned to the Abyss.

{20:1} I saw a mighty angel come down from the sky. He had the key to the Abyss and a great chain in his hand. {2} He seized the dragon, that ancient serpent, who is the devil, or Satan, and bound him for a thousand years. {3} He threw the devil and his angels back into the Abyss (the spirit world). He then locked and sealed the Abyss so there could be no escape. Lucifer and his angels will be incarcerated for 1,000 years. They will not deceive the nations

he deceived them that had received the mark of the beast, and them that worshipped his image. These both were cast alive into a lake of fire burning with brimstone. And the remnant were slain with the sword of him that sat upon the horse, which sword proceeded out of his mouth: and all the fowls were filled with their flesh.

Rev. 20:1

And I saw an angel come down from heaven, having the key of the bottomless pit and a great chain in his hand.

> **Rev. 20:2-3**
> *And he laid hold on the dragon, that old serpent, which is the Devil, and Satan, and bound him a thousand years, And cast him into the bottomless pit, and shut him up, and set a seal upon him, that he should deceive the nations no more, till the thousand years should be fulfilled: and after that he must be loosed a little season.*

(because no one is alive on Earth) and they will not be able to leave Earth. The devil and his demons will be confined in solitude, to contemplate their past, their present, and their future.

Many people believe that verse 3 indicates that people will be living on Earth during the 1,000 years. In other words, they reason that nations must exist on Earth if Lucifer is prevented from deceiving them. This conclusion is faulty because it does not align with other facts. Remember, the carnal nature makes every sinner a miniature of Lucifer. Even if sinners were alive on Earth during the 1,000 years, the curse of sin would still remain! The devil has been invisible to mankind ever since he was cast out of Heaven. From his prison (the Abyss), he has successfully deceived billions of people. So, whether in the Abyss or out of the Abyss, the devil has been (and will be) able to deceive the nations.

Please consider four points: First, Prophecy 9 teaches that all who reject the testimony of the Two Witnesses will be condemned to death. All of the wicked who live on Earth during the Great Tribulation will receive the mark of the beast and commit the unpardonable sin, so there would be no point in allowing them to live after the Second Coming. They cannot possibly be saved later on. Second, Prophecy 12 teaches that Jesus will pass eternal judgment on the dead and the living prior to the Second Coming, so again, there would be no point in allowing the wicked to live after the Second Coming. Third, Revelation 19:19,20 teaches that *all* of the wicked of Earth will be destroyed at the Second Coming. Some will be destroyed in the lake of fire; others will drop dead on command and the birds will eat their flesh. Fourth, Revelation 16 teaches that the seven bowls (the third woe) will be poured out on those having the mark of the beast. In other words, there will only be two groups of people at the Second Coming. The wicked will be destroyed and the saints will meet the Lord in the air and be taken to Heaven.[39] These events leave Earth in a desolate state during the 1,000 years. After the 1,000 years are over, the Holy City, New Jerusalem, will descend from Heaven (containing the saints) and, at that time, God will resurrect the wicked of all ages. Only then will the devil and his angels be set free for a short time to deceive the wicked one last time. (See verses 7 and 8 for further discussion.)

{4} After Jesus and the saints arrived in Heaven, I saw the redeemed sitting on thrones. God gave the saints authority to judge the wicked. The purpose of this judgment is to determine the amount of restitution that will be required of the wicked when they are resurrected. I saw those who had been beheaded because of their testimony for Jesus and their obedience to the Word of God. These martyrs had not worshiped the beast or his image and had not received his mark on their foreheads nor on their hands. Jesus resurrected them at the Second Coming and they reigned with Him for a thousand years so that they might judge their murderers.

> John particularly noticed the martyrs who had not worshiped the beast or received the mark. His comment does not exclude the saints from all ages; instead, he focuses on the numberless multitude who came out of the Great Tribulation. In 1 Corinthians 6, Paul states the saints will review the lives of their assailants and they will judge each person according to the demands of the golden rule. Jesus, insisting that justice be served, has determined that each wicked person will suffer in direct proportion to the suffering that he inflicted on others. Therefore, the saints will reign with Christ and judge the wicked according to this rule: "As you do unto others, the same shall be done unto you."[40]

{5} (The wicked killed at the Second Coming did not come to life until the thousand years were completed.) The resurrection that occurs at the Second Coming is called the first resurrection. {6} Blessed and holy are those who have part in the first resurrection because the second death, which will be imposed on the wicked at the end of the 1,000 years, will have no power over them. They will be priests of God and of Christ and will reign with Him during the thousand years.

> There is some confusion about who will be priests of God throughout eternity. The Bible teaches that all saints will be appointed as priests of God. In fact, the first verses of Revelation say, **"To him who loves us and has freed us from our sins by his blood, and has made us to be a kingdom and priests to serve his God and Father – to him be glory and power for ever and ever! Amen."**[41] The 144,000 will also serve as priests of God. I believe they will be given special recognition for their faithful service.[42]

Rev. 20:4

And I saw thrones, and they sat upon them, and judgment was given unto them: and I saw the souls of them that were beheaded for the witness of Jesus, and for the word of God, and which had not worshipped the beast, neither his image, neither had received his mark upon their foreheads, or in their hands; and they lived and reigned with Christ a thousand years.

Rev. 20:5-6

But the rest of the dead lived not again until the thousand years were finished. This is the first resurrection. Blessed and holy is he that hath part in the first resurrection: on such the second death hath no power, but they shall be priests of God and of Christ, and shall reign with him a thousand years.

> **Rev. 20:7-8**
> And when the thousand years are expired, Satan shall be loosed out of his prison, And shall go out to deceive the nations which are in the four quarters of the earth, Gog and Magog, to gather them together to battle: the number of whom is as the sand of the sea.

{7} When the wicked of all ages are resurrected, Jesus will show each person why He could not save them. After the wicked realize their fate and receive their sentences (which the saints determined during the 1,000 years), Satan will be released from the Abyss. He will become fully visible to everyone as he really is – a huge fallen angel – once a majestic being now deformed by sin's degenerate curse. The comparison between Lucifer and his demons and Jesus and his angels will be stark. The devil and his demons, knowing that only a few hours remain {8} will prey upon the condemned sinners. Full of loathing for Jesus, they will go out to deceive the nations in the four corners of the earth, Gog and Magog, to gather them for a final battle. In number they will be like the sand on the seashore.

The Father predetermined long ago that when the thousand years are over, He will resurrect the wicked of all ages (starting with Cain) at the end of sin's drama. I can think of several reasons for this. First, the Father wants every sinner to see the reality of the Holy City and the joy of eternal life that the saints will enjoy. Second, the Father wants every sinner to have a meeting with Jesus so that Jesus can explain why He could not grant them eternal life. Finally, the Father wants each sinner to consider the tremendous effort He made to save the lost. The Father wants the story of redemption to be told so that each sinner will realize what true love is, what it has accomplished, and what it must do. Once these steps are accomplished, every wicked person will understand God did not determine that person's eternal fate. Instead, each sinner determined his or her own fate. Every sinner will kneel before Jesus admitting that He has been generous and fair beyond measure.

The phrase "Gog and Magog" is borrowed from Ezekiel 38 and 39 and it is important to understand why it is used in this context. The end of sin under Plan A runs parallel to the end of sin under Plan B. Under Plan A (old covenant), the end of sin and sinners would have occurred when Lucifer (Gog) and his forces (Magog: the nations aligned with him) came up against Jerusalem to destroy the holy city. Under Plan A, God would have brought Lucifer's conquest to an end by sending fire down from Heaven.[43] Under Plan B (new covenant), a similar event will occur. When the wicked discover there is no possibility of survival, the devil and his forces will be released. They will prey on the wicked (as the devil and his demons did with ten kings prior to the Second Coming) and rally them to make war against God.

{9} Believing the devil's deception, the wicked marched across the breadth of Earth and surrounded the camp of God's people, the city He loves, but fire came down from heaven and devoured them. {10} And the devil, who deceived them, was thrown into the lake of burning sulfur, where the beast and the false prophet had been thrown. They will be tormented day and night for ever and ever (until the amount of restitution predetermined by the saints is fulfilled).

> God declares that vengeance is His to repay. This is why He allows the victims who suffered the crime to determine the amount of suffering that is appropriate for those who committed the crime.[44] Men who have been particularly violent will burn and suffer longer than those who were not so evil. The Bible teaches that there is a "lingering" hell. Justice demands that every person be treated as he treated others. God guarantees that restitution will be made: a life for a life, an eye for an eye, a tooth for a tooth, a wound for a wound and a bruise for a bruise.[45]

The Rules of Interpretation

Consider how the Rules of Interpretation (discussed in the Introduction of this book) are observed in this prophecy:

Rule One says an apocalyptic prophecy has a beginning point and ending point in time and the events within the prophecy occur in the order given. This prophecy conforms to Rule One because chronological order is self evident. The chronological order in this prophecy is easy to follow:

1. John saw a rider on a white horse, the armies of Heaven follow Him. He wears the title, "King of kings and Lord of lords."
2. A mighty angel calls for the birds to come to the great supper of God.
3. The composite beast and the kings of Earth make war against Jesus at the Second Coming.
4. The beast and the false prophet are captured and thrown into a lake of fire.
5. The rest of the wicked drop dead upon command (the sword that comes out of Jesus' mouth).

Rev. 20:9-10

And they went up on the breadth of the earth, and compassed the camp of the saints about, and the beloved city: and fire came down from God out of heaven, and devoured them. And the devil that deceived them was cast into the lake of fire and brimstone, where the beast and the false prophet are, and shall be tormented day and night for ever and ever.

6. The devil and his angels are returned to the Abyss for 1,000 years.
7. The saints are taken to Heaven where Jesus gives authority to those who suffered death and torture to determine the amount of restitution (suffering) which murderers must pay.
8. At the end of the 1,000 years, the Holy City descends and the wicked are resurrected. When they see their impending doom, the devil preys on their hopeless situation.
9. Inspired and deceived by Lucifer, the wicked march against the Holy City with the intent to destroy it.
10. Fire comes down from God and burns them up.

Rule Two says a fulfillment only occurs when all of the specifications are met, and this includes the order stated in the prophecy. When these events occur, this prophecy will be fulfilled.

Rule Three says that apocalyptic language can be literal, analogous, or symbolic. To reach the intended meaning of a prophecy, the reader must consider (a) the context, (b) the use of parallel language in the Bible, and (c) if an element is thought to be symbolic, the Bible must interpret the symbol with a *relevant* text. The language used in this prophecy is not symbolic because there are no relevant texts defining a symbol. On the other hand, we do find an extensive use of analogous and literal language. Even though all three types of language are used in this prophecy, the intended meaning is easy to discern if a person has carefully examined the previous prophecies in Revelation. In terms of language, the only thing new in this prophecy is Gog and Magog. These are parallel references from Ezekiel and provide the meaning to the prophecy.

Rule Four says the presence or absence of the Jubilee Calendar determines how God measures time. The 1,000 years are 1,000 literal years because this time period occurs after the Jubilee Calendar expired (1994).

References:

1. Revelation 6:16,17
2. John 14:1-3
3. Compare Revelation 19:19 with Revelation 16:12-16.
4. Matthew 24:30
5. Revelation 16:21
6. Revelation 19:20
7. Revelation 2:16; 19:15
8. Daniel 12:12
9. 1 Thessalonians 4:16
10. 1 Thessalonians 4:15-18
11. John 14:1-3
12. Psalm 111:10
13. Luke 12:5
14. Revelation 1:7, italics mine
15. 1 Thessalonians 4:15-17
16. Ezekiel 30:3, italics mine
17. Joel 2:1-11
18. Amos 5:20
19. Obadiah 1:15 Notice the declaration of restitution.
20. Zephaniah 1:14-18, italics mine
21. Revelation 6:14-17
22. Notice the same results in both cases. See Zephaniah 1:14-18 for the outcome under Plan A. See Revelation 19:19-21 for the outcome under Plan B.
23. 1 Thessalonians 4:15-17
24. John 14:3, insertions mine
25. John 5:22

26. See Revelation 2:17. Evidently, Jesus and the saints will use new names throughout eternity. Perhaps this is done by the Father to show specific interest in each person or reflect their personal experience while living on Earth. Ancient kings often renamed their captives when they gave them a position of authority within their kingdom. See Genesis 17:5, Daniel 1:7 and Luke 1:13,31,35.
27. Isaiah 53:5
28. John 14:9-11
29. Revelation 1:18
30. Psalm 2:9; Revelation 2:27; 12:5
31. Malachi 1:14; John 18:37-19:3; Psalm 2:12
32. Revelation 17:12,16; 16:10-16
33. Revelation 6:14-17
34. See Revelation 1:10 for a parallel text.
35. Revelation 13:13,14.
36. Revelation 16:13, 19:20, 20:10
37. Revelation 13:13,14; 2 Thessalonians 2:8-12
38. Revelation 20:3,10
39. John 14:1-3; 1 Thessalonians 4:15-17
40. Golden Rule: Matthew 7:12; Luke 6:31; Matthew 5:26; 2 Peter 2:13; Revelation 2:23; 2 Timothy 4:14; Joel 3:4,7; Ezekiel 22:31; Jeremiah 23:19,20; Deuteronomy 32:35; Hebrews 10:30
41. Revelation 1:5,6
42. Revelation 14:1-5
43. Ezekiel 38:22; 39:6,7
44. 1 Corinthians 6:2,3; Matthew 19:28
45. Exodus 21:23-27

Prophecy 16

The Earth Purified

Revelation 20:11-21:1

Beginning Point in Time: When the 1,000 Years Are Over and New Jerusalem Rests on Earth

Ending Point in Time: Soon after the Creation of a New Heaven and Earth

Summary

This prophecy describes the end of sin and sinners. God will resurrect the wicked at the end of the 1,000 years to hear the reason why they are doomed and then destroy them. After sinners and the curse of sin are consumed by fire, Jesus will create a new Heaven and a new Earth and the saints will inherit the new Earth.

Introduction

Through the centuries, many people have been puzzled by the contents of Revelation 20. Consider these issues:

1. Many Christians believe that a person goes immediately to Heaven or hell at death.[1] What is God's purpose for resurrecting the righteous dead at the Second Coming[2] if they already exist in Heaven? Even more, why would God resurrect the wicked a thousand years later if they are already burning in hell?

2. Other people have wondered why God would even want to resurrect the wicked at the end of the 1,000 years. Why not leave the wicked to rot in their graves and move on with the creation of a new Heaven and a new Earth?

3. Some Christians are frustrated with Revelation 20 because this chapter contradicts the idea that a New Testament God would punish people with hell fire, and annihilate people that He loves.

These three issues can be resolved. Many people have not taken the time to examine and absorb *all* that the Bible has to say about various aspects of God's ways and plans so they often reach a

Prophecy 16 - The Earth Purified

conclusion based on an inadequate number of data samples. For example, if a person's view of God is limited to Matthew, Mark, Luke, and John, his view of God will be incomplete. If a person thinks the God of the Old Testament is unlike the God of the New Testament, his conclusions about God are incorrect because the God of the Old Testament is the God of the New Testament and He is changeless.[3] Consider this:

The God who created Adam and Eve and put them in the Garden of Eden is the same God who drove them out of the Garden of Eden. In fact, consider these events recorded in Bible history. He is:

- the God who caused the whole world to drown in Noah's day
- the God who burned up Sodom and Gomorrah
- the God who killed the first born, both man and beast in every Egyptian family, and drowned Pharaoh's army
- the God who destroyed the wicked city of Jericho
- the God who sent Nebuchadnezzar to utterly destroy Jerusalem in 586 B.C
- the God who sent the Romans to utterly destroy Jerusalem in A.D. 70
- the God who will kill 25% of Earth's population during the first four trumpets
- the God who will destroy all of the wicked at the Second Coming
- the God who will burn the Earth with fire at the end of the 1,000 years
- the God who will create a new Earth and hand it over to His children!

God has given mankind sixty-six books (the Bible) to study. When properly aligned, these books describe God's actions over a period of approximately 7,000 years. Because God is eternal, a thousand years might go by before He decides to do something new or unusual. A thousand years contains many human generations, so it may *appear* that God has changed from one generation to another. For example, Noah's flood occurred approximately 1,656 years after Creation week. Noah's flood was not out of character for a God of love. God did not suddenly change in Noah's generation. God is so huge in terms of timing that large samples of time are required to properly understand Him and His actions. The Bible declares that God is love.[4] This means that God defines and demonstrates what love is and is not. If we are willing to examine all that the Bible has to reveal about God over a large span of time, many questions will disappear because there is One Constant in this dynamic universe. He is the Creator of the Universe, Almighty God.[5]

The Big Picture

Please consider the following questions for a moment. Why has God told us *in advance* about the 1,000 years that will occur *after* the Second Coming? Why has God told us in advance about the resurrection of the wicked and their annihilation at the end of the 1,000 years? Why has God told us in advance about the great white throne and the judgment process that goes with it? Why has God told us in advance about the destruction of the wicked by fire at the end of the 1,000 years? Why has God told us in advance about the creation of a new Heaven and a new Earth? Why has God told us in advance about the devil leading the wicked against New Jerusalem?

The simple answer to all these questions is that God has given us this information so we can understand His plans. He wants us to know where the drama with sin is going. *God wants His children to align Bible history with Bible prophecy so that we can see and understand His love for us."* Understanding principles of divine love is not as simple as you might think! (Ask a child if he understands the principles involved when his parent's discipline him.) God's love is larger and more inclusive than we can fathom and this makes God's behavior seem mysterious at times. God's love for oncoming generations is no less than His love for the current generation. This simple fact explains, in part, why He destroyed the world in Noah's day. He destroyed the world to protect oncoming generations from the decadence and degeneracy of the previous generations. God's actions are always consistent with principles of love, therefore, consider the following statements:

1. According to infinite wisdom and unfailing love for mankind, long ago God predetermined that the saints would judge the wicked during the 1,000 years. The golden rule is a fundamental building block in the law of love. The golden rule demonstrates a perfect balance between mercy and justice. "Extend mercy and kindness to others as you would have them extend mercy and kindness to you because God

will ensure that every kindness and injustice is fully repaid."[6] God knows that no one is better suited to determine how much suffering occurred during the commission of a crime than the victim. Therefore, at the appointed time, God will allow the redeemed to determine (to judge) the amount of suffering which predators must suffer by fire.[7] Love functions in a perfect balance and God loves mercy and justice equally. With God, there is no statute of limitations and this is one reason why the wicked must be resurrected at the end of the 1,000 years. God cannot conclude the drama of sin without justice being served. Bruise for bruise, eye for eye, tooth for tooth, and life for life.

2. According to infinite wisdom and love for all mankind, the Father predetermined that Jesus should speak to all of the wicked at the same time at the end of the 1,000 years. Therefore, all of the wicked will be resurrected at the end of sin's drama. First, they will see the glory of the city, New Jerusalem, whose builder and maker is God, filled with an innumerable multitude of saints. The wicked will also observe the brilliant white throne of Jesus Christ, the Creator and Honorable Judge of all mankind. He will meet face to face with each wicked person and show them a complete record of their lives; as recorded by angels.[8] Jesus will explain to each wicked person why he could not be saved and why he is not allowed to enter the New Jerusalem. The Father predetermined that each wicked person must understand that Jesus was righteous and more than fair in His judgment. This meeting with Jesus will silence every argument that God is or has been unfair.[9] Of course, God could easily ignore His enemies by leaving them in their graves, but this is not the way of love. God will confront the enemies of love so that rebellion and selfishness can be fully exposed.

3. According to infinite wisdom and love, the Father predetermined that each saint should see for himself why wicked people could not be saved. Therefore, God will give the saints 1,000 years to examine the record of any wicked person they wish to investigate. This is extremely important because God does not want one saint to question His judgment throughout eternity. For example, suppose you are taken to Heaven, but a loved one is not there. You begin

to wonder why your loved one could not be saved, so you examine the record of their life. This openness will silence and resolve any notion that Jesus judged unfairly; all this occurs *before* a single person is destroyed in the fire.

4. According to infinite wisdom and love, the Father predetermined that fire is the best tool to accomplish two purposes at the end of the 1,000 years. First, fire produces suffering and it will be used to extract the suffering which predators must repay. The suffering of the wicked will not cease until justice is satisfied. Once justice is achieved, each wicked person will die the second death (a death from which there is no recovery). Second, fire is useful in that it sterilizes as it purifies. After Jesus has destroyed Lucifer and his angels, the wicked who rebelled against the laws of love, and the curse of sin itself (death and the grave), Jesus will reuse this sterilized orb called Earth as the foundation for a new Earth.

5. According to infinite wisdom and unfailing love for new worlds that will be created millions of years later, the Father wants to prove a point at the end of sin's drama that is very important. The Father wants everyone to see what He foreknew before the creation of life. Therefore, He will break the seventh seal and display the contents of The Book of Life at the end of the 1,000 years. The universe will see that The Book of Life is a perfect mirror of the record books which angels recorded in real time. This amazing revelation will prove two points. First, the Father has perfect foreknowledge. He knows the end from the beginning. Before any life was created, He foreknew who would choose salvation and who would not, both in Heaven and on Earth, and He wrote it down. Second, God can be trusted to separate His foreknowledge from His love. In other words, the Father will not use His perfect foreknowledge to protect the Godhead from harm and He will not manipulate the choices of His children to satisfy His objectives. He will prove to the universe that He will not violate the will of His children even though He foreknows the outcome. God can be trusted completely! His commitment to the principles of love prevents Him from using His foreknowledge to manipulate His subjects.

6. According to infinite wisdom and love, God predetermined that Lucifer and his demons should remain alive until the end of the 1,000 years. By allowing them to live, the fruits of sin will be allowed to mature. Eventually, God will address each argument that Lucifer used to lead one-third of the angels into rebellion. (Remember, the drama with sin is far more encompassing than events on Earth.) The demons that followed Lucifer will clearly see that Lucifer lied to them. Even when they were confronted with the truth, they willfully chose to believe Lucifer's lies rather than surrender to God's authority and truth. Going forward through eternity, it will be necessary and important to review this confrontation so that sin's ugly pall never rises again. Pure, sinless, holy beings can fall and have fallen twice because rebellion falsely promised short term gains. Submission to God's infinite wisdom is not always easy for intelligent beings, but finite beings must remember who is infinite and who is not.

When these six issues are considered, we find that God wants His people to understand His love, plans, and actions. There is no hint of evil in God. To know God is to love God. He has generously provided a thousand answers about Himself and His plans if we are willing to search for them.

The Sequence

{11} At the end of the 1,000 years, the Holy City will descend from Heaven. Shortly afterwards, every wicked person that once lived on Earth will be resurrected and restored to life. I saw a great white throne and Jesus was seated on it. His glory was so great that Earth and sky were not visible. {12} The wicked were speechless. They stood before Jesus and His throne, both great and small, and a record of each life was opened for review and the wicked were informed of their sentence. Each was sentenced according to what he had done.

> During the 1,000 years, the saints will sit in judgment with Jesus. They will review the records of the wicked and determine the amount of suffering that each will have to suffer. Please notice that the saints do not determine who will be saved and lost. Jesus, according to the authority given to Him, made this determination prior to the Second Coming. Therefore, the judgment conducted by the saints during the 1,000 years has nothing to

---

Rev. 20:11

And I saw a great white throne, and him that sat on it, from whose face the earth and the heaven fled away; and there was found no place for them. And I saw the dead, small and great, stand before God; and the books were opened: and another book was opened, which is the book of life: and the dead were judged out of those things which were written in the books, according to their works.

do with salvation. The judgment is limited to the matter of restitution. When the wicked are raised from their graves, they will be given the sentences which the saints determined. Later, another book will be opened. The seventh seal will be broken on The Book of Life and the contents will be made known to everyone. Amazingly, The Book of Life (written by the Father before life was created) will perfectly mirror the books of record (written by the angels in real time).

This great day will never be duplicated again. Everyone who lived on Earth during its 6,000 year history will be alive and present. *Sin's drama will come to a close with every sinner in attendance.* The saints (those who overcame sin through faith in Jesus) will observe the Great White Throne event from the walls of the Holy City. Down below and surrounding the Holy City, there will be a numberless multitude of wicked people. The wicked surrounding the city will include those who were thrown alive into the lake of fire (a sea of fire) at the Second Coming,[10] and everyone else whom God could not save.

{13} Hades (the grave) gave up every person who had died. Thus, everyone who lived on Earth during the 6,000 years of sin was present and accounted for. After Jesus explained why he could not save each wicked person, each of the wicked was sentenced according to what he had done to others. {14} Then, all of the wicked (including Lucifer and his demons) were thrown into the lake of fire and the lake of fire burns them up. The wicked die the second death, a death from which there is no hope of resurrection. {15} If anyone's name was not found written in The Book of Life, he was thrown alive into the lake of fire – by a God of love!

> At this point, we should briefly review four concepts: First, the Bible says that the penalty for sin is death, not living in hell forever.[11] Death is a state of silence, where there is no thought, action or awareness.[12] Second, a God of love is always just and fair. He will not punish someone with infinite torture because no crime merits infinite torment. His law of love limits punishment to a life for a life, a bruise for a bruise, an eye for an eye, and a tooth for a tooth. God will not exceed them. Third, the fires of hell cannot burn forever![13] After restitution has been extracted from the wicked, they must die. Mercifully, it is the second death that will last forever because, never again, will there be a place for sin and sinners in God's universe. Finally, it is important to understand that the saints will not see their loved ones writhing around in the flames of hell for eternity because

---

Rev. 20:13-15
And the sea gave up the dead which were in it; and death and hell delivered up the dead which were in them: and they were judged every man according to their works. And death and hell were cast into the lake of fire. This is the second death. And whosoever was not found written in the book of life was cast into the lake of fire.

the wicked will perish and become "ashes." The fires of hell will come to an end and Jesus will create a new Heaven and Earth. The former things will pass away and Jesus will establish a new world order. He will wipe away all tears. All attachments with the wicked will end. The meek will inherit the Earth and live happily ever after, yes forever and ever!

> Rev. 21:1
>
> *And I saw a new heaven and a new earth: for the first heaven and the first earth were passed away; and there was no more sea.*

{21:1} Then I saw Jesus create a new Heaven and a new Earth, for the first Heaven and the first Earth had passed away, and there was no longer any sea (or lake of fire).[14]

The Rules of Interpretation

Consider how the Rules of Interpretation (discussed in the Introduction of this book) are observed in this prophecy:

Rule One says an apocalyptic prophecy has a beginning point and ending point in time and the events within the prophecy occur in the order given. This prophecy conforms to Rule One because Revelation 20:11 starts a new prophecy. Chronologically speaking, verse 11 does not follow verse 10, so a new prophecy begins. The chronological order in this prophecy is self evident.

1. A great white throne becomes visible
2. The wicked of all ages stand before Jesus
3. The wicked are burned up
4. God creates a new Heaven and a new Earth

Rule Two says a fulfillment only occurs when all of the specifications are met, and this includes the order stated in the prophecy. There is a profound point in this prophecy that many people overlook. A lake of fire will be created at the Second Coming.[15] This lake of fire will burn during the 1,000 years.[16] At the end of the 1,000 years, God will cast the wicked of all ages alive into this fire.[17] No one is in hell today. The wicked are not punished before the saints pass judgment on them and they are resurrected to face their Creator![18]

Rule Three says that apocalyptic language can be literal, analogous, or symbolic. To reach the intended meaning of a prophecy, the reader must consider (a) the context, (b) the use of parallel language in the Bible, and (c) if an element is thought to be symbolic, the Bible must interpret the symbol with a *relevant* text. The language used in this prophecy is not symbolic because there are no relevant texts defining a symbol. On the other hand, we find liberal use of analogous and literal language. For example, death and Hades (the grave) will be thrown into the lake of fire.[19] Personification is used to describe the end of sin's curse. Paul says, "The last enemy to be destroyed is death."[20] Of course, when death is no more, the grave will not be necessary. Thus, death and the grave will be destroyed in the lake of fire.

Rule Four is not used in this prophecy.

References:

1. Without realizing it, many Christians treat Luke 16:19-31 as a fact instead of a parable. This puts the Bible in a state of internal conflict because the Bible does not teach opposing concepts.
2. 1 Thessalonians 4:15-17
3. Deuteronomy 6:4; Malachi 3:6; 1 Timothy 2:5,6
4. 1 John 4:8,16; John 3:16
5. Malachi 1:14; 3:6; Hebrews 13:8
6. Luke 6:30; Obadiah 1:15; Romans 12:19
7. 1 Corinthians 6:1-3; Revelation 20:6
8. Ecclesiastes 12:14; 2 Corinthians 5:10 The Bible indicates that angels in Heaven record every aspect of human behavior. (Daniel 7:9,10; Malachi 3:16; Revelation 20:12.) This explains why books of record are used to judge the dead prior to the Second Coming. Jesus will also use these same books to silence any discrepancy a wicked person might have when he receives his sentence at the end of the 1,000 years. In other words, if a wicked person claims that God's judgment of him is unfair, Jesus will present the evidence that He used when making His determination. Since these records exist, God has evidently enabled certain angels to be impartial observers and chroniclers of human conduct. Their job is to record the words, thoughts, and actions of every person (including Lucifer and the angels that were cast out of Heaven) and their work is represented in the Bible as books of record. (I am sure Heaven uses a technology that is far greater than books or video duplication, but I am sure you understand the concept.) If such angels do not exist and God Himself is the recorder of human conduct, a conflict of interest occurs, because the Judge uses records that He wrote as the basis for His judgment. Therefore, it seems fair and reasonable to conclude that God has assigned intelligent angels to serve as third-party observers of human conduct. If so, these angels have nothing to gain or lose. Their job is to simply record the facts. This

arrangement aligns with a generous God of light who exalts principles of love, who does nothing shady, who has nothing to hide, and has done everything possible to save each sinner.

9. Isaiah 45:18-24
10. Revelation 19:20; 20:10
11. Romans 6:23
12. Ecclesiastes 9:5-6; Psalm 115:17
13. Malachi 4:3
14. John says "there was no more sea" after the first Heaven and first Earth passed away. John uses two different Greek words *thalassa* (sea) and *limne* (lake) in two consecutive verses and this has caused some confusion. (Revelation 20:15; Revelation 21:1) Evidently, John uses the word *thalassas* (sea) in Revelation 21:1 instead of *limne* (lake) because the lake of fire engulfs the whole world at the very end. Thus, the first Earth passes away and is totally destroyed by fire. John's use of two different words can be seen as progressive, that is, the lake (of fire) becomes a sea (of fire). This fire destroys the elements of the first Heaven and the first Earth. (2 Peter 3:12) Compare the use of *thalassas* and *limne* in Matthew 4:18, Mark 1:16 and John 6:17 with Luke 5:1 and 8:22,23.
15. Revelation 19:20
16. Revelation 20:10
17. Revelation 20:15
18. For more information on what happens when a person dies, please see Chapter 13 in my book, *Jesus: The Alpha and The Omega* or download this chapter at: http://www.wake-up.org/Alpha/Chapter13.htm.
19. Revelation 20:14
20. 1 Corinthians 15:26

Prophecy 17

The New Heaven and New Earth
Revelation 21:2-21:8

Beginning Point in Time: At the End of the 1,000 Years

Ending Point in Time: When the Old Order Has Passed Away

Summary

This short prophecy introduces three interesting topics. First, a loud voice announces that God's throne will be relocated to this planet. The eternal and universal ramifications of this move are very interesting. Second, this prophecy indicates the saints will weep when they see their friends and loved ones destroyed in the fire. (I am sure the Godhead will weep as well.) However, Jesus will wipe away the tears of the saints. As strange as it may seem, the records of the wicked will remain forever in Heaven's library. They will be preserved as "case studies" of rebellion for new beings to examine and study. The memory of the wicked will not pass away, but the emotions and attachments (the source of the tears) will be eliminated. Finally, this prophecy indicates that overcoming our natural rebellion against God's authority and will is a prerequisite for eternal life.

The Sequence

{2} I saw the Holy City, the new Jerusalem, coming down from God in Heaven, prepared as a bride beautifully dressed for her husband. {3} And I heard a loud voice from the throne saying, "Now the dwelling of God is with men, and he will live with them. They will be his people, and God himself will be with them and be their God. {4} He will wipe every tear from their eyes. There will be no more death, mourning, crying, or pain, for the old order of things has passed away."

Rev. 21:2-4

And I John saw the holy city, new Jerusalem, coming down from God out of heaven, prepared as a bride adorned for her husband. And I heard a great voice out of heaven saying, Behold, the tabernacle of God is with men, and he will dwell with them, and they shall be his people, and God himself shall be with them, and be their God. And God shall wipe away all tears from their eyes; and there shall be no more death, neither sorrow, nor crying, neither shall there be any more pain: for the former things are passed away.

Jesus' Final Victory

Prophecy 17 - The New Heaven and New Earth

Rev. 21:5-8

And he that sat upon the throne said, Behold, I make all things new. And he said unto me, Write: for these words are true and faithful. And he said unto me, It is done. I am Alpha and Omega, the beginning and the end. I will give unto him that is athirst of the fountain of the water of life freely. He that overcometh shall inherit all things; and I will be his God, and he shall be my son. But the fearful, and unbelieving, and the abominable, and murderers, and whoremongers, and sorcerers, and idolaters, and all liars, shall have their part in the lake which burneth with fire and brimstone: which is the second death.

{5} I saw Jesus seated on a great white throne. He said, "I am making everything new!" Then He said to me, "Write down my words, for they are trustworthy and true." {6} Again He spoke to me: "The plan of redemption is finished. I am the Alpha and the Omega, the Beginning and the End. To him who is thirsty (for righteousness and joy) I will give to drink without cost from the spring of the water of life. {7} He who overcomes (the cravings of the carnal mind, the lust of the eyes and the boasting of what he has and does[1]) will inherit all this, and I will be his God and he will be my son. {8} But the cowardly (those who are unwilling to do what is right), the unbelievers (those who defy the Word of God and blaspheme the Holy Spirit), the vile (those who glorify degenerate behavior), the murderers (those who are predators), the sexually immoral (those who are controlled by sexual passions), the sorcerers (those who practice magic arts, including divination and the paranormal), the idolaters (those who are greedy; loving and indulging self) and all liars (those who bear false witness); their place will be in the fiery lake of burning sulfur. This is the second death.

Rules of Interpretation

Consider how the Rules of Interpretation (discussed in the Introduction of this book) are observed in this prophecy:

Rule One says an apocalyptic prophecy has a beginning point and ending point in time and the events within the prophecy occur in the order given. Chronological order is easy to see in this short prophecy:

1. Holy City descends
2. A loud voice declares God's throne is on Earth
3. (Implied) The world is destroyed by fire (this is the second death for the wicked)
4. God wipes away the tears
5. Jesus creates a new Heaven and Earth
6. The wicked have no part in the Earth made new

Rule Two says a fulfillment only occurs when all of the specifications are met, and this includes the order stated in the prophecy. Obviously, this prophecy awaits fulfillment.

Rule Three says that apocalyptic language can be literal, analogous, or symbolic. To reach the intended meaning of a prophecy, you must consider (a) the context, (b) the use of parallel language in the Bible, and (c) if an element is thought to be symbolic, the Bible must interpret the symbol with a *relevant* text. The language used in this prophecy is not symbolic. The phrase, "To him who is thirsty I will give to drink without cost from the spring of the water of life" is considered parallel language. Consider these two passages:

"Come, all you who are thirsty, come to the waters; and you who have no money, come, buy, and eat! Come, buy wine and milk without money and without cost. Why spend money on what is not bread, and your labor on what does not satisfy? Listen, listen to me, and eat what is good, and your soul will delight in the richest of fare."[2]

"Then the angel showed me the river of the water of life, as clear as crystal, flowing from the throne of God and of the Lamb down the middle of the great street of the city. On each side of the river stood the tree of life, bearing twelve crops of fruit, yielding its fruit every month. And the leaves of the tree are for the healing of the nations."[3]

Rule Four is not used in this prophecy.

References
1. 1 John 2:16
2. Isaiah 55:1,2
3. Revelation 22:1,2

The Angel's Second Visit

Revelation 21:9-22:21

Introduction

You may recall in our study on Revelation 17 that Jesus sent one of the angels having the seven bowls to explain what John had seen previously. In that setting, John was carried away in the Spirit into a desert and while there, he saw a richly adorned harlot sitting upon the composite beast which was covered with blasphemous names. The beast had seven heads and ten horns.[1] The final verses in Revelation are similar to Revelation 17. Once again, Jesus sends one of the seven angels to John with more information. However, this time John is not carried into a desert, but instead he is carried to a high mountain where the angel shows him the bride of Christ, New Jerusalem.

Many Bible students do not agree whether Christ's bride in Revelation 21:9 is His church (the saints) or His city (New Jerusalem). The solution to this confusion is the dual role of Jesus. Jesus is King of kings (the Ruler of the city) and Lord of lords (the Head of His church). In terms of kinship, affection, and worship, the bride of Christ is His church (the saints).[2] In terms of a kingdom and government, the bride of Christ is a glorious city filled with happy and holy citizens.[3]

The Sequence

{9} One of the seven angels of the seven last plagues said, "Come with me John, I will show you the bride. The wife of the Lamb is the glorious kingdom which the Father has given to Him."[4] {10} He carried me away in the Spirit to a great, high mountain. He showed me the Holy City, Jerusalem, coming down from Heaven where Jesus lives.

Rev. 21:9-10

And there came unto me one of the seven angels which had the seven vials full of the seven last plagues, and talked with me, saying, Come hither, I will show thee the bride, the Lamb's wife. And he carried me away in the spirit to a great and high mountain, and showed me that great city, the holy Jerusalem, descending out of heaven from God,

---

Jesus' Final Victory

The Angel's Second Visit

Rev. 21:11-14

Having the glory of God: and her light was like unto a stone most precious, even like a jasper stone, clear as crystal; And had a wall great and high, and had twelve gates, and at the gates twelve angels, and names written thereon, which are the names of the twelve tribes of the children of Israel: On the east three gates; on the north three gates; on the south three gates; and on the west three gates. And the wall of the city had twelve foundations, and in them the names of the twelve apostles of the Lamb.

Rev. 21:15

And he that talked with me had a golden reed to measure the city, and the gates thereof, and the wall thereof.

{11} The city shone with the glory of God, and its brilliance was like that of a very precious jewel, like a jasper, clear as crystal. {12} It had a great, high wall with twelve gates, and with twelve angels welcoming visitors at its gates. The names of the twelve tribes of Israel were written on the city's gates. {13} The city faced north, south, east, and west. There were three gates on the east, three on the north, three on the south, and three on the west. {14} The wall of the city had twelve foundations, and on them were the names of the twelve apostles of the Lamb.

{15} The angel who talked with me had a measuring rod of gold to measure the city, its gates and its walls. {16} The city was laid out in a square, as long as it was wide. The angel measured the city with his measuring stick and found it to be 12,000 stadia (1,420 miles) on each side. The city was as tall as it was wide. The city is a giant cube! {17} The angel measured its wall and according to the Roman cubit, it was 216 feet thick. {18} The wall was made of jasper, and the city of pure gold, as pure as glass.

Physical Size

I believe that God revealed the physical dimensions of New Jerusalem to John to insure that human beings would understand the *physical* nature of the Holy City. The Holy City is not a mirage or a ghost town; it is a three dimensional reality. The New Jerusalem is 12,000 stadia or furlongs in length, width, and height and the city wall is 144 cubits thick. A Roman furlong was 625 feet in John's day and a cubit was 18 inches. Therefore, 12,000 furlongs is approximately 1,420 miles and a wall 144 cubits thick is approximately 216 feet thick. Even though we have to accept the measurements given at face value, I do not have a perfect solution for the enormous dimensions of the Holy City in terms of Earth's size and mass. It is hard to imagine a 1,420 mile cube sitting on Earth's surface. For the sake of comparison, Earth's diameter is 8,000 miles. Earth's atmosphere is 62 miles high and the International Space Station orbits Earth about 200 miles up. Can you imagine living about half way up the Holy City (say, at mile marker 710) and looking *down* on the International Space Station 500 miles below?

In an effort to rationalize the size of the Holy City and the physical parameters of Earth, please consider two suggestions. First, suppose planet Earth could be expanded to the size of

Saturn at the end of the 1,000 years. If so, a 1,420 mile cube sitting on the surface would not be such a problem. The diameter of Saturn is about ten times the size of Earth. To put this in perspective, 764 planets the size of Earth can fit within Saturn.

The second possibility is one that I favor. I have wondered if the shape of Earth will be changed at the end of the 1,000 years from that of a sphere to that of a toroid. (A toroid looks like a doughnut with a hole in the middle.) Suppose that when the New Jerusalem descends from Heaven, the Mount of Olives splits from East to West as the Scripture says, and a great valley (actually, a large hole) opens up through the middle of the Earth to accommodate the city of God.[5] In this scenario, Earth would flatten out to look something like a huge doughnut revolving around the celestial Cube of God which faces north, south, east, and west. This physical arrangement would insure that everyone is close to God's throne, no matter where on Earth he lived!

We know that the holy city will not need the light of the Sun or the moon, for the glory of God will be its light.[6] The Bible also says that God Himself will live among men.[7] I mention these two facts because Jesus might have a special purpose for planet Earth. Jesus may take Earth out of its orbit around the Sun, since the Sun will not be needed. Jesus could use this planet as a giant "motor home" that travels throughout the universe. If so, the saints would see and visit an infinite number of galaxies and worlds which the Lamb will create during eternity to come. Think about this, New Jerusalem could become something like a huge "RV" where happiness and joy, homes and gardens, animals and victorious human beings will live forever with God. I know this is wishful speculation, but the Bible says we cannot conceive the wonderful things that God has prepared for His children.[8] Nevertheless, I like the idea of the redeemed being known throughout the universe as "happy campers."

The Sequence Continues

{19} The foundations of the city walls were decorated with every kind of precious stone. The first foundation was jasper, the second sapphire, the third chalcedony, the fourth emerald, {20} the fifth sardonyx, the sixth carnelian, the seventh chrysolite, the eighth beryl, the ninth topaz, the tenth chrysoprase, the eleventh jacinth, and the twelfth amethyst. {21} There were twelve gates and each gate was made of a single pearl. The great street in the city was

---

Rev. 21:16-18

And the city lieth foursquare, and the length is as large as the breadth: and he measured the city with the reed, twelve thousand furlongs. The length and the breadth and the height of it are equal. And he measured the wall thereof, an hundred and forty and four cubits, according to the measure of a man, that is, of the angel. And the building of the wall of it was of jasper: and the city was pure gold, like unto clear glass.

Rev. 21:19

And the foundations of the wall of the city were garnished with all manner of precious stones. The first foundation was jasper; the second, sapphire; the third, a chalcedony; the fourth, an emerald;

> **Rev. 21:20-22**
>
> The fifth, sardonyx; the sixth, sardius; the seventh, chrysolyte; the eighth, beryl; the ninth, a topaz; the tenth, a chrysoprasus; the eleventh, a jacinth; the twelfth, an amethyst. And the twelve gates were twelve pearls: every several gate was of one pearl: and the street of the city was pure gold, as it were transparent glass. And I saw no temple therein: for the Lord God Almighty and the Lamb are the temple of it.
>
> **Rev. 21:23-24**
>
> And the city had no need of the sun, neither of the moon, to shine in it: for the glory of God did lighten it, and the Lamb is the light thereof. And the nations of them which are saved shall walk in the light of it: and the kings of the earth do bring their glory and honour into it.

made of pure gold that looked like transparent glass. Words cannot describe the beauty and glory of God's city.

{22} I did not see a temple in the city, because the Lord God Almighty and the Lamb are its temple. People in the Holy City will not worship in a temple because they will worship the living God, wherever He happens to be!

> A temple became necessary in Heaven when sin began. The plan of salvation required a command and control center and this made it necessary for God to establish a temple in Heaven. Before sin existed, there was no need for altars and atonement. When the work of the Two Witnesses is completed on Earth, there will be no need for altars and atonement. Thus, the temple in Heaven will be vacated.[9] During the 1,000 years, the saints will return to Heaven and they will sit (reign) with Jesus in Heaven's courtroom to determine the amount of restitution which must be extracted from the wicked. After this phase of judgment is completed, the temple will be forever eliminated. It will have no further purpose because the problem of sin will be concluded. When the Holy City descends at the end of the 1,000 years, it will not have a temple in it. The Father and Son will be worshiped wherever they present themselves.

{23} The city does not need the sun or the moon to shine on it, for the glory of God gives it light, and the Lamb is its lamp. {24} The redeemed of all nations will walk by their light, and the 144,000 (the kings of the new Earth) will bring their splendor into it. {25} The gates of Heaven will never be closed, for there will be no darkness or fear there. {26} God will bring the glory and honor of all the redeemed from every nation, kindred, tongue, and people into Heaven. {27} Nothing impure will ever enter the Holy City, and no one who does anything shameful or deceitful will be permitted to enter. Only those people whose names are found written in the Lamb's Book of Life will live in this city.

{22:1} Then the angel showed me the river of the water of life that is clear as crystal. It flows from the throne of God and of the Lamb, {2} down the middle of the great street of the city. On each side of the river stood the tree of life, bearing twelve crops of fruit, yielding its fruit every month. The leaves of the tree will be for the healing of the redeemed from all nations.

> Because of rebellion and sin, God separated mankind at the Tower of Babel. God imposed different languages on Noah's descendants and language caused the people to distance themselves from one another. As time progressed, differences in cultures separated the human family and differences in religion produced a "wall of separation" that is very difficult, even to this day, to overcome. After Jesus destroys the sin problem, the shade provided by the leaves on the Tree of Life will become a joyful meeting place. A diverse human family will become acquainted with one another and united as one family again.

Rev. 21:25-17
And the gates of it shall not be shut at all by day: for there shall be no night there. And they shall bring the glory and honour of the nations into it. And there shall in no wise enter into it any thing that defileth, neither whatsoever worketh abomination, or maketh a lie: but they which are written in the Lamb's book of life.

Rev. 22:1-2
And he showed me a pure river of water of life, clear as crystal, proceeding out of the throne of God and of the Lamb. In the midst of the street of it, and on either side of the river, was there the tree of life, which bare twelve manner of fruits, and yielded her fruit every month: and the leaves of the tree were for the healing of the nations.

Rev. 22:3-5

And there shall be no more curse: but the throne of God and of the Lamb shall be in it; and his servants shall serve him: And they shall see his face; and his name shall be in their foreheads. And there shall be no night there; and they need no candle, neither light of the sun; for the Lord God giveth them light: and they shall reign for ever and ever.

Rev. 22:6-7

And he said unto me, These sayings are faithful and true: and the Lord God of the holy prophets sent his angel to show unto his servants the things which must shortly be done. Behold, I come quickly: blessed is he that keepeth the sayings of the prophecy of this book.

{3} The curse of sin will not exist in the holy city. Everywhere, there will be joy and life! The throne of God and of the Lamb will be in the city, and His 144,000 servants will serve Him. {4} They will see the face of Jesus,[10] and His name and the Father's name[11] will be written on their foreheads. {5} Never again will there be darkness. God's people will not need a lamp or light produced by the Sun, for the Lord God will give them light; and they will reign as priests and kings forever and ever.[12]

{6} I saw Jesus standing in Heaven as the captain of a mighty host. Appearing as Michael, the archangel, whom I had seen earlier[13] he said to me, "The words you have heard and what you have seen are trustworthy and true. I am the Lord of hosts, the God of the spirits of the prophets, and I have sent my angel to show you and my servants the events that must soon occur. {7} Behold, I am coming soon! Blessed is he who keeps the words of the prophecy in this book in his heart and mind."

{8} When I heard and saw these things, I fell down to worship at the feet of the angel who had come to explain these things to me. {9} But he said, "Do not do it! I am a fellow servant with you and with your brothers the prophets and of all who keep the words of this book. Worship God!"

> **Rev. 22:8-9**
> *And I John saw these things, and heard them. And when I had heard and seen, I fell down to worship before the feet of the angel which showed me these things. Then saith he unto me, See thou do it not: for I am thy fellowservant, and of thy brethren the prophets, and of them which keep the sayings of this book: worship God.*

{10} Then He (Michael, the archangel) spoke to me again, "Do not seal up the words of the prophecy of this book, because the time is near. {11} Let him who does wrong continue to do wrong; let him who is vile continue to be vile; let him who does right continue to do right; and let him who is holy continue to be holy.

> **Rev. 22:10-11**
> *And he saith unto me, Seal not the sayings of the prophecy of this book: for the time is at hand. He that is unjust, let him be unjust still: and he which is filthy, let him be filthy still: and he that is righteous, let him be righteous still: and he that is holy, let him be holy still.*

> **Rev. 22:12-13**
>
> *And, behold, I come quickly; and my reward is with me, to give every man according as his work shall be. I am Alpha and Omega, the beginning and the end, the first and the last.*

{12} Behold, I am coming soon! My reward is with me, and I will give to everyone according to what he has done. {13} I am the Alpha and the Omega, the First and the Last, the Beginning and the End."

Several times in the book of Revelation, the return of Jesus and the end of the age is described as "near" and "soon."[14] At first glance, Jesus' use of these two words seems to indicate an imminent return and this has puzzled Bible students for two thousand years. Because two thousand years have passed since Jesus uttered these words, some scholars have concluded that the words "near" and "soon" should be understood from God's point of view, that a day is as a thousand years.[15]

I believe there is a better explanation. The book of Revelation was given to benefit mankind, *especially* those who would live at the end of the age. John was told in A.D. 95, "Do not seal up the words of the prophecy of this book," because there are many profound truths about Jesus in the book of Revelation that are timeless. (See Appendix D) However, the words "near" and "soon" do indicate an imminent return and they should be taken at face value. *When the time of fulfillment arrives, the words "soon" and "near" will mean what they say.* This solution is timing is supported in verse 11 on the previous page. Jesus said to John, "Let him who does wrong continue to do wrong; let him who is vile continue to be vile; let him who does right continue to do right; and let him who is holy continue to be holy." If Jesus' words are taken at face value starting with A.D. 95, this means no one can change his behavior and the words of Jesus in verse 17 are in conflict with His words in verse 11. Jesus says in verse 17, "whoever is thirsty and whoever wishes, let him come and take the free gift of the water of life." The solution to the *apparent* conflict is simple. If verse 11 is understood to be a benediction of redemption's offer (that is, it occurs at the end of the 1,260 days granted to His Two Witnesses), the benediction makes perfect sense *when the proper time arrives.*

> **Rev. 22:14-16**
>
> *Blessed are they that do his commandments, that they may have right to the tree of life, and may enter in through the gates into the city. For without are dogs, and sorcerers, and whoremongers, and murderers, and idolaters, and whosoever loveth and maketh a lie. I Jesus have sent mine angel to testify unto you these things in the churches. I am the root and the offspring of David, and the bright and morning star.*

{14} Michael/Jesus, the archangel continued to speak, "Blessed are those who wash their robes, that they may have the right to the tree of life and may go through the gates into the city. {15} Outside are the dogs, those who practice magic arts, the sexually immoral, the murderers, the idolaters and everyone who loves and practices falsehood. {16} I have sent my angel to give you this testimony for the seven churches. I am the Root and the Offspring of

David, and the bright Morning Star. {17} The Spirit and the bride say, 'Come!' And let him who hears say, 'Come!' Whoever is thirsty, let him come; and whoever wishes, let him take the free gift of the water of life. {18} I warn everyone who hears the words of the prophecy of this book: If anyone adds anything to them, God will add to him the plagues described in this book. {19} And if anyone takes words away from this book of prophecy, God will take away from him his share in the tree of life and in the holy city, which are described in this book." {20} He who speaks these things says, " Yes, I am coming soon. Amen."

"Yes!" John added, "Come, Lord Jesus. {21} The grace of the Lord Jesus be with God's people. Amen, so be it."

> **Rev. 22:17-21**
>
> *And the Spirit and the bride say, Come. And let him that heareth say, Come. And let him that is athirst come. And whosoever will, let him take the water of life freely. For I testify unto every man that heareth the words of the prophecy of this book, If any man shall add unto these things, God shall add unto him the plagues that are written in this book: And if any man shall take away from the words of the book of this prophecy, God shall take away his part out of the book of life, and out of the holy city, and from the things which are written in this book. He which testifieth these things saith, Surely I come quickly. Amen. Even so, come, Lord Jesus. The grace of our Lord Jesus Christ be with you all. Amen.*

Adding to and Subtracting from the Book of Revelation

God promises a blessing for everyone who will read and attempt to understand the book of Revelation.[16] He also promises to put a curse on anyone who adds or subtracts anything from this book. This curse can be viewed on two different levels. First, in ancient times, there were no copy machines. Everything had to be copied by hand. Therefore, God's warning could be understood as a promised curse for anyone who might distort or change the wording on this mysterious book. Perhaps Jesus said this to ensure that the final generation would have a perfect copy of John's original document.

The second view of the curse is larger and more complex. This view involves the interpretation of Revelation's story. A day is coming when the 144,000 will present the book of Revelation to the people of Earth *as a testing truth*. At that time, anyone adding to or subtracting from the book of Revelation will be cursed.

Of course, God knows that down through the ages, honest and sincere people have tried to understand the amazing books of Daniel and Revelation. Today, there is a great deal of *honest* confusion about apocalyptic prophecy. Even though most of what is presently said about Revelation is wrong (according to Daniel's four rules), God does not hold a person accountable for ignorance unless he knows better and continues to do evil anyway or he rejects the clearest evidences of truth or the prompting of the Holy Spirit. In other words, the curse pronounced in Revelation 22:18,19 will only occur when people knowingly and willingly alter the book of Revelation to justify their rebellion against God's laws. This time has not yet occurred because the world has not been confronted with a testing truth. Soon, the 144,000 and the Two Witnesses will proclaim the story contained in Revelation in the clearest of terms and those who willfully attempt to distort or change the story will be cursed.

Remember, Holy Spirit power will rest upon the 144,000 and they alone will present the four angel's messages to the world. (See Prophecies 12 and 14.) For 1,260 days every nation, kindred, tongue, and people will hear from the book of Revelation in their own language. The world will hear a pure gospel, the eternal gospel of Jesus Christ. The gospel of Jesus given today is highly contaminated with human doctrine. If you disagree, just step back and look at the confusion that is called Christianity.

The Bible says no lie will be found in the mouths of the 144,000.[17] The 144,000 will challenge the lies (and laws) of Babylon. Babylon will intensely persecute anyone who opposes its lies. Do not forget, Babylon will wield great power because the devil will give Babylon its great power and authority. To counteract God's 144,000 servants, the devil will empower a large number of false prophets. Of course, I do not know the actual number of the devil's false prophets, but I do recall that one true prophet (Elijah) faced down 450 false prophets on Mount Carmel.[18] I am looking forward to the day when God's 144,000 servants will present the book of Revelation to the world with power and authority and God's penetrating truth will separate the sheep from the goats. Many will refuse to believe the truth,[19] but many will also embrace the two laws of love and be saved!

Final Words

I cannot adequately explain the love, grace, mercy, or patience of God as He deals with sinners (including me) within the pages of this book. I cannot adequately explain the dimensions of the plan of redemption which the Father designed before the world was created and put into motion on the day that sin began. I cannot adequately explain the joy and peace that comes from knowing and abiding in Christ. I cannot explain the comforting companionship of the Holy Spirit. Even after forty years of Bible study, I cannot adequately explain the Bible or the books of Daniel and Revelation because I consider myself still a beginner. As I wrote this book, there were times I wanted to quit because there is so much to the story of redemption that it is overwhelming. Where does one start? How does one organize an overwhelming number of facts? What are the best words to use and when should certain details be presented? My desire has been to write the facts so that readers can easily follow the story. I have done my best and the book is finished, even though I consider it an inadequate product.

I am so thankful that God gave us the books of Daniel and Revelation. They provide a wonderful roadmap for the end time scenario. We have a chance to understand Jesus' coming actions. As I have explained, I believe the revealing of Jesus Christ began in 1798 and that it will quickly accelerate during the Great Tribulation. I eagerly anticipate the revelation of Jesus (the breaking of the fourth seal) because the human race desperately needs to reconnect with its Creator. The curse of sin has placed the world in darkness and rebellion. The curse of sin has caused endless sorrow, suffering, violence, illness, and death. The curse of sin has spawned predators who prey upon children, the elderly and anyone who they can overpower. The curse of sin has led man to put his faith in money and his love to be displaced by lust. Man's character is corrupt and loyalty to ennobling principles has vanished. It is the curse of sin that causes God's wrath to come, and it surely will come.

The curse of sin left Jesus to face several challenges. First, Lucifer's jealous hatred focused on Jesus in Heaven, and the it focused on Adam and Eve, two people who Jesus loved enough to die in their place. Then, Lucifer's attention moved toward the destruction of the world, but Jesus saved eight souls in Noah's day. As time progressed, Lucifer focused on Israel, but Jesus saved a remnant (His Church) out of Israel. Lucifer focused on Baby Jesus, only to have His parents be given a warning to escape. Lucifer tried again by sealing Jesus in the tomb of death, only to have Jesus released. Lucifer fought against Jesus in Heaven on Resurrection Sunday, but Jesus prevailed. Thrown to Earth, Lucifer focused on the woman, the bride of Christ, but she too, escaped. Let me be clear, Lucifer will soon persecute the remnant of the woman, but a remnant will live to see Jesus appear at the Second Coming! In his attempt to conquer Jesus and His creation, Lucifer will lead the kings and armies of Earth to make war on Jesus, but Jesus will destroy them. Finally, at the end of the 1,000 years, Lucifer will lead a numberless multitude against New Jerusalem, but fire will come down from God, out of Heaven, and burn them up.

A day is coming when Satan will make his last stand and Jesus will rise up and annihilate the devil and all who are like him. Yet, there is one final victory that I am sure Jesus is anxious to complete – to destroy death itself. When Jesus destroys the curse of sin, death will no longer exist in God's universe. Finally, God's house will be free of the cancer of sin!

"Then the end [of sin's drama] **will come, when he** [Jesus] **hands over the kingdom to God the Father after he has destroyed all** [earthly] **dominion, authority and power. For he** [Jesus] **must reign** [as Sovereign God] **until he has put all his enemies under his feet. The last enemy to be destroyed is death. For he** [the Father] **'has put everything under his feet.' Now when it says that 'everything' has been put un-**

der him [Jesus], **it is clear that this does not include God** [the Father] **himself, who put everything under Christ. When he** [Jesus] **has done this** [that is, destroyed death itself]**, then the Son himself will be made subject to him who put everything under him, so that God** [the Father] **may be all in all."**[20]

Most people do not realize that the final victory of Jesus has a surprise ending. Instead of remaining on the throne of God and basking forever in the glory of His incredible accomplishments, Jesus will become a subject (a son) of God all over again because His greatest joy is living among those He has created. What humility! What kindness and compassion! What love! And here I go again, having no words to adequately describe our Savior and friend, Jesus.

References
1. Revelation 17:3,4
2. Revelation 19:7
3. Isaiah 9:6; Revelation 11:2; 21:9
4. Psalm 2:7-12; John 17:6,7; Daniel 7:13,14
5. Zechariah 14:4-6
6. Revelation 21:23
7. Revelation 21:3
8. 1 Corinthians 2:9
9. Revelation 15:5-8
10. Evidently, the Father's face cannot be seen and will not be seen throughout eternity. See John 6:46; 1:18; and 1 Timothy 6:15,16. Daniel saw a representation of the Father (Daniel 7:9,10) and John saw His hand (Revelation 5:7).
11. Revelation 14:1
12. Revelation 1:6
13. Revelation 1:1; 10:1
14. Revelation 1:1; 1:3; 3:11; 22:6,10,20
15. 2 Peter 3:8
16. Revelation 1:3
17. Revelation 14:5
18. See Revelation 13:4; 1 Kings 18:20-22.
19. 2 Thessalonians 2:9-12
20. 1 Corinthians 15:24-28, insertions mine

Epilogue
A Chronological Outline

In the Introduction to this book I wrote that my conclusions are derived from five essential Bible doctrines (discussed at length in the book, *Jesus: The Alpha and The Omega*) and four self-evident rules of interpretation which are found in the book of Daniel.

Chronological order is a critical part of apocalyptic prophecy because God Himself has declared the order of events within each prophecy. The human challenge is to properly divide the books of Daniel and Revelation into distinct prophecies so that religious bias or personal whim does not manipulate God's chronology. God has declared the divine order in the books of Daniel and Revelation. If God's declaration is not true, two insurmountable problems would arise. First, there is no authority on Earth who can tell the whole world what the order of coming events will be. Second, without God providing His chronological order, confusion would reign and Bible students would not have confidence in "the more sure word of prophecy." Some people claim that God gave us prophecy so that we can see His providence *after* prophecy has been fulfilled. My response to this argument is, "What is the point of understanding the mark of the beast after it is imposed?" Jesus told His disciples, "I have told you now *before it happens*, so that when it does happen you will believe." (John 14:29, italics mine)

Over the years, people have asked for charts and outlines of coming events. I have many charts available showing the relationships between the seventeen prophecies. (See http://www.wake-up.org/Charts/ChartIndex.htm.) Because of the huge quantity of information and the small paper size in this book, a *comprehensive* chart showing the alignment of all seventeen prophecies is not possible, but a simple, abbreviated chart is provide on pages 4-5. I have also compressed the seventeen prophecies into two short verbal outlines. Section I (taken from the book of Daniel) starts with the ancient empire of Nebuchadnezzar and extends to the Second Coming. Section II (taken from the book of Revelation) starts with the birth of Jesus and extends to the end of the 1,000 years.

Section 1 - Daniel

Event	Kingdom	Date
1. Head of gold / Lion	Babylon	538 B.C.
2. Chest of silver / Bear / Ram	Medo-Persia	538 - 331 B.C.
A. 2,300 years begin		457 B.C.
B. 70 weeks begin		457 B.C.
C. Israel caught between kings in the north and south		457 B.C.
3. Things of brass / Leopard / Goat	Grecia	331 - 168 B.C.
4. Legs of iron / Monster	Rome	A.D. 168 - 476
A. Messiah's ministry and death		A.D. 27 - 30
B. Rome utterly destroys Jerusalem		A.D. 70
5. Little horn rises and persecutes saints 1,260 years	Papal Rule	538 B.C. - 1798
6. Cleansing of Heaven's temple begins at the end of the 2,300 years		1844 to present
7. Horn power from the north / Stern faced king appears -- this horn power is the physical appearing of Lucifer (fifth trumpet)		Shortly before the Second Coming
8. Michael stands up / Time of great trouble (seven bowls)		
9. Resurrection at the end of the 1,335 days		

Section 2 - Revelation

Event	Date
1. War occurs between Christ and Satan before world was created	
2. Satan attempts to kill Jesus at birth	4 B.C.
3. During His time on Earth, Jesus is victorious over sin – redeems mankind	
The devil is cast out of Heaven a second time	A.D. 30
4. Jesus is found worthy to receive a kingdom and The Book of Life	1798
5. Jesus breaks open the first three seals (the revealing of Jesus begins)	
First seal 1798 / Salvation through Jesus alone	
Second seal 1800 / The translation and distribution of the Bible	
Third seal 1844 / Judgment of the dead begins	
6. God's patience ends / Jubilee Calendar expires	
The seven angels were given the seven trumpets	1994
7. A delay – waiting for appointed time to arrive (we are currently living in this delay)	1994 to present
8. Nuclear war breaks out on earth? / World leaders call for peace and safety	
9. The 144,000 are selected, sealed, and empowered	
10. Censer is cast down / Global earthquake / God's wrath begins	
Two Witnesses begin work / 1,260 days	
11. 144,000 proclaim first message: "Fear God, worship the Creator"	
12. Fourth seal broken / 25% of Earth's population is destroyed	
First four trumpet judgments occur / Fiery hailstorm, two asteroid impacts, darkness	
13. Crisis government is formed and given power	
Babylon persecutes the saints for 42 months	
Babylon is the composite beast with seven heads and ten horns	

14. 144,000 proclaim second message: "Babylon is false, it is the work of the devil"

15. Fifth trumpet occurs 890 days into the Great Tribulation

    The devil physically appears masquerading as God

    The devil is the lamblike beast who deceives the whole world

16. 144,000 proclaim third message: "If you worship the devil, God will punish you"

17. Sixth trumpet occurs 148 days later

    The devil sets up a one world church state (theocracy)

    The devil rules as king of kings and lord of lords

    Fifth seal broken / Martyrdom

    The devil kills one-third of mankind / Imposes tattoo / Mark of the beast

18. Two Witnesses are slain on the 1,260th day / 144,000 are dead for 3.5 days

19. 144,000 resurrected / Taken to Heaven

    Seventh trumpet sounds / Ark of the Covenant shown in sky

    First four bowls poured out / Those having the mark suffer greatly

20. Fifth bowl / Lucifer unmasked / His officials and employees blinded

21. Sixth bowl / Lucifer gathers the kings of Earth to make war against Jesus

22. Seventh bowl / Jesus appears / All of the wicked are destroyed

    Saints meet the Lord in the air / Earth is desolate / No life on Earth

23. Jesus takes the saints to the Holy City, New Jerusalem for 1,000 years

    The devil is bound in the abyss during the 1,000 years

24. The saints reign with Jesus in Heaven

    Victims determine the amount of suffering the wicked must suffer (restitution)

25. At the end of the 1,000 years, Holy City descends from Heaven

26. The wicked of all ages are resurrected to meet their Creator and receive their sentence

27. Every knee bows admitting that God has been more than fair in His judgment

28. Seventh seal broken open, contents of The Book of Life exposed

>   God completely exonerated

29. The devil urges the wicked to attack the Holy City

30. Fire comes down from God and burns them up

31. Jesus wipes away the tears

32. Jesus creates a new Heaven and a new Earth

33. The meek inherit the Earth

Appendix A

The Importance of 1994

> "And I saw the seven angels who stand before
> God, and to them were given seven trumpets."
> (Revelation 8:2)

Revelation 8:2 and 1994

For those who are willing to invest the time to study, the following sections explain why I believe that 1994 is the date the seven angels were given the seven trumpets, as described in Revelation 8:2. For a more thorough study on this topic, please refer to my paper, *Great Clocks from God* which can also be downloaded at http://www.wake-up.org/daystar/ds2000/Great%20Clocks.htm.

1. Two Different Ways of Measuring Time

In apocalyptic prophecy, God *sometimes* measures time according to the operation of the Jubilee Calendar in which a day is translated as a year. For example, the seventy weeks in Daniel 9:24 contain 490 days (seventy weeks x seven days/week = 490 days). The 490 days are *translated* as 490 years because they occur during the operation of God's Jubilee Calendar. History confirms that this translation is warranted and correct. On the other hand, other instances of apocalyptic prophecy are found when God does not translate time as a day for a year. Examples when a day is to be understood as literal time include the 1,000 years in Revelation 20:2, the five months in Revelation 9:5, the 1,260 days granted to the Two Witnesses, and the forty-two months in Revelation 13:5. One significant challenge to interpreting apocalyptic prophecy is understanding when God uses a day for a year or literal time.

I believe there is a rule in Scripture that answers this question. The fourth rule governing the interpretation of apocalyptic prophecy says, "The presence or absence of the Jubilee Calendar determines how God measures time in apocalyptic prophecy." In other words, when the Jubilee Calendar is operating, God wants us to translate a day for a year according to His Calendar. On the other hand, when the Jubilee Calendar is not operating, there is no translation.

A rule of interpretation has no exception. As an example, the "seven times" imposed on King Nebuchadnezzar does not require translation because the prophecy directed at him is not an apocalyptic prophecy, and the king could not eat grass for 2,520 years (360 x 7 = 2,520 years). The prophecy concerning King Nebuchadnezzar was a "local prophecy" directed at a specific person. Each type of prophecy has its own rules, and they cannot be mixed or merged without putting the Bible in a state of internal conflict. There are five types of prophecy in the Bible and these were discussed in detail in the Introduction.

2. The Jubilee Calendar

God created the Jubilee Calendar. It is incredibly precise and God put this calendar in motion two weeks *before* the Exodus in 1437 B.C. By divine decree, God forced Israel to abandon their use of the Egyptian calendar (a summer-to-summer calendar) when He imposed His spring-to-spring Jubilee Calendar.[1] Three topics within the Jubilee Calendar need to be discussed to show how 1994 connects with the book of Revelation.

   A. Even though God required Israel to let the land rest from cultivation every seventh year, Israel did not observe the seventh year Sabbath rest while in the desert. (This makes sense since they did not grow crops in the desert.) However, the wording in Leviticus 25:2-4 causes some people to think that cycles of seven years began when Israel entered Canaan. This understanding is incorrect. God started counting cycles of seven years at the time of the Exodus and the proof only takes two steps. First, we have to align the date of Christ's death with the middle of the seventieth week and second, we have to identify one Jubilee year.

   For reasons beyond the scope of this study, it can be proven beyond reasonable argument that Jesus died on Friday, April 7, A.D. 30. (For a comprehensive study on this topic, see my book, *Daniel, Unlocked for the Final Generation*, pages 196-208 or go to this link http://www.wake-up.org/Daniel/DanChap6.htm.) Once the date of the crucifixion is determined, we learn the *synchrony* of the weekly cycle of years because Daniel 9 declares that Messiah would die in *the middle of the seventieth week*. Therefore, A.D. 30 has to be a Wednesday year because Wednesday is always the middle day of the week. By knowing A.D. 30 was a Wednesday year, we can identify all Sunday years forward and backward. For example, A.D. 27 and 457 B.C. were Sunday years.

The second step requires the identification of one Jubilee year. If one Jubilee year is known, then Jubilee cycles can be calculated forward and backward like days of the week. Fortunately, there is one Jubilee year that is easily identified. It occurred during the fifteenth year of Hezekiah's reign.[2] Since Jubilee years always fell on Sunday years, this forces Hezekiah's Jubilee year to be 702 B.C. All other dates have to be eliminated because known historical events do not align with that Jubilee year. (Many scholars, knowing nothing about the synchrony of the weekly cycle of years and the operation of the Jubilee Calendar, date Hezekiah's Jubilee at 701 B.C. This shows that good scholarship can get close to the truth, but sometimes there are limitations. History can resolve questions to a point, but sometimes, history cannot precisely pinpoint the specific year.) Jubilee years are forty-nine years apart and because Jubilee years are always Sunday years, we can precisely identify the Jubilee year during Hezekiah's reign. By counting forward or backward in forty-nine year intervals from 702 B.C., we find that God started the Jubilee Calendar on Abib 1, 1437 B.C., two weeks before the Exodus! No other date is historically possible. (This topic is discussed at length in my booklet, *Great Clocks from God* or go to this link http://www.wake-up.org/daystar/ds2000/Great%20Clocks.htm.)

B. God treats the synchrony of time in a different way than we commonly treat time today. First, God counts time inclusively. Any portion of a unit of time counts as a whole unit of time. For example, Jesus spent a portion of Friday, all of Sabbath, and a portion of Sunday in the tomb. Jesus counted this as three days and three nights.[3] All prophetic time periods are counted this way. This explains how Luke counted A.D. 27 as the fifteenth year of Tiberius Caesar, even though Tiberius took office on September 17, A.D. 14.[4]

History records that Augustus died on August 19, A.D. 14. Tiberius maneuvered the Senate for a few weeks and did not allow it to name him emperor for almost a month. On September 17, A.D. 27, Tiberius became Emperor of Rome at age 56. This means that Luke followed the Jewish tradition of inclusive dating and counted the ascension year of Tiberius as "year 1," even though the ascension year was just a few days in length before a new civil year began on Tishri 1. Josephus also followed this practice when he dated the reigns of the Herods.[5] The Mishnah further confirmed this method of Jewish regnal reckoning.[6]

During the time of Christ, the Jews also observed a fall-to-fall civil calendar. The first month of this calendar was the seventh month of the religious year called Tishri. Tiberius ascended to the throne on September 17, A.D. 14, during a Jewish civil year that ended about two months later (November 11, A.D. 14.) So, Luke counted September 17 to November 11 as "year 1" because Tiberius, counting inclusively, ascended to the throne that year. Therefore, the Jews regarded the following civil year Tishri 1 to Tishri 1 (November 12, A.D. 14 to October 31, A.D. 15), as the second year of Tiberius' reign.

Luke's Account: The Reign of Tiberius Caesar

Year 1 = A.D. 14/14 (September 17 - November 11)
Year 2 = A.D. 14/15 (Tishri 1 to Tishri 1)
Year 3 = A.D. 15/16 (Tishri 1 to Tishri 1)
Year 4 = A.D. 16/17 Etc.
Year 5 = A.D. 17/18
Year 6 = A.D. 18/19
Year 7 = A.D. 19/20
Year 8 = A.D. 20/21
Year 9 = A.D. 21/22
Year 10 = A.D. 22/23
Year 11 = A.D. 23/24
Year 12 = A.D. 24/25
Year 13 = A.D. 25/26
Year 14 = A.D. 26/27
Year 15 = A.D. 27/28 (Jesus baptized after Tishri 1, A.D. 27)

God also treats His weekly cycle in a different way than we commonly do. For example, God starts a *week* with Sunday, the first day of the *week*. We casually define a week as any period of seven days, but this is *never* the case in God's calendar. When it comes to God's clocks, there is a big difference between seven days and a week. God's seventh day Sabbath and God's seventh year rest for the land are determined by the first day of Creation and the first year of the Exodus, respectively.

C. One Jubilee cycle contained seven full weeks of seven years each. Thus, a Jubilee cycle was forty-nine years in length. The forty-ninth year always fell on a Sabbath year that was synchronous with Israel's deliverance from Egypt.[7] *The weekly cycle is the basis for translating time – "a day for a year."*[8] The Year of Jubilee (the fiftieth year) always fell on the Sunday year that followed the forty-ninth Sabbath year. This may seem strange at first, but the fiftieth year of the old Jubilee cycle and the first year of the new Jubilee cycle occurred simultaneously. This method of counting time is confirmed by the Feast of Pentecost.

The Feast of Pentecost (the fiftieth day) was always celebrated on Sunday (the first day of the week). This is how the countdown to Pentecost occurred: Passover fell on different days of the weekly cycle (like our birthdays). The priests waited until the first Sunday following Passover to start counting off forty-nine days (seven full weeks).[9] Then, on the fiftieth day, which was the first day of the eighth week, Israel celebrated the Feast of Pentecost.

Many Bible students believe each Jubilee cycle was fifty years in length. However, Jubilee cycles were forty-nine years in length because (a) the weekly cycle of seven years was not interrupted, (b) the weekly cycle of years remained synchronous with the year of the Exodus (year 1), and (c) the seventy weeks in Daniel 9 totaled 490 years. If Jubilee cycles were fifty years in length as some people claim, it would be mathematically impossible to make the seventy weeks equal 490 years. The seventy weeks are 490 years (70 x 7) and 490 years are ten Jubilee cycles (49 x 10).

You may wonder what the Jubilee Calendar has to do with Revelation 8:2. The Jubilee Calendar appears to be important to Revelation 8:2 because God's patience with mankind appears to be limited to seventy Jubilee cycles. In other words, from the Exodus in 1437 B.C. to 1994, there are seventy Jubilee cycles. I believe that in 1994 the Jubilee

Calendar *ended and Jesus handed the seven trumpets to the seven angels.* I believe that God's patience with sin on Earth ended in 1994 at the close of seventy Jubilee cycles. Jesus gave seven trumpets to the seven angels, and before the angels could release their harm on Earth, He told them to wait. So, Jesus has delayed the first four trumpets from causing the overwhelming destruction that is soon to occur.

Thirty Jubilee Cycles

Because of Abraham's friendship and faithfulness, God chose Abraham's descendants to serve as trustees of His gospel. Unfortunately, for about 800 years, the children of Israel failed to live up to the covenant they made with God at Mt. Sinai. After God exiled Israel to Babylon, He gave the nation a second chance to become the model nation that He wanted to make of them. He graciously granted the Jews ten Jubilee cycles or seventy weeks, which is 490 years!

Bible history reveals that during the Sunday year of the seventieth week (A.D. 27), Messiah began His ministry.[10] However, Israel rejected Messiah's message of love, truth, and righteousness. Instead, they crucified Him.[11] When we examine Israel's history in light of the Jubilee Calendar, we discover a stunning fact: God granted to Israel, down *to the very day*, a total of thirty Jubilee Cycles. (1437 B.C. to A.D. 34) This precision reminds me of Israel's deliverance from Egypt. **"At the end of the 430 years, *to the very day*, all the Lord's divisions left Egypt."**[12] This precision also highlights the fact that the Second Coming will occur on *the very day* which God has predetermined. **"Blessed is the one who waits for and reaches the end of the 1,335 days."**[13]

Forty Jubilee Cycles for the Gentiles

When Israel's thirty Jubilee cycles ended, God started over. He wanted to give the Gentiles their chance as trustees of His gospel. God raised up a brilliant young Jew, Saul of Tarsus, and made him an apostle to the Gentiles in A.D. 34. As a result, the Christian church soon had more Gentile believers in it than Jewish converts. Because there is a New Covenant, the Christian church did not displace Israel; it replaced Israel as trustee. God abolished the Old Covenant by creating a New Covenant. This redefined Israel. Believers in Jesus are now the heirs of Abraham.[14] History confirms that God granted forty Jubilee cycles to the Gentiles! (A.D. 34 to 1994) The proof of this assertion requires three steps:

First, the Jubilee Calendar could not end at the cross because Jesus' death occurred during the *middle* of the seventieth week (A.D. 30 was a Wednesday year), and from our study in Daniel 8 we know that the 2,300 days began *before* the cross and they continue uninterrupted until A.D. 1844. This means the 2,300 days are translated (a day for a year) past the date of the cross, without interruption, *until* 1844. So, at a minimum, we are forced to recognize that the Jubilee Calendar with its day/year translation continued until the Thursday year of 1844. However, the Jubilee Calendar could not end in 1844.

This brings us to the second step. The Jubilee Calendar is divided into three units of time: (a) a week of seven years, (b) seven weeks of seven years, and (c) seventy weeks of seven years. Since history indicates that God granted the Jews thirty Jubilee cycles to the very day, this indicates that the seventy weeks in Daniel 9 is one Great Day (seventy weeks), one unit of time.

The Great Week

I have concluded there are seven Great Days of seventy weeks each. I like to call this week of seven Great Days, the Great Week. If this structure truly exists, the seventy weeks in Daniel 9 becomes the Great Day of Tuesday. It is interesting to note that from the Exodus in the Sunday year of 1437 B.C. to the dedication of Solomon's temple in the Sunday year of 947 B.C., there are exactly seventy weeks or 490 years. (I call this seventy weeks the Great Day of Sunday.) Then, from the dedication of Solomon's temple to the decree of Artaxerxes in the Sunday year of 457 B.C., there is another Great Day of seventy weeks or 490 years. I call this Great Day, Monday. Then, from the decree of Artaxerxes to restore and rebuild Jerusalem to Saul's conversion in the Sunday year of A.D. 34, there is another seventy weeks or 490 years. I call this Great Day, Tuesday. I believe this information provides evidence that a Great Week exists. If so, it would seem reasonable that there are four more Great Days to make up the Great Week since the prophecy describing the 2,300 days does not end until 1844. If we fill the Jubilee Calendar with four more Great Days of seventy weeks each, we end up with The Great Week having seven Great Days. Each Great Day has seventy weeks each, totaling 3,430 years. (1437 B.C. - 1994) So, the Great Week for the Jubilee

Calendar began on Sunday, Nisan 1, 1437 B.C. and it ended 3,430 years (490 x 7) later on Sabbath, Adar 29, 1994.

Once the Great Week ends, the Jubilee Calendar with its weekly template of seven Great Days expires. This leads us to an amazing discovery: All remaining apocalyptic time periods *after* 1994 can occur without the translation of a day for a year. If you can accept the premise that all prophetic time periods occurring *after* 1994 are to be treated as literal units, then everything stated in Scripture will perfectly fold into an even larger calendar called the "Grand Week," a calendar where a day translates into 1,000 years!

The Grand Week

The Grand Week is a week of millenniums totaling 7,000 years. Each day in the Grand Week represents 1,000 years. When all of the genealogical records, historical events, and prophetic time periods mentioned in the Bible are assembled together, it appears that the Bible only speaks of 7,000 years for the duration of sin. I call these seven millenniums the "Grand Week." In other words, the 1,000 years of Revelation 20 will be the seventh millennium and during this Sabbath millennium, Earth itself will rest from the works of sin. There is no time period throughout all eternity, past or future, that reveals the love of God like the time He has spent resolving the sin problem! I do not have words to describe the grandeur of this incredible process. I am sure saints and angels will study the drama of the Grand Week throughout eternity.

Full Cup Principle / Jubilee Language

The final step to connect the Jubilee Calendar with Revelation 8:2 concerns the operation of the full cup principle as it pertains to timing. Notice how this works. God's patience with the nation of Israel ended when Israel violated *seventy* Sabbath years. When this limit was reached, God swiftly raised up King Nebuchadnezzar to take His people into Babylonian exile before another Sabbath year could be violated![15] The Bible says God exiled Israel to Babylon for *seventy* years because Israel violated *seventy* Sabbath years.[16] After the Babylonian exile was over, God granted Israel a second chance with respect to time. God granted the Great Day of Tuesday to Israel using Jubilee language. He used Jubilee language so that if His people (who should have understood the Jubilee Calendar) had been observing the Sabbaticals, they could have determined *which* decree would start the countdown to Messiah's appearing. The timing of the first advent of Jesus *was not* supposed to be a surprise.

"Know and understand this: From the issuing of the decree to restore and rebuild Jerusalem until the Anointed One, [Messiah] **the ruler, comes, there will be seven 'sevens,' and sixty-two 'sevens'. . . ."**[17]

Many Bible students do not understand why God stated the sixty-nine weeks in two parts. The statement, "seven weeks" and "sixty-two weeks" is confusing when God could just as easily have said, "sixty-nine weeks." Once we understand the Jubilee Calendar, the reason for a description of "sixty-two weeks" and "seven weeks" becomes apparent.

(Note: The Hebrew word *shabuwa'* translated as "weeks" or "sevens" means "the cycle of the seven" or commonly "the week." Compare Daniel 9:24 with Daniel 10:3. Millions of people have read the words in Daniel 9:25 without realizing what they actually say. Perhaps the easiest way to explain this text is to use interlaced commentary: "[Israel] **Know and understand this:** [There will be a total of four decrees to restore and rebuild Jerusalem, however] **From the issuing of the decree to restore and rebuild Jerusalem** [that will occur during the Jubilee year, 457 B.C.] **until the Anointed One** [Jesus, Messiah]**, the ruler, comes** [in A.D. 27]**, there will be** [one cycle of] **seven 'sevens,'** [a Jubilee cycle of forty-nine years. In other words, Israel, watch for the one and only decree that will be granted during a Jubilee year] **and** [after that Jubilee cycle of forty-nine years ends, count off] **sixty-two 'sevens.'** [That is, count off sixty-two more weeks of years – 434 years. Then, watch for Messiah's appearing. John the Babptist will baptize Messiah in the Sunday year of A.D. 27, the first year of His ministry and the first year of the seventieth week.]" [Daniel 9:25, insertions mine])

Think about this. God could have granted any number of probationary weeks to Israel. Why did He deliberately choose seventy weeks? God could have established any time frame for the appearing of Messiah. Why did He select "seven weeks and sixty-two weeks"? Even more, God could have used the words "490 years" instead of saying "seventy weeks." God could have started counting the years to the appearing of Messiah from a contemporary event such as the victory of the Romans over the Grecians in 168 B.C. or

He could have dated the appearing of Messiah from the date Antiochus Epiphanes IV desecrated the temple on Kislev 15, 167 B.C.

The more a person understands about God's timing, the more profound this topic becomes. I conclude that God set the time and He chose the descriptive words "seventy weeks" for two reasons. First, a week of years always begins with a Sunday year. Second, seventy weeks makes up *one day* in His Great Week. In other words, God graciously granted Israel one more "day" to accomplish His objectives. If God had said "490 years" instead of "seventy weeks," the Jews would not have been able to determine which decree "to restore Jerusalem" God used to start His count. (There were four decrees.) The language "seventy weeks" should have been a huge clue because the first day of a week always begins on Sunday in God's calendar. It is as though God was shouting to Israel's coming generations, "Watch for the decree that will be issued to restore and rebuild Jerusalem in a *Sunday year!*" This is precisely what happened in the Sunday year, 457 B.C.[18]

(**Note:** Of the four decrees issued to rebuild and restore Jerusalem, only **one** occurred in a Sunday year and interestingly, it was also a Jubilee year. Since this alignment only occurs every forty-nine years, Israel had no excuse for missing the appearing and ministry of Jesus. One of the remarkable features of the Jubilee Calendar is that during the Year of Jubilee, the land was returned to its original owners free of charge. God did no less! He moved the heart of King Artaxerxes to return the land of Judah to the Jews free of charge! He even gave them many resources to help rebuild Jerusalem.)

To be more precise, God divided the sixty-nine weeks into two parts of seven weeks and sixty-two weeks because He wanted His people to know and understand that the decree to restore and rebuild Jerusalem would not only occur in a Sunday year, but it would also occur in a Jubilee year! Since each Jubilee cycle is forty-nine years in length, God used the *first seven weeks* (the first forty-nine years) of the sixty-nine weeks to help Israel determine which decree was important to determine the appearing of Messiah. Every Jew knew that King Artaxerxes issued the all important decree on or about Nisan 1, 457 B.C., and as you might expect, 457 B.C. just happened to be a Jubilee year. Remember, 457 B.C. was a Jubilee year because 702 B.C. is a proven Jubilee year. It is as though God gave Israel every hint possible about the timing of

Messiah's appearance and yet, Israel's learned scholars, pompous Pharisees and pious scribes, did not have a clue when the actual time arrived.

The arrogance and ignorance Israel exhibited at the time of Christ's birth is no different than the attitude of Christians today. This darkness cannot be measured. *There is no darkness like stubborn religious darkness.* Jewish authorities were speechless when the wise men showed up in Jerusalem to worship the newborn King. How sad, you say, but the same problem exists today. The second appearing of Jesus is imminent. Bible prophecy has never been clearer and more understandable, yet the books of Daniel and Revelation are treated by many Christians as though they are full of darkness, gloom, and doom. Open your eyes, and you will see that the darkness is gone! The book of Daniel has been unsealed. The rules that lead us toward understanding the ways, plans, character, and love of God are shining brightly! **"But when *the time had fully come*, God sent his Son, born of a woman, born under law, to redeem those under law, that we might receive the full rights of sons."**[19]

Seventy: A Random or Deliberate Number?

Is the number *seventy* important to God or is it just a random number? I am generally opposed to numerology because it is based on the notion that numbers have hidden or obscure meanings. Since there are no defined rules regarding numerology, it is a nose of wax as far as I am concerned. It has taken time for me to come to terms with the fact that certain numbers might have special meaning to God, but I have concluded that from God's perspective, the number seven appears to represent completion. There are seven colors in the rainbow. There are seven continents and seven oceans. There are seven days in the week. Jesus spoke seven times on the cross. In the book of Revelation, there are seven angels, seven lamps, seven churches, seven seals, seven thunders, seven trumpets, seven heads, seven hills, seven thousand people, and seven bowls. Furthermore, God's Jubilee calendar is based on recurring and expanding units of seven. After reading this paragraph, I hope you see the significance to God's use of *seven*.

Unlike God, man uses many numbering systems. For example, computers use a binary system of zeros and ones, but to program them, programmers use compilers that translate ordinary words into binary numbers. Perhaps the most common numbering system that man uses is based on units of ten. (Maybe ten fingers and ten toes got human beings going in this direction.) The nice thing about base ten is that each time a count of ten is *completed*, the count continues expanding or shrinking by simply moving the decimal point one place to the left or right. It is interesting to me that God's numbering system and man's numbering systems have one thing in common. They express completion at intervals and in order to continue counting, expansion becomes necessary. In God's case, He *translates* a day as a year, whereas man moves the position of the decimal.

When God multiplies His "seven" with man's "ten," we find the limits of divine forbearance and human completion. In other words, *seventy indicates that God has gone as far as He will go and man has gone as far as God will let him go!* Multiplying seven and ten to determine completion helps us understand, in part, why God was moved to action when Israel violated *seventy* Sabbath years. This seems to be the reason why God put Israel in Babylon for *seventy* years.[20] Again, the idea of completion helps us understand why God granted *seventy* weeks to Israel. God is just too deliberate and purposeful for a person to maintain that God's use of seven and ten is random and meaningless.

God has also used the numbers seven and ten in two other ways. First, the annual Day of Atonement always fell on the *tenth* day of the *seventh* month. The Day of Atonement was the most important day in Israel's religious year because God required Israel to assemble and face His judgment on that day. It was a somber day that included fasting. It was *the annual day* of reckoning, and everyone in Israel was concerned whether God had accepted their individual efforts to make atonement. Remember, *the seventh month indicates that God's justice has gone as far as He will go and the tenth day indicates that man's behavior has gone as far as God will let him go!* So, the tenth day of the seventh month was judgment day.

Second, the great red dragon in Revelation 12, the leopard-like beast in Revelation 13, and the scarlet beast on which the whore rides in Revelation 17, all have *seven* heads and *ten* horns. The seven heads on these beasts represent the same thing, namely the seven religious systems of the world. The ten horns represent ten kings (political pawns) which the devil himself will appoint during the sixth trumpet. When the time comes, the seven heads and ten horns indicate *completion* – a world whose leadership is *full* of theological and political evil.

A final interesting point regarding the numbers seven and ten involves the Great Week and the Grand Week. The Great Week consists of seven Great Days and each Great Day consists of ten Jubilee cycles (seventy weeks). Likewise, the Grand Week consists of seven Grand Days and each Grand Day consists of ten centuries (1,000 years). When we add up the genealogical records given in Scripture, when we put historical events in their rightful places, when we place the seventeen prophetic time periods found in Daniel and Revelation in their proper places according to Rule Four, the dates and numbers will perfectly align so that everything neatly folds into a Grand Week of 7,000 years (seventy centuries)!

The Bottom Line

I believe there is a definite connection between the number "seventy" and 1994, and there is also a definite connection between the number "seventy" and the duration of sin. We can see that from Creation, God allotted a total of 7,000 years for sin. I call this time period, the Grand Week (each day of the week translates as 1,000 years[21]). From the beginning, God foreknew the limits of His patience with sin and He deliberately set the duration of sin to be seventy (7 x 10) centuries or 7,000 years! When God's use of seventy is further synthesized, I believe that God's forbearance with mankind ended in 1994. Seventy Jubilee cycles ended in 1994 and there is no further need to translate apocalyptic time as a day for a year. In 1994, God gave the seven angels the seven trumpets and they are armed and ready, waiting for the divine command to harm Earth.

Because the second and third trumpets involve asteroid impacts, I do not think it is coincidental that God gave the whole world a "prophetic sample" of coming events in 1994. You may recall the implosion of Comet Shoemaker-Levy 9 into Jupiter during July 1994. That marvelous event was televised and published worldwide. Those impact craters on Jupiter for the past fifteen years have been a harbinger of coming asteroid impacts on Earth. The comet, Shoemaker-Levy 9, broke up into a string of twenty-one chunks as it approached Jupiter and as these chunks accelerated into Jupiter's gravity, they created the most powerful explosions ever witnessed by mankind. In fact, one impact crater is so large that three planets the size of Earth can fit in it!

Appendix A - The Importance of 1994

Summary

When I conclude that 1994 is the date the seven angels were given the trumpets, a fair amount of skepticism is appropriate. Nevertheless, I believe that a synthesis of the topics just discussed will rule out any other date. In summary, here are five major points:

1. **Two Different Ways of Measuring Time** – There has to be a valid rule governing the interpretation of apocalyptic time because it is clear that some prophetic time periods are to be translated as a day for a year and other time periods are not. Based on the information presented previously, I believe the dividing line is 1994. Consequently, prior to 1994, an apocalyptic day should be translated as a year. After the Jubilee Calendar expired in 1994, the translating time as a day for a year is not permitted or justified.

2. **The Jubilee Calendar** – The Jubilee Calendar did not end at the cross for two reasons. First, Jesus died in *the middle* of the seventieth week; therefore, the seventieth week was unfinished at the cross. Second, the 2,300 days of Daniel 8:14 operate both before and after the cross; therefore, the Jubilee Calendar and the translation of a day for a year exist before and after the cross. In this case, the 2,300 day year prophecy extended from 457 B.C. to A.D. 1844.

3. **The Great Week** – The time between the Exodus in 1437 B.C. and the date Solomon's temple was dedicated in 947 B.C. was 490 years. Later, the time between the dedication of Solomon's temple and the decree of King Artaxerxes in 457 B.C. was another 490 years. In addition to this, the seventy weeks in Daniel consisted of 490 years. Since these three units are 490 years each, it suggests an ongoing pattern is present. Today, we know that God gave the Jews exactly thirty Jubilee cycles of grace to the very year. It also appears that God gave the Gentiles forty Jubilee cycles of grace (A.D. 34-1994). These two periods of grace total seventy Jubilee cycles in all. Using the weekly template and aligning each unit of 490 years as a Great Day, we find the presence of a Great Week. When the Great Week ends, so does the translation of apocalyptic time.

4. **Full Cup Principle** – Evidently, God uses the numbers seven and ten to express the limits of divine forbearance. When Israel violated *seventy* Sabbath years, God exiled

them to Babylon for *seventy* years. When God gave Israel a second chance, He gave the nation *seventy* weeks. We also see God's use of seven and ten used during Israel's annual judgment day, the Day of Atonement. This special day occurred on the tenth day of the seventh month. Furthermore, the dragon and the leopard-like beast in Revelation 12 and 13 have seven heads and ten horns. The heads and horns represent the sum of religious and political powers on Earth. Finally, the whole drama of sin fits neatly into *seventy* centuries (7,000 years). In other words, when the millennial Sabbath rest ends (the seventh millennium), Earth will be made new and life will resume!

5. **God's Timing Is Perfect** – We find throughout the Bible that God's timing is always perfect. He knows no haste or delay. Given this fact, two things stand out very prominently. First, if we translate the apocalyptic prophetic time periods prior to 1994 according to God's calendar (a day for a year) and if we treat all apocalyptic time periods after 1994 as literal time periods, everything written about timing in apocalyptic prophecy harmoniously aligns with a 7,000 year picture for the duration of sin. (Sin is destroyed at the end of the 1,000 years in Revelation 20.) Second, now that we understand what the seven trumpets are all about, we can align Revelation 8:2 with the end of seventy Jubilee cycles. This seems likely because Jesus could give the seven trumpets to the seven angels because God's patience with mankind ran out at that time. This means we are now living on borrowed time. In fact, *to my knowledge, there is no other way to determine a date for the delay imposed on the four angels in Revelation 7.*

When all of the items discussed in this appendix are aligned with a working knowledge of God's Jubilee Calendar and the precision of God's actions, there appears to be only one "biblically reasoned" date for Revelation 8:2 and 1994 is that date. I believe these conclusions are accurate, because there appears to be perfect harmony coming from the sum of the parts.

References

1. Exodus 12:1,2
2. Isaiah 37:30
3. Matthew 12:40
4. Luke 3:1
5. Antiquities xv. 5.2; xvii. 8.1
6. Mishnah Rosh Hashanah 1.1
7. Leviticus 25:8
8. Numbers 14:34
9. Leviticus 23:15,16
10. Luke 3
11. Acts 10:39
12. Exodus 12:41, italics mine
13. Daniel 12:12
14. Galatians 3:28,29
15. Jeremiah 25:7-11
16. Leviticus 26:31-35; 2 Chronicles 36:21
17. Daniel 9:25, insertion mine
18. Ezra 7
19. Galatians 4:4,5, italics mine
20. 2 Chronicles 36:21-23
21. Psalm 90:4; 2 Peter 3:8

Appendix B

The Israel of God

"... For not all who are descended from Israel are Israel. Nor because they are his descendants are they all Abraham's children.... If you belong to Christ, then you are Abraham's seed, and heirs according to the promise." (Romans 9:6,7; Galatians 3:29)

Part I

God's plan for the redemption of sinners is intricate and beautiful. His plan involves two aspects of salvation: Justification and sanctification. Justification is an administrative process. God justifies sinners and when they appear in His courtroom, they appear to be clean and sinless (just as though they never sinned). On the other hand, sanctification is a lifelong process that involves transforming a rebellious sinner so that he can enjoy being close to God and living with the holy angels.

There is no question that God loves every person on Earth. We are His creation. The plan of redemption is huge, intricate, and beautiful. God determined from the beginning of sin that certain people whom He has chosen to be trustees of His gospel will broadcast His gospel to the world. Because the plan of redemption has transforming power, because it is enormous in scope and purpose, because billions of human beings would appear and disappear on Earth before the plan of redemption is completed, God determined that His trustees would be well-informed about His plan and representatives of His love.

God Established a Trust

In simple terms, a living trust is an arrangement in which one person (the grantor) transfers something of value to a second person (the beneficiary) through the efforts of a third person (a trustee). Trusts are used to distribute assets for a variety of reasons. If a grantor is too busy with other matters, if he is out of the country, or if he is too ill to take care of matters himself, that grantor can establish a living trust and turn the distribution of his assets over to his trustee. Of course, when a trustee agrees to serve a trust, he makes a promise to the grantor to carry out the grantor's wishes. Usually, the grantor's desires are clearly stipulated in the trust so that there can be no misunderstanding between the grantor and trustee. Typically, a trustee is well paid for his services because the fiduciary responsibility imposed upon the trustee is significant.

A living trust is different from a testamentary will. A testamentary will is a document in which one person declares that his assets are to be given to another person or persons after he dies. The major difference between a testamentary will and a living trust is that a will takes effect upon a grantor's death, whereas a living trust can become effective immediately, while the grantor is alive.

I have presented the essential differences between a testamentary will and a living trust so that you can see why God established the plan of redemption as a living trust instead of a testamentary will.

God designed the plan of redemption as a living trust for two reasons. First, God is changeless[1] and His gospel is eternal.[2] *Although faith in God is expressed in different ways and at different times, the foundation of redemption never changes. Faith in God is an eternal prerequisite because there is no other way that finite beings can honor, love and worship an infinite God of love.*[3] God established the plan of redemption as a living trust so that the enormous blessings and benefits of His eternal gospel* could be disbursed immediately to all mankind (the beneficiaries).

Second, God, in His infinite wisdom, foreknew that "servant leadership" was the best way to disburse *the light* of His eternal gospel to those in darkness. Servant leadership occurs when one brother (that is, an enlightened trustee) serves another brother (the beneficiary who lives in darkness) on behalf of a grantor (God). It was God's plan for the whole world to witness a practical representation of His love, as well as a proclamation of light through His servants (His trustees). God wanted the world to discover that whenever people see one of His humble trustees, they see a

---

***Note:** The eternal gospel is defined as a comprehensive body of knowledge that includes the truth about the Father, Jesus Christ and the Holy Spirit, their love for created beings, their judicial processes, the offer of redemption, and the principles underlying the wise and righteous laws of God Almighty.

glimpse of God Himself.[4] To make His living trust viable, God gave His trustees many advantages (intellectual, spiritual, and physical). He also paid them well and gave His trustees wealth to carry out their task. From the beginning of sin, God has used trustees to disburse the benefits of His gospel to His beneficiaries who are in spiritual poverty and darkness.[5] Unfortunately, Bible history indicates that as a body of people, God's trustees have been very poor performers. They typically end up in a hopeless state of arrogance and ignorance.

Before we get into the meat of this topic, please keep this thought in mind. This study consists of two segments. The first segment focuses on God's use of trustees. The second segment focuses on the importance of being an heir of Abraham. These two topics are intimately related and very important. I find these copies are much easier for most people to understand if "the big picture" concerning trusteeship is told first, making the concept of God's elect easier to understand. Therefore, the first part of this study will focus on "the big picture" concerning God's use of trustees.

Look at the list below and notice seven groups of trustees. After sin is destroyed and Earth is made new, the redeemed of all ages will serve as trustees of God's eternal gospel. In other words, the benefits that God (the Grantor) wants distributed to His beneficiaries (the whole universe) will never end and the trustees who will deliver God's assets to the universe will be those who overcame the temptations of the world through faith in God! Please consider this list of trustees for a moment:

Seven Groups of Trustees

1. The patriarchs
2. The family of Abraham
3. The nation of Israel
4. The Christian church
5. The Protestant movement
6. The 144,000
7. The redeemed of all ages

1. The Patriarchs

Ironically, the first trustee of the plan of redemption was Adam, the same man who brought sin and condemnation upon all mankind! God revealed to Adam the essential elements of redemption. In turn, Adam was commissioned to teach his offspring about sin and God's plan for redemption. The firstborn male of each generation inherited the privilege of becoming a servant leader of the gospel. If each trustee carried out his responsibility, every household on Earth would hear the gospel and benefit from its provisions. But Cain, Adam's firstborn son, did not want to be a servant leader. Cain was arrogant and he followed the inclinations of his carnal heart. Cain showed disrespect for God by deciding, for himself, how God should be worshiped. He offered fruit instead of the prerequisite lamb and God showed no respect for Cain's offering. When God acknowledged Abel's offering, Cain was outraged that God gave Abel higher honor than "the firstborn of mankind." Later, Cain killed his younger brother out of jealousy.

When Adam and Eve were 130 years old, Eve gave birth to Seth.[6] By studying Adam's ancestry down to the time of Noah and the flood, we learn that with the exception of Cain, the trusteeship of the gospel was passed down to the firstborn of each generation. These trustees are called the patriarchs (or the elders) because a patriarch is respected as a person of experience, a person having acquired wisdom and understanding. Evidently, many of Adam's offspring followed in Cain's footsteps.[7] The Bible indicates that the trustees began to preach the Word of the Lord (that is, they began to preach to those who should not have been living in darkness) when Enosh was born to Seth.[8] Corporately speaking, the behavior of the world went from bad to worse. By the time Noah was born, most of the people on Earth wanted nothing to do with God or His redemption. When the flood occurred, only one trustee remained on Earth and ironically, Noah's family was the only beneficiary.[9]

Notice the lineage of the ten patriarchs who lived between Adam and Noah's flood:

Adam - Seth - Enosh - Kenan - Mahalalel - Jared - Enoch - Methuselah - Lamech - Noah

Two interesting facts emerge about the patriarch's trusteeship. First, there were ten patriarchs. According to the genealogical records given in Scripture, the lifetimes of these ten men covered a period of approximately 1,656 years. Ten linear trustees suggest that the Earth's population before the flood was quite small – perhaps a few hundred thousand.

The second element that stands out about the trusteeship of the patriarchs is the significance of being a firstborn son. Evidently, God used the special joy and affection given to the *firstborn* son as an object lesson to teach mankind that one day, His only begotten Son, the faithful and true Trustee of Redemption, would come to Earth and redeem us with His blood. As a practical matter, the firstborn was especially honored because they practiced the maxim, "age before beauty." It was understood in Bible times that the firstborn would be more experienced and wiser than his siblings and the family gave a certain level of respect to the eldest sibling.

God Abandons the Patriarch Policy

Noah was the last of the pre-flood patriarchs. As far as we know, Noah's sons did not walk with God as did their father. It is astonishing that within a mere 150 years after the flood, Noah's descendants built a tall tower to protect themselves from another flood. It seems incongruous that people did not believe God's promise that He would never again destroy the world with a flood! Noah's descendants even ignored frequent sightings of the rainbow! God saw the rapid degeneration caused by man's rebellion and He deliberately separated the people of Earth into groups by language. This simple act caused mankind to disperse throughout the world. Shortly after the dispersion, God divided the Earth. He pulled one land mass into several continents and this further isolated mankind from one another.[10]

The Bible traces the birth of Abraham from Noah through Shem, Japheth's younger brother.[11] If I have calculated correctly, Abraham was about seven years old when Noah died. If Noah lived out the remainder of his life in the area around the mountains of Ararat, then it seems likely that Abraham did not meet with the ancient patriarch. Noah died at the age of 950 years and so did the trusteeship and legacy of the patriarchs that began with Adam.

2. God Started Over With Abraham

After Noah's flood, God skipped over nine generations that descended from Noah to start over with a new set of trustees. He looked down on the Earth and found an open-hearted man named Abram. Abram favorably responded to God's call and invitation to be a trustee.[12] It is important to also note that Abram (later called Abraham) was not in a biological line to receive a trusteeship passed down to the firstborn. In fact, it is highly doubtful that

Abraham was the firstborn of his father, Terah, but God was starting over and Abram was, for the most part, an honest man.[13]

Abraham walked with God and he became a friend of God. After testing Abraham's faith, God purposed to make Abraham's "nonexisting" descendants into a family of trustees. In other words, God "dusted off" the trusteeship of the eternal gospel He originally gave to Adam and implemented it again. This time, however, the trusteeship would not be passed along to the firstborn son, but instead, the trusteeship would be passed along to Abraham's family. Abraham can be called "the father of the faithful" because every descendant who trusted in God as did Abraham would be considered a trustee of the gospel. Faithfulness was far more important to God than genealogical order. Notice the progression of trustees traced from Abraham:

These were Abraham's seven sons. Notice that Ishmael was not considered a trustee:

> Abraham - Ishmael - Isaac - Zimran - Jokshan - Medan,
> - Midian - Ishbak - Shuah

His Wives:

> (Hagar) (Sarah) (Keturah)

Notice again that the trusteeship was not passed to Isaac's firstborn son:

> Isaac - Esau - Jacob

Notice again, the trusteeship skipped over Reuben, Simeon, and Levi and passed down to Judah:

> Jacob - Reuben - Simeon - Levi - Judah

Notice again, the trusteeship was not passed to Er, the firstborn of Judah, for God killed Er.

> Judah - Er

Even a casual study of Bible history reveals the degenerating consequences of sin. In a sin filled world, it is unnatural to have faith in God. Beginning with Abraham and Sarah, we read how they became weary of waiting on God for a son. They took matters into their own hands and Ishmael was the result. Esau was Isaac's firstborn, but Jacob tried to steal the birthright through deceit only to discover that God would not accept his treachery. Reuben, Jacob's firstborn son, was emotionally unstable and he did not conduct himself in a way worthy of the sacred trust granted to the firstborn. Jacob denied him the birthright for his sexual promiscuity.[14] Jacob also denied the privileges of birthright to his next sons, Simeon and Levi, because of their violence and cruelty. So, Jacob gave paternal rights and the sacred trust to his fourth born son, Judah. In the next generation, God killed Judah's firstborn, Er, for his wickedness.[15] From that time, God's efforts to have Abraham's family deliver the plan of redemption to the inhabitants of Earth fell apart.

When trustees fail to discharge the terms of the trust set by the grantor, the beneficiaries cannot receive the assets or gifts the grantor wants them to have. As a consequence of their delinquency, God sent Abraham's family into Egypt. It is ironic that Joseph, a faithful "grandson of Abraham," was the one who set the stage for his family to become slaves.[16] Because of faithless living, God permitted Abraham's family to become slaves of Pharaoh and they lost the exalted opportunity to serve as trustees of the gospel for the next 400 years.

3. God Starts Over – Calls Moses

One day at a burning bush in the Arabian desert, God called Moses to be a trustee of the gospel.[17] Moses was neither the firstborn of his family nor was he a member of the tribe of Judah. At this time, lineage no longer mattered because God was starting over. Adam and the patriarchs had failed. Abraham and his immediate descendants had failed. However, God, in keeping with His promises to Abraham, started over with a distant descendant of Abraham. He needed a man to deliver the Hebrews from Egyptian bondage so that He could start over. So, Moses, the murderer turned shepherd, became a trustee of the eternal gospel.

At Mount Sinai God offered the nation of Israel the opportunity to become trustees of the plan of redemption and they accepted.[18] Meanwhile, the population of the world had multiplied significantly since the flood. Many tribal nations were scattered around Earth, and most of them did not know about the God of Heaven, nor His amazing gospel. So, working through His newly appointed trustees, Moses and his brother, Aaron, God set out again to make Abraham's descendants a family of trustees.

At Mount Sinai, God also promoted the tribe of Levi above the tribes to be a group of special trustees for His family of trustees. After a few centuries, however, it became impossible to tell who was leading who. The Levites were no different than members of the other tribes. They did the same evil things in the sight of the Lord. Time after time, God sent prophets to the kings and priests of Israel to remind the nation the conditions required for God's blessings, but the Israelites hated the prophets and killed most of them. Century after century, the prophets chastised and rebuked the Israelites for their rebellion. In 605 B.C., God sent the whole nation to Babylon as captives for their rebellion, but the captivity did not produce repentance. The story of Israel ends on a sad note. God tried everything possible for 1,470 years (thirty Jubilee cycles), but His trustees did not measure up to the terms and conditions of being trustees of His gospel. Finally, God sent the Roman army against Jerusalem and completely destroyed the nation. All this happened just as He had warned from the very beginning.[19]

4. God Starts Over Again

After Jesus was on Earth, He concluded that Israel was beyond redemption, so He created a new covenant with a new group of trustees. Jesus chose men who already knew God's ways and character. This allowed the gospel of Jesus to spread rapidly throughout the world. He chose twelve men who, when the time was right, would step out of Judaism and become known as Christians. It is amazing, given the failure of previous trustees, that all but one of the original twelve disciples lived up to His calling!

The trusteeship Jesus gave to Christians does not have any qualifications except faith in Christ. Biological lineage, paternal rights, race, and culture are all meaningless. Remember, the ultimate purpose of a living trust is to benefit the beneficiaries. Therefore, God opened the floodgates after the cross and anyone who wants to be a trustee of His gospel can do so. There are many titles describing this new arrangement, but Christians generally call it "the priesthood of the believer." In effect, it means that any person, male or female, Jew or Gentile, can now serve as a trustee of the gospel.[20]

Remember, the duty of a trustee is to carry out the wishes of the grantor. God still wants the world to hear and witness the power of His gospel. God wants the world to know about His efforts to save mankind from the penalty for sin. God wants everyone in the world to know that victory over sin is possible. God wants the world to know that lasting joy, happiness, and peace will come if men and women obey His laws and commands. God wants His trustees to be living examples of His gospel because "seeing is believing."

The history of the Christian Church is not wholesome or glorious. About 500 years after Jesus returned to Heaven, the Christian Church morphed from "the persecuted" into "the persecutor of the saints." Corporately speaking, the Christian Church repeated the rebellious history of the Jewish nation. Christian leaders became focused on power and wealth. They forgot God and they hated those who loved His gospel. During the Dark Ages, the church destroyed many people who firmly stood for God's truth. Sin consistently ruins God's trustees, because the carnal nature is hostile toward the eternal gospel. The carnal nature is self-seeking and self-important. Bible history confirms that God's trustees always fail because mankind is cursed with the carnal nature. When the carnal nature rules, there is an irresistible temptation to redirect the assets that belong to the grantor's beneficiaries to self. It is naturally easier to keep (hoard) wealth than to give it away, remaining a humble conduit through which wealth might flow.

5. God Starts over Again

The iron grip of the Roman Catholic Church in Europe was finally broken in 1798, and the resulting freedom allowed a new group of people to take the gospel commission seriously. Just as Christianity rose out of the cradle of Judaism, Protestantism arose from the soil of Catholicism. Once again, God renewed and extended the privilege of trusteeship to anyone willing to proclaim and demonstrate His eternal gospel. Keep in mind that the basic trust remains intact. The Grantor (God) wants everyone in the world (the beneficiaries) to benefit from His eternal gospel. To do this, the Grantor continues to search for faithful trustees who will accomplish the terms and conditions of His trust.

Unfortunately, Protestantism has also floundered and become derelict in fulfilling its God given duties. Protestantism has lost its vision and her purpose. It has grown indifferent to the eternal gospel because of materialism and humanism. Prosperity has robbed Protestantism of its momentum. The spiritual awakening that propelled 18th century Protestantism is dead. Many people still claim they are protestors, but few Protestants remember the protest.

6. God Starts Over Again

Just in case you have forgotten, a living trust is an arrangement whereby a grantor transfers something of value to His beneficiaries using the services of a trustee. We are now living 2,000 years after Jesus lived on Earth, and Catholics and Protestants combined represent only 25% of the world's population. The world now has more people living on it than at any other time in its history. As a percentage of people on Earth, it would be fair to say that very few people within this 25% actually know and understand the terms and conditions contained in the eternal gospel.

The seven trumpets of Revelation will sound very soon and the whole world will discover God's great displeasure with mankind. Jesus will select and empower a new group of 144,000 people as trustees of the eternal gospel before the Great Tribulation begins. These faithful men and women will come from all nations, languages, and religions. Jesus will give the 144,000 an understanding of the eternal gospel and He will empower them with Holy Spirit power so they can tell the world about redemption. This group of 144,000 people will accomplish in 1,260 days all that God desires. The 144,000 will confront each person in the world with the eternal, unchanging gospel of Jesus Christ and every person will have to make a decision for or against it. The 144,000 will not fail. They will accomplish all that the Lord wants done.

7. God's Final Trustees Will Live Forever

This study on God's trustees does not end with the Second Coming. The people who are redeemed will serve as trustees of the eternal gospel throughout eternity. They will serve God as priests and kings. Because the redeemed have shown themselves to be faithful and obedient to the King of kings, He will greatly honor them in the ages to come just as they honored Him on Earth. It is interesting that the redeemed are the seventh and final group of trustees. As the number seven signifies a full and complete number, so the redeemed will testify of God's endless love forever.

Seven Groups of Trustees

1. The patriarchs
2. The lineage of Abraham
3. The nation of Israel
4. The Christian church

5. The Protestant movement
6. The 144,000
7. The redeemed of all ages

Summary

When sin began, God implemented the plan of redemption as a living trust. God determined that "enlightened brothers" should humbly labor for their "brothers in darkness." God also determined that His trustees should be living examples of living by faith, displaying His love and grace. The foundations of the eternal gospel never change although expressions of faith do change. In other words, there is no other way to please an infinite God than through faithful obedience. Through the ages, God's trustees have proven to be a failure. This is why the final trustees of the eternal gospel will be sealed (carnal nature removed) before they begin their work. This will enable the 144,000 to accomplish all that God wants. Hopefully, this study illuminates the fact that God's trustees are only that – trustees. They are not the Grantor of redemption. In fact, trustees cannot save anyone and they cannot condemn anyone. This is God's work. The only thing that God's trustees have to offer is enlightenment. Through word and action, their lives will reflect the light of the eternal gospel. Because salvation does not come through a church or a tribe, a numberless throng of saints will sing together on Heaven's shore: "**. . . Salvation belongs to our God who sits on the throne, and to the Lamb.**"[21]

Part II

Now that we have considered the concept of a living trust, we can examine another important topic. Many Christians do not realize the necessity or importance of being counted an heir of Abraham. They read this verse, "**If you belong to Christ, then you are Abraham's seed** [Greek: sperma]**, and heirs according to the promise**",[22] without understanding the profound importance of the verse. Here is the problem: Long ago God promised to give the world to Abraham and his descendants. If Christians are not counted as heirs of Abraham, then Christians will have no place to spend eternity.

Appendix B - The Israel of God

We will examine this interesting topic in just a moment. For now, please consider this. When two people get married, it is said that six people are involved.

1. There is the guy he thinks he is.
2. There is the guy she thinks he is.
3. There is the guy he really is.
4. There is the girl he thinks she is.
5. There is the girl she thinks she is.
6. There is the girl she really is.

Normally, after two years of marriage, only two of the original six people remain alive: The guy he really is and the girl she really is. The death of four people is announced one solemn day when one spouse says to the other, "You have changed! You are not the person I married!" I have used this marriage illustration to demonstrate that two spouses can *appear* to be six different people. Similarly, two groups of people, sheep and goats, can be described as twelve different types of people in God's sight! With this thought in mind, please consider the following definitions and notice the name of the variable that identifies each group because these variables will be used throughout this study:

1. Jews

$J1$ = A Jew (an individual who descended from Abraham, loves God, lives by faith - a saint)

$J2$ = A Jew (an nonreligious individual who has Jewish parents, heritage or culture)

$J3$ = A Jew (a religious zealot who is an ignorant, arrogant, unloving, hardheaded individual whose God is his religious opinion)

$J4$ = Israel (corporately speaking, all Jews)

2. Christians

$C1$ = A Christian (a born again Jew or Gentile who loves Jesus, lives by faith - a saint)

$C2$ = A Christian (a nonreligious individual who has no interest in God but has Christian parents, heritage, or culture)

$C3$ = A Christian (a religious zealot who is an ignorant, arrogant, unloving, hardheaded individual whose God is his religious opinion)

$C4$ = Christians (corporately speaking, all Christians)

3. Gentiles

G1 = A Gentile (an individual like Cornelius whose knowledge of the truth about God is nonexistent or limited, but for all he knows, loves God and walks obediently with God according to the Holy Spirit who guides him – he lives up to all that he knows to be right and true - a saint)

G2 = A Gentile (a non-religious individual who has no interest in God)

G3 = A Gentile (a religious zealot who is neither Christian or Jew, who is ignorant, arrogant, unloving, a hardheaded individual whose God is his religious opinion)

G4 = Gentiles (corporately speaking, all who are not Jews and Christians)

God Looks on the Heart

Many Christians inherently understand these twelve definitions without giving them much thought. For example, when you hear someone say, "I believe there are sheep and goats in every religious body," that person is affirming that he believes that God *primarily* looks upon the heart and what matters most to God is honesty, integrity, fidelity, love, and faithfulness.

We need to examine these twelve definitions because there is a great deal of confusion about the end time role of modern Israel. To be frank, I do not find anything in Scripture concerning an end time role for modern Israel. There is an Israel of God during the end time, but it is not the modern nation of Israel. We will learn in the following study that the end time Israel of God consists of J1 + C1 + G1. This explains why the twelve definitions of sheep and goats are important. The words "Christian," "Jew," and "Gentile" are used throughout Scripture. Knowing which definition is appropriate within a given text is highly important and if you want to reach the intended meaning of Scripture.

Example 1: Selections from Romans 9 and Romans 2

Paul wrote, **"I have great sorrow and unceasing anguish in my heart. For I could wish that I myself were cursed and cut off from Christ for the sake of my brothers, those of my own race, the people of Israel,** [J4]. [In other words, I would forfeit eternal life if it would mean that my people would receive Christ and be saved. Look at the gifts that God has generously bestowed on J4:] **Theirs is the** [promised] **adoption as sons; theirs the divine glory** [the Shekinah glory that dwelt within the Most Holy place], **the covenants** [the offer of serving as trustees of the eternal gospel], **the receiving of the law** [at Mount Sinai], **the temple worship** [with its ceremonial shadows], **and the promises** [of earthly recognition spoken through the prophets]. **Theirs are the patriarchs** [Abraham, Moses and David], **and from them is traced the human ancestry of Christ, who is God over all, forever praised! Amen.**

[There is no question that J4 has been blessed above all nations, therefore J4's rejection of Christ is devastating.] **It is not as though God's word** [His promises] **had failed** [because all Israel [J1] will be saved. However, we must consider the problem that J4's rebellion has created for the eternal gospel and God's solution to this problem. First, remember that] **For not all who are descended from Israel are Israel.** [That is, J2 and J3 are not counted as sons of Jacob.] **Nor because they are his descendants are they all Abraham's children.** [God used Abraham's first born son to demonstrate this point. God declared that Ishmael was unacceptable in His sight as Abraham's heir even though he was Abraham's first born son. God rejected Abraham's request that Ishmael be counted as his heir and inheritor of God's promise, but God said:] **On the contrary,'It is through Isaac** [the child that came when it was humanly impossible to conceive, the child that came through patience and enduring faith] **that your offspring** [J1] **will be reckoned.' In other words, it is not the natural** [born] **children who are counted as God's children, but it is the children of the promise** [that is, people who believe God's promises and wait upon the Lord as Abraham did] **who are regarded as Abraham's offspring** [heirs]."[23]

God rejected Ishmael as Abraham's firstborn because Ishmael came as a result of abandoning faith in God. From the beginning, God wanted the impossible birth of Isaac to parallel the impossible birth of Christ. Contrary to what some people claim, God did not reject Abraham's firstborn son, Ishmael, because the child was born out of wedlock. If this were the case, there would not be twelve tribes in Israel. The twelve tribes of Israel came through two marriages and two slave women. Jacob's first wife, Leah, produced seven sons and his second wife, Rachel, produced two sons. Bilhah, Leah's slave woman, produced two sons from Jacob and Zilpah, Rachel's slave woman, also produced two sons for him.[24]

In Romans 2, Paul confronts some Jews [J3's] who were causing trouble among early Christians in Rome. These Jews [J3] were trying to merge Christianity into Judaism. Paul wrote: **"Now you, if you call yourself a Jew** [that is, if you consider yourself the elect of God]**; if you rely on the law** [to demonstrate that you are righteous] **and brag about your relationship to God; if you know his will and approve of what is superior because you are instructed by the law; if you are convinced that you are a guide for the blind, a light for those** [G4's] **who are in the dark, an instructor of the foolish, a teacher of infants, because you have in the law the embodiment of knowledge and truth – you, then, who teach others,** [why] **do you not teach yourself? You who preach against stealing,** [so why] **do you steal? You who say that people should not commit adultery,** [so why] **do you commit adultery? You who abhor idols,** [so why] **do you rob temples** [and take their gold and silver]**? You who brag about** [obeying] **the law,** [so why] **do you dishonor God by breaking the law?** [You well know that Israel [J4] has a terrible reputation among the Gentiles as an arrogant and rebellious people. Israel has a long history of being hated and scorned by its neighbors because of the way it exalts itself as the elect of God and yet, treats the Gentiles as though they were less than dogs. As a people [J4], the Old Testament constantly condemns them.] **As it is written: 'God's name is blasphemed among the Gentiles because of you.'**

[Let us reason together for a moment.] **Circumcision has value if you** [believe that obedience will produce salvation. You conscientiously] **observe the law, but** [you should know that] **if you break the law** [just once], **you have become as though you had not been circumcised** [because the penalty for one sin is death and how can you recover from the penalty of sin after committing one sin? Circumcision will not save you from death!]. **If those who are not circumcised** [and uninformed like Cornelius - G1] **keep the law's requirements** [out of a deep desire to walk with God], **will they not be regarded as though they were circumcised** [by God]**? The one who is not circumcised physically** [and knows nothing about the written code] **and yet obeys the** [intent of the] **law** [which is love, because love is written in his heart through the Spirit, he] **will condemn you who, even though you** [are a Jew, J4, and] **have the written code and circumcision, are a lawbreaker.**

Appendix B - The Israel of God

[Be assured. God reads the heart and in His sight] **A man is not a Jew [J1]** **if he is only one outwardly, nor is circumcision merely outward and physical. No, a man is a Jew [J1]** **if he is one inwardly; and circumcision is circumcision of the heart, by the Spirit, not by the written code. Such a man's praise is not from men, but from God."**[25]

[Consider God's treatment of sincere Gentiles [G1] who know nothing about Him.] **"Indeed, when Gentiles [G1], who do not have** [any knowledge of] **the law, do by nature things required by the law, they are a law for themselves, even though they do not have** [knowledge of] **the law, since they show that the requirements of the law are written on their hearts,** [even in the absence of the written code, they [G1] know through the Holy Spirit what is right from wrong because] **their consciences** [influenced by the Holy Spirit] **also bearing witness** [in matters of right and wrong], **and their thoughts now accusing** [that is, their thoughts producing guilt when they violate the Spirit within them], **now even defending them** [that is, their thoughts producing peace when doing what is right according to the Holy Spirit]."[26]

Example 2: Ephesians 2 and Galatians 3

"**For we** [all mankind, C4 + J4 + G4] **are God's workmanship, created in Christ Jesus to do good works, which God prepared in advance for us to do. Therefore, remember that formerly you who are Gentiles by birth [G4] and called** [the ignorant and] **'uncircumcised'** [dogs] **by those who call themselves** [the enlightened and] **'the circumcision' [J3] – (those who insist that you must also be circumcised by the hands of men) – remember that at that time** [prior to hearing the gospel of Christ that] **you were separate from Christ,** [and as pagans [G4] you were] **excluded from citizenship in Israel and foreigners to the covenants of the promise, without hope and without God in the world.**

But now in Christ Jesus you who once were far away have been brought near through the blood of Christ. For he himself is our peace [He is our means to reconciliation because He], **who has made the two** [groups – J1 and G1 into] **one** [church body - C1] **and has destroyed the** [religious] **barrier** [that kept us apart], **the dividing wall of hostility** [religious antagonism], **by abolishing in his flesh the** [Levitical] **law with**

its commandments and regulations. [When God abolished the Levitical system, God destroyed Judaism [J4] As a race of people we no longer have a valid religious system that uniquely separates us from the Gentiles. [G4] Our religious system, delivered by Moses, has been made void.] **God's purpose** [in doing this] **was to create in himself one new man** [C1] **out of the two** [groups of people – Jews, J1 and Gentiles, G1]**, thus making peace** [between us]**, and in this one body** [of believers, that is, the church - C1] **to reconcile both of them to God through the cross, by which he put to death their hostility. He** [Jesus] **came and preached peace** [reconciliation with God through faith] **to you who were far away** [G4] **and peace** [reconciliation with God through faith] **to those** [of us] **who were near** [J4]. **For through him we** [J1 + G1] **both have** [equal] **access to the Father by one Spirit.**

Consequently, you [born again Gentiles - G1's] **are no longer foreigners and aliens, but** [now you are] **fellow citizens with God's people** [J1's] **and members of God's** [unified] **household** [C1]**, built on the foundation of the apostles and** [Old Testament] **prophets, with Christ Jesus himself as the chief cornerstone. In him the whole building** [the church - C1] **is joined together and rises to become a holy temple in the Lord."**[27]

[God planned from the beginning to justify the Gentiles through faith.] **"Consider Abraham: 'He believed God, and it was credited to him as righteousness.'** [The Scripture says that God's righteousness 'was credited to him,' because the righteousness credited to Abraham did not exist when Abraham was alive. The righteousness of Christ was produced when Jesus lived on Earth. He overcame every temptation and His righteousness is imputed to every person who lives by faith. This is why the righteousness of Christ was credited to Abraham.] **Understand, then, that those who believe** [as Abraham believed] **are children of Abraham** [and this now includes Gentile believers]. **The Scripture foresaw that God would justify the Gentiles by faith, and announced the gospel in advance to Abraham: 'All nations will be blessed through you.' So those who have faith are blessed along with Abraham, the man of faith. All who rely on observing the law** [to achieve righteousness] **are under a curse, for it is written: 'Cursed is everyone who does not continue to do everything written in the Book

of the Law.' Clearly no one is justified before God by the law, because, [all have sinned] **and' 'The righteous will live by faith.' "**[28]

Four Facts

The two passages above illuminate four topics that should become clearer as this study unfolds:

1. From God's perspective, there are three different kinds of Jews (J1 + J2 + J3). Paul says that some Jews are considered the offspring of Abraham (J1) and the others (J2 + J3) are not.

2. From God's perspective, there are three different kinds of Gentiles (G1 + G2 + G3). Paul says that even though G1's may know nothing about the true God, they are considered His children because they honestly live up to all they know to be right and true. Living by faith means doing what is thought to be pleasing to God and leaving the consequences with Him.

3. When Jesus came to Earth, He abolished the Levitical code[29] which terminated Judaism. He established a new covenant and appointed new trustees. Speaking to Jewish and Gentile believers, Paul made clear that it was Christ's purpose to unite J1 and G1 to create C1. Of course, as time progressed, C1 fractured into corporate Christianity (C4) which has nothing to do with living by faith.

4. God views the sheep and goats as twelve distinct groups of people.

Abraham's Inheritance

Now, we come to an interesting question that confuses millions of Christians. Why is it important to God that Christians (C1) be counted as heirs of Abraham today? The answer to this question is that God made three unilateral (one sided) promises to Abraham. A unilateral promise is a standalone promise, whereas a bilateral promise has two sides. Marriage is a bilateral promise when two people promise to love, honor, and cherish one another for as long as they live. If one party in the marriage fails to keep the vow, the covenant is broken and it becomes void. Conversely, nothing is required of a person when a unilateral promise is given to him. For example, God promised all mankind that He would never destroy the world with a flood again.[30] This is a unilateral promise. Mankind is not required to do anything for the promise to be fulfilled.

Now you can appreciate the three unilateral promises which God made to Abraham:

1. "He [God] took him [Abraham] outside and said, 'Look up at the heavens and count the stars if indeed you can count them.' Then he said to him, 'So shall your offspring be.' "[31]

2. "The whole land of Canaan, where you are now an alien, I will give as an everlasting possession to you and your descendants after you; and I will be their God."[32]

3. God said, **"Abraham will surely become a great and powerful nation, and all nations on Earth will be blessed through him. For I have chosen him, so that he will direct his children and his household after him to keep the way of the Lord by doing what is right and just, so that the Lord will bring about for Abraham what he has promised him."**[33]

Of course, God knew that Abraham *would not live long enough* to see these promises fulfilled,[34] but God's view of the future is not limited. God foreknew that He would resurrect Abraham someday and at the appointed time, these three promises would be fulfilled. Abraham also realized that he would not live long enough to see the promises fulfilled and this is why he looked forward to a city whose Builder and Maker is God.[35]

If a majority in Israel (J1) had been faithful to God's covenant, Plan A would have been fulfilled and the promises God gave to Abraham would have been fulfilled long ago. But Israel fractured into J4 and J1 and became a minority. Corporately speaking, Israel became unfaithful and God implemented Plan B. Christianity has mirrored Israel's footsteps. Corporately speaking, Christianity is unfaithful; therefore, God will raise up 144,000 from all the tribes of Israel (J1 + C1 + G1)!

God will fulfill the unilateral promises He made to Abraham. God will fulfill them on a scale that is larger and more glorious than Plan A could have ever been! (With God, Plan B is always larger and better!) Consider how God fulfilled each promise to Abraham under Plan B.

Unilateral Promises Fulfilled

1. God promised Abraham that he would be the father of many nations and his offspring would be as numerous as the stars. At the end of the 1,000 years, the faith-full saints (children of Abraham = J1 + G1 + C1) will be as numberless as the stars! How many nations down through history will be represented? Hundreds, if not thousands!

2. God promised the land of Canaan to Abraham. If a majority in Israel had been faithful (J1), Plan A would have been fulfilled. Jesus would have established the kingdom of God on Earth after His death and over time, the whole land of Canaan would have become "the land promised to Abraham." Since Israel became rebellious [J4] and unfaithful, God had to implement Plan B. At the end of sin's drama, "the promised land" will fill "the whole Earth." Jesus will create a new Heaven and a new Earth. The holy city, New Jerusalem (whose Builder and Maker is God) will descend. God will move His throne to Earth and He will dwell here with Abraham and his descendants [J1 + G1 + C1] forever!

3. Finally, God promised Abraham that all nations on Earth would be blessed through him. In the Earth made new, the people who were saved will see the fulfillment of this promise. The saints will see a barren man with more descendants than he can count. The saints will see a barren man who received a son by faith. Through this son, Jesus came and through Jesus, all nations have been blessed (J1 + G1 + C1). Throughout the endless ages of eternity, the nations will rejoice to see and worship Jesus. The saints will cast their crowns before Him and marvel at His amazing love for sinners. They will never tire of singing, "Salvation belongs to the Lamb who came to Earth through the seed of Abraham and redeemed us with His blood!"

When these three promises are fulfilled, I am sure Abraham will weep for joy as he worships at Jesus' feet. Abraham looked for a city whose Builder and Maker is God, but he never dreamed the city would be 1,420 miles cubed with walls 216 feet thick. He never dreamed the world would someday become "the promised land!"

I hope the importance of being an heir of Abraham makes sense. If a person is not counted as an heir of Abraham [J1 or G1 or C1], he has no future and no place to live!

References
1. Malachi 3:6
2. Revelation 14:6
3. Genesis 15:6; Romans 4:3; Hebrews 11
4. Philippians 2:11-15; Daniel 12:3
5. Isaiah 42:6,7
6. Genesis 4:25; 5:3
7. Genesis 4:17
8. Genesis 4:26
9. Hebrews 11:7
10. Genesis 10:25
11. Genesis 10:21
12. Genesis 12:1-4
13. Genesis 20
14. Genesis 49:4;35:22
15. Genesis 38:7
16. Genesis 47:21
17. Hebrews 3:5-4:2
18. Exodus 19:4-8
19. Deuteronomy 28; 1 Thessalonians 2:14-16
20. Galatians 3:28,29
21. Revelation 7:9,10
22. Galatians 3:29, insertion mine
23. Romans 9:2-8, insertions mine
24. Genesis 35:23-26
25. Romans 2:17-29
26. Romans 2:14,15
27. Ephesians 2:10-21, insertions mine
28. Galatians 3:6-11, insertions mine
29. Colossians 2:14-17
30. Genesis 9:11
31. Genesis 15:5; Revelation 7:9
32. Genesis 17:8, Revelation 21:7

33. Genesis 18:18,19; Revelation 1:6; 5:10
34. Genesis 15:13
35. Hebrews 11:10

Appendix C

The Seven Churches

"Write, therefore, what you have seen, what is now and what will take place later." (Revelation 1:19)

Introduction

It may seem surprising that I have included a discussion on the seven churches at the end of this book. There are two reasons for this. First and foremost, I have saved the best for last. If you want to have an intimate relationship with Jesus, a proper understanding of the messages to the seven churches will put you on the right track. Few Christians appreciate that the testimony of Jesus to the seven churches stands as a divine summation of what is important to Him. Second, the seven churches are presented at the end of this commentary because they do not contain apocalyptic prophecy. They do not conform to the four rules that govern apocalyptic interpretation. They are not chronological in nature and they are not limited by a starting point or ending point in time. Even more, the messages to the seven churches are not given in any discernable order. In fact, the messages to the seven churches can be rearranged in any order, there is no dilution or consequence, and there is no conflict with the seventeen apocalyptic prophecies found in Daniel and Revelation.

Some expositors on prophecy insist on treating the seven churches as though they represent seven periods of time or seven dispensations since Jesus was on Earth. This treatment of the seven churches is not supported by the text. All seven churches simultaneously existed when Jesus addressed them in A.D. 95. Antipas (the martyr) had recently died in Pergamum and Jezebel (the harlot) lived in Thyatira. Forcing the seven churches into seven time periods creates a number of unnecessary problems. For example, why should access to the Tree of Life be limited to overcomers living during the "so-called" period of Ephesus?[1] This is not a rhetorical question because the Bible plainly teaches that all overcomers will be granted access to the Tree of Life.[2] Therefore, any effort to impose seven time periods on the seven churches will put the Bible in a state of internal conflict. The specific promise made to overcomers in each church will be granted to all overcomers at the Second Coming.

Appendix C - The Seven Churches

The messages to the seven churches are timeless and universal. At any given time, the experiences of the seven church experiences are simultaneously taking place within Christianity. Some Christians are having the Ephesus experience right now and others are having the Laodicean experience. *When viewed in their totality, the seven churches represent the whole of Christianity at any time.*

When Jesus selected the seven churches identified in Revelation 2 and 3, other Christian churches in Asia Minor existed at the same time. However, He specifically chose these seven churches because, corporately speaking, they sum up the Christian experience. Please consider three points:

1. The number seven indicates completion and fullness in the book of Revelation (e.g., seven churches, seven seals, seven trumpets, seven heads, seven bowls, seven thunders, etc.). Generally speaking, Christianity in Asia Minor in A.D. 95 was teetering between apostasy and discouragement. Years of suffering and martyrdom had taken a heavy toll and many Christians were either giving up or compromising. This brink of extinction explains why Jesus spoke to the seven churches. The testimony of Jesus is not an ordinary event. Jesus had something extremely important to say and nothing is sharper or clearer than the truth spoken from God's own lips! Many Christians do not realize this, but Jesus speaking to the seven churches from Patmos is the equivalent of Jesus speaking to Israel from Mount Sinai. Jesus commended the seven churches for the good things they were doing, but He also condemned those churches who had compromised with evil. As we proceed with this study, keep this thought in mind: *Overcoming evil is an essential part of redemption.* Jesus emphasized this point seven times.

2. In A.D. 95, the original apostles and the apostle Paul were dead, all but John. Jerusalem had been in ruins for twenty-five years and Rome continued to persecute Christians because they were thought to be a sect of Jews. Therefore, when Jesus spoke to the seven churches, He spoke to the second and third generation of the Christian faith. Few of these people, if any, were alive when Jesus walked on Earth. Because each generation has to rediscover God for itself, religious behavior and beliefs constantly mutate. The

carnal nature is insatiable, restless, rebellious, and hostile toward God's laws, and Jesus intervened to ensure His gospel could grow. Christianity in Asia Minor was on the brink of apostasy or abandonment.

3. As a practical matter, Jesus commanded John to send copies of the book of Revelation to each of the seven churches. History records that Rome destroyed the seven churches by the third century A.D. and if seven copies of the book of Revelation had not been sent, two things might have happened. First, it is possible that Christianity might have deteriorated to the point where it could no longer survive as a religious body. Second, the book of Revelation might have been lost and what a loss that would have been for the final generation!

Christians Evicted From Judaism

An explanation about the origin of the seven churches might help us understand the true meaning of what John wrote nearly two millennia ago. During His brief ministry on Earth (A.D. 27-30), Jesus established a new religion that stood, and continues to stand, in direct opposition to all other religions. At first, this religion was called "The Way" because Jesus said of Himself, **"I am *the way* and the truth and the life."**[3] As the movement grew in size and notoriety, the Jews and other religious people found the name of the movement to be inflammatory because their title, "*The Way*," inferred there was *no other way* to God.

During His ministry, Jesus made many claims that were impossible for most Jews to accept. For example, what would you have thought if you were a devout Jew and heard a young carpenter from Nazareth say, **"I am the way and the truth and the life. No one comes to the Father except through *me*."**[4] What would you have thought if you were a member of the Sanhedrin and heard Peter, a young fisherman from Galilee say, **"Salvation is found in no one else** [than Jesus Christ]**, for there is no other name under heaven given to men by which we must be saved."**[5] The controversial nature of the title, "The Way," during those early years, eventually led the believers to be called "Christians."[6]

Even though the Jews hated and persecuted members of "The Way," Jerusalem served as the defacto headquarters of Christianity for forty years (A.D. 30 to A.D. 70). The Romans considered Christians to be a sect *within* Judaism because of similarities between the two religions.[7] To the Roman mind, Pharisees, Sadducees, Essenes, and Christians were all Jewish sects. When the Romans destroyed Jerusalem in A.D. 70, they destroyed the temple of the Jews, as well as "the command and control center" of Christianity. This was God's plan. Jesus eliminated Jerusalem as the headquarters of Christianity for at least four reasons:

1. Fleeing Christians carried the gospel of Christ throughout the Roman Empire.
2. Christianity became a standalone religious body that was separate and distinct from Jerusalem and Judaism.
3. Christianity (unlike Judaism) proved that it is not concerned with ethnic origin or nationalism. Anyone within any nation could become a Christian.
4. After Jerusalem was destroyed, Jewish influence and paradigms on Christianity became less powerful.

God is so wise. Everything He does is timely and comprehensive. He held back the destruction of Jerusalem for forty years after Jesus ascended, so the Christian movement could have time to mature. If God had destroyed Jerusalem too soon, Christianity might have disbanded. If He had waited too long, Jewish paradigms and customs could have engulfed Christianity.

Shortly after Jesus returned to Heaven, God sent the apostle Paul throughout the Roman Empire among the Gentiles to establish Christian churches.[8] God foreknew that Christians living in Jerusalem would need help outside of Jerusalem. Paul's efforts were fruitful and his tireless labor proved to be a great blessing for Christians when the Romans destroyed Jerusalem in A.D. 70. Christians fleeing from Jerusalem found an established network of helpful brothers and sisters in the cities where Paul had established a church. The seven churches in Asia Minor were largely the result of Paul's theological and missionary endeavors and they were ready to help fellow Christians escaping from Jerusalem.

Complexity

Christianity is a complicated religion because the plan of redemption has ten integrated elements that operate in perfect harmony. Look over this list:

1. Law
2. Grace
3. Faith
4. Obedience
5. Sin
6. Righteousness
7. Justification
8. Sanctification
9. Judgment
10. Restitution and Reward

Putting all of these elements together properly so that the Bible is not put into a state of internal conflict is a difficult exercise. While the Bible perfectly harmonizes all ten elements, it takes considerable effort to sort and synthesize the elements. I think one reason Christianity is so difficult to understand is because everything that God makes is complex. Consider the intricate functions of the human body, the constellations in the starry heavens, the diversity of life in the ocean, the diversity and balance within the animal kingdom, the diversity and importance of the plant kingdom, and how all of the elements of creation relate to life itself. God is never simple, but certain things about God can be simplified so that even a child can understand something about God's ways.

The Bible says that God is love. This is a simple concept that has enormous depth. The depth of God's love is found in details describing God. When a Bible student studies and synthesizes the details of God's actions and ways, the interwoven tapestry is beautiful and awe inspiring. Every action of God springs from love. To know God is to love God! If we examine a flower, a hummingbird, a whale, a polar bear or a newborn child, a DNA chain, or a picture taken with the Hubble Telescope, we marvel at God's attention to detail. All of His creations are intricate and deliberate and so are His actions. God has infinite wisdom and every design and action that He takes reflects His wisdom. Christianity is complex because God is rich in detail!

Sorting through the details and harmonizing the ten elements of Christianity listed above is an educational experience that transforms everyone who participates in it. There is nothing more fulfilling than understanding God's plan of redemption. There is enormous beauty in Plan A and there is even greater beauty in Plan B! Studying God's creation and actions is life changing. He designed it this way because the more we understand about God and His love, the more we will want to please Him. After meeting with God, Moses was totally thrilled! He said, **"If you are pleased with me, teach me your ways so I may know you and continue to find favor with you."**[9] There is nothing in the whole universe that is as interesting, as intricate, as loving, as magnificent, as powerful, and as wise as God.

God's attention to detail is worth our attention because God's complexity provides a number of exits for those who want to deviate from God's will. In other words, the Bible can be easily distorted and made to say whatever you want it to say because the Word of God is not simple. This problem happened in the seven churches and it continues today. Our response to God's complexity reveals far more about us than you might think. A person may claim to be a Christian and behave like the devil (this took place in Pergamum) or a person may claim to be a Christian and behave like Christ (this took place in Philadelphia). Both churches claimed to be Christian! You might think that the gospel of Jesus is all about Jesus, but the gospel of Jesus also reveals who and what we really are. The gospel of Jesus can be compared to pressing your fist into a lump of clay. If the clay is soft, a perfect reflection of your fist will occur. If the clay is hard, the clay will remain unchanged. The gospel of Jesus reveals who we really are.

An honest-hearted person will seek out God's truth even when the truth is contrary to what he wants to believe. Whenever a person comes to a point in his life where he is willing to believe that God's truth is *always* beneficial, he will pursue truth, regardless of the consequences, because he knows that result will produce a higher plane of living. The truth seeker wants to walk more closely with God and like Moses, he prays, **"teach me your ways so I may know you and continue to find favor with you."** The prayer and experience of honest-hearted people goes something like this: "Lord, I don't care what the truth is, what it costs or where it may lead. Please open my eyes that I may understand it and subdue the natural stubbornness in my heart so that I may live it."

"Getting Saved"

Much can be written about the topic of "getting saved." For purposes of discussion, let us consider two alternative views of salvation. Individuals holding one view claim that salvation is punctiliar, that is, it comes at a specific moment in time. The textual basis for this group is Romans 10:9,10: **"That if you confess with your mouth, 'Jesus is Lord,' and believe in your heart that God raised him from the dead, you will be saved. For it is with your heart that you believe and are justified, and it is with your mouth that you confess and are saved."** Other people claim that salvation takes a life time. They believe that if you do everything that God commands for the rest of your life, you will be saved. The textual basis for this group is Romans 2:13: **"For it is not those who hear the law who are righteous in God's sight, but it is those who obey the law who will be declared righteous."** While these texts appear to be in conflict on the surface, further study reveals there is no conflict between them. When all of Paul's words are properly put together, both texts in Romans are harmonious with the whole Bible because the Bible is not internally conflicted. (If the Bible is factually conflicted, then the Bible cannot be true because truth is proven by the harmony that comes from the sum of its parts.)

Many people put the Bible in a state of internal conflict without realizing what they are doing. This error occurs when a person advocates a position which the whole Bible does not advocate. Even though the two positions mentioned above are theologically opposed, both views actually harm the gospel of Jesus! The gospel of Jesus teaches that salvation is both a punctiliar event <u>and</u> a lifetime process.

A quick survey of the seven churches reveals that most of the churches had drifted away from the importance of holiness or they had degenerated into legalism. The first group distorted the importance of sanctification and the second group distorted the gift of Christ's righteousness. Naturally, the second group was smaller than the first because freedom from obedience is more attractive to our rebellious nature[10] than the demands of legalism.

Remember, the seven churches were second and third generation Christians. This means that in A.D. 95, the seven churches had been around long enough to see where their theology was going. If a surveyor is off by one-half of a degree when surveying one acre, the consequence will not be very dramatic. However, if a surveyor is off by one-half of a degree when surveying ten sections (ten square miles), the consequences will be dramatic! A small error at the beginning will have drastic results given enough distance or time. The seven churches existed in A.D. 95, sixty years after the time Jesus ascended, and the subtle consequences of early errors had become crystal clear. According to Jesus, six of the seven churches were in serious trouble and they needed to repent of their toxic faith and evil behavior.

Three Types of People

Human beings can be divided into three groups. There are "right brained" people and "left brained" people and a few people who can use both sides of their brain. In the United States, there are Republicans, Democrats, and Independents. There are rich people, poor people, and a middle class. There are healthy people, sick people, and people whose physical condition is determined by the amount of work to be done. There are good people, bad people, and careless people. There are young people, old people, and middle-aged people. You may recall from our study on the fifth trumpet that there are saints, religious wicked, and non-religious wicked people, too.

Three groups also have varied understandings of salvation. There are people wanting to be saved *in* their sins (the group avoiding obedience) and those wanting to be saved for doing what is right (the group insisting on obedience). However, there is also a middle group. From the beginning, there has been a small group of people genuinely interested in knowing and walking with God.[11] Many people become a Christian to avoid hell. This motive will not yield good results because it usually develops into an attitude of doing the absolute minimum to avoid hell. In other words, many Christians will only go as far as necessary to be saved. Anything beyond meeting the minimum prerequisites is rejected as legalism. The gospel of Jesus is not about loving the Giver to earn the gift of eternal life. The gospel of Jesus is about having communion with God here and now. If eternal life is the goal of your Christian experience, you have missed the essential purpose of the gospel of Jesus. However, if walking with God is your objective, the gospel of Jesus will show you how. You will often repeat the precious words of Moses: **"Teach me your ways so I may know you and continue to find favor with you."**

The Bible declares this verdict: A person controlled by the carnal mind cannot walk with God, our carnal nature will not permit it! **"Those who live according to the sinful nature have their** minds set on what that nature desires; but those who live in accordance with the Spirit have their minds set on what the Spirit desires. The mind of sinful man is death, but the mind controlled by the Spirit is life and peace, the sinful mind is hostile to God. It does not submit to God's law, nor can it do so. Those controlled by the sinful nature cannot please God."[12]

The Greek word *nikao* means to conquer, to subdue, to overcome. The idea expressed in *nikao* is infinite – something ongoing forever. Jesus used *nikao* seven times when speaking to the seven churches because true Christianity involves a lifelong struggle with the carnal nature. When people understand the true gospel of Jesus, they learn that salvation is a two-sided coin. Redemption includes justification. When we surrender our heart to Jesus, to go - to be - to do as He directs, God sees us as though we never sinned. This is the punctiliar moment that salvation begins. Redemption also includes sanctification. Because we are naturally rebellious, we have to re-surrender to Jesus and His gospel each day and this involves the huge struggle of overcoming our inherent rebellion toward God's way of love. Overcoming the power of sin is humanly impossible. This is why Jesus sends the Holy Spirit to each person seeking transformation. If we are willing to be transformed, we have the privilege of walking with God. This is the work of a lifetime.

Bottom line: Unless we surrender to the gospel of Jesus, there is no justification. Unless we are overcomers, there is no sanctification, and consequently, no justification. Seven times Jesus stated the relationship between justification and sanctification to the seven churches.

Horse First, Cart Follows

Every born again Christian has to be on guard that he does not put "the cart before the horse." Sanctification does not merit salvation or eternal life because the law declares that everyone sins. In fact, no sinner can live for long without sinning. Sinning (violating the gospel) is in our nature. Overcoming temptation and sin is a tiring and difficult experience and many Christians give up on it after a few years. However, those who press on, fighting "the good fight of faith," do experience a series of amazing victories! In fact, the reality of Jesus Christ is renewed each time Christ performs a miracle within an overcomer. There is nothing quite like this experience.

There is nothing that proves the existence of Jesus Christ better than personally experiencing your life changed by His power!

Our challenge is to fight the good fight of faith year after year without becoming exhausted and discouraged. If a person attempts to sanctify himself in his own strength, he will soon give up because victory will be illusive, too difficult, and ultimately, impossible. Many Christians give up on the sanctification process shortly after joining a church, but they are ashamed to openly admit it. Instead of standing before the church and confessing defeat, one of two scenarios usually plays out when a person gives up. The first scenario goes something like this: The Christian continues to attend church services, sing praises, give offerings, and appear respectable. He maintains *a form of godliness* by publicly staying within "church boundaries," but he remains a slave to sin. He has no victory in his life over sin and lives a double life. In the presence of other Christians he acts like a Christian, but in the darkness he has a demon. The second scenario is just as bad: A Christian will change his theology in order to end the struggle with sanctification. He will justify his behavior by distorting Bible texts that permit him to fulfill the desires of his carnal nature. Both behaviors are fatal and clearly identified in the seven churches.[13]

If an honest-hearted person asks Jesus for enlightenment (a greater understanding of truth) and strength to overcome the demands of the carnal nature (greater conformity to God's will). Jesus will hear his petition and that person will prevail and be changed! (Addicts usually require special help to do this.*) When Jesus sees that a sinner is humble (teachable) and repentant (wants to be

---

*Note: An addict, by definition, is a slave to his addiction. He has no will power to overcome his addiction. God understands the slavery of addiction and He has given caring people insight on ways to help addicts who want to be set free. A properly balanced recovery involves a physical component (including diet, exercise, and the use of medication if or as required), a mental component (behavior modification therapy, accepting and respecting boundaries, accountability, etc.), and a spiritual component (learning how to love others, discovering God's power, finding healing, peace, joy and wholeness through Jesus). Of course, an addict can have the assurance of salvation (punctiliar moment) before he is free of his

Continued on following page.

changed), He sends the Holy Spirit to that sinner and the battle with a particular temptation is *miraculously* neutralized. The strength to overcome sin comes from Christ. He alone is able to neutralize our attraction for wrong doing. This is a profound truth that every Christian must personally experience. The life of Jesus was an outstanding success because Jesus asked the Father for strength to do what He could not do. **"During the days of Jesus' life on Earth, he offered up prayers and petitions with loud cries and tears to the one who could save him from death,** *and he was heard because of his reverent submission.* **Although he was a son, he learned obedience from what he suffered and, once made perfect, he became the source of eternal salvation for all who obey him."**[14]

Many people think Jesus was a success in overcoming sin because He was God. He is God, but Jesus came to Earth as a God without any power of His own! Jesus laid aside His divine powers and prerogatives before He came to Earth. He could only do whatever the Father gave Him the power to do! Jesus said, **"I tell you the truth, the Son can do nothing by himself . . . By myself I can do nothing . . . for I seek not to please myself but him who sent me."**[16]

Paul clearly understood the intricate relationship between justification and sanctification. Think about Paul's words in Romans: **"For in the gospel a righteousness from God is revealed, a righteousness that is by faith from first to last** [For in the gospel of Jesus there is a righteousness which has been created by God Himself. The righteousness created through the perfect life of Jesus enables God to save man from the beginning of redemption

---

addiction, but the addict must also understand that the assurance of salvation is based on overcoming (the work of a lifetime). As long as the addict is engaged in an effort to overcome his addiction, he is justified in God's sight through Christ's righteousness. This point is emphasized because the law of sin is at work in the lives of all sinners. As long as addicts and non-addicts alike are engaged in an effort to overcome sin, God's grace (justification) covers our deficiencies and His promise to neutralize sin's power is unwavering.[15] Remember, the essential difference between addicts and non-addicts is the depth of slavery to sin.

to the end of redemption], **just as it is written: 'The righteous will live by faith'** [in other words, the righteous will forever live in a "go-be-do" state, going as God directs, doing as God commands, being all that God requires of them – even throughout eternity!] **. . . For we maintain that a man is justified by faith apart from observing the law.** [Staying within the boundaries is essential, but obeying the law cannot save anyone! Sinners cannot possibly manufacture the righteousness needed for salvation.] **Is God the God of Jews only? Is he not the God of Gentiles too? Yes, of Gentiles too, since there is only one God, who will justify the circumcised by faith and the uncircumcised through that same faith.** [This means that people who do not know the law, but live up to the demands of the Spirit and those who know the law and live up to the demands of the Spirit are saved through the same faith. Everyone who obeys the Spirit of God will be sanctified and saved.] **Do we, then, nullify the law by this faith? Not at all! Rather, we uphold the law** [because the law of God is perfect, righteous and true. The law of God has been given to accelerate our knowledge of where the Spirit will lead]."[17]

Saul as J3, Paul as C1

If you have read Appendix B, you will recall that mankind can be divided into three basic groups and each group has four divisions. When Saul was a J3, that is, an arrogant Jew who worshiped his religion as though it were God, he was self-righteous according to the law and without fault in his own eyes.

"For it is we [born again believers in Christ - C1] **who are the circumcision, we who worship by the Spirit of God, who glory in Christ Jesus, and who put no confidence in** [the circumcision of] **the flesh – though I myself have reasons for such confidence. If anyone else thinks he has reasons to put confidence in the flesh, I have more: Circumcised on the eighth day, of the people of Israel, of the tribe of Benjamin, a Hebrew of Hebrews; in regard to the law, a Pharisee; as for zeal, persecuting the church; as for legalistic righteousness, faultless.** But [the Lord showed me the errors of my gross behavior and beliefs and] **whatever was to my profit I now consider loss for the sake of Christ. What is more, I consider everything a loss compared to the surpassing greatness of knowing Christ Jesus my Lord, for whose sake I**

have lost all things. [I am not sad about this!] **I consider them rubbish, that I may gain Christ and be found in him, not having a righteousness of my own that comes from** [obeying] **the law, but that which is through faith in Christ– the righteousness that comes from God and is by faith."**[18]

After Paul's experience on the road to Damascus, he understood that the righteousness required by God for our salvation cannot be produced by a sinner. This does not mean that the law of God is imperfect! It means that unless God provides the righteousness required for salvation, no one can be saved. Justification does not eliminate the necessity for sanctification! Sanctification is the process that reveals genuine faith! Analyze Paul's words in the following text and remember, he had been a Christian for more than twenty years when he wrote them. **"I know that nothing good lives in me, that is, in my sinful nature. For I have the desire to do what is good, but I cannot carry it out. For what I do is not the good I want to do; no, the evil I do not want to do– this I keep on doing. Now if I do what I do not want to do, it is no longer I who do it, but it is sin living in me that does it. So I find this law at work: When I want to do good, evil is right there with me. For in my inner being I delight in God's law; but I see another law at work in the members of my body, waging war against the law of my mind and making me a prisoner of the law of sin at work within my members. What a wretched man I am! Who will rescue me from this body of death?** [There is only one solution.] **Thanks be to God** – [victory is possible] **through Jesus Christ our Lord! So then, I myself in my mind am a slave to God's law, but in the sinful nature a slave to the law of sin."**[19]

Near the end of his life, Paul wrote these inspiring words, **"I have fought the good fight** [of sanctification, overcoming my sinful nature]**, I have finished the race, I have kept the faith. Now there is in store for me the crown of righteousness, which the Lord, the righteous Judge, will award to me on that day– and not only to me, but also to all who have longed for his appearing."**[20]

Repeat Seven Times: Overcoming Is Essential!

The gospel of Jesus declares that sinners cannot overcome every temptation to sin on their own. The gospel of Jesus also declares that Jesus will purify us of our sins if we confess our sins to Him. **"If we confess our sins, he is faithful and just and will forgive us our sins and purify us from all unrighteousness."**[21] When we claim this promise, Jesus may not neutralize the temptation or remove the power of a particular sin for a period of time (perhaps a lifetime) because He wants to see if we love Him more than the sin that besets us. In such a case, the sinner might think that Jesus is not listening because he remains caught in a dreadful torment. Like Paul, the sinner wants the power to overcome, but his sinful nature demands satisfaction. What will the sinner do? Will he endure the torment while waiting on the Lord to give him victory or will he throw in the towel, give in and sin again? Our choices reveal our desires. If the sinner loves the Lord more than he loves the sin, he may stumble around for a bit, but he will keep pestering the Lord for purification until the Lord neutralizes the power of that sin and delivers Him from it. This is where the battle of faith occurs and what it means to "wrestle with the Lord" as did Jacob.[22]

Many Christians reject the idea that sanctification is an inseparable component of salvation. Such Christians do not think it necessary to be saved *from* their sins. They want to be saved *in* their sins. But Jesus makes it perfectly clear to the seven churches that justification and sanctification are inseparable by stating seven times that overcoming is a mandatory attitude for salvation. Paul adds, **"If you are not disciplined (and everyone undergoes discipline), then you are illegitimate children** [that is, you have no father who loves you, who trains you and prepares you for the challenges of life] **and** [if you have no father you are] **not true sons. Moreover, we have all had human fathers who disciplined us and we respected them for it. How much more should we submit to the Father of our spirits and live! Our fathers disciplined us for a little while as they thought best; but God disciplines us** [while having this carnal nature] **for our good, that we may share in his holiness.** *No discipline seems pleasant at the time, but painful.* Later on, however, it produces a harvest of righteousness and peace for those who have been *trained* by it. Therefore, strengthen your feeble arms and weak knees. 'Make level paths for your feet,' so that the lame may not be disabled, but rather healed. Make every effort to live in peace with all men and

to be holy; without holiness [sanctification] **no one will see the Lord."** [23]

Bottom line: A pseudo-Christian is a person who *pretends* to be a Christian. He sings praises and says all of the right words, but he prays without receiving power because he is unwilling to go-be-do. His heart and affections are elsewhere.[24] The essential difference between a pseudo-Christian and a genuine Christian is not intellectual ascent to truth, it is the direction of love. A born again Christian loves in an outward direction – he loves God and His Word with all his heart, mind and soul, and his neighbor as himself.[25] A pseudo-Christian loves in an inward direction – he is self-centered, he loves personal comfort, religious traditions, his assets, and the admiration or approval of others.[26] Keep these two distinctions in mind as we examine the seven churches because Jesus requires His followers to fight against the selfish demands of the carnal nature until death or the sealing occurs and God removes the carnal nature.

(**Note:** For further discussion on the topics of justification, sanctification and the seal of God, please see my book, *Jesus: The Alpha and The Omega*, Chapters 4-8. These chapters may be freely downloaded over the internet at: http://www.wake-up.org/Alpha/Subjindex.htm.)

Ephesus

"To the angel of the church in Ephesus write: These are the words of him who holds the seven stars in his right hand and walks among the seven golden lampstands: I know your deeds, your hard work and your perseverance. I know that you cannot tolerate wicked men, that you have tested those who claim to be apostles but are not, and have found them false. You have persevered and have endured hardships for my name, and have not grown weary. Yet I hold this against you: You have forsaken your first love. Remember the height from which you have fallen! Repent and *do the things you did at first*. If you do not repent, I will come to you and remove your lampstand from its place. But you have this in your favor: You hate the practices [behaviors] **of the Nicolaitans, which I also hate. He who has an ear, let him hear what the Spirit says to the churches. To him who overcomes, I will give the right to eat from the tree of life, which is in the paradise of God."**[27]

Appendix C - The Seven Churches

The salutation to Ephesus begins with "To *the angel* of the church in Ephesus." The message to Ephesus is directed *to the angel* of the church in Ephesus because a specific angel was assigned the task of overseeing the needs of the church at Ephesus. Notice how this unfolds. When this vision begins, John saw Jesus walking among seven candlesticks and Jesus had seven stars in His right hand.[28] Each candlestick represents a church and each star represents an angel assigned to a church.[29] These seven angels stand before God[30] and they are delighted to do whatever God commands. In this particular case, Jesus had assigned seven angels to serve the seven churches and each angel had the responsibility of seeing that each church received "the testimony of Jesus." This process is not unusual because God uses angels to accomplish specific tasks. The apostle Paul wrote, **"Are not all angels ministering spirits sent to serve those who will inherit salvation?"**[31]

Jesus identified Himself to the church at Ephesus as the One "who holds the seven stars in His right hand and walks among the seven golden lampstands." Jesus used this descriptive language to show that He is the Head of the Church.[32] "Walking among the lampstands" means that Jesus is directly involved with His church family on Earth. He intimately knows the condition of each member.

Jesus commended the people at Ephesus for their perseverance and fidelity to righteousness in the face of persecution. Jesus also commended the church at Ephesus for testing those who claimed to be apostles but found that they were infiltrators sent by the devil. Jesus scolded the church because they had lost their first love for Him. The joy and enthusiasm of their first love had died. The church at Ephesus had become cold and indifferent and Jesus threatened to remove Ephesus (their lampstand) from His presence if they did not repent of this apostasy. Did you notice that losing your first love for Jesus is an apostasy?

What causes a Christian to lose his first love for Jesus and become a pseudo-Christian? When we love anyone or anything more than Jesus, our first love for Jesus *evaporates*. The following text explains how we can tell if we love Jesus foremost. **"A new command I give you: Love one another. As I have loved you, so you must love one another. By this all men will know that you are my disciples, if you love one another. . . . You are my friends if you do what I command. This is my command:**

Love each other. . . . If you love me, you will obey what I command."[33]

A genuine Christian loves in an outward direction whereas a pseudo-Christian loves in an inward direction. This is a critical difference and every Christian needs to be aware that he faces two deadly forces each day. Our first enemy is our fallen sinful nature and our second enemy is the devil. Our carnal nature is a self-resurrecting monster that selfishly demands first place in everything every day. The devil knows this and he preys on this natural inclination.[34] Paul clearly understood the problem. He knew that if he allowed his sinful nature to take over, he too would become a pseudo-Christian in no time. This is why he wrote, **"I die every day – I mean that, brothers –** [I have to crucify my carnal nature every day] **just as surely as I glory** [rejoice] **over you in Christ Jesus our Lord."**[35] The carnal nature can only be put to death through a daily charge of Holy Spirit power. If a Christian does not pray and drink in God's Word, his spiritual battery will die, his spiritual radio will go silent, and he will lose communion with God. If a Christian becomes too busy to pray, if he doesn't have some quiet time with God, he will soon become weak in resolve and purpose. *The Christian experience cannot be sustained without reconnecting to Jesus on a daily basis.*[36] This simple truth can be summed up as follows: "One week without Bible study and prayer makes one weak."

Jesus was unhappy with the members at Ephesus because the loss of first love is fatal. Left unchecked, the Christian church at Ephesus would become a pseudo-Christian church. Think about this. Jesus told the church that He would abandon them if they did not repent. Do you think that Jesus has abandoned any church groups over the past 2,000 years? I do. Do you think it is possible for people to attend a worship service and Jesus (through the Holy Spirit) is not present? I do. The message sent to Ephesus is a timeless message for all Christians. If we lose our first love for Jesus, we lose Jesus. **"As the Father has loved me, so have I loved you. Now remain in my love."** [37]

Jesus said to the church at Ephesus, **"But you have this in your favor: You hate the practices of the Nicolaitans, which I also hate."** Nicolas, of Alexandria, Egypt was a brilliant philosopher who lived during the first century A.D. and he distorted Christ's teachings by merging gnostic ideas with them. This caused a subtle but steady departure from the truth that Jesus came to reveal about the Father. In terms of behavior, Gnosticism contaminated the importance of sanctification and this robbed the gospel of its transforming power.

Long before Jesus came to Earth, Gnosticism began as a school of thought in the hedonistic philosophies of the Greeks and Romans and it included the creeds of Plato and Philo. As time passed, Gnosticism also included concepts taken from mystical religions in India and Persia. The Gnostics at Ephesus treated the Word of God as though it was an allegory (a parable having many different shades of meaning). Even though various schools of thought existed within Gnosticism, gnostic philosophy might be summed up as a collection of clever ideas that speak about right and wrong, good and evil, life and death, but the result is always the same. Self becomes self's savior. Today, Gnosticism has morphed into modern concepts that include "higher learning," "moral relevancy," and "humanism." Gnosticism belittles man's need for Jesus and it overrides God's commandments with human traditions. The church at Ephesus hated the Nicolaitan *practices* so Jesus commended the Ephesus church on this point.

Jesus closed His remarks to the church at Ephesus saying, **"He who has an ear, let him hear what the Spirit says to the churches. To him who overcomes, I will give the right to eat from the Tree of Life, which is in the paradise of God."** The phrase "He who has an ear." means there is a hidden message which pseudo-Christians cannot appreciate. The hidden message is this: Those who walk in the Spirit each day and overrule the carnal nature through the indwelling power of the Holy Spirit can enjoy the Tree of Life *right now*. In a spiritual sense, those who abide in Christ have life already![38] They do not have to wait to reach the paradise of God to receive the fullness of life. We can spiritually eat from the Tree of Life (the Word of God) and the joy and peace that comes from communion with God goes beyond human understanding.

God did not allow Adam and Eve to eat from the Tree of Life after they sinned because access to the fruit of this tree sustains life indefinitely.[39] In a spiritual way, all who have the first love experience will joyfully obey the teachings of Jesus and they will live forever.[40] Even more, Jesus would not ask us to be an overcomer if overcoming was impossible. All things are possible through

God and overcoming is only possible through God! The gospel of Jesus includes the power to be transformed (sanctified). Through the indwelling power of the Holy Spirit, the carnal nature can be temporarily neutralized so the spiritual nature might flourish. (Remember, Peter temporarily walked on water so that he might come close to Jesus.) I cannot think of anything better than being victorious over my carnal nature and living with Jesus forever.

Smyrna

"To the angel of the church in Smyrna write: These are the words of him who is the First and the Last [Alpha and Omega]**, who died** [for you] **and came to life again. I know your afflictions and your poverty – yet you are rich** [in the two things that really count, love and faith]**! I know the slander** [lies and distortions] **of those who say they are Jews** [the chosen people] **and are not, but are a synagogue of Satan. Do not be afraid of what you are about to suffer** [for I am with you]**. I tell you, the devil will put some of you in prison to test you, and you will suffer** [deadly] **persecution for ten days. Be faithful, even to the point of death, and I will give you the crown of** [eternal] **life. He who has an ear, let him hear what the Spirit says to the churches. He who overcomes** [who does not capitulate] **will not be hurt at all by the second death."**[41]

Three points in this message invite further analysis.

1. Early Christians (remember, this message was given to the church at Smyrna in A.D. 95) saw themselves as the Israel of God, a remnant which had been called out of apostate Israel.[42] The trouble in Smyrna was that some Jewish converts were determined that Jewish traditions be imposed on all church members. (The apostle Paul constantly faced this issue in his day. Jewish converts to Christianity wanted to bring their Jewish bondage and baggage into the church.) Jesus bluntly addressed this apostasy. He called the advocates of Judaism members of "the *synagogue* of Satan."

   Theologically speaking, there is a world of difference between a synagogue and a church. A church consists of followers of Christ. They believe that salvation comes through faith in Him. He is the Savior of all who repent of their sins and follow His teachings. A synagogue on the other hand, consists of people who believe that salvation comes through the observance of the law. Jesus understood the conflict between Christianity and Judaism for He had lived among the Jews. In fact, He had been condemned to death by Jewish authorities for blasphemy.[43] Jesus told the church, **"I know the slander of those who say they are Jews and are not, but are a synagogue of Satan."**

There was intense conflict in Smyrna between Jewish converts and Gentile converts. The conflict centered around the fact that Christianity declared Judaism to be obsolete. The obsolescence of Judaism was a very hard thing for Jewish converts to accept. Can you imagine being told that Jesus terminated your religious views *and culture*? The differences between Jews and Christians are insurmountable. Christians do not have a high priest on Earth, they do not need animal sacrifices, they do not need to attend feasts or participate in temple services, and they do not need circumcision. In fact, they do not need *anything* that Judaism has to offer. *Redemption: Plan B stands on its own two feet because it has an entirely different covenant.*

Freedom from Judaism was a endless source of conflict in Smyrna because Jewish converts wanted to observe their Jewish traditions and Gentile converts refused to go along. (Of course, Gentiles had religious baggage, so they too, were not without fault.) The conflict between Jewish and Gentile believers became so great during the first half of the first century A.D. that the church almost perished before it got started. Thankfully, God chose a young zealous Jew to deal with this problem. After God showed the apostle Paul the truth about Christianity and the falsehoods of Judaism, He sent Paul around the empire to tell everyone. It has been said that one man separated Christianity from Judaism. Paul wrote fourteen of the twenty-seven books of the New Testament. However, it was Jesus who delivered Christians from the Jews through Paul. It was also Jesus who delivered Israel from Egyptian bondage through Moses.

2. Jesus identified Himself to the church at Smyrna as "**the First and the Last** [Almighty God], **who died and came to life again** [for your sakes]." Jesus described Himself with this language so that His followers might remember that the servant is not greater than the Master.[44] Jesus

knew there would be many martyrs for His sake in the church at Smyrna. In A.D. 95, Christianity was an illegal religion in some parts of the Roman Empire. The evil Emperor Domitian (A.D. 81-96) put many Christians to death before he was murdered. Then, Nerva (A.D. 96-98) ascended to Domitian's throne. However, Nerva became ill shortly after he became emperor and died within two years. Then, Trajan (A.D. 98-117) came to power and even though he did not actively seek Christians to kill them, he mandated that if a Christian was found, he was to be arrested and executed unless he immediately renounced his faith. The ten days of persecution mentioned by Jesus evidently referred to a purge that would take place in Smyrna. Roman governors frequently used loyalty tests and purges to maintain control over their subjects, for no governor wanted to be charged with treason against Caesar and lose his head. Jesus warned the Christians in Smyrna of the coming purge and He encouraged them to remain faithful "even to the point of death," because those who are put to death for His sake would, like Him, live again.

One more point. You need to understand the significance of loyalty tests used in Roman times. A non-Roman citizen did not have to do anything wrong to be arrested. He could be arrested for no other reason than to question his loyalty to Caesar and his government. Loyalty arrests and tests were used in Asia Minor to keep sedition and revolt to a minimum. Non-Roman citizens would be brought before a magistrate and questioned. If they regarded Caesar as God, worthy of loyalty, obedience and worship, there was no problem. On the other hand, anyone showing less than 100% loyalty to Caesar as a God was punished with sudden death. The Romans reasoned, "Why should the security and power of the empire be threatened by people who do not love Caesar?" The use of "loyalty tests" makes Paul's words to the Romans perfectly clear, **"That if you confess with your mouth, 'Jesus is Lord,' and believe in your heart that God raised him from the dead, you will be saved."**[45] You can see that saying "Jesus is Lord" before a Roman magistrate in Smyrna would mean sudden death and within this context, doing so at a moment's notice required a great deal of faith in God each day.

3. Jesus also added, "**He who has an ear, let him hear what the Spirit says to the churches. He who overcomes will not be hurt at all by the second death.**" There is a hidden message in this phrase. Overcoming the fear of torture and death is not a normal human instinct. We instinctively do everything possible to protect ourselves from suffering and death. The hidden message that comes through the Spirit is this: God will give a martyr's courage when a martyr's courage is required. In other words, overcoming the fear of death is possible through God's grace because God's grace is more powerful than our fears! So, Jesus' words contain a wonderful promise when He said, "Be firm in your stand for truth and remain loyal to me, even to the point of death, and you will not be hurt at all by the second death." This is good news because the second death is a death for which no grace will be given nor will there be any recovery!

Pergamum

"**To the angel of the church in Pergamum write: These are the words of him who has the** [deadly] **sharp, double-edged sword** [that comes from His mouth]. **I know where you live – where Satan has his throne. Yet you remain true to my name. You did not renounce your faith in me, even in the days of Antipas, my faithful witness, who was put to death in your city – where Satan lives. Nevertheless, I have a few things against you: You have people there who hold to the teaching** [lies] **of Balaam, who taught Balak to entice the Israelites to sin by eating food sacrificed to idols and by committing sexual immorality. Likewise you also have those who hold to the teaching** [lies] **of the Nicolaitans. Repent therefore! Otherwise, I will soon come to you and will fight against them** [the advocates of Nicolaitan doctrine] **with the sword of my mouth. He who has an ear, let him hear what the Spirit says to the churches. To him who overcomes, I will give some of the hidden manna. I will also give him a white stone with a new name written on it, known only to him who receives it.**"[46]

When Jesus spoke these words, Pergamum was the cultural and religious center of Asia. Pergamum was an old, highly respected city. At one time, Pergamum had been the Roman capital of

Asia. The practice of worshiping the Roman emperors began at Pergamum. The city had many pagan temples and Eastern Mysticism was very popular. Pergamum was a big city and it had a large class of educated and wealthy people. In His message to the church at Pergamum, Jesus said twice that Satan had his throne in Pergamum because as a city, Pergamum was the undisputed queen of false religion. Pergamum was the ivory tower of false religion for Asia and as a city, it hated Christians. Jesus observed this hatred when He mentioned the death of faithful Antipas. The hatred expressed toward Christians explains in part, why some Christians in Pergamum were willing to make so many compromises with the devil.

Gentile converts brought pagan baggage, such as their practices of sexual immorality and eating meat offered to idols, into the Christian church at Pergamum. Jesus referred to Balaam in His message to Pergamum because Balaam was an Old Testament prophet who agreed to put a curse on Israel for a sum of money. However, when Balaam attempted to speak curses, blessings came out of his mouth instead. Finally, the distraught prophet revealed to King Balak (the enemy who hired Balaam to curse Israel) that Israel could only be defeated if Israel was enticed into sexual immorality. After learning this, King Balak conspired with a number of Moabite women to become sexually involved with the Israelites. Soon, the Israelites were lured into sexual immorality with these women. Then, the women invited the Israelites to participate in sacrifices offered to their gods. Food and wine was offered to Baal and many Israelites joined with the Moabites in worshiping Baal. As a result, God became furious with His people and He punished Israel with a plague that killed 24,000 Israelites.[47] The parallel is that sexually immoral people infiltrated the church at Pergamum. Their sinful ways caused the church to lose its connection with Christ. The devil promoted this behavior because he knows that when our connection with Jesus is broken, the power to overcome sin is gone.[48]

You may recall that the apostles imposed four specific rules upon Gentile converts at the first general conference of the Christian Church in A.D. 49. At that meeting the apostle James said, **"It is my judgment, therefore, that we should not make it difficult for the Gentiles who are turning to God. Instead we should write to them, telling them to abstain** (a) **from food**

polluted by idols, (b) **from sexual immorality,** (c) **from the meat of strangled animals and** (d) **from** [drinking] **blood."**[49]

When Jesus spoke to the church at Pergamum, He affirmed the Spirit led decision of the apostles by promising to destroy the sexually immoral unless they repented. Jesus' words leave no room for debate. He forbade sexual immorality and eating food offered to idols. Eating food polluted by idols was a superstitious ritual which was supposed to give the consumer the powers of the god to whom the food was first offered. The devil merged this pagan practice with the words of Jesus to create a distortion of His words. When Jesus was on Earth He said, **"Whoever eats my flesh and drinks my blood has eternal life, and I will raise him up at the last day. For my flesh is real food and my blood is real drink. Whoever eats my flesh and drinks my blood remains in me, and I in him. Just as the living Father sent me and I live because of the Father, so the one who feeds on me will live because of me. This is the bread that came down from heaven. Your forefathers ate manna and died, but he who feeds on this bread will live forever."**[50] Jesus made these remarks within the context of eating the Passover feast. His words were a metaphor. The lamb (the flesh) eaten at the feast *represented* Jesus, the wine *represented* His blood, and the bread *represented* His broken body.[51] Some members of the Pergamum church, who had pagan backgrounds, ate food offered to idols. The devil used these people and their pagan background to distort Jesus' words making it *appear* that Jesus justified eating food offered to idols. Very clever.

Jesus also mentioned that some Christians in Pergamum had accepted the teachings of Nicholas. This should not come as a surprise because Pergamum was a center for Gnostic training. The Gnostics treated Scripture as though it were "spiritual" or allegorical. In other words, the Gnostics put a layer of "philosophical fuzz" between the Word of God and its obvious meaning so that ordinary people could not be confident about the meaning of God's Word (that is, separating right from wrong). This has been (and continues to be) one of the devil's best tools for leading Christians astray. How many times have you heard it said, "The Bible does not mean what it says?" Or even worse, how many times have your heard a Bible passage quoted out of context? The devil is a master at putting the Bible in a state of internal conflict. When lay people begin to believe the lie that "ordinary people cannot understand

God's Word," or "we have to trust the opinions of godly experts and the traditions of the church," the devil has gained control of the church. There is no substitute for "a plain thus saith the Lord." Jesus was furious with those Christians who had become advocates of Nicolaitan doctrine. They were leading the church astray. Jesus warned, **"Repent therefore! Otherwise, I will soon come to you and will fight against them with the sword of my mouth."** (Incidently, this is the same sword that kills the wicked at the Second Coming.[52])

In His closing remarks, Jesus offered a special reward to those who would overcome the devil's deceptions. Jesus said, **"To him who overcomes, I will give some of the hidden manna. I will also give him a white stone with a new name written on it, known only to him who receives it."** The hidden message for those who have ears to hear is that overcomers may spiritually partake of Heaven's manna right now! Currently, the physical food of angels is not available to us. Unlike ordinary food offered to meaningless idols, the Word of God is real food.[53] God's Word provides the energy and vitality we need. Jesus is the source of life, strength, joy, and peace.

The promised white stone will be a precious stone that bears the inscription of a secret name. This secret name is an affectionate name which the Father will give to each saint. The white stone will serve as a password enabling the overcomer to enter into God's glorious throne room. Think about it. Every overcomer will be permitted to enter into God's presence *to hear truthful answers to any of his questions*. Contrast this privilege with the Gnostic's pursuit of "higher knowledge" that leads to darkness and separation from God. Standing in the presence of the brilliant light that engulfs the Father, an overcomer will have the opportunity to commune with the Father.[54] I can think of no higher privilege.

Thyatira

The church at Thyatira had a serious problem. Review the words of Jesus and consider what He said: **"To the angel of the church in Thyatira write: These are the words of the Son of God, whose eyes are like blazing fire and whose feet are like burnished bronze. I know your deeds, your love and faith, your service and perseverance, and that you are now doing more than you did at first. Nevertheless, I have this against you:** *You tolerate* **that woman Jezebel, who calls herself a** prophetess. By her teaching she misleads my servants into sexual immorality and the eating of food sacrificed to idols. I have given her time to repent of her immorality, but she is unwilling. So I will cast her on a bed of suffering, and I will make those who commit adultery with her suffer intensely, unless they repent of her ways. I will strike her children dead.

Then all the [seven] churches will know that I am he who searches hearts and minds, and I will repay each of you according to your deeds. Now I say to the rest of you in Thyatira, to you who do not hold to her teaching and have not learned [from gnosticism] Satan's so-called deep secrets (I will not impose any other burden on you): Only hold on to what you have until I come. To him who overcomes and does my will to the end, I will give authority over the nations – 'He will rule them with an iron scepter; he will dash them to pieces like pottery' – just as I have received authority from my Father. I will also give him the morning star. He who has an ear, let him hear what the Spirit says to the churches." [55]

Did Jesus Really Say This?

Jesus spoke to church members at Thyatira with words of comfort and condemnation – comfort for the believers who were doing right and the promise of death – that is right, death for those who were doing wrong. The BIG problem in Thyatira (as in Pergamum) was sexually immoral leadership. Jesus was angry with church leaders at Thyatira because they tolerated a woman named Jezebel in their church![56] The devil is particularly gratified when an immoral person holds a position of religious authority because they can do enormous damage. During the first decade of the twenty-first century, more than 5,000 Catholic priests have been charged or found guilty of sexually abusing children. These revelations have cost the Catholic church more than two billion dollars, as well as a membership decline that is measured by the thousands. In Thyratira's case, a prominent woman named Jezebel* was openly advocating sexual immorality and this made Jesus very angry.

*Note: The Jezebel in Thyatira should not be confused with Jezebel, the wife of King Ahab who lived about a thousand years earlier.

Jezebel must have been a very bright and capable woman. She called herself a prophetess, but she was not a prophetess of God. She prostituted Jesus' teachings by leading others to do the very things that Jesus condemned! She justified sexual immorality through Gnostic logic and philosophy. Jezebel taught that sex was not limited to the confines of marriage and she freely engaged and encouraged others to participate in sexual immorality. She also endorsed the popular belief that eating flesh offered to idols insured the blessings of *all* gods.

The Bible does not itemize everything that Jezebel taught, but we know enough to determine why Jezebel was successful within a Christian church. Jezebel promoted and endorsed ideas that gratified the sensual passions of carnal members. It is amazing what ignorant people will do (or will not do) when someone presuming to speak for God defines right and wrong for them! How unfortunate it is that millions of Christians would rather follow a charismatic pastor than search the Scriptures for themselves. As a recent example of this problem, consider the Worldwide Church of God, whose founder, Herbert W. Armstrong died in the 1990's. His successor eventually informed the church that several core doctrines of the church were factually wrong. Within a few weeks, most of the lay members agreed and the church imploded. Today, Armstrong's church has all but disappeared. How could this happen? Here are two questions to think about. Were the members of the Worldwide Church of God following a religious leader or the changeless gospel of Jesus? Did the Bible suddenly change when Mr. Armstrong died?

Jezebel skillfully merged contemporary pagan practices with Christian ideals. This made the commitment threshold for Christian converts so low that pagans could join the church at Thyatira without having to renounce their pagan ways! This is an area where Christians have particular vulnerability. In fact, many Christians today teach that Jesus will unconditionally accept any person who believes in Him. This claim is false because it is not entirely true.[57] The Bible does teach that Jesus will accept any *repentant* sinner who comes to Him seeking forgiveness, but the key words are "repentant sinner." The devil believes there is a God and he trembles, but he has not stopped or repented of his evil deeds.[58] Because Jezebel lowered the threshold of what it meant to be committed to Jesus, members in the church of Thyatira were not required to forsake their sinful habits and ways. Thus, false teachings and lower standards gave the illusion that the church was growing and prospering. Membership swelled and the church was packed, but the members of the church were not growing in sanctification. In fact, many of the members in Thyatira were becoming more like the devil instead of Jesus.

Jesus condemned Jezebel for using "the mysteries of religion" (Satan's dark secrets or superstitions) to manipulate and control an uninformed laity. The "mysteries of religion" is a catchall phrase that describes meaningless rituals and traditions. I call this phrase "religious bamboozle." Religious leaders have used religious bamboozle for millenniums to sway and control laymen. Invariably, television documentaries about primitive tribes show a witch doctor conducting a meaningless, but grossly expensive ritual to invoke healing or the blessings of some tribal god. Do not laugh at the poor heathen; similar traditions occur in Christianity today. For varied reasons, many lay people do not study their Bible to understand God's truth for themselves. The result is that they end up playing "follow the expert." Since religious bamboozle does not make sense to anyone, somehow this lack of understanding makes the "mysteries of religion" (Satan's dark secrets) special and sacred. It is very sad. Religious leaders maintain respect, authority, and dominion over their subjects using religious bamboozle and Jezebel was no exception.

Jesus Exposed Jezebel's Nakedness

Jesus knew Jezebel's motives and the results. He condemned her for: (a) leading others to commit sexual immorality; (b) leading others to eat food sacrificed to idols; (c) defending her actions with religious bamboozle – Satan's "deep secrets," and (d) her defiant attitude concerning her sins. Evidently, Jezebel was confronted with her errors, but she refused to repent and the religious leaders of the church were not willing to throw her out of the church. (Every time someone is removed from church membership, certain members become angry and rebellious. The social consequences surrounding church discipline can be long lasting and pervasive. For this reason, many church leaders are reluctant to do what is right in God's sight.) Jesus clearly expressed His position on Jezebel's actions and the church's tolerance. Because she refused to repent and because church leaders had not addressed Jezebel's evil behavior, Jesus said that He would turn her bed of pleasure into a "bed of suffering." Jesus also promised to inflict great suffering on those who followed her example. In fact, Jesus promised to strike her children dead. Whether the children mentioned in verse 23 were biological offspring or spiritual offspring, the Bible does not say. In either case, Jesus made His point radiantly clear: Death to all Christians who participate in sexual immorality.[59]

Don't Give Up!

Jesus closed His remarks to the church at Thyatira saying, **"To him who overcomes and does my will to the end, I will give authority over the nations – 'He will rule them with an iron scepter; he will dash them to pieces like pottery' – just as I have received authority from my Father. I will also give him the morning star. He who has an ear, let him hear what the Spirit says to the churches."**

Jesus encouraged the church at Thyatira with two wonderful promises for those who have ears for what the Spirit says. First, overcoming sin is possible through repentance and the indwelling power of the Holy Spirit.[60] People who persevere and fight the fight of faith will reign with Jesus! They will share in His awesome authority and at an appointed time, the redeemed will sit in judgment on those who harmed them.[61] Second, Jesus says that every overcomer will be given "the Morning Star." The Morning Star is Jesus Himself.[62] Jesus offers every repentant and faithful sinner His perfect righteousness.[63] This is a gift that is beyond measure because His righteousness is the ticket to eternal life! I cannot think of any gift more wonderful than this.

Sardis

"To the angel of the church in Sardis write: These are the words of him who holds the seven spirits of God [the seven angels] **and the seven stars** [in His hand]**. I know your deeds; you have a reputation of being alive, but you are dead. Wake up! Strengthen what remains and is about to die, for I have not found your deeds complete in the sight of my God. Remember, therefore, what you have received and heard; obey it, and repent.** *But if you do not wake up,* **I will come like a thief, and you will not know at what time I will come to you. Yet you have a few people in Sardis who have not soiled their clothes. They will walk with me, dressed in white, for they are worthy. He who overcomes will, like them, be dressed in white. I will never blot out his name**

from the book of life, but will acknowledge his name before my Father and his angels. He who has an ear, let him hear what the Spirit says to the churches."[64]

The church at Sardis was known for its religious zeal. Something was taking place at the church all of the time. They met together several times each week. They prayed, worshiped, worked and played together as one big family. So, what could be wrong with that? Jesus told them, **"I know your deeds; you have a reputation of being alive, but you are dead. Wake up!"**[65] Jesus said, **"Remember, therefore, what you have received and heard; obey it, and repent."**[66] The church at Sardis was on the wrong track. An active church life is not a substitute for spiritual growth. It takes a trained eye and spiritual discernment to distinguish between the two. The devil was at work in Sardis. The church was active and busy, but it was dead spiritually because it was not focused on the Word. Instead, Sardis was focused on "church life."

Church life is the social interaction that involves a group of people having similar religious views, whereas spiritual life is the process of maturing in God's truth under the firm, but loving discipline of Christ. Church life is important and what is sweeter than genuine fellowship with like believers? Unfortunately, the basis for church life should not be the joy of socializing fellowship, but a love for the discovery of truth. There is much to learn about Jesus and His gospel. Many Christians think church life is synonymous with spiritual life, but attending church services and listening to inspiring music and preaching is no substitute for personal study, meditation, and prayer. Nothing can take the place of actually doing your own homework! Spiritual life requires time with God and His Word and *there is no substitute for this*. For many people, worship is a social occasion and they go to church to be entertained with a good sermon and being told what to believe. On the other hand, walking with God and obeying His Word at all costs is the worship that God seeks. Jesus said, **"God is spirit, and his worshipers must worship in spirit and in truth."**[67] If church life does not continually put worshipers through the essential truths of the Bible, and if church life does not teach worshipers how to study the Bible and ask questions, and if church life does not produce Christians who love the Lord with all their heart, mind, and soul and their neighbors as themselves, the result will be a congregation that seems active and alive, but in reality, is spiritually dead! This was the situation in Sardis.[68]

The Christian Church has two objectives: Soul winning (the preaching of justification) and soul building (the teaching of sanctification). The carnal nature does not mind hearing about justification (that is the free part of the gospel), but it hates to hear about sanctification (that is the hard part of the gospel). Putting Jesus' Sermon on the Mount into daily practice is the hardest thing on Earth to do! Living by faith is very difficult. When the doctrines of justification and sanctification are out of balance, church life becomes a substitute for spiritual life.

Church members at Sardis were sure of their salvation. They accepted the gospel of justification. They loved the freedom in Christ which justification offers. They were happy to hear that Jesus had paid the price for their salvation, but they were not maturing spiritually, that is, they were not becoming Christ-like. Jesus reminded them of the necessity of sanctification saying, **"Remember, therefore, what you have received and heard; obey it, and repent."**

Thousands of churches today have disconnected the gospel of justification from the power and necessity of sanctification. Churches like Sardis are everywhere! Many Christians deceive themselves with self-assured salvation even though they are spiritually dead! On the other hand, when the cart is put in front of the horse, there is an equally serious problem. When sanctification is disconnected from the importance and necessity for justification, Christians enter a toxic and destructive experience consisting of legalism and self-righteousness. The narrow road leading to Heaven has two big ditches on each side and the devil is constantly trying to push Christians into the ditch of legalism or the ditch of presumption. Both ditches have the same result, spiritual death. Jesus warned the dead church at Sardis, **"But if you do not wake up, I will come like a thief, and you will not know at what time I will come to you."**

To Him That Overcomes

There were some faithful members in Sardis. Jesus said, **"Yet you have a few people in Sardis who have not soiled their clothes** [soiled by sinful deeds]**. They will walk with me, dressed in white, for they are worthy. He who overcomes will, like them, be dressed in white. I will never blot out his name from the book of life, but will acknowledge his name**

before my Father and his angels. He who has an ear, let him hear what the Spirit says to the churches."

There is a hidden message in these words and it is different than what you might think at first. The faithful people in Sardis knew that church life was no substitute for spiritual life. Throughout history, people who have had an intimate fellowship with God understand the rigors and failures involved with discipleship. Every disciple of Jesus has to be corrected and disciplined to grow. Jesus described His disciples as people having clothes that are unsoiled. In other words, the faithful saints in Sardis were examples of His life. They were willing to "go-be-do" as Jesus directed and He promised that overcomers will, like them, be dressed in His flawless righteousness someday.

The Book of Life

Jesus also gave a message to the church at Sardis that is widely misunderstood. He promised that He would never blot out the names of the overcomers from The Book of Life. Most Christians interpret these words of Jesus in one of two ways:

1. Some Christians believe that once a person receives Christ as Savior, his name is written in The Book of Life at that time. Therefore, he cannot be lost because Jesus will not blot out any name found in The Book of Life. This means that once a person is saved, he is forever "saved."

2. Other Christians believe that a person must overcome every sin in order to be saved. This implies that people who give up or fail to achieve perfection will be blotted out of The Book of Life.

There are several problems with both views.

The doctrine of "once saved, always saved" is disputed by the text itself. Jesus says seven times in Revelation 2 and 3 that salvation belongs to overcomers. This means there is a distinct relationship between our behavior and salvation. On the other side of the coin, and equally important, Jesus indicates that salvation is not based on human perfection or human righteousness. Even though some of the saints in Sardis had not soiled their garments, they still needed to be dressed in the white garment (the wedding garment) of Christ's righteousness.

The Bible teaches that a person can live and walk with God while having *the assurance of salvation* and then lose it by turning away from the Lord and doing wicked things![69] Conversely, the Bible teaches that a wicked person can repent and be saved![70] Consider Lucifer's fall along with a third of the angels. Also, consider Adam and Eve's fall. At one time all of these beings were perfect, but they turned away from righteousness by committing sin. By sinning, they fell under the penalty of God's law which demands death. On the other hand, consider the numberless multitude that will come out of the Great Tribulation and be saved![71] In both cases listed above, salvation is dynamic, that is, salvation will be granted to everyone who overcomes whatever the Holy Spirit requires them to overcome. This explains why rejecting the Holy Spirit becomes unpardonable.[72] When a new challenge comes into our lives that needs to be overcome, the Holy Spirit provides the power to overcome it. If we refuse to cooperate with the Holy Spirit, it is impossible to overcome because there is no power to overcome and non-overcomers have no place in Heaven.

Promises Made

Jesus made a promise to the overcomers in Sardis that is often distorted by people who insist that once saved means always saved. Jesus said, **"He who overcomes will, like them, be dressed in white. I will never blot out his name from the Book of Life, but will acknowledge his name before my Father and his angels."**[73] We know from Prophecy Six that The Book of Life is the book sealed with seven seals. We know The Book of Life is not used in judgment and it is not opened until the end of the 1,000 years.[74] Knowing these things, let us take a moment and review each of the rewards Jesus offers to the overcomers in the seven churches. As you review each reward, ask yourself *when* will the rewards be distributed.

> Ephesus: The right to eat from the tree of life
>
> Smyrna: The second death will not hurt you
>
> Pergamum: The right to eat hidden manna and the receipt of a white stone
>
> Thyatira: You will receive authority over the nations and the Morning Star
>
> Sardis: I will never blot our your name from The Book of Life

> Philadelphia: I will write on you the name of my God and the name of His city
>
> Laodicea: I will grant you the right to sit with Me on My throne

Clearly, these rewards will be given to overcomers *after* the saints are taken to Heaven at the Second Coming. The same timing applies to the church of Sardis. The problem for most people with Revelation 3:5 is timing. Jesus was not talking about manipulating The Book of Life when He spoke to the church at Sardis. (Remember, The Book of Life was written and sealed up before the world was created. Revelation 17:8) Rather, Jesus promised the overcomers in Sardis that He would never blot out their names from The Book of Life *after* they arrive in Heaven. This means overcomers will live forever with Jesus!

Jesus does not require sinless behavior for salvation! If He did, then no one could be saved. No one other than Jesus has lived a perfect life and no sinner can live a sinless life until the carnal nature is removed and the sealing takes place! The good news is that John tells us there is a sin that does not lead to death. This sin is accidental sin.[75] If we say we are without sin, the Bible says we are liars.[76] So, the promise Christ gave to the overcomers in Sardis has to be kept within the context of His words to all seven churches. What did the church at Sardis need to overcome? They had substituted church life for spiritual life and as a result, they had become spiritually dead. Jesus insisted they wake up so that He might walk among them and make disciples of them! Everyone who overcomes this temptation will never have his name blotted out of The Book of Life.

Philadelphia

"To the angel of the church in Philadelphia write: These are the words of him who is holy and true, who holds the key of David. [Jesus holds the key to everything.] **What he opens no one can shut, and what he shuts no one can open.** [Jesus said,] **I know your deeds. See, I have placed before you an open door that no one can shut. I know that you have little strength, yet you have kept my word and have not denied my name. I will make those who are of the synagogue of Satan, who claim to be Jews though they are not, but are liars – I will make them come and fall down at your feet and acknowledge that I have loved you.**

Since you have kept my command to endure patiently, I will also keep you from the hour of trial that is going to come upon the whole world to test those who live on the earth. I am coming soon. Hold on to what you have, so that no one will take your crown. Him who overcomes I will make a pillar in the temple of my God. Never again will he leave it. I will write on him the name of my God and the name of the city of my God, the new Jerusalem, which is coming down out of heaven from my God; and I will also write on him my new name. He who has an ear, let him hear what the Spirit says to the churches."[77]

The church in Philadelphia struggled with the synagogue of Satan just like the church at Smyrna. In fact, the seven churches were beset with all kinds of problems. Ephesus had lost its first love. Pergamum was beguiled with the devil's lies and Gnosticism. Thyratira was corrupted with Jezebel's teachings about sexual immorality. Smyrna was threated by ongoing persecution and Sardis was an active church, but it was spiritually dead. Philadephia was weak, but hanging on and Laodecia had grown indifferent. As Jesus looked down from Heaven upon His seven churches, no wonder He was not very happy.

Unfortunately, many Christians distort the message to the church at Philadelphia because they want some texts to support a pretribulation rapture. However, Jesus' words to Philadelphia do not imply a pretribulation rapture. Because the church in Philadelphia was weak and suffering from persecution, Jesus told the members at Philadelphia that He had made a way for them to go through their suffering. This is the point of the open door. By His grace they could *go through* this experience and overcome it. He also told them that He would keep them during the hour of trial that was going to come upon the whole world. This promise belongs to everyone having the Philadelphia experience.

Think about this for a moment. Did Jesus offer to protect the people in Philadelphia from the Great Tribulation and allow the other six churches to go through the Great Tribulation? Of course, not! The words of Jesus have to be understood within context. They were spoken to the people living in Philadelphia in A.D. 95. *Jesus directed His words to them because their experience will become the experience of those living during the Great Tribulation.* Jesus

Appendix C - The Seven Churches

encouraged the suffering members in Philadelphia to hold fast to their faith because He would never leave them or forsake them.

When Jesus spoke to the church at Philadelphia, the members were very weary and discouraged by persecution. Early Christians knew from Jesus and Paul that the end of the age would be marked with persecution and death. Jesus did not add to their discouragement by telling them about the end of the world, but instead, Jesus attempted to cheer them up with these words: **"Since you have kept my command to endure patiently, I will also keep you from [through] the hour of trial that is going to come upon the whole world to test those who live on the earth. I am coming soon. Hold on to what you have, so that no one will take your crown."** You will notice that I crossed out the word "from" and inserted the word "through." The Greek preposition used in Revelation 3:10 has many different meanings. In today's English, the word "through" is a better translation, but they mean the same thing in this sentence. If I take something *from* you, the word "from" indicates origin. If I take some candy *from* the dish, again the word "from" indicates origin. Translators used the word "from" in Revelation 3:10 because Jesus means, "I will also keep you "from the origin of" the hour of trial that is going to come upon the whole world...." In today's English, the word "through" implies from beginning to end a little more clearly. For example, if I went through four years of residency to become a medical specialist, this implies that I was there from beginning to end.

Jesus promised to sustain the beleaguered church at Philadelphia during the Great Tribulation that would come upon the world. This promise is interesting for two reasons. First, Jesus assures those who are suffering from persecution that He sees their pain and in His strength, they can endure and be victorious over it. Second, Jesus indicates that some Christians will have the Philadelphia experience at the end of the age because the Great Tribulation only occurs at the end of the age. Jesus encouraged the church at Philadelphia saying, **"Hold on to what you have..."** These words are inspiring when the fires of persecution are hot. It's human nature to give in or give up to stop the pain, but those who overcome will be rewarded beyond their wildest imagination!

By the way, there is also a secret message to Philadelphia: All overcomers will be given a special name tag when they get to

Heaven. Jesus said, "**I will write on him the name of my God... the name of the city of my God, and I will also write on him my new name.**" This name tag will permit its owner to travel anywhere in God's universe. You will be recognized throughout God's universe as a very special person because YOU overcame the temptation to give up, and YOU were trained through suffering on Earth for the exalted role that God has given you throughout eternity. Those who endured much will be rewarded with much. Those who endured little will be rewarded accordingly. Your life and your situation determines your victory over the curse of sin and your reward will be appropriate! Jesus wants everyone to know who YOU are throughout eternity, so He will give you a glorious name tag.

Laodicea – Avoiding Conflict

Since conflict and war is at the forefront of current events and the topic of spiritual warfare is paramount for Christian living, this is a perfect time to examine the church of Laodicea. The church at Laodicea was full of Christians *avoiding* war. The church had a deadly problem. They had muted the power of the gospel.

The gospel of Jesus Christ is like a sword, it always causes war.[78] Jesus was a victim of this war! The gospel of Jesus is an advancing gospel of love, but God's love condemns the carnal heart which loves itself. Truth condemns people who reject it and it saves people who receive it. The gospel of Jesus liberates people who love truth and their victory over darkness produces persecution by those in darkness. Few things can tear families or nations apart like differences in religion. War erupts when the advancing gospel of Jesus confronts the establishments and traditions of religion. The church at Laodicea, even though it was less than 40 years old, did everything possible to avoid conflict. Wealth and affluence had compromised the advancement of the gospel in Laodicea. Church members had muted the gospel to protect their jobs and positions of respect in a pagan community. *History proves that the gospel of Jesus mutates into various forms of pseudo-Christianity when Christians are not persecuted.* In fact, this explains why God handed the saints over to the little horn power in Daniel 7 for 1,260 years![79] Throughout the Dark Ages, the church in the wilderness maintained faith in Christ because of persecution.

Ancient Israel also proved that faith in God mutates into false religion when there is no persecution. Moses warned the children of Israel at the gates to the Promised Land, **"Be careful that you do not forget the Lord your God, failing to observe his commands, his laws and his decrees that I am giving you this day. Otherwise, when you eat and are satisfied, when you build fine houses and settle down, and when your herds and flocks grow large and your silver and gold increase and all you have is multiplied, then your heart will become proud and you will forget the Lord your God, who brought you out of Egypt, out of the land of slavery. . . . For I know that after my death you are sure to become utterly corrupt and to turn from the way I have commanded you. In days to come, disaster will fall upon you because you will do evil in the sight of the Lord and provoke him to anger by what your hands have made."**[80] The Old Testament confirms that Israel repeatedly abandoned God every time it became militarily secure, wealthy, and affluent and the same behavior is documented throughout Christian history. What does this say about the carnal nature of man?

When the church at Laodicea compromised its faith, the church died spiritually. Like the church at Sardis, they thought they were doing just fine even though their condition made Jesus almost vomit! Christians in Laodecia did not recognize their true condition before God. They were not focused on the cause of Christ or the objectives of the gospel. They did not detect the ongoing war over their souls. They could not see the sophistry of the devil's warfare. They were preoccupied with making money and spending it. They were affluent and enjoyed the good life.

The gospel of Jesus wars against acquiring riches and selfish indulgence because the carnal nature is selfish. Unfortunately, many Christians are living the Laodicean experience today. The gospel of Jesus has become an intellectual assent to truth rather than a life of service for God and man. Many Christians are willing to give money to promote the gospel, but they are unwilling to give themselves.

"To the angel of the church in Laodicea write: These are the words of the Amen, the faithful and true witness, the ruler of God's creation. I know your deeds, that you are neither cold nor hot. I wish you were either one or the other! So, because you are lukewarm – neither hot nor cold – I am about to spit you out of my mouth.

You say, 'I am rich; I have acquired wealth and do not need a thing.' But you do not realize that you are wretched, pitiful, poor, blind and naked. I counsel you to buy from me gold refined in the fire, so you can become rich; and white clothes to wear, so you can cover your shameful nakedness; and salve to put on your eyes, so you can see. Those whom I love I rebuke and discipline [torment]. **So be earnest, and repent.**

Here I am! I stand at the door and knock. If anyone hears my voice and opens the door, I will come in and eat with him, and he with me. To him who overcomes, I will give the right to sit with me on my throne, just as I overcame and sat down with my Father on his throne. He who has an ear, let him hear what the Spirit says to the churches." [81]

The church at Laodicea was full of "rich young rulers."[82] They mistook their affluence and wealth as evidence of God's approval when in fact, God condemned them for misusing His wealth. The value of money is determined by the good it produces. When God gives wealth to people, He also imposes accountability for its use. This will prove to be a big surprise for many on Judgment Day! The carnal heart loves money because money brings power, gratification, and selfish satisfaction. Money can buy almost anything. When people have too much money, few will desire or wait to see God's providence. Money can rob us of faith in God because there is no need to seek or wait upon the Lord. Money can shut out Christ's discipline and rebuke. Money can distort justice and ruin integrity. Money is harmful and this is why Jesus said, **"It is easier for a camel to go through the eye of a needle than for a rich man to enter the kingdom of God."**[83] Self-indulgence and money are brother and sister in the carnal heart. This is why Jesus said, **"No one can serve two masters. Either he will hate the one and love the other, or he will be devoted to the one and despise the other. You cannot serve both God and Money."**[84]

The "rich young ruler test" wars against the core of our carnal nature. Jesus gave up everything He owned in order to save us and He does not ask less of His disciples.[85] Carefully notice in Matthew 19 that Jesus did not ask the rich young ruler to donate his wealth to the temple. Rather, Jesus told the rich young ruler to sell his possessions and give the proceeds to the poor. Can you imagine the joy of finding poor people needing financial help? Jesus hit the rich young ruler where it hurt most. He did not want to give his wealth away. He loved money. His wealth meant more to him than God or those who lived in poverty. This was the basic problem in Laodicea. The Christians at Laodicea were happy with their riches. They did not realize that they were serving money rather than God and this made Jesus nauseous. Money is so deceitful! No one but Jesus could have told the church at Laodicea their true condition. Who would have believed His threat unless He spoke it Himself?

The Tables Turned

Overcomers who pass "the rich young ruler test" will reign with Jesus as "rich young rulers" throughout His universe.[86] Jesus can offer no greater reward than what He offered to the Laodiceans. Think about this. Jesus not only gave His life for us, He offers to share His throne with us! What amazing love! Overcomers will be exalted because they loved God and their neighbors more than money *while living with a carnal nature*! Holy angels cannot experience such a test for they do not have a carnal nature. When properly understood, the gospel of Jesus transforms an egocentric heart into a theo-centric heart. The gospel of Jesus subdues the selfish nature so that the spiritual nature can grow stronger. Jesus assures victory to every person who keeps his eyes on Jesus and keeps his heart open to the Holy Spirit. **"For everyone born of God overcomes the world. This is the victory that has overcome the world, even our faith."**[87]

Conclusion

We have examined the seven churches. We have considered their faults and their strengths. We have also considered the admonition of Jesus to each church. If there is anything that you should remember about this study it is this: Salvation is a two-sided coin. The minute you totally surrender your life to Jesus and are willing to go - be - do as He directs, the assurance of salvation is yours! To keep this assurance alive and intact, you must begin to fight the fight of faith. You must overcome temptation and be transformed through the imparted power of Christ. This process will last a lifetime. As long as you allow Jesus to discipline you (disciple you), you are justified in God's sight. That is, God sees you as though you never sinned. The righteousness of Jesus covers you. The primary objective of redemption is not eternal life. The primary object is walking with God each day throughout the rest of eternity.

Seven times, Jesus made it clear to the seven churches that overcoming temptation is not optional. Sanctification is both necessary and possible through His power. After showing John the Great Tribulation story including the persecution of the saints for forty-two months, the martyrdom of the saints during the fifth seal, the physical appearing of the devil, and the mark of the beast, Jesus emphasized the necessity of overcoming an eighth time. **"He who was seated on the throne said, 'I am making everything new!' Then he said, 'Write this down, for these words are trustworthy and true.' He said to me: 'It is done. I am the Alpha and the Omega, the Beginning and the End. To him who is thirsty I will give to drink without cost from the spring of the water of life.** *He who overcomes will inherit all this, and I will be his God and he will be my son.* **But the cowardly, the unbelieving, the vile, the murderers, the sexually immoral, those who practice magic arts, the idolaters and all liars--their place will be in the fiery lake of burning sulfur. This is the second death.' "**[88] Isn't it interesting that the book of Revelation ends where it began? Believers in Christ can be overcomers through the strength that Christ imparts. Paul knew about the miracle of having our desire for sin neutralized. He wrote, **"I can do everything through him who gives me strength."**[89] If we are willing to walk with the Lord, He will be our God and we will be His children.

Remember the seven rewards promised to overcomers:

1. To him who overcomes, I will give the right to eat from the tree of life, which is in the paradise of God.

2. He who overcomes will not be hurt at all by the second death.

3. To him who overcomes, I will give some of the hidden manna. I will also give him a white stone with a new name written on it, known only to him who receives it.

4. To him who overcomes and does my will to the end, I will give authority over the nations – 'He will rule them with an iron scepter; he will dash them to pieces like pottery' – just as I have received authority from my Father.

5. He who overcomes will be dressed in white. I will never blot out his name from The Book of Life, but will acknowledge his name before my Father and his angels.

6. To him who overcomes I will make a pillar in the temple of my God. Never again will he leave it. I will write on him the name of my God and the name of the city of my God, New Jerusalem, which is coming down out of Heaven from my God; and I will also write on him my new name.

7. To him who overcomes, I will give the right to sit with me on my throne, just as I overcame and sat down with my Father on his throne.

These rewards mean very little to those who are spiritually dead. Jesus deliberately worded His remarks this way. If the rewards of Heaven appealed to our carnal nature, Heaven would be filled with selfish people intent on *getting* their free reward, instead of walking with God and serving others! By obscuring these eternally magnificent rewards with spiritual words, Jesus ensured the carnal nature would not be attracted to them. This is why Jesus says seven times that those who have ears to hear, let him hear what the Spirit is saying. Everyone who follows the Holy Spirit can understand the messages to the seven churches. They do not require a Greek expert or a great deal of study. They do require an endless struggle against the carnal nature. The seven messages also contain a warning that any deviation from the gospel of Jesus must be corrected as quickly as possible. If a deviation is not corrected quickly, the damage only gets worse with the passage of time.

One day, each overcomer will be exalted as a hero. The angels will honor those who overcame sin through Christ's imparted strength. Jesus will honor every saint because He overcame the world and won the war for his soul. The Bible predicts a time is coming when all of God's saints will stand before His throne. I cannot think of anything more wonderful and more joyful than falling on our faces before the Father and the Lamb and praising them for the priceless gift of redemption they freely offered.

References
1. Revelation 2:7
2. Revelation 22:14
3. John 14:6; italics mine See also Acts 9:2; 19:9.
4. John 14:6
5. Acts 4:12, insertion mine
6. Acts 11:26
7. Acts 24:14
8. Acts 13:2; Ephesians 3:8,9
9. Exodus 33:13
10. Romans 8:7
11. Genesis 5:22,24; 6:9
12. Romans 8:5-8
13. Revelation 2:14,15; 3:9
14. Hebrews 5:7-9, italics mine
15. Romans 6:14-18
16. John 5:19, 30
17. Romans 1:17; 3:28-31, insertions mine
18. Philippians 3:3-9, insertions mine
19. Romans 7:18-25, insertion mine
20. 2 Timothy 4:7,8
21. 1 John 1:9
22. Compare Genesis 32:24-30 with Ephesians 6:12.
23. Hebrews 12:8-14, insertions and italics mine
24. Isaiah 29:13
25. Matthew 22:36-40
26. Matthew 23:28
27. Revelation 2:1-7, insertion and italics mine
28. Revelation 1:12-16
29. Revelation 1:20
30. Revelation 8:2
31. Hebrews 1:14
32. Ephesians 1:22, Colossians 1:18

33. John 13:34,35; 15:14,17; 14:15
34. Galatians 5:19-21; 1 John 2:15-17
35. 1 Corinthians 15:31, insertion mine
36. John 15:5
37. John 15:9
38. 1 John 5:12
39. Genesis 3:23,24
40. John 8:51
41. Revelation 2:8-11, insertions mine
42. James 1:1; 2:1; Ephesians 2; Romans 11:25
43. Mark 14:61-64
44. John 15:20
45. Romans 10:9
46. Revelation 2:12-17, insertions mine
47. Numbers 22-25
48. 1 Corinthians 5:11; John 15:5,6
49. Acts 15:19,20, insertions mine
50. John 6:54-58
51. Luke 22:19,20
52. Revelation 19:21
53. Matthew 4:4; John 4:32-34
54. See 1 Timothy 6:15,16
55. Revelation 2:18-29
56. Compare Numbers 25:1-9 with 1 Corinthians 5:11.
57. Ezekiel 14:6-8
58. James 2:19
59. See also Colossians 3:5,6 and Revelation 22:15.
60. Romans 6
61. 1 Corinthians 6:1-3; Revelation 20:4
62. Revelation 22:16
63. Romans 1:17
64. Revelation 3:1-6
65. Revelation 3:1

66. Revelation 3:3
67. John 4:24
68. Compare the situation in Sardis with Matthew 7:21-23.
69. Ezekiel 18:24-26
70. Ezekiel 18:27,28
71. Revelation 7:9,10
72. Matthew 12:31,32
73. Revelation 3:5
74. Revelation 20:12
75. 1 John 5:16,17; Romans 7:19
76. 2 Chronicles 6:36; 1 John 1:10
77. Revelation 3:7-13, insertion mine
78. Matthew 10:34; Hebrews 4:12
79. Daniel 7:25
80. Deuteronomy 8:11-14; Deuteronomy 31:29
81. Revelation 3:14-22
82. Luke 18:18-23
83. Mark 10:25
84. Matthew 6:24
85. Matthew 10:37,38
86. Revelation 1:6; 20:4; 21:24
87. 1 John 5:4
88. Revelation 21:5-8, italics mine
89. Philippians 4:13

Appendix D

God Does Not Give Up
(A Discussion on Plan A/Plan B)

The concepts presented in this chapter should be important to you because every student of Bible prophecy is overwhelmed by the sheer volume of data in the Bible. It has been said that a person has to know everything before he can properly understand anything! While this concept is not entirely true, the more we do know about the Bible, the better and richer the story of redemption becomes.

God is never simple, but there are simple truths about God that help us understand Him! I would like to introduce you to a larger picture of God than you would normally see if your study of apocalyptic prophecy is limited to the books of Daniel and Revelation. Apocalyptic prophecy is difficult to understand at first because there are so many details that surround and encompass the plan of redemption. Therefore, I hope a few general concepts about the plan of redemption will prove to be helpful.

The Living Trust

The Bible teaches that God created a living trust to redeem mankind when Adam and Eve sinned. The term, living trust, comes from two Latin words, *inter vivos,* which mean "between the living." A living trust is a very practical tool. For example, it permits a wealthy grantor to distribute his assets to his beneficiaries over a long period of time without being present or having to micro manage the day-to-day process himself. Therefore, when a grantor establishes a living trust, he appoints a trustee or someone to stand "between the living."

When a person agrees to serve as a trustee of a living trust, he enters into a covenant with the grantor. The trustee promises to carry out the will of the grantor at all costs. This is a solemn responsibility and trustees are usually paid very well for their services. If a trustee fails to keep his promise to the grantor and steals the assets instead of distributing them to the beneficiaries, two things will soon happen. (Remember, the grantor is alive.) First, the grantor will see that his beneficiaries are not receiving the assets he wants them to have and understandably, he will become angry. Second, the grantor will confront the trustee, charging the trustee with dereliction of duty. The grantor may give the trustee a second chance to do the job that he wants done or the grantor may fire the trustee and choose someone else. After all, the object of a living trust is *the distribution of the grantor's assets* to his beneficiaries and any trustee who thwarts this purpose must be disciplined or eliminated.

Hopefully, this explanation helps you appreciate the overriding concept that the redemption of mankind is built on a living trust. God is the grantor and He chooses trustees to distribute His riches. He has chosen the whole world to be the beneficiaries of His riches.[1] God originally created a living trust when Adam and Eve sinned because sin separated mankind from God. Consequently, sinners can no longer see God, so He chose to establish a living trust. God appointed trustees to be His representatives on Earth. His plan was that His trustees would be living examples of His character and love. Through their example, God wanted His beneficiaries (the whole world) to see Him.[2] In other words, God's plan was designed so His truth and grace would flow to mankind through His trustees. His trustees were to stand between a living God and the people living on Earth.

God has faithfully carried out everything necessary to make our redemption possible. He has done everything that He said He would do. Unfortunately, God's trustees have not fulfilled their responsibilities. Bible history reveals that every time God chose a particular group of trustees to distribute the riches of His grace to the world, His trustees eventually failed. They either became distracted from their mission or they rebelled against God. When His trustees become utterly useless, God has no other option than to start over. After selecting a new group of trustees, He moves forward. This process will end with the 144,000. They will be the last group of God's trustees.

Plan A / Plan B

The process of starting over and over with new trustees will take a few paragraphs to explain. For purposes of discussion, let us assume that Plan A describes God's first plan for mankind and Plan B is a followup plan that God put into motion when the trustees responsible for Plan A failed. God's living trust is intact and He will accomplish all that He intends to do with or without man's cooperation.[3] God will not terminate His living trust until He redeems all sinners who choose to follow Him. Consider the following scenario:

1. God gave Adam and Eve possession of the Garden of Eden. It was God's plan that they should live there forever and Adam should serve as "the father" of mankind! (Plan A) However, Adam and Eve sinned and had to be evicted from the Garden of Eden.

2. Plan B: God started over. He made Adam and the patriarchs who followed him trustees of His gospel. The trusteeship of the patriarchs lasted about 1,600 years (from the fall of man to the flood). It failed miserably because the patriarchs lost sight of God.[4] In fact, during the operation of this plan, the world became hopelessly evil and God destroyed all but eight people in Noah's day.

3. Plan C: About four hundred years after the flood, God started over. He called Abraham out of Ur to be "the father" of the *faith-full*. Then, God chose Abraham's descendants to be the trustees of His gospel and He entered into a covenant with them.[5] This 1,500 year plan (1437 B.C. - A.D. 70) failed because Israel would not remain loyal to God long enough to get the job done. Therefore, God destroyed Israel in A.D. 70 because of rebellion.

4. Plan D: During the seventieth week, God started over. Because He made some unconditional promises to Abraham, God had to raise up another group of trustees to keep moving forward. Many Christians do not understand why it is important that believers in Christ are counted as the heirs of Abraham. The heart of this issue involves a promise. God promised Abraham that He would someday give the whole world over to Abraham's descendants. Thankfully, God considers Abraham's descendants to be those people who love and trust God as Abraham did! Carefully study this passage and notice that biology does not determine the descendants of Abraham:

    " 'Abraham is our father,' they answered. 'If you were Abraham's children,' said Jesus, 'then you would do the things Abraham did. As it is, you are determined

to kill me, a man who has told you the truth that I heard from God. Abraham did not do such things. You are doing the things your own father does.' 'We are not illegitimate children [we have a father],' they protested. 'The only Father we have is God himself.' Jesus said to them, 'If God were your Father, you would love me, for I came from God and now am here. I have not come on my own; but he sent me. Why is my language not clear to you? Because you are unable to hear what I say. You belong to your father, the devil, and you want to carry out your father's desire. He was a murderer from the beginning, not holding to the truth, for there is no truth in him. When he lies, he speaks his native language, for he is a liar and the father of lies. Yet because I tell the truth, you do not believe me!' "[6]

When the nation of Israel passed a point of no return, God rejected Israel as the trustees of His covenant. Consequently, every one who loves and trusts in Christ for salvation becomes Israel, the heir of Abraham. **"If you belong to Christ, then you are Abraham's seed, and heirs according to the promise."**[7] God raised up a new set of trustees for His living trust. He created a *new* covenant because He needed a *new* set of trustees. However, this 2,000 year plan (A.D. 30 - 1994) has failed, too. Corporately speaking, God will abandon Christianity and eventually it will be destroyed. (This matter is addressed in Prophecy 7. See also Appendix B.)

5. Plan E: God will soon start over again, but for the last time. He will select 144,000 people as trustees of His living trust. To ensure the success of their mission, He will first remove their carnal natures. This wonderful miracle will ensure their success. (Incidently, the fallen nature of man explains why all of the previous trustees failed.) The 144,000 will proclaim the riches of God's grace and His offer of redemption to the whole world during the Great Tribulation. The 144,000 will not deviate or fail to accomplish their mission. When they complete their mission, everyone on Earth will either have the mark of the beast or the seal of God.

I have listed five examples showing that God does not quit. When one group of trustees refuses to cooperate with Him, God moves them out of the way to keep moving forward. God chooses new trustees because He cannot be thwarted! The repetitive process of starting over with new trustees has been synthesized in this book to what I call Plan A and Plan B. Rather than identify each successive plan, I prefer to simplify the concept of starting over by identifying Plan A as a previous plan and Plan B as the plan that follows. I like to do this so that I can make certain categorical statements about Plan B.

For example, Plan B is always better and more glorious than Plan A. Some people, upon hearing this comment say, "You make it sound as though God's first plan was imperfect!" Actually, God's earlier plan (Plan A) was perfect because God's ways are always perfect. However, Plan B is better and more glorious because God uses the failure in Plan A to reveal more about Himself than He previously revealed. Here is an example: If Adam and Eve and their offspring had lived in the Garden of Eden without sinning, Earth would have been "a perfect place" to live. God's original plan was perfect, but Adam and Eve sinned and God's infinite love for mankind moved Him to redeem the guilty pair (and their offspring). Plan B was put in motion and as a result, we now see a component of God's love for sinners that would not be seen if sin had not occurred. Plan A was perfect, but Plan B reveals new things about God which could not be seen in Plan A. This makes Plan B better and more glorious than Plan A.

A Much Different World History

According to the Old Testament, world history would have been much different over the past 2,000 years if the nation of Israel had embraced Jesus as the Messiah at His first advent. If this had occurred, Jesus would not have returned to Heaven.[7] There would have been no need for a second advent. There would have been no need for a New Testament and *there would have been no need for the books of Daniel and Revelation because* these two prophetic books contain Plan B!

For the sake of discussion, let us lump all of the promises and prophecies ancient Israel received into Plan A. Bible history records how Israel rebelled time and time again. God could not carry out His redemptive trust for the whole world because His trustees refused to do the very things that He wanted done. Therefore,

God had no choice but to *fire* Israel for dereliction of duty during the seventieth week.[9]

When it became clear that Israel would not receive Him as Messiah, Jesus selected a new set of trustees. He implemented a new covenant[10] between Himself and His new trustees. Keep in mind that the living trust (God's offer for salvation) remains unchanged.[11] The only element that changes are the trustees.

A Faithful Model

When Jesus selected Israel to be the trustee of the gospel, Jesus gave Israel many laws and regulations. These statutes were perfect[12] because God thoughtfully and deliberately designed them. One set of laws pertained to an intricate ceremonial system (including animal sacrifices), but most people today misunderstand the purpose for this intricate system. God gave the ceremonial system to Israel as a faithful model. This model reveals the dimensions of the plan of redemption.[13] Each process the priests conducted in the earthly ceremonial system faithfully parallels a real process that occurs in Heaven.[14]

When Jesus died on the cross, He abolished the ceremonial system along with its perfect laws because the purpose for which the ceremonial system had been created had been fulfilled.[15] This does not mean that the ceremonial system is unimportant today. In fact, the ceremonial system God gave to Israel is profoundly important today because it was a faithful "model" that reveals the plan of redemption. In other words, every theological idea concerning the salvation of mankind has to be evaluated to see if it is in compliance with the ceremonial system God gave to ancient Israel because it is a perfect explanation of redemption's process.

I like to think of the ceremonial system in this way. Suppose a group of grade school students act in a skit that illustrates the separation of the United States from Great Britain. The children thoroughly research the topic and portray the events of history. When the skit is over, we could say two things: First, since this was a skit, when the fifth graders "signed" the Declaration of Independence, they did not sign a valid document. In terms of reality, the skit is just a depiction of the actual events. In terms of "representing" actual events that occurred, their actions were perfect. Second, assuming the skit was a faithful representation of what actually happened, the skit was valuable because everyone could quickly see how the facts fit together. The skit portrayed the truth even though it was just a shadow of the truth.

The ceremonial system is like a skit revealing God's living trust. The ceremonial system shadows events that began in Heaven when Adam and Eve sinned. These events will continue to function in Heaven until the sin problem is resolved on Earth and the redemption of sinners is finished. The ceremonial system God gave to Israel was not a reality, but Israel had to faithfully carry out the skit because it was a faithful representation of God's living trust. The Bible clearly says in Hebrews 10:1-4 that sinners were not redeemed by the blood of animals because the ceremony was not a means to salvation. The ceremonial system has enormous value today because it can be used to test every concept concerning redemption.

Unconditional Promises

When Abraham obeyed the Lord and left his home, he showed great faith in God. God was pleased with Abraham and He promised this childless man that he would become the father of many nations.[16] Abraham believed God with childlike simplicity and to honor Abraham's faith, God made some unconditional promises to Abraham. For example, God promised to give Abraham and his descendants the land of Canaan as an everlasting possession.[17]

There has been a great deal of misunderstanding about the promises God gave to Abraham. For example, God took the descendants of Abraham into Canaan (the promised land), but Israel could not remain there because God had promised that He would expel Israel from Canaan if they become hostile and rebellious toward Him. After God exiled Israel to Babylon for seventy years, He returned Israel to Canaan. He gave Abraham's descendants one more chance to faithfully serve as the trustees of His covenant. Centuries later (during the seventieth week), Abraham's biological descendants (God's trustees) rejected Messiah and God, in turn, abandoned Israel. God moved forward with Plan B by making a new covenant and choosing new trustees (Christians). The new covenant did not change the terms and conditions of the living trust. In fact, since sin began, the terms and conditions for salvation have not changed. Salvation always comes through faith in God.[18]

Because God promised to give Abraham's descendants the land of Canaan, God redefined the "heirs of Abraham" when Israel became a hopeless case. **"If you belong to Christ, then you are Abraham's seed** [Greek: sperma]**, and heirs according to the promise."**[19] At the end of the 1,000 years, the holy city, New Jerusalem, will descend from Heaven. After God purifies Earth with fire, He will create a new Heaven and a new Earth. God will give this new Canaan "that flows with milk and honey," a new Canaan that is not defiled with sin, bloodshed, or death, to Abraham's descendants forever. **"By faith Abraham, when called to go to a place he would later receive as his inheritance, obeyed and went, even though he did not know where he was going. By faith he made his home in the promised land like a stranger in a foreign country; he lived in tents, as did Isaac and Jacob, who were heirs with him of the same promise. For he was looking forward to the city with foundations, whose architect and builder is God."**[20]

Today, the heirs of Abraham are believers in Christ.[21] Plan B is built on a better set of promises and prophecies than Plan A.[22] Many Christians are hopelessly confused when they study the Bible because they keep trying to make Plan A (Old Testament promises and prophecies) fit into Plan B (New Testament promises and prophecies) and the two cannot be mixed. Over the years, many pastors and scholars have recognized this problem and one popular "solution" requires a combination of two false doctrines. The first is a doctrine of dispensations. This teaches that the terms and conditions for redemption change over time. Each change is called a dispensation, that is, salvation is dispensed in a different way than it was previously. The second is the doctrine of a pretribulation rapture. This doctrine teaches that God will remove Christians from Earth prior to the time the Great Tribulation begins so that God can fulfill His promises to Israel, who will not be raptured.

These two doctrines have deeper roots than most people realize. The notion of being snatched from Earth prior to the Great Tribulation is a wonderful idea. After all, no one wants to be on Earth when God's horrific wrath is released. Going to Heaven before God's wrath breaks out is a sweet pill to swallow even though this cannot be substantiated biblically. Be aware that sweet ideas (like Santa Claus) can travel far and wide on the merits of apparent goodness, even when the idea has no basis in fact.

A Serious Problem

When Bible students carefully identify and examine the promises and prophecies given to Israel in the Old Testament, a serious problem arises. The problem is that Bible students cannot reconcile why God gave so many promises and prophecies concerning Israel that have not been fulfilled. During the nineteenth century, a few Christians concluded that the pretribulation rapture theory could "solve" this problem. They reasoned that if the church is taken to Heaven just before the Great Tribulation begins, and if 144,000 Jews suddenly become believers in Christ when they see the church taken to Heaven, then God could proceed to fulfill the promises and prophecies (Plan A) given to ancient Israel. Unfortunately over time, this concept has gained traction among evangelicals because it sounds like a good idea to a thorny problem. Moreover, when Israel was established in 1948 as a nation, many Christians rejoiced because they believed this development confirmed the idea that God would soon remove (rapture) the church so that His original plan (Plan A) for Israel could be fulfilled.

Unfortunately, there are huge problems with this scenario. The Bible neither teachs a pretribulation rapture nor different dispensations for redemption.[23] Actually, the Bible teaches that the saints will be on Earth during the Great Tribulation[24] and it also teaches that redemption has always come through faith in God![25] A great day for Bible truth is coming soon. The Great Tribulation is near. When future events force millions of people to admit that there is no pre or mid tribulation rapture, many religious people will become very bitter toward their clergy and their church for being misled.

Of Course, God Has Perfect Foreknowledge

Some people argue, "God is omniscient, He has perfect foreknowledge, therefore, He cannot have a secondary plan. From the beginning, He has had one plan and there is no room or need for another." This argument has no merit because it humanizes God. There is a big difference between God's foreknowledge and God's love because they are not remotely connected! *God does not have a carnal nature. He does not use His foreknowledge in the same way that sinners would use foreknowledge if they had access to it.* If sinners had foreknowledge, we would use it for personal benefit because the carnal nature always puts self first. God, on the other hand, does not have a carnal nature. He is not tempted to use His

Appendix D - God Does Not Give Up

foreknowledge for personal benefit because He loves us more than He loves Himself.

Jesus' death on the cross proves that God did not use His foreknowledge to save Jesus from death! The Father foreknew that Jesus would die on the cross, but He did nothing to avoid it. The Father foreknew that Adam and Eve would sin, but He gave them the power of choice and they chose to sin. There is an infinite gap between God's foreknowledge and His love for His children. God will not use His foreknowledge to protect Himself from rebellion, insurrection, or death. His love for us eclipses His foreknowledge. The purpose of God's foreknowledge is a component of infinite wisdom. His wisdom cannot be limited, which means our Father *always* knows what is best. Because His wisdom is infinite, God can be difficult to understand. Knowing this explains why we must always have a non-negotiable faith in God.

Consider the contrast between God's foreknowledge and His love. As you read the following passage from Jeremiah, you will see that God's heart is very sad. Keep in mind that God has perfect foreknowledge: **"This is what the Lord Almighty, the God of Israel, says: Go ahead, add your burnt offerings to your other sacrifices and eat the meat yourselves! For when I brought your forefathers out of Egypt and spoke to them, I did not just give them commands about burnt offerings and sacrifices, but I gave them this command: Obey me, and I will be your God and you will be my people. Walk in all the ways I command you, that it may go well with you. But they did not listen or pay attention; instead, they followed the stubborn inclinations of their evil hearts. They went backward and not forward. From the time your forefathers left Egypt until now, day after day, again and again I sent you my servants the prophets. But they did not listen to me or pay attention. They were stiff-necked and did more evil than their forefathers. When you tell them all this, they will not listen to you; when you call to them, they will not answer. Therefore say to them, 'This is the nation that has not obeyed the Lord its God or responded to correction. Truth has perished; it has vanished from their lips.' "**[26]

Obviously, there is a wide gulf between God's foreknowledge and God's love. God foreknew from the beginning that Israel would become rebellious and when they did, it was heartbreaking for

Him. How could He be heartbroken if He foreknew this was going to happen before He chose Israel to be His trustees? Please understand that God's foreknowledge and God's love do not cross over. They serve different purposes. One characteristic does not affect the other because God is pure in heart; He is love personified.

Plan B Means God Does Not Give Up

Under the "new" covenant, there is a "new" Israel. A "new" sequence of prophetic events will culminate with a second advent. The prophecies in Daniel and Revelation concern "Plan B." Mixing and/or merging different types of prophecies produces insurmountable confusion. Prophecies belonging to Plan A will not mix with Plan B prophecies. Plan B is a bigger and better plan. Plan B contains a brighter set of promises and prophecies and unlike Plan A, Plan B is unconditional! This time around, God will not wait for a group of people to get their act together and He will not depend on a particular religious body of people to accomplish the gospel commission. At the appointed time, He will complete His work by hand picking 144,000 people from all over the world. These trustees of God, having Abraham's faith and love for Him, will accomplish all that God wants done in a mere 1,260 days!

God has done a very clever thing by creating Plan B using parallels from Plan A. Remember that Plan A and Plan B cannot be mixed or merged. However, to appreciate Plan B, it is very helpful to understand some of the building blocks in Plan A. In this sense, the prophecies and promises in the Old Testament remain indispensable. By studying the Old Testament carefully, we can understand God's plans better because there are many parallels between Plan A and Plan B.

Many people have asked if I think the Jews will rebuild the temple in Jerusalem because the Old Testament indicates the temple would be rebuilt. The Old Testament does indicate the temple would be rebuilt, but the Old Testament is not refering to a third temple. Nebuchadnezzar destroyed the first temple (Solomon's temple) in 586 B.C. and four decrees were issued to rebuild it. The Romans completely destroyed the second temple in A.D. 70. There is no prophecy in the Bible indicating that a third temple will be built. The reason for this silence is because God abandoned the nation of Israel at the end of the seventy weeks. He destroyed Jerusalem and the temple because He had installed a new covenant and created a new Israel. God has no need for a third temple.

Jesus told the Jews, **"Look, your house** [your temple] **is left to you desolate. For I tell you, you will not see me again** [I will not live among you] **until you say, 'Blessed is he who comes in the name of the Lord.' "**[27] These two sentences are easy to understand. Jesus declared the temple of Israel, which was designed to be His dwelling place, would be left empty. Jesus declared this benediction on the temple because Israel had rejected Him, and as a result, He then rejected Israel. Second, Jesus made it perfectly clear in this text that *He would never dwell in Israel again.* Israel will not see Jesus again until the Second Coming, and then the Jews will be forced to say, **"Blessed is he** [Jesus] **who comes in the name of the Lord."**[27]

Historically speaking, the Roman army destroyed the second temple in A.D. 70. Later, a Moslem mosque (the Dome of the Rock) was built on the temple mount in A.D. 684. The presence of this mosque keeps the temple mount from Jewish control. God gave the site to the Moslems so that a third Jewish temple could not be built. Many Christians who do not understand Plan B are frustrated that a mosque now sits on the temple mount, but they should not be frustrated. There will not be a third temple. The temple that we should be focusing on and studying about is in Heaven![28] That is where Jesus lives and intercedes for us. Soon, Jesus will call for the seven trumpets of Revelation to begin![29] When that day arrives, the present confusion over rebuilding a third temple in Jerusalem will vanish.

Plan B Sealed Up

Now that we have discussed Plan A and Plan B at some length, please consider two statements:

1. God foreknew that Plan B would be necessary from the beginning and He began preparing for Plan B during the Babylonian captivity. The book of Daniel contains visions that pertain to Plan B.

2. God loved Israel as much as any father could love a child. He desperately wanted His trustees to do the work that He had chosen them to do. During the Babylonian captivity, God spoke to Ezekiel and Jeremiah. Through them, He gave Israel many encouraging prophecies and promises that would come to pass *if* Israel would cooperate with Him during the seventy weeks (Plan A). *At the same time*, God

spoke to Daniel. Even though God revealed Plan B to Daniel, the information He gave to Daniel was sealed until the end of the world. If Israel had been faithful and Plan A was realized, the book of Daniel would not have been needed.

The Final Generation

The prophecies of Daniel and Revelation tell a story that covers many centuries. It gradually builds in intensity until it reaches the time of the final generation. This story contrasts the powers of sin and rebellion with the power of Jesus, revealing all who He really is. God hid this story from previous generations by hiding four rules in the book of Daniel. This process helped to keep prophetic matters a secret until the time arrives for fulfillment.[30] God does this for two reasons. First, when the time for fulfillment comes, those who love truth move forward. They are spiritually renewed when they see God's Word fulfilled with their own eyes, and in the process, those moving forward are separated from those who prefer darkness and tradition. This response to truth explains why some people were overjoyed when Jesus was born and others were deeply offended by His ministry. Second, as knowledge increases, man's knowledge of God increases. God reveals new information about Himself in an orderly way so that His children can spiritually mature.[31] Jesus told His disciples, **"The knowledge of the secrets of the kingdom of heaven has been given to you, but not to them** [unbelievers].**"**[32] If being a part of the kingdom of Heaven is important to you, then the secrets of the kingdom of Heaven will be *very* important to you. On the other hand, when people are spiritually dead, secrets about the kingdom of Heaven are not important.

From the beginning, God predetermined the number of days allotted to Earth's existence.[33] I believe the appointed time of the end has come because the book of Daniel has been unsealed. The architecture that has been hidden for twenty-six centuries has been discovered and the intended meaning of Daniel and Revelation is now available!

References
1. John 3:16
2. John 15:20-27
3. Luke 19:40; Matthew 3:9
4. Hosea 6:6,7
5. Exodus 19:4-8
6. John 8:39-45, italics and insertion mine
7. Galatians 3:29
8. Isaiah 9:6,7; 2 Chronicles 6:16; Jeremiah 33:17-22; John 12:12-16; Matthew 3:1-3
9. Hosea 8:1-3; Daniel 9:26; Matthew 23:1-39
10. Luke 22:20; Hebrews 8:8-13
11. Malachi 3:6-18
12. Psalm 19:7-11
13. Hebrews 8:1-5; 10:4-9
14. Colossians 2:13-17
15. Hebrews 7:12-22; Galatians 3:24
16. Genesis 17:2-7
17. Genesis 17:8
18. Genesis 15:6; Hebrews 11:1-29; Ephesians 2:8,9; Hebrews 10:1-29
19. Galatians 3:29, insertion mine
20. Hebrews 11:8-10
21. Romans 2:28,29; Galatians 3:28,29
22. Hebrews 11:40
23. For a comprehensive discussion on the topics of salvation, judgment, and the rapture, please read my book, *Jesus: The Alpha and The Omega*. This book may be freely downloaded at this web address: http://www.wake-up.org/Alpha/Subjindex.htm.
24. Revelation 13:7; 17:6; 18:24
25. Hebrews 11
26. Jeremiah 7:21-28
27. Matthew 23:38,39

28. Hebrews 8:1-5
29. Revelation 8 and 9
30. Acts 1:7; Ephesians 3:9
31. Hebrews 1:1,2
32. Matthew 13:11, insertion mine
33. Daniel 8:19; Revelation 9:15

Supplemental Helps

Books

Books available from Wake Up America Seminars

- **Warning! Revelation is about to be fulfilled**

    Written in an easy to read format, this book gives an overview of events described in Revelation. An excellent book to share with other people, regardless of denomination.

- **Bible Stories with End Time Parallels**

    This book is a "real faith builder." Even though the Bible stories are familiar, they "snap" with new perspective, highlighting significant end time parallels for Earth's final generation.

- **Jesus - The Alpha and The Omega**

- **Daniel Unlocked for the Final Generation**

- **A Study on the Seven Seals and the 144,000**

- **A Study on the Seven Trumpets, Two Witnesses and Four Beasts**

For a catalog with pricing, contact:

Wake Up America Seminars, Inc.
(800) 475-0876
www.wake-up.org

Other Materials

Recorded Seminars

- **Daniel Unlocked for the Final Generation - Series 213**
- **The Book of Revelation - Series 214**
- **Highlights of the Second Coming - Series 215**

Study Materials

- **The Jubilee Calendar - God's Template**
- **Great Clocks from God**
- **Overview Charts of Danel and Revelation's Story**

New materials are continually added so call Wake Up America Seminars at the number below to obtain a catalog listing the latest materials available.

Wake Up America Seminars, Inc.
P.O. Box 273
Bellbrook, OH 45305
(800) 475-0876
www.wake-up.org

Notes

Notes

About the Author

Larry Wilson, Director of Wake Up America Seminars, became a born again Christian after returning from a tour of duty in Vietnam. His understanding of the gospel, the plan of salvation, and the atonement of Jesus Christ has thrilled his soul ever since. He has spent more than forty years intensely studying the prophecies of Daniel and Revelation.

In 1988, he published the book *Warning! Revelation is about to be fulfilled* and since then, he has written several books (over 900,000 books in circulation throughout the world). Along with writing books, Larry Wilson gives seminar presentations, produces video programs which have been broadcast from various locations throughout the United States, and is a guest on radio talk shows.

About the Organization

Wake Up America Seminars (WUAS) is both a non-profit and a non-denominational organization. With God's blessings and the generosity of many people, WUAS has distributed millions of pamphlets, books and tapes around the world since it began in 1988. WUAS is not a church, or is it affiliated or sponsored by any religious organization. WUAS does not offer membership of any kind. Its mission is not to convert the world to a point of view. Although WUAS has well defined views on certain biblical matters, its mission is primarily "seed sowing." It promotes the primacy of salvation through faith in Jesus Christ, His imminent return, and is doing its best to encourage people with the good news of the gospel. People of all faiths are invited to study the materials produced by WUAS.